Augustine's Cyprian

Brill's Series in Church History and Religious Culture

Edited by

Wim Janse (*Vrije University Amsterdam, The Netherlands*)
Fred van Lieburg (*Vrije University Amsterdam, The Netherlands*)

In cooperation with

Jan Wim Buisman (*Leiden University, The Netherlands*)
Paul van Geest (*Vrije University Amsterdam/ Tilburg University, The Netherlands*)
Alastair Hamilton (*University of London, UK*)
R. Ward Holder (*Saint Anselm College, Manchester (NH), USA*)
Scott Mandelbrote (*University of Cambridge, UK*)
Andrew Pettegree (*University of St Andrews, UK*)
Karla Pollmann (*University of Kent, Canterbury, UK*)

VOLUME 73

The titles published in this series are listed at *brill.com/bsch*

Augustine's Cyprian

Brill's Series in Church History and Religious Culture

Edited by

VOLUME 73

The titles published in this series are listed at *brill.com/bsch*

Augustine's Cyprian

Authority in Roman Africa

By

Matthew Alan Gaumer

TUTA SUB AEGIDE PALLAS · 1683 ·

BRILL

LEIDEN | BOSTON

Cover illustration: Roman ruins of Gens Septimia temple in Cuicul (Djémila), Algeria (by Lidiia Akimova, under license from Shutterstock). Ancient Cuicul was a typical late Roman African city featuring a Roman military garrison and a thriving Christian community of Donatists and Catholics, and survived well into the sixth century. It was never resettled by Arabs as they swept through Africa centuries later.

Library of Congress Cataloging-in-Publication Data

Names: Gaumer, Matthew Alan, author.
Title: Augustine's Cyprian : authority in Roman Africa / by Matthew Alan Gaumer.
Other titles: Brill's series in church history ; d. 73.
Description: Boston : Brill, 2016. | Series: Brill's series in church history and religious culture ; volume 73 | Includes bibliographical references and index.
Identifiers: LCCN 2016000263 (print) | LCCN 2016001884 (ebook) | ISBN 9789004312630 (hardback : alk. paper) | ISBN 9789004312647 (E-book)
Subjects: LCSH: Augustine, Saint, Bishop of Hippo. | Cyprian, Saint, Bishop of Carthage. | Church--History of doctrines--Early church, ca. 30-600. | Africa, North--Church history. | Church history--Primitive and early church, ca. 30-600. | Donatists. | Authority--Religious aspects--Catholic Church.
Classification: LCC BR65.A9 G33 2016 (print) | LCC BR65.A9 (ebook) | DDC 270.2--dc23
LC record available at http://lccn.loc.gov/2016000263

Typeface for the Latin, Greek, and Cyrillic scripts: "Brill". See and download: brill.com/brill-typeface.

ISSN 1572-4107
ISBN 978-90-04-31263-0 (hardback)
ISBN 978-90-04-31264-7 (e-book)

This book is printed on acid-free paper and produced in a sustainable manner.

For Eva

Contra Donatistas auctoritate beatissimi episcopi et martyris Cypriani se defendere molientes septem libros de baptismo scripsi in quibus docui nihil sic ualere ad refellendos Donatistas et ad eorum prorsus ora claudenda, ne aduersus Catholicam suum scisma defendant, quomodo litteras factum que Cypriani. Ubicumque autem in his libris commemoraui ecclesiam non habentem maculam aut rugam.

AUGUSTINE OF HIPPO REGIUS, *Retractationes* 2,18

Contents

Preface

Amongst the ruins of ancient Carthage, outside the centre of modern Tunis, Tunisia, one is able to see, touch, and walk along a maritime promenade that was once the lively scene of robust economic activity and disembarkation for seafarers from ports of call throughout the known world in the late antique *imperium romanum*. In 383 (or 1,136 years after the founding of the *urbs romae*, as contemporaries would have counted time), somewhere in that ancient commercial district, a certain aspiring African nobody was confronting his mother over his desire to take leave of his homeland and set sail for greater horizons, an experience not uncommon for people throughout history. His mother, Monnica, a widow since 370, feared the bereavement of losing her cherished son. Her son, unequivocally determined to pursue and develop his intellectual gifts, was committed to reaching the Italian peninsula. Faced with such an impasse Aurelius Augustinus, aged twenty-nine, surreptitiously left his mother behind:

> ...I deceived her, pretending that I did not want to take leave of a friend until a favorable wind should arise and enable him to set sail. I lied to my mother, my incomparable mother! But I went free, because in your mercy you forgave me. Full of detestable filth as I was, you kept me safe from the waters of the sea to bring me to the water of your grace...At the time, however, she refused to go home, and it was only with difficulty that I persuaded her to spend the night in a place very near our ship, a memorial chapel built to Blessed Cyprian [*in memoria beati Cypriani*]. The same night I left by stealth...the wind blew for us and filled our sails, and the shore dropped away from our sight as she there at morning stood mad with grief.[1]

1 Augustine, *Conf.*, 5,15, *WSA* I/1, intro., trans., notes M. Boulding, ed. J. Rotelle (Hyde Park, NY: New City Press, 1997, 124), (*CCSL* 27, 65): 'Sed quare hinc abirem et illuc irem, tu sciebas, deus, nec indicabas mihi nec matri, quae me profectum atrociter planxit et usque ad mare secuta est. Sed fefelli eam uiolenter me tenentem, ut aut reuocaret aut mecum pergeret, et finxi me amicum nolle deserere, donec uento facto nauigaret. et mentitus sum matri, et illi matri, et euasi, quia hoc dimisisti mihi misericorditer seruans me ab aquis maris plenum execrandis sordibus usque ad aquam gratiae tuae, qua me abluto siccarentur flumina maternorum oculorum, quibus pro me cotidie tibi rigabat terram sub uultu suo. Et tamen recusanti sine me redire uix persuasi, ut in loco, qui proximus nostrae naui erat, memoria beati Cypriani, maneret ea nocte. Sed ea nocte clanculo ego profectus sum, illa autem non; mansit orando et flendo.'

This passage from his most popular work, *Confessiones*, is noteworthy because of its scarce appreciation by modern scholars and literati. It signifies crucial themes that would reverberate throughout Augustine's life, writings, and subconscious thought. More than being an example of parent–child psychology, it speaks of the inseparability of Augustine from his *africanitas* and of his complex identification with Roman North Africa's most venerated religious figure: Cyprian of Carthage.

Indeed in virtually every decade of Augustine's life as a Christian, from convert, to presbyter, and then bishop, he would be unable to escape the gravity of the prestige and authority of the third-century martyr-bishop from Carthage. This is especially the case as pertains to the myriad controversies Augustine found himself engaged in during the duration of his ministerial career.

These same events, in turn, occasioned the course of the evolution of his theology as a whole. Therefore, if Augustine of Hippo's impact upon history is as significant as commonly stated,[2] one only perceives a partial reality if one neglects to take into account the impact, sometimes pronounced, other times latent, of Cyprian in the development and outcome of Augustine's intellectual experiences. However, this relationship is, unfortunately, often perceivable only to a well-trained eye.

But this book is not only about Augustine or Cyprian, nor the relation between the two. Instead this book is concerned primarily with the authority and influence of Cyprian in late antique Roman Africa and the battles that occurred in a long struggle over the right for various Christian factions and their government allies to stake an exclusive claim to orthodoxy and tradition, of who has the truth and who is in error. In short, about who could claim to be successor to the name, legitimacy, and authentic faith of an indisputable North African authority; that is, Cyprian.

There is perhaps no better example from late antiquity or from the early church, and certainly not as well documented, than the sustained multi-decade campaigns to vanquish theological/ideological opponents over the question of who was the proper heir of Cyprian's teaching. This is especially clear when evaluating Augustine's confrontations with the 'Donatist' and 'Pelagian' Christians. But this situation is superlatively interesting not merely because of that; rather, the fight to claim the inheritance of Cyprian is intriguing and relevant precisely because it assumed the character of being a

---

2 But one such reference is Oliver O'Donovan and Joan Lockwood O'Donovan, *From Irenaeus to Grotius: A Sourcebook in Christian Political Thought 100–1625* (Grand Rapids, MI/Cambridge: Wm. Eerdmans Publishing, 1999), 104.

trans-continental, trans-ecclesial, trans-century, trans-cultural, and cross-controversy phenomenon. Even more, this historical event is germane to us in the twenty-first century. This is so for a number of reasons.[3] Perhaps, the clearest reason that comes to mind for the reader is the January 2011 Arab Spring that exploded, seemingly out of the blue to most casual observers, in Tunisia and spread by wild-fire throughout other places as well like Libya, Egypt, Morocco, and shortly in Algeria. In the time that elapsed it has become abundantly clear to anyone who watches the news that North Africa is an important geo-political region that will have a significant role in the twenty-first century.

Not only does this ancient convergence elucidate the complexities inherent in theological, doctrinal, and historical rationales and methodologies, but it also calls into question the ideological assurances that buttress opposing schools of thought in today's religious movements which are often based on exclusivist claims to the truth or authority. Of purely secular concern, this example is a learning event for those in the West struggling to reconcile the growing disputes over the legitimate role of religion in a post-Christian culture,[4] of the nature of religious extremism, but also for those attempting to find deeper sources of commonality between the east and west, north and south.[5] In a world hurriedly moving towards greater inter-communication, globalisation, and assimilations of various sorts, it helps to clearly perceive the ways in which our histories are alike, and also, paradoxically, the aspects that make our

3 This is summarised quite well in the new go-to edition for North African/Maghreb studies by Phillip Naylor, *North Africa: A History from Antiquity to the Present* (Austin, TX: University of Texas Press, 2009), 1: 'Studying North Africa offers students and scholars an exceptional opportunity to appreciate the formative and transformative role of historical transcultural relations. Transcultural history studies and emphasizes the significance of encounters and interactions within and among societies and civilizations.'

4 This is a matter consistently being addressed, three relevant examples are: Joseph Ratzinger and Marcello Pera, trans. M.F. Moore, *Without Roots: The West, Relativism, Christianity, Islam* (New York: Basic Books, 2007); J. Ratzinger, *Europa: I suoi fondamenti oggi e domani* (Milan: Edizioni San Paolo, 2004); Goulven Madec, 'Augustinus- Ist er der genius malignus Europas?,' in P. Koslowski (ed.), *Europa imaginieren. Der europäische Binnenmarkt als kulturelle und wirtschaftliche Aufgabe, Studies in Economic Ethics and Philosophy* (Berlin: Springer-Verlag, 1992), 298–312.

5 Again, see Naylor, 1–2: 'North Africa is one of those rare regions of the world that serves as an axis of cultures and civilizations…North Africa is like and island located between two seas, the Mediterranean and the Sahara. Waves of human encounters and interactions have swept ashore and shaped the 'island's' rich cultural and historical morphology. Accordingly, extraordinary peoples and histories have fashioned an impressive transcultural legacy.'

cultures unique and diverse.[6] The illustration of the battle for Cyprian's authority is special precisely because it sheds light on and provides us a greater context for those concerns and many more.

6 The importance of studying the Maghreb countries is paramount for these reasons as well as a means of arranging a more certain strategic approach to its people and governments in the coming decades, with the 'Arab Spring' of 2011 as one recent example. Current projections indicate that North Africans countries will be in a strong position, based on its youthful demographic, for greater economic and social development and international weight in the next twenty to thirty years. Literature abounds in this area, but for a concise breakdown, see *Global Trends 2025: A Transformed World* (Washington, D.C.: Office of the Director of National Intelligence, National Intelligence Council, 2008), esp. 18, 64–65, 69.

List of Figures and Tables

Figures

Tables

Abbreviations

1 Augustine's Works

Adult. conj.	*De coniugiis adulterinis* (*On Adulterous Marriages*)
An. et or.	*De anima et eius origine* (*On the Soul and its Origin*)
De bapt.	*De baptismo* (*On Baptism, against the Donatists*)
Brev.	*Breviculus conlationis cum Donatistis* (*A Summary of the Meeting with the Donatists*)
Cath.	*Ad Catholicos fratres* (*To Catholic Members of the Church*)
C. ep. Parm.	*Contra epistulam Parmeniani* (*Against the Letter of Parmenianus*)
Civ. Dei.	*De civitate Dei* (*City of God*)
Conf.	*Confessiones* (*Confessions*)
C. Don.	*Contra Partem Donati post Gesta* (*Against the Donatists after the Council*)
C. ep. Pel.	*Contra duas epistulas Pelagianorum* (*Against Two Letters of the Pelagians*)
Cont.	*De contentia* (*On Continence*)
Correct.	*De Correctione Donatistarum* (*On the Correction of the Donatists* [*Ep.* 185])
Corrept.	*De correptione et gratia* (*On Admonition and Grace*)
Cresc.	*Ad Cresconium grammaticum partis Donati* (*To Cresconius, a Donatist Grammarian*)
Doc. Chr.	*De doctrina Christiana* (*On Christian Teaching*)
Emer.	*Gesta cum Emerito*(*Proceedings with Emeritus*)
En. Ps.	*Enarrationes in Psalmos* (*Expositions of the Psalms*)
Ep.	*Epistula/Epistulæ* (*Letter/Letters*)
*Ep.**	*Epistula/Epistulæ* (*Newly Discovered Letters*)
C. Gaud.	*Contra Gaudentium* (*Against Gaudentius*)
Gr. et pecc. or.	*De gratia Christi et de peccato originali* (*On the Grace of Christ and Original Sin*)
Gr.lib. arb.	*De gratia and libero arbitrio* (*On Grace and Free Will*)
Gest. Pel.	*De gestis Pelagii* (*The Deeds of Pelagius*)
Haer.	*De haeresibus* (*Arianism and Other Heresies: Heresies, Memordandum to Augustine, To Orosius in Refutation of the Priscillianists and Origenists, Arian Sermon, Answer to an Arian Sermon, Debate with Maximianus Answer to Maximianus, Answer to an Enemy of the Law and the Prophets*)
Ioh.ev. tr.	*In Iohannis euangelium tractatus* (*Tractates on the Gospel of John*)
C. Iul.	*Contra Iulianum* (*Answer to Julian*)

C. Iul. imp.	*Contra Iulianum opus imperfectum* (*Unfinished Work in Answer to Julian*)
C. litt. Pet.	*Contra litteras Petiliani* (*Answer to the Letters of Petilian*)
Nat. et grat.	*De natura et gratia* (*On Nature and Grace*)
Nupt. et con.	*De nuptiis et concupiscentia ad Valerium* (*On Marriage and Concupiscence*)
Pecc. Mer.	*De peccatorum meritis et remissione peccatorum et de baptismo paruulorum*(*On the Merits and Forgiveness of Sins and On Infant Baptism*)
Perf. iust.	*De perfectione justitae hominis* (*On the Perfection of Human Righteousness*)
Persev.	*De dono perseverantiae* (*On the Gift of Perseverance*)
Praed. sanct.	*De praedestinatione sanctorum* (*On the Predestination of the Saints*)
Ps. c. Don.	*Psalmus contra partem Donati* (*Psalm against the Donatists*)
Retract.	*Retractationes* (*Retractions*)
s.	*Sermo/Sermones* (*Sermon/Sermons*)
Spir. et litt.	*De spiritu et littera* (*On the Spirit and the Letter*)
Un. bapt.	*De unico baptismo contra Petilianum ad Constantinum* (*On the One Baptism, against Petilian*)

2 Cyprian's Works

Ep.	*Epistulæ* (*Letter/Letters*)
Lapsis	*De lapsis*
De Unit.	*De ecclesiae catholicae unitate* (*The Unity of the Catholic Church*)

3 General Abbreviations

ACW	*Ancient Christian Writers*
AugLex	*Augustinus-Lexikon*
BA	*Bibliothèque Augustinienne*
CAG	*Corpus Augustinianum Gissense*
CLCLT	*Cetedoc Library of Christian Latin Texts*
CCSL	*Corpus Christianorum Series Latina*
CSEL	*Corpus Scriptorum Ecclesiasticorum Latinorum*
CTh	*Codex Theodosianus*
MA	*Miscellanea Agostiniana*
PL	*Patrologia Latina, Cursus Completus*
SC	*Sources Chrétiennes*
WSA	*The Works of St. Augustine: A Translation for the 21st Century*

Timelines

1 Anti-Donatist Works

Title	Date	Edition		
	Fitzgerald[1]—Monceaux[2]	CSEL/CCSL	WSA	BA/SC
Ps. c. Don.	393/94—393	51, 3–15	I/21*	28
C. ep. Don. Her.	393/95—end 393 or early 394	Lost	—	—
C. ep. Parm.	400—early 400	51, 19–141	I/21*	28
De bapt.	400/01—early 400	51, 145–325	I/21*	29
C. quod attulit Cent. a Don.	401/02	Lost	—	—
C. litt. Pet.	400/03—400/01/02	52, 231–322	I/21*	30
Ad Cath. ep. c. Don. [*Ep. ad Cath.*]	401/03 (after *C. litt. Pet.*)	Lost	—	—
Cath. [*De unit. eccl.*]	402/05—end 401	52, 231–322	I/21*	28
Prob. et testim. c. Don.	405—early 406	Lost	—	—
C. Nescio quem Don.	405—early 406	Lost	—	—
Cresc.	405/06—end 405	52, 325–582	I/22*	31
Adm. Don. de Maxim.	406—early 406	Lost	—	—
Un. bapt.	late 410/11—early 410	53, 3–34	I/22*	31
Brev.	June 411—end 411	53, 97–162	I/22*	32
Gest. Con. Carth.	Summer 411	CCSL 149A	—	SC 194, 195, 224, 373
C. Don.	412—early 412	53, 97–178	—	32
De Max. c. Don.	412—early 410	Lost	—	—
Ad. Emer. Epics. Don. post Conl.	415—early 416	Lost	—	—
Correct. [*Ep. 185*]	417—early 417	57, 1–44	II/3	
Serm. Caes.	418—Sept. 18, 418	53, 167–78	—	32

Title	Date	Edition		
	Fitzgerald[1]—*Monceaux*[2]	CSEL/CCSL	WSA	BA/SC
Emer.	Sept. 20, 418—Sept. 20, 418	53, 181–96	—	32
C. Gaud.	419—early 420	53, 201–74	I/22*	32

* The Anti-Donatist Works are slated to be released by New City Press in the WSA series as volumes I/21-22. It is anticipated that they will be released starting in 2016–17.

1 Anti-Donatist works: Allan Fitzgerald (ed.), *Augustine through the Ages. An Encyclopedia* (Grand Rapids, MI/Cambridge: Wm. Eerdmans Publishing, 1999), xliii–il.
Epistulae: Robert Eno, 'Epistulae,' in A. Fitzgerald (ed.), *Augustine through the Ages. An Encyclopedia* (Grand Rapids, MI/Cambridge: Wm. Eerdmans Publishing, 1999), 299–305.

2 Paul Monceaux, *Histoire littéraire de l'Afrique chrétienne: depuis les origines jusqu'a l'invasion arabe, tome septième, Saint Optat et les premiers écrivains Donatistes* (Paris: Éditions Ernest Leroux, 1923), 275–278.

2 'Sermones' Closely Connected with the Donatist Controversy

Title	Dates				
	Kunzelmann[1]	*Verbraken*[2]	*Hombert*[3]	*Rebillard*[4]	*Gryson*[5]
s. 3 PL 38, 32–33	407–408	before 420	—	407/08 or 420(?)	405/08
s. 4 CCSL 41, 20–48	410/19	before 420	—	410/19	403
s. 10 41, 153–59	411	—	405/10	c. 412	412
s. 33 41, 413–16	405/11	—	405/10	405/11	413/16
s. 37 41, 446–73	410	before 420	400/10	397	400/10
s. 45 41, 515–26	408/11	before 420	407/08	408/11	408/11
s. 46 41, 529–70	409/10	410/11	407/08	410/11	407/08
s. 47 41, 572–604	409/10	410/11	—	401/11	407/08
s. 71 PL 38, 444–67	417	before 420	419/20	417(?)	419/20

(*cont.*)

Title	Dates				
	Kunzelmann[1]	*Verbraken*[2]	*Hombert*[3]	*Rebillard*[4]	*Gryson*[5]
s. 88 38, 539–53	400	—	c. 404	c. 400	404
s. 90 38, 559–66	412/16	—	—	411/16	411
s. 129 38, 720–25	393/405	—	405/09	393/405	405/09
s. 137 38, 754–63	400/05	before 404	410/20	408/11	—
s. 138 38, 763–69	411/12	—	—	411/12	411
s. 147A *MA* 50–55	—	—	—	409/10	409/10
s. 159B *Dol.* 21	—	—	—	403/04	—
s. 162A *MA* 98–111	—	—	—	404	404
s. 164 *PL* 38, 895–902	end 411	—	—	411	411
s. 182 38, 984–88	416	—	—	416/17	417
s. 183 38, 988–94	416	—	—	416/17	417/19
s. 197 38, 1021–26	400	—	—	—	—
s. 198 38, 1024–26	January 1	January	—	—	—
s. 202 38, 1033–35	405/11	—	—	405/11	400/10
s. 223 38, 1092–93	Easter Vigil 400/05	—	—	400/05 or 412	412
s. 252 38, 1171–79	April 18, 396	Friday before Easter	—	c. 395	396[3]
s. 266 38, 1225–29	May 28, 410	May 23, 397	403/08	397	403/08
s. 269 38, 1234–37	May 14, 411	—	405/10	411	405/10

Title	Dates				
	Kunzelmann[1]	*Verbraken*[2]	*Hombert*[3]	*Rebillard*[4]	*Gryson*[5]
s. 271 38, 1245–46	393/405	—	—	393/405	393/405
s. 275 38, 1254–55	410/12	—	—	410/12	410–12
s. 292 38, 1319–27	393/405	—	402/05	393/405	402/05
s. 293A *MA* 223–26	—	—	—	June 24	—
s. 295 *PL* 38, 1348–52	405/11	—	400/10	405/11	400/11
s. 313E *MA* 535–43	—	—	—	410	393/96
s. 327 *PL* 38, 1450–51	405/11	—	—	405/11	405/11
s. 340A *MA* 563–75	—	—	—	—	411
s. 357 *PL* 39, 1582–86	May 17, 411	—	—	411	411
s. 358 *SPM* 144–49	end May 411	May 31, 411	—	411	411
s. 359 *PL* 39, 1590–97	end 411	—	—	411/12	411/12
s. 359B *Dol.* 2	—	—	—	404/05	—
s. 360 *PL* 39, 1598–99	411	—	—	411	—
s. 360A *Dol.* 24	—	—	—	—	—
s. 360C *Dol.* 27	—	—	—	—	—
s. 400	—	—	—	—	—

* The dating of individual Sermons is still a matter of debate and scholarly exploration. Therefore, the five most referred-to sources are used in order to provide as comprehensive a reference as is currently feasible. As a disclaimer, because of the tendentious nature of dating the Sermons, one must use caution in assuming the theoretical dates provided. Also, use of '—' does not necessarily indicate that the source has no opinion, but could also mean it was not treated.

1 A. Kunzelmann,'Die Chronologie der Sermones des Hl. Augustinus,' in J. Wilpert, et al. (ed.), *Miscellanea Agostiniana: testi e studi publicata a cura dell'ordine eremitano di S. Agostino nel XV centenario dalla morte del santo dottore, vol. II, Studi Agostiniani* (Rome: Tipografia Poliglotta Vaticana, 1931), 417–520.
2 P.-P. Verbraken, *Études Critiques sur les Sermons Authentiques de Saint Augustin, Instrumenta Patristica 12* (Steenbrugge, Bel. : Abbatia S. Petri/Martinus Nijhoff, 1976).
3 P.-M. Hombert, *Nouvelles Recherches de Chronologie Augustinienne, Collection des Études Augustiniennes, Série Antiquité* 163 (Paris: Institut d'Études Augustiniennes, 2000).
4 É. Rebillard, 'Sermones,' in A. Fitzgerald (ed.), *Augustine through the Ages. An Encyclopedia* (Grand Rapids, MI/Cambridge: Wm. Eerdmans Publishing, 1999), 773–792.
5 R. Gryson, *Répertoire Général des Auteurs Ecclésiastiques Latins de l'Antiquité et du Haut Moyen Âge, Tome I* (Freiburg: Verlag Herder, 2007).
N.B.: P. Monceaux (1923) posits additional Sermones to be numbered in the anti-Donatist works of Augustine. In terms of extra Sermones, he also lists: 99, 112, 238, 249, 265, 268, 285, 325.

3 'Epistulae' Closely Connected with the Donatist Controversy

Title	Date	Edition		
	Fitzgerald[1], Monceaux[2], Teske[3]	CSEL	WSA	BA[4&6]/LSA[5]
Ep. 21	390–91[1], —[2], 391[3]	34/1,49–54	II/1, 55–57	40,[4]
Ep. 22	early 391[1], —[2], 391/93[3]	34/1,54–62	II/1, 58–62	40,[4]
Ep. 23	ca. 392[1], early 392[2], 391/95[3]	34/1, 63–73	II/1, 63–68	40,[4]
Ep. 29	Spring 395[1], 395[2], 395[3]	34/1,114–22	II/1, 95–100	40,[4]
Ep. 32	—[1], —[2], 396/97[3]	34/2, 8–18	II/1, 108–14	1,[5]
Ep. 33	before 396[1], early 396[2], 396[3]	34/2, 18–23	II/1, 115–17	1,[5]
Ep. 34	396/97[1], late 396/97[2], 396/97[3]	34/2,23–27	II/1, 118–20	1,[5]
Ep. 43	396/97[1], late 397[2], 396/97[3]	34/2, 85–109	II/1, 156–72	1,[5]
Ep. 44	before Ep. 43[1], late 398[2], 396/97[3]	34/2,109–21	II/1, 173–81	1,[5]
Ep. 49	398[1], before 398[2], 398[3]	34/2, 140–42	II/1, 195–96	1,[5]
Ep. 51	399/400[1], early 399[2], 399/400[3]	34/2, 144–49	II/1, 198–201	1,[5]
Ep. 52	after 398? [1], before 400[2], 399/400[3]	34/2,149–51	II/1, 202–03	1,[5]

Title	Date	Edition		
	Fitzgerald[1], Monceaux[2], Teske[3]	CSEL	WSA	BA[4&6]/LSA[5]
Ep. 53	398–400[1], before 400[2], ca. 400[3]	34/2,152–58	II/1, 204–08	1,[5]
Ep. 56	396–410[1], before 400[2], likely 400[3]	34/2,213–15	II/1, 237	1,[5]
Ep. 57	396–410[1], before 400[2], likely 400[3]	34/2,215–16	II/1, 238	1,[5]
Ep. 58	after 410[1], —[2], 401[3]	34/2,216–19	II/1, 239–40	1,[5]
Ep. 61	late 401[1], —[2], 401/02[3]	34/2,222–24	II/1, 245–46	1,[5]
Ep. 66	before 401[1], 400/01[2], 400[3]	34/2, 235–36	II/1, 257–58	1,[5]
Ep. 70	after 397/400[1], before 402[2], 397 or 400[3]	34/2,246–47	II/1, 264–65	1,[5]
Ep. 76	404[1], end 403[2], end 403[3]	34/2,324–28	II/1, 297–300	1,[5]
Ep. 86	406/09[1], early 413[2], 406/09[3]	34/2,396–97	II/1, 343	2,[5]
Ep. 87	405/11[1], 405/11[2], 405/11[3]	34/2, 397–406	II/1, 344–50	2,[5]
Ep. 88	406/11[1], 406[2], 406/11[3]	34/2, 407–19	II/1, 351–58	2,[5]
Ep. 89	406/09[1], before 406[2], 405/11[3]	34/2, 419–25	II/1, 359–63	2,[5]
Ep. 93	407/08[1], before 408[2], 407/08[3]	34/2, 445–96	II/1, 376–408	2,[5]
Ep. 100	late 408[1], 408[2], end 408[3]	34/2, 535–38	II/2, 15–16	2,[5]
Ep. 105	August 408[1],early 409[2], 406[3]	34/2, 595–610	II/2, 54–64	2,[5]
Ep. 106	409[1], ca. 410[2], 409[3]	34/2, 610–11	II/2, 65	2,[5]
Ep. 107	—[1], —[2],409[3]	34/2, 611–12	II/2, 66	2,[5]
Ep. 108	late 409/10[1], ca. 410[2], 409/10[3]	34/2, 612–34	II/2, 409/10	2,[5]
Ep. 111	late 409[1], late 409[2], end 409 [3]	34/2, 642–57	II/2, 88–94	2,[5]
Ep. 128	ca. May 411[1], 411[2], 411[3]	44, 30–34	II/2, 175–77	2,[5]
Ep. 129	ca. May 411[1], 411[2], 411[3]	44, 34–39	II/2, 178–82	2,[5]
Ep. 133	late 411[1], late 411[2], 411[3]	44, 80–84	II/2, 203–04	2,[5]
Ep. 134	late 411[1], late 411[2], 411[3]	44, 84–88	II/2, 205–07	2,[5]
Ep. 139	411/12[1], 412[2], 411/12[3]	44, 148–54	II/2, 238–41	2,[5]

(*cont.*)

Title	Date	Edition		
	Fitzgerald[1], Monceaux[2], Teske[3]	CSEL	WSA	BA[4&6]/LSA[5]
Ep. 141	May 14, 412,[1] 412[2], 412[3]	44, 235–46	II/2, 290–97	3,[5]
Ep. 142	ca. 412[1], before 412[2], 412[3]	44, 247–50	II/2, 298–300	3,[5]
Ep. 144	before 411? [1], late 412[2], before 411[3]	44, 262–66	II/2, 308–10	3,[5]
Ep. 173	411/14[1], early 412[2], 411/14[3]	44, 640–48	II/3, 124–29	3,[5]
Correct. [*Ep. 185*]	417[1], early 417[2], 417[3]	57, 1–44	II/3, 178–207	3,[5]
Ep. 208	422/23? [1], before 423[2], ca. 423[3]	57, 342–47	II/3, 389–92	4,[5]
*Ep. 28**	415–17[1], —[2], 418[3]	88, 133–37	II/4, 330–32	46,[6]

* The criteria used for labeling Augustine's 'epistulae' are as follows: the majority of the document concerns Donatist beliefs or believers, contains anti-Donatist themes, or is a legalistic document with an anti-Donatist purpose. Also, use of '—' does not necessarily indicate that the source has no opinion, but could also mean it was not treated.

1 Anti-Donatist works: Allan Fitzgerald (ed.), *Augustine through the Ages. An Encyclopedia* (Grand Rapids, MI/Cambridge: Wm. Eerdmans Publishing, 1999), xliii-il.
Epistulae: R. Eno, 'Epistulae,' in A. Fitzgerald (ed.), *Augustine through the Ages. An Encyclopedia* (Grand Rapids, MI/Cambridge: Wm. Eerdmans Publishing, 1999), 299–305.

2 Monceaux, *Histoire littéraire de l'Afrique chrétienne: depuis les origines jusqu'a l'invasion arabe, tome septième*, 279–286.

3 Augustine, Letters 1–99, *WSA* II/1, trans. R. Teske, ed. J. Rotelle (Hyde Park, NY: New City Press, 2001); Letters 100–155 (Epistulae), *WSA* II/2, trans. R. Teske, ed. B. Ramsey (Hyde Park, NY: New City Press, 2003); Letters 156–210 (Epistulae), *WSA* II/3, trans. R. Teske, ed. B. Ramsey (Hyde Park, NY: New City Press, 2004); Letters 211–270, 1*-29* (Epistulae), *WSA* II/4 trans. R. Teske, ed. B. Ramsey (Hyde Park, NY: New City Press, 2005).

4 Augustine, Lettres 1–30, *BA* 40A, trans. S. Lancel (Paris: Études augustiniennes, 2011).

5 Augustine, Lettres de Saint Augustin 1: Lettre 1–84, trans. F. Poujoulat (Paris: Lefort, 1858); Lettres de Saint Augustin 2: Lettre 85–139, trans. F. Poujoulat (Lille: Lefort, 1858); Lettres de Saint Augustin 3: Lettre 140–185, trans. F. Poujoulat (Lille: Lefort, 1858) ; Lettres de Saint Augustin 4: Lettre 186–270, trans. F. Poujoulat (Lille: Lefort, 1858).

6 Augustine, Lettres 1*-29*, *BA* 46B, trans. J. Divjak (Paris: Études augustiniennes, 1987).
N.B.: P. Monceaux (1923) posits additional Epistulae and Sermones to be numbered in the anti-Donatist works of Augustine. In terms of extra Epistulae, he also lists: 29, 33–34, 41, 44, 49, 52–53, 55–58, 61, 69, 70, 76, 78, 83, 85, 87, 89, 97, 106, 108, 111–12, 128–29, 133–34, 139, 141–42, 144, 151, 155, 204, 208–09, 245.

4 'Ennarationes in Psalmos' Closely Connected with the Donatist Controversy

Title	Date	Edition		
	Dekkers/Fraipont[1], Boulding[2], Müller/Fiedrowicz[3], Monceaux[4]	CCSL	WSA	PL
En. in Ps. 10	—[1], —[2], —[3], 395–98[4]	38, 74–82	III/15, 160–69	36, 131–38
Ex. 2 of Ps. 18	25 Aug 403[1], —[2], —[3], before 420[4]	38, 105–13	III/15, 204–14	36, 157–64
Ex. 2 of Ps. 21	2 Sep 403[1], —[2], —[3], early 397[4]	38, 121–34	III/15, 227–43	36, 170–82
Ex. 3 of Ps. 30	—[1], —[2], 29 Jun—[3], before 420[4]	38, 212–22	III/15, 334–46	36, 247–56
Ex. 3 of Ps. 32	—[1], —[2], Sep[3], 403[4]	38, 257–73	III/15, 406–24	36, 286–300
Ex. 2 of Ps. 33	—[1], —[2], Sunday[3], before 420[4]	38, 281–99	III/16, 23–44	36, 307–22
Ex. 2 of Ps. 36	411/12[1], late 403[2], —[3], 403[4]	38, 347–68	III/16, 103–28	36, 363–83
Ex. 3 of Ps. 36	411/12[1], —[2], late 403[3], 403[4]	38, 368–82	III/16, 129–45	36, 383–95
En. in Ps. 54	—[1], —[2], —[3], 396–96[4]	39, 655–76	III/17, 53–80	36, 493–514
En. in Ps. 57	412[1], Sep 403[2], —[3], early 396[4]	39, 707–29	III/17, 120–47	36, 532–43
En. in Ps. 67	412[1], —[2], —[3], 415[4]	39, 868–900	III/17, 324–63	36, 812–40
En. in Ps. 85	412 [1], 13 Sep 401 or 416[2], 13/14 Sep[3], before 420[4]	39, 1176–97	III/18, 220–45	37, 1081–1100
Ex. 2 of Ps. 88	412[1], 14 Sep 399–411[2], 13/14 Sep[3], before 420[4]	39, 1220–44	III/18, 289–302	37, 1120–41
En. in Ps. 95	412[1], 406/07[2], —[3], before 405[4]	39, 1342–53	III/18, 423–37	37, 1227–37
Ex. 2 of Ps.101	Jan 413[1], —[2], —[3], early 406[4]	40, 1438–50	III/19, 63–77	37, 1305–16

(*cont.*)

Title	Date	Edition		
	Dekkers/Fraipont[1], Boulding[2], Müller/Fiedrowicz[3], Monceaux[4]	CCSL	WSA	PL
En. in Ps. 119	414/15[1], 406/07[2], —[3], before 420[4]	40, 1776–86	III/19, 497–509	37, 1596–1605
En. in Ps. 145	—[1], —[2], —[3], 405–10[4]	40, 2105–21	III/20, 400–19	37, 1884–98
En. in Ps. 147	—[1], Dec 403[2], —[3], 412–20[4]	40, 2138–65	III/20, 441–75	37, 1913–37

* The criteria used for labeling Augustine's Ennarationes in Psalmos are as follows: the majority of the document concerns Donatist beliefs or believers, contains anti-Donatist themes, or is a legalistic document with an anti-Donatist purpose. Also, use of '—' does not necessarily indicate that the source has no opinion, but could also mean it was not treated.

1 Augustine, *Enarrationes in Psalmos, Corpus Christianorum Series Latina* 38–40, ed. E. Dekkers and J. Fraipoint (Turnhout: Brepols, 1956).

2 Augustine, *Exposition of the Psalms* 1–32, *WSA* III/15, trans. M. Boulding, ed. J. Rotelle (Hyde Park, NY: New City Press, 2000); *Exposition of the Psalms, WSA* III/16, trans. R. Teske, ed. J. Rotelle (Hyde Park, NY: New City Press, 2000); *Exposition of the Psalms, WSA* III/17, trans. R. Teske, ed. J. Rotelle (Hyde Park, NY: New City Press, 2001); *Exposition of the Psalms, WSA* III/18, trans. R. Teske, ed. J. Rotelle (Hyde Park, NY: New City Press, 2002); *Exposition of the Psalms, WSA* III/19, trans. M. Boulding, ed. B. Ramsey (Hyde Park, NY: New City Press, 2003), *Exposition of the Psalms, WSA* III/20, trans. M. Boulding, ed. B. Ramsey (Hyde Park, NY: New City Press, 2004).

3 H. Müller and M. Fiedrowicz, 'Enarrationes in Psalmos,' in C. Mayer (ed.), *Augustinus-Lexikon*, vol. 2 (Basel: Schwabe & Co., 2001), 804–858.

4 P. Monceaux, *Histoire littéraire de l'Afrique chrétienne: depuis les origines jusqu'a l'invasion arabe, tome septième*, 287–292.
N.B. 1: P. Monceaux (1923) posits additional *Ennarationes in Psalmos* to be numbered in the anti-Donatist works of Augustine (dates are from Monceaux): 25 (early 393), 35 (early 396), 39 (before 420), 49 (before 420), 69 (before 420), 75 (before 420), 124 (early 396), 132 (before 405), 139 (before 405).

Map

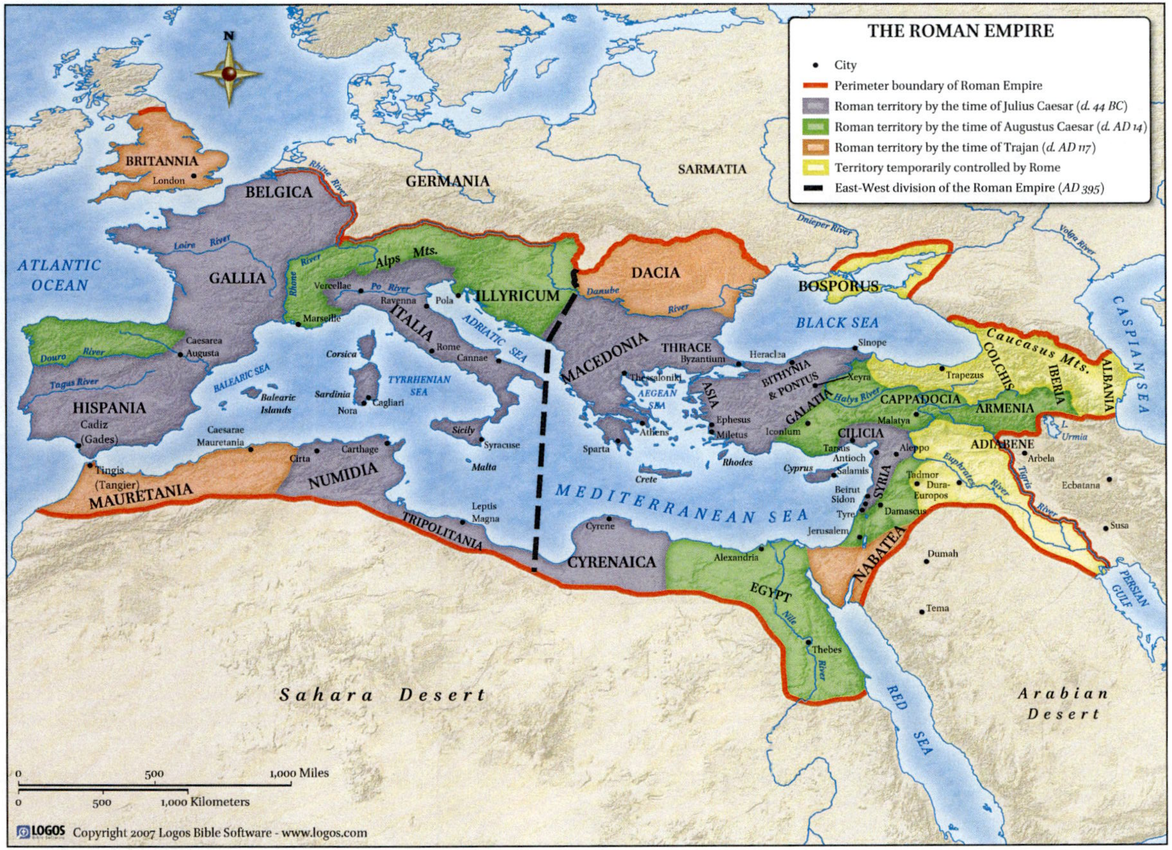

The Roman Empire.

Introduction

In 388, after some years spent abroad in Rome and Milan, Augustine again set foot on African soil. Whilst it is impossible to know this with any certainty, the Roman citizen, now aged 34, must have been bewildered by thoughts of where his life had taken him thus far, and even more so by his future path.[1] Although the years after his homecoming are sparsely recorded, either by Augustine or his biographer, Possidius, one can nevertheless sense the flurry of activity that surrounded that period. Hoping to find the serenity of a provincial lifestyle, characterised by calm, study, and discernment, Augustine found himself instead in an uncertain retirement. Hoping for peace, he was instead surrounded by eager followers and demands on his time from the broader Christian community in this Roman province of Numidia.

By 391, the man who had wished to spend the rest of his life enjoying a contemplative existence, was inducted, reluctantly apparently,[2] into public ministry as a presbyter of the Hippo Regius diocese.[3] His Church, which he would probably have been familiar with as a boy, as an adolescent, and throughout his Manichean period, was part of the same community that he had come to know through his sojourns on the Italian peninsula. Yet this branch of the Church, the one he had long known, and which he had also seen during his forays abroad, was not the sole group in Africa claiming to be the Christian Church.

All around him, in Hippo Regius and elsewhere in Roman North Africa, there were other Christians who created an environment of uneasy peace at the best of times, and palpable tension, if not outright provocation, when

1 One need only consider how drastic were the 'vocational' changes Augustine had already undergone in the 380s: first as an aspiring instructor of rhetoric who had to leave his native North Africa (after relocating to bigger, more influential cities like Carthage), then as an imperial teacher of rhetoric, a semi-established member of the late antique 'bourgeois' class. There followed a period as an uncomfortable *philosophe* dabbling in the tenets of Mani, and a period of neo-Platonism, until eventually he found himself a bewildered catechumen, with his world turned upside down within the walls of the Christian basilica in Milan, in the presence of its most famous bishop, Ambrose.

2 Augustine recounted a degree of trepidation about this, see: *s.* 355,2. One biographer has identified this under-reported event as the most important of the 'conversions processes' Augustine would undergo. See James O'Donnell, *Augustine: A New Biography* (New York: HarperPerennial, 2006), 26.

3 Hippo Regius (or Hippo), known as Bône before independence from France, is now called Annaba and is located in north-eastern Algeria.

 | DOI 10.1163/9789004312647_002

disagreements escalated. Augustine, and the group he ministered to, were Christians who overtly embraced (and were affirmed by) other communities of co-religionists throughout their known world, to which they were linked by common apostolic origins. The rival North African group likewise enjoyed a flourishing membership, but saw life and the rest of the world through the prism of their own African assuredness. This group would have been ever before the eyes of Augustine the priest; even in the midst of liturgical acts he could not escape their reality.[4]

Augustine, with Optatus of Milevis, a predecessor of the same Church, came to call their own community 'Christians', and more specifically 'Catholics'. The rival group also called themselves 'Christians' and 'Catholics', but through the process of history became known as 'Donatists', the label applied by Optatus, Augustine and their Church.[5] Since mention of 'Donatist' Christians had already appeared in Augustine's writings by 392,[6] it is inconceivable that the presbyter from Hippo was not already intimately knowledgeable about the two

4 Aug., *Ep.* 29,11.

5 The Donatists were a majority group in Hippo Regius and its environs with strong backing from the citizenry; Aug., *Ioh. evang. tract.* 6,25 (CCSL 36,66); *C. ep. Parm.* 1, 17–18 (CSEL 51, 38–41); *C. litt. Pet.* 1,26 (CSEL 52, 20–21); 2,184 (CSEL 52, 112–15); Possidius, *Vita Augustini* 7,2 (PL 32, 446–53). On the diffusion of Donatist Christianity see also P. MacKendrick, *The North African Stones Speak* (Chapel Hill, NC: University of North Carolina Press: 1980), 261–83. Catholics were reportedly often threatened by Donatist Circumcelliones; *En. in Ps.* 10,5 (CSEL 93/1A, 225–28); *C. ep. Parm.* 2,4 (CSEL 51, 52–54); *C. litt. Pet.* 1,26 (CSEL 52, 21–22); 2,65 (CSEL 52, 98); *Cresc.* 3, 15–16 (CSEL 52, 424–26); *Ep.* 43,24 (CSEL 34/2, 106); 76,3 (CSEL 34/2, 327–28); 87, 4–5 (CSEL 34/2, 400–02).

6 Augustine's first indirect reference to the Donatists is found in *En. in Ps.* 10,1. He makes the first descriptive reference in *En. in Ps.* 10,5 (WSA III/15, 164–65): 'How can I feel sure for instance, that those who were in communion with you yesterday, in communion with you today and in communion with you tomorrow, have committed no sin during these three days? But if neither you nor I are defiled because we do not know, what reason have you for rebaptising those who know nothing of the treachery and reproach of the days of Marcarius? As for the Christians hailing from Mesopotamia who have never so much as heard the names Caecilian and Donatus, how can you dare to rebaptise them on the plea that they are not Christians?' (CCSL 38, 78): 'Unde ergo confido in eis quibus heri communicasti, et hodie communicas, et cras communicabis, utrum uel isto triduo nihil mali commiserint? Quod si nec te nec me polluit quod nescimus, quae causa est ut rebaptizes eos qui tempora traditionis et Macarianae inuidiae non nouerunt? Quae causa est ut christianos de Mesopotamia uenientes, qui Caeciliani et Donati nec nomen audierunt, rebaptizare audeas, et neges esse christianos?'. Finally, in *Ex.2 in Ps.* 21,2 (WSA III/15, 228) he will refer explicitly to the 'parte Donati': 'I wonder, brethren, whether this Psalm is being read among the Donatists?'

rival churches and the deep rift that separated them. But most of this period in Augustine's life is lost to history and we therefore cannot tell for certain.

It was during the emergence from this somewhat silent stage that the trajectory for Aurelius Augustine's recorded life was set. Starting in the early 390s, and largely without pause, after ordination first as presbyter and then as bishop, he was caught up in a maelstrom of actions which changed the nature of Christianity in Africa and the West. As we shall see, Augustine the priest initiated a campaign that was pastoral, intellectual, political, and polemical in nature, and which would occupy his time in one form or another until his death in 430. This was the opening salvo of a battle and process which he never really resolved: i.e., how to find a foundation in Christian tradition, while at the same time refining his resulting theological and ideological positions as necessitated by his experience as a minister and thinker. The solution to this paradox, in short, was that Augustine settled upon a customised and uneasy juxtaposition of views that allowed him to anchor them locally or universally, specifically or broadly, as required, even if this resulted in an apparent self-contradiction. Two of the most striking demonstrations of this process are Augustine's drives to secure foundational authority in support of his views during the crossfire of the Donatist (c. 392–429) and Pelagian (c. 412–429) controversies.[7] Though the two controversies seem on the surface to be unrelated, when seen through the narrative of Augustine's search for an authority source, they are not. And the one constant throughout the two disputes, one that has gone essentially unremarked in previous literature, is the overshadowing and disproportionate influence of that African Christian icon, Cyprian of Carthage.

Already as a priest, and into the first decade of his episcopacy, Augustine understood that his pastoral work and desire to conform to a life of service would be for naught unless he proactively endeavoured to construct a firmer foundation for his own fledgling Church. As we shall see later, the foremost objective for the man from Thagaste was to shield and refine the very *raison d'être* of his small Christian sect against an entrenched North African viewpoint that traditionally considered a Church that was favoured (or tolerated) by the *imperium* inherently bogus. Augustine's own persuasions and experiences early on

7 The dating of these desperate controversies differs from other chronologies previously used. Casually speaking, the Donatist controversy is thought to have ended with its suppression in 411 at the Council of Carthage. The Pelagian confrontation is thought to have slowly developed afterwards and with barely any overlap. I challenge this perception throughout this book, being especially mindful of the later writings of Augustine discovered in the Divjak Letters, which are concerned with Donatism and the theological continuity between the two controversies.

motivated him to consider his Church otherwise, however. His was a Church imbued with the truth, and this was evidenced by its prophetic expansion throughout the *terra cognita* and beyond. Unfortunately for Augustine, most of the inhabitants of his city and North Africa generally held an opposing perspective. For the majority of North Africans, Christianity was lived out in a way that was intertwined with their culture, a culture that was both proud and resilient. Theirs was a Church whose heroes were Cyprian of Carthage and the martyrs. Moreover, these same heroes were more than simply casualties of imperial aggression; they were concrete role-models for the seriousness and fidelity with which Africans came to cherish and safeguard their tradition. Much like the difficulties encountered throughout their history, North Africans had a way of life adapted to constant threats to their homeland: invasions, Roman cultural pressure, environmental instability, and routine raids along the imperial frontier. Their religions had always mirrored this rugged reality. It was within this perilous context that Augustine would have to make the identity and purpose of his Church relevant, and hence only afterwards credible to the native populace. This credibility would be possible only with the involvement of Cyprian of Carthage, North Africa's favourite son.[8]

Skipping ahead some thirty years to near the end of Augustine's prodigious life, the bishop of Hippo found himself in a situation both alike and utterly different from that which had begun his career. The same Donatist Church, which had been the target of his opposition at the onset of his career, was reeling from a potent mix of legal setbacks, errant leadership, Catholic immigration from the north shores of the Mediterranean (caused by the incursions of Germanic groups, especially the *Vandali*), and a sustained pastoral initiative by Augustine's resurgent Church. The bishop's familiar Roman world was showing signs of increasing contraction in the form of economic deterioration and military retreat.[9] Even as this failing regime was looking ever more to the Catholic

8 Geoffrey Willis referred to Cyprian in this case as 'the great national martyr of Africa…'; *Saint Augustine and the Donatist Controversy* (London: SPCK, 1950), 121.

9 Throughout this book the decline of the Roman Empire and civilization is interpreted through a lens advocated by Peter Heather, *The Fall of the Roman Empire* (London: Pan Books, 2006) and 'Why Did the Barbarian Cross the Rhine?', *Journal of Late Antiquity* 2/1 (2009), 3–29; Bryan Ward-Perkins, *The Fall of Rome and the End of Civilization* (Oxford: Oxford University Press, 2005); and Niall Ferguson, 'Complexity of Collapse: Empires on the Edge of Chaos', *Foreign Affairs* 89/2 (2010), 18–32. The central argument within this school of thought is that rather than positing Rome's gradual, multi-centennial decline, as popularised by authors such as Edward Gibbons and even scholars of North African Christianity, such as William Frend and Robert Markus, the decline was a sudden event for Roman citizens. It was precipitated by political-impasse, military defeat, uncontrollable immigration from the north

Church for order and solace, peace within the Christian religion was still an aspiration, and Augustine was locked into a bitter exchange against Christians he called 'Pelagians'. This new threat was unlike that which Augustine had experienced with his African compatriots. No longer was it a matter of who was most in line with Cyprian and his teaching, nor of who was corrupting the tradition and thought of the native population and Church in North Africa. At stake was an ideological/theological conflict with the potential to disrupt the entire Church of the early fifth century, as it would grow to include the input of leaders from places as far dispersed as Asia Minor, Rome, Jerusalem, Carthage, and Ravenna. Now being debated were topics as varied as original sin and its transmission, mortality, human goodness, the possibility for human improvement/perfection, religious life, Christology, sacramentology, and the role and ranking of individual churches and their corresponding relation to the world. At the same time, the Pelagian controversy became in some ways a rehashing of topics that had already been considered in the previous dispute with the Donatist Christians: the usefulness of baptism; Christology; ecclesiology; the possibility of human perfection; the relation between the world and the Church; and biblical exegesis.

What undoubtedly remained constant throughout this period was each side's need (though for different reasons) for a validating authority anchored in Christian tradition. The new threat placed Augustine in the defensive posture of having his Church considered 'rustic', peopled by provincially-minded 'Africans' and nasty 'Punics', with his enemies accusing him of attempting to impose his sectarian innovations on the rest of the catholic world. Again it was Cyprian of Carthage who would be employed by the respective camps to retake the high ground in the debate.

These were the two intense controversies separated by time, geography, theology, ideology, and name, that marked the beginning and end of Augustine's long career. At each turn, and in order to have his voice taken seriously, he would come to rely on an earlier Carthaginian bishop who had preceded him in life by 96 years. And so too would his opponents.

My aim in this book is therefore to examine Augustine within the context of the Donatist and Pelagian controversies and determine how his reactions, approaches, and methodologies changed throughout these conflicts. Central to this investigation is the legacy of Cyprian of Carthage and whether or how

---

and east, a collapse of trade, and extreme indebtedness and taxation levels. Thus the fall of the Roman Empire can be placed within the two generations or so beginning in the winter of 406 and the subsequent Germanic-tribe invasions, and 429–452, when Africa, Spain, Gaul (France), and Britain were lost and most economic/social exchanges ground to a virtual halt.

in each instance Augustine was required to modify this legacy depending on its reception by the opponent at hand. Augustine's appropriation of Cyprian was in each case prefaced by the fact that the Donatist Christians in the first controversy and the so-called Pelagians in the latter, both regarded Cyprian as a worthy example, vested with authority (*auctoritas*), and invaluable in corroborating a stance on doctrinal matters. In each case the parties involved equally claimed legitimate representation of Christian tradition as evinced by that singular authority, Cyprian of Carthage.

This point flows smoothly into the underlying focus of this book, namely: in the Donatist controversy (against those who claim to be the genuine heirs of the African Cyprianic tradition), Augustine distances himself from Cyprian at times and thus simultaneously upends traditional North African thinking. Yet in the Pelagian crisis (against the more 'Greek' or 'Eastern' theology of the Pelagians), he appeals unreservedly to and claims to speak exclusively for the Cyprian tradition. Where or how is Cyprian's patrimony similar or different in the two controversies with their respective camps? Likewise, where or how is Augustine's Cyprian identical or different in each controversy? Where is the legacy of Cyprian contiguous and where is there discontinuity? Does Augustine appeal to Cyprian during the Pelagian controversy in a way that he rejected in the Donatist controversy? Where and by whom is Cyprian most accurately interpreted? And where and by whom is he most incorrectly interpreted? What elements and situational factors play a role in these similarities or differences? Can we observe an interpretative evolution amongst the warring sides? And lastly, does a comparative analysis of the two controversies teach us anything about the elasticity or rigidity of the concepts of authority, innovation, tradition and orthodoxy in the ancient world? In other words, from the characters and groups involved, how were these concepts interpreted and applied by thinkers in the ancient world, both in terms of their own beliefs and ideas as well as those of others? The above set of questions frames the overall thrust of this study, which is to provide a first-ever content-minded and systematic analysis of the claims asserted by Augustine and his allies versus those of the Donatists and the Pelagians, in the endeavours of both sides to claim the authenticity of Christian tradition through the personage of Cyprian of Carthage.

In Part 1, three chapters are dedicated to assessing the beginning of Augustine's appropriation of Cyprian of Cathage's authority in the first decade of his ordained career, and the related events that helped shape the course of the anti-Donatist and Pelagian debates. Chapter 1 provides an overview of Augustine's first years as a priest and then as a young bishop in the 390s. As far as these can be determined from extant sources, I identify central early writings (letters, sermons, and tracts) that evince proto-themes that will endure through Augustine's polemic stylisations for the rest of his career. Chapter 2 is an analysis of Augustine's realisation of a need for an authority for his dealings with the Donatist Church leadership. Particular emphasis is placed on identifying what Augustine considered adequate authority in this heated environment, a discussion which branches into biblical authority; the approval of the universal Church and the continuity entailed therein; and lastly into his need for concrete North African ideas and personas in which to ground his argumentation. In Chapter 3 I analyse the oft-neglected impact of the intra-Donatist schism occasioned by the episcopal election of Primian of Carthage. This experience was central to Augustine's polemical development.

Part 2 is composed of three chapters that explore the substance of Augustine's campaign against Donatist Christianity and how he succeeded in applying rhetorical themes such as '*gratia*' and the role of the Holy Spirit to imperial legislation via the appropriated authority of Cyprian, for the suppression of his enemies. Chapter 4 is dedicated to exploring the stage that was set in the 400s when Augustine produced his first major anti-Donatist works, *Contra epistulam Parmeniani* (*C. ep. Parm.*) and *De baptismo* (*De bapt.*). Chapter 5 provides a comprehensive account of the way Augustine appropriated Cyprian and also the themes that Augustine coupled with this appropriation. Chapter 6 uses three cornerstone themes to analyse how Augustine sustained his appropriation of Cyprian: religious coercion (correction by man), divine grace, and the Holy Spirit. Chapter 7 and the Conclusion comprise Part 3 and provide the necessary appraisal of the way Augustine applied the newly-asserted authority of Cyprian against his Pelagian interlocutors.

Throughout the book, a number of emphases are present that must be disclosed straight away. First is the focus on the anti-Donatist and anti-Pelagian campaigns, which is mostly construed through the surviving accounts of Augustine. Though inevitably not entirely fair and balanced, this work is not intended to re-create the worldviews of those respective groups. Instead, it is an account of Augustine's approach to authority and how that changed his approach to the two groups. This work could be enriched in the future, however, by a more thorough reconstruction of Donatist Christianity as the Donatists understood themselves. Because of the reliance on Augustine and various biased Catholic sources, this endeavour is still somewhat tricky and will only be achieved through much labour. Also proffered throughout the work is a thematic analysis of Augustine's appropriation of Cyprian. What this means is that the various sources are viewed chiefly for their thematic content. This means that the contextual backgrounds of the sources and their impact upon the content are not in general accounted for. That task would offer much substance for future researches and publications. Third, considerable emphasis is placed on numerical data as a means of comparing important themes throughout the two controversies. This method is pursued for two reasons: it allows for a clear comparison in this particular book, but also provides material for future research. Likewise throughout, especially with original Latin texts, spelling matches the respective critical editions as closely as possible. A final comment is that in the course of the book, there is a greater emphasis on the impact of the Donatist controversy than on the Pelagian. There is a two-fold reason for this. It is not intended to downgrade the importance of the Pelagian controversy, but rather to provide a basis for a sequel to this work, and also to provide a new approach to themes that are found in the Pelagian controversy and their background in the Donatist controversy.

Reconsidering Donatism and Pelagianism in Light of Historical and Recent Approaches

Any entry into a discussion about the schisms, heresies, and Church infighting of late antiquity must be prefaced with caution, some general exegetical guidelines, and an analytical mindset. This is especially true for a reader who is new to this period of history. The Donatist and Pelagian controversies require a similar, if not greater, level of vigilance when under discussion, because neither shares a history free from biased interpretation and spin, having often been used as weapons in the Catholic/Protestant polemical arsenals or in prejudiced scholarship. This was just as true in the fifth century as it is in the modern era. Accordingly, this section of the introduction provides a review of the historical interpretation of the Donatist and Pelagian movements as well as that of current research, and offers some preliminary clarifications and 'rules of the road' with which to proceed.

All of the major characters and groups with whom I am concerned have been the objects of considerable research and documentation in the past century and half. What was for centuries the domain of Church apologists and sectarian enthusiasts blossomed in the mid-nineteenth century into the greater Western emphasis on empirically-based scientific methods over traditional scholarship. This period saw the beginning of a veritable flood of revised critical editions (including many vernacular translations), articles, and monographs. This outpouring is significant because before that time materials concerning Cyprian, Augustine, and Donatist and Pelagian Christians were sparse and were composed and kept for employment in various argumentative initiatives. The most classical examples that come to mind are Gotschalk of Orbais

(9th cent.); Erasmus and Jean Driedo (16th cent.); Martin Luther and Jean Calvin (16th cent.); and the *De Auxiliis* (1580s–90s) and Jansenist (esp. 17th cent.) controversies.[10] Works (in Latin and vernacular languages) on ancient North African Christianity and collections of Augustine's polemical works produced before the nineteenth century (in chronological order), include from the 16th century: Franciscus Balduinius, *Delibatio Africanæ historiæ ecclesiasticæ, sive Optati Mileuitani libri VII. ad Parmenianum de schismate donatistarum. Victoris Vticensis libri III. de persecutione Vandalica in Africa. Cum annotationibus ex Fr. Balduini,... Commentariis rerum ecclesiasticarum* (Paris, 1569) and *Historia Carthaginensis Collationis sive disputationis de ecclesia, olim habitae inter Catholics et Donatistas* (Paris, 1566);[11] Jacques de Foigny, *Epistre ou le Livre de St. Augustin de l'Unité de l'Eglise, contre Petilien, Evesque Donatiste, avec certaines observations pour entendre les lieux plus difficiles* (Rhiems, 1567);[12] and the first work printed outside of France: Caesar Baronius, *Annales Ecclesiastici*, tomes 3–5 (Cologne, 1601–08).[13]

The 17th century saw growth in this area, perhaps as a reaction to the Jansenist controversy, or due to the continued interest in mining polemical firepower from patristic sources. Among the works from this century are: Karl Schönmann, *S. Augustini liber sex Epistola de Unitate Ecclesiae contra Petiliani Donat. Epistolam, Argumentiis, Notis atque Analysi illustrata, studio Justi Caluini* (Leipzig, 1792–94);[14] the first work printed outside of continental Europe: Merici Casaubonus, *Optati Mel. de schismate Donatistarum libri VII.*

10 The entirety of the *De Auxiliis* affair is still unknown to most and is an area of only occasional research. This is important because of the number of countries, university faculties, religious orders, and highly ranked clerics (not least of whom was the future saint Robert Bellarmine) involved in this pan-European debate, as well as the relevance of the controversy to the theological trajectory that it influenced for centuries afterwards. One might consult E.J.M. van Eijl's exhaustive background treatments in: 'La Controverse Louvaniste Autour de la Grâce et du Libre Arbitre à la Fin du XVIe Siècle', in M. Lamberigts (ed.), *L'Augustinisme à l'Ancienne Faculté de Théologie de Louvain, Bibliotheca ephemeridum theologicarum Lovaniensium* 111 (Leuven: Peeters, 1994), 207–82, and 'Michael Baius (1513–1589)', *Louvain Studies* 5 (1975), 287–91. Also helpful are *L'Augustinisme à l'Ancienne Faculté de Théologie de Louvain* and A. Vanneste, 'Le «De prima hominis justicia» de M. Baius. Une relecture critique', 123–66, and M. Biersack, 'Bellarmin und die «Causa Baii»', 167–78.

11 Both of these were theological-historical tractates by the author. They were reprinted in the 18th century in the edition by Ellies du Pin, *Historia Donatistarum* (Paris: 1700).

12 This appears to be a very early, if not the earliest, vernacular treatment of Donatism in French; it is a theological-historical tractate.

13 A theological commentary.

14 A Latin edition of Augustine's texts.

In eosd. notae et emendationes Merici Casauboni (London: 1631). This text would be reprinted in E. Du Pin in 1690 (see below). The text that would cause a great stir via the Jansenist controversy was by Cornelius Jansenius: *Augustinus, sive doctrina S. Augustini de humanae naturae sanitate, aegritudine, medicina, adv. Pelagianos et Massilienses* (Leuven: 1640). The first in the Low Countries were Gerhard Johannes Vossius, *Historia Pelagiana sive Historiae de controversies quas Pelagius ejusque reliquiae moverunt* (Amsterdam, 1618); and Georgius Callistus, *SS. Cypriani et Augustiniani de unitate Ecclesiae tractatus* (Helmstedt, 1657).[15] From France there came, Henricus Valesius, *Historia ecclesiastica Eusebii Pamphili, Socratis scholastici, Hermiae Sozomeni, Theodoriti episcopi Cyri et Evagrii scholastici* (Paris: 1659), which had embedded in it his dissertation entitled *De schismate Donatistarum*. Then there was Jean Garnier, *Dissert. vii. quibus integra continentur Pelagianorum hist. Opera quaecumque extant/prodeunt nunc primum studio Joannis Garnieri...qui notas etiam ac dissertationes addidit* (Paris, 1673), the result of Garnier's effort to provide a complete history of Pelagianism with stronger emphasis on Julian of Aeclanum.[16] From Belgium came a work by the Augustinian monk Henry de Noris, *Historia Pelagiana et dissert. de Synodo Quinta Oecumen.* (Leuven, 1673, reprinted in 1702); and the first English work on Donatism is found in Thomas Long, *History of the Donatists* (London, 1677). These are followed by Emmanuel Schelstrate, *Ecclesia Africana* (Paris, 1679, reprinted in Antwerp: 1780); Melchior Leydecker, *Aurelii Augustini, Episcopi Hipponensis, Liber de Unitate Ecclesiae contra Donatistas* (Utrecht, 1690);[17] also by Leydecker, *Historia Ecclesiastica Africana* (Utrecht, 1690); Thomas Ittig, *De Haeresiarchis Aevi Apostolici Et Apostolico Proximi* (Leipzig, 1690–1703); the vernacular (French) work of Louis Ellies Du Pin, *Nouvelle bibliotheque des auteurs ecclesiastiques* [...]. *Tome III. Des auteurs ducinquiéme siecle de l'eglise* (Paris, 1690) contains a collection of works by Augustine. Du Pin is also credited with an edition of Optatus's *De schismate Donatistarum*

15 The last half of the original Latin title is: *Accedit Georgii Calixti, S. Theo. Doct. et in Acad. Julia Prof. primarii, in eorundem librorum lectionem Introductionis fragmentum edente Frid. Ulrico Calixto.*

16 Josef Lössl, 'Augustine, "Pelagianism", Julian of Aeclanum, and Modern Scholarship', *Zeitschrift für Antikes Christentum* 11 (2007), 148.

17 The last half of the Latin title, omitted above for brevity's sake, is: *Ext. cum Commentariis uberrimis et utillisimis in Melchioris Lydeckeri Historia illustrata Ecclesiae Africanae, cujus totum paene tomum secundum constituit inscriptum*: *Tomus secundus ad Librum Augustini de Unitate Ecclesiae contra Donatistas, de principiis Ecclesiæ Africanæ, illiusque fide in Articulis de Capite Christo et Ecclesia, de Unitate et Schismate, plurimisque Religionis Christianae capitibus agit. Ultrajecti apud viduam Guil. Clerck.*

libri septem, ad...codices et veteres editiones collati... Quibus accessêre Historia Donatistarum...nec non geographia episcopalis Africae (Paris, 1700); Hermann Witsius, *Miscellaneorum Sacrorum libri* (Amsterdam, 1692), contains his *Dissertatio de schismate Donatistarum*; Nikolaus Berg, *Divi Augustini liber de moderate coercendis haereticis ed. Bonifacium Comitem. Nic. Bergius Revalensis Holmiae* (Leipzig, 1696).

The 18th century followed roughly the same trajectory as previous centuries. However, towards the end of the century, at roughly the same time as the Enlightenment, there came the gradual emergence of a new type of source-study which integrated an approach to writing in an objective manner (for example, see Walch, 1768, below). A list from this period includes: the first vernacular Italian work by Domenico Bernino, *Historia di tutte l'heresie descritta da Domenico Bernino* (Venice, 1711), which contains a section on Donatist history; Ellies du Pin, *Monumenta vetera ad Donatistarum Historiam pertinenta* (Paris, 1700); the German vernacular work of J. Ph. Storren, *Asführlicher und gründlicher Bericht von den Namen, Ursprung, v.s.w. der Donatisten* (Frankfurt-am-Main: 1723); Louis Sebastien Le Nain de Tillemont, *Memoires pour servir a l'histoire Ecclésiastique, Tom. I, Histoire du schisme des Donatistes, où l'on marque aussi tou ce qui regarde' l'Eglise d'Afrique depuis l'an 305, jusques en l'an 391 que S. Augustin fut fait Prestre* (Paris, 1732) and also in: *Tom. XIII. La Vie de Saint Augustin, dans laquelle on trouvera l'histoire des Donatistes de son temps, et celle des Pelagiens* (Paris, 1732), and again in: *Mémoires pour servir à l'histoire ecclésiastique des six premiers siècles jusfifiez par les citations des auteurs originaux*, vol. 13 (Brussels, 1732), which contains an account of the life and work of Augustine; Henricus Norisius, *Opera omnia nunc prim. collecta et ordinata*, four vol. (Verona, 1729–32); Giuseppe Agostino Giuseppe Orsi, *Della Istoria Ecclesiastica descritta da F. Guiseppe Agostino Orsi*, vols. 4–5 (Rome, 1741–49) records a history of Donatism; Christian Wilhelm Franz Walch, *Entwurf einer vollständigen Historie der Ketzereien, Spaltungen und Religionsstreitigkeiten, bis auf die Zeiten der Reformation*, see Section 4 (Leipzig, 1768) initiates a new critical approach to ancient sources; Christian Wilhelm Franz Walch, *Ketzerhistorie*, Sections 4 and 5 (Leipzig, 1770); such a critical approach is continued in: Johann Mattheus Schröckh, *Christliche Kirchengeschichte*, see Sections 6 and 11 (Leipzig, 1784–86).[18]

18 For more detailed information on the historical background of Augustine/Cyprian/Donatist/Pelagian research see the bibliographical data in J. Lössl, 'Augustine, "Pelagianism", Julian of Aeclanum', 147–50; P. Schaff (ed.), J.R. King (trans.), *Nicene and Post-Nicene Fathers, Volume IV, St. Augustine: Writings against the Manicheans and against the*

The beginning of the 19th century marked the last decades of traditional source-reading and set the stage for the eventual emergence of an invigorated scientific approach in the middle part of the century. Authors and works from the first half of this century are: Stefano Antonio Morceli, *Africa christiana in tres partes distribute* (Brescia, 1816–17); Gustav Friederich Wiggers, *Versuch einer pragmatischen Darstellung des Augustinismus und Pelagianismus* (Hamburg, 1833), later translated into English (Andover, 1840); Adrianus Roux, *Dissertatio de Aurelio Augustino, adversario Donatistarum* (Leiden, 1838), a brief summary of the works and doctrine; Julius Müller, *Die christliche Lehre von der Sünde* (Wroclaw, 1838, published in English in Edinburgh, 1868); Justus Ludwig Jacobi, *Die Lehre des Pelagius* (Leipzig, 1842); Georg Friedrich Böhringer, *Die Kirche Christi in Biographien*, see Section 3 (Zürich, 1845); Johann Karl Ludwig Gieseler, *Kirchengeschichte*, vol. 2 (Bonn, 1845), which is more favourable towards Pelagianism; Neander, *Kirchengeschichte*. vol. 4 (1847, more Augustinian); P. Schaff, 'The Pelagian Controversy', in *Bibliotheca Sacra* 18 (1848); Theodore Gangauf, *Metaphysische Psychologie des heiligen Augustinus* (Augsburg, 1852); Carl Bindemann, *Der heilige Augustinus*, Sections 2–3 (1844–1869), which contain analyses of anti-Donatist works and a history of Augustine's life; Julius Müller, *Der Pelagianismus* (Berlin: 1854); Ferdinand Ribbeck, *Donatus und Augustinus oder der erste entscheidende Kampf zwischen Separatismus und Kirche. Ein Kirchenhistorischer Versuch von Ferdinand Ribbeck* (Elberfeld, 1857), which remains in the tradition of polemical writing; Henry Hart Milman, *History of Latin Christianity*, vol. 1 (New York, 1860), the first work on Augustine and Pelagianism/Donatism to come from the Americas; Friedrich Wörter, *Der Pelagianismus nach seinem Ursprung und seiner Lehre* (Freiburg, 1866); and Nourrisson, *La philosophie de S. Augustin*, 2 vols. (1866).

The watershed came not from one particular monograph but rather in an outburst of contributions. Works that stand out from the mid-nineteenth century include the initiation of J.-P. Migne's *Patrologiae cursus completus* series which covers most Greek and Latin patristic sources, and also the *Corpus Christianorum* series. (W. Hartel's CSEL editions of Cyprian were published between 1868–71 but Augustine's works were not put into new critical editions until 1891 with I. Zycha's first translations.) At this time English translations also began to appear, such as C. Thornton, *The Treatises of S. Caecilius Cyprian* (1839); and R.E. Wallis, *The Writings of Cyprian* (1868). A comprehensive effort also began to introduce the majority of patristic works into English in P. Schaff's,

---

Donatists (Grand Rapids, MI: Wm. Eerdmans Publishing, 1887, repr. 1996), 369–72; and John Chapman, 'Donatists', in C. Herbermann, et al. (eds.), *The Catholic Encyclopedia*, vol. 5 (New York: Robert Appleton Co., 1909), 129.

Nicene and Post-Nicene Fathers of the Christian Church series and the *Oxford Library of the Fathers*. Such serial projects were supported in Martin Deutsch, *Drei Actenstücke zur Geschichte Donatismus. Neu herausgegeben und erklärt von Martin Deutsch* (Berlin: 1875), the first work on the textual and historical criticism of the sources; D. Benedict's *History of the Donatists* (1875), however, would display a lingering tendency to integrate a polemical objective in related research.[19] Such polemicisation would be equalled by other promising works, such as Voelter, *Der Ursprung des Donatismus, nach den Quellen untersucht und dargestellt von Lic Dr. Daniel Voelter* (Freiburg/Tübingen: 1883), which attempts to portray Donatists more fairly. This period is remarkable overall in that a standard was set whereby texts began to be utilised less for ideological arguments and instead as objects of value and focus in themselves, demonstrating a concern for the contexts in which they were created.

By the advent of the twentieth century, numerous studies arrived on the scene whose authors are familiar to us today: e.g., Benson (1897), Monceaux (1901–23), Leclercq (1904–10s), and Martroye (1904–14). Additionally, ground was being gained in accelerating the release of more *CSEL* editions, especially concerning Augustine, at the same time as attention was being focused anew on his *Sermones* by A. Kunzelmann in the 1930s. Another major breakthrough was G. De Plinal's research filtering out Pelagian writings from Augustine's. At this stage in the history of Augustinian research an important trend emerged, the impact of which is felt even today. Patristics and late antiquity studies began to be pursued alongside archaeology in the Maghreb countries. Not only that, but greater emphasis was beginning to be placed on new disciplines such as sociology and group psychology. What remained constant through this rapid expansion was the premier position of French-language literature (followed by German and English), no doubt enhanced by the Republic's colonial involvement in North Africa, and, in the run up to the Second Vatican Council, an overall increased interest among scholars within French Catholicism, especially within the *Nouvelle Théologie* movement, in an enhanced understanding of the traditions and teachings of the early Church.[20]

---

19 David Benedict, *History of the Donatists with Notes* (Providence, RI: Nickerson, Sibley & Co., 1875).

20 Catholicism in Europe in the early to mid-twentieth century witnessed a blossoming of interest in research into the early Church and particularly in Augustine, which culminated at the Second Vatican Council (1962–65). See Jürgen Mettepenningen, 'Más allá del déficit de téologia (1930–1965): La "nouvelle théologie" y el redescrubrimiento de Agustín', *Augustinus* 55 (2010), 165–84 and *Nouvelle Théologie – New Theology: Inheritor of Modernism, Precursor of Vatican II* (London: T&T Clark, 2010).

By the 1960s, study of the ancient North African Church had attained a level of sophistication hitherto unknown. By this time some of the most paradigm-setting individuals had emerged, including such well-known scholars as G. Willis, P. Brown, M. Bévenot, T.J. van Bavel, Y. Congar, H. Chadwick, C. Mayer, W.H.C. Frend, R. Crespin, R. Evans, E. Tengström, S. Lancel, P.-P. Verbraken, V. Grossi, and G. Bonner. This generation opened up a previously unimagined array of different areas for late antique research by penetrating deep into the texts and upending assumptions, as evidenced in the bountiful numbers of articles, anthologies, and monographs from that period. Also noteworthy was the inauguration of serials (which are still being added to today) such as the *Sources chrétiennes*, *Ancient Christian Writers*, *Bibliothèque Augustinienne*, and the *Corpus Christianorum Series Latina*. At the same time new journals and research centres were springing up. Energy was invested in understanding Pelagians, Donatists, and Catholics, not as heretics, schismatics, or nemeses, but as subjects with integral historical backgrounds. The study of Augustine and Cyprian had moved beyond hagiography and proof-texting and into comprehending their real identities, motivations, and legacies. This same generation's work is the essential condition for today's level of knowledge in the area.

In the decades since, and now well into the 21st century, there has been a steady growth in just about all matters touching upon Augustine, Cyprian, the Pelagians and Donatists, and indeed the whole context of late antique Christianity, which it is not possible to summarise here. One need only look at the considerable projects (some still in progress) on the product end of research, such as the *Augustinus-Lexikon*, *Augustine Through the Ages*, *Augustin Handbuch*, the *Cetedoc Library of Christian Latin Texts* and the *Corpus Augustinianum Gissense* databases, the new interactive, multi-lingual online system available at www.findingaugustine.org, as well as the myriad vernacular translations underway, such as *The Works of St. Augustine: A Translation for the 21st Century* (English), and the *Augustinus Opera-Werke* and *Fontes Christiani* (German). Most spectacular, however, was the uncovering in the 1980s of the *Dolbeau Sermons* and *Divjak Letters* (1970s). It is not easy to convey the rarity of finding previously forgotten/lost works of Augustine (or any other ancient writer for that matter). Their introduction has been a considerable boost for Augustinian studies and enhances our understanding of late antique Africa, and naturally they are utilised in this work.

In this period specialisation has been achieved in the study of persons as disparate as Optatus of Milevis, Pelagius, Tyconius, Julian of Aeclanum, Possidius of Calama, Tertullian, Primian and Parmenian, and Cyprian. Categories and themes as varied as religious coercion, divine grace, Augustine's *Sermons*, episcopal elections, biblical exegesis, cross-maritime ecclesial and political relations, the development of orthodoxy, and Christian architecture, have been and continue to be taken up. Energy continues to pour into the task of perceiving Augustine and Cyprian and their interlocutors, their thought and context, more clearly and intricately than ever before.[21] So too Pelagians and Donatists have been (and are still) investigated in order to better situate them in their own proper historical realities, rather than as suspects in a criminal investigation[22] English-language students of Donatism and Augustine will be given an inestimably valuable tool in 2016–2017 when the anti-Donatist works will be published in their entirety for the first time in English.[23] Nonetheless, despite the focus on the topics that are discussed here, not everything that demands closer examination has been approached and many areas await further treatment. One area remains open to question and that is the reception of Cyprian by Augustine, the Donatists, and the Pelagians. A detailed study of Augustine's appropriation of Cyprian has never been attempted before and that is what makes this particular work the logical next step.[24]

21 A few of the scholars associated with Augustinian studies: J.J. O'Donnell, C. Harrison, R. Dodaro, F. van Fleteren, A. Fitzgerald, J. Van Oort, A. De Veer, D. Weber, R. Eno, A. Di Bernardino. On Cyprian: M. Sage, P. Burns, E. Dassmann, and G. Dunn.

22 For studies of Pelagianism, a few of the authors that stand out are: J. Lössl, O. Wermelinger, T. De Bruyn, G. Greshake, N. Cipriani, and M. Lamberigts. For works on Donatism: M. Tilley, A. Mandouze, J. Merdinger, C. Lepelley, B. Kriegbaum, S. Their, B.R. Rees, J.-L. Maier, and A. Schindler.

23 New City Press anticipates *WSA* volumes I/21 and 22, translated by Maureen Tilley, to be available in 2016–17.

24 This initiative was called for explicitly in G. Dunn, 'The Reception of the Martyrdom of Cyprian of Carthage in Early Christian Literature', in Johan Leemans (ed.), *Martyrdom and Persecution in Late Antique Christianity: Festschrift Boudewijn Dehandschutter, Bibliotheca ephemeridum theologicarum Lovaniensium* 241 (Leuven: Peeters, 2010), 76.

PART 1

Augustine's Early Years as a Church Leader and Initial Reactions to Donatist Christianity

CHAPTER 1

Augustine's First Years of Ministry, the 390s

Augustine returned to Africa from the Italian peninsula in 388 and by 390/91 had entered ministry in Hippo as a presbyter (priest). This move also marked a period of transformation from an energetic newly-ordained with a view of humanity as capable of self-mastery and spiritual satisfaction, to a man with an increasingly negative view of humanity as totally reliant on grace.[1] It is helpful to recount how this occurred.[2]

Upon entering the priesthood, Augustine faced dealing with the deeply-entrenched Donatist Church and an intimidated Catholic minority,[3] a reality he was less prepared to deal with than he expected,[4] particularly in light

1 This was a matter which has been treated before in Maureen Tilley, 'Augustine's Unacknowledged Debt to the Donatists', in ed. P.-Y. Fux, J.-M. Roessli, O. Wermlinger (eds.), *Augustinus Afer: Saint Augustin: africanité et universalité. Actes du colloque international, Alger-Annaba, 1–7 avril 2001* (Paradosis 45/1), (Fribourg: Éditions Universitaires Fribourg, 2003), 141–48. See esp. 141: '[Augustine] moved from being a man who firmly believed and hoped that Christians could reach a sort of perfection in this life to one who doubted the possibility'.

2 It is important to state here that Augustine of the 380s/390s was not completely different or 'other' from the Augustine of the 410s/420s as is sometimes suggested in the literature. C. Harrison has demonstrated persuasively that many of the themes in Augustine's 'mature' theology are in fact traceable to the time of his conversion in 386 and his earliest writings afterwards; 'The early works (386–96)', in T.J. van Bavel (ed.), *Saint Augustine* (Brussels: Mercatorfonds/Augustinian Historical Institute, 2007), 165–80. My contention adds to Harrison's: before his intensive exegesis of Paul, Augustine was propelled to develop theologies of original sin and grace under the influence of his pastoral/personal experiences with the Donatist Church.

3 This realization was probably immediate for Augustine; Willis, *Saint Augustine and the Donatist Controversy*, 26. The Donatists were the majority religion in Hippo Regius and its environs, with strong backing from the citizenry; Aug., *Ioh ev. tr.* 6, 25; *C. ep. Parm.* 1, 17–18; *C. litt. Pet.* 1, 24, 26; 2, 83, 184; Poss., *Vita Aug.* 7, 2. On the diffusion of Donatist Christianity, see also Paul MacKendrick, *The North African Stones Speak* (Chapel Hill, NC: University of North Carolina Press, 2000), 261–83. Catholics were reportedly often threatened by Donatist Circumcelliones; *En. in Ps.* 10, 5; *C. ep. Parm.* 2, 4; *C. litt. Pet.* 1, 26; 2, 65; *Cresc.* 3, 15–16; *Ep.* 43,24; 76, 3; 87, 4–5, but it is important to recall this is reported by a less-than-objective Augustine whose perspective is nonetheless indispensible.

4 Poss., *Vita Aug.* 5.4; Augustine relates in *Ep.* 21,2 that he became tearful and overcome at the time of his ordination on realising the burden of priesthood: '[T]his was the reason for those tears that some of the brothers noticed that I shed in the city at the time of my ordination…'; English translation taken from R. Teske, WSA II/1, (trans.), J. Rotelle (ed.), (Hyde Park,

 | DOI 10.1163/9789004312647_003

of what he had experienced in his initial adult faith formation in the Italian churches of Milan and Rome.[5] On the one hand, Augustine would be pitted against the African, or Donatist, Church, which was particularly dominant in his region of Africa (Numidia).[6] On the other hand, the Catholic Church in Africa had its own traditions which were unique within the empire and with

NY: New City Press, 2001), 55. The largely neglected role and impact of Valerius of Hippo in the life of Augustine is a topic receiving renewed interest in recent years with a number of groundbreaking articles; Edward Smither, 'An Unrecognized and Unlikely Influence? The Impact of Valerius of Hippo on Augustine', *Irish Theological Quarterly* 72 (2007), 251–64; Michael Cameron, 'Valerius of Hippo: A Profile', *Augustinian Studies* 40/1 (2009), 5–26; and Allan Fitzgerald, 'When Augustine Was Priest', *Augustinian Studies* 40/1 (2009), 37–48.

Not only did Augustine not know 'Punic' but he also did not know 'Libyan' (though these languages were nevertheless vaguely understood); William Frend, *The Donatist Church: A Movement of Protest in Roman North Africa* (Oxford: Clarendon Press, 1952, reprinted 1970), 233. This fact would surface in Augustine's disputation with Petilian of Constantine later (the target of his *C. litt. Pet.*), see Frend, *The Donatist Church*, 255. Examples of Augustine's lack of familiarity with Numidia include statements indicating he did not know where the dominant Auras Mountains were, or that olives were a major export, when Numidia was the largest exporter in the Mediterranean; *s.* 46, 39. This lack of knowledge also seems to indicate that his area of travel and pastoral work was chiefly in the precincts of the Romanised areas along the coast and in inland Proconsularia. To be objective, however, as a Catholic priest and then bishop, his travels would necessarily only have required him to visit liminal cities (especially Carthage) because those were the Catholic population centres. This point is thoroughly covered in O. Perler and J.L. Maier, *Les voyages de saint Augustin* (Paris: Études Augustiniennes, 1969).

These rather minor details would have been highly symbolic to the Numidians and Mauretanians, who would have identified Augustine's ignorance with the condescension that they had come to expect from Roman elites. This perhaps explains Augustine's naïveté in dealing with Donatist cultural sensitivities, such as his notion that he could somehow 'wake-up' the Donatists a bit with some mild persecution, *Cresc.* 2, 25; *Ep.* 93,5.

5 Gerald Bonner, 'Christus Sacerdos: The Roots of Augustine's Anti-Donatist Polemic', in *Signum Pietatis 40. Festgabe für Cornelius Petrus Mayer OSB zum 60 Geburtstag* (Cassiciacum 40), ed. A. Zumkeller (Würzburg: Augustinus Verlag, 1989), 327; M. Tilley, 'Augustine's Unacknowledged Debt to the Donatists', 144.

6 Donatist Christians were often found to take pride in their isolation, see F. Martroye, 'Une tentative de révolution sociale en Afrique. Donatistes et circoncelliones', *Revue des questions historiques* 76 (1904), 389–90; Serge Lancel, *Saint Augustine*, ed. A. Nevill (London: SCM, 2002), 162. There has been some question through past decades about the proper name for the Church that Augustine was opposed to in Africa. I use the term Donatist because this was a polemical term affected by the Catholics, although for the purpose of accuracy I side with Brent Shaw's distinction that they should nonetheless be labelled the Donatist Church in an imperialistic sense; see *Sacred Violence: African Christians and Sectarian Hatred in the Age of Augustine* (Cambridge: Cambridge University Press, 2011), 5–6.

which he would have to contend.[7] Added to this complication was the fact that the Roman Empire maintained an ever-changing relationship with the Donatist Church. Sometimes the Donatist Church had the support of the government; sometimes it was opposed and persecuted.[8]

The Donatists created one of the greatest challenges to the first decades of Augustine's ministry as they applied pressure on a pastoral/theological basis, as well as in terms of day-to-day objectives.[9] Not only were the Donatists the majority Church and intensely eager to defend the wellbeing of their communities and culture, but more important was their powerful claim to be the only authentic and genuinely rooted Church in North Africa, confident heirs of the heroic martyr-bishop, Cyprian of Carthage.[10] For Augustine to presume any level of authority in his efforts, he would have the task of tapping into the Donatist claim to being sole possessors of the North African tradition. This task could be performed most effectively by usurping the Donatists' exclusive hold on the teachings and legacy of Cyprian, and then refining these teachings when

---

7 Among these variances was the North African penchant for maintaining a position of equality with other sees in the western Mediterranean, even with Rome, although this tendency declined towards the end of Augustine's life, as attested to in the Divjak Letters; see Jane Merdinger, *Rome & the African Church in the Time of Augustine* (New Haven, CT: Yale University Press, 1997), esp. 43–49, 205; for unique para-liturgical rites, Aug., *s.* 311, 5 (*PL* 38, 1415); and the distinction (within North Africa at least) of the Catholic Church as concentrated in liminal cities with more Latinised populations and less successful in the African interior. For the sociological underpinnings of this phenomenon, see Frend, *The Donatist Church*, esp. pp. 1–93; Peter Brown, 'Christianity and Local Culture in Late Roman Africa,' *Journal of Roman Studies* 58 (1968), 85–95, reprinted in Peter Brown, *Religion and Society in the Age of Augustine* (London: Faber & Faber, 1972), 283; and Maureen Tilley, 'North Africa', in *The Cambridge History of Christianity, Volume 1, Origins to Constantine*, ed. M. Mitchell and F. Young (Cambridge: Cambridge University Press, 2006), 383.

8 The main historical examples are: Constantine's scrutiny of Donatism (312–37), the Marcarian persecution (346–48), toleration by Julian (361–63), and the uprising of Gildo and Optatus of Thamugadi (late 390s).

9 Among his central priorities in this period were adapting himself to being a theologian *and* a pastor; speaking about the truth; revising the mission and accentuating the importance of the unity of the Church; and emphasising the role of the bible in interpreting daily activities in the life of the Church and in the world. This is succinctly recapped in Vittorio Grossi, 'Gli Scritti di Agostino Prosbitero (391–96),leMotivazioniPrincipali', http://www.cassiciaco.it/navigazione/scriptorium/settimana/1991/grossi.html, (L'Associazione storico-culturale Sant' Agostino, 1991).

10 Lancel stipulates in this regard that: 'Actually, the Donatists had remained faithful to the doctrine of St Cyprian in this matter [i.e., rebaptism] whereas the rest of the African Church had renounced it following the council of Arles in 314', *Saint Augustine*, 172.

doing so was advantageous for the Catholic position, while at the same time disregarding elements that seemed irreconcilable. It would be to Augustine's credit that he managed to implement such a strategy, and this section covers the way Augustine came to identify his criticisms of the Donatist Church and his eventual arrival at the need for an authority source such as Cyprian.

What Augustine's Earliest Writings Tell Us

Writings from the first years of Augustine's ministry provide key insights into the way in which he developed his approach to the Donatist Church. An analysis of his *epistulae*, *sermones*, and *ennarationes in psalmos*, from roughly the years 390–400, provides the appropriate background information for what appears to be a transformation from hopeful young cleric to one readily crafting new polemical themes to use against rivals unwilling to enter into dialogue.

Augustine's *epistulae* from the years 391–395 provide the most comprehensive early insights, with his anti-Donatist *sermones* and *ennarationes in psalmos* coming more into focus in the years 395–400. These earliest letters provide important evidence of the emotional and attitudinal approach Augustine initially took towards Donatist leaders. This evidence offers another dimension in interpreting Augustine's approach in these formative years, complementing what we can glean from his engagement with two specifically anti-Donatist works of the period 391–95, *Psalmus contra partem Donati* (393) and the now lost *Contra epistulam Donati heretici* (393/94).[11]

Two times in *Ep.* 19 and *Ep.* 20, written in 390/91, Augustine reveals his central concern for the truth or *veritas*,[12] and his willingness to share his excitement in his faith with anyone who will listen to him. He expresses joy in encouraging others to 'seek the truth'[13] which he describes intimately: 'For everything that is alive in you has been revealed to me in a short time, almost as if the covering of the body had been torn open'.[14] Already, however, there is some indication Augustine is becoming knowledgeable about the division within African Christianity. Still, in *Ep.* 20, he discusses his hope that the 'one faith

11 Aug., *Retract.* 1, 21.

12 In *Ep.* 19,1, Augustine describes the arrival of the truth in the following way (*WSA* II/1, 52): 'No one, after all, sees in the book itself or in the author he reads that what he reads is true, but sees it rather in himself, if a certain light of truth is impressed upon his mind, a light which is bright in the ordinary way and is most far removed from the impurity of the body'.

13 *Ep.* 19,1 (*WSA* II/1, 52).

14 *Ep.* 19,1 (*WSA* II/1, 52).

and devotion, which is the Catholic faith alone, may also come to your house'. This may be achieved, he adds, through a 'reasonable fear of God…by reading the word of God and by serious conversation'.[15] In a manner relevant to themes Augustine would develop in subsequent years, he declares these approaches prevent the error that he was beginning to understand more fully day-to-day in Hippo: 'For there is hardly anyone concerned about the state of his soul and, for this reason, intent upon seeking the will of the Lord without any stubbornness who by using a good guide does not distinguish the difference between some sect and the one Catholic Church'.[16]

These first two letters, then, provide the correct preface with which to discern the rather dramatic internal revolution Augustine would experience in that same period after his ordination. An example of the young priest's reaction is contained in *Ep.* 21 to his bishop Valerius (dated 391):[17]

> …I suffered violence because of the merits of my sins…But I think that my Lord wanted to correct me in that way precisely because I dared…to reprimand the mistakes of many sailors before I had experienced what is involved in their work. And so, after I was launched into the middle of the sea, I began to feel the rashness of my reprimands though even earlier I judged this ministry to be filled with perils. And this was the reason for those tears…I have experienced this much more, very much more extensively than I thought…[18]

It seems quite clear from such passages that Augustine is reacting to a complete lack of responsiveness from those in his outlying city. And more importantly than simply feeling defeated, this turn of events seems to herald for

15 Ep. 20,3 (*WSA* II/1, 54).

16 *Ep.* 20,3 (*WSA* II/1, 54).

17 *Ep.* 21 is touched upon in Peter Brown, *Augustine of Hippo: A Biography* (Berkeley/Los Angeles: University of California Press, 1967/2000), 132. William Babcock takes up a more thorough examination in 'Augustine's Interpretation of Romans (A.D. 394–96)', *Augustinian Studies* 10 (1979), 55–74. A more recent reconsideration is observable in Fitzgerald, 'When Augustine Was Priest', 41–43, and Matthew Gaumer, 'The Development of the Concept of Grace in Late Antique North Africa', *Augustinianum* 50/1 (2010), 163–88.

18 Aug., *Ep.* 21,1–2 (*WSA* II/1, 55–56), (*CCSL* 31, 48–49): '…rito peccatorum meorum…Sed arbitror dominum meum propterea me sic emendare uoluisse, quod multorum peccata nautarum, antequam expertus essem, quid illic agitur, quasi doctior et melior reprehendere audebam. Et hinc erant illae lacrimae…Sed multo, ualde multo amplius expertus sum, quam putabam'. For more background also see Allan Fitzgerald, 'Augustine the Preacher', in *Saint Augustine*, ed. T.J. van Bavel (Brussels: Mercatorfonds/Augustinian Historical Institute, 2007), 143–50, esp. 143.

Augustine an existential crisis from which he will not easily be able to escape. We can gain yet further insight of this in the years directly after his ordination as presbyter. *Ep.* 23, composed c. 391–95, continues to define Augustine's angst. The letter is ostensibly to Maximinus, the Donatist bishop of Sinti (Numidia), on the question of the rebaptism of a Catholic deacon. Concerning this rebaptism, Augustine records, 'I was deeply saddened both over his wretched fall and over your unexpected crime, my brother.'[19] The second part of Augustine's description occasions greater interest as it seems to reveal the true source of his pain.[20] Here he writes, 'But you are unaware that we are commanded by God to call you "brother," so that we say even to those who deny that they are our brothers, "You are our brothers"...'[21] But this desire is dashed by the Donatists' refusal to go along with Augustine and the realisation that the Donatist Church is much mightier and more entrenched than he ever thought possible: '...seize the freedom of Christ...seize it, I beg you'.[22] He then continues, 'In the sight of Christ do not fear the reproach or do not be terrified at the power of any human being. The honour of this world is passing; its pride is passing'.[23] In a sense then, it is easy to see Augustine as distraught by the disunion with Maximinus as by the status of his deacon: 'I was aroused by the tortures of the bitterest sorrow over the true death of a brother. By the help of the Lord's mercy and providence, some compensation will perhaps soothe this pain of mine'.[24]

Further evidence of Augustine's Donatist predicament can be found in 395 in *Ep.* 29. The evidence from this letter is among the most revealing in terms of what Augustine understood his mission to be at that time, that is, to be an apologist for the Catholic Church seeking dialogue with the Donatist Christians. He reveals here why he thinks his mentor Valerius was so keen to ordain him: '[Valerius] did not hesitate to lay upon my shoulders the very dangerous burden of commenting on the words of truth on their [the Donatists'] account,

19 *Ep.* 23,2 (*WSA* II/1, 64).

20 This angst or pain seems to be located in Augustine's desire for communion with Donatist leaders. A lack of success in that pursuit leads him to record stoically: 'For you are not unaware, nor is any human being who knows us unaware, that you are not my bishop and that I am not your priest'; *Ep.* 23,1 (*WSA* II/1, 63). And yet Augustine's zeal to reach out remains obvious to the reader.

21 *Ep.* 23,1 (*WSA* II/1, 64).

22 *Ep.* 23,3 (*WSA* II/1, 65), (*CCSL* 34, 66): 'Arripe libertatem christianam, frater Maximine, arripe, quaeso te'.

23 *Ep.* 23,3 (*WSA* II/1, 65), (*CCSL* 34, 66): 'In contemplatione Christi aut reprehensionem uerearis aut exhorreas potestatem. Transit honor huius saeculi, transit ambitio'.

24 *Ep.* 23,8 (*WSA* II/1, 68).

and he often said to them that his prayers were answered when we arrived'.[25] Again he comments later in his *Confessions* on his sense of being overwhelmed by this mission in a way that mirrors his account in *Ep.* 21 and *Ep.* 23 (see below). Therefore, it is appropriate to quote here at length:

> In this appeal [to the Donatists] I acted as our protector and ruler which gave me the energy and power for the magnitude of the problem and the danger. I did not evoke their tears, but when I said such things, I admit, I was caught up in their weeping and could not hold back my own. And when we had both equally wept, I brought my sermon to an end with the fullest hope of their correction.[26]

We learn from writings of only a few years later that this issue was still resonating with Augustine. From the *Confessions*, namely the section written between 397–401, we gather that the bishop was not only grappling with the issue of grace (particularly pertaining to his own life and narrative), but possibly also that his Donatist rivals were the effective cause behind the memoir since he was, and would continue throughout his career, to be challenged for being a crypto-Manichean.[27] Augustine was nevertheless able to invoke a stirring

25 *Ep.* 29,7 (*WSA* II/1, 98).

26 *Ep.* 29,7 (*WSA* II/1, 98), (*CCSL* 34, 118–19): 'In qua conquestione sic actum, ut pro negotii atque periculi magnitudine tutor et gubernator noster animos facultatemque praebebat. non ego illorum lacrimas meis lacrimis moui, sed cum talia dicerentur, fateor, eorum fletu praeuentus meum abstinere non potui. Et cum iam pariter fleuissemus, plenissima spe correctionis illorum finis sermonis mei factus est'.

27 For the hypothesis that the *Confessiones* was an *apologia pro vita sua* against Donatist adversaries, consult P. De Labriolle, 'Pourquoi saint Augustin a-ti-il rédigé des Confessiones?', *Bulletin de l'Association Guillaume Budé* (1926), 34–39; Max Wundt, 'Zur Chronologie augustinischer Schriften', *Zeitschrift für die neutestamentliche Wissenchaft und die Kunde der älteren Kirche* 21 (1922), 128–35; M. Wundt, 'Augustins Konfessionen', *Zeitschrift für die neutestamentliche Wissenchaft und die Kunde der älteren Kirche* 22 (1923), 161–206. The emphasis on the Confessions as a theological/spiritual-growth biography is advocated in Aimé Solignac, 'Introduction aux Confessions', *BA* 13, *Les Confessions* I–VII (Paris: Desclée de Brouwer, 1962), 45–54. This is further examined in (and in notations from): Mathijs Lamberigts, 'Augustinus' Confessiones. Enkele beschouwingen', *Kleio* 23 (1993), 24–46. Indeed, this matter is still debated today, with one camp arguing that there is a discernible rupture in Augustine's position before the Pelagian controversy, and another arguing that there is more continuity than novel deployment. Scholars inclined towards the 'rupture thesis' include Brown, *Augustine of Hippo: A Biography*; J. Patout Burns, *The Development of Augustine's Doctrine of Operative Grace*, Collection des Études Augustiniennes, Série Antiquité 82 (Paris: Études augustiniennes, 1980); Kurt Flasch, Logik *des Schreckens.*

rhetorical refrain, accusing the Donatists of vindicating themselves by their pride. It was this same pride that so affected Augustine he would later be led to describe it in the following way:

> Filled with terror by my sins and my load of misery I had been turning over in my mind a plan to flee into solitude, but you forbade me, and strengthened me by your words. *To this end Christ died for all,* you reminded me, *that they who are alive, may live not for themselves, but for him who died for them* [2 Cor. 5:15]...[Christ] has redeemed me with his blood. Let not the proud disparage me, for I am mindful about my ransom. I eat it, I drink it, I dispense it to others, and as a poor man I long to be filled with it among those who are fed and feasted...Those who seek him praise the Lord.[28]

Augustinus von Hippo, De diversis quaestionibus ad Simplicianum 1, 2. Deutsche Erstübersetzung von Walter Schäfer. Herausgegeben und erklärt von Kurt Flasch. Zweite, verbesserte Auflage mit Nachwort—Excerpta classica 8 (Mainz: Dieterichsche Verlagsbuchhandlung, 1995); Gaetano Lettieri, *L'altro Agostino. Ermeneutica e retorica della grazia dalla crisi alla metamorfosi del De doctrina christiana* (Brescia: Morcelliana, 2001); and Athanase Sage, 'Péché originel. Naissance d'un dogme', *Revue des Études Augustiniennes* 13 (1967), 211–48. Those defending the 'continuity thesis' include: Nello Cipriani, 'L'altro Agostino di G. Lettieri', *Revue des Études Augustiniennes* 48 (2002), 249–65; Volker Drecoll, *Die Entstehung der Gnadenlehre Augustins.* Beiträge zur historischen Theologie 109 (1999); Anthony Dupont, 'Continuity or Discontinuity in Augustine? Is There an "Early Augustine" and What Does He Think on Grace?', *Ars Disputandi* 8 (2008), 67–79; Carol Harrison, *Rethinking Augustine's Early Theology: an Argument for Continuity* (Oxford: Oxford University Press, 2006); Pierre-Marie Hombert, *Gloria gratiae. Se glorifier en Dieu, principe et fin de la théologie augustinienne de la grâce.* Collection des Études Augustiniennes, Série Antiquité 148 (Paris: Études augustiniennes, 1996); Goulven Madec, 'Sur une nouvelle introduction à la pensée d'Augustin', *Revue des études augustiniennes* 28 (1982), 100–11; and T. Ring, 'Bruch oder Entwicklung im Gnadenbegriff Augustins? Kritische Anmerkungen zu K. Flasch, Logik des Schreckens. Augustinus von Hippo, Die Gnadenlehre von 397', *Augustiniana* 44 (1994), 31–113.

28 Aug., *Conf.* 10,70 (*WSA* I/1, 283), (*CCSL* 27, 193): 'Conterritus peccatis meis et mole miseriae meae agitaueram corde meditatus que fueram fugam in solitudinem, sed prohibuisti me et confirmasti me dicens: ideo christus pro omnibus mortuus est, ut qui uiuunt iam non sibi uiuant, sed ei qui pro ipsis mortuus est. ecce, domine, iacto in te curam meam, ut uiuam, et considerabo mirabilia de lege tua. tu scis imperitiam meam et infirmitatem meam: doce me et sana me. ille tuus unicus, in quo sunt omnes thesauri sapientiae et scientiae absconditi, redemit me sanguine suo. non calumnientur mihi superbi, quoniam cogito pretium meum et manduco et bibo et erogo et pauper cupio saturari ex eo inter illos, qui edunt et saturantur: et laudant dominum qui requirunt eum'.

A final clue to Augustine's disposition entering into his anti-Donatist campaign is found in *Ep.* 52, dated to 399–400. In this letter he writes to his Donatist relative Severinus as follows:

> [The Donatists] cut themselves off from the unity of Christ by a most wicked schism... But some sort of carnal habit, brother Severinus, holds you there, and long have I grieved, long have I groaned, and long that I desired to see you in order to speak with you about this topic. After all, what good does temporal health and relationship do if we scorn in our thinking the eternal heritage of Christ and everlasting salvation?[29]

This passage in *Ep.* 52 is essential for understanding Augustine's state of mind as he approached the year 400, the year that his anti-Donatist campaign would emerge with full force. Among the topics at the forefront of his mind were that the flesh (*caro/carnis*) lay at the source of the schism, and was causing his anguish. The ending is also quite telling for it reappears in his other letters and can be interpreted as a swipe at the material and institutional supremacy that the Donatist Church enjoyed during this specific period. It was the perceived pride of the Donatist leaders Augustine encountered that led him to assert that they rejected the truth because they had displaced Christ from the centre of their faith.[30] This was a radical realisation for him, especially in terms of his rhetorical approach, one that would eventually stimulate Augustine to directly question the Donatist belief in their purity and holiness as baptised of the 'rightful' Church. This issue would resurface later when Augustine would advocate initial baptismal grace and personal will were insufficient for salvation over a lifetime. These matters became not only theological talking points, but also areas where Augustine increasingly came to realise the Donatist Church was vulnerable.

---

29 *Ep.* 52,3–4 (*WSA* II/1, 203), (*CCSL* 34, 151): 'ne partem Donati conscinderent, et non dubitauerunt illo tempore falsas suspiciones suas obicientes pacem Christi unitatemque disrumpere et uos uidetis. Sed nescio quae carnalis consuetudo, frater Seuerine, ibi uos tenet; et olim doleo, olim gemo maxime prudentiam tuam cogitans et olim te uidere desidero, ut de hac re tecum loquerer. Quid enim prodest uel salus uel consanguinitas temporalis, si aeternam Christi hereditatem salutemque perpetuam in nostra cognitione contemnimus?'

30 To this effect, Augustine noted: 'Si et uos toleratis malos, quare non in unitate, ubi nemo rebaptizat nec altare est contra altare? Malos tantos toleratis, sed nulla bona mercede, quia quod debetis pro Christo, pro Donato uultis ferre'; *Ps. c. Don.* 293–94 (*CSEL* 51, 14–15).

The Gradual Emergence of Anti-Donatist Themes

The shock that Augustine experienced as a newly ordained, described in *Ep.* 21 and later expressed in his *Confessions,* is only the opening chapter in the development of his polemic during this period. This same period is also central in understanding how Augustine's approach to Donatist Christianity changed, and how he would arrive at the authority of Cyprian as the bulwark of his campaign against the Donatists and then later against the Pelagians. The first group of documents to be analysed here are his letters written between 391 and 400/401: *Ep.* 22, 23, 29, 32, 33, 34, 35, 43, 44, 49, 51, 52, and 53, which signal the lead-up to the maturation of Augustine's anti-Donatist effort.

Among the central themes to emerge early on, I identify three broad groupings within Augustine's letters. The first thematic group is the attestation of his personal experience, which feeds into a theological anthropology that was to greatly influence the course of his subsequent works. The second is his articulation of a difference between the Catholic faith he immersed himself in whilst in Italy, and the African Church that now surrounded him. And the third is his arrival at theological principles intended to create a distinction between the Catholic and Donatist positions.[31]

The Pride of the Donatists

Beyond Augustine's initial reaction to the Donatist leaders, which he expressed with a deep level of angst, is his interpretation of Donatist behaviour in light of an enhanced anthropology that sees humankind marked by corrupted flesh. Augustine would later answer this view with a theology of grace: the grace of Christ, and grace via the sacraments within the one, true Church. This development centred on a consideration of pride, or *superbia*, which he saw in the Donatist leaders' refusal to enter into any dialogue about the truth; and in *Ep.* 22 (to Aurelius, Catholic bishop of Carthage), 33 (to Proculiean, Donatist

31 It is necessary to clarify how important it was from Augustine's standpoint to identify areas of difference, since the two communities shared many practices and beliefs in common; see M. Tilley, 'Theologies of Penance during the Donatist Controversy', *Studia Patristica* 35 (2001), 330–37, esp. 330. Perhaps one of the greatest historical oversights in Donatist studies is that too little emphasis has been placed on the formative influence of Optatus on Augustine's anti-Donatist polemical style. Indeed, criticisms of the Donatists for their ecclesiology, their alleged 'African' isolation from the rest of the Catholic Church, and their appeal to Cyprian as the defender of the Church's unity and peace, were all points that Augustine quite evidently inherited from Optatus of Milevis, the original 'Anti-Donatist'. For more on this, see Chapter 4.

bishop of Hippo), 43 (to a group of Donatist leaders), 53 (to Generosus, a Catholic layman in Constantina, Numidia) he comes back to this point repeatedly.

Already in 391 Augustine reports to Aurelius in Carthage his disgust at the local African practice of superficial 'feasting and drunkenness' at the tombs of the martyrs.[32] He observes that this behaviour is an indication of carnal weakness[33] and is greatly manifest in the peculiar status of the African Church.[34] This behaviour indicates the influence of *superbia*,[35] the 'mother of these vices',[36] since the Donatists honour the saints not out of true faith in God but out of 'pride and the eagerness for human praise, which also often leads to hypocrisy'.[37] Augustine recommends the cure for such pride as correct faith in God, exemplified in patience and humility.[38] It is interesting to note what Augustine considers the authority for patience and humility here: 'the books of God'.[39] This detail stands out, as Augustine specifically chooses scripture as a basis for right living over the subject at hand, martyr veneration. Though this can be partly explained by the fact that Augustine is writing to the Catholic primate of Carthage and not an overtly critical Donatist audience, it does show that his criticism of martyr veneration in this period places him outside the mainstream North African tradition of incorporating martyr stories into identity construction.[40]

In 396, when Augustine entered into dialogue with Proculiean (his Donatist counterpart in Hippo) this sentiment was again re-stated. Augustine makes his focus the truth, which he thinks Proculiean (as a symbol for all Donatists) should embrace '...once it had been shown to you'.[41] His approach is still a

---

32 *Ep.* 22,3 (*WSA* II/1, 59).

33 *Ep.* 22,2–3; 22, 6 (*WSA* II/1, 59–60).

34 *Ep.* 22,2 & 4 (*WSA* II/1, 59–60).

35 *Ep.* 22,6 (*WSA* II/1, 60).

36 *Ep.* 22,7 (*WSA* II/1, 61).

37 *Ep.* 22,7 (*WSA* II/1, 61).

38 *Ep.* 22,7 (*WSA* II/1, 61).

39 *Ep.* 22,7 (*WSA* II/1, 61).

40 This observation corresponds with the timeline put forth for Augustine's acceptance of martyr veneration (390–401, new to Africa and against it; 401–15, Augustine becomes more favourably inclined as a result of the Donatist influence; 415-death, proves himself to be a genuine adherent to the cult, thus showing one way in which the African tradition rubbed off). See T.J. van Bavel, 'The Cult of the Martyrs in St. Augustine: Theology versus Popular Religion?' in M. Lamberigts and P. Van Deun (eds.), *Martyrium in Multidisciplinary Perspective. Memorial Louis Reekmans*, Bibliotheca Ephemeridum Theologicarum Lovaniensium 117, (Leuven: Peeters, 1995), 351.

41 *Ep.* 33,3 (*WSA* II/1, 116).

pastoral one, imploring his reader to be loving 'as much…as he commanded who loved us up to the ignominy of the cross'.[42] In such a spirit Augustine even asks that his ally, Evodius, be excused for his forceful argumentation for the Catholic side, which 'should not be called arrogance, but confidence'.[43] Two points stand out here. For one, Augustine articulates the idea that love, *caritas*, evokes truth or *veritas*, whilst the Donatists' pride is a byproduct of error. He illustrates this point by using a traditional Donatist typology: 'The righteous man will correct me with mercy and rebuke me, but the oil of the sinner will not anoint my head' (Ps. 141, 5).[44] To explore this further, Augustine explains the Psalm's meaning in the following: '[Evodius] wanted to engage in a discussion [about truth] with arguments, not simply to offer flattering agreement'.[45] In other words, flattering agreement is opposed to the truth, which is Christ: 'I am the truth' (Jn. 14, 16),[46] and flattery and error are actually what are meant by the oil of sinners, with which the prophet does not want his head anointed. Mirroring Augustine's critique of the desire of pride for human praise in *Ep*. 22, is the 'harsh truth of correction' that remedies pride, likewise called a 'swollen head…fattened by the oil of the sinner…the smooth falsity of praise'.[47] This usage of the Donatist 'oil of sinners' motif is impressive, because it signals that by the year 396 Augustine had become familiar and comfortable with popular North African biblical exegesis, to say nothing of his willingness, already by that time, to turn the North African tradition on its head. The traditional interpretation of this Psalm, 141, 5 is based on Cyprian's exegesis in *Ep*. 70, 2–2, 3 (ACW 47, 47):

> The Holy Spirit has here given us this advance warning in the Psalms, not wishing that any wanderer who might stray away from the path of truth should receive anointing among heretics and the enemies of Christ… Besides, can a man give what he does not have himself? How can a man who has himself lost the Holy Spirit perform actions of the spirit? That is why those who come uninitiated to the Church are to be baptised and renewed; within the Church they may accordingly be sanctified by men who are themselves holy…

42 *Ep*. 33,3 (WSA II/1, 115).
43 *Ep*. 33,3 (WSA II/1, 116).
44 *Ep*. 33,3 (WSA II/1, 116).
45 *Ep*. 33,3 (WSA II/1, 116).
46 *Ep*. 33,3 (WSA II/1, 116).
47 *Ep*. 33,3 (WSA II/1, 116).

M. Fahey interprets Cyprian's intention as 'clear proof that the baptismal anointing undertaken by the heretic is invalid.'[48] Therefore, the Donatists appear to have upheld Cyprian's intended view more accurately than the Optatian-Augustinian rendering.

In *Ep.* 43 (c. 396–97) and *Ep.* 53 (c. 398–400) the theme of pride features again, which is significant considering the two letters provide the fullest expression of Augustine's anti-Donatist sympathies before his polemical trilogy, consisting of *Contra epistulam Parmeniani* (400), *De baptismo* (400/01), and *Contra litteras Petiliani* (400/03), which were to mark the pinnacle of the campaign. In *Ep.* 43 we see again the connection between pride and error, which Augustine proposed earlier in *Ep.* 33. He writes of the Donatists' 'stubborn animosity', 'brazenness of presumption', and says they are 'swollen with odious pride and insane with the stubbornness of evil strife'.[49] Also noteworthy in *Ep.* 43 is the way that Augustine by this time intertwines methods. Unlike *Ep.* 33, where Augustine wrote in exasperation to a Donatist reader, here he manages to maintain a pastoral sense in order to lure his Donatist opponent to the Catholic truth: '[T]hose who hold different views should be rebuked with moderation, *in case*,' he says, '*God may perhaps give them repentance to know the truth and they may escape from the snares of the devil...*' (2 Tm. 2, 26).[50]

At the same time as maintaining his overall pastoral approach he also manages to call his Donatist readers heretics, but without doing so directly. Here it is helpful to quote him at length:

> But people like yourselves should by no means be considered to be heretics. For you defend your view, though false and erroneous, without any stubborn animosity, especially since you did not give rise to it by the brazenness of presumption, but have received it from your parents, who were seduced and fell into error, and you seek the truth with a cautious concern, ready to be corrected when you find it. If I did not believe you that you were such people, I would perhaps not be sending you a letter.

---

48 M. Fahey, *Cyprian and the Bible: A Study in Third-Century Exegesis*, Beiträge zur Geschichte der Biblischen Hermeneutik 9 (Tübingen: J.C.B. Mohr (Paul Siebeck), 1971), 155.

49 *Ep.* 43,1 (*WSA* II/1, 157). In order to contrast the Donatist Church with his own Catholic one, Augustine explains in his preaching around the same time that his own Church is a 'refuge for the poor' or humble, 'who do not presume on their own virtue', in comparison with the 'haughty and ostentatious Donatists'; *En. in* Ps. 10, 8 (*WSA* III/15, 167); En. 2 of Ps. 21, 25 (*WSA* III/15, 236).

50 *Ep.* 43,1 (*WSA* II/1, 157).

> And yet, just as we are warned that we should avoid the heretic swollen with odious pride and insane with the stubbornness of evil strife for fear that he may deceive the weak and little ones, so we do not deny that we have to correct him in whatever ways we can.[51]

A reading of *Ep.* 53, written only a few years later, seems to call into question Augustine's sincerity when addressing the same subject to a Catholic audience. Concerning 'these wretched Donatists who throw many false and empty accusations against innocent Christians' there are numerous documents that alone disprove their legitimacy if they are 'willing to avoid being quarrelsome and to listen to wisdom.'[52] If the Donatists would surrender their pride and listen 'and cease plotting against the truth'[53] then would their 'proud tongue fall silent and acknowledge their crimes in order that it may not rave with madness'.[54]

This episode brings an additional element into question, that is, in what sense is Augustine tailoring his approach to his audiences at this point in time? As much as Augustine in this earlier period is laboring as a servant priest (and then as a bishop), he is also a trained/skilled rhetor, which means that when debating he argues to get his point across and win. Yet paradoxically, Augustine is to be constrained by his rhetorical capacity, the same facility that normally benefited a skilled Roman patrician in late antiquity. Specifically, as Carol Harrison has shown,[55] Augustine finds himself limited by the fact that by his own reckoning rhetoric or *eloquentia* is to be used in a way that is subordinate to and evocative of the truth. Writing in 396, he adds that this is even the case if one's writing or speaking becomes necessarily subdued and without flourish:

---

51 *Ep.* 43,1 (*WSA* II/1, 157), (*CCSL* 34, 85): 'Sed qui sententiam suam quamuis falsam atque peruersam nulla pertinaci animositate defendunt, praesertim quam non audacia praesumptionis suae pepererunt, sed a seductis atque in errorem lapsis parentibus acceperunt, quaerunt autem cauta sollicitudine ueritatem corrigi parati, cum inuenerint, nequaquam sunt inter haereticos deputandi. Tales ergo uos nisi esse crederem, nullas fortasse uobis litterasmitterem, quamquam et ipsum haereticum quamlibet odiosa superbia tumidum et peruicacia malae contentionis insanum sicut uitandum monemus, ne infirmos et paruulos fallat, ita non abnuimus, quibuscumque modis possumus, corrigendum'.

52 Here Augustine is implying that the Donatists are stubborn; *Ep.* 53,5 (*WSA* II/1, 206).

53 *Ep.* 53,5 (*WSA* II/1, 207).

54 *Ep.* 53,4 (*WSA* II/1, 206).

55 Carol Harrison, 'The Rhetoric of Scripture and Preaching: Classical decadence or Christian aesthetic?', in *Augustine and His Critics: Essays in Honour of Gerald Bonner*, ed. R. Dodaro and G. Lawless (London: Routledge, 2000), 214–29, esp. 220–22; and also: *Christian Truth and Fractured Humanity* (Oxford: Oxford University Press, 2000), 74.

> And who would be willing to listen to him, unless he also held the hearer's attention with some pleasantness of style?...It frequently happens, though, that when the most difficult problems are being solved in the calm, plain mode, and something is demonstrated with unexpected clarity...from heaven knows what...the speaker hauls up and displays the shrewdest judgments, convicting his opponent of error...it frequently happens [that] spontaneous applause breaks out on an occasion of this kind that you would scarcely suppose the calm, plain mode was being employed. Just because this style, after all, does not enter the arena either dressed up or armed, but engages the opponent as it were naked, it doesn't follow that it fails to grapple him with its sinewy arms, and to overthrow the falsehood resisting it, and to reduce it to nothing by its sheer strength of muscle.[56]

Rhetoric is not for mere titillation, but serves to implant an understanding, delight in, and love for the truth. And even with the aim of teaching and instilling a love for the truth, Augustine is further channeled in his polemic by the standards of decorum or appropriateness of grammar and rhetoric of his time.[57] Grammar provides boundaries in argumentation, and Augustine will indeed use such boundaries to limit his own positions, by labeling the Donatists' positions as improprieties, whilst upholding his own to be supported by contemporary usage and attested to as authoritative.[58]

Attacking 'Africa'

The previous section provided an overview of the way Augustine reacted to Donatist leaders in the first years of his ministry. The negative consequences of those interactions, both in person and epistolary, provoked a seemingly personal dilemma, since Augustine felt ineffective in sharing his zeal for the Catholic

56 Aug., *Doct. Chr.* 4, 56 (*WSA* I/11, 236–37), (*CCSL* 32, 162): 'Quid etiam quaerit nisi credi, qui aliquid, licet submisso eloquio, discentibus narrat?...plerumque autem dictio ipsa submissa, dum soluit difficillimas quaestiones et inopinata manifestatione demonstrat, dum sententias acutissimas de nescio quibus quasi cauernis, unde non sperabatur, eruit et ostendit...ipsis rebus extorta numerositas clausularum, tantas acclamationes excitat, ut uix intellegatur esse submissa. non enim quia neque incedit ornata neque armata, sed tamquam nuda congreditur, ideo non aduersarium neruis lacertis que conlidit et obsistentem subruit ac destruit membris fortissimis falsitatem'.

57 This was the focus of research by Robert Dodaro, 'The Theologian as Grammarian: Literary Decorum in Augustine's Defense of Orthodox Discourse', *Studia Patristica* 38 (2001), 70–83.

58 Dodaro, 'The Theologian as Grammarian', 77.

truth with other Christians. And as the years passed, this self-described 'pain' was channelled into a critique of Donatist pride (*superbia*), even as Augustine had to temper the rhetorical pride he was entitled to. At around the same time Augustine was articulating his cutting criticisms of Donatist theological positions, or at least the ones he portrayed negatively to his advantage. These were criticisms that would mature during the peak of the anti-Donatist campaign in the early 400s, and can readily be categorised into two groups: (1) ecclesiological, and (2) foundational.

Augustine's ecclesiological criticisms centred on his observation of Donatism as isolated from the Latin Christianity he had been immersed in whilst in Italy. In a sense, feeling *persona non grata* in Hippo and Donatist Africa as a whole, these views would have come easily, and this probably explains their proliferation in the earlier epistles. Augustine crafted three general lines of attack for the Donatists' ecclesiology, which he associated rhetorically with Africa for polemical purposes: (1) the Catholic Church is present in all nations; (2) Donatist 'Africa' is stained by its schism from the catholic world; and (3) the African Church is in conflict with churches across the Mediterranean Sea. These lines of attack remained throughout Augustine's earlier letters, alongside themes such as the 'pride of the Donatists'.

In *Ep.* 22 and *Ep.* 23 we can see these efforts at work. In both epistles Augustine decries the fact that there are 'many carnal diseases and illnesses that the African Church suffers'.[59] Whilst in *Ep.* 22 this criticism was focused more on the North African custom of gathering and feasting at the tombs of the martyrs, in *Ep.* 23 it is a direct assault on rebaptism and the splitting of the Church. Curiously, though, *Ep.* 22 was directed to his ally Aurelius in Carthage, whilst *Ep.* 23 is intended for the Donatist leader Maximian, yet both feature parallel language. Augustine is equally enthusiastic about comparing Donatist Africa with Catholic Italy in both:

> If Africa were first to try to eliminate [feasting at martyr's tombs], it would deserve to be worthy of imitation by the other lands but since through the greater part of Italy and in all or almost all the churches across the sea—in part because they were never practiced, in part because, when they had just sprung up or when they had been established, they were destroyed and wiped out by the diligence and attention of holy bishops [as opposed to the ambitious Donatist forefathers] who truly had the life

59 *Ep.* 22,2 (*WSA* II/1, 59).

> to come in mind—how can we hesitate to correct so great a moral defect, at least with so widespread an example set before us?[60]

In *Ep.* 23 he maintains this theme by describing Africa's contagion of erroneous customs (rebaptism and separation from the world) that need purification in order to 'heal the other members that lie miserably wasting through the whole of Africa...'[61] He is also careful to contrast such a deprived state with churches elsewhere: '[D]o not repeat the baptism of the Catholic Church, but rather approve it as the baptism of the one truest mother, who offers her breast to all the nations for their rebirth and who, as the one possession of Christ that stretches out to the ends of the earth...'[62]

By 396/97, Augustine is ready to fully contrast Africa and the Catholic Church, to demonstrate the wrong and right ways, respectively, of operating a church. In *Ep.* 43 and *Ep.* 44 this argumentation comes to the fore. In these letters there are multiple themes at work. On one level, there is the plea that the 'leaders of the Donatists' have irrationally 'turned away from the Catholic unity, which is spread through the whole world'.[63] Here again, throughout

---

60 *Ep.* 22,4 (*WSA* II/1, 59–60). Augustine continues in this section with another affront to Africa, implying its moral inferiority: 'And we, of course, have as bishop [Valerius], something for which we thank God. And yet he is a man of such modesty and gentleness and also of such prudence and solicitude in the Lord, that, even if he were African, he would quickly be convinced from the scriptures that he must cure the wound that had been inflicted by a custom that is unbridled and free in a bad sense'; (*CCSL* 34, 57): 'Haec si prima Africa temptaret auferre, a ceteris terries imitatione digna esse deberet; cum uero et per Italiae maximam partem et in aliis omnibus aut prope omnibus transmarinis ecclesiis, partim quia numquam facta sunt, partim quia uel orta uel inueterata sanctorum et uere de uita futura cogitantium episcoporum diligentia et animaduersione extincta atque deleta sunt, ...dubitare quo modo possumus tantam morum labem uel proposito tam lato exemplo emendare'.

61 *Ep.* 23,5 (*WSA* II/1, 66).

62 *Ep.* 23,4 (*WSA* II/1, 65), (*CSEL* 34/1, 67): 'Si tamen facis, ut ecclesiae catholicae baptismum non iteres, sed adprobes potius tamquam unius uerissimae matris, quae omnibus gentibus et regenerandis praebet sinum et regeneratis ubera infundit tamquam unius possessionis Christi sese usque ad terrae terminos porrigentis'. Augustine also uses this motif in *Ep.* 23,2 (*WSA* II/1, 64) 'The nations are the heritage of Christ, and the possession of Christ is the ends of the earth'.

63 *Ep.* 43,1 (*WSA* II/1, 157). Augustine repeats an excerpt from *Ep.* 23,2 (*WSA* II/1, 64) '...the madness of schism, the insanity of rebaptising, and the wicked separation from the heritage of Christ, which is spread through all nations'. Augustine refines this further from a previous position: 'We read out, not merely from our books, but also from theirs, the names of the

the whole world, 'across the sea',[64] there are churches in existence, which is another way of saying rightful Catholics 'preserve throughout the world the order of succession from the apostles and are established in the most ancient churches'.[65] For Augustine, apostolicity and antiquity equal authenticity.

On another, and new level, Augustine is introducing in these two letters a new technique of levelling a charge against the Donatist Church via the theme of 'Africa.' Altogether Augustine invokes 'Africa' seventeen times in *Ep.* 43, followed by three more occurrences in the much shorter *Ep.* 44. His purpose in doing so varies. To a Latinised audience identifying with the Roman Empire, emphasis on *africanitas* or being called *Punic* carried a loaded ethnographic message: implying greed, physical inferiority, mendacity, cowardice, and crudity.[66] This implication can be detected in Augustine's usage where he implies the inferiority of the African Church to overseas churches, especially those of Italy.[67]

Likewise, 'Africa' is used to denote sin and treachery. In fact, Augustine connects the schism with the 'carnal ways' of Africans, with Carthage as the head of the viper. 'Carthage…a large and famous city, from which the evil that arose there might pour down, as if from its head, over the whole body of Africa'.[68] He adds to this imagery by portraying the city of Carthage as the nerve centre

---

churches that they read today and with which they are today not in communion'. (*Ep.* 43,21 (*WSA* II/1, 168), (*CSEL* 34/2, 103)): 'De codicibus non tantum nostris sed etiam eorum recitamus ecclesias, quarum nomina hodie legunt et quibus hodie non communicant'.

64 He repeats the 'transmarine' or 'across the sea' theme frequently in the letter under consideration, *Ep.* 43,18 & 19, and implies the theme in *Ep.* 43,4 & 7, where it is enunciated that authority and authenticity come from outside of Africa, not from within.

65 *Ep.* 44,5 (*WSA* II/1, 175).

66 As H. Sidebottom explains, Romans would direct the insult 'Poenulus' or 'little Phoenician', with the same pejorative meaning as calling an African-American 'boy' in the modern, southern United States; *Ancient Warfare: A Very Short Introduction* (New York: Oxford University Press, 2001), 12.

67 Augustine is keen to note how African bishops resort to Rome for various approvals; *Ep.* 43,4. Also, Augustine adds, the gospel came to Africa via Rome; *Ep.* 43,7. Continuing, the 'overseas judges' are a seal of authority for the Church and Africa avoids such authority intentionally; *Ep.* 43,8–9. And as a final insult, Africans tend to have a narrow worldview and peculiar behaviour; *Ep.* 43,11 & 14. Augustine deliberately spells out that he sees the African Church as subordinate to other churches: 'The African church is incomparably less in authority and in number if it is compared to the others of the world. And it is far smaller, even if there were unity here, far smaller compared to all the other Christian peoples than the sect of Maximian compared to the sect of Primian', *Ep.* 43,26 (*WSA* II/1, 171).

68 *Ep.* 43,7 (*WSA* II/1, 160).

of the schism, for 'the bishops [at the start of the schism] were bribed in the Church of Carthage, the capital of Africa, by Lucilla's money,[69] altar was erected against altar'. It is at the head of Africa, where its members are in 'anguish from the swelling of pride',[70] that the 'unity of Christ is torn in two; the heritage of Christ is blasphemed; the baptism of Christ is subjected to the rite of exsufflation',[71] resulting in the 'groaning of the whole of Africa…'[72]

A final method for concentrating polemically on the Donatist's 'African peculiarity' was to fuse a discussion of the isolation of African Christians from the rest of the world with an identification of the Donatist schism with sin and selfishness. Indeed, Augustine draws out the accusation of African isolation and the schism as a whole to prove the Donatists violate the scriptures with their insistence on a unified body of Christ, personified in the oldest churches. In this way, antiquity is equated with authority: 'I asked how these people had justly separated themselves from the innocence of other Christians who preserve throughout the world the order of succession from the apostles and are established in the most ancient churches, though they were ignorant about

69 Lucilla was an alleged conspirator of the Donatist partisans, and her name was deployed routinely in anti-Donatist literature, thus implying that the schism was a kind of wrath on her part. See A. Mandouze, *Prosopographie de l'Afrique Chrétienne (303–533)*, Prosopographie Chrétienne du Bas-Empire 1 (Paris: Éditions du CNRS, 1982), s.v. 'Lucilla 1', 648–49. *Ep.* 43,17 (*WSA* II/1, 165). Augustine notes how Carthage cut Africa off from the rest of the world, *Ep.* 43,24 (*WSA* II/1, 170) 'on account of their altar over against our altar, on account of their separation from the heritage of Christ spread throughout the world, as it was promised so long ago'. It must also be asked if Augustine's use of the phrase 'altar against altar' was directly borrowed from Optatus who crafted the catchy anti-schism slogan. See Optatus, *Against the Donatists* [De Schismate], trans., ed. Mark Edwards, Translated Texts for Historians 27 (Liverpool: Liverpool University Press, 1997), 1, 15 (Edwards, 15). *Ep.* 43,17 (*WSA* II/1, 166). *Ep.* 43,21 (*WSA* II/1, 167). *Ep.* 43,24 (*WSA* II/1, 169). *Ep.* 44,5 (*WSA* II/1, 175). *Ep.* 44,3 (*WSA* II/1, 174–75). *Ep.* 43,25 (*WSA* II/1, 171). *Ep.* 43,27 (*WSA* II/1, 171). *Ep.* 49,2 (*WSA* II/1, 169).19; *Gesta apud Zenophilium* 6 & 17–18 & 20; Augustine, *Ep.* 43,6 & 9; s. 46, 15; *C. Cresc.* 3, 28, 32 & 3, 29, 33; *Ad cath. de secta Don.* 3 & 18 & 25; *C. ep. Parm.* 1, 3, 5; *C. litt. Pet.* 2, 108, 247. By targeting a female Donatist leader, Augustine and others were able to tap into a Roman stereotype of African women as 'dangerous seducers, like the mythical Queen Dido', H. Sidebottom, *Ancient Warfare*, 9. Augustine makes a particularly cutting remark about Lucilla again in *Ep.* 43,25 (*WSA* II/1, 171) in a way that argues this point well: 'Or has the world lost the light of Christ because Caecilian offended Lucilla in Africa?', thus again implying that the schism was a kind of wrath on her part. See Mandouze, *Prosopographie de l'Afrique Chrétienne (303–533)*, s.v. 'Lucilla 1', 648–49. Also see Ch. 7.

70 *Ep.* 43,17 (*WSA* II/1, 166).

71 *Ep.* 43,21 (*WSA* II/1, 167).

72 *Ep.* 43,24 (*WSA* II/1, 169).

who were *traditors* in Africa.'[73] This argument was used before as well: 'Then we began to seek which was that church in which one ought to live, whether one which, as the holy scriptures foretold so long ago, would spread over the whole earth [Ps. 2, 7–8] or that one which a small part of Africa or of the Africans would contain'.[74] Augustine develops this line further with the intention of signifying Africans not only cut themselves off, but offend the honour of the ancient, apostolic churches. 'What has the church of the Corinthians done to you, O sect of the Donatist, what has it done to you?'[75] He then adds, 'no one wipes out from the earth the Church of God'.[76] In opposition to the Donatist way, Augustine argues that their intolerance and geographic narcissism should be replaced with reconciliation 'for the sake of unity, sparing the weeds on account of the wheat…'[77] Using the writings of Paul (Eph. 4, 3) in support, he repeats the plea to 'preserve the unity of the Spirit in the bond of peace'.[78]

On the Eve of the Full Anti-Donatist Campaign, 398–400

At this juncture it is fruitful to examine the letters written on the eve of 400 and the initiation of Augustine's full anti-Donatist effort in *Ep.* 49, 51, 52, and 53. *Ep.* 49, written in 398, bears the theme of Africa's isolation and inferior status. From this point on, Augustine increasingly refers to Paul to force his point that Africa is not in the same league of authoritativeness as the apostolic churches:

> And before the word of God arrived in Africa, the apostle Paul wrote… *Through whom we have received grace and apostleship to bring about*

73 *Ep.* 44,5 (*WSA* II/1, 175), (*CSEL* 34/2, 113): 'Sed tamen sequestrata ista dubia quaestione quaerebam, quo modo se isti iuste separassent ab innocentia ceterorum christianorum, qui per orbem terrarum successionis ordinem custodientes in antiquissimis ecclesiis constituti penitus ignorarent, qui fuerint in Africa traditores'.

74 *Ep.* 44,3 (*WSA* II/1, 174–75), (*CSEL* 34/2, 111): 'Deinde quaerere coepimus, quaenam illa esset ecclesia, ubi uiuere sic oporteret, utrum illa, quae, sicut sancta tanto ante scriptura praedixerat, se terrarum orbe diffunderet, an illa, quam pars exigua uel Afrorum uel Africae contineret'.

75 *Ep.* 43,25 (*WSA* II/1, 171). Augustine will incorporate this argumentation in his preaching of this period as well. 'What justification have you for rebaptising those who know nothing of the days of betrayal [at the start of the Donatist schism] or the bitterness of Macarius' time? Why do you presume to rebaptise Christians coming from Mesopotamia who have not so much as heard the names of Caecilian and Donatus, and to deny they are Christians?'; *En. in Ps.* 10, 5 (*WSA* III/15, 165).

76 *Ep.* 43,27 (*WSA* II/1, 171).

77 *Ep.* 49,2 (*WSA* II/1, 169).

78 *Ep.* 43,23 (*WSA* II/1, 169).

> *obedience to the faith in all nations for the sake of his name* (Rom. 1:48). Then he himself preached the gospel from Jerusalem…through all of Asia up to Illyricum. He established and founded the churches, not he himself, but the grace of God with him [1 Cor. 15, 10]… But how can anything be seen with greater evidence than when we find the names of regions and of cities in his letters? He writes to the Romans, to the Corinthians, to the Galatians, to the Ephesians, to the Philippians, to the Thessalonians, and to the Colossians. John also writes to the seven churches…and we understand that the universal Church is also indicated in these by the number seven, namely, Ephesus, Smyrna, Sardis, Philadelphia, Laodicea, Pergamum, and Thyatira [Rev. 1, 11].[79]

Augustine concludes this passage with a rhetorical flourish aimed at his reader, the Donatist bishop, Honoratus: 'And it is evident that we are today in communion with all these churches, just as it is evident that you are not in communion with these churches'.[80]

Augustine takes a different direction in preparing *Ep.* 51 (ca. 399–400). In this specimen, the novice bishop of Hippo is diverted from comparing Donatist 'smallness' to a somewhat wide array of polemical attacks. Here he uses critiques that are short, effective, and will be recognisable in later writings. Among such linguistic manoeuvres are the following: 'You are accustomed to toss about false statements…perhaps not because you want to lie, but because you are mistaken'.[81] This is effectively a means of labeling Bishop Crispinus a liar, but only indirectly so. Other accusations include Donatists preaching 'to the ignorant' and taking advantage of the less educated,[82] making declarations

---

79 *Ep.* 49,2 (WSA II/1, 195–96), (CSEL 34/2, 141): 'Iesus Christus dicit euangelium suum in omnibus gentibus futurum et apostolus Paulus, antequam sermo dei in Africam peruenisset, in ipso capite epistulae, quam scribit ad Romanos: per quem accepimus, inquit, gratiam et apostolatum ad obaudiendum fidei in omnibus gentibus pro nomine eius. Deinde ipse ab Hierusalem in circuitu per totam Asiam usque in Illyricum euangelium praedicauit, ecclesias constituit atque fundauit, non ipse sed gratia dei cum eo, sicut ipse testatur. Quid autem euidentius apparere potest, quam cum in eius epistulis nomina etiam regionum uel ciuitatum inuenimus? Ad Romanos, ad Corinthios, ad Galatas, ad Ephesios, ad Philippenses, ad Thessalonicenses, ad Colossenses scribit; Iohannes etiam scribit ad septem ecclesias, quas commemorate in illis partibus constitutas, in quibus etiam uniuersis ecclesiam septenario numero intellegimus commendari, Ephesum, Smyrnam, Sardis, Philadelphiam, Laodiciam, Pergamum, Thyatiram'.

80 *Ep.* 49,2 (WSA II/1, 196).

81 *Ep.* 51,1 (WSA II/1, 198).

82 *Ep.* 51,2 (WSA II/1, 199).

'pompously stated', and committing 'the terribleness of so great a sacrilege [receiving back Maximianists, whilst rejecting Caecilianist Christians at the start of the Donatist schism]'[83] and a 'far greater crime of schism than that which you boast to have condemned in the Maximianists'.[84] Two additional notes on the language he uses here are illuminating.

First, when discussing the Donatists' 'terribleness of so great a sacrilege', Augustine's full remark is, 'You likewise often raise as an objection to us that we persecute you by earthly powers. On this point I do not want to discuss either what you deserve for the terribleness of so great a sacrilege or how much Christian kindness restrains us.'[85] This excerpt is interesting in that it presents two problems: Augustine seems to be demonstrating an early inclination for religious coercion either as a just punishment or as a correction. At the same time he evinces the frustration of needing to correct theological error, yet with the mandate to do so charitably, and for the express purpose of proclaiming the truth. Secondly, Augustine is now enlisting openly polemical techniques whilst also maintaining language which on the surface appears to demonstrate a spiritual concern for his opponents, that is, exercising pastoral charity.[86] He seems to argue that the schism between the two churches can be solved 'not with the strength of the word, but with that of the heart!'[87] He even concludes his letter with 'May the peace of Christ win out in your heart'.[88] Augustine has by now learned to attack Donatist competitors more directly, whilst not losing a shepherd's sense.

Epistle 51 is also important for revealing the nuances of Augustine's polemic. In it he clearly formulates argumentative refrains, which are used only sporadically and in an uncoordinated manner, but which will reappear for years afterwards in his later works. Among such refrains are: (1) that schism is worse than idolatry;[89] (2) that personal sins are to be tolerated for the sake of ecclesial unity;[90] (3) that Donatists wrongly criticise cooperation with secular

83 *Ep.* 51,3 (*WSA* II/1, 199–200).
84 *Ep.* 51,5 (*WSA* II/1, 201).
85 *Ep.* 51,3 (*WSA* II/1, 199).
86 One might understandably posit that this is a hybridisation of efforts used by Augustine in the 390s, with his *Ps. c. Don.* on one side demarcating a straightforward polemical approach, and with *Ep.* 21 on the other as an example of an overtly pastoral concern, although only introspectively so, through the reflection of Augustine to his bishop Valerius.
87 *Ep.* 51,2 (*WSA* II/1, 199).
88 *Ep.* 51,2 (*WSA* II/1, 199).
89 *Ep.* 51,1.
90 *Ep.* 51,2.

authorities, especially since Donatist leaders rely upon these authorities for their objectives;[91] (4) that Africa/African Christianity contrasts with the rest of the world/Catholic Church;[92] (5) that Donatist bishops repudiate the theological grounding for rebaptism in the course of the Maximian schism;[93] and (6) that Christ rather than the minister is the unique source and channel of grace in sacraments.[94] Augustine even seems to indicate a desire, or willingness, to elaborate on baptismal theology more singularly.[95]

In *Ep.* 52 Augustine returns to channel this thought, insisting the Catholic Church is dispersed throughout the whole world, unlike the sect of Donatus, which is 'found only in Africa' and which 'slanders the world and does not consider that by that sterility, because of which it refuses to bear the fruits of peace and love, it is cut off from that root of the Eastern churches, from which the gospel came to Africa. If a bit of soil is brought to them from those lands, they reverence it, but if a believer comes to them from there, they subject him even to exsufflation and rebaptise him'.[96] Again, Augustine is careful to indicate that the Church in Africa is subservient to those across the sea. If, however,

91 *Ep.* 51,3.

92 *Ep.* 51,2 (WSA II/1, 199) 'You would, of course, see how the peace of Christ should not be violated by any slanders throughout the world, if it permissible in Africa that men condemned even for sacrilegious schism are received back in the very same episcopacy to maintain the peace of Donatus'. Another worthwhile example is found in *Ep.* 51,5 (WSA II/1, 201): 'The baptism, then, of the Maximianists is accepted, and the baptism of those apostolic churches is subjected to exsufflation, though baptism belongs neither to these nor to those, but to him of whom it was said, This is he who baptises' (Jn. 1, 33).

93 *Ep.* 51,4.

94 *Ep.* 51,5.

95 *Ep.* 51,4 (WSA II/1, 200): 'You are also accustomed to say that we do not have the baptism of Christ and that it exists nowhere outside of your communion. I could on this issue speak more at length'.

96 *Ep.* 52,2 (WSA II/1, 202). To advance this comment, Augustine draws on a biblical typology from Jn. 14, 6 & 15, 2. *Ep.* 52,2 (WSA II/1, 202–03): 'The Son of God who is the truth… foretold this when he said that he was the vine, his children the branches, and his Father the farmer. He said, My Father will destroy the branch that does not bear fruit in me, but he will trim the branch that does bear fruit in me in order that it may bear more fruit. It is, therefore, not surprised if they who refused to bear the fruit of love were cut off from that vine which grew and filled their lands'. (CSEL 34/2, 150): 'Hoc enim praedixit filius dei, qui ueritas est, se esse uitem, suos autem filios esse sarmenta et patrem suum agricolam: sarmentum, inquit, quod in me non dat fructum, pater meus tollet illud; sarmentum autem quod in me dat fructum, purgat illud, ut maiorem fructum adferat [Jn. 15, 2]. Non ergo mirum est, si de illa uite, quae creuit et omnes terras impleuit [Ps. 79, 10], praecisi sunt illi, qui fructum caritatis adferre noluerunt'.

the same Donatists know the true crimes of their African colleagues and neglect to point them out and prove themselves to the churches overseas, they cut themselves off from the unity of Christ by a most wicked schism.[97]

The final letter providing evidence of Augustine's frame of mind leading up to his fully-fledged anti-Donatist assault in 400 is *Ep.* 53 (ca. 398–400). The letter contains the summation of his ridicule of the Donatists' exclusivity up to that point with elements now familiar to the reader. The 'hopelessly stupid'[98] Donatists are arrogant, speaking with a 'proud tongue'[99] and are actively 'plotting against the truth'.[100] And by plotting against the truth, Augustine means that the Donatists reject the view that the Church is established in all nations,[101] and that it contains both sinners and righteous believers. 'These people who have been separated by wicked schism hurl accusation against the straw in the Lord's harvest, which is mixed with the wheat and must be tolerated up to the end when the whole threshing floor will be winnowed at the last judgment'.[102] Their 'African crimes', 'African sins',[103] and 'clever vanity'[104] cut them off from the root of Christ and the Church; thus they prepare themselves and their victims for the fire, 'like dried branches'.[105] And even though, as Augustine rhetorically insinuates, the 'African' Donatists themselves have early on acknowledged their lack of authority compared to Rome by appealing to the emperor and the bishops north of the Mediterranean for legitimacy, they are nonetheless 'blown away'[106] by the scriptural mandate forbidding separation from other believers in the body of Christ. To this effect, as the classical rhetorician, Augustine does not hold back: 'Even if, then, an angel from heaven said to you…"Abandon the Christianity of the whole world, and hold onto that of the sect of Donatus"…that angel ought to be anathema, because he tried to cut you off from the whole, shove you into a part, and separate you from the promises of God'.[107]

---

97 *Ep.* 52,3 (*WSA* II/1, 203).
98 *Ep.* 53,1 (*WSA* II/1, 204).
99 *Ep.* 53,4 (*WSA* II/1, 206).
100 *Ep.* 53,5 (*WSA* II/1, 207).
101 Or, as Augustine would alternately put it, 'the Lord's grain, which must continue to grow through the whole field, that is, through the world, up to the end of the world…' *Ep.* 53,6 (*WSA* II/1, 207).
102 *Ep.* 53,6 (*WSA* II/1, 207).
103 *Ep.* 53,6 (*WSA* II/1, 207).
104 *Ep.* 53,1 (*WSA* II/1, 204).
105 *Ep.* 53,1 (*WSA* II/1, 204).
106 *Ep.* 53,3 (*WSA* II/1, 205).
107 *Ep.* 53,1 (*WSA* II/1, 204).

At this point the bishop of Hippo interjects a new reproach that is likewise significant. He mentions the full succession of the bishop of Rome. 'After all, we must consider the order of bishops in succession, how much more certainly and in a way truly conducive to salvation would we begin from Peter himself, who symbolised the whole Church and to whom the Lord said, *Upon this rock I shall build my Church*...(Mt. 16, 18)'.[108] What is most significant about this appeal to Peter and the bishop of Rome is that it marks a high point, to this date, in the resort to a deeply ensconced Christian authority, external to Africa, in order to refute the provincially-minded 'few Africans'.[109] It also marks a profound division between Augustine and the North African tradition encapsulated by Cyprian, and even, in this case, by Optatus of Milevis. R. Eno has quite adequately shown that until Augustine's initiatives, Peter and Rome were intimately bound up with terms signifying the unity and wholeness of the Church, such as *origo, radix, matrix, caput, ratio*.[110] Optatus continued Cyprian's usage, claiming that the Donatists had severed themselves from the root by their schism from the universal Church. But as it happened, in Augustine's time, the Donatists adhered more assiduously to the Cyprianic tradition, which made Augustine's appropriation problematic. It should therefore come as no surprise that Augustine channelled this line of argumentation into a greater concern with 'geographic catholicity',[111] which largely explains his repetitive use of the theme of African Donatist isolation from the rest of the world.

Although *Ep.* 53 is written to a Catholic reader, Generosus of Numidia, it is revealing that Augustine's apologetic weaponry is still conditioned for use by a non-African, or at least by someone who is critical of the African way of doing business, and who invokes authorities from beyond the shores of Africa. So even though he is writing to a fellow Catholic, he is still missing something that will allow his opinions to resonate more profoundly with African audiences. That is, he still lacks an authority to enhance his positions, one

108 *Ep.* 53,2 (*WSA* II/1, 205). Augustine's canon of the bishops of Rome very closely mimics that of Optatus of Milevis, found in his work *Against the Donatists* 2, 3 (Edwards 33).

109 *Ep.* 53,2 (*WSA* II/1, 205). The fact is that Augustine steers the argument towards the superiority of the bishop of Rome in relation to any African see presenting what he considers an innovation. This is so because while he took over this argument from Optatus of Milevis, he actually changed the intention in employing it, and re-thematised what Cyprian had originally intended in claiming Peter and Rome as the symbol of unity between churches; Ulrich Wickert, *Sacramentum Unitatis: Ein Beitrag zum Verständnis der Kirche bei Cyprian* (Berlin: Walter de Gruyter, 1971), 108–134.

110 Robert Eno, 'The Significance of the Lists of Roman Bishops in the Anti-Donatist Polemic', *Vigiliae Christianae* 47/2 (1993), 160.

111 Eno, 'The Significance of the Lists of Roman Bishops', 166.

who is held in high regard by both sides in the African Church. Some time after composing this letter Augustine seems to have realised this deficiency, but we do not know exactly when or how. Despite the later significance of popular African figures in his writing, it is suprising Augustine does not reveal his arrival at their importance. Was it because of familiarity, or was it perhaps because of the suggestion of an ally, or the provocation of a Donatist interlocutor? Regardless, we do know why he needed an African authority for his side to rally around in order to deprive the Donatist hierarchy of motivation: his anti-Donatist efforts had been largely impotent and had been received neither widely nor well up to that time.[112]

Pre-400 Anti-Donatist Sermons: Inconclusive Evidence or *Locus Cypriani*?

Whilst *Ep.* 21, 22, 23, 29, 32, 33, 34, 35, 43, 44, 49, 51, 52, and 53 contain a staggering amount of data concerning the first years of Augustine's ministry and involvement with the Donatist leadership, those epistles come up rather short in demonstrating the mechanism by which Augustine moved from being a reactionary episcopal upstart from Hippo's minority Caecilianist Church, to a highly disciplined and combative campaigner able to strike North African custom at the point where he disliked it, whilst also managing to incorporate allies in other sees to effect a total, African solution to the schism. We can observe this development unfolding in his anti-Donatist sermons written before 400: *s.* 37, 252, 271, 292, 313E,[113] *En. in Ps.* 10,[114]

112 This assessment is made after evaluating other polemical works-to-date of Augustine, as well as the popularity of his non-Donatist related works. One is left with the impression he was not only struggling to find his niche within the African context, but was also desperate to find his voice in the Church outside of Africa.

113 The dating of 313E is particularly troubling as will be seen towards the end of this chapter. Gryson places 313E at 393/96 (*Répertoire général des auteurs ecclésiastiques latins de l'antiquité et du haut Moyen âge, Tome 1* (Freiburg: Verlag Herder, 2007), while Rebillard places it at 410; É. Rebillard, 'Sermones', in *Augustine through the Ages*, 786. Hill dates the sermon to 395/96 (*WSA* III/9, 116), which is roundly criticised by J. Yates, 'The Use of the Bible in the North African Martyrological Polemics of Late Antiquity', in J. Leemans (ed.), *Martyrdom and Persecution in Late Antique Christianity: Festschrift Boudewijn Dehandschutter*, Bibliotheca ephemeridum theologicarum Lovaniensium 241 (Leuven: Peeters, 2010), 405.

114 Monceaux places En. in Ps. 10 between 395–98. All other sources (Dekkers/Fraipoint, Müller/Fiedrowicz, and Boulding) are silent on a probable date.

Ex. 2 *in Ps.* 21,[115] *Ex.* 2 *in Ps.* 33,[116] *En. in Ps.* 54,[117] *En. in Ps.* 57.[118] But doing so entails confronting a large obstacle to identifying the seminal moment of Augustine's appropriation of Cyprian. Either these sermons show contemporaneous complementarities with his letters or his other efforts of the period, or their inconclusive dates of origin show his arrival at Cyprian remains 400 and after.[119]

For an assessment of the pre-400 sermons it is helpful at this stage to analyse thematic continuities with the letters. The reader will find familiar references to Donatist pride,[120] arrogance,[121] and a lack of humility concerning the schism.[122] Again, '*caro*'[123] is used by the bishop as an explanation for Donatist

115 Dekkers/Fraipoint (CCSL 38–40, Turnhout: Brepols, 1956) place this sermon at 403, while Monceaux puts it at early 397.

116 Monceaux places it at 420, whilst H. Rondet ('Bulletin d'histoire de la théologie, études augustiniennes', Recherches de Science Religieuse 37 (1950), 619–33) puts it at late 403; La Bonnardière ('*Les Enarrationes in Psalmos préchées par saint Augustin* a l'occasion des fêtes de martyrs', Recherches Augustiniennes 7 (1971), 73–104) fixes it at 403; T. De Bruyne ('*Enarrationes in Psalmos* préchées à *Carthage*', Miscellanea Augustiniana II (1976), 321–25) at 403 and S.M. Zarb (*Chronologia Enarrationum s. Augustini in Psalmos* (Valetta: St. Dominic's Priory, 1948), 125–27.162) at 403. The general consensus of this having been written after 400 is complicated by the fact that its content so closely mirrors other sermons of the period dated before 400. The date of this sermon is therefore particularly inconclusive.

117 Monceaux places it at early 396, and Zarb places it during Eastertide 395 (*Chronologia Enarrationum*, 197–205.213). H. Rondet ('Essais sur la chronologie des «Enarrationes in Psalmos» de saint Augustin', *Bulletin de Littérature Ecclésiastique* 61 (1960), 199–202) finds it to be at 408, with A.-M. La Bonnardière ('La Prédication d'Augustin sur les Psaumes à Hippone', *AEPHE.R* 86 (1977), 340) at 400–11.

118 Dekker/Fraipoint place it at 412, Monceaux places it at 396, and R. Teske/J. Rotelle (Exposition of the Psalms, trans. R. Teske, ed. J. Rotelle, WSA III/17 (Hyde Park, NY: New City Press, 2001) in September 403.

119 As seen directly beforehand, placing a date on the sermons and *ennarationes in psalmos* is incredibly problematic, with the date of origin often relying on the judgment of the redactor. With the selections I have made for documents produced before 400, I have had to rely on at least one corroborative time period from a reliable secondary work, as well having to decipher a similar thematic maturity to determine if the specimen is pre- or post-400. This makes any calculation quite probably inaccurate to a certain degree.

120 *s.* 292, 2 (*WSA* III/8, 138); *En. in Ps.* 10, 1 (*WSA* III/15, 160); *En. in Ps.* 54, 19 (*WSA* III/17, 71); *En. in Ps.* 57, 16 & 18–20 (*WSA* III/17, 138 & 140–43).

121 *s.* 292, 6 (*WSA* III/8, 142).

122 *s.* 292, 2 & 5 (*WSA* III/8, 138 & 41).

123 *s.* 252, 4 (*WSA* III/7, 135); *s.* 37, 1 (*WSA* III/2, 184); *En. in Ps.* 10, 2 & 4 (*WSA* III/15, 161 & 164); *En. in Ps.* 54, 16 (*WSA* III/17, 69); *En. in Ps.* 57, 5 & 10 & 19 (*WSA* III/17, 127 & 132 & 142).

error, that is, their rejection of the truth,[124] unity[125] and peace,[126] and of the reality of 'wheat and chaff' existing in the earthly Church, till Christ's final

124 *En. in Ps.* 57, 5–6 (*WSA* III/17, 126 & 128) 'Alienated from what? From the truth. Alienated from their homeland, from a life of blessedness'.

125 *s.* 252, 11 (*WSA* III/7, 140); *s.* 271 (*WSA* III/7, 298–99); *s.* 313E,3 & 5 (*WSA* III/9, 110 & 13); *Ex.* 2 *of Ps.* 33, 7 (*WSA* III/16, 28). Augustine portrays the Donatist rejection of unity eloquently in *En. in Ps.* 10, 7 (*WSA* III/15, 166): 'The Lord is in his holy temple...God's temple is holy, and that temple is yourselves. If anyone violates God's temple, God will destroy that person (1 Cor. 3, 17). Whoever violates unity violates God's temple, for he does not keep hold of the Head, from whom the whole body is united and consolidated through every kind of mutual service, so that as each constituent joint plays its due part, the whole body grows and builds itself up in love. The Lord is in this holy temple. It consists of many members, each carrying out its own duties and functions, built together by love into one structure. Any who separate themselves from this Catholic fellowship for the sake of their own pre-eminence violate its unity'. (*CCSL* 38, 79): 'Dominus in templo sancto suo [Ps. 10, 5]. Ita uero, sicut apostolus dicit: templum enim dei sanctum est, quod estis uos. quisquis autem templum dei uiolauerit, disperdet illum deus [1 Cor. 3, 17]. Templum dei uiolat, qui uiolat unitatem. non enim tenet caput, ex quo totum corpus connexum et compactum per omnem tactum subministrationis, secundum operationem in mensuram uniuscuiusque partis incrementum corporis facit, in aedificationem sui in caritate. In hoc templo sancto suo dominus est; quod constat multis membris suis, sua quaeque officia gerentibus, in unam aedificationem caritate constructis. Quod uiolat, quisquis causa principatus sui a catholica societate disiungitur'.

126 Augustine develops this rhetorically to signify that the Donatists have fully assaulted Christ himself by their actions, 'He said, My peace I give to you, my peace I leave with you (Jn. 14, 27), but you have besmirched that peace with your unspeakable schism. What did Christ do to you?' *En. in Ps.* 10, 6 (*WSA* III/15, 166). In the same paragraph Augustine launches into a rather full explication of Christ's example of toleration in distinction to the Donatists. 'It was Christ who endured his own betrayer with such patience that he gave him the first Eucharist consecrated with his own hands and blessed with words from his own lips, as he gave it to the other apostles. What did Christ do to you? It was Christ who sent his own betrayer with the other disciples to preach the kingdom of heaven, that same betrayer whom he called a devil, who even before his treason could not be trusted with the Lord's purse. And he sent him out to preach in order to show that the gifts of God come to those to receive with faith, even if those through whom they receive are like Judas.' (*CCSL* 38, 79): 'Christus quid uobis fecit, qui traditorem suum tanta patientia pertulit, ut ei primam eucharistiam confectam manibus suis et ore suo commendatam, sicut ceteris apostolic traderet? Quid uobis fecit Christus, qui eumdem traditorem suum, quem diabolum nominauit, qui ante traditionem domini nec loculis dominicis fidem potuit exhibere, cum ceteris discipulis ad praedicandum regnum caelorum misit, ut demonstraret dona dei peruenire ad eos qui cum fide accipiunt, etiamsi talis sit per quem accipiunt, qualis Iudas fuit?'

judgment and separation.[127] Augustine refers back to the isolation of the African Church,[128] of its being cut off from the rest of the catholic world, which exists in all nations.[129]

Beyond those themes which already proliferate in his letters, Augustine also manages to incorporate new criticisms. These are easily divisible into two categories: (1) stinging characterisations, and (2) substantive theological critiques, both of which are likely to have had the result of titillating the listener or any third party to whom they were repeated.

Since the sermons were delivered in person to crowds in tense, mixed communities,[130] the impact of Augustine's preaching must have been powerful. 'Mr. Heretic', 'Mr. Backtracker', 'Mr. Proud man', 'Mr. Lamp-put-out',[131] 'Mr. Donatist',[132] are all names Augustine attaches to his enemies to drive home

---

127 s. 252, 4–5 (*WSA* III/7, 135–36); *En. in Ps.* 10, 4 (*WSA* III/15, 164); *Ex. 2 of Ps.* 21, 1 (*WSA* III/15, 227); *En. in Ps.* 54, 19 (WSA III/17, 71–72); s. 252, 7 (*WSA* III/7, 137).

128 *Ex. 2 of Ps.* 21, 1–2 & 24 & 26 & 28 (*WSA* III/15, 228, 236–38); *En. in Ps.* 54, 21 (*WSA* III/17, 74); 'Africa' as a polemical attack theme reappears, though it is interesting how Augustine tempers this approach in comparison to his letters. This can be partly explained by a consideration of his largely indigenous African audience in the respective basilicas.

129 *En. in Ps.* 54, 22 (*WSA* III/17, 74); *En. in Ps.* 10, 4 (*WSA* III/15, 164); *Ex.* 2 of Ps. 21 (*WSA* III/15, 237); *En. in Ps.* 54, 16 & 20 (*WSA* III/17, 70 & 73); *En. in Ps.* 57, 6 & 9 (*WSA* III/17, 128 & 131).

130 It is certainly not the case that this was always true. There are two examples from this group of sermons that illustrate Augustine preached to diverse groups, either mostly friendly Catholic audiences, or to audiences with Donatists mixed in. It is logical to suppose this, given that Donatists were the majority element in Hippo Regius and Numidia. *S.* 271 (*WSA* III/7, 299) provides evidence of Augustine preaching to a mixed congregation: 'And so it is that those people [Donatists] have absolutely no share in this gift of the Holy Spirit, who hate the grace of peace, who do not hold on to the fellowship of unity. Yes, they too may come flocking to the solemnity of this day [Pentecost], may hear these readings in which the Holy Spirit was promised and sent; but their hearing brings judgment on them, not reward'. *S.* 313E,2 (*WSA* III/9, 110) offers an example of Augustine speaking before a strictly Catholic crowd: 'Faith is something great—and where is it? After all, we can see each other's faces, our figures, our clothes, finally, we perceived each other's voices and words in our ears. But where is the faith which I'm talking about now? Let it be shown to our eyes. Look here, faith can't be seen; and yet the whole of this crowd, which can be seen here in God's house, was drawn here by faith, which cannot be seen'. (*MA* 1, 536): 'O quam magna, quam mirabilis est fides! aliquid magnum est fides, et ubi est? Uidemus enim nos inuicem facies nostras, formam nostram, uestes nostras, uerba denique nostra uocesque aure percipimus; fides ubi est, de qua nunc loquor? Demonstretur oculis nostris. Ecce fides non uidetur: et tamen totam istam multitudinem, quae hic in domo dei uidetur, ipsa fides attraxit, quae non uidetur'.

131 s. 292, 8 (*WSA* III/8, 145).

132 s. 313E,5 (*WSA* III/9, 113).

his view of the Donatists as inconsistent in terms of their beliefs and practices. Meanwhile, Augustine makes the charge of Donatist 'deafness', based on their refusal to hear the truth and their compensation for such by 'yellowing' their own version of it.[133] Augustine continues by arguing that the Donatists, who so 'strangely praise Christ' in claiming to be the exclusive 'progeny of Jacob',[134] are not only deceitful and impatient 'flatterers' and 'rogues',[135] but are even more consequentially hypocrites for demanding justice for themselves while living in a way that opposes justice. Continuing, Augustine calls the Donatists snakes who will not listen,[136] 'hypocritical 'Pharisees' who refuse to hear what the Lord says,[137] or 'lions' and 'Jews' for 'roaring' their own version of the truth with lethal rampage.[138] Nonetheless, he continues, the Donatists have their 'mouths shut' by the Lord,[139] their 'teeth smashed' by the truth',[140] and through God's grace they are 'bent like bows'.[141]

Whilst Augustine's polemical delivery-style in his preaching is somewhat new at this point, he does have recourse to familiar ways too. In Augustine's recapitulation of the North African tradition of rebaptism, he argues that the Donatists conceive of grace as emanating from the minister, thus claiming the position of Christ.[142] As opposed to his own Catholic Church, the Donatists

133 *Ex. 2 of Ps.* 21, 2 & 29 (*WSA* III/15, 228 & 239); *En. in Ps.* 57, 6 (*WSA* III/17, 128).

134 *Ex. 2 of Ps.* 21, 24 (*WSA* III/15, 236).

135 *En. in Ps.* 57, 1 & 5 (*WSA* III/17, 120 & 126–27).

136 *En. in Ps.* 57, 9 (*WSA* III/17, 131).

137 *En. in Ps.* 57, 11 (*WSA* III/17, 133).

138 *En. in Ps.* 57, 14 & 15 (*WSA* III/17, 134–35). Augustine made a practice of tying the Donatists to violence, such as with his repetitive use of the Circumcelliones in the controversy as in 'the daily acts of violence perpetrated by the Circumcelliones under the leadership of bishops and priests, how their gangs roam around and call their terrifying cudgels Israels'. *En. in Ps.* 10, 5 (*WSA* III/15, 64).

139 *En. in Ps.* 57, 14 (*WSA* III/17, 135).

140 *En. in Ps.* 57, 20 (*WSA* III/17, 143).

141 *En. in Ps.* 57, 16 (*WSA* III/17, 138).

142 *s.* 292, 6 (*WSA* III/8, 142) 'Yes, we certainly do find these people saying, "I am the Christ," not in these very words, but what is worse, in their deeds. Not with the effrontery of these words. Who would listen to them, after all? Who would be taken in and admit such foolish people to their ears and hearts? If the one who was about to baptise them said, "I am the Christ," they would turn away from him, abandon the man's blatant arrogance, seek instead the grace of God'. *PL* 38, 1323–24): 'Prorsus inuenimus istos dicentes, ego sum Christus: non his uerbis, sed quod peius est, factis. Non audacia uerborum istorum. quis enim eos audit? Quis ad aures uel ad cor, tam insipientes deceptus admittit? Si dicat ei qui eum baptizaturus est, ego sum Christus: auertit faciem suam ab illo, relinquit hominis

appeal to the doctrine of Donatus and thereby displace Christ.[143] They do this by manifestly rejecting the 'body of Christ, the unity of Christ'.[144]

Augustine's other set of enhanced criticisms can be considered more substantial attacks upon Donatist theology. The purpose of such attacks was to call into question the core principles which Augustine thrust into the debate, thereby making the controversy largely something of his own design.[145] A first example is located in *s.* 292 where he attempts to centralise rebaptism as the chief error of the Donatists.[146] Here his rhetorical abilities are seen in

---

arrogantiam manifestam, quaerit dei gratiam'. The claim of Augustine that the Donatists clamour to be Christ is used again in *En. in Ps.* 10, 5 & 7 (WSA III/15, 160 & 164).

143 The figure of Donatus would be revisited by Augustine through the controversy, and in this sampling of sermons as well: *Ex. 2 of Ps.* 21, 24 (WSA III/15, 236).

144 *En. in Ps.* 54, 17 (WSA III/17, 70–71) 'I cried out to the Lord. The body of Christ, the unity of Christ, is crying out in its anguish, its weariness, its affliction, in the distress of its ordeal. It is one single person, a unity grounded in an individual body, and in the distress of its soul it cries from the bounds of the earth…It is one, but the oneness is a unity made from many; it is one, but not because of confinement to any one place, for this is one person crying out from the ends of the earth. How could one individual cry out from the ends of the earth, unless that individual were one formed from many? I cried out to the Lord. Yes, do just that: you cry out to the Lord, not to Donatus'. (CCSL 38, 669): 'Ego ad dominum exclamaui [Ps. 54, 17]. Corpus Christi et unitas Christi in angore, in taedio, in molestia, in conturbatione exercitationis suae; ille unus homo, in uno corpore posita unitas, cum taederet animam eius exclamans a finibus terrae: a finibus terrae ad te clamaui, inquit, cum angeretur cor meum [Ps. 60, 3]. Ipse unus, sed unitas unus; et ipse unus, non in uno loco unus, sed a finibus terrae clamat unus. Quomodo a finibus terrae clamaret unus, nisi in multis esset unus? Ego ad dominum exclamaui [Ps. 54, 17]. Recte. Tu exclama ad dominum, noli ad Donatum'.

145 I take as my point of departure Tilley's assertion that there was much more in common between the Donatist and Caecilianist parties than Augustine alluded to; 'Theologies of Penance during the Donatist Controversy', 330–37. In this sense, items that Augustine harp on are largely figurative divisions and not really concrete divergences. It seems that this partly explains why African Christianity moved along fine until government involvement or because of propagandists like Optatus of Milevis or Augustine. Augustine himself passively attests to the similarities that both sides would have had in common at that time in *En. in Ps.* 54, 16 (WSA III/17, 69). 'Suppose you say to someone, "What's the matter, brother? We are brothers and sisters, we call upon the one God, we believe in the one Christ, we listen to the same gospel, we sing the same psalm, we respond with the one 'Amen,' we ring out the one 'Alleluia' [possible reference to their Liturgy?], we celebrate the one Easter"'.

146 *En. in Ps.* 54, 16 (WSA III/17, 69): 'You go further and admonish him: "Isn't the disaster of separation bad enough? Must you compound it by repeating baptism? Acknowledge in me the reality you have yourself; and even if you hate me, be kind to the Christ in me."

full flourish as he reduces the Donatist insistence on their ecclesial integrity and doctrinal continuity by placing themselves in the role of Christ,[147] as the one who justifies.[148] He recasts their position as follows: '[Christ] foresaw that many people were going to puff themselves up [*superbia*] about the ministry of baptism, and to say, "It's I who baptise," and "The sort of person I am as I baptise, is the sort I make the person whom I baptise"'.[149] But interestingly, Augustine himself is quick to note that no particular Donatist has opined such a thing![150] However, the polemical effect sank in, especially with a friendly Catholic audience. Imagine then, how a battered Catholic would have responded upon hearing their bishop summarise and belittle the Donatists as asserting 'I am the Christ',[151] 'I am the one who baptizes',[152] or 'Believe in me for I am the good tree',[153] and 'You are justified by me'.[154] And whilst it is difficult to know for certain how the audience reacted to the implications of this line of reproach, it is reasonable to assume that such rhetoric fast developed into a personal arsenal for Augustine's eventual Christological and sacramental teachings, as well as for his understanding of grace.

Donatist Ecclesiology in the Cross-Hairs of the Sermons

That this polemical context was informing Augustine's own long-range theological capabilities seems even more likely when we see his rhetoric being utilised against Donatist ecclesiology as he characterised it.[155] He accuses the Donatists of freely choosing schism over Christ's intention that the Church

This pernicious practice is often the most grievous point of all to them, and they will admit, '"Yes, it's true; this does happen. How we wish it did not! But what can we do about the statutes our ancestors handed down to us?"'

147 *s.* 292, 5–6 (*WSA* III/8, 141–42).

148 *s.* 292, 6 (*WSA* III/8, 142).

149 *s.* 292, 5 (*WSA* III/8, 141). Hill is careful to note that this was an erroneous rhetorical affront to the Donatists, see footnote 16, *WSA* III/8, 147.

150 *s.* 292, 6 (*WSA* III/8, 142).

151 *s.* 292, 6 (*WSA* III/8, 142).

152 *s.* 292, 5 (*WSA* III/8, 141).

153 *s.* 292, 5–6 (*WSA* III/8, 141–42).

154 *s.* 292, 6 (*WSA* III/8, 142–43).

155 On a purely polemical level, one of Augustine's greatest credits was his success in permanently tagging the Donatist Church as obsessed with the purity of its members, and of imitating the deaths or martyrs, regardless of the fact that there were several streams of thought about ecclesiology amongst the Donatists, and not a single 'Donatist' ecclesiology as such. Consult James Alexander, 'Donatism', in P.F. Esler (ed.), *The Early Christian World*, vol. 2 (New York/London: Routledge, 2000), 952–74; R. Eno, 'Some Nuances in the Ecclesiology of the Donatists', *Revue des études augustiniennes* 18/1–2 (1972), 46–50.

to be one body for all nations; for believing that theirs is a 'Church of Donatus' that exists solely in Africa.[156] By doing so they in fact lose the Holy Spirit and its gift of unity.[157] Augustine even attempts to stake his claim over traditional African biblical typologies for his own Church, such as the ones that refer to lilies and thorns, or to fishing nets full of sinners and the righteous.[158] But Augustine's perspective is this: by their insistence on schism, the Donatists are wounding the body of Christ, and causing it anguish, weariness, affliction, and distress:[159] 'Donatus arrived, and tore Christ's Church apart. Christ's body is whole and complete on the cross in the hands of his persecutors, but in the hands of Christians [Donatists] his body, the Church, is not whole'.[160] Yet despite the Donatists' weakness of flesh,[161] God will be victorious as his unity and peace will never be broken;[162] the Holy Spirit will never fail to heal disunity.[163]

Following this reasoning, Augustine's rhetorical overtures evolve into a whole new level of scathing reproach. What follows next will be the end-result of years of experimentation in his letters, sermons, and other works, probing to see which criticisms are most effective in arousing Catholic partisans and deflating the Donatists. Perhaps most important is that this next step will occasional battle-cries that will be carried forth as both sides wage war for the soul of the African Church.

The first trick was one Augustine had been cultivating cautiously. His move from labelling the Donatist Church a schismatic group to calling it a heretical one was an entry into undiscovered country. Doing so was new in the Catholic-Donatist debate and was indeed a novelty on Augustine's part. Optatus of Milevis, from whom Augustine drew much of the framework for

156 *En. in Ps.* 54, 21 (*WSA* III/17, 74). As just one prefiguring of themes to come in the Pelagian controversy, Augustine uses the term, 'freedom of choice', *liberum arbitrium,* here to argue that the Donatists draw an inside/outside (*intus/foris*) contrast that seems to disregard the capacity for humanity to opt for a life of grace or to indulge in their carnal side, and that they pay little attention to the action of grace in effecting these choices. In this sense a direct comparison is easily made with Augustine's later argument against the Pelagians; that those heretics hold that humans can pursue whatever course in life they wish, without accounting for divine grace; *En. in Ps.* 54, 6 (*WSA* III/17, 136).

157 *s.* 271 (*WSA* III/7, 298–99).

158 *s.* 37, 27 (*WSA* III/2, 198–99); *s.* 252, 7 (*WSA* III/7, 136–37).

159 *En. in Ps.* 54, 17 (*WSA* III/17, 70–71).

160 *En. in Ps.* 33, 7 (*WSA* III/16, 28–29).

161 *s.* 37, 1 (*WSA* III/2, 184).

162 *s.* 252, 11 (*WSA* III/7, 140).

163 *s.* 271 (*WSA* III/7, 298).

his anti-Donatist campaign, more or less only accused Donatists of being schismatics.[164] Using Tilley's method of assessing Donatist-Catholic differences and similarities, it is quite safe to assert that the two rival groups squared with each other in terms of doctrine. This is where Augustine's innovation becomes evident.

Starting in 391–95, Augustine claims that by cutting themselves off from the rest of the catholic world, the Donatists are claiming 'Africa alone has been worthy of this grace through Saint Donatus',[165] and that those with 'right opinions have been tested and approved'.[166] What he means by 'right opinions' is a belief in Christ and his Church, and a covenant of '*your seed,*' *which is Christ* (Gal. 3, 15–16). What then was the covenant promised in this seed, in Christ? *In your seed all nations shall be blessed.*'[167] Augustine channels this argument into a full-scale assault, claiming through a clever rhetorical bombardment that the Donatists actually reject Christ's words and Passion:

> *All the ends of the earth will be reminded and will turn to the Lord* [Ps. 21, 28]. In view of that, brothers and sisters, why ask me how we may reply to the Donatists? Look at the psalm, this same psalm that is read here today and is being read to them as well [possible clue to a similarity in liturgical calendars]. Let us write it on our foreheads! Forward march, everyone! Let not our tongues fall silent, let us shout, "Look, Christ suffered, the merchant offered his price. The money he handed over was his blood, the blood he shed. He carried our ransom-money in a purse; he was pierced with a spear, the purse spilled out, and the price of the whole world gushed out." What have you to say to me, you heretic? That it was not the ransom-price of the whole world? That Africa alone was redeemed? You dare not say, "The whole world was redeemed, but perished later." Who attacked Christ, and robbed him of what was his own? Look what the psalm says: *All the ends of the earth will be reminded and will turn to the Lord.* Let this satisfy you, and let the psalmist have the last word. Had he said, "The ends of the earth," rather than *all the ends of the earth*, they might have said, "Fine; as far as we are concerned, the earth ends at Morocco." But *all the ends of the earth* [Ps. 21, 28] is what he said, you

---

164 Opt., *De Schismate* 1, 10 (Edwards 9–10).

165 *En. in Ps.* 54, 21 (*WSA* III/17, 74).

166 *En. in Ps.* 54, 22 (*WSA* III/17, 74).

167 *En. in Ps.* 54, 21 (*WSA* III/17, 74).

> heretic; *all* is the word he used. Where are you off to, to hide from further questioning? You have no way out, only a way in.[168]

Since the Donatists deny this, that is, 'let slip the unity of all nations and clung to a part only…' they deny Christ, thus violating the faith of the Church. To which Augustine adds, 'Could heretics be more clearly indicated?'[169] He continues by identifying a silver lining in this heretical disgrace:

> Thanks to the heretics, the Catholic faith has been clearly enunciated, and in reaction to people with wrong opinions, those with right opinions have been tested and approved? Many truths were contained in the scriptures in an obscure way; and the heretics, after being cut off, rocked God's Church with their questions. But this served to lay open hidden truths, and so God's will came to be understood better.[170]

Augustine even cleverly modifies his 'African isolation' attack to show Donatists are in league with other transmarine churches after all, the Arians, the Novatianists, and right there amongst those heretics, the Donatists.[171]

---

168 *Ex.* 2 *of Ps.* 21, 28 (*WSA* III/15, 238–39), (*CCSL* 38, 130–31): 'Et conuertentur ad dominum uniuersi fines terrae. Eia fratres, quid quaeritis a nobis quid respondeamus parti Donati? ecce Psalmus, et hic legitur hodie, et ibi legitur hodie. Scribamus illum in frontibus nostris, cum illo procedamus, non quiescat lingua nostra, ista dicat: ecce Christus passus est, ecce mercator ostendit mercedem, ecce pretium quod dedit, sanguis eius fusus est. in sacco ferebat pretium nostrum; percussus est lancea, fusus est saccus, et manauit pretium orbis terrarum. quid mihi dicis, o haeretice? Non est pretium orbis terrarum? Africa sola redemta est? Non audes dicere: totus orbis redemtus est, sed periit. Quem inuasorem passus est Christus, ut perderet rem suam? Ecce commemorabuntur, et conuertentur ad dominum uniuersi fines terrae. Adhuc satiet te, et dicat. si diceret fines terrae, et non diceret uniuersi fines terrae, dicere habebant: ecce habemus fines terrae in Mauritania. Uniuersi fines terrae dixit; O haeretice, uniuersi dixit; qua exiturus es, ut euadas quaestionem? Non habes qua exeas, sed habes quo intres'.

169 *En. in Ps.* 54, 21 (*WSA* III/17, 74).

170 *En. in Ps.* 54, 22 (*WSA* III/17, 74), (*CCSL* 39, 672–73): 'Etenim ex haereticis asserta est catholica, et ex his qui male sentiunt probati sunt qui bene sentiunt. Multa enim latebant in scripturis; et cum praecisi essent haeretici, quaestionibus agitauerunt ecclesiam dei: aperta sunt quae latebant, et intellecta est uoluntas dei'.

171 Augustine singles out each 'heretical group' as aiding in the indirect elucidation of Catholic truths, *En. in Ps.* 54, 22 (*WSA* III/17, 74–75) 'Thanks to heretics, the Catholic faith has been clearly enunciated…this served to lay open hidden truths… Among God's people there were many individuals capable of explaining the scriptures with excellent

In 395/96, with *s.* 252, Augustine repeats this line of attack, merging Donatist provincialism into a localised heresy, as well as evidence for his belief in a mixed body or *corpus permixtum*![172] At this point it is beneficial to quote at length to see how he blends this argument at this point in time:

> In this very city, my brothers and sisters, didn't we experience what your holiness can recall as vividly as I can, what risks we ran when God expelled drunken celebrations from the basilica? Wasn't the ship almost sunk, along with us its crew, by the rowdy behavior, the rioting of worldly people? Again, it also says there that the nets were breaking. When the nets broke, heresies and schisms occurred. The nets indeed enclosed them all; but some impatient fish, being unwilling to come to be the Lord's food, hurl themselves against the nets and break them, and get away. Those nets, indeed, are spread out through the whole world; those who break them, though, do so locally. Donatists have broken them in Africa, Arians have broken them in Egypt, Photinians have broken them in Pannonia, the Cataphrygians broke them in Phrygia, the Manichees broke them in Persia. How many places, in which that seine has been broken![173]

discernment, but they were unknown. There was no occasion for them to put forward a solution to difficult questions as long as nobody arose to make false claims. Was any complete account of the Trinity offered, before the Arians began to bay at it? Was there any satisfactory treatment of penitential practice, before the Novatianists challenged it? In the same way we had no complete teaching on baptism until the "rebaptisers" [Donatists] had put themselves outside the church'. (CCSL 39, 672–73): 'Et cum praecisi essent haeretici, quaestionibus agitauerunt ecclesiam excludantur… Ergo multi qui optime possent scripturas dignoscere et pertractare, latebant in populo dei; nec asserebant solutionem quaestionum difficilium cum calumniator nullus instaret. numquid enim perfecte de trinitate tractatum est, antequam oblatrarent Ariani? Numquid perfecte de paenitentia tractatum est, antequam obsisterent Nouatiani? Sic non perfecte de baptismate tractatum est, antequam contradicerent foris positi rebaptizatores'.

172 To support this theological insight further, Augustine integrates a poetic allegory of the moon to illustrate his view that the church contains both sinners and righteous; *En. in Ps.* 10, 3 (WSA III/15, 162–63).

173 *s.* 252, 4 (WSA III/7, 135), (PL 38, 1174): 'In ista ciuitate, fratres mei, nonne experti sumus, quod recordatur nobiscum sanctitas uestra, quanto periculo nostro de ista basilica ebriositates expulerit deus? nonne seditione carnalium paene mergebatur nobiscum nauis? unde hoc, nisi de illo numero piscium innumerabili? deinde etiam illud ibi dictum est, quia retia rumpebantur. disruptis retibus, haereses et schismata facta sunt. retia quidem omnes concludunt: sed impatientes pisces, nolentes uenire ad cibum domini, ubi possunt, impingunt se, et rumpunt, et exeunt. et retia quidem illa per totum expanduntur:

The consequences of making allegations of heresy could be severe, and to pursue such charges was bold, especially given that heresy was a status punishable in the Roman Empire as of the 390s.[174] In fact, just as this manoeuvre was coming into focus for Augustine, he was aided by the ongoing Maximianist schism which allowed him the opportunity to press the accusation of heresy officially (see Chapter 2). But even more bold, given Donatist fortune in surviving persecutions, was that the charge of heresy was an outright denial of the Donatist Church's legitimacy and authority. To claim the Dontatists were heretical, or schismatic even, was to say that they were the newcomers, that they were the ones not steeped in North African tradition, with its martyrs and saints such as Cyprian. Obviously the Donatists based their entire identity otherwise and would pursue the Caecilianists' accusation by turning it against them.[175] And it was exactly the act of re-writing history and tradition that would result in the most significant event in the anti-Donatist campaign: the appropriation of Cyprian of Carthage.

The Early Texts, a Window and an Obstruction to the Early Campaign

To review, a careful analysis of the works Augustine produced in the 390s, his earliest years of ministry, led to the legitimate conclusion that he had been quickly thrust into an anti-Donatist posture already as a presbyter, something which only escalated when he became bishop. This overview showed how his reaction was multi-faceted, evoking a clear sense of angst and emotional investment in the outcome of his dialogue with Donatist leadership. By having as his focal point for conversation, the *veritas*, or truth of the Catholic faith, he was readily perplexed and bewildered by the reaction of the North African populace, leading him to form personal insights to explain such. This process led Augustine to craft a theological anthropology with implications for theologies of *concupiscentia carnis* (the weakness of the flesh), *superbia* (pride), and *arrogantia* (Donatist arrogance).

As the campaign accelerated through the decade of the 390s, Augustine targeted Donatist stances, especially those that he defined largely for polemical engagement. This tactic allowed Augustine to depict a controversy where it is

---

qui rumpunt autem, per loca rumpunt. Donatistae ruperunt in Africa, Ariani ruperunt in Aegypto, Photiniani ruperunt in Pannonia, Cataphryges ruperunt in Phrygia, Manichaei ruperunt in Perside. quot locis sagena illa disrupta est?'

174 *Cod. Theo.* 16, 64. Augustine also makes ready use of the accusation of heresy a in *En. in Ps.* 10, 1 (WSA III/15, 160–61); *Ex. 2 of Ps.* 21, 28 (WSA III/15, 239); *En. in Ps.* 57 (WSA III/17, 135).

175 *C. litt. Pet.* 2, 218; *C. litt. Pet.* 2, 91; *Gest. Con. Carth.* 3, 193.

questionable there had been one previously. The topics of Augustine's intra-Africa controversy would hinge upon his criticism of local traditions. Foremost was an attack on North African 'rebaptismal' rites, which occasioned an all-out attack from Augustine, leading to charges of an African refusal to commune with more venerable overseas sees, a preference for local tradition over universal practices, and a bastardised ecclesiology that opted for a paranoid purity over communion. The charge of mandatory purity allowed Augustine the flexibility to say that the Donatists had redefined the way the Church is described in the scriptures, i.e., as containing 'wheat and tares'. Moreover, their insistence on such purity meant that they had disregarded unity and peace within the body of Christ. Eventually Augustine was able to transform his critique of the Donatist rejection of peace and unity into an argument that they had rejected the example and tradition of Cyprian of Carthage.This present work continues by pin-pointing this revolution in Augustine's polemical engagement.

But before moving on to the next component of Augustine's appripriation of Cyprian, and his overall approach to an anti-Donatist polemical campaign, a few more observations have been made which warrant further consideration. In terms of these observations, firstly Augustine seems to have re-branded Donatist approaches to ecclesiology as a *single, sole* theology inherently opposed to the world. Second, Augustine appears to have exaggerated the existence and threat of the Circumcelliones, making an across-the-board accusation that even moderate North Africans were militantly-oriented.[176] Third, it is likely that Augustine personally cultivated the appellation of Donatists as *heretics* given that there was no prior tradition of Catholics doing so, not even in the significant contribution of Optatus of Milevis. And, as a last observation, by making the Donatist schism a referendum on an alleged 'African isolationism', Augustine created a narrative that their Church was, in their view, opposed or superior to other sees. The purpose here was evidently the goal of polemically isolating the Donatists from the transmarine churches.

Two questions arise. Could Augustine actually have been the one who was out of step with tradition? This suggestion refers not only to his intention of branding Donatists as heretics, but also to his re-orientation of the theology of sin. The African Church was historically preoccupied with concerns of ecclesial and communal sin introduced by corrupt leaders, whilst Augustine's obsession with the flesh evinced a prioritisation in the direction of personal sin and personal choice in coordination with divine grace. (Donatists were more concerned with 'group grace'.) An addition to Augustine's possible novelties

176 See Peter Kaufman, 'Donatism Revisited: Moderates and Militants in Late Antique North Africa', *Journal of Late Antiquity* 2/1 (2009), 313–142.

was a view of the martyr *cultus* that fell outside the African norm. His disapprobation towards martyr veneration and African martyrs specifically, placed him clearly outside the mainstream, at least in the 390s.

A final question, and the concern of the following chapter, is whether or not Augustine's accusation of Donatist hypocrisy was affected by the fallout from the Maximian schism that had unfolded simultaneously with his earliest anti-Donatist endeavours. Was the willingness of the Donatists, under Primian of Carthage in particular, to reconcile lapsed 'Maximianists' the spark that lit the fuse? Following on from this, was Augustine likewise encouraged by the contemporaneous actions of the army commander Gildo and the Donatist bishop, Optatus of Thamugadi, along with the apparent zeal of Donatists in having recourse to the Roman administration when it was to their advantage to do so?

CHAPTER 2

The Need for Authority, Why Did Augustine Need Cyprian?

To this point the focus has been on tracking Augustine's response to Donatist leaders in the first decade of his ministerial career. His personal interactions with friendly Catholic readers and listeners to his letters and sermons, as well as with Donatist readers and those Donatists who might have heard him in the basilica, provoked both a personal response and a theological development from the presbyter turned bishop, which played out as the 390s progressed. At the same time, the Donatist Church was torn asunder by the fallout from the election in 392 of Primian of Carthage as the new Donatist primate. (This election was simultaneous with Augustine's entrance into ecclesiastical politics.) Augustine did not hesitate to chide the Donatists with his rhetoric for the inconsistencies he observed in their willingness to readmit dissidents back into their numbers.

The fact of the matter is, whilst Augustine was stumbling towards the articulation of a polemical strategy against the Donatists in this period, essentially defining the Donatist controversy as such, he was still missing a strategy for endearing himself to North African believers, whether Catholic or Donatist. Part of Augustine's dilemma on the threshold of 400 and beyond, was that he was still experimenting with ways of making himself credible in the African context. He lacked a way of establishing his own pastoral and theological sincerity, which was a pronounced difficulty, because many of his theological positions had their origins outside the traditions of Roman Africa.

Added to the novel approaches and opinions of Augustine, was the fact that his efforts at distinguishing the Catholic from the Donatist positions often brought him to the point of belittling Africa and its ways (as discussed in Chapter 1). This tendency contributed also to the probable perception of Augustine as an insincere patrician/rhetorician.[1] In addition to this frustrating situation was the fact that up to the year 400 Augustine was struggling for a breakthrough

1 One of the factors that would propel Augustine to seek a corroborating authority who would give his voice legitimacy, was the sincere regard in which figures such as Cyprian of Carthage were held, based on their example of martyrdom. Augustine's success in this matter is still debatable, however. See P. Van Geest, 'Pectus ardet Evangelica pietate, et pectori respondet oratio: Augustine's Neglect of Cyprian's Striving for Sincerity', in H. Bakker, P. van Geest,

 | DOI 10.1163/9789004312647_004

in his anti-Donatist campaign. The anti-Donatist works that Augustine produced in the 390s, *Psalmus contra partem Donati* (393) and *Contra epistulam Donati heretici* (393/94), apparently failed to make any real waves either with Catholic partisans or against the Donatists.[2] Whilst they were voluminous, it is impossible to know how effective his sermons and letters were in stirring up Catholics and humbling Donatists. In a very real sense, for the better part of a decade, Augustine was waging a losing battle in the attempt to set his ecclesial body apart from that of the majority in North Africa.

But fortuitously for Augustine, his lack of success in convincing the African audience under his own auspices was to be offset by affairs that were external to his own initiative. Propelling the search for an adequate authority for use in the anti-Donatist campaign was a revolution in pastoral affairs resulting from the effort to admit converted Donatists into the Catholic Church, a process instigated by the intra-Donatist Maximianist schism. This pastoral situation, with Donatists willing to leave their communion to escape the conflict between the pro-Primian and pro-Maximian sides, was addressed by Church councils three times: in October 393, August 397, and June 401.[3] That converting congregations would retain their ministers in their respective ranks, meant children of ex-Donatists could be ordained and ex-Donatist clergy could keep their status. This in turn meant that the African tradition (and therefore the legacy of Cyprian), of separating the ritually impure from the Church, was to come under attack in an unprecedented way. Augustine reports that this practice even occasioned a violent reaction from the Circumcelliones, requiring the attention of Emperor Honorius, who, as a result of the turbulence, sought to repress the Donatist Church with a series of anti-schism laws in the early 400s.[4]

H. Van Loon (eds.), *Cyprian of Carthage: Studies in His Life, Language, and Thought*, Late Antique History and Religion 3 (Leuven: Peeters, 2010), 203–25.

2 The effectiveness of the earliest anti-Donatist works is measured by the lack of references Augustine himself makes to them. He only recalls the existence of *Contra epistulam Donati heretici* towards the end of his life, in five different references in *Retract.* 1,21–33, hardly a boastful usage of the work throughout this career. His recourse to *Psalmus contra partem Donati* was even more remarkably subdued, with only one reference in total in his later extant writings, found in *Retract.* 1,20.

3 J. Patout Burns, 'Appropriating Augustine Appropriating Cyprian', *Augustinian Studies* 36/1 (2005), 116–17. These early African councils have been the subject of investigation in F.L. Cross, 'History and Fiction in the African Canons', *Journal of Theological Studies* 12/2 (1961), 227–247; and Jane Merdinger, 'On the Eve of the Council of Hippo, 393: The Background to Augustine's Program for Church Reform', *Augustinian Studies* 40/1 (2009), 27–36.

4 *Cod. Th.* 16,38; 6,3–5; 11,2.

Overcoming Optatus

Because the entire polemical playbook Augustine used in response to this rapidly developing and unstable pastoral situation was taken from Optatus of Milevis, Augustine was handicapped from the outset in his dealing with African Christianity and in overcoming his lack of African affiliation. Considering the real stature of the institutional Donatist Church up to the late 390s, it seems clear that Optatus' efforts between 360 and the 380s had rung hollow. Whether this was because his voice was only representative of a minority group, or whether because his flock found his proposals created unnecessary distinctions between their side and the more numerous group is unclear. But what is discernible is a lack of efficacy on the part of Optatus and the emerging 'Catholic' party. Likewise, Optatus' anti-Donatist efforts were a failure, especially in comparison with the breakthrough Parmenian of Carthage was achieving in adapting the traditional African ecclesiology of a closed society of martyrs and heroes to a changing Roman world in which the majority were increasingly Christianized, and to an Africa where African Christians, that is, Donatists, controlled the culture. As it happened, Donatist leaders had to constantly redefine their Church, especially the notion of separateness from the world and from the worldly Catholics (rather than the traditional emphasis on martyrdom), and this redefining process would become *sine qua non* for the survival of the Donatist Christians.[5]

Despite Optatus' shortcomings in the African world, Augustine would have recourse to his writings upon his own ordination to the priesthood almost by default, and would inherit many of the same themes and arguments. From Optatus, Augustine would make front and centre considerations of the isolation of Africa from the rest of the catholic world (i.e., the geographical seclusion of Africa from the rest of the world); the dubiousness of the origin of the schism; the fault of the Donatists in rejecting the Catholic lineage; the proper relationship between Church and imperial government; and scrutiny of the African practice of rebaptism (the notion that grace is conferred through sin-tainted ministers).[6]

The question that arises is whether Augustine adopted these very same themes out of a sense of panic and because of their ready availability. In other

5 Tilley, *The Bible in Christian North Africa*, 93; Maureen Tilley, 'Donatus, Donatism', in *Augustine Through the Ages: An Encyclopedia*, ed. A. Fitzgerald (Grand Rapids, MI: Wm. Eerdmans Publishing, 1999), 286.

6 Robert Eno, 'Optatus of Milevis', in A. Fitzgerald (ed.), *Augustine through the Ages. An Encyclopedia* (Grand Rapids, MI/Cambridge: William B. Eerdmans Publishing, 1999), 596–597.

words, were Optatus' arguments the typical approaches of Catholics up to the 390s? Regardless of the answer, Augustine would be just as unsuccessful in the short-to-medium term as Optatus had been. Augustine would also encounter Optatus' problem of authority, in terms of which his condemnation of historic African traditions and heroes largely stigmatised the Catholic side as un-African and elitist. Indeed, given the known Donatist reverence for martyrs and for Cyprian of Carthage specifically, it is shocking that Optatus only refers to the martyr-bishop of Carthage twice! Both occurrences are noticeably lacking in affection:

> But I see you are as yet ignorant that the schism of Carthage was created by your leaders. Inquire into the origin of these affairs, and you will find that you have pronounced this judgment on your own party, as you have numbered heretics with schismatics. For it was not Caecilian who seceded from Majorinus your grandfather, but Majorinus from Caecilian; nor did Caecilian secede from the see of Peter or Cyprian but Majorinus. It is his see that you occupy, which before that same Majorinus had no existence.[7]

Optatus adds to that rather dispassionate reference to Cyprian another equally mild appropriation of his authority:

> The church [in Carthage] was filled by the populace, the episcopal see was filled, the altar was in its place, in which previous peaceable bishops—Cyprian, Lucian and others—had made their offerings in the past.[8]

Both excerpts leave one with the unavoidable impression that Augustine could scarcely have adopted Cyprian as an authority directly from Optatus. However, at work in the background is a central question about the interpretation of the authority of Cyprian, even if he is not mentioned specifically more than

7 Opt., *De Schismate* 1,10 (Edwards, 10), (*CSEL* 26, 12): 'Sed uideo te adhuc ignorare schisma apud Carthaginem a uestris principibus factum. Quaere harum originem rerum et inuenies te hanc in uos dixisse sententiam cum schismaticis haereticos sociasti. Non enim Caecilianus exiuit a Maiorino auo tuo sed Maiorinus a Caeciliano. Nec Caecilianus recessit a cathedra Petri uel Cypriani sed Maiorinus cuius tu cathedram sedes, quae ante ipsum Maiorinum originem non habet'.

8 Opt., *De Schismate* 1,19 (Edwards, 19), (*CSEL* 26, 12): 'Conferta erat ecclesia populis, plena erat cathedra episcopalis, erat altare loco suo in quo pacifici episcopi retro temporis obtulerant, Cyprianus, Carpoforius, Lucilianus et ceteri'.

twice by Optatus.[9] For the Donatists, Cyprian proves that traitor Catholics are cut off from the vine that is Christ, whilst for Catholics, the Donatists have proved themselves to be in schism and cut off from the chair of Cyprian and therefore the true Church.[10] So whilst this very short but significant example of a reference to Cyprian is evidence of a preceding critique of Donatism, it clearly lacks the depth that Augustine would require for his efforts. The question then remains: from where and when, or from whom and for what reason, did Augustine learn to appropriate Cyprian for the purpose of his anti-Donatist campaign?

Identifying Authority

The answer to identifying from whence reference to Cyprian's character and authority entered Augustine's fray with the Donatists can be found somewhere at the end of the 390s. As noted previously, Augustine had already familiarised himself with the positions of opposition leaders and had already more-or-less stumbled into his own theological trajectory. Augustine was also struggling to give resonance to his views within the African theatre, since not even his adoption of Optatus' anti-Donatism had granted him the currency he needed for an effective polemical strategy.

This all seems to have changed, however, when Augustine underwent an evolution in his conception of the role of authority in establishing orthodoxy and tradition. Augustine realised that his views could not be considered evident to everyone, and that he would have to appeal to sources and symbolisms more powerful than his own pre-existing rhetorical machinations. This movement towards an association with authority was multi-faceted; it incorporated the message of scripture, the weight of the Church, the outcome of the governance processes of the Church, and the backing of important Christian personages, all to argue that Augustine stood on the right side of the matter. His was becoming an argument based less on the truth as he understood it and expected others to do, and more on authority attested to with strong numbers.[11]

9 Dunn, 'The Reception of the Martyrdom of Cyprian', 78.

10 Opt., *De Schismate* 1,10 (Edwards, 10).

11 Curiously, Augustine's movement towards authority complemented his overall fatigue and impatience with dealing with Manichean and Donatist interlocutors in his early career phase. This in part explains his emphasis on authority as an aid to humanity's flawed capability for reason and the role of divine grace in supporting the 'perversity of men',

Augustine's appeal to authoritative sources emerged over time, surfacing first in his earliest known (philosophical) works, then becoming forged into the Manichean and Donatist campaigns, until finally coming to maturity in his anti-Pelagian efforts. Although identifying the origins of Augustine's understanding of authority is difficult,[12] it was an essential part of his thinking as the means of gaining right knowledge and beholding the truth.[13] This process of grasping the truth, the purpose of authority, was particularly useful since Augustine believed there were two groups of human beings, the erudite (*eruditi*) and the uneducated masses,[14] who could be moved to right knowledge through a combination of reason, grace and the attestation of sound *auctoritas*.[15] In this construction, grace acts upon authority to lead to full faith through its connection with human freedom,[16] making any authority a medium between humanity (via *ratio*/reason) and God (via *fides*/faith).[17]

---

conflicting opinions, and the problem of heresy; J. O'Donnell, 'The Authority of Augustine', *Augustinian Studies* 22 (1991), 9.

12 One would be remiss in failing to mention that appealing to authority and tradition was a long established practice for learned Romans of the period; see T.G. Ring, 'Auctoritas bei Tertullian, Cyprian und Ambrosius', *Cassiciacum* 29 (Würzburg: Augustinus-Verlag, 1975), 3–32.

13 Karl-Heinrich Lütcke, 'Auctoritas', in C. Mayer (ed.), *Augustinus-Lexikon*, Vol. 1 (Basel: Schwabe & Co., 1996), 499. However, some of his earlier works do reveal some sort of joint-emergence of an '*auctoritas* theme': (386/87) *Contra Academicos* 3,42; (386/87) *De ordine* 2,26; (387/88) *De moribus ecclesiae catholicae et de moribus Manichaeorum* 1,3. There also appear to be undertones throughout *De vera religione* (390–91).

14 (c. 387/88) *De animae quantitate* 12; (c. 391/92) *De utlilitate credendi* 31,33–34.

15 On the role of reason, as a way of arriving at knowledge for *eruditi* and the unlearned, see *De ordine* 2,26: '…ad discendum item necessario dupliciter ducimur, auctoritate atque ratione. Tempore auctoritas, re autem ratio prior est. Aliud est enim, quod in agendo anteponitur, aliud, quod pluris in appetendo aestimatur. Itaque quamquam bonorum auctoritas imperitae multitudini videatur esse salubrior, ratio vero apitor eruditis, tarnen, quia nullus hominum nisi ex imperito peritus fit, nullus autem imperitus novit, qualem se debeat praebere docentibus et quali vita esse docilis possit, evenit, ut omnibus bona magna et occulta discere cupientibus non aperiat nisi auctoritas ianuam'.

On the role of grace, as the agent that allows for the proper use of reason against human infirmity or '*infirmitas*', *Conf.* 13,18 and *Cresc.* 2,40. See Lütcke, 'Auctoritas', in C. Mayer (ed.), *Augustinus-Lexikon*, 501–04.

16 E. Dassmann, 'Glaubenseinsicht—Glaubensgehorsam. Augustinus über Wert und Grenzen der „auctoritas" ,' in H. Waldenfels et al. (eds.), *Theologie—Grund und Grenzen. Festgabe für Heimo Dolch zur Vollendung des 70 Lebensjahres* (Paderborn: Schöningh, 1982), 262.

17 E. Dassmann,'Glaubenseinsicht—Glaubensgehorsam', 263 and 270.

As the 390s gave way to the 400s, Augustine's authority concept manifested itself most decisively in his claim that authority was classifiable as either *auctoritas divina* or, via select persons, *auctoritas humana*.[18] Having two forms of authority, divine and human, meant that he was able to sustain the core of his authority model, which consisted of a vertical scale, beginning with (1) scripture,[19] and then descending to (2) the tradition and faith of the Church,[20] (3) the workings of the 'organs' of the Church (such as councils, liturgical practices, and institutions),[21] and lastly (4) to the personal authority and assent of individuals. Emphasising such a hierarchy gave Augustine a powerful tool in arguing for his views, and this would increasingly be the case against the Donatists. By placing scripture as the foremost source of authority, a position agreed upon by the Donatists,[22] Augustine would be able to subordinate virtually any argument he would encounter from his Donatist opponents. This tactic would become invaluable as Augustine undoubtedly ran up against the universal African veneration for the authority of Cyprian.[23] In principle, Augustine should have been able to successfully mitigate any rival position put forth by the Donatist leadership, based on the fact that any figure the Donatist used to defend their position would have been kept in line by the weight of the authority of scripture. However, Augustine's trump card was kept from play by the reality that the African appreciation of Cyprian was complemented by a uniquely African approach to biblical exegesis. This meant that Augustine's intention to advance his arguments under the assumption that scripture would keep the authority of Cyprian from validating Donatist claims

18 This distinction was already under construction as early as 386/87 with Augustine's *De ordine* 2,26–27. The indispensable source for Augustine's development of a conception of authority, especially in its division into divine and human, remains K.-H. Lütcke, *„Auctoritas" bei Augustin* (Stuttgart: W. Kohlhammer Verlag, 1968).

19 Robert Eno, 'Doctrinal Authority in Saint Augustine', *Augustinian Studies* 12 (1981), 136–141; R. Eno, 'Authority', in A. Fitzgerald (ed.), *Augustine Through the Ages. An Encyclopedia* (Grand Rapids, MI, Cambridge: Wm. Eerdmans Publishing, 1999), 80; Dassmann, 'Glaubenseinsicht—Glaubensgehorsam,' 265; Lütcke, *„Auctoritas" bei Augustin*, 128–35; Lütcke, 'Auctoritas', in C. Mayer (ed.), *Augustinus-Lexikon*, 507.

20 Eno, 'Doctrinal Authority in Saint Augustine', 157–72; R. Eno, 'Authority', 80–81; Dassmann,'Glaubenseinsicht—Glaubensgehorsam', 268; Lütcke, „Auctoritas" bei Augustin, 136–41; Lütcke, 'Auctoritas', in C. Mayer (ed.), Augustinus-Lexikon, 508.

21 Eno, 'Doctrinal Authority in Saint Augustine', 157–72; R. Eno, 'Authority', 81; Dassmann, 'Glaubenseinsicht—Glaubensgehorsam', 265; Lütcke, *„Auctoritas" bei Augustin*, 136–41; Lütcke, 'Auctoritas', in C. Mayer (ed.), *Augustinus-Lexikon*, 508.

22 Eno, 'Doctrinal Authority in Saint Augustine', 139. This is as least according to the polemical reporting of Augustine in *Gest. coll. Carth.* 3,101 (*CCSL* 149A, 205); Cresc. 1,37 (*CSEL* 52, 356); *Ep.* 129,3 (*CSEL* 44, 35).

23 Eno, 'Doctrinal Authority in Saint Augustine', 138.

was rendered useless. We see this reality most clearly in Augustine's inevitable movement towards Cyprian, a movement that was at the same time an outcome of his manoeuvring as much as it was an abrupt polemical realisation.

Identifying the Origin of Cyprian's Influence

Since Augustine never explicitly states in any of his writings or sermons that he has now happened upon the writings of Cyprian, the only way of isolating the moment of Augustine's appropriation comes from an overall assessment of his writings in the late 390s/early 400s. Even then it is difficult to draw certain conclusions, as the dating of Augustine's myriad works is in itself an unsettled affair.

The period 396–399 provides the earliest examples of an appeal to Cyprian by name. *De doctrina Christiana* (396), *Confessiones* (397), and *Contra Faustum Manicheaum* (397/99) are three works not conventionally associated with the Donatist polemic. Yet, as we saw clearly in the first chapter, in Augustine's labours the entire decade of the 390s was permeated by the Donatist controversy, and there is little way of separating out Augustine's thoughts, even if the writing or preaching he was undertaking was for an altogether different purpose. Because of this overlap, we find an increasing affinity with and gradual ease of use of Cyprian's authority in these three earlier works.[24] In a sense, these works can be affirmed as having been written between 396–399, and thus the origin of Cyprian's influence in Augustine's corpus can be located in *De doctrina Christiana* 2,61 with the following passage:

> For what else, after all, have so many of our good believers done? Can we not see how much gold and silver and fine raiment Cyprian was crammed with as he came out of Egypt, that loveliest of teachers and most blessed of martyrs [*doctor suavissimus et martyr beatissimus*]? Or Lactantius, or Victorinus, Optatus, Hilary, not to mention the living? Or countless Greek writers?[25]

24 *Doct. Chr.* 2,61 (CCSL 32, 162–64): 'Nam quid aliud fecerunt multi boni fideles nostri? Nonne aspicimus quanto auro et argento et ueste suffarcinatus exierit de Aegypto Cyprianus et doctor suauissimus et martyr beatissimus? Quanto Lactantius? Quanto Victorinus, Optatus, Hilarius, ut de uiuis taceam? Quanto innumerabiles Graeci?'; 4,31; 4,45; 4,47; 4,48; Conf. 5,15; C. Faust. 5,8; 13,4; 20,21. Another work of this time, *De agone christiano* 29,31, should not be overlooked. Though it lacks a direct appropriating reference to Cyprian, it does frame the increasingly acerbic tone Augustine was by then taking. In the passage, he slams the Donatist Church for believing that only their church, of which Cyprian would have been considered a member, contains legitimate Christians.

25 *Doct. Chr.* 2,61 (WSA I/11, 160). It is interesting to note how Augustine assigns Cyprian a pre-eminent ranking amongst the other African/Latin-speaking authorities in this passage.

Continuing with this premier sourcing of Cyprian in *De doctrina Christiana*, Augustine sustains his bold trend. In the fourth chapter of *De doct. Chr.* he establishes what he has begun in 2,61 and what he will continue to do for the rest of his career: that is, he makes references to Cyprian's writings to support his own arguments, accords flattering accolades to the martyr-bishop, and situates Cyprian amongst other heavy-weight authorities. So, already in Augustine's earliest Cyprian references in *De doct. Chr.*, he refers to Cyprian's *Ad Don.* 1 (*De doct. Chr.* 4,31), *Ep.* 63, 2–4 (*De doct. Chr.* 4,45), *De habit. virg.* 3; 15 and 23 (*De doct. Chr.* 4,47 and 49) in order to situate Cyprian on the same level as Ambrose in terms of efficacy and holiness of teaching (*De doct. Chr.* 4, 45–49). He employs terms that will become routine in subsequent years: '*beatissimi Cypriani*',[26] '*beatus Cyprianus*',[27] and 'martyr Cyprianus'.[28]

Beyond these achievements in *De doctrina Christiana*, Augustine could claim to his credit to have furthered his African portfolio with his references in *Confessiones* and *Contra Faustum*. Augustine's reference in *Conf.* reveals a great deal when placed under enhanced scrutiny. In the passage, *Conf.* 5,15, Augustine passively mentions the point where he left his native Africa and his mother Monnica near 'a memorial chapel built to Blessed Cyprian [*in memoria beati Cypriani*]'.[29] This minor utterance provides a significant clue to the identification Augustine would make with Cyprian throughout his life, although always in the background and cultivated slowly at first. Augustine's references to Cyprian in *C. Faustum* will only solidify this point as he uses Cyprian's authority to argue with his Manichean opponents. Here Augustine deploys Cyprian to stand a sign of orthodoxy. He 'whose writings teach us that he believed in Christ who was born of the Virgin Mary',[30] is an authority by virtue of being 'foremost of martyrs',[31] a prophet and apostle of Africa,[32] and a martyr of equal rank with Peter and Paul.[33]

26 *Doct. Chr.* 4,31.

27 *Doct. Chr.* 4,45.

28 *Doct. Chr.* 4,48.

29 *Conf.* 5,15 (WSA I/1, 124).

30 *C. Faust.* 5,8 (WSA I/20, 90).

31 *C. Faust.* 5,8 (WSA I/20, 90): 'Let thousands of martyrs come to your mind, and especially Cyprian himself…'

32 *C. Faust.* 13,4 (WSA I/20, 160): 'Your Mani, after all, was not a prophet of the Christ who was to come. It is in fact by a most impudent lie that he refers to himself as his apostle, for it is well known that this heresy arose not only after Tertullian, but even after Cyprian'.

33 *C. Faust.* 20,21 (WSA I/20, 279): 'After all, what bishop, while standing at the altar in the places where their holy bodies are buried, ever said, "We offer this to you, Peter or Paul or Cyprian"?'.

That Augustine was already so keen in the late 390s to overtly align himself with a celebrity martyr, quite some years before he is thought to have associated himself with the martyr-cultus,[34] does reveal to some extent the pressing nature of his need to connect with a workable African application that would allow him to present his theology to the local audience. There was, at this stage, a bit of a disconnection, however. Given that Augustine's appeal to Cyprian was contextually and pastorally conditioned by the requirement to apply his Catholic orientation to a Donatist region, one might have expected more abundant evidence of an appropriation of Cyprian in his letters and *sermones ad populum*. What this lack shows is that either the three non-Donatist works containing Cyprian references before 400 were isolated phenomena, or that these were Augustine's experimental cases in which he was fielding Cyprian to see how adaptable such an authority might be to his own theological and polemical techniques. This might partly explain why it is that up to that point in time, Augustine had not used Cyprian live against the Donatists.

Indeed, when an accounting is made of where Cyprian appears earliest in Augustine's letters and sermons, it seems as if there is a gap of some four to six years before Augustine has more regular recourse to the martyr. In fact, when an analysis is provided of the all-important letters and sermons, the evidence seems only to show a lack of continuity in Augustine's approach. It appears as if Augustine first mentions Cyprian by name only once in one of his letters in *Ep.* 82 (ca. 404/05),[35] and only by the time of *Ep.* 93 (407/08)[36] has he made Cyprian a recurring character in his letters. A total reckoning shows the overall late nature of this development: *Ep.* 98 (408/14), *Ep.* 108 (409/10), *Ep.*140 (411/12), *Ep.* 151 (?), *Ep.* 157 (414/15), *Ep.* 166 (415), *Ep.* 180 (416), *Ep.* 215 (426/27), *Ep.* 217 (426/28), *Ep.* 259 (429/30).[37] The pastoral disjunction is reflected also in the available evidence from Augustine's sermons: *s.* 8 (418), *s.* 13 (418), *s.* 49 (418), *s.* 114 (423), *s.* 138 (411/12), *s.* 163B (?), *s.* 197 (?), *s.* 294 (413), *s.* 309 (?), *s.* 310 (?), *s.* 311 (405), *s.* 312 (417), *s.* 313 (?), *s.* 313D (?), *s.* 313G (410/12), *s.* 335K (?), *s.* 341 (?), *s.* 359B (404/05).[38]

34 Placed between 401–410; see Van Bavel, 'The Cult of the Martyrs in St. Augustine', 351.

35 *Ep.* 82,24; 82,30; 82,36.

36 *Ep.* 93,15; 93,31; 93,35; 93,37(x3); 93,39(x3); 93,40; 93,41; 93,42; 93,45(x4); 93,47.

37 *Ep.* 98,3(x2); *Ep.* 108,9; 108,10(x2); 108,11(x2); 108,12; 108,20; *Ep.* 140,13; *Ep.* 151,6, *Ep.* 157,6; 157,34; *Ep.* 166,23; 166,24; Ep. 180,5; *Ep.* 215,3(x2); *Ep.* 217,2; 217,3; 217,6; 21,22; 217,26; *Ep.* 259,4 (x2).

38 *s.* 8; 8,16; *s.* 13; *s.* 49; *s.* 114; *s.* 138,1; 138,3; *s.* 163B,5,6; *s.* 197,26,3; 197,26,60; *s.* 294,19(x19); *s.* 309,2(x3); 309,3; 309,5(x3); 309,6(x3); *s.* 310,1(x2); 310(x8); *s.* 311,1; 311,3; 313 7; 311,10; *s.* 312,3(x6); 312,4; 312,6;(x2); *s.* 313,1; 313,2(x6); 313,5; *s.* 313D; *s.* 313G,2,3 (x2); *s.* 335K,21,5; *s.* 341,22,4; *s.* 359B,2,5: 359B,2,16.

Curiously, however, within the margin of error, there is a series of sermons that throws this timeline into doubt. *S.* 37 (c. 397–410), *s.* 305A (c. 401), *s.* 313A (c. 401), *s.* 313B (c. 400), *s.* 313C (403), and *s.* 313E (c. 399–410) all present something of quandary for unravelling the emergence of Cyprian in Augustine's anti-Donatist efforts. Of those six sermons, *s.* 305A, *s.* 313A, and *s.* 313B are most accurately dated to 10 August 401, 14 September 401, and 14 September 400 respectively.[39] Since these sermons were delivered virtually simultaneously with Augustine's anti-Donatist polemic reaching full force, and along with *C. ep. Parm.* and *De bapt.* in 400/01, and since all fall within the margin of error in terms of dating them precisely, they do furnish an important insight into Augustine's early appropriation of Cyprian.

In *s.* 313B Augustine clearly accentuates the exemplary role of Cyprian as the most revered martyr-hero of all Africa: '[W]hen the blessed martyr shed his blood in this place [in Carthage], I don't know whether there was such a big crowd here raging against him, as there now is a multitude of people praising him'.[40] More importantly, he goes on to compare Cyprian with Peter and with Christ, going so far as to suggest that 'Saint Cyprian, Christ's holy martyr'[41] is an '*alter Christus*,' and to compare Christ's crucifixion and its converting effect on the Jews with Cyprian's martyrdom in the arena:

> The Jews who killed Christ, who wagged their heads at him as they abused him hanging on the cross, and exulted as they said whatever words they liked against him, afterward came to believe in the very Lord they had crucified. It was impossible, after all, for the voice of the doctor to be without effect, as he hung on the cross and made a medicine of health and sanity out of his blood for them in their frenzied madness…The same sort of thing, clearly, is in no way to be doubted about the blessed Cyprian, Christ's holy martyr; that many of those who impiously watched him killed came to believe in his Lord, and perhaps even came to imitate him by shedding their blood for the name of Christ.[42]

---

39 É. Rebillard places the three at 10 AUG 401/14 Sep 401/14 SEP 400, in 'Sermones', in A. Fitzgerald (ed.), *Augustine through the Ages*, 785–86. E. Hill places the three at 401; WSA III/9, 90 and 96.

40 *s.* 313B,1 (*WSA* III/9, 96).

41 *s.* 313B,4 (*WSA* III/9, 99).

42 *s.* 313B,4 (*WSA* III/9, 99), (*MA* 1, 74): 'Iudaei Christi interfectores, qui pendente illo caput agitauerunt insultantes, et in illo uerba quae uoluerunt dixerunt, exultantes postea in ipsum dominum, quem crucifixerunt, crediderunt. Nec enim poterat uacare uox medici in cruce pendentis, et medicamentum sanitatis freneticis de suo sanguine facientis…Hoc plane et de beato Cypriano Christi sancto martyre nullo modo est dubitandum, quod

To allay any doubts about what Augustine was intimating in these lines, compare that passage with Augustine's further rendering of Cyprian's passion below:

> How many of the persecutors, who saw the blessed Cyprian shed his blood, saw him kneel down, offer his neck to the sword, saw it here, watched it here, exulted it here as such a spectacle, here, here heaped abuse upon him as he died; how many of them, which I have no doubt about, later came to believe! It's not be doubted, it's to be believed without a shadow of a doubt.[43]

Revealing that this comparison was no passing fancy for the bishop of Hippo, Augustine portrays Cyprian's action even more specifically as a sacrificial act of heroism in the Christian combat against the sin of the world. He frames Cyprian's worldly enemies thus:

> So the raging crowd has departed, and the praising multitude has taken its place. Let them say…*Blessed is the Lord, who has not given us as a quarry to their teeth* [Ps 123,6]. Whose teeth? The teeth of the enemies, the teeth of the godless, the teeth of those persecuting Jerusalem, the teeth of Babylon, the teeth of the enemy city, the teeth of a crowd gone stark, staring mad in their villainy, the teeth of a crowd persecuting the Lord, forsaking the creator, turning to the creature, worshipping things made by hand, ignoring the one by whom they were made.[44]

Against so formidable an opponent, the stakes were astronomically high, just as they were for Christ's world-redeeming passion. And with this opportunity, Augustine makes one of his most colourful and unambiguous comparisons

---

plurimi eorum, qui occisum impie spectauerunt, in eius dominum crediderunt, et forte etiam ipsi imitando pro Christi nomine sanguinem fuderunt'.

43 *s.* 313B,4 (*WSA* III/9, 99), (*MA* 1, 74): 'Qui percussum in isto loco sanctum Cyprianum uiderunt, incertum sit utrum crediderint: certe isti omnes, aut paene omnes, quorum uoces audio exultantium, filii sunt insultantium'.

44 *s.* 313B,1 (*WSA* III/9, 96), (*MA* 1,70–71): 'Nescio utrum tanta hic fuerit turba furentium, quanta nunc est multitudo laudantium. sed et si fuit…benedictus dominus, qui non dedit nos in uenationem dentibus eorum. Dentibus quorum? Dentibus inimicorum, dentibus impiorum, dentibus persecutorum Hierusalem, dentibus Babyloniae, dentibus ciuitatis inimicae, dentibus turbae in sceleribus insanientis, dentibus turbae dominum persequentis, creatorem deserentis, ad creaturam se conuertentis, manu facta colentis, a quo facta est contemnentis'.

between Cyprian and Christ, concerning the import of the success of both passions, and the specifically beneficial result of that of Cyprian:

> What a fat prey, what a juicy quarry would godless Babylon have fed on, if the Lord had been denied by Cyprian the bishop! What a full meal would godless Babylon had had, what a quarry, what a choice prey would it have fed on, if Cyprian the bishop, the teacher of nations, the smasher of idols, the unmasker of demons, the winner of pagans the strengthener of Christians, the man who fired the weal of the martyrs [*si a Cypriano episcopo, doctore gentium, frustratore idolorum, proditore daemoniorum, lucratore paganorum, confirmatore Christianorum, inflammatore martyrium*]; so if such and so great a man were to deny the Lord, what a noble quarry would godless Babylon have rejoiced over!...Let them rage they would, persecute, torture, imprison, bind, strike burn, toss to the wild beasts; Christ was not denied, the confessor of the Lord [Cyprian] was crowned.[45]

When we take the assertions made in Augustine's *s.* 313B and compare them with *s.* 305A and *s.* 313A, written scarcely one year later, the difference in tone and style is remarkable. Whilst we again see conventional accolades such as 'holy martyr Cyprian' (sancti martyris Cypriani),[46] 'blessed Cyprian',[47] 'most blessed martyr',[48] 'the glory of so great a martyr',[49] what is more noticeable is that Augustine is by this point combining his pre-existing theology with an appropriation of Cyprian, thereby attempting to lay a claim to Cyprian's authority for himself. Specifically, Augustine makes this bold interpretation by arguing that more than being victorious through his loss of life for Christ, Cyprian's most important accomplishment is his overcoming, through grace

45 *s.* 313B,2 (*WSA* III/9, 97), (*MA* 1, 72): 'Quali sagina praedae, quali pinguedine uenationis Babylon impia pasceretur, si a Cypriano episcopo dominus negaretur. quali sagina, quali uenatione, quam optima praeda Babylon impia pasceretur, si a Cypriano episcopo, doctore gentium, frustratore idolorum, proditore daemoniorum, lucratore paganorum, confirmatore christianorum, inflammatore martyrum; si ergo a tali et tanto uiro dominus negaretur, quali uenatione Babylon impia laet...Saeuierint, persecuti fuerint, torserint, incluserint, alligauerint, percusserint, incenderint, bestiis subrexerint: non est Christus negatus, confessor domini est coronatus'.

46 *s.* 305A,4 (*WSA* III/8, 326).

47 *s.* 305A,2 (*WSA* III/8, 325); s. 313A,3 (*WSA* III/9, 92); 313A,5 (*WSA* III/9, 94).

48 *s.* 313A,1 (*WSA* III/9, 90).

49 *s.* 305A,1 (*WSA* III/8, 324).

of 'the pleasures of the flesh, the lust of the eyes, worldly ambition'.[50] In fact, Augustine continues, Cyprian is worthy of imitation precisely because he overcame pride (*superbia*),[51] endured the 'rage of the pagans',[52] and escaped the pull of 'sordid and carnal pleasures'[53] by his gentleness and humility in obedience to Christ,[54] made possible through God's grace: 'When could [Cyprian] have done so, if the Lord had not come his aid? When could he have been victorious, if the spectator, who was preparing a crown for him in his victory, had not provided him with the necessary strength for his toils?'[55] This new conception of Cyprian put forth by Augustine postulates Cyprian's authority was derived from his obedience, his infusion of grace, and his humility:

> But the human mind has a natural tendency to self-importance. Then self-importance should be checked. The one who sits in judgment on human beings must recognise he is only human himself. There's a disparity of rank, but a common share of human frailty. Anyone who thinks about this in a godfearing and religious way can both exercise authority and avoid lapsing into self-importance. Cyprian overcame all these things.[56]

Indeed, Augustine uses Cyprian here as a model of holiness, focused less on the loss of one's life and more on obedience and humility towards God in ordinary circumstances. In this sense, Augustine is in agreement with Cyprian's original intention that the quality of martyrdom consists in responses to both persecution and peacetime. To explicate this here, Augustine says a Christian should be 'crazy about Cyprian'[57] because of Cyprian's humility and patience before God and God's grace in return. Augustine uses Cyprian as the ultimate African authority in this regard: 'You heard the blessed Cyprian, both example and trumpet of the martyrs: "In persecution," he said, "it is the soldiering that is crowned, but in peacetime it is the conscience" [*audistis beatum Cyprianum, martyrum et exemplum et tubam: in persecutione, inquit, militia,*

50 *s.* 305A,2 (*WSA* III/8, 325).
51 *s.* 305A,4 (*WSA* III/8, 326–27).
52 *s.* 305A,3 (*WSA* III/8, 326).
53 *s.* 305A,4 (*WSA* III/8, 93).
54 *s.* 305A,4 (*WSA* III/8, 326–27).
55 *s.* 305A,5 (*WSA* III/8, 327).
56 *s.* 313A,4 (*WSA* III/9, 93), (*MA* 1, 69): 'Sed humana mens pergit in elationem? Frenetur elatio: hominem se esse cognoscat, qui de homine iudicat. dispar est dignitas, sed communis est ipsa fragilitas. Hoc qui pie sancteque cogitat, et habet potestatem, et non pergit in elationem. uicit ista omnia Cyprianus'.
57 *s.* 313A,3 (*WSA* III/9, 92).

in pace conscientia coronatur] So none of you should think that it isn't the time for you. It isn't always the time for suffering death, but it is always the time for devoting one's life to God'.[58]

This argument had the effect of placing Augustine squarely on the side of Cyprian in terms of recognising the dignity of 'white martyrs' who suffer in faith, even without accompanying loss of life.[59] The question remains whether Augustine drew this distinction as a way of distancing himself from the Donatist interpretation of Cyprian, or more for the purpose of placing himself squarely within the Cyprianic tradition.

Sermons 37 & 313E: A Problem?

Among the sermons that most complicate the timing of the appropriation, two sermons in particular, 37 and 313E, present the most acute problem in pinpointing the breakthrough moment when Augustine arrived at Cyprian for use as an authority against the Donatists. Due to inconclusive dating of these two sermons, they either present evidence Augustine's breakthrough occurred between the years 393–97, or, more likely, that the breakthrough only really occurred between 397–400, on the threshold of Augustine writing his anti-Donatist trilogy. If the latter scenario proves correct, then *s.* 37 and *s.* 313E are likely to have been produced closer to 410, at the junction of the Donatist and Pelagian controversies.

But, what would the slight chance that the two sermons (or even one of them) can be traced back to before 400 entail? If they were produced before 400, it would mean Augustine had already designed almost the entire platform that he would use against the Donatists: the nature of the Church, a rival sacramentology (especially concerning baptism), an understanding of operative grace, and perhaps most importantly from the perspective of a listening African audience, a balanced array of authority sources through which to validate proposals. If this group of sermons is pre-400, it would also mean conditions between Augustine and Donatist leaders had deteriorated much more precipitously in the earliest years of his career than has been previously thought.

Even determining which sermon was prepared first is difficult. Only by analysing what each contains and lacks is any hypothesis possible. Both of the sermons were delivered for the purpose of commemorating martyrs' feast days before friendly audiences. According to Van Bavel's timeframe of Augustine's favouring of the martyr cult, this detail would indicate a creation date of

58 *s.* 305A,2 (*WSA* III/8, 325).

59 Allen Brent, *Cyprian and Roman Carthage* (Cambridge: Cambridge University Press, 2010), 275–281.

between 401–410. Both sermons contain themes identified in the more precisely-dated letters and sermons. *S.* 37 refers to the weakness of the flesh, the global span of the Church (in all nations), the problem of heresies, and typologies of the Church commonly used in North Africa. *S.* 313E contains repetitious pleas to the audience not to be afraid (of an external enemy?), ideas of the absolute importance of peace and unity, of Donatist obedience to Donatus instead of Christ, of the damnation attendant upon separation from Christ's Church and of the Donatists being cut off from grace.

But what can be said about which sermon was produced first? Whilst this too is difficult to determine exactly, one feature of *s.* 37 would make it a solid candidate for being earlier: it lacks the ascription of Cyprian as a martyr, which became a very important rationale for his authority. Whilst this can be explained partly by the fact that the excerpt is found within a sermon on the African Scillitan Martyrs, the fact remains that here Augustine emphasises Cyprian's doctrinal importance and not his martyrdom:[60]

> There are precious stones in the Church, and always have been, learned, well endowed with knowledge and eloquence and all the teaching of the laws. Precious indeed are these stones. But of their number there are some who have gone astray from the jewelry of this woman. In terms of his brilliant doctrine and eloquence such a precious stone—he shines so brilliantly, doesn't he, with the doctrine of the Lord—such a precious stone was Cyprian, but he was one that remained among the woman's jewels. Such a precious stone, too, was Donatus—but he burst out of this collection of jewellery. The one who remained wanted to be loved in her. The one who shook himself loose sought a name for himself apart from her. The one who remained with her gathered others to her; the one who popped out was eager not to gather but to scatter.[61]

60 This aspect is itself something of an innovation on Augustine's part. North Africans in the third and fourth centuries clearly lionised Cyprian because of his heroic stature as a martyr. It was only as a later development that Cyprian's doctrinal insights began receiving any emphasis. See G. Dunn, 'The Reception of the Martyrdom of Cyprian of Carthage in Early Christian Literature', 65.

61 *s.* 37,3 (*WSA* III/2, 186), (*CCSL* 41, 449): 'Sunt in ecclesia lapides pretiosi, et semper fuerunt, docti, abundantes et scientia et eloquio et omni instructione legis. pretiosi plane isti lapides sunt. Sed ex eorum numero quidam aberrauerunt ab ornamento mulieris huius. quantum enim pertinet ad doctrinam et eloquium unde fulget, lapis pretiosus—doctrina enim dominica fulget—lapis pretiosus erat Cyprianus, sed mansit in huius ornamento. Lapis pretiosus erat Donatus, sed resiliuit a compage ornamenti. Ille qui mansit, in ea se amari uoluit. Ille qui inde excussus est, praeter illam nomen sibi quaesiuit'.

Dating this passage to an earlier period would mesh more neatly with Augustine's earlier ease in highlighting the weight of an authority based on his preeminence as a teacher within the Church. This held also for Augustine's initial gravitation towards employing the scriptures, the judgment of councils, venerable primatial sees like Rome, and biblical figures (especially Paul). However, when determining the origin of *s.* 37, it cannot be overlooked that the language of the sermon differs strikingly from that of *s.* 305A and *s.* 313A. Absent in s. 37 is terminology referring to martyrdom, to obedience to Christ, and to Cyprian overcoming sin and worldly temptations. In their place we find references to Cyprian's doctrinal authority in which he is described as 'learned, well endowed, with knowledge and eloquence and all the teaching of the law'.[62] These are all terms that would surface more prominently during the Pelagian controversy, when Augustine had recourse to various authority figures based on their erudition and holiness (see Chapter 7), an argument that might suggest a later date. As an additional note, it is worth bearing in mind that even though *s.* 37 is considerably longer than *s.* 313E, the appeal to Cyprian is noticeably abbreviated, consisting of less than a paragraph.

Situating Sermon 313E

Given the dynamics involved in placing *s.* 305A, *s.*313A, and *s.* 37, it should come as no surprise that a definitive placement of *s.* 313E is also a difficult endeavour. Even today there is a wide array of views as to when s. 313E originated. As examples, E. Hill posits 395/96[63] and O. Perler-J.-L. Maier suggests 395/96–399,[64] whilst A. Kunzelmann holds 410,[65] as does J. Yates, who is critical of a date of origin before 400.[66] G. Dunn acknowledges the historical tendency has inclined towards 410, but finds Augustine's concerns with cliff-jumping and coerced martyrdom to be more fitting for the pastoral situation in 395/96.[67]

Adding to the diversity of scholarly estimates is the outcome of a close analysis of the text of *s.* 313E which reveals commonalities with the other sermons under discussion, but which also reveals advancements which make situating the source more doubtful. Insofar as Augustine's appreciation of Cyprian goes,

62 *s.* 37,3 (*WSA* III/2, 186).

63 Augustine, *Sermons* III/9 (306–340A), On the Saints, ed. J.E. Rotelle, trans., notes E. Hill, *WSA* (Hyde Park, NY: New City Press, 1994), 116.

64 Perler and Maier, *Les Voyages de Saint Augustin*, 280 and 455.

65 Kunzelmann, 'Die Chronologie der Sermones des Hl. Augustinus', 455.

66 Yates, 'The Use of the Bible in North African Martyrological Polemics of Late Antiquity', 405.

67 G. Dunn, 'The Reception of the Martyrdom of Cyprian of Carthage in Early Christian Literature', 82–83.

it is not surprising to see common appellations once again: 'blessed Cyprian',[68] 'martyr Cyprian',[69] and 'Saint Cyprian'.[70] Likewise, we see a fascinating convergence of Cyprian-related themes which Augustine had been modelling in the late 390s and early 400s. Augustine's insistence was at first on the need for Catholics to be unafraid of the Donatists and other heretics because Cyprian would have been: 'The blessed Cyprian wasn't afraid of the worshippers of demons; we shouldn't be afraid of the gatherings of heretics, we shouldn't be afraid of the assemblies of cliff jumpers [Circumcelliones]'.[71] Another example is the way he contrasts the worldly and ambitious Donatists with the example of Cyprian, who he claims the Catholics follow more authentically through their obedience;[72] through their preference for peace in society and in the Church;[73] and by not wanting to place themselves in the limelight for the sake of celebrity.[74] In another related example, Augustine re-uses a comparison of Cyprian with Christ and Peter.[75] Other themes, which are by now familiar,

68 *s.* 313E,1 (*WSA* III/9, 109); *s.* 313E,5 (*WSA* III/9, 113); *s.* 313E,6–8 (*WSA* III/9, 114–116).

69 *s.* 313E,2 (*WSA* III/9, 110).

70 *s.* 313E,7 (*WSA* III/6, 114).

71 *s.* 313E,7 (*WSA* III/9, 115). The theme of 'fear' reappears throughout *s.* 313E: 1; 4; 6; 7(x3).

72 *s.* 313E,1 (*WSA* III/9, 109); *s.* 313E,6 (*WSA* III/9, 114).

73 *s.* 313E,3 (*WSA* III/9, 110): 'The Donatist or heretic is not a disciple of Christ; the enemy of peace is not a disciple of Christ'; *s.* 313E,5 (*WSA* III/9, 113), (*MA* 1, 537): 'Non est Christi discipulus Donatista aut haereticus; non est Christi discipulus pacis inimicus'.

74 This is perhaps most powerfully displayed in *s.* 313E,6 (*WSA* III/9, 114): 'So then, observe the branches that have been cut off, those heretics the Donatists. Why do you people say you belong to this man, this man who bore the fruit of peace and unity, who was pruned by the pruning hook of martyrdom, to obtain his crown of eternal salvation? Why do you compare yourselves to this man, heretics and Donatists, cut off from the vine by separation, defiled by your habit of headlong self-destruction? The blessed Cyprian takes his stand, he confesses Christ, he does not consent to what he is being compelled to do; he accepts the temporal judicial sentence, he come, with Christ, a judge for eternity. He accepts the sentence, and quite rightly says "Thanks be to God," because he has quite rightly confessed Christ'; (*MA* 1, 541): 'Attendite sarmenta amputata, haeretici et Donatistae. Quid uos ad istum dicitis pertinere, ad istum ferentem fructum pacis et unitatis, purgatum falce martyrii ad percipiendam coronam aeternae salutis? Quid uos huic comparatis, haeretici et Donatistae, separatione concisi, praecipitatione coinquinati? Stat beatus Cyprianus, Christum confitetur, non consentit ad id quod cogitur; accipit iudiciariam sententiam temporalem, fit cum Christo iudex in aeternum. Accipit sententiam, et Deo gratias recte, quia recte confessus est'.

75 *s.* 313E,3 (*WSA* III/9, 110): 'Let us consider…the case of Christ teaching and Cyprian following him; and then these people shouting contradiction and claiming to be Christians, to belong to Cyprian [Consideremus, fratres dilectissimi, docentem Christum, sequentem Cyprianum; et istos de transuerso clamantes se esse christianos, se ad Cyprianum

and found in *s.* 313E, are his insistence on Cyprian's option for unity and peace over paranoia about ritual purity;[76] Cyprian's graced-state, which was bestowed by God;[77] blistering polemical attacks against the Donatists as pawns of Satan;[78]

pertinere]... Listen to what Christ teaches: My peace I give you, my peace I leave you (Jn. 14,27). The Donatist or heretic is not a disciple of Christ; the enemy of peace is not a disciple of Christ [non est Christi discipulus Donatista aut haereticus; non est Christi discipulus pacis inimicus]...Just see whether the Lord our God said this and didn't do it—the one who said My peace I give you, my peace I leave you. He tolerated Judas the devil among his disciples, he didn't set him apart. He was admitted to the Lord's supper, when he had already accepted the Lord's price. He wanted to sell Christ, you see, he refused to be redeemed by Christ. This was how our Lord and Savior Jesus Christ taught that separation is to be avoided, and division to be outlawed, peace and unity to be loved'. For more Christ-Cyprian comparisons also see, s. 313E,5 (*WSA* III/9, 113) and s. 313E,6 (*WSA* III/9, 114). For a Peter-Cyprian comparison, see s. 313E,8 (*WSA* III/9, 116).

76 *s.* 313E,1; 313E,3–5.

77 *s.* 313E,1 (*WSA* III/9, 109): 'He won God's favor by a twin grace, grace of course which he received from the one who was pleased with him [gemina gratia commendatus deo, ea utique gratia, quam sumpsit ab illo cui placuit]. He pleased God because of God's gift to him; as far as concerned him in himself, you see, he had that which would displease God, not that which would please him [human sin and weakness via caro] But, as it is written, where sin abounded, grace abounded all the more (Rom 5,20). He himself, a trustworthy and truthful martyr and servant of God, truthful by God's gift, confesses in his writings what he had been like previously; he doesn't forget what he had been like, in order not to be ungrateful to the one through whom he ceased to be like that'.

78 Augustine attempts to contrast Cyprian as teacher of the Catholics with Donatus and Satan as teachers of the Donatists; *s.* 313E,4 (*WSA* III/9, 111): 'Well, the Donatists aren't false Christians, they're quite simply not Christians at all [Donatistae enim non falsi christiani, sed omnino christiani non sunt], since they listen to what the devil suggested, and don't listen to the answer Christ gave him...This, you see, is exactly what the devil is also suggesting to the Donatists, saying, "Hurl yourselves down, the angels are there to catch you; with such a death you don't go to punishment, but you win through a crown" [of martyrdom]. They would be Christians if they gave an ear to Christ and didn't trust the devil, who first separated them from the peace of the Church, and later on gave them cliff-jumpers'. See also, s. 313E,5 (*WSA* III/9, 113): 'If they were in their right minds, they would shrink in horror from throwing themselves over cliffs, and wouldn't commit murder. This is what they do, what their father the devil has taught them, and their teacher Donatus has instructed them on. As against them, the blessed Cyprian manfully defended both unity and peace'. (*MA* 1, 540): 'Ad hunc articulum uenis: martyrem te esse ideo dicturus es, ut facias aut homicidium aut homicidam; ut et ad homines ueniant, et eos in se arment, et terrendo occidere cogant. Qui si sanum cor haberent, et praecipitium horrerent, et homicidium non facerent; sed hoc faciunt, quod eos pater suus diabolus docuit, et magister suus Donatus instruxit. Contra quos beatus Cyprianus et unitatem et pacem fortiter

and the subtly recurring idea that there was actually very little separating Donatists from Catholics besides pride, stubbornness, and sin.[79]

Nevertheless, *s.* 313E displays some strong new developments in Augustine's anti-Donatist campaign. Whilst Augustine elaborates on Cyprian's dignity, arising from his being an erudite teacher-bishop (which he transfers from *s.* 37) as well as a martyr, we see here for the first time Augustine using Cyprian's warrior example as a battle cry to stir his Catholic audiences against the Donatists, a true breakthrough in the polemical timeline. We witness here for the first time, in front of an assembled and frightened Catholic audience,[80] Augustine's unequivocal denial of the Donatist claim to Cyprian's authority:

> So it's not surprising if out of faith which cannot be seen, this life is despised which can be seen, in order to obtain the life which cannot be seen. This was the faith Saint Cyprian was filled with, this the faith that fills, not false, but true Christians, who believe and trust God with their whole heart and an unshaken faith. The heretics, though, and the Donatists [E. Hill treats this distinction as actually one group and not two; see *WSA* III/9, 116], who falsely boast that Cyprian belongs to them, should pay attention to the way he exercised his office of bishop, and then they wouldn't break away; they should pay attention to the way he went to his martyrdom, and then they wouldn't throw themselves over cliffs. The heretic breaking away in heresy, the Donatist jumping deliberately to

defendit'. Beyond the Cyprian (Catholic) vs. Satan (Donatist) contrast, Augustine seems at this point to have become quite skilful in applying the right polemical tone to the debate. One can see this in his resort to phrases such as 'rabid dogs', *s.* 313E,6 (*WSA* III/9, 114); 'insane Donatists', *s.* 313E,6 (*WSA* III/9, 114); 'unhappy and miserable wenches', *s.* 313E,4 (*WSA* III/9, 112); and 'Mr. Donatist, so keen to kill yourself, you shun the traitor's noose; why don't you shun the devil's precipice', *s.* 313E,4 (*WSA* III/9, 112).

79 *s.* 313E,4 (*WSA* III/9, 111); *s.* 313E,5 (*WSA* III/9, 113).

80 *s.* 313E,2 (*WSA* III/9, 110): 'But where is the faith which I'm talking about? Let it be shown to our eyes. Look here, faith can't be seen; and yet the whole of this crowd, which can be seen here in God's house, was drawn here by faith, which cannot be seen. So it's a grand thing, is faith, as the Lord also says in the gospel…So it's not surprising if, out of faith which cannot be seen, this life is despised which can be seen, in order to obtain the life which cannot be seen'. (*MA* 1, 536): 'Fides ubi est, de qua nunc loquor? Demonstretur oculis nostris. Ecce fides non uidetur: et tamen totam istam multitudinem, quae hic in domo dei uidetur, ipsa fides attraxit, quae non uidetur. Magna ergo fides, sicut et dominus in euangelio dicit…non ergo mirum est, si per fidem quae non uidetur contemnitur uita quae uidetur, ut acquiratur uita quae non uidetur'.

> his death, is certainly not one of Christ's disciples; certainly not one of Cyprian's comrades.[81]

To emblazon this rather bold assertion, Augustine capitalises on his denial of the Donatist appropriation of Cyprian and introduces a clever three-stage re-appropriation for the Catholic side. The first stage involves a rejection of the Donatist claim to Cyprian via the polemical assault that they reject Christ/Cyprian's premium on peace and unity in the Church: 'Let us consider, my dearest brothers and sisters, the case of Christ teaching and Cyprian following him; and then these people shouting in contradiction and claiming to be Christians, to belong to Cyprian. Listen to what Christ teaches: *My peace I give you, my peace I leave you*'.[82]

Next, Augustine moves to entice his Catholic listeners to take the teaching of Christ and Cyprian to heart and cease being afraid:

> As for us though, we pay attention to the authoritative teaching of Christ; so let us take example of Cyprian to heart, beseeching the Lord God, with the assistance too of the prayers of the saints, to preserve us from fearing such people, and from keeping quiet to them about the faith and the hope that is in us. So let us confess Christ, and not be afraid of men, nor keep quiet out of fear. Because the blessed Cyprian too spent his life among persecutors and the heathen, and though finding himself among the worshippers of idols, he had no fear of the temporal authority of the empire, and he didn't keep quiet either about idols not being gods.[83]

In the last step, Augustine maintains the symbol of Cyprian as brave in the face of vile enemies and as a model of speaking out for Christ without regard for self-interest. Perhaps more fundamentally, Augustine uses this opportunity to

---

81 s. 313E,2 (*WSA* III/9, 110), (*MA* 1, 536): 'Non ergo mirum est, si per fidem quae non uidetur contemnitur uita quae uidetur, ut acquiratur uita quae non uidetur. Hac fide plenus erat sanctus Cyprianus: hac fide implentur non falsi sed ueri christiani, qui ex toto corde et fide. Inconcussa deo credunt. haeretici autem et Donatistae, qui se ad Cyprianum falso iactant pertinere, si episcopatum eius attenderent, non se separarent; si martyrium, non se praecipitarent. Non est omnino discipulus Christi, non est comes Cypriani'.

82 s. 313E,3 (*WSA* III/9, 110), (*MA* 1, 537): 'Pacem meam do vobis, pacem meam relinquo vobis'.

83 s. 313E,7 (*WSA* III/9, 114), (*MA* 1, 541): 'Sed nos attendentes magisterium Christi, exemplum Cypriani ponamus in cordibus nostris, deprecantes dominum deum, adiuuantibus etiam orationibus sanctorum, ut tales homines non timeamus, et eis non taceamus de fide et spe quae in nobis est. confiteamur ergo Christum, et homines non timeamus, neque timendo taceamus. Nam et beatus Cyprianus inter persecutores et gentiles uitam agens, cum esset inter idolorum cultores'.

show that since Cyprian is on the side of Catholic theology, Catholics should not only not fear the Donatists, but actually receive grace, since the model of Cyprian's courage brings the vigilant Catholic's heart and mind to the truth.[84] With this technique Augustine sets the tone for virtually the entire duration of his career when it comes to dealing with Donatist leaders and later the Pelagian 'threat'. But as much as this denial of Cyprian for the Donatists, and appropriation for the Catholic side marks a breakthrough in the course of the Donatist and Pelagian controversies, it is important to note how it also set the stage for how he would interact with future enemies. Whilst before this point he had placed a premium on dialogue for the truth, this series of sermons marks a radical change towards an aggressive offensive that seeks to overwhelmingly deny his opponents access to any validating authority source, thus making any opposing view a rogue one and an anti-Christian threat.

At the same time as identifying Augustine's rather systematic accession of Cyprian, more questions abound, especially concerning the dating of *s.* 313E as either before 400 or closer to 410. On the one hand, there are many apparent reasons that make 410 seem more likely: (1) Augustine's free emphasis on martyrdom (in keeping with van Bavel's timeline); (2) more abundant mentions of grace; and (3) a hard-line attitude towards Donatists as heretics rather than mere schismatics. On the other hand, one cannot escape evidence that strongly suggests delivery in the late 390s/early 400s, since firstly, the anti-Donatist campaign ignited Augustine's efforts to arouse his Catholic audience to take on the Donatists head on, as well as convince them to use the model of Cyprian that they might not be afraid of retribution. Second, whilst *s.* 313E does present a coalescence of anti-Donatist themes and an obvious ease in using Cyprian's name, the fact remains that the use of Cyprian is still rather fresh at this point and not bound up with meatier theology as would happen by 410/411. Finally, there is as yet minimal utilisation of Pauline sources in combination with the appeal to Cyprian (only three are used in *s.* 313E: Rom. 5,20, 8,32, and Gal. 2,20). Pauline sources will become a trademark of Augustine's appropriation as the campaign matures.

Regardless of the remaining uncertainties, what is clear is that in the run-up to 400, Augustine had entered a phase of frantic efforts against the Donatist Church in a way that would endure throughout the rest of his career, with Cyprian as his banner in the charge to assert the dominance of the Catholic religion in Africa. And now our attention turns to the 400s, by which time Augustine had waded into a full-scale controversy with his self-proclaimed Donatist enemies.

84 *s.* 313E,7 (*WSA* III/9, 115).

CHAPTER 3

The Election of Primian and Its Consequences, Mid 390s

Whilst Augustine, as a young bishop in the mid-390s, was briskly acquiring status as a veteran anti-Donatist campaigner, history was presenting the Catholic side with an event that would define the internal dynamics of the Donatist Church in the 390s and early 400s, and this largely in a negative sense. This event was the ascension of Primian of Carthage,[1] successor to the famed Donatist bishop, Parmenian. Primian would go on to serve as Donatist primate in a period of transition perhaps unmatched in the history of that Church. Under his tenure, he would oversee a decade (the 390s) in which Donatism would consolidate its hegemony, ecclesiastically and politically, almost making it the undisputed Church in Roman North Africa,[2] much to the displeasure of Augustine and other nascent Catholic insurgents.

But by the first decade of the fifth century, the Donatist Church had suffered a number of setbacks at the hands of Roman imperial authorities and also because of the proselytising efforts of the Catholics, essentially putting the Donatist Church in a defensive posture concerning its own existence. One therefore cannot help asking how this series of events transpired so quickly and how the Donatist fortunes reversed so rapidly. Was there a link between the leadership of Primian and the gradual eradication of Donatism as a structured organisation distinguishable from the Catholics?

To answer these questions, in this chapter I examine contemporary evidence that might shed light on the reception of Primian's election as bishop of Carthage within the context of Augustine's anti-Donatist campaign. Specifically, I discuss the degree to which the controversy over Primian's election was a polemical gateway (*locus polemicus*) for Augustine, the main opponent of the Donatists, as he embarked on his own prolonged anti-Donatist agenda. As a corollary, I analyse whether, as suggested by B. Kriegbaum,[3] Primian can be

1 Reigned c. 392–411/12(?); Mandouze, *Prosopographie de l'Afrique Chrétienne*, s.v. 'Primianus 1', 905–13.

2 Frend referred to this epoch as the 'culminating point' in Donatist history in *The Donatist Church*, 223.

3 B. Kriegbaum, 'Die Donatistischen Konzilien von Cebarsussa (393) and Bagai (394)', *Zeitschrift für Katholische Theologie* 124 (2002), 267.

 | DOI 10.1163/9789004312647_005

considered responsible for the decline of Donatism, and whether his election as Donatist primate ushered in the beginning of the end of Donatism as an entity independent of the Christianity found in other parts of the empire at that time.

But first some preliminary remarks are in order. Any discussion of the circumstances surrounding Primian's election is rendered tendentious in view of the fact that the historical record is rather limited. The evidence we do have, such as a number of surviving specimens of Donatist literature and ideas, are tainted by the pro-Catholic bias of Augustine, Donatism's greatest historical definer.[4] This bias likewise extends to overly-negative descriptions of Primian himself found in modern research and literature, making him the quintessential cad of antiquity.[5] Also, whilst at this stage I endeavour to identify the causal relationship between the election of Primian and the suppression of Donatism, it is disingenuous to assign complete blame to the bishop[6] and infelicitous to

4 James Alexander, 'Donatistae', in *Augustinus-Lexikon*, vol. 2, ed. C. Mayer (Basel: Schwabe & Co., 1999), 631.

5 A plethora of examples exist and a few examples from recent research are as follows (author followed by abbreviated title): (1) those summarising Primian with a highly negative tone: Gerald Bonner, 'a man of violence rather than a leader or diplomat', *St Augustine of Hippo: Life and Controversies* (Norwich: Canterbury Press, 1986), 247; Frend, 'man of extreme views and ruthless violence', (*The Donatist Church*, 213); Kriegbaum, 'Zu einem guten Teil scheint Primian selbst für den Niedergang des Donatismus um die Wende vom 4. zum 5. Jh. Verantwortlich gewesen zu sein,' 'Die Donatistischen Konzilien von Cebarsussa (393) and Bagai (394),' 267; and then (2) those who posit a neutral assessment of Primian (the majority view): Willis, *Saint Augustine and the Donatist Church*, 31–35; Arne Hogrefe, *Umstrittene Vergangenheit: Historische Argumente in der Auseinandersetzung Augustins met den Donatisten* (Berlin: Walter de Gruyter, 2009), 24–37 & 102–06, Jean. Louis Maier, *Le dossier du Donatisme. 1: Des origines à la mort de Constance II (303–61), Texte und Untersuchungen zur Geschichte der altchristlichen Literatur* 134 (Berlin: Akademie Verlag, 1987), 73–92; Mandouze, *Prosopographie de l'Afrique Chrétienne*, 905–11; Matthew Gaumer, 'The Evolution of Donatist Theology as Response to a Changing Late Antique Milieu', *Augustiniana* 58/3–4 (2008), 216–18, Erika Hermanowicz, *Possidius of Calama: A Study of the North African Episcopate* (New York: Oxford University Press, 2008), 126; no mention is made to Primian in the most popular works of Brown (*Augustine of Hippo: A Biography*) nor O'Donnell (*Augustine: A New Biography*; and (3) those with a positive rendition of Primian's career: Pamela Bright, 'learned and passionate', ('Donatist Bishops' in *Augustine Through the Ages, An Encyclopedia*, ed. A. Fitzgerald (Grand Rapids, MI: Wm. Eerdmans Publishing, 1999), 283); Tilley, 'a talented orator and gifted theologian (though not enough to counterbalance his lack of pastoral sensitivity)', (*The Bible in Christian North Africa*), 133.

6 There were a number of external factors that led to the decline of Donatism (laid out in Chris Botha, 'The Extinction of the Church in North Africa', *Journal of Theology for Southern Africa* 57 (1986), 24–25), such as: Donatism could not overcome the tension between indigenisation

maintain the age-old categorisation of Donatists as usurpers, rebel-rousers, and innovators, and Catholics as the Church of Cyprianic-continuity in North Africa. Though the matter is still debated, R.A. Markus has argued forcefully to the contrary.[7] Therefore, in this chapter the question that remains throughout is not necessarily how Donatism upstaged the Catholic Church, but rather which factors, best exemplified in the polemical efforts of Augustine, contributed to the eventual success of Catholics over Donatists.[8]

The Councils of Cebarsussa and Bagaï

The actual process and events surrounding the election of Primian in 392 are lost to history. However, some inferences can be drawn regarding the context of his election. He succeeded Parmenian (r.362–391/92),[9] a non-African (Spaniard) and popular leader, who never faced a serious challenge to his authority and who made considerable advances in the Donatist *raison d'être* in the face

---

and catholicity (the central thesis of Botha); diocesan structure was ill-suited to the Berber, i.e. nomadic lifestyle; there appears never to have been a Berber or Punic translation of the Bible; there was a certain superficiality in the Christianity the Berbers accepted, etc.

7 Refer to Robert Markus, 'Christianity and Dissent in Roman North Africa: Changing Perspectives in Recent Work', in *Schism, Heresy, and Religious Protest, Studies in Church History* 9, ed. D. Baker (Cambridge: Cambridge University Press, 1972), 21–35, esp. 35; as well as: *Saeculum: History and Society in the Theology of St. Augustine* (Cambridge: Cambridge University Press, 1970), 110. It is noteworthy that even the titles 'Donatist' and 'Catholic' remain ambiguous at the least and tentative at best, given the fact that Donatists saw themselves as 'Catholics' in that they contained the wholeness of truth; see: Kevin Coyle, 'The Self-identity of North African Christians in Augustine's Time', in P.-Y. Fux, J.-M. Roessli, O. Wermlinger (eds.), *Augustinus Afer: Saint Augustin: africanité et universalité. Actes du colloque international, Alger-Annaba, 1–7 avril 2001* (*Paradosis* 45/1), (Fribourg: Éditions Universitaires Fribourg Suisse 2003), 69.

8 This is further elaborated upon in Robert Markus, 'Africa and the Orbis Terrarum: The Theological Problem', in F.E. Bouyaed (ed.), *Le philosophe Algérien Saint Augustin africanité et universalité: actes du premier colloque international Alger—Annaba, 1–7 avril 2001, Tome 2* (Fribourg, 2004), 101–02. This was further explored in an abbreviated version of this chapter found in Matthew Gaumer, 'The Election of Primian of Carthage: The Beginning of the End of Donatist Christianity?', *Zeitschrift für Antikes Christentum* 17 (2012), 290–308.

9 Aug., *s.* 46,17 (*CCSL* 41, 543), (*WSA* III/2, 273): 'Extulit se superbia donati, fecit sibi partem. Subsequens Parmenianus illius confirmauit errorem'. (And my sheep were scattered, and strayed over every mountain and every hill (Ez. 34,6). The beasts of the mountains and hills are earthly haughtiness and the pride of the world. The pride of Donatus reared up, he formed himself a party. Parmenian followed, and compounded his error.)

of ever-changing circumstances.[10] Parmenian's progress in developing more openness to non-Donatists was considerable, especially his adoption of a theology of 'dotes' or 'gifts of the church', which moved Donatist thinking away from seeing their Church as the 'Church of the pure' towards the 'collecta of Israel'.[11] For Parmenian then, personal disposition was unimportant compared to belonging to the right, authentic Church.[12]

It seems plausible that the election problems for Primian found their origin in the innovative nature of his predecessor's theology. Donatists prided themselves on a strict interpretation of their theology, which they believed had remained undiluted from Cyprian's time. It does not take an over-imaginative mind to see such rigidity would not have welcomed much theological latitude. I find evidence of this in the rejection of Tyconius by the Donatist leadership in 385[13] for taking Parmenian's lead a step further in crafting a church model

---

10 This was the subject of study in Gaumer, 'The Evolution of Donatist Theology', 201–33.

11 See Tilley, *The Bible in Christian North Africa*, 101–03, 106, 179.

12 Tilley, *The Bible in Christian North Africa*, 106 'The significant advance Parmenian made was to provide a well-articulated form of what had been heretofore only latent in Donatist ecclesiology, that is, it is not the personal holiness but the ecclesial affiliation of the minister of the sacrament that is necessary for validity'.

13 For the positions he put forward, Tyconius was excommunicated by Parmenian and the Donatist college of bishops at a Carthaginian council in 385. This is recorded in Aug., *C. ep. Parm.* 1,1 (CSEL 51, 19): 'Multa quidem alias aduersus Donatistas pro uiribus quas dominus praebet partim scribendo partim etiam tractando disserui. Nunc autem, quoniam incidit in manus nostras Parmeniani quondam episcopi eorum quaedam epistula quam scribit ad Tychonium, hominem quidem et acri ingenio praeditum et uberi eloquio, sed tamen Donatistam, cum eum arbitraretur in hoc errare quod ille uerum coactus est confiteri, placuit petentibus, immo iubentibus fratribus, ut hic eidem Parmeniani epistulae responderem propter quaedam maxime quae de scripturis testimonia non sicut accipienda sunt accipit. Tychonius enim omnibus sanctarum paginarum uocibus circumtunsus euigilauit et uidit ecclesiam dei toto terrarum orbe diffusam, uidelicet in Africa Christianos pertinere ad ecclesiam toto orbe diffusam, qui utique non istis ab eiusdem orbis communione atque unitate seiunctis, sed ipsi orbi terrarum per communionem conecterentur. Parmenianus autem ceterique Donatistae uiderunt hoc esse consequens et maluerunt suscipere obstinatissimum animum aduersus apertissimam ueritatem, quam Tychonius asserebat, quam ea concessa superari ab Africanis ecclesiis, quae illius unitatis quam Tychonius asseruit communione gauderent, unde se isti separassent. et Parmenianus quidem primo eum per epistulam uelut corrigendum putauit; postea uero etiam concilio eorum perhibent esse damnatum. Epistulae itaque Parmeniani quam scripsit ad Tychonium reprehendens eum, quod ecclesiam praedicaret toto orbe diffusam, et ammonens ne facere auderet, hoc opere statuimus respondere sicut de illa tanto ante per corda et ora sanctorum praeuisum atque praedictum est. Quo perspecto suscepit aduersus ipsos suos hoc demonstrare et adserere, nullius hominis quamuis sceleratum et immane

of a mixed body or '*corpus permixtum*', which, incidentally Augustine and the Catholics would later adopt.[14] Afterwards, a gradual narrowing of outlook can be traced among Donatist thinkers.[15]

This narrowed perspective is on display in 392/93 when opposition to Primian early became manifest. As one of his first acts, Primian brought the Donatist Claudian party back into communion without any known rites of penance.[16] He seems to have also alienated the influential laity, or *seniores laici* in Carthage and support began to coalesce around a Carthaginian deacon named Maximian,[17]

---

peccatum praescribere promissis dei nec id agere quorumlibet intra ecclesiam constitutorum et quamlibet impietatem, ut fides dei de ecclesia futura diffundenda usque ad terminos orbis terrae, quae in promissis patrum retenta et nunc exhibita est, euacuetur. Hoc ergo Tychonius cum uehementer copioseque dissereret et ora contradicentium multis et magnis et manifestis sanctarum scripturarum testimoniis oppilaret, non uidit quod consequenter uidendum fuit, illos'; *Ep.* 93,44.

14 Tyconius not only acknowledged the reality of sin among members of the Church, but went so far as to argue the existence of sin as a characteristic of the Church, in that it has a 'bipartite' nature: Tyconius, *Liber Regularum*, Texts and Translations 31. Early Christian Literature Series 7, trans. William Babcock (Atlanta: Scholars Press, 1989), 7 (72–75); Pamela Bright, '"The Preponderating Influence of Augustine": A Study of the Epitomes of the *Book of Rules* of the Donatist Tyconius', in P. Bright (ed., trans.), *Augustine and the Bible* (Notre Dame, IN: University of Notre Dame Press, 1986), 109–28.

15 This development has been described rather harshly as 'the violent and narrow mind of Donatism'; Bonner, *St Augustine of Hippo: Life and Controversies*, 249.

16 This was a para-Donatist group based in Rome, with Claudian as its bishop; see: Optatus of Milevis, *De Schismate* 2,4 (Edwards, 33–35). Claudian was ejected from the city of Rome in 378 through the initiative of Pope Damasus, and upon returning to North Africa, broke away from communion with Parmenian and Carthage; Aug., *Ex. 2 in Ps.* 36,20 (CCSL 38, 364): '…ut Claudianenses uel quid aliud appellent quos Claudianistas appellauerunt, cum eos Primiano in communionem receptos inter alia quibus eum et praedamnauerunt et damnarunt crimina posuerunt'. Also confer with Aug., *Cresc.* 4,11 and Willis, *Saint Augustine and the Donatist Controversy*, 31.

17 Maximian was a Carthaginian deacon, apparently an heir of Donatus, and the leader of the breakaway Donatist group, the *Maximianists*, who protested against the election of Primianus as the new bishop of Carthage; Mandouze, *Prosopographie de l'Afrique Chrétienne (303–533)*, s.v. 'Maximianus 3', 719–22. The exact reasons for the beginning of the Maximian rift are not known today nor is the exact start of the schism. A.C. De Veer postulates that Maximian may have possibly been an heir apparent, or that there was some sort of personal feud between the two: 'Les origines du maximianisme', in *BA* 31, *Traités Anti-Donatistes IV* (Paris: Desclée de Brouwer, 1968), 825–26. Another possibility, though relatively un-researched, is that this rift was a result of geographic tensions. The Numidian and Mauretanian bishops would have probably favoured one type of primate, while

purportedly a descendent of Donatus the Great.[18] This resulted in Primian excommunicating the deacon and three of his colleagues.[19] An oppositional council was called, to be held in short order in the Byzacène town of Cebarsussa.[20] The council, convened 24 June 393, reported Primian's alleged offences as follows:

> 'Blocked the doors to the basilicas…in order to deny us the possibility of entering and celebrating the liturgy [Eucharist]'…'pass[ed] sentence on the deacon Maximian, an innocent man, as everyone knows'…'had caused Fortunatus [a pro-Maximian presbyter] to be thrown into a sewer for bringing comfort to sick persons and baptising them'…'sent out a gang to damage Christian homes'…'has caused [opposing] bishops and clerics to be besieged and later stoned by his minions'…and 'has caused elders of the community [*seniores laici*] to be beaten in the basilicas because they objected to Claudianists being admitted to communion'.[21]

---

the more mainstream bishops from Tripolitania and Byzacènia potentially preferred another type. This is briefly alluded to in Frend, *The Donatist Church*, 215–16; Mandouze, *Prosopographie de l'Afrique Chrétienne*, s.v. 'Maximianus 3', 719–22.

18 The ancestry of Maximian is recorded in Aug., *Ep.* 43,26 (CSEL 34, 108): 'Qui dicitur esse Donati Propinquus'. However, it is essential to point out that the reason for indicating this familial connection is still unclear. It is possible that Augustine was attempting to make this a detail in the construction of his polemic against the Donatists.

19 Aug., *Ep.* 93,20; *En. in Ps.* 36,20.

20 The precise location of Cebarsussa is not known, but is believed to have been in modern-day southern Tunisia.

21 These accusations are recorded in the Cebarsussa council minutes in Aug., *Ex.2 in Ps.* 36,20 (CCSL 38, 363–64): 'Atque impetrates officialibus, basilicarum ianuas obsedissent, – et cum recitaret idem dixit: ne intrarent episcopi. et cum tractaret idem sequentia recitauit: qui ingrediendi nobis atque agendi sollemnia interdicerent facultatem…usque adeo ut in Maximianum diaconum, uirum, sicut omnibus notum est, innocentem, sine causa, sine accusatore, sine teste, absentem ac lecto cubantem, sententiam putaret esse promendam…quod *supra* dictus Primianus multitudinem miserit, quae christianorum domos euerteret; quod obsessi sint episcopi simul et clerici, et postea ab eius satellitibus lapidati…quod Fortunatum presbyterum in cloacam fecerit mitti, cum aegrotantibus baptismo succurrisset…quod in basilica caesi sint seniores, quod indigne ferrent ad communionem Claudianistas admitti'; also J.L. Maier, *Le Dossier du Donatisme. Tome II. De Julien L'Apostat à Saint Jean Damascène (361–750)* (Berlin: Akademie Verlag, 1989), 77–78. English translation from *The Works of St. Augustine: A Translation for the 21st Century* III/16 (trans. by R. Teske, ed. by J. Rotelle; Hyde Park, NY: New City Press, 2000), 123–24.

What is even more interesting is that even though the record of this council survived because of Augustine's use of it for polemical purposes, a fair number of Donatist themes are found interspersed within:

> 'If the people sin, the priest will pray for them; but if the priest sins, who will pray for him? [1 Sam. 2,25]'; 'he admits to sacrileges against the communion of saints, contrary to the Law and priestly rules';[22] '[Primian] is condemned in perpetuity…lest through contact with him the Church of God be defiled by any contagion or accusation. The apostle Paul urges this duty upon us when he warns, "In the name of the Lord Jesus Christ we command you, brethren, to keep clear of any brother whose conduct is irregular" [2 Thess. 3,6] [and be] therefore, not unmindful of the Church's purity'.[23]

It seems that the 54 bishops (mostly from Tripolitania and Byzacènia) who signed the declaration of the council were inadvertently articulating a traditional Donatist perspective, in contrast to the theologies so recently encountered from Parmenian, Tyconius, and now their successor Primian. The moral accusations levelled against Primian are serious, but also questionable. Since it has survived through the auspices of Augustine's writing, one might credibly theorise this condemnation is an example of a localised manifestation of intra-African polemics, in this case eastern (Tripolitania, Byzacènia) versus western (Numidia, Mauretania) Roman North Africans. Was this a critique of Parmenian in the person of Primian, who was closely identified with his predecessor?

Regardless of such theoretical suggestions, the fact remains that those who rallied around Maximian found cause to condemn Primian in the following way: 'Mindful of the purity of the church…take all conscientious efforts in the refusal of communion with this man by reason of his condemnation'.[24] And in expanding their rationale for such a course of action they used ideas that

---

22 Aug., *Ex.2 in Ps.* 36,20 (*CCSL* 38, 362), (*WSA*, 122); J.L Maier, *Le Dossier du Donatisme. Tome II*, 76.

23 Aug., *Ex.2 in Ps.* 36,20 (*CCSL* 38, 364): 'Perpetuo esse damnatum, ne eo palpato, dei ecclesia aut contagione aut aliquo crimine maculetur. Quod idipsum Paulus apostolus exhortatur et admonet: praecipimus autem uobis, fratres, in nomine domini nostri Iesu Christi, ut discedatis ab omni fratre inordinate ambulante atque adeo non im puritatis ecclesiae'. J.L Maier, *Le Dossier du Donatisme. Tome II*, 79. (English taken from *The Works of St. Augustine: A Translation for the 21st Century* III/16,124 Teske); J.L Maier, *Le Dossier du Donatisme. Tome II*, (see note 22), 79.

24 Aug., *Ex.2 in Ps.* 36,20 (*CCSL* 38, 364), (*WSA* III/16, 124); J.L Maier, *Le Dossier du Donatisme. Tome II*, 79.

were comfortable for a Donatist: avoid sacrileges towards the saints, avoid sinful clergy, fear contact with ecclesial stain/defilement, and walk not with fallen brothers and sisters.

What becomes interesting is a comparison between the approach of the pro-Maximianists at Cebarsussa and the pro-Primianist response almost a year later at a 'universal council' at Bagaï.[25] Whereas the Maximianists tended to use words such as 'sacrilege', 'incest', and 'crime' particularly, Primianists seemed to place greater emphasis on 'schism' and 'ecclesial crime'. Further, whilst scriptural references were employed at both councils, there is a discernable difference between the two in their utilisation. At the earlier councils Ex. 23,7, 1 Sam. 2,25, and 2 Thess. 3:6 were used to support the Maximianist position that there needs to be a physical separation between those with guilt and those who are pure. However, at the Primianist council, OT (Ps. 7,15, 85,11, Ex. 6, Num. 16,32) and NT sources (Rom. 3,13–18, 1 Tim. 7,15) were used in order to emphasise that their opponents were causing their own demise and toxicity by their act of schism.

In a tradition well embedded in North African Christianity, the authors at Bagaï drew on Old Testament typologies to portray schismatics as the doomed Egyptian charioteers in pursuit of the fleeing Israelites at the Red Sea, or as servants of Dathan, Core, and Abrian (Num. 16),[26] or again as snakes and vipers injecting their poison.[27] These are examples of the sermon technique, whereby a brief biblical passage is followed up with further illustrative condemnation, well exemplified in this use of Paul: 'They have venom of asps under their lips... They have no fear of God before their eyes'.[28] This pattern of scripture used to describe the threat of schism seems in keeping with the overall Donatist

25 The Council of Bagaï took place on 24 April 394. Bagaï (Ksar Baghai) is located in modern-day central Algeria, not far from Thamugadi (Timgad).

26 *Emer.* 10; *Cresc.* 3,22; 3,24; 3,59; 4,2; 4,5; *Ep.* 108,5; 108,13; J.L. Maier, *Le Dossier du Donatisme. Tome II*, 87.

27 *C. litt. Pet.* 1,21; *Cresc.* 4,30; *Ep.* 108,5; J.L. Maier, *Le Dossier du Donatisme. Tome II*, 88.

28 *Cresc.* 3,22; 4,5; J.L. Maier, *Le Dossier du Donatisme. Tome II*, 88–89. This was a technique that the Catholic side often accused the Donatists of engaging in. A fine earlier example is from Optatus, *De Schismate* 4,5 (Edwards, 87) 'You begin to read the Lord's text and you expound treatises in our despite; you produce the Gospel, and you reproach your absent brother; you pour hatreds into the souls of hearers, you persuade them to feel enmity by your teaching, by saying all this you put stumbling-blocks in our way'. (Nullus uestrum est qui non conuicia nostra suis tractatibus misceat, qui non aut aliud initiet aut aliud explicet. Lectiones dominicas incipitis et tractatus uestros ad nostras iniurias explicatis. Profertis euangelium et facitis absenti fratri conuicium.)

concern for the integrity of the Church as a body, a body of ritualistic purity free from ecclesiastical sin (primarily betrayal or *traditio*).[29]

The self-understanding of Donatists as the body was the means by which they sustained their group viscosity in the long years after martyrdoms had ceased. Among the great fears the Donatists harboured in safeguarding their assembly was ritualistic contamination from *traditores* (betrayers) which they thought could spread like a disease.[30] A favourite verse in this regard became, 'Let not the oil of the sinner anoint my head'.[31] What distinguished the Maximianists from Primianists, since they both appeared to use language supporting that particular conceptualisation, is that the party of Primian made reference to explicit concerns about schism and its effects. By the end of the Bagaï council, Maximian had been condemned; clergy aligned with him had been ordered back into the Donatist fold, and those who did so were to be allowed re-admission without reconciliation, with the sacraments they had conferred whilst separated considered legitimate. All of these steps were intended to restore unity to the Donatist Church.

And it is this development—Primian's acceptance of schismatics back into communion and his emphasis on schism as a problem in itself—coupled with a concerted appeal to the Roman administration to validate his authority as bishop of Carthage, which would create one of the most significant legacies for the Catholic polemic of Augustine.

Legal Force and Catholic Polemic

The evidence indicates that after Bagaï and the proscription of Maximian and his colleagues, Primian led an effort to use the proceedings from Bagaï before imperial authorities so that they would enforce re-unification and the end of

29 Tilley, *The Bible in Christian North Africa*, 106; this is corroborated in Gaumer, 'The Evolution of Donatist Theology', 217.

30 Aug., *Emer.* 11 (CSEL 53, 195): 'Eos autem, quos sacrilegi surculi non polluere plantaria, hoc est qui a maximiani capite proprias manus uerecundo fidei pudore retraxerunt, ad matrem ecclesiam redire permisimus'. Pro-Primian Donatists would actually expand their *collecta* concept into a means of criticism of the Maximianists, referring to them as '*collecta faeculentia*' or 'body of crap (or filth)' 12 times (using the CLCLT *Library of Latin Texts, version 7*, ed. P. Tombeur (Turnhout: Brepols, 2008); *Cresc.* 3,22; 3,25; 3,59; 4,5; 4,15; 4,21; 4,38–39; *Gesta cum Emer.* 11; *C. Gaud.* 2,7. I am also in debt to M. Tilley for this extract in her article, 'Sustaining Donatist Self-Identity: From the Church of the Martyrs to the collecta of the Desert', *Journal of Early Christian Studies* 5/1 (1997), 34.

31 Optatus, *De Schismate* 4,7 (Edwards, 92); Aug., *Ep.* 108,6 (WSA *II/2*, 72).

the schism. Primian's legal strategy appears to have been focused on two fronts in order to reconcile the Maximianist schism: (1) to be recognised as the legitimate Church in Africa by classifying the Maximianists as heretics,[32] and (2) to disrupt the structure of the Maximianists by liquidating their assets, namely churches.[33]

The central line of argumentation against the Maximianists was that they were heretics (as attested to by the proceedings of Bagaï) and therefore punishable under imperial legislation.[34] Though Primian would initially run into some turbulence in being recognised as the authentic Church in Africa,[35] he and his loyalists would repeatedly appeal, with success, to Roman officials between the conclusion of Bagaï in 394 and 397.[36] The pinnacle of Primian's

---

32 This was apparently not the first time Primian had attempted to use the Roman legal system to his advantage. At the beginning of his struggle with Maximian, Primian appealed to the imperial legate to regain possession of a house claimed and used by Maximian's allies; *Cresc.* 4,57; *Ex.2 in Ps.* 36,19 (WSA III/16, 118). Augustine notes this Donatist legal strategy by suggesting, through a twist of Donatist argumentation, that Primian taunted his opponents with imperial edicts, while Catholics only brought with them the Gospels; Aug., *Ad Don. post Coll.* 1,53.

33 This was a strategy implemented roughly between 394–97; Aug., *Cresc.* 3,58; 3,62; 4,3; *Brev.* 3,22; *Ep.* 108,5.

34 The specific jurisprudence used by Primian against the Maximianists is unclear. It is not unrealistic to surmise that Primian, being as astute as he was, was knowledgeable about the Theodosian anti-heresy laws of 392, and perhaps used this knowledge to his advantage. It is also important to note that the 392 law instituted by Emperor Theodosius was rarely used at first, especially in North Africa; R. Malcolm Errington, *Roman Imperial Policy from Julian to Theodosius* (Chapel Hill, NC: University of North Carolina Press, 2006); Peter Brown, 'Religious Coercion in the Later Roman Empire: 283–305', *History* 48 (1963), 83–101, reprinted in Peter Brown, *Religion and Society in the Age of Augustine* (London: Faber & Faber, 1972), 283–305. Augustine records that the Donatist leadership applied a comprehensive approach to winning favour with the Roman juridical system by simultaneously pursuing local councils, vicars, and proconsuls; *C. litt. Pet.* 2,132; *En. in Ps.* 57,15.

35 This was recorded in Aug., *En. in Ps.* 21,31.

36 On 23 March 395, Primian's attorney, Nummasius, submitted a brief against Bishop Salvius of Membressa to Proconsul Herodes, arguing for foreclosure on all Maximianist property and that it should be returned to the Primian coalition given that Maximian had been condemned as a heretic at Bagaï. Herodes sided in favour of Primian; *Cresc.* 3,65; *Codex Theodosianus* (*The Theodosian Code and Novels and the Sirmondian Constitutions*), trans. C. Pharr (Princeton: Princeton University Press, 1952) 16,9, 'Letter to Hierius, Vicarius Africae'. This procedure was probably repeated against Salvius three more times as he refused to submit to the intervention. Primian appealed twice to Proconsul Theodorus in December 396 (*Cresc.* 3,62), and then to Proconsul Seranus in 397, who decided in favour

projection of temporal strength came with his alliance with Optatus, the bishop of the Donatist-stronghold, Thamugadi,[37] and with Gildo, the Roman count in Africa.[38] This was particularly evinced by the forced submission of Felicianus and Praetextatus, the bishops of the Byzacèan towns of Musti and Assuras. The two leaders were pro-Maximian holdouts against Primian and refused to be replaced by their rival's loyalists.[39] This situation ended when Optatus led an *ad hoc* force of professional Roman infantry and Berber Circumcelliones into Byzacène and caused a general panic among the public with the result that they yielded to Primian and swore their allegiance.[40] This show of joint ecclesial-civil strength was perhaps best demonstrated upon Optatus's return to his see city arm-in-arm with Primian.[41] There they celebrated Optatus's ten-year jubilee with great triumphalism at their newly-uncontested authority over ancient North Africa.

The zenith of power held by Primian and his closest allies was short-lived however. A combination of factors coalesced in the 390s and 400s, sending Donatist Christianity into an existential contraction. Among those factors were the imperial response to immigration from Germania and beyond, which required greater resources for securing North Africa as an agricultural and trade resource hub;[42] greater collaboration between the holders of power in Milan, Ravenna, and Constantinople and the Catholic hierarchy in the

---

of the Primianists and the edicts of Bagaï; *En. in Ps.* 21,31; *Cresc.* 4,58. This process is also reviewed in Hermanowicz, *Possidius of Calama*, 127–29 and Frend, *The Donatist Church*, 219–20.

37 Died c. 398; Mandouze, *Prosopographie de l'Afrique Chrétienne*, s.v. 'Optatus 2', 797–801.

38 We have limited knowledge about the details of the life of Gildo, and also about the effect he had overall: B. Kriegbaum, 'Die Donatistischen Konzilien von Cebarsussa (393) and Bagai (394)', 274; Mandouze, *Prosopographie de l'Afrique Chrétienne*, s.v. 'Gildo', 539.

39 *Cresc.* 3,66; see also A.C. De Veer, 'L'exploitation du schisme maximianiste par saint Augustin dans sa lutte contre le Donatisme', *Recherches augustiniennes* (1965), 226; E. Lamirande, 'Argument tiré par Augustin du schisme des Maximianistes', BA 32, *Traités Anti-Donatistes V* (Paris : Études augustiniennes, 1965), 692.

40 *Cresc.* 4,32.

41 *Ep.* 108,5 (WSA II/1, 70–71); Willis, *Saint Augustine and the Donatist Controversy*, 41.

42 This development became ever more acute in the first decade of the 400s, as Alaric entered Rome and other Germanic tribal groups infiltrated the imperial borders. As a result, Emperor Honorius pulled out all of the stops in getting North Africa in order, even if by 'blood and proscription' (*Cod. Th.* 16,51). Indeed, to ensure Africa remained a refuge for the wayward Italians, Honorius made North Africa a top policy issue.

post-Theodosian milieu;[43] and perhaps most manifest, the new generation of Catholic bishops[44] in North Africa, beginning in the 390s, who led a successful effort to reassert the position of their Church. Augustine was the foremost of such bishops and it was with him that the Catholic resurgence found its epicentre.

Despite a problematic beginning to his ordained career due to his lack of preparation in dealing with Donatist leaders, Augustine worked prodigiously, perhaps obsessively even,[45] in his early years as a priest, and then as bishop, at gradually interpreting the narrative of the Maximianist schism to the advantage of the Catholic party in Africa. In this sense, one can trace the cleaving of the Maximianist schism alongside the arrival of Augustine (and the start of his anti-Donatist works).[46] The bishop of Hippo would go on to identify three aspects of the Maximianist controversy for the benefit of his polemic against Donatist positions: (1) Primian had refuted the central Donatist belief

43 This is a tedious topic to summarise here, though we can agree with some certainty that at least in the Western Empire '[t]he great churchman was often a leader of society in temporal as well as spiritual matters'; Willis, *Saint Augustine and the Donatist Controversy*, 133. But this is not to say that bishops in this period had become autocrats such as in later European history. In *s.* 302,7, Augustine revealed 'the limits of Christianisation in Africa at the beginning of the fifth century, or more exactly, the limits of a bishop's actual power on the face of a completely "lay" administration, in the sense we give the word, whose representatives, even when they themselves were Christians, were jealous of the their autonomy relative to another hierarchy'; Lancel, *Saint Augustine*, 261.

44 The placement of Augustine's peers into North African Catholic dioceses guaranteed a pool of bishops who would be team-players with Augustine in attacking the Donatists and also in counter balancing the Donatist episcopate bishop-for-bishop, especially in strategic places. In 394, Augustine's close friend Alypius was installed as Bishop of Thagaste. In 397, another of his friends, Severus, was elevated to the bishopric of Milevis simultaneously with his other friend, Profuturus, who was elected as the bishop of Constantine. In 400, Profuturus was replaced by yet another friend, Fortunatus. Finally, in the same year, Augustine's biographer was installed at Calama.

45 Poss., *Vita Aug.* 9.

46 Lamirande, 'Argument tiré par Augustin du schisme des Maximianistes', 693. A short excursus on Augustine's usage of Maximian for polemical purposes is warranted here. The database *CLCLT 7* reveals the following: explicit and unique references are made to 'Maximian' x446 in the *corpus Augustinianum*. In the *Gesta collationis Carthaginiensis* (of 411), a further x22 references are locatable. To put this into perspective, Augustine refers to 'Cyprian', a cornerstone of his argumentation with the Donatists, 589 times in all of his works. It is evident Augustine places a great deal of importance on Maximian as a polemical tool.

in the necessity of rebaptism by readmitting the Claudianists and Maximianists without penance; (2) the Donatists had (again) violated their insistence on the separation of Christians from the secular sphere through their recourse to the imperial powers for validation; and (3) Primian and the Donatists were guilty of committing the same 'crimes' as Caecilianus at the beginning of the Donatist controversy, but yet refused to show any sense of conciliation with the Catholics, preferring instead to remain in schism.

Critique of Rebaptism

Augustine's polemical attack on the Donatist precept of rebaptism was aimed at strategically refuting a central pillar of Donatist theology. Rebaptism was traditional North African praxis, with Donatists considering it to be rooted in their earliest history and ratified by their martyr-hero Cyprian. This ritual was for them the *sine qua non* for those entering their Church if the person had been baptised elsewhere. The intention behind this practice was the quarantining of ecclesial infection that had spread in the '*traditor*' Catholic Church from the time of the Great Persecutions (303–05). This view was heavily dependent on a Christology and an understanding of sacramental grace that placed tremendous weight on the worth and mediation of the minister. It was likewise a method of reinforcing the Donatist consideration of the Church as being utterly 'other' in relation to the world. Therefore, when Augustine argued that the Maximian struggle 'forced them [the Primianists] to recognise that the baptism of Christ can also be administered outside their Church',[47] he was attempting to completely overhaul the contemporary North African view of the way grace is conferred. And the means by which Augustine argued for this was to reiterate that the Primianists permitted both the Claudianists and Maximianists back into the Donatist fold without penance:

> After all, they [the Primianists] readmitted some of them, along with those whom they had baptised outside their church, to their positions of honour without in any case repeating baptism.[48]

47 Aug., *De Haeresibus* 69,5 (*Arianism and Other Heresies: Heresies, Memordandum to Augustine, To Orosius in Refutation of the Priscillianists and Origenists, Arian Sermon, Answer to an Arian Sermon, Debate with Maximianus Answer to Maximianus, Answer to an Enemy of the Law and the Prophets*, WSA *I/18*, trans. R. Teske (Hyde Park, NY, 1995), 51).

48 Aug., *Haer.* 69,5 (WSA I-18, 51), (CCSL 46, 333): 'Nam quosdam ex eis cum eis quos extra eorum ecclesiam baptizauerant in suis honoribus sine ulla in quoquam repetition baptismatis receperunt'.

Augustine made a case-in-point, in this regard, the contentious forced submission of Felicianus of Musti and Praetextatus of Assura (which, it will be recalled, was only solved acrimoniously by Optatus of Thamugadi's military efforts).[49] Augustine would follow through this line of argumentation rhetorically, by asking, 'If you are willing to readmit a guilty person for the sake of Donatian peace, can you not be as accommodating to all nations for the sake of the peace of Christ?'[50] By readmitting the two hold-outs, and reinstating them in their episcopal functions without the requirement for penance and rebaptism (arguably for the sake of Donatist unity),[51] Primian handed Augustine a prime example of what appeared to be a renunciation of Donatist discipline and doctrine and a focus for Augustine's systematic anti-Donatist polemic.[52]

Criticism of Donatist Legal Strategy

Augustine used a second polemical tool which was no less effective, which was to focus on Primian's recourse to Roman legal authorities:

> [T]hey neither stopped trying to correct them [the Maximianists] through public powers, nor did they have any fear of contaminating their communion by the crimes of these persons which the sentence of their own council strongly denounced.[53]

---

49 Aug., *Ep.* 51,2 (*WSA II/1*, 199): 'As many as they baptised at that time, they now have them with you...those people who were baptised outside their sect [the Donatist Church] in the crime of schism, and for none of these was baptism repeated'.

50 Aug., *Ex. 2 in Ps.* 36,22 (*WSA* III/16, 126), (*CCSL* 38, 367): 'Aut nocens receptus est, aut innocens damnatus est. Si ergo nocentem recipis pro pace Donati, cede omnibus gentibus pro pace Christi'.

51 Aug., *Ep.* 51,2 & 4 (*WSA* II/1, 199–200) '[W]hat defence remains for why they were received back into the same episcopacy except that, by emphasising the benefit and salutariness of peace, you show that even these crimes should be tolerated to maintain the bond of unity?...if these people had to be baptised again, those bishops [Felicianus and Praetextatus] had to be ordained again. After all, they lost their episcopacy in withdrawing from you if they were not able to baptise outside of your communion...they, then, ought to have been ordained upon their return in order that what they had lost might be restored to them'.

52 De Veer, 'L'exploitation du schisme maximianiste par saint Augustin dans sa lutte contre le Donatisme', 226: 'Catholics found in this abandonment of principles a weapon that in the hands of Augustine would become formidable' (translation my own).

53 Aug., *Haer.* 69,5 (*WSA* I/18, 51), (*CCSL* 46, 333): 'Nec eos ut corrigerent per publicas potestates agere destiterunt, nec eorum criminibus per sui concilii sententiam uehementer exaggeratis communionem suam contaminare timuerunt'.

This was, for Augustine, a further repudiation of Donatist theology by the actions of the pro-Primian party.[54] Besides rebaptism, hardly any other issue carried as much gravitas for Donatists than their insistence on being a pure enclave, free from ecclesial sin and fortified against secular powers and their associated evils. For the Donatists, the Roman Empire had nothing to do or say within the Church, a view recognisable in their favoured refrain: *quid est imperatori cum ecclesia*?[55] How powerfully, then, could the bishop of Hippo rhetorically savage his opponent Primian for his legal recourse, especially in attempting to persuade the imperial powers to coerce the Maximianists by force. Thus not only were the Donatist Primianists guilty of blurring the border between their Church and the world by allying themselves with the secular regime, they were also guilty of committing '*crimen persecutionis*' according to Augustine. This was the same offence perennially levelled against the betraying Catholics (or *traditores*) by the Donatists. Furthermore, Augustine accused the Donatists of masquerading as Catholics in order to garner favour from the magistrates and to make use of the Theodosian anti-heresy laws:

> Now tell me, you Donatist: why do you call yourself a Catholic in order to get a heretic ejected, rather than really being a Catholic, so as not to be excluded as a heretic yourself? You are temporarily a Catholic, only to bolster your case and oust a heretic.[56]

To this Augustine added a rhetorical flourish as to why Primian and the Donatists seemed unable to explain their own about-face:

> They have nothing to say in reply, because *God has smashed the teeth in their mouths*. Unable to slither in like asps with their slippery lies, they

54 Lamirande referred to the Donatist legal strategy retrospectively as a 'dangerous precedent'; 'Argument tiré par Augustin du schisme des Maximianistes', 692; William Frend, 'Augustine and State Authority. The Example of the Donatists', *Agostino d'Ippona 'Quaestiones Disputatae'* (Palermo: Augustinus, 1989), 49–73.

55 Optatus of Milevis, *De Schismate* 3,3 (Edwards, 62). Augustine uses the familiar Donatist refrain rhetorically in *En. in Ps.* 57,15 (*WSA* III/17, 136): '"What have kings to do with us" they ask. "What do emperors matter to us? You are basing your argument on imperial authority." Yes, but I will counter that with a similar point: why do you have recourse to proconsuls sent by emperors? Why do you appeal to the law, when emperors have legislated against you?'

56 Aug., *En. in Ps.* 57,15 (*WSA* III/17, 136), (*CCSL* 39, 720–21): 'Egerunt legibus publicis, ad iudices uenerunt, dixerunt se catholicos, ut possent excludere haereticos. quare te dicis catholicum, ut excludatur haereticus, et non potius es catholicus, ne sis exclusus haereticus?'

> take to rampaging like lions with open violence [referring to the attack against Felicianus and Praetextatus]. But *the Lord has shattered the jawbones of the lions too.*[57]

The Maximian crisis opened for Augustine another rhetorical gold mine: the criticism that Primian and Maximian had re-presented the conditions of the origins of the Donatist break-away in 311/12.[58] In this case, Primian was Caecilian and Maximian was Majorinus (respectively the presiding Catholic and Donatist bishops who had led their camps into schism):

> We have, then, an amazing and incontrovertible example of history repeating itself: the Maximianists are bringing the same complaints against Primian as those others against Caecilian.[59]

In this situation, Augustine sought to have Donatist leaders recognise that the condemnation by the early Donatists was in error, much as the condemnation of Primian at Cebarsussa had been. This was the case because, as Augustine phrased it, 'there were others better qualified to judge…'[60] But if, in this polemical scenario, Primian was to say he was innocent, whilst upholding the Donatist condemnation of Catholics, then Primian would not only be refuting himself, but drawing a guilty verdict against his Church,[61] whilst at the same

---

57 Aug., *En. in Ps.* 57,15 (*WSA* III/17, 136), (*CCSL* 39, 721): 'Non est quod respondeant: Deus contriuit dentes eorum in ore ipsorum. Ideoque ubi non possunt lubrica fallacia serpere ut aspides, aperta uiolentia fremunt ut leones. Prosiliunt et saeuiunt armatae turbae Circumcellionum; dant stragem quantam possunt, quantamcumque possunt. Sed et molas leonum confregit dominus'.

58 Eno, 'Some Nuances in the Ecclesiology of the Donatists', 49; Hogrefe, *Umstrittene Vergangenheit*, 104.

59 Aug., *Ex.2 in Ps.* 36,19 (*WSA* III/16, 120), (*CCSL* 38, 360): 'Quia reuera facta maiorum suorum ipsi imitati sunt. Sic enim erexerunt Maximianum aduersus Primianum, quomodo illi erexerunt Maiorinum aduersus Caecilianum'.

60 Aug., *Ex.2 in Ps.* 36,19 (*WSA* III/16, 120). This element of Augustine's argument, that the bishops who caused the Donatist and Maximian schisms were unsuitable to judge because of a lack of presence and inadequate knowledge, is deployed readily by the bishop, especially again in 36,2,19 and 36,2,23.

61 Aug., *Ex.2 in Ps.* 36,21 (*WSA* III/16, 126) '[D]o you prefer to maintain that those who originally condemned Caecilian were in the right? In that case, they condemn you as well. No, the ruling of those opposed Caecilian had no validity then, not will it have in the future. But be careful not to give a verdict against yourself'.

time ratifying the isolation of Donatism from the other Christianities of the world.[62] Here Augustine attempted to pin Primian down and in doing so made it clear that if he wished to be found right in the eyes of Christians elsewhere in the world, then he must reconsider the Donatist condemnation of Caecilian, which was the very *raison d'être* for Donatism.

The Catholic Ascendancy

With the disappearance of Gildo and Optatus by 398–99, Primian would be, to a certain extent, much more isolated in fending off a resurgent Catholic Church and their mimicking of the Donatist legal strategy, a process which resulted in a sudden shrinking in Donatist temporal influence. Primian (who by this time had found his most efficient ally in Petillian),[63] would have to deal with enhanced Catholic proselytisation, and use of the 392 anti-heresy laws, a combination that apparently resulted in diminished membership of his Church.[64]

By 403, the Catholics succeeded in filing suit in court against the Donatists, which was decided in favour of the Catholics, itself a first for the Catholic party.[65] This taste of success would continue: Proconsul Septimus again ruled

62 Augustine centralised his criticism of Donatism as being apart, secluded, and theologically disjointed from the rest of the Church here in the Maximian debate. This would of course become an important argument for Augustine in his mature anti-Donatist writings as well as in the Pelagian controversy. A few examples are as follows: 'Think now about Caecilian: you have kept Numidia for yourself, but he has kept the whole world'. *Ex.2 in Ps.* 36,19 (*WSA* III/16, 120): 'Keep before your eyes the unity of the whole world at that time [beginning of the Donatist schism]…from which unity they split off in their opposition to Caecilian.' *Ex.2 in Ps.* 36,19 (*WSA* III/16, 119): 'Why have you separated yourself from the innocent? Some baptised person comes to you from elsewhere in the world and you want to rebaptise him or her'. *Ex.2 in Ps.* 36,23 (*WSA* III/16, 128).

63 Mandouze, *Prosopographie de l'Afrique Chrétienne,* s.v. 'Petilianus', 855–68.

64 Aug., *C. litt. Pet.* 2,225; *s.* 252,4–5; *Ep.* 93,3.

65 In the 390s, the Catholics were largely unsuccessful in bringing forth litigation in the Roman court system; Emin Tengström, *Donatisten und Katholiken: soziale, wirtschaftliche und politische Aspekte einer nordafrikanischen Kirchenspaltung* (Göteborg: Elanders Boktryckeri Aktiebolag, 1964), 102–04. The first time Catholic advocates attempted to use the Theodosian Law of 392 was in 395, which set the precedent for nearly a decade in which it was found that the 392 anti-heresy law was incredibly difficult to apply concretely; *Cont. litt. Pet.* 2,184. Therefore, before 404, the Catholics' only grounds were the anti-Manichean laws from 381 and the 392 Theodosian anti-heresy laws (*Cod. Th.* 16,21). The challenge was, therefore, to convince the Roman administrators that Donatists were heretical. 'The gap between the intent of the law and how (and against whom) the Catholics wanted that law

in favour of the Catholics shortly after using the 392 anti-heresy laws (the first time the Theodosian legislation was successfully used against the Donatists).[66] It is interesting to point out that by this time Primian had opted away from the Roman legal system by rejecting such cooperation with the '*sons of traditores*.'[67] By 405 the western Emperor Honorius had implemented an edict of ecclesial unity for North Africa as a stop-gap measure to assuage general unrest caused by the 403 decisions. Therefore some clergy were exiled, Donatist property rights were suppressed,[68] rebaptism was outlawed,[69] and Primian fled his see for Numidia and Mauretania.[70]

By 411, a council was called for in Carthage, through which Honorius wanted to finally settle the Donatist-Catholic affair.[71] At this council what stood out concerning Primian, was that although he was a member of the seven-person panel representing the Donatist side,[72] the bishop was particularly subdued,[73] playing second-fiddle to his colleague Petillian. [74]

The council saw, among other things, debates over whether or not Caecilian had been rightfully condemned,[75] separation of the Church from the world

applied necessitated intense rhetorical persuasion, a legal swimming against the current'; Hermanowicz, *Possidius of Calama*, 102.

66 Septimus was a Roman loyalist installed after the uprising spurred on by Gildo.

67 Primian made ready use of the traditional Donatist slogan, such as used here against the Catholics who 'offered letters of the emperors as opposed to the Gospels offered by the sons of martyrs', *Ad Don. post Coll.* 1,31.

68 *Cod. Th.* 16,2; 16,37–38; 16,4–5.

69 *Cod. Th.* 16.,4.

70 Aug., *Ep.* 88,10.

71 The intent of the 411 Carthaginian Council was ostensibly to sequester the Donatist Church and to 'confirm the Catholic faith', *Gesta collationis Carthaginiensis* [*Actes de la Conférence de Carthage en 411*], *Sources chrétiennes* 195, ed. S. Lancel (Paris: Les Éditions du Cerf, 1972), 1,4. This fact was reinforced by the threat of imperial condemnation *in absentia* if a Donatist bishop failed to attend. The 411 council is thoroughly analysed in S. Lancel, *Saint Augustine*, 287–305 and in Maureen Tilley, 'Dilatory Donatists or Procrastinating Catholics: The Trial at the Conference of Carthage', *Church History* 60/1 (1991), 7–19.

72 *Gest. coll. Carth.* 1,31 (SC 195, 626–29).

73 *Gest. coll. Carth.* [*Actes de la Conférence de Carthage en 411*], SC 224, ed. S. Lancel (Paris: Les Éditions du Cerf, 1975) 3,104; *Brev.* 2,30. Primian resisted convening the council, saying the sons of martyrs should not mingle with the sons of *traditores; Gest. coll. Carth.* 3,116 (SC 224, 1074–76)*; Brev.* 3,4.

74 *Gest. coll. Carth.* 3,247 (SC 224, 1184–86).

75 *Gest. coll. Carth.*, 3,539–40; 3,584.

(sinners from the righteous);[76] and rebaptism;[77] that is, matters that were explicitly formulated by Augustine during the Maximian controversy! The final verdict was unsurprisingly in favour of the Catholics,[78] and the organisational side of the Donatist Church was quickly confiscated and suppressed. In the end, it was the legal strategy improvised by the Donatists themselves that led to eventual Catholic supremacy in North Africa.[79] With this paralysing blow to the Donatist Church, its now-nominal head disappeared from history[80] and what had been the roar of a vibrant, endemic Christianity was reduced to a whimper, barely distinguishable from the so-called Catholic Church in Africa.

Conclusions about Primian and the Maximianists

In this chapter I sought to ascertain whether or not the election of Primian as bishop of Carthage served as the gateway through which Augustine's

76 *Gest. coll. Carth.* 3,275–77 (SC 224, 1234). Marcellinus elucidated that the parable of the wheat and the tares (a favoured parable of the Donatists) signifies the nature of the constitution of the Church within itself and has little to say about the Church's relationship or opposition to the world. This is in opposition to the Donatist view that the parable signified the diametric opposition between the fallen world and the saintly Church. The Donatists attempted to defend this hermeneutical rationale repeatedly throughout the council. A few examples are as follows: 'inter mundum et inmundum non diuidebant et inter sanctum et pollutum non separabant. Ad hanc parabolam illud quoque aduersarii subiungunt, paleas cum frumentis debere simul in ecclesia permanere. Quod Hieremias repercutit dicens: quid paleis ad frumentum? Et Paulus apostolus: quae particula est fideli cum infideli aut quae communio luci ad tenebras?'; (*Gest. coll. Carth.* 3,258 (SC, 224), 1200): 'Secundum hanc igitur rationem frustra dixerunt bonos propter malos sacrilega separatione non deseri, sed malos propter bonos pia unitate tolerari, cum propter hanc profanam permixtionemconmoueri et seiunctionem maximam prouocare alio loco dominus indignatus ostendat: *pro eo, inquit, quod facta est mihi omnis domus Israel permixtio, omnes aeramentum, argentum, ferrum, stagnum et plumbum in medio camini ardentis permixtum, propterea haec dicit Dominus: propter quod facti estis omnes in permixtione una, ideo ego recipio uos in medio Hierusalem. Sicut recipitur aeramentum et argentum et ferrum et stagnum et plumbum in medio camini ad insufflandum in igni ut confletur, ita recipiam uos in ira mea, et concremabo, et insufflabo in uos insufflationem ignis irae meae, et conflabimini in medio eius; et scietis quia ego sum Dominus qui effudi iram meam super uos*', (*Gest. coll. Carth.* 3,258 (SC 224, 1202–04), 1203–04).

77 *Gest. coll. Carth.* 1,16 (SC 195, 593–601); 1,18 (SC 195, 603–17); 1,55 (SC 195, 643–71); 3,258 (SC 224, 1195–1219).

78 *Gest. coll. Carth.* 3,587; Aug., *Ad Don. post Coll.* 12,16; 35,58.

79 Hermanowicz, *Possidius of Calama*, 129.

80 Tilley, *The Bible in Christian North Africa*, 134.

anti-Donatist campaign gained traction and efficacy. Despite a scarcity of information about Primian himself, and an exclusive reliance on Augustine, it was possible to examine the religious context of North Africa in the 390s and early 400s. The Maximian crisis, of which it seems Primian's election was a contributing factor, signalled a serious foundational shift within the Donatist Church and handicapped Primian's mandate to lead his co-religionists, especially at a time when the Catholic Church was reorganising itself in North Africa and when the Roman Empire was beginning to be much more assertive in enforcing orthodoxy. I analysed how the Maximianist accusations against Primian were a stimulant for Augustine, who used this intra-Donatist affair[81] as a springboard for his own anti-Donatist campaign. This is evident from the recurring themes of his polemical writings in the 390s and later into the 400s, which were particularly focused on rebaptism, the legitimacy of Caecilian's condemnation, and the separation of the Church from the world. We lastly saw Primian's stature was diminished even before 411, as the Catholic party repeatedly succeeded in drafting the imperial powers into condemning the Donatists, using the Donatists' own legal-appeals method.

From what has been gauged here, an important question can be raised: was Primian's behaviour so vicious as to have caused Donatism's structural collapse because of his allegedly scandalous ways and unscrupulous use of secular power to condemn his enemies? In other words, is Kriegbaum right in asserting Donatism ended more-or-less as a result of Primian's actions as the Donatist primate? This suggestion leads me to assert a conclusion in the negative, albeit a qualified negative.

I surmise that whilst there is much reason to accept the legitimacy of the Maximianist condemnation of Primian's conduct (and that it was not solely a polemical contrivance), this was not in and of itself enough to bring down the house. Mindful that the Donatists themselves considered the Maximian schism to be a family matter, it would have likely been sorted out in-house. In this case, it seems feasible this could simply have been a squabble over regional tensions or a reaction to the theological liberalisation under Parmenian and Tyconius. Even Primian's recourse to the Roman legal system was not in and of itself enough to cause the decline of Donatist Christianity. There are repeated examples from North African history where Donatist bishops had recourse to

81 It is important to reiterate that the Donatists considered the Maximian rift an internal affair. For this reason, you never saw the pro-Primianists or the pro-Maximianists attempting to ally themselves with the Catholics whom they both saw as *traditores*. See Bonner, *St Augustine of Hippo: Life and Controversies*, 249; Frend, *DC*, 224.

Rome for its imperial validation,[82] but those occurrences never crushed their organisations' fecundity. The fact that it was the Catholic usurpation of the same legal strategy implemented by Primian that eventually brought down the heavy-fire needed to suppress Donatism is less a matter of calculation than the simple fact that Donatists had the forces of history stacked against them.

Primian is not to be let off of the hook completely, however. Whilst it is true there were movements at work beyond his control, the case must nonetheless be made that Primian's initial failures and inability to hold together his rambunctious Church, as his predecessors did in similar circumstances, set the stage for Augustine's polemical technique to ripen. One need only consider how Augustine's initial anti-Donatist works rang hollow in North Africa.[83] Indeed, it was only after Bagaï that as a bishop Augustine could capitalise on the theological opportunities of the Maximian crisis. Perhaps it is this that explains, at least in part, the intensification in Augustine's writings and the increased efficacy of his arguments?

Nonetheless, what is particularly noteworthy in this earlier phase is that Augustine took advantage of an increasingly volatile Donatist situation and adapted his efforts to take advantage of numerous polemical openings. It is in this context that the investigation continues into the way Augustine brought about this fully-fledged anti-Donatist campaign.

---

82 The most noteworthy occurrences were: the appeal to Constantine in 313, which resulted in the Council of Arles siding with Caecilian and the Catholics; Donatus the Great's appeal to Constans in 346, which resulted in the Marcarian persecutions; and the *détente* between Parmenian and Julian (the Apostate) in 363; see Frend, *The Donatist Church*, 141–92.

83 Augustine's first anti-Donatists works made their debut in 393: *Psalmus contra partem Donati* and the *Contra Epistulam Donati haeretici* (now lost). Particularly with the first work, one can see Augustine was attempting to find the right note with which to criticise Donatist leaders and ideas. In this period he also tried direct contact with Donatist bishops, as seen in *Ep.* 23.

PART 2

The Maturation of the Anti-Donatist Campaign

CHAPTER 4

De Baptismo and the Escalation of the Controversy, 400–01

As the fourth century gave way to the fifth, a new chapter in Augustine's career opened up, one that would allow him to leave behind the experience of his initial anti-Donatist efforts and his failure to effect the change he wanted through his earliest *ad hoc* works, i.e., *Ps. c. part. Don.* (393), *C. ep. Donati heretici* (393/94),[1] and *C. partem Donati* (397).[2] At this point he was perhaps feeling a surge of confidence as his efforts were coming to fruition, with successes like *s.* 37, *s.* 305A, *s.*313A, *s.* 313E (c. 397–01) evincing the fact that he was at last gaining ground with a winning approach against the Donatist Church. At the heart of this approach was the authority of Cyprian of Carthage. Though Augustine's arrival at Cyprian—at least in the sources that survive—was relatively cumbersome, and a number of uncertainties remain in precisely targeting the starting point of Cyprian's influence, an overall picture emerges that Augustine nonetheless came to realise that tapping into such a widely-recognised African hero as Cyprian was the surest method for undermining Donatist claims to authenticity.

And it was within this new situation of increasing comfort in wielding the name and brand of Cyprian that Augustine entered the 400s, which date marks his full engagement in the Donatist controversy. The first surviving document marking Augustine's entry into the mature stage of the anti-Donatist campaign is *Contra epistulam Parmeniani*, written at the earliest in 398 but more likely in 400.[3] Cyprian's name is drawn upon ten times across the entirety of *C. ep. Parm.*[4] Though numerically unimpressive, an analysis of those occurrences

1 *Retract.* 1,21.

2 *Retract.* 2,5.

3 Willis, *Saint Augustine and the Donatist Controversy*, 42. Alfred Schindler makes a convincing argument for more appropriately placing the date of *C. ep. Parm.* at late 404/early 405 due to its situatedness in the heresy vs. schism questions apparent in the work; 'Die Unterscheidung von Schisma und Häresie in Gesetzebung und Polemik gegen den Donatismus (mit einer Bemerkung zur Datierung von Augustinus' Schrift: Contra epistulam Parmerniani', in E. Dassmann and K. Suso Frank (eds.), *Pietas: Festschrift für Bernhard Kötting, Jahrbuch für Antike und Christentum Ergänzungsband* 8 (Münster: Aschendorf, 1980), 228–36, esp. 232.

4 Using the *CLCLT-7* and *CAG-2* search algorithms, 'Cyprianus' is identifiable in the following segments of *C. ep. Parm.*: 1,6; 3,8(x4); 3,9; 3,11(x2); 3,16; 3,25.

 | DOI 10.1163/9789004312647_006

indicates a highly nuanced use of the Cyprianic theology and identity, combined with themes already familiar in Augustine's works pre-400, namely that the Church is world-wide and not exclusive to Africa, and that the Church is likewise composed of a mixture of good and evil members.[5] Augustine used Cyprian's example as a blessed martyr[6] to argue against what he saw as the Donatist insistence on the exclusion of those they considered to be contaminated with ecclesial or personal sin, and as a result, the exclusion of the heirs of the Caecilianist Christians (Catholics). Augustine's Cyprian here actively reconciles those in schism or who are lapsed[7] and tolerates them, because he values the unity of the Church above all else.[8] Furthermore, any Donatist who insists on maintaining separation from the Catholic Church is committing an affront to Cyprian[9] and tarnishes his legacy, thus going against the example of pastoral charity that is attested to in scripture.[10] And lastly, as Augustine rhetorically puts it, if the Donatists insist on separation, why is it that Cyprian did not teach likewise? Continuing, he asks, 'Do you Donatists believe yourselves to know more than the blessed Cyprian?'[11] Obviously this is a rhetorical manoeuvre to check-mate Donatist leaders on claims to Cyprian's legacy, by emphasising their contradiction of the bishop of Carthage and thereby asserting that Augustine's own stance is the one rooted in catholic authority. Because of this polemical breakthrough, one may reasonably consider this seminal anti-Donatist volume to signal the fully-blown anti-Donatist campaign in Augustine's works. By this I mean that it was the first occurrence of a finely formulated Cyprian-based charge against Donatist authority in a large-scale anti-Donatist treatise.

---

5 *C. ep. Parm.* 1,1; 1,6–9; 1,10; 1,11.

6 We see this refrain used throughout *C. ep. Parm.* 1,6 (*CSEL* 51, 26): 'martyr Cyprianus'; 3,8 (*CSEL* 51, 109): 'beatissimi Cypriani'; and 3,16 (*CSEL* 51, 114): 'beatus Cyprianus'.

7 *C. ep. Parm.* 1,6; 3,8; 3,9; 3,11.

8 *C. ep. Parm.* 3,8 (*CSEL* 51, 109): '...dicant ergo isti meliorem nunc esse ecclesiam suam et no se habere tales collegas, quales habuit in ipsa unitate Cyprianus'.

9 *C. ep. Parm.* 3,8 (*CSEL* 51, 109): 'Quando ille vir tantus episcopus Carthaginiensis ecclesiae Cyprianus de tam malo collegio testimonio liberae vocis usque ad ea scripta quae posteris etiam proderentur ingemuit, erat ecclesia christi an non erat'.

10 *C. ep. Parm.* 3,8 (*CSEL* 51, 109): 'Si erat, quaero quemadmodum Cyprianus et ceteri similes eius implebant quod praecepit apostolus: si quis frater nominatur aut fornicatur aut idolis serviens at avarus aut maledicus at ebriosus aut rapax, cum eiusmodi ne quidem cibum simul sumere, quando cum his avaris et rapacibus, qui esurientibus in ecclesia fratribus habere argentum largiter vellent, fundos insidiosis fraudibus raperent, usuris multiplicantibus faenus augerent, panem domini manducabant et calicem domini bibebant'.

11 *C. ep. Parm.* 3,11 (*CSEL* 51, 112): '...si enim dicunt per talium communionem perire ecclesiam, cur eam non dicut iam Cypriani perisse temporibus?'

This incorporation of arguments drawing on the authority of Cyprian marks a watershed in Augustine's approach to the Donatist Church.[12] His previous works, in the form of letters, sermons, and *Ps. c. part. Don.*, *C. ep. Donati heretici*, and *C. partem Donati,* contain considerable theological positioning,[13] but lack a level of concreteness necessary to penetrate the hearts and minds of North African Christians. Now it seems in *C. ep. Parm.* that Augustine is beginning to draw on the technique tested in the 390s during his anti-Manichean debates and against the Donatists in *s.* 37, *s.* 305A, *s.*313A, *s.* 313E, that is, using a recognised form of authority, which at the beginning was the scriptures, but which became increasingly focused on the name of Cyprian. In this new, more threatening context, it had to be an authority specifically tailored and evident to North Africans, 'Donatist' and 'Catholic' alike. There was no more obvious choice for Augustine and his allies than Cyprian of Carthage.[14]

That Augustine began in this work to heavily integrate Cyprian into his literary schema is not surprising, given the overall purpose of *C. ep. Parm.* As opposed to his previous works against the Donatist leadership, which were mostly rebukes,[15] this treatise was intended to offer a systematised attestation to Augustine's orthodoxy, whilst at the same time undermining the views of his opponents. In short, this new form of anti-Donatist writing was intended to

---

12 R. Crespin refers to Augustine's appropriation of Cyprian as nothing less than brilliant, 'Saint Augustin devra déployer des prodiges d'ingéniosité – notamment dans le *De baptismo* – pour démontrer que l'illustre martyr, apôtre de l'unité, condamne leur attitude au lieu de la justifier'. *Ministère et sainteté: pastorale du clergé et solution de la crise donatiste dans la vie et la doctrine de saint Augustin* (Paris: Études augustiniennes, 1965), 38.

13 Augustine records in *Retract.* 2,5 that the now-lost *C. partem Donati* contained his early thoughts on the legitimate appeal to the Roman Empire for the purpose of forcing the Donatist Church into re-unification. As seen in the Primian-Maximian crisis, this was realised and would again be so in the 400s/10s when Augustine would successfully have the imperial powers intervene against the Donatist Church.

14 Towards the end of his life, Augustine would recount that he penned *De baptismo* and gave Cyprian such an emphatic role therein because it was simply the best way to invalidate the claims of the Donatists and likewise conveniently provide extra advantage in his ongoing struggles with the Manicheans: *Retract.* 2,2: 'Contra Donatistas auctoritate beatissimi episcopi et martyris Cypriani se defendere molientes septem libros de baptismo scripsi.' Indeed, it was pastoral necessity that precipitated Augustine's active recourse to Cyprian; Burns, 'Appropriating Augustine Appropriating Cyprian', 113–30.

15 I am again making reference to the myriad formats (letters, sermons, and short tractates) Augustine used in the 390s to discuss and move forward the controversy with the Donatist leaders. Even before the production of *C. ep. Parm.*, this approach was beginning to change, however, with Augustine's more pronounced efforts in the anti-Manichean affair.

dissuade and convert the Donatist and in turn motivate the Catholic listener. And in this same document, which was dedicated to questions on the nature of the Church, Augustine made a promise to provide a comprehensive guide to understanding baptism in what would become his second major anti-Donatist treatise: *De baptismo*.[16]

Laying the Foundation for *De Baptismo*

Emerging from his successes with *s.* 37, *s.* 305A, *s.*313A, *s.* 313E and in composing *C. ep. Parm.*, Augustine is seen to be broadening the use of themes with which he could address contemporary challenges, such as his Manichean debate, his own personal theological questions, and most critically, relations with the Donatist Church. But what is of interest at the moment of creating *De baptismo* is the evident incorporation of a whole array of theological themes he had tested intermittently in the years 392–400. During these early years, the surviving anti-Donatist documents (and others contemporaneous with them) attest to a proliferation of such themes which Augustine would conspicuously enlist in his writings throughout the Pelagian controversy. Among the examples that reveal an immediate intensification leading into *De baptismo*,[17] are overtly theological themes such as 'truth' (*veritas*),[18] 'flesh' (*caro*), 'concupiscence' (*concupiscentia*),[19] 'pride' (*superbia*),[20] 'grace' (*gratia*),[21] 'ignorance'

16 *C. ep. Parm.* 2,32. In this passage Augustine promises a fully-fledged treatment of Donatist rebaptism, which would come about in *De baptismo*.

17 A more rigorous analysis of the following themes is offered in Chapter 5 immediately following.

18 '*Veritas*' occurs in the following pre-*De baptismo* writings: x2 in *Ps. c. part. Don.*; x41 in *C. ep. Parm.*; in *De bapt.* the theme '*veritas*' will occur x129!

19 '*Caro, carnis*' occurs, sometimes jointly with '*concupiscence*', in the following pre-*De baptismo* writings: x0 in *Ps. c. part. Don.*; x50 in *C. ep. Parm.*; *Ep.* 1(x3), 22(x11), 23(x8), 29(x18), 34(x5), 36(x30), 43(x5), 47(x3), 52(x5), 55(x27), 82(x3), 87(x2). In *De bapt.* the themes will occur x100! An interesting variation of this word combination can be found when one pairs '*caro*' with 'Cyprian.' Augustine would make this combination in *s.* 310 (x1), *De bapt.* (x3), *C. duas ep. Pel.*(x3), *c. Iul.* (x1), *c. Iul. imp.* (x2).

20 '*Superbia*' occurs in the following pre-*De baptismo* writings: x1 in *Ps. c. part. Don.*; x16 in *C. ep. Parm.*; in *De bapt.* the theme '*superbia*' will only occur x10.

21 '*Gratia*' occurs in the following pre-*De baptismo* writings: x0 in *Ps. c. part. Don.*; x9 in *C. ep. Parm.*; in *De bapt.* the theme '*gratia*' will occur x40. '*Gratia*' and 'Cyprian' will be used by Augustine altogether x7 in his works.

(*ignorantia*),[22] 'stubbornness' (*pertinacia*),[23] 'rebaptism',[24] 'martyr',[25] 'Africa',[26] the Church and its relation with the world (*mundus*),[27] theological 'innovation' (*novitas*),[28] and most centrally 'authority' (*auctoritas*).[29] Augustine paired such theological terms with concrete interests which were immediately intelligible to his audience: Maximian,[30] the apostles Peter and Paul, Donatus, and most pertinently, Cyprian.

It comes as no surprise, then, that the stage was set for Augustine to funnel his energies into a prolonged theological assault in the seven long books that make up his third surviving anti-Donatist work *De baptismo* (after *Ps. c. part. Don.* and *C. ep. Parm.*).[31] This major anti-Donatist treatise deserves pride

22 '*Ignorantia*' occurs in the following pre-*De baptismo* writings: x0 in *Ps. c. part. Don.*; x0 in *C. ep. Parm.*; in *De bapt.* the theme '*ignorantia*' will occur a modest x5.

23 '*Pertinacia*' occurs in the following pre-*De baptismo* writings: x0 in *Ps. c. part. Don.*; x3 in *C. ep. Parm.*; in *De bapt.* the theme '*pertinacia*' will occur x5.

24 '*Rebaptizare*' occurs in the following pre-*De baptismo* writings: x10 in *Ps. c. part. Don.*; x13 in *C. ep. Parm.*; in *De bapt.* the theme '*rebaptizare*' will occur x32.

25 'Martyr' occurs in the following pre-*De baptismo* writings: x0 in *Ps. c. part. Don.*; x15 in *C. ep. Parm.*; in *De bapt.* the theme 'martyr' will occur x19.

26 'Africa' occurs in the following pre-*De baptismo* writings: x2 in *Ps. c. part. Don.*; x33 in *C. ep. Parm.*; in *De bapt.* the theme 'Africa' will only occur x7.

27 '*Mundus*' occurs in the following pre-*De baptismo* writings: x2 in *Ps. c. part. Don.*; x21 in *C. ep. Parm.*; in *De bapt.* the theme '*mundus*' will occur x5.

28 '*Novitas*' occurs in the following pre-*De baptismo* writings: x2 in *Ps. c. part. Don.*; x41 in *C. ep. Parm.*; in *De bapt.* the theme '*novitas*' will occur x129.

29 '*Auctoritas*' occurs in the following pre-*De baptismo* writings: x2 in *Ps. c. part. Don.*; x41 in *C. ep. Parm.*; in *De bapt.* the theme '*auctoritas*' will occur x46. Within the *corpus augustinianum* the first time that '*auctoritas*' is paired with 'Cyprianus' (e.g., *auctoritas Cypriani*) occurs in *De bapt.* altogether x25: *De bapt.* 1,29 (*beati Cypriani auctoritatem*); 2,1 (*auctoritate beati Cypriani*); 2,2(x4) (*auctoritas Cypriani*); 2,12(x2); 2,13(x2); 2,14(x4); 2,15; 3,1; 3,4(x2); 3,5; 3,6(x2); 3,7; 3,14; 4,29(x2).

30 Due to how fresh a controversy the Maximianist rebellion was at the time of authoring *De bapt.*, it should be no surprise that 'Maximian' comes into play heavily here: *De bapt.* 1,2; 1,8; 2,11; 2,15; 2,16; 2,17; 3,3; 3,5; 5,5; 5,7.

31 *De baptismo* and the discussion over Augustine's (and the Donatists') baptismal theology is a well-trodden field and for that reason a full treatment of baptism is not rendered here. Instead, consult the recognised benchmarks: J. B. Bord, 'L'autorité de saint Cyprien dans la controverse baptismale, jugée d'après saint Augustin', *Revue d'Histoire Ecclésiastique* 18 (1922), 445–68; Maria Cenzon-Santos, *Baptismal Ecclesiology of St. Augustine: A Theological Study of his Antidonatist Letters* (Rome: Athenaeum Romanum Sanctae Crucis, 1990); Vittorino Grossi, 'Baptismus', in C. Mayer (ed.), *Augustinus-Lexikon*, vol. 1 (Basel: Schwabe & Co., 1996), 583–91; Maureen Tilley, 'Baptismo, De', in A. Fitzgerald (ed.), *Augustine Through the Ages. An Encyclopedia* (Grand Rapids, MI/Cambridge: Wm. Eerdmans

of place, not only as Augustine's most bulky anti-Donatist text, or because it really sets the operational tone for the Catholic party in Africa's fully-fledged confrontation with their Donatist counterparts (after the initiation of the campaign in *C. ep. Parm.*). Rather, the importance of *De baptismo* derives from the overall anti-Donatist strategy it presents: a blistering theological and historical cascade (using the themes just mentioned above) coupled with the concretely discussable authority sources for an African audience: scripture and Cyprian.[32]

Augustine's new operational tempo is clear straight away in *De baptismo,* where he declares:

> Wherefore in this treatise we have undertaken, with the help of God, not only to refute the objections which the Donatists have been wont to urge against us in this matter [the nature of baptism is referred to] but also to advance what God may enable us to say in respect of the authority of the blessed martyr Cyprian, which they endeavour to use as a prop, to prevent their perversity from falling before the attacks of truth. And this we propose to do, in order that all whose judgments is not blinded by party spirit [i.e., Donatists] may understand that, so far from Cyprian's authority being in their favour, it tends directly to their refutation and discomfort.[33]

There it is, a two-fold method based on a sustained theological/thematic critique and a direct and forceful appropriation of an authority (in this case Cyprian), which had the effect of inserting this perspective whilst also situating

---

Publishing, 1999), 91–92; Garcia Mac Gaw, *Le problème du baptême dans le schisme donatiste* (Paris: De Boccard, 2008); Everett Ferguson, *Baptism in the Early Church: History, Theology, and Liturgy in the First Five Centuries* (Grand Rapids, MI/Cambridge: Wm. Eerdmans Publishing, 2009).

32 Monceaux, *Histoire littéraire de l'Afrique chrétienne: depuis les origines jusqu'a l'invasion arabe, tome septième.* In the quest to enunciate Augustine's flirtations with Cyprian, it is important to point out that scripture, Church councils, and Church fathers always retained the highest magisterial bearing for Augustine. See Jochen Eber, '*De Baptismo – Über die Taufe Augustinus*', book review in *European Journal of Theology* 16/2 (2007), 124.

33 *De bapt.* 1,1 (*CSEL* 51, 145): 'Quapropter in hoc opera adiuvante domino suscepimus non solum ea refellere, quae de hac re nobis Donatistae obiectare consuerunt, sed etiam de beatissimi martyris Cypriani auctoritate, unde suam perversitatem, ne veritatis impetus cadat, fulcire conantur, quae dominus donaverit dicere, ut intellegant omnes, qui non studio partium caecati iudicant, non solum eos non adiuvari auctoritate Cypriani, sed per ipsam maxime convince adque subverti'.

himself into the African psyche through an unambiguous affiliation with their most popular hero.

But this new two-fold method required a level of statesmanship such that Augustine had to navigate very carefully between claiming allegiance with Cyprian and his theology whilst at the same time handily criticising the Donatists' positions, which were rather more in line with Cyprian's original intent.[34] A first instance of this careful balancing act can be found in Augustine's bid to controvert the Donatist understanding of baptism:

> [O]n the subject of baptism we should believe what the universal Church maintains, apart from the sacrilege of schism [the Donatist Church]. And yet, if within the Church different people still held different opinions on that, without violating the peace in turn, then until a clear decree should be issued by a universal council, it is right for the love [*caritas*] that opts for unity to throw a veil over the error of human sin [that has led to the rebaptismal practice].[35]

In this way Augustine is laying the groundwork for a modification of Cyprian's own teaching on rebaptism. He does this firstly by distinguishing the bishop of Carthage from the Donatists, whom he insists violently affront the unity of the Church with their petulant insistence on rebaptising all non-Donatists. By contrast, Augustine's Cyprian at all times insists on peace and unity [*pax et unitas*]. Secondly, Augustine exempts what he finds to be Cyprian's error in the lack of a universal ruling in that earlier period. There can be no doubt who Augustine is referencing in this regard when he writes as follows:

> There is great evidence on the part of the blessed martyr Cyprian, found in his letters, regarding whose authority it is that they [the Donatists] carnally flatter themselves with, while they are actually overthrown by him. For at that time [Cyprian's episcopacy] before the faith of the universal Church had been authoritatively proclaimed, by the decree of an

34 See introduction of G. Bavaud in Augustine, *Sept Livres sur le Baptême*, trans. G. Finaert, intro., notes G. Bavaud, *BA* 29 (Brugge: Desclée de Brouwer, 1964), 10; C. Mayer, 'Taufe und Erwählung—Zur Dialektik des sacramtentum-Begriffes in der antidonatistischen Schrift Augustins: De baptismo', in C. Mayer and W. Eckermann (eds.), *Festschrift: P. Dr. theol. Dr. phil. Adolar Zumkeller OSA zum 60. Geburtstag*, *Cassiciacum* 30 (1975), 26.

35 *De bapt.* 1,27 (*CSEL* 51, 170): 'Restat ut hoc de baptismo pie credamus, quod universa ecclesia a sacrilegio schismatis remota custodit. In qua tamen si aliud alii, et aliud alii adhuc de ista quaestione salva pace sentirent, donec universali concilio unum aliquid eliquatum sincerumque placuisset, humanae infirmitatis errorem cooperiret caritas unitatis'.

> ecumenical council [Nicaea], concerning what baptismal practice should be followed, it seemed to Cyprian, jointly with eighty fellow bishops of African churches, that every person who had been baptised outside the communion of the Catholic Church, should be baptised anew. And, I take it, that the reason why the Lord did not reveal this error to such a man of eminence, was so that his pious humility and charity concerning the peace and well-being of the Church might be manifest, and be heeded as such, so as to serve as an example of healing power, not only for Christians then, but also for those later on.[36]

In writing this, Augustine has himself introduced an innovation to the tradition. For one thing, it is clear Augustine is re-calibrating the Donatist/North African understanding of rebaptism, as this was traditionally only sought when someone who was baptised in a sect outside of the Church sought to enter into the Church. Then, although Augustine acknowledges Cyprian was wrong, it is still the Catholic party that maintains organic lineage with the Cyprianic tradition, by virtue of the Catholic option for peace and unity over sin, as opposed to the Donatists who, Augustine claims, bastardise Cyprian's belief. Two other minor trends are apparent, namely (1) that Augustine was by this time aware of the value of martyrdom status as carrying an unsurpassable authoritativeness, a view he would maintain throughout the anti-Donatist/Pelagian campaign. Also, (2) Augustine had begun strongly to introduce the eventual vocabulary of original sin into the debate with his repeated references to carnality opposing grace.

Redefining the African Debate

In *De baptismo*, Augustine quite sensibly included as his first priority a redefinition of the debate over baptism/rebaptism. In this regard Augustine was less

36 *De bapt.* 1,28 (*CSEL* 51, 170–71): 'Extant beati martyris Cypriani in eius litteris magna documenta, ut ad illium iam veniam cuius sibi auctoritate isti carnaliter blandiuntur, cum eius caritate spiritualiter perimantur. Nam illis temporibus, antequam plenarii concilii sententia quid in hac re sequendum esset, totius ecclesiae consensio confirmaret, visum est ei cum ferme octoginta coepiscopis suis africanarum ecclesiarum, omnem hominem qui extra ecclesiae catholicae communionem baptizatus fuisset, oportere ad ecclesiam venientem denuo baptizari. Quod non recte fieri tanto viro nimirum propterea dominus non aperuit, ut eius pia et humilitas et caritas in custodienda salubriter ecclesiae pace patesceret, et non solum illius temporis christianis, sed etiam posteris ad medicinalem, ut ita dicam, notitiam signaretur'.

at a loss in face of the considerable historical depth which lay beneath the theology of the Donatists.[37] The application of 'rebaptism' to those who had never been baptised in the Catholic Church, but who had instead been baptised by ministers in apostasy/schism, was a practice that pre-dated Cyprian and had been continuously implemented by North African Christians. In fact it was the Donatists who adhered to the African tradition more exactingly;[38] it was Christians in league with Caecilian who only later diverged from this practice.[39] The overall integrity of the North African practice of rebaptism is already well attested to and need not be recapitulated here.[40] But in short, if Augustine was to overcome the reality that the Donatists stood in closer continuity with Cyprian in this matter, he needed to acknowledge the historicity of rebaptism and then re-formulate Cyprian's acquiescence as a sacrifice for the good of the Church. On this basis, Augustine notes the following:

> Cyprian [the Donatists claim], whose great merits and considerable learning we all know, decreed at a council, with his bishop colleagues of differing opinions, that all heretics and schismatics, that is, all cut-off from the communion of the one Church, are without baptism; and therefore,

---

37 One of the most rigourous treatments of the historical background of North African theology and rebaptism can be found in Joseph Fischer, 'Die ersten Konzilien im römischen Nordwest-Afrika', in E. Dassmann and K. Suso Frank (eds.), *Pietas: Festschrift für Bernhard Kötting, Jahrbuch für Antike und Christentum Ergänzungsband* 8 (Münster: Aschendorf, 1980), 217–27. Equally strong is Anne-Lene Fenger, 'Zur Beurteilung der Ketzertaufe durch Cyprian von Karthago und Ambrosius von Mailand', in E. Dassmann and K. Suso Frank (eds.), *Pietas: Festschrift für Bernhard Kötting, Jahrbuch für Antike und Christentum Ergänzungsband* 8 (Münster: Aschendorf, 1980), 179–97.

38 G. Bavaud, *Sept Livres sur le Baptême*, BA 29 (Brugge: Desclée de Brouwer, 1964), 12.

39 J. Alexander, 'Donatism', in P. Esler (ed.), *The Early Christian World, Volume II* (London: Routledge, 2000), 972. R. Markus adds to this definition, that 'what we call "Donatism" is in reality nothing else than the Christianity of North Africa as it continued to survive into the fourth century…', 'Africa and the Orbis Terrarum: The Theological Problem', 321.

40 Authors who have invested significant time in studying the historicity of rebaptism in the third/fourth centuries are Robert Evans, *One and Holy: The Church in Latin Patristic Thought* (London: SPCK, 1972); Maurice Bévenot, 'Cyprian's Platform in the Rebaptism Controversy', *Heythrop Journal* 19/2 (1978), 123–42; Geoffrey Dunn, 'Validity of Baptism and Ordination in the African response to the "Rebaptism" Crisis: Cyprian of Carthage's Synod of Spring 256', *Theological Studies* 67 (2006), 257–74; J. Patout Burns, 'On Rebaptism: Social Organization in the Third Century Church', *Journal of Early Christian Studies* 1/4 (1993), 367–03. Also see J. Patout Burns, *Cyprian the Bishop* (London/New York: Routledge, 2002), esp. 166–76.

> whosoever joined the communion of the one Church after being baptised by [heretics or schismatics] must be baptised in the Church.[41]

Interestingly, while simultaneously re-quoting a direct statement of the Donatists, Augustine is actually laying out the actual view of Cyprian and the Donatists, that is, that anyone who has been baptised outside of the Church, even in a separated Church, is not considered actually baptised. In this sense, that person, when coming over to the true Church, would be baptised for the first time. But Augustine does realise he is explaining their proper view, so he moves straight away to a nuanced view of Cyprian's intention, in order to validate what he himself is putting forth:

> The authority of Cyprian does not cause me alarm, because I am affirmed by his humility. We know, truly, the great merit of the bishop and martyr Cyprian; but is it in any way superior to that of the apostle and martyr Peter [who relented to the apostle Paul over the matter of circumcising Christians converts; quoting Cyp., *Ep.* 71]. In this example, Cyprian writes what we are also shown in the scriptures, that the apostle Peter, through whom the primacy of the apostles shines with the most brilliant grace, was corrected by the apostle Paul, when he adopted a custom [circumcision of non-Jews] at variance with the demands of the truth.[42]

Knowing the solidity of the African tradition, Augustine made the original idea of rebaptism a referendum on Cyprian. Indeed, Cyprian held an idea that would serve as the basis for the later Donatist baptismal theology, and because of this Cyprian was wrong. But what makes the Donatist wrong and Augustine right in the end is that Cyprian, who was driven by humility, tolerance, and a love of unity, maintained that no Christian should be found 'judging others...

---

41 *De bapt.* 2,2 (*CSEL* 51, 174): 'Cyprianus, inquiunt, cuius tantum meritum novimus tantamque doctrinam, cum multis coepiscopis suis sententias proprias conferentibus, in concilio statuit haereticos vel schismaticos, id est omnes qui extra unius ecclesiae communionem sunt, baptismum non habere; et ideo quisquis ab eis baptizatus ad ecclesiam venerit, esse in ecclesia baptizandum'.

42 *De bapt.* 2,2 (*CSEL* 51, 174–75): 'Non me terret auctoritas Cypriani, quia reficit humilitas Cypriani...magnum quidem meritum novimus Cypriani episcopi et martyris, sed numquid maius quam Petri apostoli et martyris?...ecce ubi commemorat Cyprianus, quod etiam nos in scipturis sanctis didicimus, apostolum Petrum, in quo primatus apostolorum tam excellenti gratia paeminet, aliter quam postulabat de circumcisione agere solitum a psoteriore apostolo Paulo esse correctum'.

or depriving any one of communion',[43] which Augustine takes from Cyprian's *Ep.* 71. Cyprian's opinion was subject to correction, according to Augustine, because of his abundance of love (*caritas*),[44] much like the apostle Peter who was willing to suffer correction by Paul.[45] In comparison, Augustine accuses the Donatists of being 'proud,' of having 'swollen necks', and of being 'arrogant',[46] since they will not concede to the teaching of the universal Church, as Cyprian would have done,[47] which means they do not possess the authority and spirit of Cyprian: 'For, indeed, so holy and peaceful a soul would have been most ready to assent to the argument of any single person who would prove to him the truth'.[48]

At this point Augustine tries to strip Cyprian out of the hands of the Donatists, whom he calls 'ravening wolves, seeking to be clad in a sheep's [Cyprian's] clothing' (Matt. 7,15),[49] and insists the Donatists 'seek counsel from the blessed Cyprian himself',[50] by which he intends placing unity of the Church above self-concern, or as the bishop of Hippo put it: 'Cease, then, to bring forward against us the authority of Cyprian in favour of repeating baptism, but cling with us to the example of Cyprian for the preservation of unity'.[51]

In illustrating Cyprian's desire for unity, Augustine is aided further by plentiful examples gleaned from the Maximian schism into which he had waded so enthusiastically a few short years before. This placed Augustine in a safe position from which to fire upon his Donatist listeners, even whilst accepting he was at variance with Cyprian's own views. The following is a rich example of such a rationale:

> What attitude do they [Donatists] assume, when it is shown that saint Cyprian, though he himself did not admit new members into the Church

43 *De bapt.* 2,6 and 2,7 (*CSEL* 51, 180): '...ait enim: neminem iudicantes aut a iure communionis aliquem si diversum senserit amoventes'.

44 *De bapt.* 2,5.

45 *De bapt.* 1,2.

46 *De bapt.* 1,3.

47 *De bapt.* 1,5.

48 *De bapt.* 2,5 (*CSEL* 51, 179): 'Quin profecto et uni uerum dicenti et demonstranti posset facillime consentire tam sancta anima, tam pacata'. This seems to be at variance with the nature of the debate between Cyprian and the Roman bishop at the time, Stephen, see J. Patout Burns, 'Social Context in the Controversy between Cyprian and Stephen', *Studia Patristica* 24 (1993), 38–44.

49 *De bapt.* 2,11.

50 *De bapt.* 2,18.

51 *De bapt.* 2,12.

> who were otherwise baptised in heresy or schism, still held communion with colleagues who did, under the obligation to 'Judge no one, nor deprive any of communion'? If he was polluted by communion with these types of people, why do [Donatists] follow his authority regarding baptism? But if he was not polluted by communion with them, why do they not follow his example in keeping unity?[52]

So whilst the Donatists receive Cyprian's teaching on baptism, Augustine argues that they reject his more important teaching on preserving the body of Christ. In doing so, he even blasts Donatists for protecting their baptismal theology for selfish reasons, becoming so self-concerned as to commit suicide as self-justified martyrs.[53] And it is the personally-refined Maximian schism argument that serves as his *coup de grâce*:

> What answer can they give about the adherents of Maximian whom [the Donatists] have received back into their fold, they cannot even start to explain. If they dare say, 'Those we received back were innocent,' then the response is clear, 'Then you have damned the innocent.' If they say, 'We did it out of ignorance,' then you judged hastily like you did against Caecilian and the *traditores*...For indeed the innocent could never be damned by the voice of the truth...If [the Donatists] say, 'They were received for the sake of peace,' our answer is, 'Why then do you not accept the only true and complete peace? Who urged you, who compelled you to receive a schismatic whom you had damned, to preserve the peace of Donatus, and yet to condemn the whole world, in contradiction to the peace of Christ?' Truth hems them in on every side, and they think that there is nothing left for them to do; they cannot figure out how to respond.[54]

---

52 *De bapt.* 2,15 (*CSEL* 51, 190): 'Quid autem agunt isti, cum docetur sanctus Cyprianus, etiamsi non admisit in haeresi vel in schismate baptizatos, tamen communicasse admittentibus, quod apertissime declaravit dicens: neminem iudicantes aut a iure communicationis aliquem so diversum senserit amouentes?'

53 This was in reference to Augustine's earlier problem of Donatist cliff-jumpers that he discussed in *Ep.* 22 at the start of his career.

54 *De bapt.* 2,17 (*CSEL* 51, 192–93): 'Quid de receptis Maximianistis respondeant, non inveniunt. Si dixerint: Innocentes recepimus: respondetur eis: Ergo innocentes damnaveratis. Si dixerint: "Nesciebamus: Ergo temere iudicastis (sic etiam de traditoribus sententiam temerariam protulistis)"...Si dixerint: "Pro pace suscepti sunt," respondetur, "Cur ergo veram et plenam non agnoscitis pacem?" Quis vos impulit, quis coegit pro pace Donati

In this way Augustine lays out his rationale for confronting the Donatist leadership head-on as he initiates the anti-Donatist campaign in earnest. According to Augustine, and in this new strategy, the Donatists claim to possess the authority of Cyprian, but because of their own interests actually reject Cyprian in his premier concern for Church unity. In saying this, Augustine accuses the Donatists of rejecting the truth (Augustine's obsession since his conversion), the bond of peace, and Cyprian's very authority. On a rhetorical level he adds a triumphal flourish to this line of thought:

> There was at one time a doubt about the subject of baptism; those who held different opinions but remained in unity. In the course of time, due to the gradual unfolding of the truth [ecumenical councils], any remnant of doubt was wiped away. The question, while yet unsolved, did not scare Cyprian into endorsing separation from the Church, invites you [Donatists], to return back to the fold. Come to the Catholic Church which abides in agreement, which Cyprian did not abandon even while he faced doubts; or if you are now dissatisfied with the example of Cyprian, who held communion with those who were received with the baptism of the heretics, who also declared we should 'judge no one, nor deprive anyone communion if they disagree.' What are you doing?[55]

From now on, Cyprian will be aggressively pulled from the Donatists through a process of refuting any legitimate claims they have to the bishop of Carthage. Augustine's intended objective for appropriation is clear: make the Donatists appear as if they are favouring their own theology over the 'most moderate and most truthful sermonising of Cyprian'.[56] It is a choice that would have been easy for any North African Christian caught in the middle of this tit-for-tat polemic.

---

schismaticum recipere damnatum, et contra pacem Christi orbem damnare inauditum? Urget eos utique veritas; vident se non habere quid respondeant'.

55 *De bapt.* 2,20 (CSEL 51, 196): 'Ea dubitatio procedente tempore perspecta veritate sublata est: quaestio, quae nondum finita Cyprianum non deterruit ut recederet, vos finita ut redeatis invitat...Venite ad catholicam concordantem, quam Cyprianum non deservit fluctuantem...aut si vobis exemplum Cypriani iam displicet, qui communicavit eis, qui cum baptismate haereticorum recipiebantur, aperte dicens: neminem iudicantes aut a iure communioinis aliquem si diversum senserit amouentes, quo itis, miseri, quid agitis?'

56 *De bapt.* 3,5 (CSEL 51, 201): 'Cypriani nobis mitissimo et veracissimo sermone concessum'.

Claiming 'That Loveliest of Teachers and Most Blessed of Martyrs'[57]

Arguing that *De baptismo* deserves pride of place among the extant anti-Donatist works requires more than a demonstration of its coalescence of disparate theological substrata into a sustained critique of Donatist beliefs. Indeed, more than for its comprehensive elucidation of early baptismal theology, *De baptismo* stands out as Augustine's main breakthrough document against the Donatists. And at the heart of this breakthrough is Augustine's concentrated effort to assume the title of heir of Cyprian and to displace the Donatists from that designation.[58] In short, whilst Augustine has by 400/01 become adept at utilising scripture and other external authorities as the basis for his own authority, it is in *De baptismo* where it appears he has arrived at the solution of how best to polemically address his Donatist adversaries, and this he does through such a concerted and prolonged push as to peel the 'Cyprian' authority away from them. This, along with a simultaneous re-appropriation of Cyprian's authority, places the Donatist claim in doubt, whilst making the seemingly improbable relation between the Catholic Augustine and the blessed Cyprian a self-evident fact.[59]

---

57 *De doct. Chr.* 2,61 (CCSL 32, 74): 'Cyprianus doctor suavissimus et martyr beatissimus'.

58 This proved to be an overriding concern of Augustine's throughout the controversy. Although not universally shared, the general consensus is that the Donatists did represent the communion of continuity with Cyprian, and therefore could be considered as the legitimate 'heirs' to his legacy. See Gerald Bonner, 'Dic Christi Veritas Ubi Nunc Habitas: Ideas of Schism and Heresy in the Post-Nicene Age', in W.E. Klingshirn and M. Vessey (eds.), *The Limits of Ancient Christianity: Essays on Late Antique Thought and Culture in Honour of R.A. Markus*, (Ann Arbor, MI: University of Michigan Press, 1999), 63–79, esp. 67.

59 That appropriating the Cyprian brand is Augustine's overriding concern at this particular moment is beyond doubt. The raw data speaks for itself in this regard. Of the 600+/– occurrences throughout his entire corpus where Augustine refers to Cyprian, some 214 are found in *De baptismo* alone! This is by far the largest single source of material on Cyprian in either the Donatist or Pelagian controversies. References to Cyprian in *De baptismo* are as follows: 1,1(x2); 1,28; 1,29; 2,1; 2,2(x8); 2,3(x4); 2,4(x2); 2,5; 2,6(x2); 2,7(x4); 2,8(x2); 2,9(x2); 2,11(x2); 2,12(x3); 2,13; 2,14(x3); 2,15; 2,18; 2,19(x2); 2,20(x5); 3,1(x2); 3,2(x3); 3,3(x8); 3,4(x4); 3,5(x3); 3,6(x2); 3,7(x3); 3,10; 3,13; 3,14; 3,16(x2); 3,17(x4); 3,22; 3,23; 3,26; 3,28; 4,2; 4,3; 4,4; 4,6; 4,7(x2); 4,8(x3); 4,9; 4,10(x4); 4,11(x4); 4,13; 4,16(x4); 4,17; 4,18(x4); 4,19; 4,21; 4,24; 4,28; 4,29; 5,1(x7); 5,2(x4); 5,3(x5); 5,4(x3); 5,7; 5,8; 5,12; 5,13(x2); 5,14; 5,16(x2); 5,19; 5,21; 5,22; 5,23; 5,24(x2); 5,27; 5,30(x2); 5,31(x2); 5,32; 5,34; 5,37(x2); 5,38(x2); 5,39(x2); 6,1(x2); 6,2(x2); 6,3(x5); 6,4(x2); 6,5; 6,8; 6,9; 6,10(x2); 6,12(x3); 6,19(x3); 6,24; 6,25; 6,33; 6,41; 6,43;

Before moving on to Augustine's interpretation of the Cyprian-figure and his methods of invalidating the Donatist claim to the bishop, it is helpful to clearly ascertain the benefit Augustine hoped to gain by overtly allying himself with the Cyprian name. An ensuing question would be, 'why is it even necessary for Augustine to seek out various authorities in the first place?' Considering the value that Augustine, the Donatists, and later the Pelagians, all place on the primary authoritativeness of scripture, should it not have been sufficient to resolve their respective discourses before a Christian audience through mediation of scriptural texts and typologies? Lastly, in what way does Augustine's appropriation of Cyprian in the Donatist dilemma mirror his appropriation in the Pelagian controversy?

If Augustine's extant works are any indication, he probably discovered through trial and error how to criticize well-entrenched Donatist positions. In this same way he was probably led to an intimate understanding of the potency within North Africa that came along with close association with Cyprian and his teachings. In fact, if one intended to summarise the underlying rationale motivating Augustine to create a link in the Donatist controversy, it is that in the pastoral milieu of Roman North Africa (and especially the Numidian province), one could only hope to be taken seriously by the faithful[60] (and to be physically safe)[61] if one stood ostentatiously in the tradition of Cyprian and in communion with his faithful interpreters.

But why was Cyprian so well regarded in North Africa in the first place? That he was the hometown celebrity is probably only a partial explanation. Though Africa was in some ways far removed from the imperial power centres on the northern side of the Mediterranean, it claimed a respectable number of venerable sons, such as Septimus Severus (193–11); and seminal Christian figures like Origen, Pope Victor I, Pope Miltiades, Tertullian, Lactantius, and Donatus of Nigrae.[62] A number of important factors made it stand out in the history of

6,44; 6,45; 6,47; 6,48; 6,50; 6,60; 6,68; 6,78; 6,80; 6,87; 7,1(x3); 7,3(x3); 7,5; 7,7; 7,9(x2); 7,13; 7,21; 7,23; 7,25; 7,27(x4); 7,29; 7,33(x2); 7,39(x2); 7,49(x4); 7,51; 7,89(x2); 7,96; 7,97; 7,98(x2); and 7,103(x3).

60 Augustine's *Sermones* on the feast day of Cyprian (and later of Stephen the Martyr) seem to attest to the fact that Augustine readily had to set aside his own preferred view that veneration of the martyrs tended to be supercilious and detached from right Christian belief.

61 One need only recall the open tension that Augustine was aware of towards the Church of the *traditores* from the Donatists.

62 J. Coyle summarises well the personalities associated with North African civic pride in 'Particularities of Christianity in Roman Africa', *Studia Patristica* 39 (2006), 13–26.

Western Christianity: its own distinctive architectural styling,[63] the first Latin Bible translation,[64] and its own '*lingua afra*.'[65] On top of this, Cyprian was as Roman as it was possible to be in ancient African Christian culture, leaving aside the fact that Berbers in Numidia and Mauretania found a cultural affinity with him. One must therefore consider the religious motivations for assigning Cyprian such unmatched hero-worship. He was a figure who was certainly controversial in his own time,[66] especially over the scandal involving his flight from the Decian persecution in Carthage.[67] But his martyrdom set the stage for his posthumous ascendancy, one that established him as a person who embodied every trait envied by North African Christians:[68] continuity with tradition, courage before the imperial powers and foreign bishops, resolute defence of doctrine and the integrity of the Church, and a glorious death as the ultimate indication of virtue. These types of ascriptions were what enhanced Cyprian's reputation in the eyes of later Christian generations. And for Augustine, to become associated with such a personage meant a sure source of authority.

An appropriation and usurpation of Cyprian's legacy would also provide a means of undermining virtually every Donatist position as well as their claim to legitimacy. This is abundantly clear in the myriad accusations Augustine levels against the Donatists in conjunction with his Cyprian-appropriation: (1) that Donatists interpret Cyprian accordingly to their fleshly whims and not the Holy Spirit;[69] (2) that Donatists defile Cyprian by rejecting ecclesial unity;[70] (3) that Donatists renounce Cyprian by refusing unity;[71] (4) that Donatists stand

63 J. Christern, *Das frühchristliche Pilgerheiligtum von Tebessa: Architektur und Ornamentik einer spätantiken Bauhütte in Nordafrika* (Wiesbaden: Steiner Verlag, 1976), 5–9.

64 J. Coyle, 'The Self-identity of North African Christians in Augustine's Time', 66.

65 Aug., *In epistolam Ioannis ad Parthos tractatus decem* 2,3 (*PL* 35, 1991): 'Sic honorat Christum Donatistae ut dicant illum remanisse ad duas linguas, Latinam et Puniacam, id est, Afram'.

66 This was particularly true concerning the election of Cyprian as bishop of Carthage; Geoffrey Dunn, *Cyprian and the Bishops of Rome: Questions of Papal Primacy in the Early Church, Early Christian Studies* 11 (Strathfield, NSW: St. Pauls Publications, 2007), 20–23.

67 Cyprian's biographer Pontius recorded that Cyprian fled his see for the wellbeing of his congregants; *Vita Cypriani*, in M. Pellegrino (ed.), *Ponzio: Vita e martirio de San Cipriano, Verba Seniorum* 3 (Alba: Pia Società *San* Paolo, 1955), 7.13. This is further covered in M. Sage, *Cyprian* (Cambridge, MA: Philadelphia Patristic Foundation, 1975), 191–94.

68 Van Bavel, 'The Cult of Martyrs', 260–63. This is likewise explicated in Evans, *One and Holy*, 68.

69 *De bapt.* 1,28.

70 *De bapt.* 2,9; 2,11.

71 *De bapt.* 2,14–15.

to benefit from listening to the real Cyprian;[72] (5) that Donatists hate Cyprian's example of unity;[73] (6) that Donatists posses no link with authority or tradition;[74] and (7) that the Donatists are disqualified in the first place by the choices they made in the Maximian schism.[75] These accusations convincingly illustrate the exposure of the Donatist Church, which had its theological foundation on the premise of being the sole body to authentically interpret North African tradition in the manner of Cyprian. At the heart of this vulnerability was the risk that someone might strip away from the Donatists the authority of Cyprian, which would be tantamount to completely removing any claims to historicity for Donatist theology.[76]

Similarities in Appropriation

As seen in the brief overview of the twin controversies—the Donatist and Pelagian—there were considerable contextual differences between them in terms of the need for authorities. But there were also resounding similarities in the way Augustine employed Cyprian in both situations. In both cases one finds Augustine regularly deploying Cyprian as follows: Cyprian's credentials and sanctity are reaffirmed and clearly presented. Therefore we encounter such flattering accolades as: '*beatus*', '*sanctus*', 'martyr', and 'episcopus'. This technique displays Augustine's increasing rhetorical understanding concerning the African audience. He understands in both situations that by ratifying Cyprian's prestige upfront, he is establishing a common ground on which to parley, with the additional benefit of appearing sensitive to and in line with the religiosity of the general Christian population.

There is also present Augustine's method of regularly situating Cyprian within the continuum of an episcopal corps and among noteworthy saints. This serves several functions; on the one hand, it demonstrates a collegial preference towards communion with others of the faith and towards upholding this even when disputes arise. On the other hand, it is a way of showing that Cyprian, and therefore any authentic Christian, operates within a community of believers and not on individual terms when receiving/transmitting tradition.

72 *De bapt.* 2,18.

73 *De bapt.* 2,20.

74 *De bapt.* 3,2.

75 *De bapt.* 3,3(x2).

76 The historicity of Donatist thought founded upon the legacy of Cyprian is perhaps best elucidated in Johannes Mühlsteiger, 'Donatismus und die verfassungrechtlichen Wirkungen einer Kirchenspaltung', ZRG *Kan.Abt.* 85 (1999), 1–59. Reprinted in Konrad Breitsching and Wilhelm Rees (eds.), *Tradition-Wegweisung in die Zukunft* (Berlin: Dunker & Humbolt, 2001), 681–39, esp ch. 6, pages 726–39.

Likewise, the plurality of corroborative voices in harmony with Cyprian also enhance his authority. For this reason, no-one should be surprised that Augustine routinely employs Cyprian in his writings, along with a host of other specifically-intentioned bishops, councils, and holy men. This also gives Augustine a loophole when siding with Cyprianic theology. By this I mean that times when Augustine finds Cyprian wrong, either by saying so directly or by implication, he is able to modify the apparent paradox by excusing Cyprian's error as a mutually-shared mistake with mitigated responsibility. Augustine takes this a step further when he turns a disagreement with Cyprian into a showcase for the latter's graced state; that is, instead of making the same mistakes as the Donatists or Pelagians by clinging to their error no matter what the cost, Cyprian exhibited his charity and humility by refusing to become embittered and defensive. In sum, Augustine's Cyprian reacts to personal mistakes and to error in doctrine, not with schism and rejection like the Donatists or Pelagians, but with a love that mirrors Christ's.

A final display of Augustinian rhetorical sophistication concerning Cyprian is found in his readily proliferating recognition of the bishop as a martyr. This is one of the most recognisable appellations Augustine uses in his anti-Donatist and anti-Pelagian campaigns. The inclusion of this tactic is quite ingenious on Augustine's part. In the Donatist crisis, acknowledgement of Cyprian the *martyr-bishop* situates the Catholic insurgent within a literary continuum that is popularly grounded in North Africa. A cursory reading of the Donatist martyrdom stories provides a copious amount of evidence of the value placed upon the status of martyrs in the third and fourth centuries. But Augustine's appropriation of Cyprian as a martyr serves a double purpose here. On one front, Augustine is preaching and writing in a style not only agreeable to a North African audience, but which is probably even a prerequisite. Secondly, using the 'martyrdom card' allots him a currency with which to make his points based on the inherent value and recognisable authority present in such vocabulary. To a North African, martyrdom signifies the highest level of respectability, morality, and authority possible, especially in terms of theological reflection and the modelling of everyday Christian life.[77] In essence, Augustine uses the term here against Donatist leaders because no one will talk back to a martyr!

77 The reverence bestowed upon martyrdom is reviewed in a host of researches, an example being: C. Straw, 'Martyrdom and Christian Identity: Gregory the Great, Augustine, and Tradition', in W.E. Klingshirn and M. Vessey (eds.), *The Limits of Ancient Christianity: Essays on Late Antique Thought and Culture in Honor of R.A. Markus*, (Ann Arbor, MI: University of Michigan Press, 1999), 250–66, esp. 250–52.

The Pelagian controversy will occasion a similar need. But whereas in the Donatist conflict Augustine seeks to piece himself into the fabric of Africa; in the Pelagian crisis Augustine needs to defend African tradition and identity (*africanitas*) with a universally-recognised authority. Cyprian as 'martyr' allows Augustine to perform both tasks. Proof of this is found in the frequent recurrence of Augustine defending his theological positions with the validation of the martyr Cyprian, whose teaching is codified by his Christ-like death. So, to recapitulate, in both controversies Cyprian the martyr is included as the proof *par excellence* of authentic teaching; the one following in Cyprian's way is assured orthodoxy because of that martyrdom, which is itself a symbol of God's grace.[78] Cyprian is thus a flesh-and-blood example venerated by all sides in both controversies, and whose authority summons the attention of a listener with a degree of relatability and concreteness that the more authoritative scriptures lack.

Who is Augustine's Cyprian?

By now it is evident that Augustine needed the assent of authority, specifically in the person of Cyprian. In *De baptismo* this need was met as a number of rhetorical techniques, references, and intuitions which Augustine nurtured and experimented with in the 390s came together for the first time in one central anti-Donatist opus. This work marked an important event for the bishop, who was still struggling to establish his voice among the din of other Mediterranean luminaries of the time, especially since events in the Roman Empire were becoming ever more chaotic with the society beginning to show signs of fatigue.[79] Themes that were sewn together in *De baptismo* matured in Augustine's subsequent anti-Donatist writings, and blossomed again in the anti-Pelagian effort. But what were these themes? Who was Cyprian according to Augustine?

78 *De bapt.* 4,9; Vittorino Grossi, 'Baptismus', in C. Mayer (ed.), *Augustinus-Lexikon*, vol. 1 (Basel: Schwabe & Co., 1996), 589.

79 That Augustine was so feverishly intent on embarking on a prolonged war with the Donatist Church runs counter to other Christian writers of the time, who were increasingly concerned with the practicalities of a Christian Roman Empire that was showing signs of collapse, notably his sometime pen-pal, Jerome. See Stefan Rebenich, 'Christian Asceticism and Barbarian Incursion: The Making of a Christian Catastrophe', *Journal of Late Antiquity* 2/1 (2009), 49–59.

Augustine worked strenuously to establish clearly his respect for Cyprian. Hence, in *De baptismo*, a full array of positive descriptions are used in support of this objective. His most common appellations are *beatus*[80] and *sanctus*;[81] and also 'tolerant'[82] and 'man of unity'.[83] Both sets of terms were advantageous within the general North African context, where praise for Cyprian was normative in everyday Christian life.[84] But they were also necessary terms for Augustine to argue two points in *De baptismo*, namely that his views of baptism and ecclesiology are based on the testimony not only of an authority, but also of a graced and holy figure. The second set was particularly effective in complementing Augustine's claim that the Donatists' practice of 'rebaptism',[85] and their view of the Church as an exclusive body of the pure (also a body of martyrs and later on the collective of Israel),[86] stand in stark contrast with Cyprian's theology and spirit.

The terms *beatus* and *sanctus* assumed an even more important place, because of their routine usage in earlier African Christian writings and in Augustine's later anti-Donatist and anti-Pelagian works. This evinces two aspects to *De baptismo* and beyond: by 400/01 Augustine had certainly acquired fluency in the sacral vocabulary of North Africa, a way of speaking and writing that was amenable to Donatists and Catholics alike. This means Augustine would have already had in place a practical method of drawing-upon authorities in his polemical works.

Secondly, Augustine's insistence on Cyprian's tolerance and love of unity marks the central theological refrain associated with Cyprian's authority in *De baptismo*. By emphasising Cyprian's love of unity, Augustine is drawing a connection with lines of argumentation in *C. ep. Parm.*, written shortly before on the nature of the Church. By highlighting Cyprian's tolerance, Augustine was making a move to give nuance to traditional North African baptismal theology by arguing that a decisive rupture exists between the thought and attitude of

80 *De bapt.* 1,28–29; 2,1–2; 2,6; 2,11; 2,13; 2,14; 2,18; 2,20; 3,1; 3,4; 3,17; 4,3; 4,16; 4,29; 5,1; 5,2; 5,14; 5,39; 6,1; 6,3; 6,10; 6,25; 6,48; 7,1; 7,3; 7,98.

81 *De bapt.* 1,29; 2,5; 2,12; 2,15; 3,26; 4,7; 4,8; 4,16; 5,2; 5,7; 5,22; 5,23; 5,37; 6,3; 6,19; 6,87; 7,39.

82 *De bapt.* 2,2; 2,6(x2); 2,15; 2,19; 3,3(x2); 3,4; 3,23; 3,26; 3,28; 6,43; 7,3; 7,9(x2); 7,13; 7,49; 7,51; 7,89(x2).

83 *De bapt.* 2,2; 2,6; 2,7(x2); 2,8; 2,20; 3,1; 3,2; 3,22; 3,26; 4,8; 4,11; 5,23; 5,32; 5,37; 6,1; 6,8; 7,25,49; 7,103.

84 J.-P. Brisson, *Autonomisme et christianisme dans l'Afrique romaine de Septime Sévère à l'invasion vandale* (Paris: De Boccard, 1958), 123–88.

85 *De bapt.* 1,2; 1,29; 2,2; 2,16; 2,18; 2,19(x5); 2,20(x3); 2,20(x3); 3,1; 3,16(x2); 3,23; 5,2(x3); 5,3; 5,6(x2); 5,7; 5,36; 6,2; 6,12; 6,27;6,81(x2); 6,82.

86 See Tilley, 'Sustaining Donatist Self-Identity', 21–35.

Cyprian (which Augustine makes out to be tolerant of those not in communion with the Church, and also to affirm that sinners exist in the earthly Church), and the Donatist claim to be heirs of Cyprian. In this case, Augustine argues that rather than being vindicated by Cyprian, Donatist leaders are silenced (their mouths are shut) by his example.[87] Both of these trends are remarkable in that they do represent a highly modified appropriation of Cyprian.

Augustine fortifies his most prominent descriptions of Cyprian with a number of other equally strong titles of praise: humble,[88] man of peace,[89] teacher/learned,[90] man of charity,[91] uncontaminated by the sins of others,[92] refuter of the Donatists,[93] modest,[94] great,[95] exemplary bishop,[96] non-judgmental,[97] corrector of sinners,[98] persistent,[99] patient,[100] perfected through grace/virtue,[101] merciful,[102] docile,[103] fruitful,[104] most beloved,[105] most excellent and graced,[106] having an 'abundance of love',[107] and 'Cyprian of Carthage'.[108]

A few more appellations which bear significant weight are: martyr,[109] *auctoritas*,[110] *exemplum*,[111] 'like Peter',[112] 'like Paul',[113] 'in accord with Stephen

87 *De bapt.* 7,103.
88 *De bapt.* 2,2; 2,5; 3,5.
89 *De bapt.* 2,4; 2,6; 2,19; 5,2(x2); 5,22; 6,3; 7,3; 7,103.
90 *De bapt.* 2,13; 4,7; 4,29; 5,30; 5,37.
91 *De bapt.* 1,29; 2,5; 2,12; 2,15; 3,26; 4,7; 4,8; 4,16; 5,2; 5,7; 5,22; 5,23; 5,37; 6,3; 6,19; 6,87; 7,39.
92 *De bapt.* 2,9; 3,3; 7,9; 7,27.
93 *De bapt.* 1,1; 1,23; 1,29; 2,1; 2,2; 5,1(x2); 5,39; 7,3; 7,103: 'shuts their [the Donatists'] mouths'.
94 *De bapt.* 2,13; 3,5; 5,23.
95 *De bapt.* 3,3,5.
96 *De bapt.* 2,2(x2); 3,5; 6,3; 6,12; 7,103.
97 *De bapt.* 2,3; 2,7; 3,7; 3,13; 5,23; 7,7; 3,1; 6,9; 6,10; 6,12; 6,48; 7,3(x2); 7,49.
98 *De bapt.* 4,4; 4,8; 4,11; 6,33; 7,29; 7,89.
99 *De bapt.* 2,5,6.
100 *De bapt.* 4,7; 5,23; 7,33.
101 *De bapt.* 4,9.
102 *De bapt.* 5,3(x2).
103 *De bapt.* 5,37.
104 *De bapt.* 6,2.
105 *De bapt.* 6,24.
106 *De bapt.* 6,3.
107 *De bapt.* 7,1.
108 *De bapt.* 7,96.
109 *De bapt.* 1,1; 1,28; 1,29; 2,2(x2); 2,6; 2,14; 3,5; 6,3; 7,1.
110 *De bapt.* 1,1(x2); 1,27; 1,29: 2,1; 2,2; 2,4; 2,12; 2,14; 2,15; 3,1; 4,18; 5,39; 7,1; 7,33.
111 *De bapt.* 2,4; 2,12; 2,15; 2,20; 3,1.
112 *De bapt.* 2,2(x4); 3,10; 6,3; 7,1; 7,39; 7,103.
113 *De bapt.* 4,10; 4,19; 5,13; 5,34; 6,12; 6,80; 6,87; 7,23; 7,21; 7,27.

the martyr',[114] 'validator of Augustine',[115] 'recognised throughout the world',[116] 'peaceful bishop and glorious martyr',[117] obedient to the scriptures,[118] 'truth-filled',[119] and 'guarantee of right communion'.[120] Each of these themes represents an overt attempt by Augustine to identify the Cyprian *gestalt* with a highly appreciative authority label. The recurrence of 'martyr', '*auctoritas*', and '*exemplum*', serve to make Cyprian's legacy the unambiguous indicator of orthodoxy and continuity by suggesting a value pegged to the biblical exegesis of that period, especially through a comparison with Christ, who is the ultimate example, martyr, and authority. Because the martyr Cyprian mirrors Christ, the one who can best claim Cyprian in the eyes of the public acquires a most powerful advocate.

Cyprian, Authority on the Church

A second dimension to Augustine's Cyprian-appropriation was his concrete utilisation of Cyprian's legacy in order to advance the theological and polemical objectives present in *De baptismo*. This was itself a result of Augustine first having referenced the credentials of Cyprian as being *sanctus*, *beatus*, *exemplum*, martyr, and tolerant. Specifically, Augustine needed to counter the Donatist point of view on the Church, even though *De baptismo* was intended as a discursus on baptism. Augustine had already begun addressing Donatist ecclesial and baptismal doctrines in works before *De baptismo*, but it was here that these critiques were placed in their specific formula for the first time. Among such criticisms was one that the Church is not a collective or Church of martyrs, but a mixed body that counts sinners as well righteous members. By virtue of the mixed nature of the Church, baptism retains its Christ-based potency even when delivered by a cleric who is afflicted by personal or ecclesial sin. For this reason Augustine calls upon the Cyprian *gestalt* in two major ways: Cyprian adamantly acknowledged that sinners are included in the membership of the Church here on earth,[121] and people who return to the Church from schism do not need to be rebaptised.[122]

---

114 *De bapt.* 5,31.

115 *De bapt.* 6,1.

116 *De bapt.* 4,11.

117 *De bapt.* 6,3.

118 *De bapt.* 6,5; 7,96.

119 *De bapt.* 3,5; 4,11; 5,3.

120 *De bapt.* 3,4; 3,7(x2); 6,68.

121 *De bapt.* 4,2; 4,10(x2); 4,16; 4,18(x2); 4,19; 4,21; 5,39; 6,44; 5,1; 5,3; 5,13; 5,16; 5,19; 5,24; 5,31; 5,38; 6,19; 6,41; 6,45; 6,47; 6,50; 6,78; 6,80; 7,13; 7,49; 7,89; 7,98(x2).

122 *De bapt.* 3,16; 3,17(x2); 4,6; 4,16(x2); 4,18; 4,24; 4,28; 5,1(x2); 5,2(x2); 5,14; 5,21; 5,27; 6,19; 6,44; 7,5; 7,25; 7,27; 7,96.

To advance these positions, Augustine draws upon Cyprian's writings (esp. *Sent. Episc.* and *Ep.* 73), to argue that the genuine theology and spirit of Cyprian is such that no one should presume to judge the state of grace or sin of another Christian. To this end, Augustine repeatedly enlists Cyprian's command: 'Judge no one!'[123] From Augustine's vantage point, the act of determining the sinfulness and liability to damnation of a person is reserved for Christ at the eschatological moment, far from today. To further drive home that this reflects the true belief and authority of Cyprian, Augustine challenges the notion that not believing in Cyprian's defence of the integrity of the Church via the requirement of rebaptism (regardless of whether people were originally baptised in the Church or were the recipients of schismatic baptism) places people outside of continuity with the North African tradition.

Instead, Augustine redefines Cyprian's intention to mean that tolerance of sinners for the purpose of maintaining ecclesial unity was the bishop of Carthage's paramount concern. And consequently, if this same tolerance is not exercised, then the Donatists are the ones repudiating Cyprian. Augustine supports this assertion with frequent recourse to Donatist biblical typologies concerning the Church: 'Dove',[124] 'Enclosed Garden' or 'paradise',[125] 'without spot or wrinkle',[126] 'wheat among tares',[127] 'orchard of pomegranates',[128] and 'Ark of Noah'.[129] Augustine readapts these typologies to benefit his alternative ecclesiology by arguing that Cyprian used them in the same way Augustine does now.[130] Naturally this stands in contrast with the North African scriptural tradition and requires a vast amount of energy on the part of Augustine in order to convince African Christians. Throughout, Augustine's aim remains the re-appropriation of Cyprian.

Augustine draws conclusions about Cyprian's legacy in Donatist theology for them. Among the accusations levelled against Donatists for their

123 *De bapt.* 2,7; 3,1; 4,12; 5,23; 6,9; 6,10; 6,12; 6,48; 7,3(x2); 7,7; 7,49.

124 Cant. 6,8 in *De bapt.* 1,15; 3,22; 4,4; 4,16; 5,13; 5,21; 6,5; 6,78; 7,89; 7, 97; 7,99. Augustine would use this *typologos* again in *En. in Ps.* 67,17; 141,7 and *Ioh. Evang. Tract.* 5,10; 6,6; 6,10; 6,11(x2); 6,12; 6,15; 6,26.

125 Gen. 2,8–14 and Cant. 4,12–13 in *De bapt.* 4,1,1; 4,7,11; 5,27,38; 7,51,99. 'Paradise' occurs in: 2,2; 4,1(x5); 4,29; 5,38(x3); 6,5; 6,37(x3); 6,78(x2); 7,7.

126 Cant. 6,9 in *De bapt.* 4,5; 5,21; 5,34; 5,21; 5,35; 6,5; 7,99.

127 *De bapt.* 4,14; 5,13; 5,23; 6,1; 6,78.

128 Cant. 4,12–13, *De bapt.* 5,38; 6,5; 7,99. Augustine would again use this central Donatist typology in (c. 401) *De Genesi ad litteram* 11,32; 12,56 and in (c.405/06) *C. Cresc.* 2,17.

129 Gen. 6–9, but typology used in New Testament sense of the Church found in 1 Pet. 3,20–21. Appears 17 times in *De bapt.* 5,39(x12); 6,78(x3).

130 Alfred Schindler, 'Baptismo (De-)', in C. Mayer (ed.), *Augustinus-Lexikon*, vol. 1 (Basel: Schwabe & Co., 1996), 580.

'misinterpretation' of Cyprian is that they follow him incorrectly,[131] according to the flesh and not in truth,[132] and that they defile Cyprian by the error of rejecting unity in preference to rebaptism[133] and as a result do not follow Cyprian's example.[134] The Donatists are, according to Augustine, unhappy with Cyprian's example of unity.[135] And even though they need to seek Cyprian's counsel,[136] their theology is nevertheless disqualified, because they have renounced their authority through their leaders' actions during the Maximian schism.[137]

The accusation that the Donatists misinterpret Cyprian is audacious, especially given that Augustine himself clearly calls Cyprian wrong on multiple occasions in *De baptismo*.[138] This was a technique with which Augustine found great resonance. The occurrences of Augustine's direct criticism of Cyprian revolve around the issue of Cyprian's call for the rebaptism of those entering the Church from a severed group. This seeming contradiction in claiming Cyprian's authority whilst refuting one of its core components required not only Augustine's acknowledgment of Cyprian's personal qualities, but also the redefinition of Cyprian's theology, which Augustine provided in terms of ecclesiology and sacramentology.

In *De baptismo* Augustine manages to turn this contradiction into a polemical reversal against the Donatists. He accomplishes this by recreating the narrative of Cyprian: even though Cyprian had no clear authority to fall back on concerning the question of (re)baptism, since at that time the Church had had no universal council to discuss it.[139] Instead he followed his predecessor, Agrippinus, because of his obedience, humility, appreciation of unity, and above all his love. For this reason, Augustine accuses the Donatists of acting in a way that is the exact opposite of Cyprian. And though since Cyprian's death the Church has been illuminated on correct baptismal theology,[140] the Donatists

131 *De bapt.* 3,2.

132 *De bapt.* 1,28.

133 *De bapt.* 2,9; 2,11.

134 *De bapt.* 2,14; 2,15; Paul Monceaux, *Histoire Littéraire de l'Afrique Chrétienne: Depuis les Origines Jusqu'a l'Invasion Arabe, Tome Septième*, 97.

135 *De bapt.* 2,20.

136 *De bapt.* 2,18.

137 *De bapt.* 3,3(x2).

138 *De bapt.* 2,2; 3,6; 3,17; 4,8; 4,9; 4,12; 4,17; 5,4; 5,8; 6,1; 6,2; 6,3; 7,39.

139 *De bapt.* 4,9.

140 Augustine places a certain amount of importance on 'council' in *De baptismo*. It is used variably, depending on Augustine's aim. It is used to demonstrate the global reach of the Catholic Church 'universali concilio' (83 occurrences) or 'orbis concilio' (67 occurrences)

cling to their Africa-centric belief, which is corroborated by no other Church in the world.[141] This too is unlike Cyprian. Making his argument even more intense, Augustine accuses the Donatists of protecting their theology, not out of love as Cyprian did, but out of *superbia* (pride),[142] *ignorantia*,[143] and *pertinacia* (stubbornness).[144] For this reason, Augustine feels confident enough in *De baptismo* to state rhetorically:

> The authority of Cyprian does not alarm me, because I am reassured by his humility. We know indeed, the great merit of the bishop and martyr Cyprian; but is it greater than that of apostle and martyr Peter.[145]

---

or the provincial (i.e. limited) nature of councils presided over by Cyprian which appears supportive of rebaptism 'prouinciae concilio' (22 occurrences) or 'plenorium conciliorum' (78 occurrences). By focusing on the limited nature of local councils, Augustine could also articulate how Cyprian would have yielded to the opinion of the whole Church, *De bapt.* 2,5: 'Nec nos ipsi tale aliquid auderemus adserere nisi uniuersae ecclesiae concordissima auctoritate firmati, *cui et ipse sine dubio cederet*, si iam illo tempore quaestionis huius ueritas eliquata et declarata per plenarium concilium solidaretur'. Discussing the role of councils also allowed Augustine to demonstrate the collaborative spirit of Cyprian, 'Cypriani concilium'. In all, the term 'concilio' appears x97 times in the work.

141 *De bapt.* 1,5; 5,39; *Ep. ad Cath.* 16,40 (CSEL 52, 283–84): 'Scriptum est'—inquiunt—in *Canticis canticorum* sponsa, id est Ecclesia, dicente ad sponsum: '*Annuntia mihi, quem dilexit anima mea, ubi pascis, ubi cubas in meridie*.' Hoc est unicum testimonium quod pro se isti resonare arbitrantur, eo quod Africa in meridiana orbis parte sit constituta... Interrogat fortasse quid ad eius communionem pertineat in meridie, id est ubi sponsus eius pascat et cubet in meridie, quia suos pascit et in suis cubat. Veniunt enim quaedam membra eius, id est boni fideles, ex partibus transmarinis in Africam et, cum audierint esse hic partem Donati, timentes ne incidant in manus alicuius rebaptizatoris'. This criticism, that the Donatists are stubborn, backwards, and out-of-touch, is an interesting approach for Augustine to take, given that the appeal to North Africans of Donatist-flavoured Christianity was partly due to the impression that the Church strongly upheld its tradition and values in the face of changing imperial mores: Evans, *One and Holy*, 67: 'Something, obviously, about the Donatist Church held strong appeal for African Christians. This appeal was in large measure due to the tenacious preservation among the Donatists of traditions long cherished in Christian Africa'.

142 *De bapt.* 2,4; 3,27(x2); 4,4; 4,31; 5,10; 5,23; 6,60; 6,87.

143 *De bapt.* 1,6; 1,9; 4,7(x2); 6,47.

144 *De bapt.* 1,16; 5,6–7.

145 *De bapt.* 2,2 (CSEL 51–1, 174): 'Quid ergo isti dicunt cum ueritatis uiribus praefocantur, cui consentire nolunt? Cyprianus, inquiunt, cuius tantum meritum nouimus tantamque doctrinam...non me terret auctoritas Cypriani, quia reficit humilitas Cypriani. Magnum quidem meritum nouimus Cypriani episcopi et martyris, sed numquid maius quam Petri

This appears to be a hallmark of *De baptismo*. In writings leading up to the composition of this document, Augustine demonstrates an increasing facility in making polemical use of Cyprian against the Donatist Church. This writing represents the expansion of the appeal to Cyprian to the point where Augustine appears to have made him his most authoritative choice for the refutation of Donatist theology. But that is not enough; Augustine himself needs to be the voice of Cyprian in order to be taken seriously in Africa. For that reason Augustine needs to demonstrate also that the Donatists actually refute their own supposed forefather.[146]

What Augustine Stood to Gain through Cyprian

Now that it is clear that *De baptismo* represented the point of no return for Augustine as he set forth on his anti-Donatist campaign, a more critical analysis must be rendered of the specific reasons Africans regarded Cyprian of Carthage so highly. To do this, it is essential to confront not only what Augustine might possibly have gained through a successful Cyprian-appropriation, but also the risks entailed. An obvious concern was that in breaking the Cyprian brand away from Donatist ownership, he would run into the inevitable complication that 150 years of reverence and imitation meant Cyprian's theology and that of the Donatists closely mirrored each other. The only possible way to lay claim to Cyprian, therefore, was to say that the Donatists were wrong, even with a tradition that was anchored in 150 years of history! And the key to his strategy lay in his theological undermining of key Donatist/African positions.

A first example of this undermining is the popularly known discussion on rebaptism. The North African understanding of baptism and the nature of the Church was rooted in a tradition reaching back to Tertullian or earlier, but received its enduring form with Cyprian.[147] A wealth of scholarship has been

---

apostoli et martyris?…nec despexit Paulum quod ecclesiae prius persecutor fuisset, sed consilium ueritatis admisit et rationi legitimae quam Paulus uindicabat facile consensit'.

146 *De bapt.* 5,4 (CSEL 51–1, 266): 'Eodem unitatis uinculo intellegat saluos esse potuisse quibus aliud salua caritate tunc uisum est. ac per hoc simul oportet intellegatur eos, quos nulla zizania, nulla palea, si ipsi frumenta esse uoluissent, in societate ecclesiae toto orbe diffusae poterant maculare et ideo nulla existente causa se ab eodem unitatis uinculo dirruperunt, *quodlibet illorum duorum uerum sit, siue quod Cyprianus tunc sensit siue quod catholicae uniuersitas unde ille non recessit optinuit*, foris apertissime constitutos in manifesto sacrilegio schismatis saluos esse non posse'.

147 Tertullian, *De Baptismo* 15,2 (CCSL 1/1, 1,290): 'Unus omnino baptismus est nobis tam ex domini evangelio quam et apostoli litteris, quoniam unus deus et unum baptisma et una ecclesia in caelis. sed circa haereticos sane quae custodiendum sit digne quis retractet. ad nos enim editum est: haeretici autem nullum consortium habent nostrae disciplinae,

produced in recent decades which has refined our knowledge of Cyprian's stance. So, for the sake of contextualising Augustine's task of appropriation, only a brief summary is necessary at this point.

Cyprian inherited a tradition wherein matters of baptism and offence against God and the Church were taken deadly seriously.[148] Those who were baptised into the Church and who sinned risked polluting and harming its integrity and being, and needed to be rebaptised. By 220, Cyprian's predecessor, Agrippinus, codified the position on the necessity of rebaptism for the lapsed in the presence of seventy fellow *African* bishops.[149] During his episcopate,

---

quos extraneos utique testatur ipsa ademptio communicationis. Non debeo in illis cognoscere quod mihi est praeceptum, quia non idem deus est nobis et illis, nec unus Christus, id est idem: ergo nec baptismus unus, quia non idem. quem cum rite non habeant sine dubio non habent, nec capit numerare quod non habetur: ita nec possunt accipere, quia non habent'; Cyprian, *The Letters of St. Cyprian of Carthage, Volume IV, Letters 67–82*, Ancient Christian Writers 47, trans. G.W. Clarke (Mahwah, NJ: Newman Press, 1989), introduction, 7.

148 Tert., *Apologeticum* 39,4 (*CCSL* 1, 150): 'Ibidem etiam exhortationes, castigationes et censura divina. Nam et iudicatur magno cum pondere, ut apud certos de dei conspectu, summumque futuri iudicii praeiudicium est, si quis ita deliquerit, ut a communicatione orationis et conventus et omnis sancti commercii relegetur'; Tertullian also gave an early defence of the practice of considering baptism from a heretic or other egregious sinner as invalid, see: *De Baptismo* 5 (*CSEL* 1, 281).

149 Cyp., *Ep.* 71,1 (CCSL 3/C, ed. G.F. Diercks (Turnhout: Brepols, 1996), 521); 73,1 (CCSL 3/C, 532); 75,3 (CCSL 3/C, 598); also repeated in Aug., *De bapt.* 2,14 ([*CSEL* 51/1, ed. M. Petschenig (Vienna: Tempsky, Leipzig: Freytag, 1909), 190): 'Ubi certe quid fieri soleret, etsi non fieri vellet, satis ostendit et eo ipso quod, concilium Agrippini commemorat, aperte indicat fuisse aliam consuetudinem ecclesiae. Neque enim opus erat hoc concilio velle statuere, si iam consuetudine tenebatur: et in ipso concilio nonnullae sententiae omnino declarant, eos contra ecclesiae consuetudinem decrevisse, quod decernendum esse arbitrati sunt'. According to E.W. Benson, this practice may actually only have been introduced in 213; *Cyprian: His Life, His Times, His Work* (London: Macmillan, 1897). In this matter J. Patout Burns recounts Cyprian's own uncertainty about the situation. In *Ep.* 75,19,3–4, the bishop states that while their Church had never accepted the baptism of heretics, it only later advanced the position to exclude schismatics; *Cyprian the Bishop*, 102–03, 215. This issue is further complicated by the fact that there seem to have been other traditions of rebaptism in the East attested to in Cyprian's letters. In Asia Minor, c. 230, councils in Iconium and Syanada called for the practice in response to Montanist baptism, according to Firmilian, the witness and author of *Ep.* 75. The same Firmilian mentions the practice had roots in apostolic tradition, which begs even further questions (*Ep.* 75,5 [*CCSL* 3/C, 589]. In Alexandria too, rebaptism seems to have been practised briefly during the episcopates of Heracles and Dionysius in the 230s–240s (Eusebius of Caesarea, *Historia Ecclesiastica* [*Histoire Ecclésiastique*] *II, Livres V–VII*, ed. G. Bardy (Paris: Les Éditions du

Cyprian would further develop the necessity for rebaptism as the Church in Carthage and beyond was sent into disarray following the Decian persecution in 250–51.[150] The experience of having so many of the baptised, especially clergy, renege on their baptismal vows, demanded a strong reaction to keep the Church together and to maintain its group identity.[151]

Cyprian was experienced at confronting divisions that arose in dealing with Christians who had lapsed during persecution. The divisions were between those who were angry that he had become too firm about readmitting the lapsed back into the Church and those who split to form their own Church out of disapproval of the Carthaginian bishop's handling of the matter.[152] After the Decian persecution, subsided, Cyprian faced his first test, to which he

Cerf, 1955), 7,9,1–6). Refer also to Clarke, *The Letters of St. Cyprian of Carthage, Volume IV, Letters 67–82*, introduction, 6. I am grateful to Bonner for these references to the Eastern churches, 'Christus Sacerdos', 328.

150 See Merdinger, *Rome and the African Church*, esp. ch(s). 3–4.

151 Cyprian's responses are recounted in *Ep.* 69 (CCSL 3/C, 469–96), 73 (CCSL 3/C, 529–62), 74 (CCSL 3/C, 563–80); *De rebaptismate* (CSEL 3/1, ed. W. Hartel (Vienna: C. Geroldi, 1868), 69); *Sententiae Episcoporum de Haereticis Baptizandis*, §87 (CCSL 3/E, ed. G.F. Diercks (Turnhout: Brepols, 2004), 107–09): 'Meam sententiam plenissime exprimit epistulae, quae ad Iubianum collegam nostrum scripta est, haereticos secundum evangelicam et apostilicam contestionem adversarios Christi et antichristos appellatos, quando ad ecclesiam venerint, unico ecclesiae baptismo baptizandos esse, ut possint fieri de adversariis amici et de antichristis christiani'. Two indispensable works on this issue are from Burns, *Cyprian the Bishop*, esp. 126–31; and 'On Rebaptism: Social Organization in the Third Century Church', *Journal of Early Christian Studies* 1/4 (1993), 367–03. Burns illustrates the importance of the fact that African Christians identified clear cosmological boundaries between the Church, identifiable around the bishop, and the rest of the *secular world*, including schismatics. Thus, 'Within the church, water and oil could be sanctified, the divine name could be invoked, saving faith could be professed; outside the church, water and oil were polluted by idolatry or schism, appeals to Christ were in vain, the baptismal profession contradicted…'; *Cyprian the Bishop*, 128.

152 On Cyprian's reaction to the rigorist view of denying reconciliation, see *Ep.* 55,17 (CCSL 3/B, 275–76): 'Sed quoniam est in illis quod paenitentia robur armatur, – quod armari non poterit, si quis desperatione deficiat, si ab ecclesia dure et crudeliter segregatus ad gentiles se uias et secularia opera converat vel ad haereticos et schismaticos reiectus ab ecclesia transeat, ubi esti occisus propter nomen postmodum fuerit extra ecclesiam constitutus et ab unitate adque a caritate divisus coronari in morte non poterit - et ideo placuit, frater carissime, examinatis causis singulorum libellaticos interim admitii, sacrificatis in exitu subveniri, quia exomologesis apud inferos non est nec ad paenitentiam quis a nobis conpelli potest, si fructus paenitentiae subtrahatur. Si proelium prius venerit, corroboratus a nobis inuenietur armatus ad proelium: si vero ante proelium infirmitas urserit, cum solacio pacis et communicationis abstedit'. On Cyprian's reaction to those

responded in a reliably African way: 'Let no one think that good men can leave the Church; it is not the grain that the wind carries away, nor the solidly rooted tree that the storm blows down: it is the empty chaff that is swept away by the storm, the weakening trees that are overturned by the blast of the whirlwind... '[153] This was the grounding for Cyprian's inside/outside paradigm, for which he found a further basis in Matt. 3,12: 'Thus are the faithful proved, thus the faithless discovered; thus too even before the day of judgment, already here below, the souls of the just and unjust are distinguished, and the wheat is separated from the chaff'.[154]

And it is for this reason there exists the scandal of schism, in terms of which 'certain people...seize authority for themselves without any divine sanction... assume the title of Bishop on their own authority'.[155] The result of such selfish acts committed by these 'pests and plagues of the faith, snake-tongued deceivers, skilled corrupters of the truth, spewing venom from their poisonous fangs'[156] is their separation from the Church and exclusion from salvation, 'extra ecclesiam nulla salus',[157] more specifically because:

> It is these same men whom the Lord indicates and censures when He says: 'They have forsaken me, the fountain of the water of life, and they have digged out for themselves crumbling cisterns, which cannot hold the water.' [Jer. 2,13] Whereas there can be but the one baptism, they think they can baptise; they have abandoned the fountain of life, yet promise the life and grace of the waters of salvation. It is not cleansing that men find there, but soiling; their sins are not washed away but only added to. That 'new birth' does not bring forth sons unto God, but to the devil. Born of a lie, they cannot inherit what the truth has promised; begotten by the faithless, they are deprived of the grace of faith. The reward for those 'in peace' can never come to men who have broken the peace of the Lord by the frenzy of dissent.[158]

---

who became schismatic in response, see *Ep.* 41 and 43 (CCSL 3/B, 196–98 and 200–10). It would also be advantageous to consult M. Sage, *Cyprian.*, esp. 295–36.

153 Cyp., *De Unit.*, *Ancient Christian Writers* 25, trans. M. Bévenot (Mahwah, NJ: The Newman Press, 1957), 9 (CCSL 3/A, ed. M. Bévenot (Turnhout: Brepols, 1972), 261).

154 Cyp., *De Unit.* 10 (CCSL 3/A, 256).

155 Cyp., *De Unit.* 10 (CCSL 3/A, 257).

156 Ps. 1,1 in *De Unit.* 10 (CCSL 3/A, 257).

157 Cyp., *Ep.* 73,21,2 (CCSL 3/C, 555); C. Mayer, 'Taufe und Erwählug—Zur Dialektik des sacramtentum-Begriffes in der antidonatistischen Schrift Augustins: De baptismo', 25.

158 Cyp., *De Unit.* 11 (CCSL 3/A, 257).

It is quite clear then that Cyprian identified a distinct lack of ability in those outside the Church to benefit from the salvific effects of the sacraments. Not only do those outside the Church, especially those who are so because of schism, not receive grace, but they actually accumulate more incrimination.[159]

This was to become an explosive issue again between 253–56, as the bishop of Carthage was faced with the issue of reconciling with the Church those baptised outside by schismatic groups. Cyprian condemned such a consideration in no uncertain terms. In his *Epistle* 69, Cyprian drew on African biblical exegesis to articulate his stance. There he found typologies for his opponents such as 'adversaries of the Lord and antichrists' who attempt to disperse Christ's flock, for 'he who is not with me is against me, and he who does not gather with me scatters.'[160] In like fashion, Cyprian argued for the Church's oneness and unique relationship with Christ, which the Donatists would largely draw upon later as well: the Church which is 'My dove, my perfect one, is but one; she is the only one of her mother, the favourite of her who bore her…an enclosed garden is my sister, my bride, a sealed fountain, a well of living water'.[161]

Cyprian continued in this line by articulating not only the deficiency of those outside the Church, but also the reason for the Church's authority, namely that it is imbued by Christ with the Holy Spirit:

---

159 From this reasoning, the Donatists would later draw their *raison d'être*: 'Quando alliud baptisma praeter unum esse non possuit, baptizare se opinantur; uitae fonte deserto, uitalis et salutaris aquae gratiam pollicentur. Non abluuntur illic homines sed potius sordidantur, nec purgantur delicta sed immo cumulantur, non Deo natiuitas illa sed diablo filios generat'; Cyp., *De Unit.* 11 (CCSL 3/A, 257).

160 Mt. 12,30; Lk. 11,23 in *Ep.* 69,1,2 (CCSL 3/C, 470); see also Fahey, *Cyprian and the Bible: A Study in Third-Century Exegesis*, 303.

161 Cant. 4,12 and 6,8 in *Ep.* 69,1 (CCSL 3/C, 471–72); Fahey, *Cyprian and the Bible*, 170. Cyprian would again utilize an enviable arsenal of scriptural language to reiterate his point. Among his other typologies are his use of the *Ark of Noah* (*Ep.* 69,2 (CCSL 3/C, 472), the *Passover lamb* [the paschal Christ]: 'In one household shall it be eaten; and you shall not cast from the house any of the flesh outside' (Ex. 12,46 in *Ep.* 69,1 (CCSL 3/C, 474); Fahey, *Cyprian and the Bible*, 71–72); *Moses*, who is commanded by the Lord to 'separate yourselves from the tents of these hardened sinners and do not touch anything that is theirs, for fear that you may perish along with them in their sin' (Num. 16,26 in *Ep.* 69,1 (CCSL 3/C, 483); Fahey, *Cyprian and the Bible*, 84); baptism (*Ep.* 69,2 (CCSL 3/C, 472); 70,1 (CCSL 3/C, 501–05); Christ (*Ep.* 63,6 (CCSL 3/C, 395–96); *Eucharist* (*Ep.* 63,4–6, 11(CCSL 3/C, 391–92, 92–96, 403–05); the priesthood (*Ep.* 59,5 (CCSL 3/C, 342–46); the Church (*De Unit.* 4 (CCSL 3/A, 251–52); *Ep.* 74,11 (CCSL 3/C, 578–79); 75,15 (CCSL 3/C, 595); and the relationship between God and his nation Israel, the *collecta* (*De Unit.* 2 (CCSL 3/A, 221–22); *Ep.* 58,1 (CCSL 3/C, 319–21); 63,17 (CCSL 3/C, 413–14).

> [T]he Lord asserts clearly in His Gospel that one can be forgiven only through those who possesses the Holy Spirit…[and speaking to his disciples after his resurrection said] *Just as the father sent me, so too am I sending you. And when he said this, He breathed on them and said to them: Receive the Holy Spirit. Whose sins you have forgiven, they shall be forgiven him; whose sins you have retained, they shall be retained.*[162]

In this passage Cyprian was repeating that the only one, or the only Church, capable of baptising was the one who possessed the Holy Spirit. It is clear from such source excerpts that Cyprian was more than simply opposed to reconciliation of outsiders without rebaptism, and it is beyond a doubt that he felt this issue to be of such prime importance that he convened his African episcopal colleagues to convince those who were not in accord on the matter and to protect the tradition from foreign influence. He did this through three sequential pan-African councils in 254–56.[163] The contents of *Ep.* 70–75, which cover the sentiment of the period further, reveal the rigid line that Cyprian and his contemporaries held in defending baptism as an indivisible property of the Church: "[T]here is only one baptism, but it is only found with the Catholic Church, for the Church itself is one and there cannot be baptism outside of the Church'.[164] Within the African tradition, this reasoning, buttressed by their particular biblical hermeneutic (which strongly emphasised the literal/typological imagery of the election of believers as God's collective and the demise of those not in the Church),[165] oriented the belief in a certain duality which pitted the Church as 'Paradise'[166] against the corruption and lechery of the

162 John 20,21 in *Ep.* 69,11 (CCSL 3/C, 485): '…probat et declarat in evangelio suo dominus per eos solos posse peccata dimitti qui habeant spiritum sanctum. Post resurrectionem enim discipulos suos mittens loquitur ad eos et dicit: *sicut misit me pater, et ego mitto vos. Hoc cum dixisset, insufflavit et ait illis: accipite spiritum sanctum. Si cuius remiseritis peccata, remittentur illi: si cuius tenveritis, tenebuntur*'. Fahey, *Cyprian and the Bible*, 403. See also *De Unit.* 4 (CCSL 3/A, 251).

163 These first of these councils took place in either 254 or 255 (*Ep.* 70 (CCSL 3/C, 501–18), and others in May/June 256 (*Ep.* 72 (CCSL 3/C, 523–28) and autumn 256 (*Ep.* 75 (CCSL 3/C, 581–04). This period is covered in detail in G. Dunn, 'Validity of Baptism and Ordination in the African response to the "Rebaptism Crisis": Cyprian of Carthage's Synod of Spring 256', 257–74.

164 Cyp., *Ep.* 71,2 (CCSL 3/C, 516–17).

165 The source to consult here is Tilley, *The Bible in Christian North Africa*, esp. 30, 65, 76, 78, 80, 143, 155–56, 159–60, 161, 73, 177–79.

166 'The Church is like Paradise: within her walls she encloses on the inside fruit-bearing trees…faint with a never-ending thirst'; Cyp., *Ep.* 73,3 (CCSL 3/C, 540–41).

outside world (*saeculum*), of which heretics were citizens. And it is for this reason, those who were baptised in the Church, but had lapsed, must only receive the laying on of hands and the Spirit.[167] More controversially (to those outside North Africa at least), those baptised in heresy and/or schism were to be baptised anew: 'Those who come from heresy are not being rebaptised with us, they are being baptised',[168] for their previous baptism is clearly without benefit.[169]

And, in a refrain that would recur throughout African theological sentiment in the generations after Cyprian's martyrdom,[170] the bishop gave an admonition to fight for the rightful Church: 'We conclude…that there is no need for us to suppose we have to surrender ground to heretics and betray to them that baptism which was given to the one Church and to that Church alone. It is the duty of a good soldier to defend the camp of his commander against enemies and rebels; it is the duty of an illustrious general to guard the standards entrusted to its safekeeping'. For Cyprian, as for the equally adamant Donatists who would follow, no other cause was as worthy of a soldier's *reveille* than defending the Church against corruption from the error and sin of the world, and from defilement of its sacraments and sanctity.[171]

---

167 Cyp., *Ep.* 71,2 (*CCSL* 3/C, 518–19), also see: M. Bévenot, 'Cyprian's Platform in the Rebaptism Controversy', 125–30.

168 Cyp., *Ep.* 71,3 (*CCSL* 3/C, 517).

169 Here again Cyprian drew from a hefty arsenal of scriptural exegesis to discredit the usefulness of baptism outside the Church: 'Keep away from alien water; do not drink from an alien fountain' (Prov. 9,18 in *Ep.* 70,1 (*CCSL* 3/C, 503); Fahey, *Cyprian and the Bible*, 161); 'they have forsaken me, the source of living waters; they have dug themselves cisterns, broken cisterns, that hold no water' (Jer. 2,13 in *Ep.* 70,1 (*CCSL* 3/C, 503); Fahey, *Cyprian and the Bible,* 219): 'If on the other hand, a man comes to us from heresy who was not previously baptized in the Church but who is a total stranger and outsider, then he must be baptized in order to be made sheep, and that is to be found in the holy Church. Falsehood and truth can have nothing in common, no more can darkness and light, mortality and immortality, antichrist and Christ. We must, therefore, in every way defend the oneness of the Catholic Church, we must at no point yield ground to the enemies of the faith and truth' (*Ep.* 71,3 (*CCSL* 3/C, 519); 'If a man is baptized by one who is dead, what does his washing avail him?' (Sir. 34,25 in *Ep.* 71,3 (*CCSL* 3/C, 518); Fahey, *Cyprian and the Bible*, 184).

170 Here I am referring to the distinctively North African Circumcelliones, see C. Lepelley, 'Circumcelliones', in *Augustinus-Lexikon*, vol. 1, ed. C. Mayer (Basel, Schwabe & Co., 1996), 930–36.

171 'And the tradition handed down to us is that there is one God and one Christ, one hope and one faith, one Church and one baptism appointed only in that one Church. Whoever departs from that unity must be found in company with heretics; and in defending

The Donatist Transmission of Cyprian's Theology

One of the driving forces behind much of what Donatists said and did was their trademark sense of immediacy in achieving their agenda, and this was particularly true in observing and interpreting the theology of Cyprian.[172] Because Donatist theology held that scripture was guiding their community in their contemporary experience to follow God's Law, and because of their collective experience of the unpredictability of an encounter with martyrdom, the Church must adhere faithfully to the Word of God and act as if the final hour were upon them. This perhaps explains the level of seriousness of the Donatists when defending and adhering to ways of God's revelation and will that were often questioned by outsiders.[173]

And no other theological matter in the entire Donatist saga sparked as much reaction and was as prolifically debated as the rebaptism issue. At the heart of this concern in Cyprian's time was the fear of public sin/scandal spreading through the Church,[174] which is what made an obsession with ritual pollution so central for African Christians and for the Donatists.[175] To support this primary concern, African Christians developed a vast array of baptismal typologies, which would be vigorously used by the Donatists to corroborate their view that the Catholics had faulty sacraments and thus no access to the

---

heretics against the Church, he is launching an attack upon the sacred mystery of this divine tradition' (Cyp., *Ep.* 74,1 (CCSL 3/C, 578).

'The sacred mystery of this unity we also see expressed in the person of Christ, who says in the Song of Songs [Cant. 4,12 and 15]: An enclosed garden is my sister, my bride, a sealed fountain, a well of living water, an orchard of fruits. Now if this Church is an enclosed garden and a sealed fountain, how is it possible for anyone who is not within the Church to enter that garden or to drink from its fountain?' (Cyp., *Ep.* 74,2 (CCSL 3/C, 578). R. Evans expands this further, noting that for Donatists, at least according to Augustine (*C. ep. Parm.* 3,28 and *Ep.* 93,23), being 'Catholic' meant that there was integrity within the sacraments and the Church; *One and Holy*, 88.

172 Maureen Tilley, 'When Schism Becomes Heresy in Late Antiquity: Developing Doctrinal Deviance in the Wounded Body of Christ', *Journal of Early Christian Studies* 15/1 (2007), 18. See also Robert Herrera, 'A Shattered Mirror: The Presence of Africa in Augustine's Exegesis', in F. Van Fleteren and J.C. Schnaubelt (eds.), *Augustine: Biblical Exegete* (New York: Peter Lang, 2001), 175–88, esp. 177: 'The Donatists claimed that their church was the true church in Africa'.

173 Gaumer, 'The Evolution of Donatist Theology', 189.

174 Cyprian's foremost worry about public/ecclesial sin and ritual pollution is seen in his *De lapsis* 23–26; *Ep.* 67,2–4,3 and 9,1–3; *Ep.* 70,3; *Ep.* 72,3; *Ep.* 73,1–3.

175 The foremost depiction of the social-ecclesial reality for Cyprian, the Donatists, Augustine, and the rebaptism issue is depicted in Burns, 'Appropriating Augustine Appropriating Cyprian', 113–30.

means of salvation. And what these typologies also attested to was the need for Catholics to be rebaptised as a matter of utmost urgency:

> [H]eaven abhorred the evils done by the people of God, that [sic] they forsook the fount of living water and they dug for themselves hollowed lakes, which could not hold water.[176]

The theology and biblical interpretation of the Donatists necessitated the gathering in of those Christians in the world who were baptised with 'living water which did not contain faith'.[177] The only solution, before it was too late, was to bring into the Donatist Church those outside it, into the real body of Christ where the real water of life flowed, as typified in John 19,34.[178] This Body of Christ, the ark (Gen. 6,14), the walled-in garden, the dove, the perfect one (Cant. 4,12 and 6,19)[179] was where one must be for the impending return of Christ. With the greatest possible sense of urgency, Donatist theologians motivated North Africans to bring about the conformity of all in their lands to the 'one Lord, one faith, one baptism'.[180] Without a doubt, the matter of rebaptism was given a deeper meaning when one considers how these North Africans believed themselves to have faithfully inherited and interpreted the words of Cyprian. With this it becomes possible to begin to understand the Donatist approach to many issues which were and still are ill-understood or considered idiosyncratic, such as their interaction with the secular regime, the existence of the Circumcelliones, their attitude towards other churches, and their overall theological moorings. In each of these areas, as well as in others, Donatist belief was punctuated by a literalist interpretation of scripture and their tradition.[181] This particular way of understanding led them to safeguard their religion in ways that were demonised by Optatus, Augustine, and other contemporaries then as well as today.[182]

---

176 Jer. 2,13 in Optatus of Milevis, *De Schismate* 4,9 (CSEL 26, 114): '...exhorruisse caeulum, quod duo maligna fecerit populus dei, ut derelinqurent fontem aquae vivae et foderent sibi lacus detritos, qui non possent aquam continere'. This was Optatus's critique of the theological argumentation of the Donatists in general, directed at Parmenian in book four of *De Schismate*.

177 Jer. 5,18 in Aug., *C. ep. Parm.* 2,20 (CSEL 51/1, 66); *Cresc.* 2,28 (CSEL 52/2, 387); *Ep. ad Cath.* 23,64 (CSEL 51, 312–13).

178 Aug., *Ep. ad Cath.* 24,68 (CSEL 52, 314).

179 Opt., *De Schismate*, 1,12 (CSEL 26, 14); Cyprian, *De Unit.* 4 (CCSL 3/A, 252).

180 Eph. 4:5 in Aug., *Cresc.* 1,33 (CSEL 52, 353), *Un. bapt.* 10,17 (CSEL 53, 18).

181 Tilley, 'North Africa', in *The Cambridge History of Christianity, Volume I*, 395.

182 Optatus and Augustine's polemical approaches are contained throughout their anti-Donatist writings, especially in terms of their recapitulation of Donatist theology.

Augustine's Response to the Cyprianic/Donatist Theology of Baptism

Augustine overcame the objections and positions of the Donatists by (1) moving the emphasis away from rebaptism, and (2) accentuating Cyprian's condemnation of schism.[183] To put it another way, knowing he could not engage his opponents in their own terms and on their own ground, Augustine devised a counter-attack which they were less prepared to fight.[184]

Examples of more modern treatments include: F. Van der Meer, *Augustine the Bishop: The Life and Work of a Father of the Church*, trans. B. Battershaw and G.R. Lamb (London: Sheed & Ward, 1961), 79–128; C. Lepelley, 'Circumcelliones', in *Augustinus-Lexikon*, vol. 1, 930: 'Les Circumcelliones étaient, au temps d'Augustine, l'aile extrémiste et violente de l'église donatiste', 'les circumcelliones comme des brigands et des fanatiques' (934); James Keleher, *Saint Augustine's Notion of Schism in the Donatist Controversy. Dissertationes ad Laurem* 34 (Mundelein, IL: Saint Mary of the Lake Seminary, 1961), 24, the Circumcelliones as 'terrorists'; O'Donnell, *Augustine: A New Biography*, 359 (footnote 365): 'Donatism, had it prevailed and become the Christianity of the Middle Ages, would have been far more like Islam'.

183 Cyprian, using the words of Paul: 'There is one body, and one Spirit, one hope of your calling, one Lord, one faith, one baptism, one God'; Eph. 4,4-6 in *De Unit.* 4 (CCSL 3/A, 252). For Augustine's reaction to Donatists claims, see Peter Kaufman, 'Augustine, Evil and Donatism: Sin and Sanctity before the Pelagian Controversy', *Theological Studies* 50/1 (1990), 115–26. An excellent survey on Augustine's view of schism in the Donatist controversy remains J. Keleher, *Saint Augustine's Notion of Schism in the Donatist Controversy*.

184 The Donatist theological schema would be handicapped from the very beginning of the conflict. On one hand, by pegging themselves so closely to Cyprian, the Donatists limited their view of grace and salvation to mean that only those visibly in the Church and free from sin were saved (Bonner, 'Christus Sacerdos', 328–29; for other examples where Augustine used Cyprian's words in such a way see: Burns, 'Appropriating Augustine Appropriating Cyprian', *Augustinian Studies* 36/1 (2005), 26–27). On the other hand, this meant that Augustine could positively manipulate Cyprian's literary straightforwardness to his advantage, all the while demonstrating respect and discipleship along with modification of his stance; M.F. Wiles, 'The Theological Legacy of St. Cyprian', *The Journal of Ecclesiastical History* 14/2 (1963), 142.

Mention is also required of the role Optatus of Milevis played in framing the Catholic counter-argument for Augustine, a fact which did not escape Monceaux when he referred to Optatus as 'le précurseur et le maître d'Augustin'; *Histoire littéraire de l'Afrique Chrétienne depuis les origines jusqu'a l'invasion Arabe. Tome Septième*, 306. Optatus's *De Schismate* listed a potent array of scriptural defence lines that worked well with African exegetical tradition, e.g., Donatist schismatics as branches broken from the tree, shoots cut from the vine, a spring severed from its source; II,9 (CSEL 26, 45 [also found in Cyprian, *De Unit.* 5 (CCSL 3/A, 253)]); forsakers of the font of living waters, makers of a broken cistern; 4,9 (CSEL 26, 116 [Cyp., *De Unit.* 11 (CCSL 3/A, 257]). So too, from Song of Solomon:

Augustine wasted little time in dispelling the claim to the legitimacy of rebaptism. He noted Cyprian's acquiescence to the custom set in 220, but exempted him from condoning the practice since it was clear it was not the custom before Agrippinus, who had convened the North African bishops in order to convince them of the position.[185] Augustine was thus arguing that the custom itself was an innovation not firmly rooted (a line of argument he would use regularly in his dealings with Pelagians).[186] With rebaptism removed from

'My beloved is one; one is my bride, and one my dove'; 11,13 (CSEL 26, 48 [Cyp., *De Unit.* 4 (CCSL 3/A, 252]).

185 Augustine argued that the practice of rebaptism was introduced directly by Agrippinus: 'Hanc ergo saluberrimam consuetudinem per Agrippinum prodecessorem suum dicit sanctus Cyprianus quasi coepisse corrigi; sed sicut diligentius inquisitia veritas docuit, quae post magnos dubitationis fluctus ad plenarii concilii confirmationem perducta est, verius creditur per Agrippinum corrumpi coepisse, non corrigi'; (*De bapt.* 2,12 (CSEL 51, 187); see also 2,14 (CSEL 51, 189). The practice had received recognition, not through the Spirit, but out of protest against Pope Stephen and only in 258: 'nam illud quod adiungit de episcopo Carthaginensi Agrippino, de inclito martyre Cypriano, de septuaginta praecessoribus Cypriani, quia hoc fecerunt et fieri praeceperunt, o quam detestandus error est hominum, qui clarorum virorum quaedam non recte facta laudabiliter se imitari putant, a quorum virtutibus alieni sunt!' (*De un. bapt.* 13,22 (CSEL 53, 21). Cyprian himself even seemed to indicate a variety of practices/lack of uniformity in Africa itself concerning rebaptism: 'Nescio qua etenim praesumptione ducuntur quidam de collegis nostris ut putent eos qui apud haereticos tincti sunt, quando ad nos venirent, baptizari non oportere' (*Ep.* 71,1; CCSL 3/C, 516–17). See also Mac Gaw, *Le problème du baptême dans le schisme donatiste*, ch. 4, 263.

186 With such a tag-line from dealing with the Donatists, Augustine would accuse those falling outside of the authority derived from Cyprian and the Church of being guilty of proposing or being: *novi haeretici, profana vocum novitas, error novitius, novitia deformitas, perversitas novitia, dogma novum, novitium, novellum, haeresis nova, pestis novitia, novitia pestilentia, novitiate praesumptiones*. See Aug., *De Nuptiis et Concupiscentia ad Valerium* [*Nupt. et conc.*], (CSEL 42), ed. C. Urba and J. Zycha (Prague: Tempsky, Vienna: Tempsky, Leipzig: Freytag, 1902), 1,1 (CSEL 42, 212); 1,22 (CSEL 42, 235); 2,25 (CSEL 42, 278); 2,38 (CSEL 42, 292–93); 2,51 (CSEL 42, 307); 2,55 (CSEL 42, 312); *Contra duas epistulas Pelagianorum* 1,9 (CSEL 60), ed. C. Urba and I. Zycha (Vienna: Tempsky, Leipzig: Freytag, 1962), 430; 1,11 (CSEL 60, 533); 3,15 (CSEL 60, 503); 3,25 (CSEL 60, 517); 4,4 (CSEL 60, 544); 4,12 (CSEL 60, 533); 4,20 (CSEL 60, 543); 4,24 (CSEL 60, 549); 4,26 (CSEL 60, 553); 4,32 (CSEL 60, 568); *Contra Iulianum* [*Cont. Iul.*], (*Patrologiæ Cursus Completus* [PL] 44), ed. J.-P. Migne (Paris: 1841), 1,15 (PL 44, caput V, 649); 1,8 (PL 44, caput III, 615); 3,5 (PL 44, caput I, 704); 5.24 (PL 44, caput IV, 798); *Contra Iulianum Imperfectum* [*Cont. Iul. Imp.*], *Libri I–III* (CSEL 85/1), ed. M. Zelzer (Vienna: Hoelder-Pichler-Tempsky, 1974), 1.2 (CSEL 85/1, 6); 1.6 (CSEL 85/1, 9); 1.86 (CSEL 85/1, 99); 3.94 (CSEL 85/1, 419); 4.75 (CSEL 85/2, *Libri IV–VI*), ed. M. Zelzer (Vienna: Verlag der Österreichischen Akadamie der Wissenschaften, 2004), 85/2, 77); 4,122 (CSEL 85/2, 143); 5,9 (CSEL 85/2, 177); 6,3 (CSEL 85/2, 294); 6,5 (CSEL 85/2, 297);

consideration, Augustine was free to concentrate on the issue of the schism of the Donatists, their 'devilish division'[187] and 'abominable separation'.[188] By their obstinacy in segregating themselves from the rest of the catholic world, the Catholic Augustine's position was vindicated, because it was he and his side that had remained faithful to the spirit of Cyprian in refusing to divide Carthage from Rome: 'The authority of Cyprian does not frighten me because the humility of Cyprian restores me'.[189] According to Augustine, it was the Donatists' lack of humility and charity that blinded them to the error of their prideful separation. Augustine quickly recalled how Cyprian warned how grievous a sin schism was,[190] that it was in fact worse than betrayal or *traditio*[191]

M. Lamberigts, 'The Italian Julian of Æclanum about the African Augustine of Hippo', in *Augustinus Afer: Saint Augustin: africanité et universalité. Actes du colloque international, Alger-Annaba, 1–7 avril 2001* (*Paradosis* 45/1), ed. P.-Y. Fux, J.-M. Roessli, O. Wermlinger (Fribourg, 2003), 91.

187 *De bapt.* 5,2 (CSEL 51, 263–64).

188 Aug., *Ep.* 43,21 (CSEL 34, 91).

189 *De bapt.* 2,2 (CSEL 51, 174). This style of argumentation in imitation of Cyprian's charity would recur throughout this controversy, *De bapt.* 5,23 (CSEL 51, 281–82): 'I will learn if I can, from Cyprian's writings, if my sins do not hamper me and assisted by his prayers, the peace and consolation with which the Lord governed his Church through him'.

190 Augustine lists the Donatist reasons for their separation in an obviously polemical light: they saw themselves as a small collection of saints who shunned the outside world (*saeculum*); *Cresc.* 4,63 (CSEL 52, 561): 'Si enim in paucis frequenter est veritas et errare multorum est, permitte ut Maximianenses, quanto vobis sunt inpares paucitate, tanto vos superent veritate. Non facis: noli ergo in conparatione multitudinis gentium catholicarum de vestra paucitate gloriari, sicut non vis, ut Maximianenses in comparatione multitudinis vestrae de sua paucitate glorientur'; *C. ep. Parm.* 2,1,2 (CSEL 51, 45): 'Et quid tenebrosius praesumptionibus hominum, qui propter temere obiecta et numquam probata crimina traditorum, quae si uera essent numquam deo praeiudicarent quominus quod promisit impleret, perisse dicunt christianum nomen de tot gentibus in orbe terrarum et in solo Africa remanisse?' *Cresc.* 2, 46 (CSEL 52, 406): 'Vos contagione malorum Afrorum Ecclesiam perisse dicitis de orbe terrarum, et in parte Donati eius reliquias remansisse tamquam in frumentis a zizaniis et palea separatis; contra Cyprianum apertissime sentientes, qui dicit nec malorum permixtione bonos perire in ecclesia, nec eosdem malos posse ante tempus iudicii divini a bonorum permixtione separari'. Refer also to: Cyp., *De Unit.* 20 (CCSL 3/A, 263–64); Aug., *Ep.* 208,7 (CSEL 57, 346): 'Si enim de isto saeculo exires separata ab unitate corporis Christi, nihil tibi prodesset seruata integritas corporis tui'. See also C.G. Mac Gaw, *Le problème du baptême dans le schisme donatiste*, ch. 4, esp. 260 and 262.

191 *De bapt.* 3,3 (CSEL 51, 199): 'Cum etiam si vera crimina obicerent, multo sunt maiora scelera haeresum et schismatum, unde sine Baptismo, sicut ipse sensit, venientes, et in catholicam communionem non per Baptismum recepti, non potuerunt maculare Cyprianum'.

(particularly because, in the view of the Hippo bishop, many in the Donatist leadership had refuted their claim to the proof of sanctity as a mark of the true Church by the example of their scandalously sinful lives).[192] In sum, the very line of attack Cyprian and later the Donatists used, of their Church being sole possessor of the Holy Spirit, was refuted and denied by Augustine. For Augustine, the Donatists' selfishness and hypocrisy was manifest in licentious behaviour, separation from the wider catholic communion, and an evident lack of charity in their dealings, which demonstrated an obvious absence of the Holy Spirit.[193] In other words, it was Augustine's church that could rightfully assume the title of being heirs to the 'blessed Cyprian'.[194]

---

192 Here Augustine mentions the *violence of the Circumcelliones*, (*Ep.* 185,15 (CSEL 57, 42): 'disrupters of the existing, divinely ordained, social order'; (*C. ep. Parm.* 1,19 (CSEL 51, 42): 'Ubi etiam circumcellionum mentio facta est, si more suo violenter obsisterent'; *Ep.* 185,25 (CSEL 57, 42): 'Sed in quorum regionibus aliaquas violentias a clericis vel circumcellionibus verl populis eorum ecclesia catholica paterentur…'; *drunkenness* (*C. Cresc.* 4,77 (CSEL 52, 577): 'Negas eas quas dixi tyrannicas vestrorum in fundis alienis dominationes et bacchationes ebrietatum'; and the *intrigue, violence, and political cunning* of Optatus of Thamugadi and Gildo (*C. ep. Parm.* 2,2 (CSEL 51, 45): 'Et hanc praesumptionem suam lucem dicunt, promissa vero Dei iam ipso effectu rerum inluminata mendaciorum tenebris operire contendunt et insuper adversus nos facta sua clamant dicentes: *Vae his qui ponunt lucem tenebras et tenebras lucem.* Itane lux erat Optatus et eum tota Africa tenebras appellabat, an eum potius esse tenebras tota Africa sentiebat et isti eum lucem vocabant, qui non ponunt lucem tenebras et tenebras lucem? "Sed displicebat," inquiunt, "Optatus in communione nostra omnibus bonis." Non ergo eum lucem vocabatis et tamen ei communicabatis. Eligite itaque quid velitis, aut non obesse in una communione tenebras luci, sed sufficere luci ut tenebras improbet et eas pro unitate, si expellere non potest, toleret, atque ita non fuisse causam cur ab innocentibus fratribus, quibus malos certe non potuistis ostendere, etiamsi vobis cognitos fuisse dicatis, tenebroso schismatis sacrilegio disiungeremini; aut si non sufficit luci ut improbet tenebras quas expellere non potest, id est si non sufficit bonis ut improbent malos quos excludere vel emendare non possunt, facilius unus Optatus partem Donati in una Africa notissimus et apertissimus maculavit quam quilibet Afer traditor tot gentes per orbem terrarum, etsi non dicam falsis criminibus accusatus, tamen, quod impudentissime negatur, ignotus'.

193 Aug., *Ep.* 185,46 (CSEL 57, 40): 'Apostolus Petrus quando salutorem negauit et fleuit et apostolus mansit, nondum acceperat promissum spiritum sanctum; sed multo magis isti eum non acceperunt, ubi a corporis compage diuisi, quod solum corpus uiuificat spiritus sanctus, extra ecllesiam et contra ecclesiam ecclesiae sacramenta tenuerunt et tamquam ciuili bello nostris contra nos erectis signis armisque pugnarunt'.

194 *De bapt.* 6,3 (CSEL 51, 300): 'Quapropter reddens debitam reverentiam, dignumque honorem, quantum valeo, persolvens pacifico episcopo et glorioso martyri Cypriano, audeo tamen dicere aliter eum sensisse de schismaticis vel haereticis baptizandis, quam postea veritas prodidit, non ex mea, sed ex universae Ecclesiae sententia'.

Augustine's assault on the Donatist use of Cyprian in terms of disqualifying rebaptism, and their very claims to existence based on their schism and lack of charity, left his opponents in a vulnerable position.[195] The bishop of Hippo completed his theological vanquishing with a combination of a sacramental theology less dependent on the internal dispositions of the minister, as well as an ecclesiology much more compatible with the changed reality of a Church which had become largely synchronised with the secular world after the fourth century.

Whereas the Donatists posited an intimate relation between the holiness and worthiness of a minister and his ability to effect valid sacraments and the holiness of the Church, Augustine advocated a system with Christ as the incorruptible source of grace for the Church, and the efficient cause of the salvific benefits of sacraments. Under this regime, sacraments such as baptism retain their force if the minister and recipient are outside the Church.[196] However, the salvific efficacy of sacraments at that point become fruitless because they occur outside the Church, and are thus not perfected.[197] In this sense the permanent nature of the sacraments is evoked and likened to a Roman Legion branding (*nota militaris*):[198]

> Notwithstanding, we deal with these matters lest the unity of the harvest should be deserted on account of evil dispensers of the sacraments—not their own, but the Lord's—who must, of necessity, be mixed among us, until the winnowing of the Lord's field. Now to make a schism from the unity of Christ, or to be in schism, is indeed an evil and a great evil, nor is it in any way possible that Christ should give to the schismatic what he had—not faith, but a sacrilegious error; or that Christ should be the fountain head to the schismatic. And yet, if he give the Baptism of Christ, it shall have been given and if he receive it, it shall have been received, not

195 In a monument to the resilience of the North African spirit then and now, Donatists did not back away from the Roman 'outsiders'. In fact, it would only be with the implementation of state-sponsored coercion that the Donatist Church would lose its existential strength as a movement and formal organisation; see *Actes de la Conférence de Carthage en 411. SC* 194, 195, 224, 373, ed. and intro. Serge Lancel (Paris: Les Éditions du Cerf, 1972–1991); Tilley, 'Dilatory Donatists or Procrastinating Catholics', 7–19; Matthew Gaumer and Anthony Dupont, 'Donatist North Africa and the Beginning of Religious Coercion by Christians: A New Analysis', *La Ciudad de Dios* 223 (2010), 445–66.

196 Grossi, 'Baptismus', in *Augustinus-Lexikon*, vol. 1, ed. C. Mayer, 589–90.

197 *De bapt.* 1,18 (CSEL 51, 157–58).

198 Mayer, 'Taufe und Erwählug—Zur Dialektik des sacramtentum-Begriffes in der antidonatistischen Schrift Augustins: De baptismo', 32.

> to eternal life but to eternal damnation if he shall persevere in sacrilege, not by turning a good thing into evil but by having a good thing to his evil, so long as he had it being evil.[199]

Augustine's second successful theological implementation was a two-cities model of the Church which allowed the increasing number of Christians to remain involved citizens in the secular world (a novel concept in the fourth century)[200] and which also overcame the intellectual *impasse* in reconciling the existence of good and bad Christians, 'wheat and tares',[201] 'lilies and thorns',[202] since the more zealous individuals feared the rigour of Christians had lessened after the acceptance of the religion into the mainstream by the end of the fourth century.

Augustine's two-cities theology was an understanding of the interaction of the Church with the world 'conditioned by his sense of the two ontological cities, invisible to the world'[203] and provided an explanation of the reality of sinners and saints existing in the Church as a mixed body or '*corpus permixtum*'[204] until the return of Christ and his judgment. This adjustment fundamentally

---

199 *Cresc.* 4,26 (CSEL 52, 525–26): 'Verumtamen ista tractamus, ne propter malos dispensatores non tamen suorum, sed dominicorum sacramentorum, quos necesse est usque ad tempus ventilationis areae dominicae commisceri, deseratur ipsa unitas frumentorum. Schisma autem facere ab unitate Christi aut esse in schismate profecto malum est et magnum malum, nec omnino fieri potest, ut Christus det schismatico non fidem, sed sacrilegum errorem. Aut in Christo radicem schismaticus fixerit aut schismatico Christus sit origo vel caput, et tamen baptismum Christi si dederit datum erit, si acceperit acceptum erit, non ad vitam aeternam, sed ad poenam aeternam, si in eo sacrilegio perseveraverit non in malum convertendo bonum quod habet, sed malo suo bonum habendo quamdiu malus habet'.

200 See Robert Markus, *Christianity and the Secular* (Notre Dame, IN: University of Notre Dame Press, 2006), introduction.

201 The 'wheat and tares' theme was dear to Donatist advocates, and Augustine's use of it shows his literary and polemical knack; Aug., *Ep.* 76,2 (CSEL 34, 326); 93,15 (CSEL 34, 53); *Un. bapt.* 17,31 (CSEL 53, 32–33); *Cresc.* 2,44 (CSEL 52, 404); 36,45 (CSEL 52, 405); *C. Gaud.* 1,27 (CSEL 53, 225–26).

202 *De bapt.* 5,38 (CSEL 51, 294).

203 Bonner, 'Christus Sacerdos', 330.

204 For more on the influence of the Donatist Tyconius, see Aug., *De doct. Ch.*, 3,42–56 (CSEL 32, 102–03), ed. I. Martin (Turnhout: Brepols, 1962), §92–133 [§30–56], 104–17; Tyconius, *Liber Regularum* [*The Books of Rules*]. Texts and Translations 31. Early Christian Literature Series 7, trans. W. Babcock (Atlanta: Scholars Press, 1989), §7, 72–75. This point is further investigated in a survey of Augustine's scripturally-based refutation of the Donatist's appropriation of Cyprian in N. Henry, 'The Lily and the Thorns: Augustine's Refutation of

reoriented the debate in Africa over how to understand the Church. Now stock would be placed on the individual Christian as well as on the bipartite communion which is the intimate union with Christ:[205]

> Let them understand that the one prince of the city is our Lord Jesus Christ, whose ministers are good. He is the ruler of His city Jerusalem, who citizens accord with the dignity of the ruler, not equality but according to His measure who said to them, *Ye shall be holy since I am holy*, that is, according to a certain likeness, into which we are changed *from glory unto glory as by the Spirit of God*, the gift of Him who makes us to be *conformed to the image of His Son*. But the devil is the prince of the other evil people and the ruler of the city which in an allegory is called Babylon- a prince who, with his angels, is called by the Apostle Paul *ruler of this darkness* that is, of sinners. And the devil's ministers are like him because they *transform themselves into ministers of righteousness* even as he *transforms himself into an angel of light*, and the citizens of Babylon conform to their most evil ruler by deeds resembling his. But the manifest separation of these two peoples and two cities will be when the harvest is winnowed; until which times love bears with every part of the crop, lest while those who are the grain too hastily flee from the chaff, they impiously separate themselves from others of the grain.[206]

---

the Donatist Exegesis of the Song of Songs', *Revue des Études Augustiniennes* 42/2 (1996), 255–66.

205 *C. ep. Parm.* 2,14 (CSEL 51, 59): 'Quamvis enim, in quantum ex Deo nati sumus, non peccemus, inest tamen adhuc etiam quod ex Adam sumus, quia nondum est *absorta mors in victoriam*, quod etiam in corporum resurrectione promittitur, ut omni modo beati et immaculati et incorrupti simus qui iam secundum fidem *filii Dei sumus*, sed secundum speciem *nondum apparuit quod erimus*. Nondum enim re, *sed spe salvi facti sumus. Spes autem quae videtur non est spes. Quod enim videt quis, quid sperat? Si autem quod non videmus speramus, per patientiam exspectamus*. Quamdiu autem *per patientiam exspectamus redemptionem corporis nostri*, non audeamus nos dicere carere omni vitio, ne ipsa superbia sit immanissimum vitium, et evigilemus aliquando atque videamus in sacerdotibus illius temporis, cum corporalia vitia vitabantur, illum praefigurari, qui cum esset Deus factus est homo propter nos, solus vere agnus immaculatus et sacerdos sine vitio'. See also R.A. Markus, *Saeculum: History and Society in the Theology of St. Augustine*, 117.

206 Emphases original, *C. ep. Parm.* 2,9 (CSEL 51, 54–55): 'Nam ipsi respiciant et recordentur quam multos inter se similes habeant, quorum par malitia est, sed impar notitia, et aliquando veniant ad veram sententiam istorum verborum et intellegant unum populi principem dominum nostrum Iesum Christum, cuius ministri sunt boni, et ipsum rectorem civitatis illius Hierusalem, *quae est mater nostra aeterna in caelis*. Cuius rectoris dignitati congruunt habitantes non ad aequalitatem, sed pro modo suo, quia dictum est

This theological construct was certainly not created by Augustine,[207] but was undoubtedly used by him effectively at a time when Donatist Christians faced an internal dilemma over the identity and lack of growth in their Church since the 390s, when the promising theologies of Tyconius and Parmenian, which effectively allowed for a more integrated Donatist Church, were bypassed by Primian and his contemporaries in favour of more traditional African models of ecclesiology which re-emphasised the separateness of the Church (the *collecta* or collective body) and the world.[208]

---

eis: *Sancti eritis, quoniam et ego sanctus sum*, secundum quandam scilicet imaginis similitudinem, in quam *transformamur de gloria in gloriam tamquam a domini spiritu* munere illius, qui nos facit conformes imaginis filii sui. Est et alterius mali populi diabolus princeps et rector eius civitatis, quae mystice Babylonia dicitur, quoniam principes et rectores tenebrarum harum id est peccatorum ipsum et angelos eius apostolus Paulus appellat, et illius ministri similes eius sunt, quia transfigurant se in ministros iustitiae, sicut ille in angelum lucis, et inhabitantes rectori pessimo in factis similibus congruunt. Sed istorum populorum atque civitatum tunc erit aperta separatio, cum ista messis fuerit ventilata; quod donec fiat omnia tolerat dilectio frumentorum, ne, dum grana paleam praepropere fugiunt, a consortibus granis impie separentur'.

207 *C. ep. Parm.* 1,1 (CSEL 51, 19–20): 'Tychonius enim omnibus sanctarum paginarum vocibus circumtunsus evigilavit et vidit ecclesiam Dei toto terrarum orbe diffusam, sicut de illa tanto ante per corda et ora sanctorum praevisum atque praedictum est. Quo perspecto suscepit adversus ipsos suos hoc demonstrare et adserere, nullius hominis quamvis sceleratum et immane peccatum praescribere promissis Dei nec id agere quorumlibet intra ecclesiam constitutorum et quamlibet impietatem, ut fides Dei de Ecclesia futura diffundenda usque ad terminos orbis terrae, quae in promissis patrum retenta et nunc exhibita est, evacuetur. Hoc ergo Tychonius cum vehementer copioseque dissereret et ora contradicentium multis et magnis et manifestis sanctarum Scripturarum testimoniis oppilaret, non vidit quod consequenter videndum fuit, illos videlicet in Africa christianos pertinere ad ecclesiam toto orbe diffusam, qui utique non istis ab eiusdem orbis communione atque unitate seiunctis, sed ipsi orbi terrarum per communionem conecterentur.' Tyconius, *Commentarius in Apocalypsin Ioannis*, in the compilation of Beatus of Libana (Madrid, 1772), ed. H. Florenz (American Academy of Rome, 1939), 506: 'Ecce duas civitates, unam Dei, unam diaboli…et in utrasque reges terrae ministrant'; *In Apocalypsin* (Beatus, 316): 'Diximus quator angelos bipartitos esse, et invicem mixtos, id est eccleasiam et regna mundi: cirabimus opportune commemorare mundi regna, vel maxime presens regnum, in medio esse eccleasia, per orbem in falsos fraters.' It would also be helpful to consult J. Van Oort, *Jerusalem and Babylon: A Study into Augustine's City of God and the Sources of His Doctrine of the Two Cities*, *Supplements to Vigiliae Christianae* 14 (Leiden: Brill, 1991), esp. 93–154, 199–22.

208 The use of the typology of '*collecta*' is rooted in the century after Constantine's toleration of Christianity. Donatists in this period found success in maintaining their church through stress and expansion by solidifying their use of biblical typology of the Church as a tight-knit group that obeyed the laws of God, separated from those who did not. Indeed, the watchword of Donatism had become *separatism,* with martyrdom a rare and distant

With Augustine's introduction of the two-cities model of the Church, along with a realigned sacramentology, Donatists were simply outmanoeuvred theologically. They were further at a loss when it came to mounting a sustainable reaction to Augustine and Catholics at a time when the latter had successfully begun enlisting the Roman authorities in enacting legislation aimed at religious uniformity throughout Africa and the empire. (The Roman authorities had grown impatient with religious mass-movements and other forms of dissension in the early fifth century[209] and were especially at odds with Donatism after the failed revolt of Gildo and Optatus of Thamugadi in the late 390s.) Indeed, it was the combination of these factors that gave Augustine the advantage in the debate over who interpreted Cyprian rightly in the end.[210]

Beyond *De Baptismo* and the Campaign's Beginning

By now it is clear that in 400/01 Augustine had waded headlong into a fully-fledged collision with the Donatist Church over who had the right to represent Christianity in Africa. Because of the struggles Augustine faced in his first years of ministry, in his first encounters with the Donatist Church, he created

reality by the mid-300s. This allowed the church to constantly redefine itself through the notion of separateness from the world and the worldly Catholics, the *sine qua non* for the survival of the Donatist Christians. For further data, see Maureen Tilley, 'Sustaining Donatist Self-Identity: From the Church of the Martyrs to the Collecta of the Desert', *Journal of Early Christian Studies* 5/1 (1997), 21–35; *The Bible in Christian North Africa*, 65, 73–76, 93; 'Donatus, Donatism', in *Augustine Through the Ages*, 286. Also see Maureen Tilley, 'From Separatist Sect to Majority Church: The Ecclesiologies of Parmenian and Tyconius', *Studia Patristica* 33 (1997), 260–65; Frend, *The Donatist Church*, 201 (Frend attaches the accolade to Tyconius that he was the only Donatist ever to influence Christian thought outside of Africa).

209 See R.M. Errington, *Roman Imperial Policy from Julian to Theodosius*; Brown, 'Religious Coercion in the Later Roman Empire: 283–305', 83–101, reprinted in Brown, *Religion and Society in the Age of Augustine*, 283–05.

210 J. Yates makes an insightful summary of this process: '…interesting is the fact that Augustine's first step on the path toward appropriation was an anachronistic one. Augustine seems to have presumed that the North African church's self designation as 'Catholics' vis-à-vis the (at least officially) defeated Donatists also gave him the right to drag Cyprian across more than 150 years of time and label him as a fellow, fifth-century, Catholic…Once Cyprian had been appropriated, it placed the onus on anyone who challenged Augustine on any point he could 'proof-text' via Cyprian'; 'Augustine's Appropriation of Cyprian the Martyr-bishop against the Pelagians,' in *More than a Memory: the Discourse of Martyrdom and the Construction of Christian Identity in the History of Christianity* (*Annua Nuntia Lovaniensia* 51), ed. Johan Leemans (Leuven: Peeters, 2005), 119–35.

a winning formula with which he would be able to take on Donatist interlocutors and win. At the centre of this invigorated effort was Augustine's immediate capturing of Cyprian's legacy, not least in works leading up to *De baptismo*, such as *s.* 37, *s.* 305A, *s.*313A, *s.* 313E and *C. ep. Parm.* For this reason, by the time it came to writing *De baptismo*, Augustine was fully aware of the efficacy of tapping into a universally revered African hero like Cyprian. It also became clear that this resulted in a fair amount of controversy, since Augustine's aggressive reapplication of Cyprian meant that he inevitably controverted the martyr-bishop's original meaning with regard to many theological issues. Nonetheless, this process of aggressive appropriation and resultant contradiction, led the way for Augustine's interaction with serious Donatist opposition in the future, as well as with the challenges presented by the Pelagians. In sum, 400/01 marks the genuine beginning of Augustine's full-blown campaign for Catholic orthodoxy in Africa, and, as a result, his unambiguous appropriation of Cyprian for use on the side of the Catholic party.

CHAPTER 5

The Process of Appropriation

To comprehend the total picture of Augustine's appropriation of Cyprian, it is necessary to uncover and examine the place(s) where Augustine first showed signs of using Cyprian exclusively as an authority to support his own views. This step was taken in Chapter 3, where I examined Augustine's earliest examples of appropriation: *De doct. Chr.*, *C. Faust.*, *Conf.*, and especially *S.* 37, *s.* 305A, *s.* 313A, *s.* 313B, *s.* 313C, and *s.* 313E. Then, in Chapter 4, I presented a close analysis of Augustine's first two major anti-Donatist works, *C. ep. Parm.* and *De bapt.* Yet that important analysis only told the beginning of a story that would last till Augustine's death and beyond, as North African Christianity retained its Donatist-flavour well into the Islamic period. Evidence of Augustine's most vigorous Cyprian-appropriation came only later, between 404 and 430. In this sense, we can say that what formally began in *C. ep. Parm.* and *De bapt.* really only drew to a close with Augustine's *C. Iul. imp.*, that is, with his death in 430. Tracing Augustine's long-term reinterpretation of Cyprian is really the point where the two most career-altering dramas in Augustine's life overlap, therefore actually making them into a somewhat parallel set of controversies.

So far each chapter has had as its main concern tracking the method by which Augustine entered into his anti-Donatist campaign, the influences that drove him, his own pastoral and theological responses, and the complexities that resulted. I have also tracked the way external events such as the Maximianist schism deeply altered the course Augustine would follow as the controversy dragged on. Most crucially, I have recovered in his texts his slow arrival at authoritative sources to serve as polemical fodder against the Donatists, the culmination of which was when he settled upon Cyprian of Carthage as his leading argument. I then analysed the consequences of Augustine's appropriation of Cyprian, and what stood out was that Augustine had to go to extreme lengths to reconcile Cyprian's differing views and theology (and therefore also those of North Africans/Donatists) with his own. Since he could not avoid the fact that Cyprian's theology differed from his own, Augustine had no other option but to redefine Cyprian's intention and over-accentuate Cyprian's virtues. This was in order to show that because he was so humble, charitable, and deferential, Cyprian's spirit dictated that unity and peace were the most important priorities, and that a Christian must always opt for the good of the greater Catholic Church.

With such foundational work already complete, it is now appropriate to look more deeply into the mechanics of Augustine's Cyprian-appropriation as

 | DOI 10.1163/9789004312647_007

it matured through the 400s and 410s. To facilitate this analysis, the chapter moves beyond the earliest years of the anti-Donatist campaign and launches instead into a treatment of how Augustine sustained his polemic in the decades after the conflict became a fully-fledged affair in 400/01. The first section of this chapter is primarily concerned with the 'nuts and bolts' (the fine details) of Augustine's appropriation of Cyprian. A thorough analysis and inventory is made of Augustine's post-400/01 works, and how these evince the impact of the Donatist controversy. This analysis entails a close look at recurring themes and methods Augustine used, not only to drive home his anti-Donatist message, but to associate his thought more closely with the authority of Cyprian.

Appropriation in the Medium Term

The effect of Augustine's audacious appropriating manoeuvre in *C. ep. Parm.* and *De bapt.* is most evident when one analyses the amount of times he re-used the Cyprian legacy straight after those premier anti-Donatist works and then throughout the remainder of his career. Using *Ground Theory* methodology throughout this chapter, I analyse the occurrences of important thematic terms that evidence the evolution and construction of Augustine's polemical and theological concepts.[1] When using this methodology the resulting data is startling. Consider that Augustine uses the word 'Cyprian' a grand total of 39 times before *C. ep. Parm.*! This number includes *De doct. Chr.*, *Conf.*, *C. Faust.*, *s.* 37, *s.* 305A, *s.* 313A, and *s.* 313E.[2] This total drops to just 17 if *s.* 37 and *s.* 313E are removed from consideration because of their problematic dating. This means that of the 600+/– total appearance of 'Cyprian' in the works of Augustine, only 5.8 percent of those appeared before Augustine launched his full anti-Donatist

1 *Ground Theory* methodology is particularly useful in this regard as Augustine's literary corpus is extensive, and the theory is a qualititative research methodology that allows for the exploration of concepts, the identification of relationships in raw data, and the organisation of concepts and the relationships into a theoretical scheme. The methodology of *Ground Theory* was pioneered by A. Strauss and J. Corbin in *Basics of Qualitative Research: Techniques and Procedures for Developing Grounded Theory* (Thousand Oaks, CA: Sage, 1998). This methodology is well suited to the purposes of this research, in that the theory emphasises the need for developing multiple concepts and their linkages in order to capture the central phenonomenon.

2 *Doct. Chr.* 2,61; 4,31; 4,45; 4,47; 4,48; *Conf.* 5,15; *C. Faust.* 5,8; 13,4; 20,21; *s.* 37,3; *s.* 305A,2; 4; *s.* 313B,2(x2); 4(x3); *s.* 313C,2(x2); *s.*313E,1; 2(x3); 5(x4); 6(x4); 7(x4); 8.

campaign in 400/01. This is quite strong numerical evidence demonstrating that *C. ep. Parm.* and *De bapt.* were the genuine start of Augustine's full-blown anti-Donatist initiative, when it came to using Cyprian's authority to vanquish them. In all, the word 'Cyprian' will recur 344 times in the surviving anti-Donatist works.

As covered in Chapter 4, *C. ep. Parm.* saw Cyprian referred to 10 times (1.5%),[3] and with *De bapt.*, this figure skyrocketed to an unparalleled 214 times (32%).[4] The subsequent anti-Donatist writings have the following results: *C. litt. Pet.* x1(–1%)[c.401/03];[5] *Cresc.* x66(10%)[c.405/06];[6] *Un. bapt.* x15(2.25%)[c.410/11];[7] *Brev.* x5(.75%)[c.411];[8] *Gest. Con. Carth.* x4(1%)[c.411];[9] *C. Don.* x13(2%)[c.412];[10] *Correct.* x0[c.417]; *Serm. Caes.* x0[c.418]; *Emer.* x0[c.418]; *C. Gaud.* x31(5%)[c.419/20].[11] What is most interesting about these figures is that there is a noticeable drop after Augustine wrote *Cresc.* in 405/06, which only sees some semblance of a pick-up in *C. Don.* (c.412) and *C. Gaud.* (419/20). For a breakdown, see Figure 1 below.

Only supposition can explain this phenomenon, but a credible guess is that by the time *Cresc.* was produced, Augustine had already sufficiently established his claim to the authority of Cyprian. Also probable is that Augustine reverted to his appropriation in his *epistulae* and *sermones*, which were directly

3 *C. ep. Parm.* 1,6; 3,8(x4); 3,9; 3,11(x2); 3,16; 3,25.

4 *De bapt.* 1,1(x2); 1,28; 1,29; 2,1; 2,2(x8); 2,3(x4); 2,4(x2); 2,5; 2,6(x2); 2,7(x4); 2,8(x2); 2,9(x2); 2,11(x2); 2,12(x3); 2,13; 2,14(x3); 2,15; 2,18; 2,19(x2); 2,20(x5); 3,1(x2); 3,2(x3); 3,3(x8); 3,4(x4); 3,5(x3); 3,6(x2); 3,7(x3); 3,10; 3,13; 3,14; 3,16(x2); 3,17(x4); 3,22; 3,23; 3,26; 3,28; 4,2; 4,3; 4,4; 4,6; 4,7(x2); 4,8(x3); 4,9; 4,10(x4); 4,11(x4); 4,13; 4,16(x4); 4,17; 4,18(x4); 4,19; 4,21; 4,24; 4,28; 4,29; 5,1(x7); 5,2(x4); 5,3(x5); 5,4(x3); 5,7; 5,8; 5,12; 5,13(x2); 5,14; 5,16(x2); 5,19; 5,21; 5,22; 5,23; 5,24(x2); 5,27; 5,30(x2); 5,31(x2); 5,32; 5,34; 5,37(x2); 5,38(x2); 5,39(x2); 6,1(x2); 6,2(x2); 6,3(x5); 6,4(x2); 6,5; 6,8; 6,9; 6,10(x2); 6,12(x3); 6,19(x3); 6,24; 6,25; 6,33; 6,41; 6,43; 6,44; 6,45; 6,47; 6,48; 6,50; 6,60; 6,68; 6,78; 6,80; 6,87; 7,1(x3); 7,3(x3); 7,5; 7,7; 7,9(x2); 7,13; 7,21; 7,23; 7,25; 7,27(x4); 7,29; 7,33(x2); 7,39(x2); 7,49(x4); 7,51; 7,89(x2); 7,96; 7,97; 7,98(x2); and 7,103(x3).

5 *C. litt. Pet.* 3,40.

6 *Cresc.* 1,38(x2); 2,18; 2,39(x6); 2,40(x7); 2,41(x4); 2,42(x4); 2,43(x3); 2,44(x7); 2,45(x4); 2,46; 2,47; 2,48(x2); 2,49; 3,2(x8); 3,3; 3,5; 3,35; 3,40; 3,45; 3,64; 3,73(x2); 3,78; 3,93(x2); 4,20(x2); 4,33(x2); 4,67; 4,73.

7 *Un. bapt.* 6; 22(x4); 23(x4); 24(x2); 25; 26.

8 *Brev.* 3,11(x2); 3,20(x2); 3,30.

9 *Gest. Con. Carth.* 1,55; 1,133(x2); 1,135.

10 *C. Don.* 9(x2); 11; 19(x2); 28; 37; 50(x6).

11 *C. Gaud.* 1,34; 1,40; 2,2(x3); 2,3; 2,4(x3); 2,5(x2); 2,6; 2,28(x4); 2,9; 2,10(x2); 2,14.

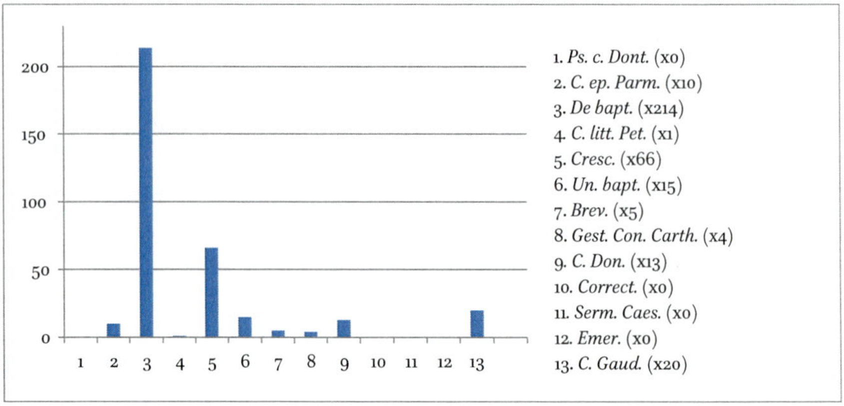

FIGURE 1 *'Cyprian' in anti-Donatist specimens*

targeted at his intended audiences, and less time-consuming to produce than his fully-fledged anti-Donatist treatises. Additionally helpful is the realisation that by 410/11 Augustine had begun to alter his Cyprian-appropriation agenda specifically to counter the self-imposed Pelagian threat.

At this point it is necessary to examine where 'Cyprian' appears in the anti-Pelagian works of Augustine. In all, 'Cyprian' is discussed by Augustine 95 times, or in 14 percent of all references in the anti-Pelagian works. Though this number is somewhat lower than the 344 occurrences in the anti-Donatist selections, it does make quite an impression when one considers that Cyprian is not usually associated with the Pelagian controversy by and large.[12]

These works, written between 411–430, present an important key for interpreting the duration of Augustine's appropriation of Cyprian. The way the anti-Donatist and anti-Pelagian numbers complement each other within the context of this timeline is significant. Take notice of how in Figure 1, the number of references flatlines after 410/11 and *Un. bapt.* Then, when one looks at Figure 2, one notices straightaway that Augustine resumes the appropriation in *Pecc. mer.*, composed in c. 411. Actually, both sets of data together present

12 This is not to say that scholarship ignores Cyprian when it comes to exploring the Pelagian controversy; this is simply not true when one considers a work such as E. Dassmann, 'Tam Ambrosius quam Cyprianus (c.Iul.imp. 4,112). Augustins Helfer im pelagianischen Streit', in D. Papandreou, W.A. Bienert, and K. Schäferdiek (eds.), *Oecumenica et Patristica. Festschrift für W. Schneemelcher* (Geneva: Metropolie der Schweiz, 1989), 258–68.

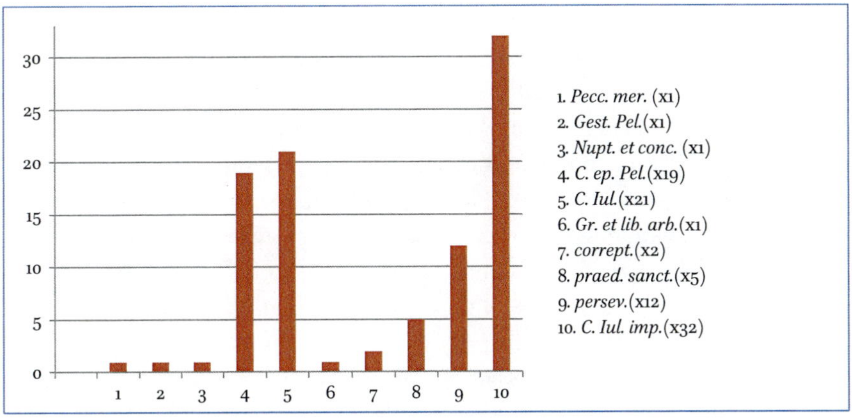

FIGURE 2 *'Cyprian' in anti-Pelagian specimens*

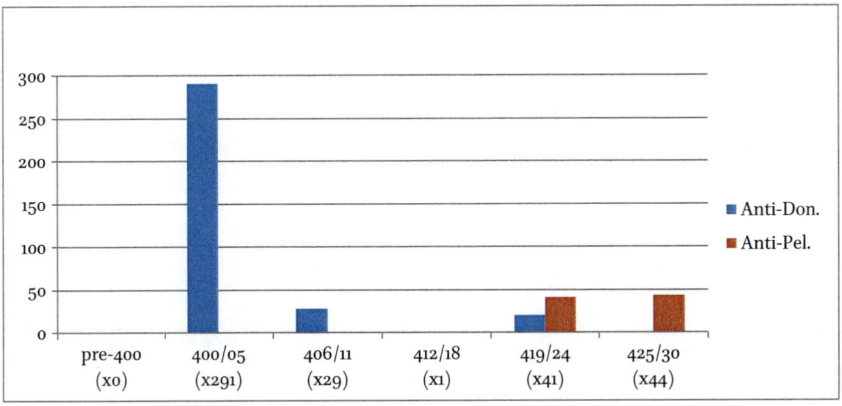

FIGURE 3 *Yearly over-lap of the controversies*

solid proof of a Cyprian-appropriation that was long-lived, and used in both controversies, Cyprian remained Augustine's most valuable asset against his opponents. But before both sets of data are overlaid in Figure 3, a brief look at each of the anti-Pelagian works is represented here, pulled from the 600+/– occurrences, with the total of 95 references as follows: *Pecc. mer.* x1(–1%) [c.411];[13] *Gest. Pel.* x1(–1%)[c.416/17];[14] *Nupt. et conc.* x1(–1%)[c.419/21];[15] *C. ep.*

13 *Pecc. mer.* 3,10.

14 *Gest. Pel.* 25.

15 *Nupt. et conc.* 2,51.

Pel. x19(2.86%)[c.421];[16] *C. Iul.* x21(3.13%)[c.421/22];[17] *Gr. et lib. arb.* x1(–1%) [c.426/27];[18] *Corrept.* x2(–1%)[c.426/27];[19] *Praed. sanct.* x5(.75%)[c.428/29];[20] *Persev.* x12(1.8%)[c.428/29];[21] *C. Iul. imp.* x32(4.8%)[c.429/30].[22]

But this data contained in Figure 3 is incomplete in a sense, especially with an obvious gap indicated in the period 412/18. This gap creates the impression that either Augustine deviated from his appropriation strategy in those lean years, or perhaps abandoned the anti-Donatist/ Pelagian campaigns for some other pursuits, such as writing his famed doctrinal works. The answer to this problem is arrived at when one includes the critical data of Augustine's *sermones* and *epistulae* from that period.

Once an account is rendered of the *sermones* and *epistulae* that contain references to the name 'Cyprian,' the complete picture emerges. This is so because these important examples represent not only the best chronological evidence, but are the most persuasive form of Augustine's *realpolitik* in Africa against his enemies bar none. Among the letters Augustine authored with direct Cyprian references (specifically anti-Donatist letters are indicated in bold) are: *Ep.* 82(c.404/05),[23] ***Ep.* 93**(c.407/08),[24] *Ep.* 98(c.408/14),[25] ***Ep.* 108**(c.409/10),[26] *Ep.* 140(c.411/12),[27] *Ep.* 151(?),[28] *Ep.* 157(414/15),[29] *Ep.* 166(spring 415),[30] *Ep.* 180(416?),[31] *Ep.* 215(c.426/27),[32] *Ep.* 217(426/28),[33] *Ep.*

16 *C. ep. Pel.* 4,21(x4); 4,23; 4,24; 4,25; 4,26(x2); 4,27; 4,28(x4); 4,29; 4,32(x3); 4,34.

17 *C. Iul.* 1,6; 1,22(x2); 1,32; 2,6; 2,8; 2,9; 2,18; 2,25(x2); 2,30; 2,33(x2); 2,37(x2); 3,31(x4); 3,32(x2).

18 *Gr. et lib. arb.* 26.

19 *Corrept.* 10; 12.

20 *praed. sanct.* 8; 15; 26; 28.

21 *persev.* 4; 7; 8(x2); 12; 36(x3); 43; 48; 49; 55.

22 *C. Iul. imp.* 1,6; 1,7; 1,9; 1,50; 1,52; 1,59; 1,72(x2); 1,106(x2); 1,117; 2,2(x2); 2,14; 2,33; 2,37; 2,73; 2,164; 4,72; 4,73; 4,109(x2); 4,112(x2); 4,113; 6,6; 6,10; 6,14(x2); 6,18; 6,21; 6,23.

23 *Ep.* 82,24; 30; 36.

24 *Ep.* 93,15; 31; 35; 36; 37(x3); 38(x3); 39(x3); 40; 41; 42; 45(x4); 47.

25 *Ep.* 98,3(2).

26 *Ep.* 108,9; 10(x2); 11(x2); 12; 20.

27 *Ep.* 140,13.

28 *Ep.* 151,6.

29 *Ep.* 157,34.

30 *Ep.* 166,23; 24.

31 *Ep.* 180,5.

32 *Ep.* 215,3(x2).

33 *Ep.* 217,2; 3(x3); 6; 22; 26.

259(c.429/30),[34] and *Ep.* 29*(c.412/13).[35] The sermons that contain references (specifically anti-Donatist *sermones* are indicated in bold) are as follows:[36] *In Ioh. ev. tr.* (406/07),[37] ***Ex. 3 of En. 36***(403),[38] *in Ps. 80*(?),[39] ***En. in Ps.* 85**(412/16),[40] *s.*8(411),[41] *s.* 13(418),[42] ***s.* 37**(397/410),[43] *s.* 49(418),[44] *s.*114(after 423),[45] ***s.* 138**(411/12),[46] *s.* 163B(410),[47] ***s.* 197**(400),[48] *s.* 294(413),[49] *s.* 305A(401)[50] *s.* 309(?)[51] *s.* 310(?),[52] *s.* 311(405),[53] *s.* 312(417),[54] *s.* 313(?),[55] *s.* 313A(401),[56]

34 *Ep.* 259,4(x2).

35 *Ep.* 29*,2.

36 The dating of the *sermones* is from a variety of sources: A. Kunzelmann,'Die Chronologie der Sermones des Hl. Augustinus', in J. Wilpert et al. (ed.), *Miscellanea Agostiniana: testi e studi publicata a cura dell'ordine eremitano di S. Agostino nel XV centenario dalla morte del santo dottore, vol. II, Studi Agostiniani* (Rome: Tipografia Poliglotta Vaticana, 1931), 417–520; P.-P. Verbraken, *Études Critiques sur les Sermons Authentiques de Saint Augustin, Instrumenta Patristica 12* (Steenbrugge, Bel.: Abbatia S. Petri/Martinus Nijhoff, 1976); P.-M. Hombert, *Nouvelles Recherches de Chronologie Augustinienne, Collection des Études Augustiniennes, Série Antiquité* 163 (Paris: Institut d'Études Augustiniennes, 2000); É. Rebillard, 'Sermones', in A. Fitzgerald (ed.), *Augustine through the Ages. An Encyclopedia* (Grand Rapids, MI/Cambridge: Wm. B. Eerdmans Publishing, 1999), 773–92; R. Gryson, *Répertoire général des auteurs ecclésiastiques latins de l'antiquité et du haut moyen âge, tome I* (Freiburg: Verlag Herder, 2007). For dating the *En. in Ps.*: H. Müller and M. Fiedrowicz, 'Enarrationes in Psalmos', in C. Mayer (ed.), *Augustinus-Lexikon*, vol. 2 (Basel: Schwabe & Co., 2001), 804–58.

37 *In Ioh. ev. tr.* 7,17.

38 *En. in Ps.* 3 of 36,13.

39 *En. in Ps.* 80,23.

40 *En. in Ps.* 85,24.

41 *s.* 8.

42 *s.* 13.

43 *s.* 37,3.

44 *s.* 49.

45 *s.*114.

46 *s.* 138,1; 3.

47 *s.* 163B,6.

48 *s.* 197,3; 60.

49 *s.* 294,19(x3).

50 *s.* 305A,2; 4.

51 *s.* 309,2(x3); 3; 5(x3); 6(x3).

52 *s.* 310,1(x2); 2,(x8).

53 *s.* 311,1; 3; 7; 10.

54 *s.* 312,3(x6); 4; 6(x2).

55 *s.* 313,1; 2(x6).

56 *s.* 313A,3(x2); 4; 5(x2).

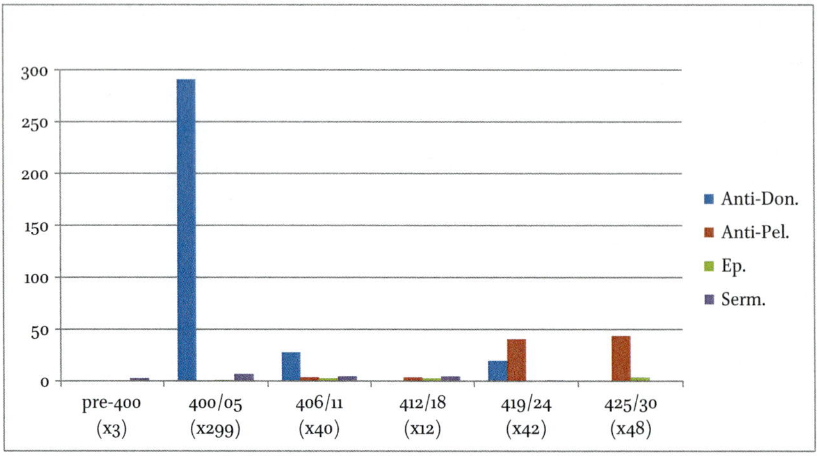

FIGURE 4 *Yearly over-lap of the controversies, including letters and sermons*

s. 313B(400),[57] *s.* 313C(403),[58] *s.* 313D(?),[59] *s.*313E(397–410),[60] *s.* 313G(410/12),[61] *s.*335K(?),[62] *s.* 341(?),[63] *s.* 359B(404/05).[64]

With this data, it is easy to conclude that Augustine maintained his appropriation of Cyprian throughout his career. But even with the inclusion of the letters and sermons, there still appears to be a relative lull between 411 and 419 as first indicated. A possible explanation for this is that after the Carthage colloquium in June 411 and the somewhat successful implementation of the imperially-mandated re-unification of the African churches, the matter died down as a matter for Augustine's reaction. The exception to this came with *C. Gaud.* when Augustine had to reactivate his slate of authorities to win the argument against a recalcitrant Donatist leader. Furthermore, it was not until his dealings with Julian of Aeclanum in the 420s that the so-called Pelagian controversy became a vicious war of words and official intrigues. So whilst Augustine's appropriation of Cyprian never really ceased in this timeline, there was certainly a period of less activity.

57 *s.* 313B,2(x2); 4(x3).
58 *s.* 313C,2(x2).
59 *s.* 313D,1(x2); 2(x2); 4(x8).
60 *s.*313E,1; 2(x3); 3(x2); 5(x4); 6(x4); 7(x4); 8.
61 *s.* 313G,3(x2).
62 *s.*335K,5.
63 *s.* 341,4.
64 *s.* 359B,5; 16.

The Long Road

The surest way to grasp the magnitude of Augustine's appropriation of Cyprian is through an assessment of the major themes that he focused on in his career, and how they helped him navigate the outcomes of his controversies. In the earlier chapters of this book great care was taken to show how over-arching concerns, or passions really, permeated Augustine's earliest dealings with the Donatists; themes like 'truth', the 'flesh', and the closed-off mentality of African Christians to the rest of the catholic world. Even personalities such as Primian and Maximian featured, as Augustine took the opportunity presented by the Maximianist schism in the 390s. Once Augustine had finally begun using Cyprian's authority in his campaign at the end of the 390s, that is, once he had virtually exhausted his 'gloves-off approach' and vehemently engaged with the Donatists, those themes never went away. As touched on briefly in the preceding chapter, the themes of *veritas*, *caro/carnis*, *concupiscentia*, *superbia*, *gratia*, *ignorantia*, *pertinacia*, 'rebaptism', 'martyr', 'Africa', the Church and its relation with the world (*mundus*), theological 'innovation' (*novitas*), and authority (*auctoritas*) were all present in the lead-up to the formal beginning of the Donatist controversy in *C. ep. Parm.* and *De bapt.* But the magnitude of the Donatist controversy in terms of being a driving force behind Augustine's theological development is only evident when an analysis is provided which lays out a global picture of those themes. Only then, when those themes are broken down categorically, can one see how prominent they were for Augustine in driving his polemic.

Truth—Veritas

As seen in Chapter 1, when examining Augustine's earliest letters and writings upon his ordination as a priest, 'truth' (*veritas*) was his passion early on, and would remain so throughout his career, 'the object of his life's inquiry', if you will.[65]

The profusion of references to *'veritas'* in the *corpus augustinianum* is striking. In total, Augustine uses the term and concept *6127 times in 3658 places* throughout the entire surviving works. The following graph is a breakdown of how the term is present in the general categories of Augustine's writings:
An analysis of the use of *'veritas'* in Augustine's works throughout the entirety of his career leaves one with the unmistakeable impression that this was

65 Simon Harrison, 'Truth, Truths', in A. Fitzgerald (ed.), *Augustine Through the Ages: An Encyclopedia* (Grand Rapids, MI: Wm. Eerdmans, 1999), 852. Harrison's discussion of 'truth' shows how powerful this theme was, especially in the earliest decade of Augustine's career.

TABLE 1 *'Veritas' in Augustine's writings*

Genre	# of instances	Works where the term 'veritas' is present
Anti-Manichean (380s–390s)	414	*Mor. eccl.* (x34); *Gn. adu. Man.* (x36); *Duab. anim.* (x3); *C. Fort.* (x6); *F. et symb.* (x3); *Gn. litt. imp.* (x6); *S. dom. mont.* (x22); *C. Adim.* (x14); *C. ep. Man.* (x24); *C. Faust.* (x199); *C. Fel.* (x41); *C. Sec.* (x20); *C Prisc.* (x6)
Anti-Arian	66	*C. s. Arrian.* (x17); *Conl. Max.* (x14); *C. Max.* (x35)
Anti-Donatist (390s–420s)	563	*Ps. c. Don.* (x2); *C. ep. Parm.* (x41); *De bapt.* (x129); *C. litt. Pet.* (x66); *Cresc.* (x139); *Un. bapt.* (x48); *Brev.* (x12); *c. Don.* (x39); *Emer.* (x14); *C. Gaud.* (x43); *Cath. fr.* (x30)
Anti-Pelagian (410s–430)	600	*Pecc. mer.* (x38); *Spir. et litt.* (x11); *Nat. et gr.* (x19); *Gest. Pel.* (x16); *Gr. et pecc. or.* (x22); *nupt. et conc.* (x13); *An. et or.* (x23); *C. ep. Pel.* (x33); *C. Iul.* (x115); *Gr. et lib. arb.* (x8); *Corrept.* (x10); *Cont.* (x8); *Perf. iust.* (x9); *Praed. sanct.* (x19); *Persev.* (x30); *C. Iul. imp.* (x226)
Letters (390s–420s) [anti-Donatist works indicated in bold]	453	*Ep.* 1(x2); 3(x3); 7(x1); 11(x1); 14(x1); 15(x1); 19(x1); 20(x1); **23**(x1); 26(x1); 27(x2); 28(x3); **29**(x1); **33**(x5); **34**(x1); 36(x1); 37(x1); 40(x6); **43**(x10); 47(x1); **52**(x1); **53**(x1); 55(x7); **56**(x1); **58**(x2); **61**(x2); **66**(x2); 71(x1); 73(x2); 78(x1); 80(x2); 82(x24); **87**(x2); **88**(x3); **89**(x3); 91(x3); 92(x1); **93**(x32); 95(x2); 98(x1); **100**(x2); 101(x3); 102(x6); 104(x9); **105**(x15); **108**(x9); **111**(x3); 112(x1); 118(x34); 120(x5); **128**(x5); **129**(x1); 130(x2); 137(x7); 138(x2); **139**(x1); 140(x9); **141**(x7); **142**(x1); 143(x3); **144**(x2); 147(x4); 148(x2); 149(x9); 153(x7); 155(x4); 157(x4); 162(x1); 164(x2); 166(x2); 167(x4); 169(x2); 170(x1); **173**(x5); 176(x1); 177(x1); 178(x1); 180(x2); **185**(x21); 186(x7); 187(x2); 188(x1); 191(x1); 193(x3); 194(x14); 199(x5); 202A(x6); 203(x1); 204(x1); 217(x6); 219(x1); 220(x1); 228(x1); 229(x1); 231(x1); 232(x1); 236(x1); 237(x8); 238(x18); 241(x2); 242(x5); 243(x1); 247(x1); 258(x1); 2*(x2); 6*(x1); 20*(x1); 28*(x1).

Genre	# of instances	Works where the term 'veritas' is present
Sermons (390s–420s) [anti-Donatist works indicated in bold]	844	**4**(x6); 5(x1); 7(x1); 8(x23); 9(x2); **10**(x7); 12(x9); 15A(x1); 16(x1); 16A(x1); 20(x1); 21(x1); 22A(x1); 23(x1); 23B(x4); 26(x1); 28(x1); 28A(x3); 30(x2); 33A(x1); 35(x1); 36(x1); **37**(x1); 38(x2); 41(x1); **46**(x9); **47**(x5); 50(x1); 51(x7); 53(x2); 55(x2); 56(x1); 57(x3); 58(x1); 60(x4); 60A(x2); 61A(x3); 62(x2); 63B(x1); 64(x1); 65(x2); 66(x1); 68(x4); 70A(x1); **71**(x13); 72(x2); 72A(x7); 73(x2); 74(x1); 75(x3); 77(x1); 78(x1); 81(x4); 83(x1); 87(x1); **88**(x3); 89(x4); **90**(x5); 92(x1); 93(x1); 94A(x11); 98(x2); 99(x2); 101(x2); 103(x1); 104(x1); 105(x4); 107(x3); 110(x1); 110A(x1); 112(x1); 112A(x4); 113(x1); 113A(x1); 114(x2); 114A(x3); 115(x1); 116(x1); 121(x1); 124(x1); 125A(x1); 127(x1); 128(x8); **129**(x1); 130(x1); 130A(x1); 131(x1); 132(x1); 132A(x2); 133(x20); 134(x11); 135(x5); 136(x1); **137**(x4); 139(x2); 141(x15); 142(x3); 143(x1); 147(x1); 150(x6); 153(x5); 157(x1); 158(x3); 159(x2); **159B**(x2); 162(x1); **162A**(x1); 162C(x16); 163(x4); **164**(x7); 166(x11); 169(x1); 170(x1); 171(x2); 173(x1); 174(x1); 177(x1); 178(x2); 179(x12); 180(x1); 181(x7); **182**(x2); **183**(x4); 184(x2); 185(x12); 189(x5); 191(x3); 192(x6); 193(x3); 196A(x3); **198**(x30); 199(x1); 201(x2); **202**(x3); 210(x1); 211(x1); 213(x1); 214(x8); 215(x1); 216(x2); 217(x2); 218(x2); 218C(x1); 220(x7); 221(x1); 223A(x1); 223K(x1); 228B(x1); 229(x1); 229A(x5); 229C(x3); 229E(x1); 229F(x1); 229H(x1); 229I(x4); 230(x1); 236(x1); 237(x1); 239(x1); 240(x6); 241(x5); 242(x2); 243(x1); 244(x1); 245(x1); 246(x2); 247(x1); 250(x1); 254(x5); 255(x1); 257(x1); 260E(x1); 260C(x2); 264(x2); 265(x3); 265B(x2); 265D(x3); **266**(x2); 267(x2); 268(x2); 270(x1); 272(x1); 273(x1); 274(x1); **275**(x2); 277(x1); 277A(x1); 284(x3); 286(x2); 287(x1); 288(x1); 290(x2); 291(x1); **292**(x5); 293C(x1); 293D(x3); 293E(x1); 294(x5); **295**(x2); 296(x4); 297(x2); 299A(x2);

TABLE 1 *'Veritas' in Augustine's writings* (cont.)

Genre	# of instances	Works where the term 'veritas' is present
		299C(x1); 299E(x1); 299F(x2); 300(x3); 301(x1); 301A(x3); 302(x1); 303(x1); 304(x1); 306(x5); 306A(x1); 306E(x4); 308A(x2); 310(x1); 311(x2); 312(x1); 313(x4); 313B(x1); 313D(x1); 314(x1); 315(x6); 318(x2); 325(x4); 328(x6); 330(x2); 335A(x4); 335B(x3); 335E(x5); 337(x1); 338(x1); 339(x1); **340A**(x2); 341(x4); 343(x1); 344(x1); 346(x11); 348A(x1); 350(x3); 351(x1); 352(x2); 352A(x1); 353(x1); 354A(x1); **358**(x3); **359**(x6); 359A(x2); **359B**(x1); **360**(x1); 360B(x1); **360C**(x3); 362(x19); 369(x2); 374(x3); 375B(x1); 375C(x5); 379(x1); 380(x10); 389(x1)
Other Sermons (390s–420s) [anti-Donatist works indicated in bold]	397 43 829	*Io. ev. tr.* 2(x6); 3(x13); 5(x15); 7(x10); 8(x12); 10(x2); 11(x3); 12(x11); 13(x4); 14(x3); 15(x10); 16(x2); 17(x1); 18(x1); 19(x5); 20(x1); 21(x2); 22(x3); 23(x2); 25(x3); 26(x4); 27(x1); 29(x1); 30(x12); 31(x1); 33(x8); 34(x9); 35(x3); 36(x3); 37(x2); 38(x5); 39(x13); 40(x12); 41(x13); 42(x26); 43(x3); 45(x9); 46(x8); 47(x2); 48(x2); 50(x4); 52(x1); 54(x7); 56(x2); 57(x5); 58(x10); 59(x1); 60(x1); 61(x1); 63(x3); 64(x1); 66(x1); 69(x6); 70(x2); 71(x1); 74(x2); 80(x1); 81(x3); 83(x1); 85(x1); 89(x1); 90(x7); 91(x2); 92(x5); 93(x1); 94(x1); 95(x1); 96(x12); 97(x5); 98(x3); 99(x2); 100(x4); 105(x1); 108(x16); 111(x1); 112(x1); 113(x1); 115(x21); 117(x2); 122(x2); 123(x3); 124(x5) *Ep. Io. tr.* 1(x3); 3(x7); 4(x5); 5(x10); 6(x7); 7(x7); 8(x2); 10(x1) *En. in Ps.* 3(x3); 4(x6); 5(x11); 6(x3); 7(x5); 8(x5); 9(x4); **10**(x1); 11(x3); 14(x3); 16(x1); **18**(x2); **21**(x2); 24(x3); 25(x13); 26(x5); 27(x1); 29(x5); **30**(x14); 31(x2); **32**(x10); **33**(x4); 34(x5); 35(x12); **36**(x9); 37(x11); 38(x10); 39(x21); 41(x6); 42(x11); 44(x12); 45(x3); 46(x1); 47(x2); 48(x3); 49(x4); 50(x7); 51(x1); 52(x1); 55(x5); 56(x27); **57**(x28);

Genre	# of instances	Works where the term 'veritas' is present
		58(x5); 59(x2); 60(x17); 61(x2); 62(x4); 63(x3); 64(x6); 65(x4); 66(x7); 67(x6); 68(x4); 70(x7); 71(x1); 73(x6); 75(x9); 76(x2); 77(x1); 78(x3); 79(x4); 80(x4); 82(x3); 83(x11); 84(x27); 85(x8); 87(x5); 88(x65); 89(x1); 90(x8); 91(x11); 92(x3); 93(x2); 94(x1); 95(x6); 96(x5); 97(x8); 98(x6); 99(x8); 100(x1); 101(x4); 102(x4); 103(x12); 104(x1); 105(x4); 106(x9); 108(x5); 109(x4); 110(x4); 113(x8); 115(x9); 116(x3); 117(x1); 118(x91); 120(x4); 121(x2); 122(x2); 123(x14); 124(x1); 129(x1); 130(x2); 131(x4); 133(x1); 134(x5); 136(x5); 137(x9); 138(x1); 139(x6); 140(x5); 141(x1); 142(x4); 143(x6); 144(x8); 145(x4); 146(x1); 147(x10); 148(x2); 149(x2)
Philosophical	427	*C. acad.* (x69); *Beata vita* (x12); *Ord.* (x13); *Sol.* (x78); *Imm. anim.* (x10); *Dial.* (x5); *Reth.* (x2); *Anim. quant.* (x14); *Lib. arb.* (x72); *Vera rel.* (x63); *Div. qu.* (x41); *Mend.* (x48)
Doctrinal	727	*Util. cred.* (x27); *Ad Simp.* (x9); *De agone* (x8); *Doctr. chr.* (x62); *Disc. chr.* (x2); *Nat. bon.* (x5); *Cat. rud.* (x14); *De Trin.* (x150); *B. coniug.* (x3); *Virg.* (x12); *F. et op.* (x10); *De Civ. Dei* (x252); *Adult. coniug.* (x4); *C. mend.* (x92); *Ench.* (x16); *F. rerum invis.* (x3); *Haer.* (x11); *Symb. cat.* (x3)
Exegetical	314	*Exp. prop. Rm.* (x2); *Exp. Gal.* (x17); *Ep. Rm. inch.* (x17); *Ques. evan.* (x18); *Adn. Iob.* (x24); *Cons. evan.* (x70); *Gn. litt.* (x63); *Loc.* (x5); *Quaest.* (x42); *C. adv. leg.* (x29); *Cura mort.* (x6); *Dulc. ques.* (x7); *Ques. Mat.* (x9); *Adv. Iud.* (x5)
Dialogues	42	*Mag.* (x8); *De musica* (x34)
Others	244	*Conf.* (x142); *Op. mon.* (x4); *Div. daem.* (x4); *B. uid.* (x5); *Pat.* (x3); *Retract.* (x18); *Spec.* (x67); *Exc. urb.* (x1)

one of his enduring concerns throughout. One is not wrong in this impression. The data can be interpreted any number of ways, but a quick breakdown reveals '*veritas*' is present in every genre of Augustine's works and in each decade of his career. An interesting observation is the statistical connection between the anti-Manichean and anti-Donatist works. Since the works against the Manicheans have an earlier origin, it is interesting to see that the high number of occurrences of *veritas* in those writings is maintained once Augustine becomes fully engaged with the Donatists. Even more interesting is to match the anti-Pelagian works, which carry on the substantial use of the theme. Altogether, there seems to be some observable evidence to show a strong continuity between the anti-Manichean, anti-Donatist, and anti-Pelagian works. It is helpful to keep in mind how Augustine maintained throughout that his opponents were outside the truth, and how his relationships with all three parties moved in the end from being cordial/pastoral to openly bitter and hostile/dismissive as each group failed to 'heed' Augustine's Catholic brand of truth.

A closer look at the presence of the word *veritas* in the anti-Donatist and anti-Pelagian works shows just how comprehensive this theme was throughout both. Amongst Augustine's anti-Donatist works, this theme is presented in each period of the controversy with a total of 563 occurrences (from the first anti-Donatist work: *Ps. c. Don.*, to the last: *C. Gaud.*), further demonstrating the staying power of '*veritas*' in the mission of Augustine: *Ps. c. Don.* (x2); *C. ep. Parm.* (x41); *De bapt.* (x129); *C. litt. Pet.* (x66); *Cresc.* (x139); *Un. bapt.* (x48); *Brev.* (x12); *c. Don.* (x39); *Emer.* (x14); *C. Gaud.* (x43); *Cath. fr.* (x30). Within anti-Donatist letters, the case holds true also: 23(x1); 29(x1); 33(x5); 34(x1); 43(x10); 52(x1); 53(x1); 56(x1); 58(x2); 61(x2); 66(x2); 87(x2); 88(x3); 89(x3); 93(x32); 100(x2); 105(x15); 108(x9); 111(x3); 128(x5); 129(x1); 139(x1); 141(x7); 142(x1); 144(x2); 173(x5); 185(x21); 28*(x1). The presence of '*veritas*' in Augustine's anti-Pelagian sermons only buttresses the importance of the theme: *s.* 4(x6); 10(x7); 37(x1); 46(x9); 47(x5); 71(x13); 88(x3); 90(x5); 129(x1); 137(x4); 159B(x2); 162A(x1); 164(x7); 182(x2); 183(x4); 198(x30); 202(x3); 266(x2); 275(x2); 292(x5); 295(x2); 340A(x2); 358(x3); 359(x6); 359B(x1); 360(x1); 360C(x3).

Augustine's anti-Pelagian controversy, with 600 occurrences (not including anti-Pelagian letters and sermons), is also well-represented when considering the prevalence of the theme of '*veritas*': *Pecc. mer.* (x38); *Spir. et litt.* (x11); *Nat. et gr.* (x19); *Gest. Pel.* (x16); *Gr. et pecc. or.* (x22); *nupt. et conc.* (x13); *An. et or.* (x23); *C. ep. Pel.* (x33); *C. Iul.* (x115); *Gr. et lib. arb.* (x8); *Corrept.* (x10); *Cont.* (x8); *Perf. iust.* (x9); *Praed. sanct.* (x19); *Persev.* (x30); *C. Iul. imp.* (x226). A note should be made of the stronger numerical presence of the theme in the anti-Pelagian works; this is probably explained by the sheer length of these works, which in general were considerably longer than the anti-Donatist works.

The Flesh—Caro/Carnis

Augustine's fascination with 'the flesh' is a topic that has received much attention historically, and rightly so. In all, '*caro*' will appear with *9947 occurrences in 4214 places*, making it undisputedly one of the most expansive and dynamic themes in Augustine's output. This means it was certainly an important topic throughout both controversies and played a major part in forming the way Augustine approached both camps.[66]

TABLE 2 *'Caro/carnis' in Augustine's writings*

Genre	# of instances	Works where the term 'caro/carnis' is present
Anti-Manichean (380s–390s)	626	*Mor. eccl.* (x82); *Gn. adu. Man.* (x24); *Duab. anim.* (x2); *C. Fort.* (x20); *F. et symb.* (x26); *Gn. litt. imp.* (x2); *S. dom. mont.* (x20); *C. Adim.* (x50); *C. ep. Man.* (x4); *C. Faust.* (x341); *C. Fel.* (x22); *C. Sec.* (x32); *C. Prisc.* (x1)
Anti-Arian	104	*C. s. Arrian.* (x37); *Conl. Max.* (x27); *C. Max.* (x40)
Anti-Donatist (390s–420s)	99	*Ps. c. Don.* (x0); *C. ep. Parm.* (x16); *De bapt.* (x20); *C. litt. Pet.* (x23); *Cresc.* (x3); *Un. bapt.* (x1); *Brev.* (x4); *C. Don.* (x2); *Emer.* (x1); *C. Gaud.* (x4); *Cath. fr.* (x15)
Anti-Pelagian (410s–430)	1828	*Pecc. mer.* (x154); *Spir. et litt.* (x24); *Nat. et gr.* (x58); *Gest. Pel.* (x7); *Gr. et pecc. or.* (x26); *Nupt. et conc.* (x94); *An. et or.* (x152); *C. ep. Pel.* (x101); *C. Iul.* (x324); *Gr. lib. arb.* (x19); *Corrept.* (x13); *Cont.* (x117); *Perf. iust.* (x15); *Praed. sanct.* (x21); *Persev.* (x6); *C. Iul. Imp.* (x697)
Letters (390s–420s) [anti-Donatist works indicated in bold]	497	*Ep.* 22(x2); **23**(x3); **29**(x7); 36(x7); 47(x1); **52**(x1); 55(x13); 82(x1); 87(x1); 92(x5); **93**(x8); 95(x1); 98(x3); 102(x9); **111**(x1); 118(x4); 120(x2); 126(x2); 127(x1); **129**(x1); 130(x7); 137(x17); 138(x1); 140(x57); 143(x18); **144**(x1); 145(x3); 147(x16); 148(x6); 149(x15); 150(x1); 151(x1); 155(x3); 157(x4); 164(x39); 166(x19); 167(x1); 169(x4); 171A(x1); 177(x1); 179(x1); 180(x1); 184A(x1); **185**(x1); 186(x8); 187(x22); 188(x1); 190(x16); 194(x4); 196(x29);

66 Paul Rigby, 'Original Sin', in A. Fitzgerald (ed.), *Augustine through the Ages. An Encyclopedia* (Grand Rapids, MI/Cambridge: Wm. Eerdmans Publishing, 1999), 607–14.

TABLE 2 *'Caro/carnis' in Augustine's writings* (cont.)

Genre	# of instances	Works where the term 'caro/carnis' is present
		199(x8); 202A(x2); 205(x40); 211(x2); 217(x2); 219(x2); 220(x3); 224(x1); 228(x5); 229(x1); 236(x2); 237(x2); 238(x2); 243(x4); 262(x4); 263(x1); 264(x4); 264(x1); 266(x1); 1*(x1); 5*(x1); 6*(x15); 20*(x1)
Sermons (390s–420s) [anti-Donatist works indicated in bold]	3299	*s.* 2(x3); 3(x2); **4**(x8); 5(x6); 6(x7); 8(x7); 9(x3); **10**(x4); 11(x1); 12(x3); 13(x1); 15A(x1); 16A(x1); 17(x5); 19(x1); 20(x1); 20A(x2); 20B(x4); 21(x5); 22(x5); 22A(x4); 23A(x2); 24(x1); 25(x6); 25A(x1); 26(x1); 27(x5); 28(x3); 30(x22); 31(x1); 32(x1); 36(x3); **37**(x8); 43(x2); 45(x40); **46**(x5); **47**(x5); 50(x3); 51(x27); 52(x5); 53(x3); 53A(x10); 55(x2); 56(x10); 57(x3); 58(x10); 60A(x2); 61A(x1); 62(x5); 62A(x4); 63B(x3); 64A(x2); 65(x12); 65A(x4); 67(x7); 70(x2); 70A(x1); **71**(x18); 72(x3); 72A(x3); 75(x5); 76(x7); 77(x1); 77A(x4); 78(x2); 79A(x2); 80(x7); 81(x3); 82(x5); 84(x1); 86(x2); 87(x1); **88**(x9); **90**(x4); 90A(x2); 91(x10); 92(x1); 96(x2); 97(x1); 99(x3); 103(x7); 104(x3); 105(x4); 106(x1); 107(x4); 107A(x3); 110(x3); 110A(x6); 112(x13); 113B(x4); 114A(x3); 114B(x5); 116(x9); 117(x5); 119(x20); 121(x7); 124(x15); 125A(x4); 126(x7); 127(x11); 128(x49); **129**(x3); 130(x3); 130A(x3); 131(x4); 132(x8); 132A(x4); 134(x24); 135(x1); 136(x8); 136B(x1); 136C(x3); 138(x3); 139(x1); 142(x1); 143(x6); 144(x1); 145(x1); 145A(x5); 147(x1); 147A(x2); 150(x4); 150A(x3); 151(x12); 152(x35); 153(x22); 154(x31); 154A(x23); 155(x83); 156(x47); 157(x1); 158(x2); 159(x13); 159A(x13); **159B**(x15); 160(x7); 161(x16); 162(x7); **162A**(x1); 162C(x1); 163(x24); 163A(x15); 163B(x1); 165(x1); 166(x1); 167A(x3); 169(x18); 170(x2); 171(x1); 172(x1); 174(x6); 177(x1); 179(x1); 179A(x1); 180(x7); 181(x1); **182**(x21); **183**(x56); 184(x4); 185(x13); 187(x11); 188(x2); 189(x1); 190(x8); 191(x8); 192(x7); 193(x2);

Genre	# of instances	Works where the term 'caro/carnis' is present
		194(x2); 195(x6); 196A(x4); **198**(x30); 201(x1); **202**(x5); 204(x4); 205(x7); 207(x4); 208(x4); 209(x2); 210(x8); 213(x19); 214(x9); 215(x6); 216(x4); 218(x1); 218C(x6); 219(x3); 220(x1); 221(x3); 222(x1); 223A(x2); 223D(x1); 223G(x1); 223I(x1); 223J(x4); 224(x3); 225(x5); 228(x1); 228B(x7); 229(x2); 229B(x1); 229D(x2); 229E(x5); 229F(x1); 229G(x5); 229H(x2); 229I(x3); 229J(x8); 229K(x3); 229N(x1); 229O(x1); 229P(x1); 229S(x1); 229T(x2); 229V(x1); 230(x1); 231(x1); 232(x5); 233(x9); 234(x1); 235(x2); 237(x19); 238(x11); 239(x3); 240(x3); 241(x4); 242(x12); 242A(x10); 243(x3); 244(x3); 245(x3); 246(x4); 247(x2); 250(x2); 252(x2); 253(x3); 254(x1); 255(x7); 256(x9); 257(x3); 258(x9); 260(x2); 260A(x5); 260C(x1); 260E(x2); 261(x8); 262(x5); 264(x40); 265A(x7); 265B(x3); 265C(x2); 265D(x23); 265E(x2); 268(x1); 270(x5); 272(x1); 272A(x2); 272B(x2); 273(x6); 274(x2); **275**(x5); 276(x2); 277(x32); 277A(x1); 280(x5); 283(x1); 284(x2); 287(x5); 288(x6); 289(x9); 290(x7); 291(x7); **292**(x4); 293(x5); 293A(x6); 293B(x3); 293C(x1); 293D(x6); 294(x20); 296(x7); 297(x3); 298(x1); 299(x2); 299A(x3); 299B(x6); 299D(x5); 299E(x3); 299F(x6); 300(x2); 301(x1); 301A(x7); 304(x1); 305(x1); 305A(x12); 306(x1); 3306B(x7); 306C(x4); 306D(x2); 306E(x1); 308A(x1); 309(x3); 310(x1); 311(x1); 312(x2); 313(x1); 313A(x5); 313E(x7); 314(x3); 315(x3); 316(x2); 317(x5); 318(x1); 319(x1); 325(x4); 328(x1); 334(x2); 335A(x4); 335B(x7); 335C(x6); 335D(x10); 335E(x1); 335I(x1); 335J(x6); 335K(x12); 337(x1); 339(x2); **340A**(x1); 341(x25); 341A(x8); 342(x5); 343(x12); 344(x14); 346(x1); 348A(x8); 349(x4); 350(x5); 351(x6); 352(x1); 352A(x1); 353(x6); 354(x3); 354A(x4); **358**(x1); **359**(x7); **359B**(x1); **360**(x2); 360A(x1); 362A(x7); 360B(x6); **360C**(x4); 361(x5); 362(x95); 363(x7); 369(x6); 370(x1);

TABLE 2 *'Caro/carnis' in Augustine's writings* (cont.)

Genre	# of instances	Works where the term 'caro/carnis' is present
		373(x3); 374(x5); 375A(x2); 375B(x28); 375C(x27); 376(x3); 379(x1); 380(x4); 381(x1); 389(x3); 390(x1)
Other Sermons (390s–420s) [anti-Donatist works indicated in bold]	1224 97 1224	*Io. ev. tr.* 1(x5); 2(x21); 3(x14); 5(x3); 7(x6); 8(x12); 9(x10); 10(x13); 11(x15); 12(x6); 13(x12); 14(x10); 15(x24); 16(x5); 17(x1); 18(x13); 19(x15); 20(x12); 21(x7); 22(x1); 23(x4); 25(x5); 26(x23); 27(x43); 30(x4); 31(x5); 32(x2); 34(x10); 35(x3); 36(x14); 37(x13); 38(x2); 40(x4); 41(x18); 42(x18); 43(x8); 44(x4); 45(x4); 46(x1); 47(x43); 48(x4); 49(x15); 50(x4); 53(x2); 54(x1); 55(x1); 57(x3); 59(x1); 60(x2); 61(x2); 64(x7); 66(x3); 69(x10); 72(x1); 73(x2); 74(x1); 75(x4); 76(x1); 76(x1); 78(x8); 79(x4); 80(x2); 81(x1); 82(x1); 84(x2); 86(x1); 87(x1); 89(x1); 91(x2); 93(x1); 94(x6); 95(x3); 97(x1); 98(x6); 99(x1); 100(x2); 101(x2); 103(x1); 104(x1); 105(x7); 108(x6); 109(x4); 110(x2); 111(x4); 112(x1); 117(x1); 118(x2); 119(x1); 120(x1); 121(x3); 122(x3) *Ep. Io. tr.* 1(x17); 2(x17); 3(x4); 4(x4); 5(x4); 6(x34); 7(x7); 8(x5); 9(x6); 10(x7) *En. in Ps.* 1(x1); 3(x5); 4(x1); 6(x4); 7(x2); 8(x5); 9(x1); **10**(x2); 15(x4); 17(x2); **18**(x9); 20(x1); **21**(x9); 24(x1); 25(x1); 26(x20); 27(x2); 28(x1); 29(x20); **30**(x12); 31(x4); **32**(x4); **33**(x25); 34(x14); 35(x4); **36**(x10); 37(x27); 38(x4); 39(x7); 40(x11); 41(x6); 42(x9); 43(x3); 44(x14); 45(x1); 46(x13); 47(x6); 48(x7); 49(x16); 50(x16); 51(x2); 52(x1); 53(x3); 54(x13); 55(x19); 56(x24); **57**(x10); 58(x10); 59(x1); 60(x1); 61(x8); 62(x34); 63(x3); 64(x27); 65(x14); **67**(x19); 68(x17); 69(x5); 70(x19); 71(x10); 72(x6); 73(x8); 74(x3); 75(x19); 76(x2); 77(x18); 78(x8); 79(x6); 80(x3); 81(x5); 82(x3); 83(x20); 84(x12); **85**(x10); 86(x4); 87(x12); **88**(x27); 89(x3); 90(x14); 91(x5); 92(x6); 93(x14); 94(x1); **95**(x1); 96(x9); 97(x18); 98(x22); 99(x2); 100(x2); **101**(x23); 102(x10); 103(x17); 104(x7);

Genre	# of instances	Works where the term 'caro/carnis' is present
		105(x4); 105(x1); 106(x4); 108(x12); 109(x16); 110(x1); 112(x9); 113(x1); 114(x10); 117(x7); 118(x53); 119(x7); 120(x12); 121(x5); 122(x5); 124(x2); 125(x7); 126(x1); 127(x1); 129(x5); 130(x13); 131(x8); 132(x1); 134(x13); 135(x2); 136(x5); 137(x2); 138(x19); 139(x8); 140(x14); 141(x10); 142(x16); 143(x20); 144(x10); 145(x17); 146(x9); 147(x11); 148(x7); 149(x7); 150(x5)
Philosophical	308	*C. acad.* (x69); *Beata vita* (x12); *Ord.* (x13); *Sol.* (x78); *Imm. anim.* (x10); *Dial.* (x5); *Reth.* (x2); *Anim. quant.* (x1); *Lib. arb.* (x8); *Vera rel.* (x24); *Div. qu.* (x82); *Mend.* (x4)
Doctrinal	879	*Util. cred.* (x27); *Ad Simp.* (x9); *De agone* (x22); *Doctr. chr.* (x49); *Disc. chr.* (x5); *Nat. bon.* (x7); *Cat. rud.* (x16); *De Trin.* (x168); *B. coniug.* (x14); *Virg.* (x50); *F. et op.* (x15); *De civ. Dei* (x337); *Adult. coniug.* (x10); *C. mend.* (x0); *Ench.* (x44); *F. rerum invis.* (x3); *Haer.* (x42); *Symb. cat.* (x3)
Exegetical	611	*Exp. prop. Rm.* (x42); *Exp. Gal.* (x63); *Ep. Rm. inch.* (x15); *Ques. evan.* (x15); *Adn. Iob.* (x32); *cons. evan.* (x48); *Gn. litt.* (x186); *Loc.* (x27); *Quaest.* (x77); *C. adu. leg.* (x67); *Cura mort.* (x15); *Dulc. ques.* (x7); *Ques. Mat.* (x5); *Adv. Iud.* (x12)
Dialogues	42	*Mag.* (x8); *De musica* (x34)
Others	281	*Conf.* (x92); *Op. mon.* (x7); *Divin. daem.* (x4); *B. uid.* (x14); *Pat.* (x11); *Retract.* (x52); *Spec.* (x56); *Itil. Ieiun.* (x40); *Exc. Urb.* (x5)

Much like the term *'veritas,' 'caro'* is a major theme for Augustine, and the data demonstrates this conclusively. In all phases of Augustine's career this term is present, although there is a noteworthy disparity between the Donatist and Pelagian controversies. The term is only present 99 times in the anti-Donatist works (not including letters and sermons), whilst it features a gargantuan 1828 times in the anti-Pelagian works (not including the anti-Pelagian letters and sermons). This is evidence that while the term was being born in the anti-Donatist campaign, it was not a particularly intensively used term, as it would become in the Pelagian controversy, a phase better known for Augustine's consideration of the theme. A look at the presence of the term '*caro*' in the anti-Pelagian works is startling: *Pecc. mer.* (x154); *Spir. et litt.* (x24); *Nat. et gr.* (x58); *Gest. Pel.* (x7); *Gr. et pecc. or.* (x26); *Nupt. et conc.* (x94); *An. et or.* (x152); *C. ep. Pel.* (x101); *C. Iul.* (x324); *Gr. lib. arb.* (x19); *Corrept.* (x13); *Cont.* (x117); *Perf. iust.* (x15); *Praed. sanct.* (x21); *Persev.* (x6); *C. Iul. imp.* (x697).

Within the anti-Donatist corpus, even though numerically less in this gestation period, the term '*caro*' is nonetheless spread evenly across the doctrinal writings, sermons, and letters: *Ps. c. Don.* (x0); *C. ep. Parm.* (x16); *De bapt.* (x20); *C. litt. Pet.* (x23); *Cresc.* (x3); *Un. bapt.* (x1); *Brev.* (x4); *C. Don.* (x2); *Emer.* (x1); *C. Gaud.* (x4); *Cath. fr.* (x15); *Ep.* 23(x3); 29(x7); 52(x1); 87(x1); 93(x8); 111(x1); 129(x1); 144(x1); 185(x1); *s.* 4(x8); 10(x4); 37(x8); 46(x5); 47(x5); 88(x9); 90(x4); 129 (x3); 159B(x15); 160(x7); 161(x16); 162(x7); 162A(x1); 182(x21); 183(x56); 198(x30); 201(x1); 202(x5); 292(x4); 340A(x1); 358(x1); 359(x7); 359B(x1); 360(x2); 360C(x4). Even though the presence of '*caro*' in the anti-Donatist works is relatively small given that the term and the theology of 'the flesh' was in its infancy for Augustine at that point, with the term only occasionally used to describe the Donatists as 'carnal,' and never the subject of a prolonged theological discussion, its importance is borne out by considering the significant overlap between the anti-Donatist works, major doctrinal works, and the anti-Pelagian writings. This is perhaps best observed in Augustine's major doctrinal works, which were often influenced by, and influenced the writing of, his polemical works (879 occurrences): *Util. cred.* (x27); *Ad Simp.* (x9); *De agone* (x22); *Doctr. chr.* (x49); *Disc. chr.* (x5); *Nat. bon.* (x7); *Cat. rud.* (x16); *De Trin.* (x168); *B. coniug.* (x14); *Virg.* (x50); *F. et op.* (x15); *De civ. Dei* (x337); *Adult. coniug.* (x10); *C. mend.* (x0); *Ench.* (x44); *F. rerum invis.* (x3); *Haer.* (x42); *Symb. cat.* (x3).

Concupiscence—Concupiscentia

'*Concupiscentia*' was another of Augustine's major themes throughout his career, and it certainly features throughout the Donatist/Pelagian controversies. Altogether there are *1760 occurrences in 915 places* of this term and its variations. Obviously this shows that Augustine was indeed engaged with the theme, and as the examples below show, it was something which he worked with throughout the duration of his career, giving form to many of the theological concepts he initiated early on and pursued well into old age. As a side venture for research, it would be interesting to contrast this data with the findings of Jonathan Yates on this subject.[67]

---

67 Jonathon Yates, 'Was there "Augustinian" Concupiscence in Pre-Augustinian North Africa?' *Augustiniana* 51 (2001), 39–56. Also consult David Hunter, 'Augustine and the Making of Marriage in Roman North Africa', *Journal of Early Christian Studies* 11/1 (2003),

TABLE 3 *'Concupiscentia' in Augustine's writings*

Genre	# of instances	Works where the term 'concupiscentia' is present
Anti-Manichean (380s–390s)	47	*Mor. eccl.* (x7); *Gn. adv. Man.* (x6); *Duab. anim.* (x0); *C. Fort.* (x0); *F et symb.* (x0); *Gn. litt. imp.* (x0); *S. dom. mont.* (x8); *C. Adim.* (x3); *C. ep. Man.* (x0); *C. Faust.* (x20); *C. Fel.* (x3); *C. Sec.* (x0); *C. Prisc.* (x0)
Anti-Arian	2	*C. s. Arrian.* (x2); *Conl. Max.* (x0); *C. Max.* (x0)
Anti-Donatist (390s–420s)	10	*Ps. c. Don.* (x0); *C. ep. Parm.* (x1); *De bapt.* (x3); *C. litt. Pet.* (x3); *Cresc.* (x2); *Un. bapt.* (x0); *Brev.* (x0); *C. Don.* (x0); *Emer.* (x0); *C. Gaud.* (x0); *Cath. fr.* (x1)
Anti-Pelagian (410s–430)	852	*Pecc. mer.* (x27); *Spir. et litt.* (x17); *Nat. et gr.* (x5); *Gest. Pel.* (x6); *Gr. et pecc. or.* (x6); *Nupt. et conc.* (x83); *An. et or.* (x0); *C. ep. Pel.* (x29); *C. Iul.* (x251); *Gr. et lib. arb.* (x14); *Corrept.* (x1); *Cont.* (x37); *Perf. iust.* (x12); *Praed. sanct.* (x0); *Persev.* (x2); *C. Iul. imp.* (x362)
Letters (390s–420s) [anti-Donatist works indicated in bold]	74	*Ep.* 22(x1); **29**(x1); 55(x1); 95(x1); 102(x1); 127(x1); 130(x5); 131(x1); 137(x1); 140(x1); 143(x1); 147(x1); 149(x2); 157(x1); 164(x2); 167(x1); 175(x1); 177(x1); 184(x3); **185**(x1); 186(x1); 187(x4); 194(x3); 196(x6); 211(x1); 220(x7); 228(x1); 2*(x2); 6*(20); 13*(x1)
Sermons (390s–420s) [anti-Donatist works indicated in bold]	337	s. 2(x1); 4(x1); 8(x3); 9(x4); 13(x1); 15(x1); 21(x1); 20B(x3); 26(x1); 30(x3); 32(x1); **37**(x2); 42(x2); 51(x8); 53A(x2); 56(x1); 57(x6); 58(x5); 61(x1); 75(x2); 77A(x14); 88(x4); 96(x4); 98(x1); 99(x1); 108(x1); 110A(x3); 112(x3); 114B(x1); 121(x1); 128(x17); 132(x2); 132(x2); 136(x1); 139A(x1); 143(x1); 145(x3); 149(x2); 151(x19); 152(x5); 153(x26); 154(x19); 155(x24); 156(x1); 159B(x1); 162(x13); 163(x11); 163A(x12); 169(x1); 170(x6); 193(x1); 198(x1); 205(x3); 207(x2); 208(x2); 209(x1); 210(x3); 214(x1); 216(x1); 219(x2); 229D(x1); 229P(x1); 229V(x2); 230(x1); 231(x1);

63–85, and also his *Marriage, Celibacy, and Heresy in Ancient Christianity: The Jovinianist Controversy* (New York: Oxford University Press, 2007); Gerald Bonner, 'Nuptiis et concupiscentia, De', in A. Fitzgerald (ed.), *Augustine through the Ages. An Encyclopedia* (Grand Rapids/Cambridge: Wm. Eerdmans Publishing, 1999), 592–93.

TABLE 3 *'Concupiscentia' in Augustine's writings* (cont.)

Genre	# of instances	Works where the term 'concupiscentia' is present
		233(x2); 246(x1);250(x1); 254(x1); 260A(x1); 271(x1); 273(x1); 278(x1); 283(x2); 284(x2); 287(x1); 298(x2); 299D(x1); 302(x1); 3061(x1); 306C(x2); 311(x2); 313A(x7); 335B(x3); 335C(x1); 335J(x5); 335K(x4); 341(x2); 341A(x1); 343(x2); 345(x1); 346B(x1); 348A(x1); 351(x1); 354A(x4); 360(x3); 360B(x2); 362(x2); 363(x1); 367(x1)
Other Sermons (390s–420s) [anti-Donatist works indicated in bold]	20	*Io. ev. tr.* 3(x2); 10(x1); 14(x2); 30(x1); 41(x7); 44(x1); 60(x1); 73(x3); 107(x1); 118(x1)
	6	*Ep. Io. tr.* 1(x2); 4(x2); 7(x1); 10(x1)
	136	*En. in Ps.* 6(x1); 7(x2); 8(x3); 9(x2); **21**(x1); 25(x1); 26(x2); **30**(x1); **32**(x1); 35(x9); 39(x2); 41(x1); 44(x1); 50(x2); 54(x1); **57**(x16); 64(x1); 65(x1); **67**(x2); 70(x1); 72(x1); 75(x2); 77(x4); 80(x1); 83(x3); 84(x2); 89(x1); 93(x5); 96(x2); 100(x1); **101**(x2); 105(x3); 106(x4); 118(x37); 120(x1); 127(x2); 136(x7); 139(x1); 141(x1); 143(x1); **145**(x2); 149(x2)
Philosophical	15	*C. acad.* (x0); *Beata vita* (x0); *Ord.* (x0); *Sol.* (x0); *Imm. anim.* (x0); *Dial.* (x0); *Reth.* (x2); *Anim. quant.* (x0); *Lib. arb.* (x1); *Vera rel.* (x7); *Div. qu.* (x4); *Mend.* (x1)
Doctrinal	102	*Util. cred.* (x0); *Ad Simp.* (x25); *De agone* (x0); *Doctr. chr.* (x13); *Disc. chr.* (x0); *Nat. bon.* (x3); *Cat. rud.* (x1); *De Trin.* (x6); *B. coniug.* (x6); *Virg.* (x2); *F. et op.* (x8); *De civ. Dei* (x21); *Adult. coniug.* (x3); *C. mend.* (x1); *Ench.* (x10); *F. rerum invis.* (x0); *Haeres.* (x3); *Symb. cat.* (x0)
Exegetical	60	*Exp. prop. Rm.* (x13); *Exp. Gal.* (x7); *Ep. Rm. inch.* (x0); *Ques. evan.* (x3); *Adn. Iob.* (x7); *Cons. evan.* (x1); *Gn. litt.* (x14); *Loc.* (x1); *Quaest.* (x6); *C. adu. leg.* (x7); *Cura mort.* (x0); *Dulc. ques.* (x1); *Ques. Mat.* (x0); *Adv. Iud.* (x0)
Dialogues	3	*Mag.* (x0); *De musica* (x3)
Others	68	*Conf.* (x17); *Op. mon.* (x4); *Divin. daem.* (x0); *B. vid.* (x5); *Pat.* (x6); *Retract.* (x17); *Spec.* (x18); *Exc. urb.* (x1)

Much like the example of the theme of '*caro*', that of '*concupiscentia*' presents another clear proof of development and continuity in the thought of Augustine. The term only surfaces 10 times in anti-Donatist works, while it is present 852 times in the anti-Pelagian works. Even the 102 occurrences of the theme in the major doctrinal works are meager compared with their presence in the anti-Pelagian works. Again, as in the case of '*caro*', this theme is clearly more evident in the anti-Pelagian writings since it was amongst the foremost themes in the course of that controversy.

A systematic break-down is as follows: (anti-Donatist works) *Ps. c. Don.* (x0); *C. ep. Parm.* (x1); *De bapt.* (x3); *C. litt. Pet.* (x3); *Cresc.* (x2); *Un. bapt.* (x0); *Brev.* (x0); *C. Don.* (x0); *Emer.* (x0); *C. Gaud.* (x0); *Cath. fr.* (x1); (anti-Pelagian works): *Pecc. mer.* (x27); *Spir. et litt.* (x17); *Nat. et gr.* (x5); *Gest. Pel.* (x6); *Gr. et pecc. or.* (x6); *Nupt. et conc.* (x83); *An. et or.* (x0); *C. ep. Pel.* (x29); *C. Iul.* (x251); *Gr. et lib. arb.* (x14); *Corrept.* (x1); *Cont.* (x37); *Perf. iust.* (x12); *Praed. sanct.* (x0); *Persev.* (x2); *C. Iul. imp.* (x362); and major doctrinal works: *Util. cred.* (x0); *Ad Simp.* (x25); *De agone* (x0); *Doctr. chr.* (x13); *Disc. chr.* (x0); *Nat. bon.* (x3); *Cat. rud.* (x1); *De Trin.* (x6); *B. coniug.* (x6); *Virg.* (x2); *F. et op.* (x8); *De civ. Dei* (x21); *Adult. coniug.* (x3); *C. mend.* (x1); *Ench.* (x10); *F. rerum invis.* (x0); *Haeres.* (x3); *Symb. cat.* (x0).

Pride—Superbia

As soon as Augustine engaged with the Donatists as a young presbyter he was left disappointed about a lack of *camaraderie* and what he considered to be their rejection of the Catholic truth. A criticism of their 'pride', caused by humanity's sinful inclination was born, and would surface repeatedly with *1278 occurrences in 896 places.*

TABLE 4 *'Superbia' in Augustine's writings*

Genre	# of instances	Works where the term 'superbia' is present
Anti-Manichean (380s–390s)	42	*Mor. eccl.* (x4); *Gn. adu. Man.* (x17); *Duab. anim.* (x0); *C. Fort.* (x0); *F. et symb.* (x1); *Gn. litt. imp.* (x0); *S. dom. mont.* (x1); *C. Adim.* (x1); *C. ep. Man.* (x2); *C. Faust.* (x13); *C. Fel.* (x0); *C. Sec.* (x3); *C. Prisc.* (x0)
Anti-Arian	0	*C. s. Arrian.* (x0); *Conl. Max.* (x0); *C. Max.* (x0)
Anti-Donatist (390s–420s)	50	*Ps. c. Don.* (x1); *C. ep. Parm.* (x17); *De bapt.* (x9); *C. litt. Pet.* (x11); *Cresc.* (x6); *Un. bapt.* (x0); *Brev.* (x0); *C. Don.* (x0); *S. Caes.* (x1); *Emer.* (x1); *C. Gaud.* (x3); *Cath. fr.* (x1)

TABLE 4 *'Superbia' in Augustine's writings* (cont.)

Genre	# of instances	Works where the term 'superbia' is present
Anti-Pelagian (410s–430)	87	*Pecc. mer.* (x9); *Spir. et litt.* (x6); *Nat. et gr.* (x18); *Gest. Pel.* (x0); *Gr. et pecc. or.*(x0); *Nupt. et conc.* (x1); *An. et or.* (x0); *C. ep. Pel.* (x8); *C. Iul.* (x15); *Gr. et lib. arb.* (x2); *Corrept.* (x3); *Cont.* (x3); *Perf. iust.* (x1); *Praed. sanct.* (x2); *Persev.* (x0); *C. Iul. imp.* (x19)
Letters (390s–420s) [anti-Donatist works indicated in bold]	64	*Ep.* 22(x1); 27(x1); 31(x1); **43**(x2); 48(x1); 60(x1); 69(x1); **93**(x3); **100**(x1); 102(x2); **105**(x4); 118(x3); 130(x1); 137(x1); 140(x15); 149(x1); 153(x1); 155(x3); 157(x6); 175(x1); **185**(x1); 194(x3); 196(x1); 199(x2); 208(x1); 232(x4); 266(x1); 4*(x1)
Sermons (390s–420s) [anti-Donatist works indicated in bold]	299	*s.* 1(x1); 3(x3); **4**(x7); 9(x1); 12(x1); 14(x2); 16B(x1); 18(x1); 20A(x2); 22(x1); 26(x1); 29A(x1); 30(x1); 32(x4); 33A(x2); 36(x2); 39(x2); **46**(x5); 50(x2); 51(x1); 53A(x2); 54(x1); 58(x1); 61(x2); 62(x3); 66(x1); 67(x1); 70A(x3); 72A(x3); 77(x8); 77A(x1); 85(x2); **88**(x1); 91(x1); 97(x1); 100(x1); 101(x1); 111(x1); 112(x3); 113A(x2); 113B(x3); 114A(x1); 114B(x2); 115(x1); 123(x4); 124(x1); 125(x4); 136(x1); 141(x1); 142(x5); 150(x1); 156(x2); 159B(x14); 160(x1); 162(x2); 162A(x2); 163(x4); 166(x1); 169(x1); 174(x1); 175(x2); 177(x1); 181(x2); 185(x1); 188(x1); 197(x35); 200(x1); 211(x1); 218C(x1); 216(x2); 229A(x2); 229G(x2); 229P(x1); 250(x1); 255(x1); 259(x1); 261(x3); 263(x1); 269(x1); 270(x2); 272B(x1); 274(x1); 284(x2); 287(x1); 289(x5); 290(x3); **292**(x3); 293(x1); 293A(x1); 293B(x1); 293D(x1); 293E(x1); 299D(x1); 299E(x2); 301(x2); 304(x1); 308A(x1); 313A(x2); 323(x1); 335J(x2); 339(x1); 340A(x12); 341(x3); 341B(x1); 342(x1); 346B(x5); 348(x3); 350B(x1); 350C(x1); 351(x2); 353(x2); 354(x19); 360B(x10); 362(x1); 363(x2); 369(x1); 374(x2); 379(x1); 380(x2); 392(x2)
Other Sermons (390s–420s) [anti-Donatist works indicated in bold]	39 77 329	*Io. ev. tr.* 1(x4); 2(x1); 3(x1); 4(x1); (x6); 12(x2); 17(x1); 22(x1); 23(x1); 25(x15); 41(x1); 53(x1); 55(x1); 95(x2); 124(x1) *Ep. Io. tr.* 1(x1); 2(x1); 4(x1); 7(x1); 8(x22); 10(x1) *En. in Ps.* 1(x5); 2(x2); 3(x1); 6(x1); 7(x4); 8(x3);

Genre	# of instances	Works where the term 'superbia' is present
		9(x1); **10**(x3); 12(x1); 15(x1); 17(x2); 18(x9); 19(x1); 21(x1); 23(x1); 24(x2); 25(x1); 29(x2); 30(x15); 31(x3); **32**(x2); **33**(x8); 35(x19); **36**(x1); 37(x1); 38(x2); 41(x1); 46(x1); 47(x5); 48(x1); 50(x1); 52(x1); 53(x1); 54(x6); 55(x4); **57**(x8); 58(x29); 61(x3); 65(x4); **67**(x3); 68(x4); 70(x3); 71(x1); 72(x6); 73(x12); 74(x2); 75(x4); 77(x3); 78(x1); 81(x2); 82(x2); **85**(x8); **88**(x6); 90(x5); 91(x2); 91(x1); 92(x1); 93(x3); 94(x1); **95**(x1); 96(x1); 97(x1); 100(x5); **101**(x4); 102(x2); 103(x4); 106(x5); 110(x1); 111(x1); 112(x6); 118(x14); 119(x1); 120(x9); 121(x3); 122(x1); 124(x3); 126(x2); 130(x6); 131(x3); 134(x3); 136(x2); 137(x1); 138(x5); 139(x4); 140(x1); 141(x1); 142(x1); 143(x1); **145**(x3); 146(x2); **147**(x4); 148(x1)
Philosophical	30	*C. acad.* (x1); *Beata vita* (x1); *Ord.* (x1); *Sol.* (x0); *Imm. anim.* (x0); *Dial.* (x0); *Reth.* (x0); *Anim. quant.* (x0); *Lib. arb.* (x7); *Vera rel.* (x13); *Div. qu.* (x7); *Mend.* (x0)
Doctrinal	116	*Util. cred.* (x2); *Ad Simp.* (x0); *De agone* (x3); *Doctr. chr.* (x11); *Disc. chr.* (x1); *Nat. bon.* (x0); *Cat. rud.* (x9); *De Trin.* (x7); *B. coniug.* (x1); *Virg.* (x21); *F. et op.* (x0); *Civ. Dei* (x53); *Adult. coniug.* (x0); *C. mend.* (x0); *Ench.* (x6); *F. rerum invis.* (x1); *Haer.* (x0); *Symb. cat.* (x0); *Util.* *Ieiun.* (x1)
Exegetical	84	*Exp. prop. Rm.* (x4); *Exp. Gal.* (x12); *Ep. Rm. inch.* (x1); *Ques. evan.* (x0); *Adn. Iob.* (x17); *Cons. evan.* (x13); *Gn. litt.* (x30); *Loc.* (x2); *Quaest.* (x11); *C. adu. leg.* (x1); *Cura mort.* (x0); *Dulc. ques.* (x0); *Ques. Mat.* (x2); *Adv. Iud.* (x1)
Dialogues	9	*Mag.* (x0); *De musica* (x9)
Others	42	*Conf.* (x15); *Op. mon.* (x5); *Divin. daem.* (x1); *B. uid.* (x2); *Pat.* (x0); *Retract.* (x1); *Spec.* (x17); *Exc. urb.* (x1)

Augustine often discussed the theme of 'pride' in a polemical context and the evidence supports this trend. The term was used 42 times against Manicheans, 50 times against Donatists, 87 times against Pelagians, and was further deployed 116 times in the major doctrinal works. An important note is that this term features relatively more often in Augustine's anti-Donatist letters. This is a clear indication that *superbia* was a favourite term for Augustine when pitted in direct rhetorical/polemical combat with his most dreaded foes.

A breakdown of the presence of this term is as follows: (anti-Manichean sources) *Mor. eccl.* (x4); *Gn. adu. Man.* (x17); *Duab. anim.* (x0); *C. Fort.* (x0); *F. et symb.* (x1); *Gn. litt. imp.* (x0); *S. dom. mont.* (x1); *C. Adim.* (x1); *C. ep. Man.* (x2); *C. Faust.* (x13); *C. Fel.* (x0); *C. Sec.* (x3); *C. Prisc.* (x0); (anti-Donatist): *Ps. c. Don.* (x1); *C. ep. Parm.* (x17); *De bapt.* (x9); *C. litt. Pet.* (x11); *Cresc.* (x6); *Un. bapt.* (x0); *Brev.* (x0); *C. Don.* (x0); *S. Caes.* (x1); *Emer.* (x1); *C. Gaud.* (x3); *Cath. fr.* (x1); (anti-Donatist letters, x64): *Ep.* 43(x2); 93(x3); 100(x1); 105(x4); 185(x1); (anti-Pelagian writings):*Pecc. mer.* (x9); *Spir. et litt.* (x6); *Nat. et gr.* (x18); *Gest. Pel.* (x0); *Gr. et pecc. or.*(x0); *Nupt. et conc.* (x1); *An. et or.* (x0); *C. ep. Pel.* (x8); *C. Iul.* (x15); *Gr. et lib. arb.* (x2); *Corrept.* (x3); *Cont.* (x3); *Perf. iust.* (x1); *Praed. sanct.* (x2); *Persev.* (x0); *C. Iul. imp.* (x19); (major doctrinal works): *Util. cred.* (x2); *Ad Simp.* (x0); *De agone* (x3); *Doctr. chr.* (x11); *Disc. chr.* (x1); *Nat. bon.* (x0); *Cat. rud.* (x9); *De Trin.* (x7); *B. coniug.* (x1); *Virg.* (x21); *F. et op.* (x0); *Civ. Dei* (x53); *Adult. coniug.* (x0); *C. mend.* (x0); *Ench.* (x6); *F. rerum invis.* (x1); *Haer.* (x0); *Symb. cat.* (x0); *Util. Ieiun.* (x1).

Grace—Gratia

Coming in with *6921 occurrences in 3661 places*, 'grace' is undoubtedly another of the most significant concepts in the work of Augustine, a pervasive fascination that he nurtured throughout his career. As will become even more clear in the following chapter, '*gratia*' was at the forefront in the Donatist and Pelagian controversies, and it was in those campaigns where the proper form for 'grace' was given, as Augustine had to adjust his ideas on the subject based on the circumstances of the polemic.[68]

An interesting addition to Augustine's crafting of '*gratia*' is the way he integrated the theme into his appropriation of Cyprian. In all of his works, there are 281+/– situations where he speaks of 'Cyprian' and '*gratia*' jointly. This impressive number reveals that Augustine's discussion of grace was certainly conditioned in part by the polemical context of the Donatist and Pelagian

68 Consult Anthony Dupont and Matthew Gaumer, '*Gratia Dei, Gratia Sacramenti.* Grace in Augustine of Hippo's Anti-Donatist Writings', *Ephemerides Theologicae Lovanienses* 86/4 (2010), 307–29.

TABLE 5 *'Gratia' in Augustine's writings*

Genre	# of instances	Works where the term 'gratia' is present
Anti-Manichean (380s–390s)	193	*Mor. eccl.* (x13); *Gn. adu. Man.* (x2); *duab. anim.* (x0); *C. Fort.* (x7); *F. et symb.* (x2); *Gn. litt. imp.* (x2); *S. dom. mont.* (x21); *C. Adim.* (x5); *C. ep. Man.* (x5); *C. Faust.* (x120); *C. Fel.* (x8); *C. Sec.* (x8); *C. Prisc.* (x0)
Anti-Arian	57	*C. s. Arrian.* (x12); *Conl. Max.* (x15); *C. Max.* (x30)
Anti-Donatist (390s–420s)	131	*Ps. c. Don.* (x0); *C. ep. Parm.* (x9); *De bapt.* (x44); *C. litt. Pet.* (x21); *Cresc.* (x17); *Un. bapt.* (x2); *Brev.* (x7); *C. Don.* (x15); *S. Caes.* (x3); *Emer.* (x2); *C. Gaud.* (x1); *Cath. fr.* (x10)
Anti-Pelagian (410s–430)	2154	*Pecc. mer.* (x113); *Spir. et litt.* (x116); *Nat. et gr.* (x89); *Gest. Pel.* (x153); *Gr. et pecc. or.* (x178); *Nupt. et conc.* (x38); *An. et or.* (x28); *C. ep. Pel.* (x220); *C. Iul.* (x220); *Gr. et lib. arb.* (x135); *Corrept.* (x71); *Cont.* (x13); *Perf. iust.* (x33); *Praed. sanct.* (x99); *Persev.* (x112); *C. Iul. imp.* (x536)
Letters (390s–420s) [anti-Donatist works indicated in bold]	959	*Ep.* 3(x1); 7(x2); 20(x3); 22(x3); 27(x3); **29**(x2); 31(x3); **34**(x1); 35(x1); 38(x1); 40(x3); 41(x4); 45(x1); 49(x2X); 54(x1); 55(x6); **58**(x2); 71(x3); 73(x1); 80(x1); 82(x23); 92A(x1); **93**(x14); 95(x1); 97(x1); 98(x8); 99(x1); 101(x2); 102(x6); 104(x2); **105**(x3); 118(x1); 120(x2); 124(x2); 125(x1); 126(x5); 127(x2); **128**(x2); **129**(x1); 130(x5); 131(x2); 137(x7); 138(x2); 140(x67); **141**(x1); 143(x1); **144**(x1); 145(x7); 147(x14); 149(x13); 151(x5); 153(x4); 155(x5); 157(x64); 162(x1); 164(x1); 166(x14); 167(x7); 169(x4); 171A(x1); 173A(x1); 175(x12); 176(x8); 177(x50); 178(x5); 179(x17); 180(x2); **185**(x6); 186(x90); 187(x17); 188(x15); 189(x2); 190(x22); 191(x4); 193(x2); 194(x89); 196(x14); 199(x3); 202A(x3); 205(x3); 208(x1); 210(x1); 211(x3); 213(x1); 214(x12); 215(x29); 215A(x1); 217(x70); 218(x2); 227(x2); 228(x1); 237(x1); 238(x1); 241(x1); 242(x1); 243(x1); 246(x1); 247(x1); 248(x1); 250(x1); 256(x1); 257(x2); 258(x2); 268(x1); 1A*(x1); 2*(x4); 6*(x1); 18*(x1); **28***(x1)

TABLE 5 *'Gratia' in Augustine's writings* (cont.)

Genre	# of instances	Works where the term 'gratia' is present
Sermons (390s–420s) [anti-Donatist works indicated in bold]	1026	*s.* 2(x1); **4**(x2); 5(x1); 6(x1); 7(x1); 8(x6); 9(x3); **10**(x17); 14(x1); 16A(x10); 16B(x6); 20(x1); 20B(x3); 21(x2); 22A(x1); 23(x6); 23A(x6); 23B(x6); 24(x5); 25(x3); 26(x42); 27(x1); 28A(x4); 29A(x1); 29B(x1); 30(x8); 32(x17); 33A(x1); **37**(x4); 38(x2); 43(x2); **46**(x4); **47**(x2); 51(x6); 52(x2); 53(x4); 56(x1); 57(x1); 59(x2); 60A(x2); 61(x1); 61A(x3); 62(x2); 63B(x1); 65A(x1); 67(x6); 68(x5); 70(x1); 70A(x1); **71**(x7); 72(x1); 72A(x7); 75(x1); 76(x8); 77(x1); 77B(x1); 79(x1); 80(x1); 81(x6); 84(x5); 87(x1); **88**(x1); 89(x2); **90**(x2); 90A(x1); 91(x1); 94A(x1); 96(x2); 97A(x1); 99(x4);100(x14); 101(x3); 104(x1); 105(x2); 107(x1); 109(x1); 110(x3); 110A(x4); 111(x3); 112(x1); 112A(x4); 113A(x5); 114(x1); 114A(x3); 114B(x2); 115(x11); 117(x2); 120(x1); 121(x1); 124(x1); 125(x7); 125A(x1); 127(x1); **129**(x1); 130(x1); 130A(x3); 131(x22); 132(x1); 132A(x2); 132A(x1); 133(x2); 134(x1); 135(x1); 136(x7); 136A(x2); 136B(x3); **137**(x2); 138(x2); 139(x4); 140(x1); 141(x4); 142(x1); 143(x4); 144(x3); 145(x13); 145A(x1); 149(x4); 150(x3); 151(x4); 152(x)6; 153(x1); 154(x10); 154A(x3); 155(x6); 156(x16); 157(x1); 158(x1); 159(x2); **159B**(x4); 160(x3); 161(x1); **162A**(x2); 162C(x1); 163(x16); 163B(x4); 165(x8); 166(x3); 168(x6); 169(x6); 170(x6); 172(x1); 174(x6); 176(x10); 177(x3); 178(x2); 179(x1); 179A(x3); 180(x1); 181(x1); **182**(x2); **183**(x5); 185(x5); 188(x1); 190(x1); 192(x1); 193(x2); 196A(x3); **198**(x9); 199(x1); 200(x2); 203(x6); 204(x1); 210(x3); 212(x3); 213(x2); 214(x2); 215(x1); 216(x3); 218(x2); 218C(x2); 221(x2); 222(x1); 223(x1); 223A(x1); 223I(x1); 223K(x1); 224(x3); 227(x3); 228B(x4); 229(x1); 229A(x5); 229C(x3); 229D(x1); 229E(x1); 229F(x1); 229G(x3); 229H(x1); 229I(x4); 229M(x1); 229O(x1); 229U(x1); 229V(x2); 234(x1); 235(x1); 236(x1);

Genre	# of instances	Works where the term 'gratia' is present
		239(x3); 241(x3); 242(x1); 242A(x1); 245(x1); 246(x3); 248(x1); 250(x4); 254(x2); 255(x1); 256(x1); 258(x1); 259(x2); 260A(x1); 260C(x2); 260D(x1); 260E(x1); 261(x4); 263A(x3); 265B(x2); 265D(x3); 265E(x1); **266**(x7); 267(x2); 269(x1); 270(x14); 271(x1); 272(x1); 272B(x8); 273(x1); 277(x2); 281(x1); 283(x10); 284(x1); 285(x3); 289(x4); 290(x10); 291(x4); **292**(x6); 293(x7); 293A(x3); 293B(x3); 293C(x4); 293D(x3); 293E(x1); 294(x5); **295**(x1); 296(x1); 297(x11); 298(x9); 299(x3); 299A(x2); 299B(x8); 299C(x7); 299E(x1); 299F(x2); 301(x2); 301A(x1); 305(x1); 305A(x1); 306A(x2); 306B(x5); 306C(x2); 306E(x4); 308A(x2); 309(x2); 311(x1); 312(x1); 313(x1); 313A(x1); 313B(x1); 313C(x3); 313D(x3); 315(x2); 316(x1); 322(x2); 323(x3); 328(x1); 329(x1); 334(x1); 335A(x1); 335B(x3); 335E(x5); 335G(x1); 335I(x2); 335K(x6); **340A**(x2); 341(x1); 343(x1); 348(x1); 348A(x23); 350B(x1); 351(x5); 352(x3); 352(x3); 352A(x3); 353(x1); 354(x1); 354A(x1); 356(x3); 359A(x2); **359B**(x1); **360**(x3); 360A(x6); 360B(x2); **360C**(x3); 361(x1); 362(x6); 363(x6); 373(x2); 374(x3); 375B(x1); 375C(x5); 376A(x2); 379(x2); 380(x2); 381(x3); 389(x1); 392(x2)
Other Sermons (390s–420s) [anti-Donatist works indicated in bold]	254 17 760	*Io. ev. tr.* 2(x7); 3(x57); 4(x4); 5(x2); 6(x4); 7(x1); 8(x2); 10(x3); 12(x4); 13(x4); 14(x13); 15(x2); 17(x3); 19(x1); 20(x1); 21(x6); 22(x2); 23(x4); 24(x2); 25(x3); 26(x3); 27(x3); 28(x2); 29(x2); 30(x1); 34(x1); 35(x1); 37(x1); 38(x1); 40(x1); 41(x4); 42(x1); 44(x1); 46(x1); 48(x3); 49(x7); 50(x1); 52(x2); 53(x3); 54(x4); 55(x2); 62(x2); 73(x2); 74(x4); 75(x1); 77(1); 79(x2); 81(x3); 82(x13); 83(x1); 84(x1); 86(x9); 87(x4); 90(x1); 92(x3); 93(x1); 95(x1); 96(x1); 98(x2); 100(x1); 103(x1); 105(x1); 107(x1); 108(x1); 110(x4); 111(x7); 115(x3); 118(x3); 121(x1); 122(x7); 124(x2)

TABLE 5 *'Gratia' in Augustine's writings* (cont.)

Genre	# of instances	Works where the term 'gratia' is present
		Ep. Io. tr. 1(x3); 4(x4); 5(x1); 6(x4); 8(x4); 9(x1) *En. in Ps.* 3(x2); 5(x2); 6(x1); 7(x1); 8(x1); **10**(x1); 12(x1); 17(x1); **18**(x8); **21**(x3); 23(x1); 24(x1); 25(x1); 26(x4); 29(x4); **30**(x17); 31(x25); **32**(x5); 35(x4); **36**(x10); 37(x1); 38(x4); 39(x8); 40(x1); 41(x1); 42(x3); 43(x2); 44(x26); 45(x4); 46(x2); 47(x5); 48(x4); 49(x21); 50(x3); 52(x1); 53(x4); 54(x4); 55(x3); 56(x2); **57**(x3); 58(x6); 59(x3); 61(x1); 62(x4); 64(x2); 65(x14); 66(x4); **67**(x38); 68(x6); 69(x2); 70(x51); 71(x12); 72(x3); 73(x7); 75(x3); 77(x24); 78(x3); 79(x1); 80(x1); 81(x6); 83(x20); 84(x3); **85**(x7); 86(x1); 87(x17); **88**(x10); 89(x3); 90(x3); 91(x2); 93(x10); 94(x4); **95**(x1); 96(x1); 97(x1); 98(x2); 99(x1); 100(x2); **101**(x4); 102(x20); 103(x27); 103(x1); 104(x3); 105(x3); 106(x12); 108(x4); 109(x5); 110(x3); 111(x3); 112(x4); 113(x4); 115(x3); 117(x3); 118(x67); 121(x1); 122(x3); 123(x2); 124(x3); 125(x1); 126(x1); 127(x1); 129(x1); 130(x9); 131(x2); 132(x8); 133(x1); 134(x10); 135(x1); 136(x2); 137(x3); 138(x6); 139(x2); 140(x7); 142(x9); 143(x19); 144(x16); **145**(x3); 146(x6); **147**(x5); 148(x1); 149(x3); 150(x2)
Philosophical	89	*C. acad.* (x9); *Beata vita* (x2); *Ord.* (x3); *Sol.* (x4); *Imm. anim.* (x2); *Dial.* (x2); *Reth.* (x1); *Anim. quant.* (x1); *Lib. arb.* (x10); *Vera rel.* (x13); *Div. qu.* (x38); *Mend.* (x4)
Doctrinal	417	*Gramm.* (x1); *Util. cred.* (x8); *Ad Simp.* (x80); *De agone* (x1); *Doctr. chr.* (x31); *Disc. chr.* (x0); *Nat. bon.* (x0); *Cat. rud.* (x5); *De Trin.* (x67); *B. coniug.* (x2); *Virg.* (x19); *F. et op.* (x16); *Civ. Dei* (x117); *Adult. coniug.* (x3); *C. mend.* (x2); *Ench.* (x58); *F. rerum invis.* (x2); *Util. Ieiun* (x5); *Haer.* (x6); *Symb. cat.* (x0)
Exegetical	385	*Exp. prop. Rm.* (x60); *Exp. Gal.* (x58); *Ep. Rm. inch.* (x48); *Ques. evan.* (x18); *Adn. Iob.* (x26); *Cons. evan.* (x0); *Gn. litt.* (x61); *Loc.* (x2); *Quaest.* (x78);

Genre	# of instances	Works where the term 'gratia' is present
		C. adu. leg. (x25); *Cura mort.* (x1); *Dulc. ques.* (x5); *Ques. Mat.* (x0); *Adv. Iud.* (x3)
Dialogues	11	*Mag.* (x0); *De musica* (x11)
Others	274	*Conf.* (x55); *Op. mon.* (x15); *Divin. daem.* (x0); *B. vid.* (x13); *Pat.* (x15); *Retract.* (x79); *Spec.* (x95); *Exc. urb.* (x2)

controversies. It also means that there is a mutual interplay between the terms, as Augustine used both not only to advance the rightfulness of his claims, but to enhance the relative authority of Cyprian and the importance of grace for Christian theology.[69] This combination gave rise to a number of clever word concoctions: '*Cyprianus...exempli gratita*' (*Doct. Chr.* 4,45); '*Cyprianus...gratia praeminet*' (*De bapt.* 2,2); '*Copiae gratiarum*' (*De bapt.* 4,8); '*auctoritatem Cypriani tanti habeant—Trinitas immortalis est cuius gratia consecratur ecclesia et gratia Dei et effuse pro ea sanguine saluatoris*' (*Brev.* 3,20).

A quantitative analysis reveals that along with '*veritas*' and '*caro*', '*gratia*' belongs in an elite category among Augustine's central theological themes. The 6921 occurrences are not evenly spread out across his literary corpus. Instead, we see the same trend as with *veritas* and *caro*: the theme is clustered in specific areas, in this case in the anti-Pelagian campaign where it was used to support the theological and polemical attacks Augustine was deploying. Furthermore, there is again considerable evidence to show an overlap between anti-Donatist (131) and anti-Pelagian (2154) writings through the medium

69 *Doct. Chr.* 4,45(x2); 4,47(x2); *Conf.* 5,15(x2); *De bapt.* 1,29(x2); 2,2(x7); 2,3(x5); 3,4(x4); 3,5(x4); 3,6(x4); 3,7; 3,17(x5); 4,8(x4); 4,19; 4,20; 5,13(x2); 5,14(x2); 6,2(x2); 6,3(x5); 6,24(x2); 6,33; 6,36; 6,49; 6,50(x2); 6,68; 6,69; 6,79; 6,80(x2); 6,87; 7,1; 7,51; 7,54; 7,55; *Cresc.* 3,34; 3,35; *Un. bapt.* 22(x3); *f. et op.* 49(x2); *Brev.* 3,20(x4); *C. Don.* 28(x2); *Civ. Dei.* 8,27(x2); *Gest. Pel.* 25; 26; 4,21; *C. ep. Pel.* 4,21(x3); 4,23(x2); 4,24; 4,25(x2); 4,26(x3); 4,32; 4,33; 4,34; *C. Iul.* 1,6(x3); 1,22(x3); 2,5(x5); 2,8(x3); 2,9(x2); 2,24; 2,25(x2); 2,29(x2); 2,30; 2,32; 2,33(x2); 2,34(x2); 3,32(x3); 3,33; *Gr. et lib. arb.* 26; 27(x3); 28(x3); *Corrept.* 12(x3); *Retract.* 2,1(x3); *Praed. sanct.* 7(x6); 8(x4); 15(x3); 16; 25; 26; 27(x3); 28; *Persev.* 3; 4(x4); 36(x4); 47; 48(x4); 49(x4); 54(x3); 55(x3); *C. Iul. Imp.* 1,59(x2); 1,72(x6); 2,136; 2,164(x3); 4,113; 4,114; *Ep.* 93,47(x2); 98,2; 98,3; 140,13; 140,14; 166,23; 166,24(x2); 215,3(x5); 217,5; 217,6; *s.* 294,19(x6); 309,5(x2); 309,6(x5); 310,1; 312,2; 312,3(x6); 313,4; 313,5; 313A,4(x2); 313C,2(x3); 313D,4(x9); 313E,1(x4); 313E,6(x4); 313E,7(x5); 359B,5(x2).

of major doctrinal works (417). A breakdown of each category is as follows: (anti-Donatist) *Ps. c. Don.* (x0); *C. ep. Parm.* (x9); *De bapt.* (x44); *C. litt. Pet.* (x21); *Cresc.* (x17); *Un. bapt.* (x2); *Brev.* (x7); *C. Don.* (x15); *S. Caes.* (x3); *Emer.* (x2); *C. Gaud.* (x1); *Cath. fr.* (x10); (anti-Donatist letters): *Ep.* 29(x2); 34(x1); 58(x2); 93(x14); 128(x2); 129(x1); 141(x1); 144(x1); 185(x6); 28*(x1); (anti-Donatist sermons): *s.* 4(x2); 10(x17); 37(x4); 46(x4); 47(x2); 71(x7); 88(x1); 90(x2); 129(x1); 137(x2); 159B(x4); 162A(x2); 182(x2); 183(x5); 198(x9); 266(x7); 295(x1); 340A(x2); 359B(x1); 360(x3); 360C(x3).

Within the anti-Pelagian writings, *'gratia'* features in: *Pecc. mer.* (x113); *Spir. et litt.* (x116); *Nat. et gr.* (x89); *Gest. Pel.* (x153); *Gr. et pecc. or.* (x178); *Nupt. et conc.* (x38); *An. et or.* (x28); *C. ep. Pel.* (x220); *C. Iul.* (x220); *Gr. et lib. arb.* (x135); *Corrept.* (x71); *Cont.* (x13); *Perf. iust.* (x33); *Praed. sanct.* (x99); *Persev.* (x112); *C. Iul. imp.* (x536). The presence of the term in the doctrinal works signals the strength of the development of the term throughout Augustine's career: *Gramm.* (x1); *Util. cred.* (x8); *Ad Simp.* (x80); *De agone* (x1); *Doctr. chr.* (x31); *Disc. chr.* (x0); *Nat. bon.* (x0); *Cat. rud.* (x5); *De Trin.* (x67); *B. coniug.* (x2); *Virg.* (x19); *F. et op.* (x16); *Civ. Dei* (x117); *Adult. coniug.* (x3); *C. mend.* (x2); *Ench.* (x58); *F. rerum invis.* (x2); *Util. Ieiun* (x5); *Haer.* (x6); *Symb. cat.* (x0).

Ignorance—Ignorantia

Augustine's use of the theme of 'ignorance' is relatively small, statistically speaking, with only *352 occurrences in 270 places*. However, for the purposes of investigating the anti-Donatist polemic it is interesting to examine ignorance as one of the criticisms Augustine levelled against the Donatists, i.e., that the Donatists were aloof and often refused to accept the truth, preferring to live in ignorance rather than admit their mistake of schism.

TABLE 6 *'Ignorantia' in Augustine's writings*

Genre	# of instances	Works where the term 'ignorantia' is present
Anti-Manichean (380s–390s)	81	*Mor. eccl.* (x0); *Gn. adu. Man.* (x1); *Duab. anim.* (x0); *c. Fort.* (x0); *F et symb.* (x3); *Gn. litt. imp.* (x0); *s. dom. mont.* (x3); *C. Adim.* (x1); *C. ep. Man.* (x24); *C. Faust.* (x7); *C. Fel.* (x41); *C. Sec.* (x0); *C. Prisc.* (x1)
Anti-Arian	0	*C. s. Arrian.* (x0); *Conl. Max.* (x0); *C. Max.* (x0)
Anti-Donatist (390s–420s)	14	*Ps. c. Don.* (x0); *C. ep. Parm.* (x0); *De bapt.* (x5); *C. litt. Pet.* (x5); *Cresc.* (x0); *Un. bapt.* (x2); *Brev.* (x0); *C. Don.* (x0); *Emer.* (x0); *C. Gaud.* (x1); *Cath. fr.* (x1)

Genre	# of instances	Works where the term 'ignorantia' is present
Anti-Pelagian (410s–430)	97	*Pecc. mer.* (x15); *Spir. et litt.* (x1); *Nat. et gr.* (x7); *Gest. Pel.* (x4); *Gr. et pecc. or.* (x2); *Nupt. et conc.* (x1); *An. et or.* (x7); *C. ep. Pel.* (x4); *C. Iul.* (x18); *Gr. et lib. arb.* (x5); *Corrept.* (x1); *Cont.* (x8); *Perf. iust.* (x1); *Praed. sanct.* (x0); *Persev.* (x5); *C. Iul. imp.* (x18)
Letters (390s–420s) [anti-Donatist works indicated in bold]	34	*Ep.* 38(x1); **43**(x1); 47(x1); 78(x1); **93**(x3); 95(x1); **108**(x1); 118(x1); 126(x1); 130(x2); 147(x1); 164(x2); 166(x1); 167(x1); 177(x1); **185**(x1); 186(x1); 187(x1); 190(x1); 194(x3); 197(x3); 199(x2); 228(x1); 266(x1); **8***(x1).
Sermons (390s–420s) [anti-Donatist works indicated in bold]	33	*s.* 12(x1); 19(x1); 27(x1); **71**(x1); 72A(x2); 93(x1); 99(x1); 105(x1); 117 (x2); 178(x1); **183**(x1); 199(x1); 212(x1); 229D(x1);229E(x1); 229K(x1); 241(x1); 244(x1); 251(x1); 263(x1); 277(x1); 301(x2); 351(x4); 354(x1); 360B(x1); 362(x1); 376A(x1)
Other Sermons	6	*Io. ev. tr.* 6(x1); 15(x1); 18(x1); 53(x1); 73(x1); 114(x1)
(390s–420s) [anti-Donatist works indicated in bold]	33	*En. in Ps.* 1(x1); 24(x2); **33**(x5); 34(x1); 35(x3); **36**(x2); 41(x2); 44(x1); **57**(x1); 61(x1); 80(x2); 90(x2); **101**(x1); 105(x1); 106(x1); 113(x1); 114(x1); 118(x5)
Philosophical	25	*C. acad.* (x1); *Beata vita* (x0); *Ord.* (x0); *Sol.* (x1); *Imm. anim.* (x0); *Dial.* (x0); *Reth.* (x0); *Anim. quant.* (x1); *Lib. arb.* (x21); *Vera rel.* (x0); *Div. qu.* (x1); *Mend.* (x0)
Doctrinal	42	*Gramm.*(x1); *Util. cred.* (x0); *Ad Simp.* (x1); *De agone* (x0); *Doctr. chr.* (x6); *Disc. chr.* (x0); *Nat. bon.* (x4); *Cat. rud.* (x0); *De Trin.* (x4); *b. coniug.* (x0); *virg.* (x0); *f. et op.* (x2); *Civ. Dei* (x11); *Adult. coniug.* (x0); *C. mend.* (x6); *Ench.* (x6); *F. rerum invis.* (x0); *Haer.* (x1); *Symb. cat.* (x0)
Exegetical	124	*Exp. prop. Rm.* (x0); *Exp. Gal.* (x0); *Ep. Rm. inch.* (x8); *Ques. evan.* (x18); *Adn. Iob.* (x5); *Cons. evan.* (x70); *Gn. litt.* (x5); *Loc.* (x0); *Quaest.* (x11); *C. adu. leg.* (x7); *Cura mort.* (x0); *Dulc. ques.* (x0); *Ques. Mat.* (x0); *Adv. Iud.* (x0)
Dialogues	1	*Mag.* (x0); *De musica* (x1)
Others	18	*Conf.* (x6); *Op. mon.* (x1); *Divin. daem.* (x0); *B. uid.* (x0); *Pat.* (x0); *Retract.* (x5); *Spec.* (x6)

Augustine's use of the term '*ignorantia*' presents a clear example of terminology deployed to support his polemical endeavours. In this case the term is intensively used in polemical contexts: anti-Manichean (81), anti-Donatist (14); and anti-Pelagian (97). Interestingly, this term is also strongly present in Augustine's exegetical works (124 times). It would be a curious venture to see if it is used in such a way as to suggest heretics are 'ignorant' of scripture and therefore of genuine orthodoxy: (anti-Manichean): *Mor. eccl.* (x0); *Gn. adu. Man.* (x1); *Duab. anim.* (x0); *c. Fort.* (x0); *F et symb.* (x3); *Gn. litt. imp.* (x0); *s. dom. mont.* (x3); *C. Adim.* (x1); *C. ep. Man.* (x24); *C. Faust.* (x7); *C. Fel.* (x41); *C. Sec.* (x0); *C. Prisc.* (x1); (anti-Donatist): *Ps. c. Don.* (x0); *C. ep. Parm.* (x0); *De bapt.* (x5); *C. litt. Pet.* (x5); *Cresc.* (x0); *Un. bapt.* (x2); *Brev.* (x0); *C. Don.* (x0); *Emer.* (x0); *C. Gaud.* (x1); *Cath. fr.* (x1); (anti-Donatist letters and sermons): *Ep.* 43(x1); 93(x3); 108(x1); 185(x1); 8*(x1); *s.* 71(x1); 183(x1); (exegetical works): *Exp. prop. Rm.* (x0); *Exp. Gal.* (x0); *Ep. Rm. inch.* (x8); *Ques. evan.* (x18); *Adn. Iob.* (x5); *Cons. evan.* (x70); *Gn. litt.* (x5); *Loc.* (x0); *Quaest.* (x11); *C. adu. leg.* (x7); *Cura mort.* (x0); *Dulc. ques.* (x0); *Ques. Mat.* (x0); *Adv. Iud.* (x0).

Stubbornness—Pertinacia

One of the more sticking criticisms Augustine would level against the Donatists was that they were stubborn. It was for this reason that they adhered to their separation from the Catholic Church, and in order to validate their stubbornness and pride, they claimed only to be defending the authority of Cyprian of Carthage. That is why we see this theme of stubbornness appear in mostly overtly polemical texts, with *79 occurrences in 74 places.*

TABLE 7 *'Pertinacia' in Augustine's writings*

Genre	# of instances	Works where the term 'pertinacia' is present
Anti-Manichean (380s–390s)	12	*Mor. eccl.* (x8); *Gn. adu. Man.* (x0); *Duab. anim.* (x1); *C. Fort.* (x0); *F. et symb.* (x0); *Gn. litt. imp.* (x0); *S. dom. mont.* (x0); *C. Adim.* (x0); *C. ep. Man.* (x1); *C. Faust.* (x1); *C. Fel.* (x0); *C. Sec.* (x1); *C. Prisc.* (x0)
Anti-Arian	0	*C. s. Arrian.* (x0); *Conl. Max.* (x0); *C. Max.* (x0)
Anti-Donatist (390s–420s)	23	*Ps. c. Don.* (x0); *C. ep. Parm.* (x3); *De bapt.* (x3); *C. litt. Pet.* (x4); *Cresc.* (x4); *Un. bapt.* (x0); *Brev.* (x0); *C. Don.* (x2); *Emer.* (x3); *C. Gaud.* (x1); *Cath. fr.* (x3)

Genre	# of instances	Works where the term 'pertinacia' is present
Anti-Pelagian (410s–430)	8	*Pecc. mer.* (x1); *Spir. et litt.* (x0); *Nat. et gr.* (x0); *Gest. Pel.* (x0); *Gr. et pecc. or.* (x0); *Nupt. et conc.* (x0); *An. et or.* (x1); *C. ep. Pel.* (x1); *C. Iul.* (x1); *Gr. et lib. arb.* (x0); *Corrept.* (x0); *Cont.* (x0); *Perf. iust.* (x0); *Praed. sanct.* (x0); *Persev.* (x1); *C. Iul. imp.* (x3)
Letters (390s–420s) [anti-Donatist works indicated in bold]	9	*Ep.* 20(x1); **43**(x1); 57(x2); **88**(x1); **89**(x1); **139**(x1); 167(x1); **185**(x1);
Sermons (390s–420s) [anti-Donatist works indicated in bold]	9	*s.* 22(x1); **47**(x1); 198(x1); 209(x2); **275**(x1); 285(x1); 335G(x1); 351(x1)
Other Sermons (390s–420s) [anti-Donatist works indicated in bold]	2	*En. in Ps.* 34(x1); 146(x1)
Philosophical	8	*C. acad.* (x2); *Beata vita* (x0); *Ord.* (x0); *Sol.* (x0); *Imm. anim.* (x0); *Dial.* (x0); *Reth.* (x0); *Anim. quant.* (x1); *Lib. arb.* (x1); *Vera rel.* (x0); *Div. qu.* (x4); *Mend.* (x0)
Doctrinal	3	*Util. cred.* (x1); *Ad Simp.* (x0); *De agone* (x0); *Doctr. chr.* (x1); *Disc. chr.* (x0); *Nat. bon.* (x0); *Cat. rud.* (x0); *De Trin.* (x0); *B. coniug.* (x0); *Virg.* (x0); *F. et op.* (x0); *Civ. Dei* (x0); *Adult. coniug.* (x0); *C. mend.* (x0); *Ench.* (x0); *F. rerum invis.* (x1); *Haer.* (x0); *Symb. cat.* (x0)
Exegetical	2	*Exp. prop. Rm.* (x0); *Exp. Gal.* (x0); *Ep. Rm. inch.* (x0); *Ques. evan.* (x0); *Adn. Iob.* (x0); *Cons. evan.* (x1); *Gn. litt.* (x0); *Loc.* (x0); *Quaest.* (x0); *C. adu. leg.* (x0); *Cura mort.* (x0); *Dulc. ques.* (x1); *Ques. Mat.* (x1); *Adv. Iud.* (x0)
Dialogues	0	*Mag.* (x0); *De musica* (x0)
Others	0	*Conf.* (x0); *Op. mon.* (x0); *Divin. daem.* (x0); *B. uid.* (x0); *Pat.* (x0); *Retract.* (x0); *Spec.* (x0)

Much like the previous example of 'ignorance' that Augustine used against whatever polemical target he faced at the time, *'pertinacia'* or 'stubbornness', was a term Augustine deployed frequently and almost exclusively against his enemies, as there are few example of his use of the term outside a polemical context. For this reason one should not be surprised that he uses the term 12 times against the Manicheans: *Mor. eccl.* (x8); *Gn. adu. Man.* (xo); *Duab. anim.* (x1); *C. Fort.* (xo); *F. et symb.* (xo); *Gn. litt. imp.* (xo); *S. dom. mont.* (xo); *C. Adim.* (xo); *C. ep. Man.* (x1); *C. Faust.* (x1); *C. Fel.* (xo); *C. Sec.* (x1); *C. Prisc.* (xo); against the Donatists x23: *Ps. c. Don.* (xo); *C. ep. Parm.* (x3); *De bapt.* (x3); *C. litt. Pet.* (x4); *Cresc.* (x4); *Un. bapt.* (xo); *Brev.* (xo); *C. Don.* (x2); *Emer.* (x3); *C. Gaud.* (x1); *Cath. fr.* (x3); *Ep.* 43(x1); 88(x1); 89(x1); 139(x1); 185(x1); *s.* 47(x1); 275(x1); and against the Pelagians also x8: *Pecc. mer.* (x1); *Spir. et litt.* (xo); *Nat. et gr.* (xo); *Gest. Pel.* (xo); *Gr. et pecc. or.* (xo); *Nupt. et conc.* (xo); *An. et or.* (x1); *C. ep. Pel.* (x1); *C. Iul.* (x1); *Gr. et lib. arb.* (xo); *Corrept.* (xo); *Cont.* (xo); *Perf. iust.* (xo); *Praed. sanct.* (xo); *Persev.* (x1); *C. Iul. imp.* (x3).

Rebaptism—Rebaptizare

Of the many themes that Augustine would latch on to throughout the anti-Donatist campaign, none was as omnipresent as his scathing critique of the native African practice of 'rebaptism', for which he attacked the Donatists. Surprisingly, this theme only appears with *199 occurrences in 147 places*. Unsurprisingly, the majority of such examples are found in overtly anti-Donatist writings.

TABLE 8 *'Rebaptizare' in Augustine's writings*

Genre	# of instances	Works where the term 'rebaptizare' is present
Anti-Manichean (380s–390s)	1	*Mor. eccl.* (xo); *Gn. adu. Man.* (xo); *Duab. anim.* (xo); *C. Fort.* (xo); *F et symb.* (xo); *Gn. litt. imp.* (xo); *S. dom. mont.* (xo); *C. Adim.* (xo); *C. ep. Man.* (xo); *C. Faust.* (x1); *C. Fel.* (xo); *C. Sec.* (xo); *C. Prisc.* (xo)
Anti-Arian	0	*C. s. Arrian.* (xo); *Conl. Max.* (xo); *C. Max.* (xo)
Anti-Donatist (390s–420s)	123	*Ps. c. Don.* (x10); *C. ep. Parm.* (x13); *De bapt.* (x33); *C. litt. Pet.* (x17); *Cresc.* (x36); *Un. bapt.* (x6); *Brev.* (xo); *C. Don.* (xo); *Emer.* (x2); *C. Gaud.* (x4); *Cath. fr.* (x2)
Anti-Pelagian (410s–430)	0	*Pecc. mer.* (xo); *Spir. et litt.* (xo); *Nat. et gr.* (xo); *Gest. Pel.* (xo); *Gr. et pecc. or.* (xo); *Nupt. et conc.* (xo); *An. et or.* (xo); *C. ep. Pel.* (xo); *C. Iul.* (xo); *Gr. et lib. arb.* (xo); *Corrept.* (xo); *Cont.* (xo); *Perf. iust.* (xo); *Praed. sanct.* (xo); *Persev.* (xo); *C. Iul. imp.* (xo)

Genre	# of instances	Works where the term 'rebaptizare' is present
Letters (390s–420s) [anti-Donatist works indicated in bold]	50	*Ep.* **23**(x11); **34**(x1); 35(x3); **43**(x1); **44**(x2); **52**(x2); 66(x3); **70**(x1); 87(x4); 88(x1); **89**(x2); **93**(x2); **105**(x1); **106**(x3); **108**(x5); **111**(x2); **128**(x1); **139**(x1); **185**(x2); 204(x1); 220(x1)
Sermons (390s–420s) [anti-Donatist works indicated in bold]	5	*s.* 229U(x1); 293A(x2); **359**(x2)
Other Sermons (390s–420s) [anti-Donatist works indicated in bold]	4 8	*Io. ev. tr.* 5(x2); 6(x1); 45(x1) *En. in Ps.* **10**(x2); **32**(x1); **36**(x2); 39(x1); 54(x1); **145**(x1)
Philosophical	0	*C. acad.* (x0); *Beata vita* (x0); *Ord.* (x0); *Sol.* (x0); *Imm. anim.* (x0); *Dial.* (x0); *Reth.* (x0); *Anim. quant.* (x0); *Lib. arb.* (x0); *Vera rel.* (x0); *Div. qu.* (x0); *Mend.* (x0)
Doctrinal	5	*Util. cred.* (x0); *Ad Simp.* (x0); *De agone* (x2); *Doctr. chr.* (x0); *Disc. chr.* (x0); *Nat. bon.* (x0); *Cat. rud.* (x0); *De Trin.* (x0); *B. coniug.* (x0); *Virg.* (x0); *F. et op.* (x0); *Civ. Dei* (x0); *Adult. coniug.* (x0); *C. mend.* (x0); *Ench.* (x0); *F. rerum invis.* (x0); *Haer.* (x3); *Symb. cat.* (x0)
Exegetical	0	*Exp. prop. Rm.* (x0); *Exp. Gal.* (x0); *Ep. Rm. inch.* (x0); *Ques. evan.* (x0); *Adn. Iob.* (x0); *Cons. evan.* (x0); *Gn. litt.* (x0); *Loc.* (x0); *Quaest.* (x0); *C. adu. leg.* (x0); *Cura mort.* (x0); *Dulc. ques.* (x0); *Ques. Mat.* (x0); *Adv. Iud.* (x0)
Dialogues	0	*Mag.* (x0); *De musica* (x0)
Others	1	*Conf.* (x0); *Op. mon.* (x0); *Divin. daem.* (x0); *B. uid.* (x0); *Pat.* (x0); *Retract.* (x1); *Spec.* (x0)

'Rebaptism' is clearly a uniquely anti-Donatist term as evidenced by its nearly complete absence outside the anti-Donatist campaign. This term, though exclusively used against the Donatists, does in fact demonstrate the multi-faceted approach Augustine took in his efforts against the Donatists in combining his anti-Donatist works with sermons and letters. This representative display is seen in 123 examples in the anti-Donatists works: *Ps. c. Don.* (x10); *C. ep. Parm.* (x13); *De bapt.* (x33); *C. litt. Pet.* (x17); *Cresc.* (x36); *Un. bapt.* (x6); *Brev.* (x0); *C. Don.* (x0); *Emer.* (x2); *C. Gaud.* (x4); *Cath. fr.* (x2); and in bountiful examples in Augustine's anti-Donatist letters: *Ep.* 23(x11); 34(x1); 43(x1); 44(x2); 52(x2); 66(x3); 70(x1); 87(x4); 88(x1); 89(x2); 93(x2); 105(x1); 106(x3); 108(x5); 111(x2); 128(x1); 139(x1); 185(x2); and anti-Donatist sermons: *s.* 359(x2); *En. in Ps.* 10(x2); 32(x1); 36(x2); 145(x1). Compared to this decidedly anti-Donatist usage, there is just one example of the term 'rebaptism' used against the Manicheans (in *C. Faust.*) and none against the Pelagians.

Martyr

A large part of Augustine's assumption of the authority of Cyprian came through flattering accolades in his sermons, letters, and anti-Donatist treatises. One of the most important terms in that process was 'martyr'. In all, Augustine would use this term some *1445 times in 758* places in his work. An analysis of this record promises to reveal just how essential his consideration of martyrdom was in his own thinking, and how much the martyr cult in Africa influenced his approach.

As seen in the data above, the term 'martyr' holds a special place in Augustine's writings as it usurps the use of other terms that were often used to

TABLE 9 *'Martyr' in Augustine's writings*

Genre	# of instances	Works where the term 'martyr' is present
Anti-Manichean (380s–390s)	31	*Mor. eccl.* (x2); *Gn. adu. Man.* (x0); *Duab. anim.* (x0); *C. Fort.* (x0); *F. et symb.* (x0); *Gn. litt. imp.* (x0); *S. dom. mont.* (x6); *C. Adim.* (x0); *C. ep. Man.* (x0); *C. Faust.* (x23); *C. Fel.* (x0); *C. Sec.* (x0); *C. Prisc.* (x0)
Anti-Arian	1	*C. s. Arrian.* (x0); *Conl. Max.* (x0); *C. Max.* (x1)
Anti-Donatist (390s–420s)	100	*Ps. c. Don.* (x0); *C. ep. Parm.* (x15); *De bapt.* (x13); *C. litt. Pet.* (x9); *Cresc.* (x6); *Un. bapt.* (x2); *Brev.* (x13); *C. Don.* (x17); *S. Caes.* (x1); *Emer.* (x0); *C. Gaud.* (x22); *Cath. fr.* (x2)
Anti-Pelagian (410s–430)	41	*Pecc. mer.* (x2); *Spir. et litt.* (x0); *Nat. et gr.* (x2); *Gest. Pel.* (x1); *Gr. et pecc. or.* (x0); *Nupt. et conc.* (x0); *An. et or.* (x6); *C. ep. Pel.* (x4); *C. Iul.* (x9); *Gr. et lib. arb.* (x1); *Corrept.* (x1); *Cont.* (x1); *Perf. iust.* (x0); *Praed. sanct.* (x1); *Persev.* (x6); *C. Iul. imp.* (x7)

Genre	# of instances	Works where the term 'martyr' is present
Letters (390s–420s) [anti-Donatist works indicated in bold]	50	*Ep.* 22(x3); **29**(x1); 35(x1); 36(x2); 40(x2); 76(x1); 78(x1); 88(x2); 89(x2); **93**(x3); **105**(x1); **108**(x1); 138(x1); **139**(x1); 140(x3); 151(x1); 157(x1); 166(x1); **185**(x8); 189(x1); 193(x1); 204(x2); 215(x2); 217(x1); 243(x1); 25*(x1); **29***(x5)
Sermons (390s–420s) [anti-Donatist works indicated in bold]	780	*s.* 3(x1); **4**(x4); 20B(x2); 22(x1); 24(x1); 31(x3); 32(x2); 36(x1); **37**(x7); **46**(x2); 51(x3); 53A(x2); 56(x1); 58(x2); 61A(x1); 62(x2); 64(x6); 64A(x3); 65(x6); 65A(x2); 68(x1); 79(x1); 81(x1); 94(x1); 105A(x1); 107(x2); 107A(x1); 110(x1); 111(x1); 113A(x4); 116(x1); 128(x4); 130A(x1); **137**(x1); 138(x1); 143(x1); 149(x1); 150(x1); 155(x1); 158(x1); 159(x5); 159A(x8); 169(x2); 173(x1); 198(x21); 211(x1); 229H(x1); 229J(x2); 236A(x7); 252(x1); 256(x1); 260E(x2); 272B(x1); 273(x16); 274(x4); **275**(x7); 276(x9); 277(x7); 277A(7); 278(x1); 280(x10); 281(x4); 282(x3); 283(x7); 284(x19); 285(x10); 286(x12); **292**(x1); 294(x3); **295**(x4); 296(x2); 297(x4); 298(x2); 299(x5); 299A(x10); 299C(x1); 299D(x7); 299E(x5); 299F(x7); 300(x10); 301(x1); 301A(x2); 302(x12); 304(x5); 305A(x19); 306(x5); 306A(x3); 306B(x3); 306C(x3); 306D(x6); 306E(x18); 306F(x1); 309(x7); 310(x4); 311(x9); 312(x4); 313(x5); 313B(x10); 313C(x4); 313D(x13); 313E(x5); 313G(x4); 314(x3); 315(x6); 316(x2); 317(x6); 318(x8); 319(x3); 319A(x1); 320(x1); 322(x4); 323(x2); 324(x6); 325(x)11; 326(x7); 327(x9); 328(x23); 329(x6); 330(x3); 331(x9); 332(x3); 334(x13); 335(x9); 335A(x12); 335B(x10); 335C(x13);335D(x13); 335E(x15); 335G(x10); 335H(x6); 335I(x1); 335J(x3); 341(x1); 344(x2); 345(x6); 351(x1); 356(x2); 359B(x26); 360B(x2); 365E(x1); 373(x2); 375(x1); 375B(x5); 375C(x1)
Other Sermons (390s–420s) [anti-Donatist works indicated in bold]	23	*Io. ev. tr.* 3(x1); 5(x1); 6(x2); 11(x1); 21(x1); 27(x2); 43(x1); 47(x1); 49(x2); 84(x4); 93(x1); 94(x1); 105(x1); 133(x1); 116(x1); 123(x2)
	9	*Ep. Io. tr.* 1(x7); 6(x1); 8(x1)
	223	*En. in Ps.* **10**(x2); 26(x1); 29(x4); **32**(x3); 34(x8);

TABLE 9 *'Martyr' in Augustine's writings* (cont.)

Genre	# of instances	Works where the term 'martyr' is present
		35(x1); **36**(x2); 37(x2); 39(x3); 40(x10); 41(x1); 43(x5); 44(x2); 47(x1); 49(x2); 51(x2); 52(x1); 54(x2); 56(x3); **57**(x1); 58(x1); 59(x8); 61(x1); 63(x8); 64(x2); **67**(x2); 68(x4); 69(x19); 71(x1); 75(x1); 76(x1); 78(x8); 79(x1); 80(x3); **85**(x2); 86(x1); 87(x1); **88**(x3); 89(x1); 90(x3); 93(x3); 96(x1); 98(x1); **101**(x7); 102(x5); 103(x2); 108(x1); 110(x1); 115(x3); 117(x1); 118(x26); 121(x1); 123(x3); 125(x1); 127(x8); 129(x1); 134(x2); 136(x1); 137(x6); 139(x2); 140(x8); 141(x6); 144(x2); **147**(x2); 148(x2)
Philosophical	5	*C. acad.* (x0); *Beata vita* (x0); *Ord.* (x0); *Sol.* (x0); *Imm. anim.* (x0); *Dial.* (x0); *Reth.* (x0); *Anim. quant.* (x0); *Lib. arb.* (x2); *Vera rel.* (x1); *Div. qu.* (x1); *Mend.* (x1)
Doctrinal	94	*Util. cred.* (x1); *Ad Simp.* (x0); *De agone* (x2); *Doctr. chr.* (x3); *Disc. chr.* (x3); *Nat. bon.* (x0); *Cat. rud.* (x1); *De Trin.* (x1); *B. coniug.* (x1); *Virg.* (x2); *F. et op.* (x0); *Civ. Dei* (x73); *Adult. coniug.* (x0); *C. mend.* (x5); *Ench.* (x1); *F. rerum invis.* (x0); *Haer.* (x1); *Symb. cat.* (x0)
Exegetical	34	*Exp. prop. Rm.* (x0); *Exp. Gal.* (x0); *Ep. Rm. inch.* (x1); *Ques. evan.* (x2); *Adn. Iob.* (x2); *Cons. evan.* (x3); *Gn. litt.* (x0); *Loc.* (x0); *Quaest.* (x2); *C. adu. leg.* (x0); *Cura mort.* (x23); *Dulc. ques.* (x1); *Ques. Mat.* (x0); *Adv. Iud.* (x0)
Dialogues	0	*Mag.* (x0); *De musica* (x0)
Others	17	*Conf.* (x4); *Op. mon.* (x2); *Divin. daem.* (x1); *B. uid.* (x0); *Pat.* (x4); *Retract.* (x5); *Spec.* (x1)

develop Augustine's own theology, which tended to be concentrated in one context or controversy or another. The term 'martyr' is more evenly spread throughout the genres that Augustine used. This explains why 'martyr' appears 31 times against the Manicheans: *Mor. eccl.* (x2);*Gn. adu. Man.* (x0); *Duab. anim.* (x0); *C. Fort.* (x0); *F. et symb.* (x0); *Gn. litt. imp.* (x0); *S. dom. mont.* (x6); *C. Adim.*

(x0); *C. ep. Man.* (x0); *C. Faust.* (x23); *C. Fel.* (x0); *C. Sec.* (x0); *C. Prisc.* (x0)); then x100 against the Donatists (*Ps. c. Don.* (x0);*C. ep. Parm.* (x15); *De bapt.* (x13); *C. litt. Pet.* (x9); *Cresc.* (x6); *Un. bapt.* (x2); *Brev.* (x13); *C. Don.* (x17); *S. Caes.* (x1); *Emer.* (x0); *C. Gaud.* (x22); *Cath. fr.* (x2); *Ep.* 29(x1); 88(x2); 89(x2); 93(x3); 105(x1); 108(x1); 139(x1); 185(x8); 29*(x5); *s.* 4(x4); 37(x7); 46(x2); 137(x1); 275(x7); 292(x1); 295(x4)); and then x41 against the Pelagians (*Pecc. mer.* (x2);*Spir. et litt.* (x0); *Nat. et gr.* (x2); *Gest. Pel.* (x1); *Gr. et pecc. or.* (x0); *Nupt. et conc.* (x0); *An. et or.* (x6); *C. ep. Pel.* (x4); *C. Iul.* (x9); *Gr. et lib. arb.* (x1); *Corrept.* (x1); *Cont.* (x1); *Perf. iust.* (x0); *Praed. sanct.* (x1); *Persev.* (x6); *C. Iul. imp.* (x7)). This even spread is sharply evinced by its enumeration in major doctrinal works, x94: *Util. cred.* (x1); *Ad Simp.* (x0); *De agone* (x2); *Doctr. chr.* (x3); *Disc. chr.* (x3); *Nat. bon.* (x0); *Cat. rud.* (x1); *De Trin.* (x1); *B. coniug.* (x1); *Virg.* (x2); *F. et op.* (x0); *Civ. Dei* (x73); *Adult. coniug.* (x0); *C. mend.* (x5); *Ench.* (x1); *F. rerum invis.* (x0); *Haer.* (x1); *Symb. cat.* (x0).

As a final note about Augustine's employment of the term 'martyr', there are *388 occurrences in 98 places* ('Cyprian'+'martyr') where Augustine elaborated on Cyprian's martyr status with the express intention of siding with the authority of Africa's premier Christian hero.[70] The 388 occurrences signify a very substantial number of passages dedicated to Cyprian, showing how much of a concern this matter was during Augustine's first ten years as an ordained minister. It also shows that even if Augustine was less than ecstatic about endorsing martyrdom as an expression of spiritual devotion, he nonetheless had to confront it in real terms within the context of his priesthood and episcopacy.

70 *Doct. Chr.* 2,61(x2); 4,48; *C. Faust.* 5,8; 20,21(x6); *C. ep. Parm.* 1,6(x2); *De bapt.* 1,1(x2); 1,28; 1,29(x2); 2,1; 2,2(x11); 2,6(x4); 2,7; 2,10; 2,11(x2); 2,12(x2); 3,5(x4); 3,6; 4,18(x2); 4,28(x2); 6,3(x2); 6,4(x2); 7,1(x2); *Cresc.* 2,39; 2,40(x2); 2,48(x2); 2,49(x2); 3,2(x2); 4,33; *Pecc. mer.* 3,10(x2); *Un. bapt.* 22(x3); *C. Don.* 11; 18(x6); 28(x2); *Civ. Dei.* 8,26; 8,27(x8); *Gest. Pel.* 25; *An. et orig.* 1,11(x5); *C. Gaud.* 2,2(x4); 2,3(x2); *C. ep. Pel.* 4,21(x4); 4,24(x2); 4,28; 4,29; *C. Iul.* 1,5; 1,6; 2,18; 2,25(x2); 3,31(x5); *Corrept.* 10(x2); *Retract.* 2,1(x2); 2,18(x3); 2,28; *Praed. sanct.* 8; *Persev.* 4(x2); 12(x4); 43; 49; *C. Iul. imp.* 1,50(x2); 1,106(x3); *Ep.* 93,36; 108,9; 108,10(x2); 151,6(x2); 215,3(x3); 217,2; 217,3; 217,6(x2); 217,22; *Ep.* 29*,2(x2); 29*,3; *En. in Ps.* 80,23(x2); 85,24(x2); *s.* 138,1(x2); 138,2(x2); 138,3; 198,3(x2); 305A,1(x3); 305A,2(x2); 305A,4(x8); 309,1(x2); 309,2(x3); 309,3; 309,4; 309,5(x3); 309,6(x5); 310,1(x4); 310,2(x9); 310,3; 311,1(x6); 311,3(x2); 311,5; 311,6; 311,7; 312,3(x6); 312,4(x2); 312,5; 312,6(x3); 313,1(x2); 313,2(x7); 313,3; 313,4; 313,5(x2); 313A,3(x4); 313A,5(x2); 313B,1(x2); 313B,2(x5); 313B,4(x4); 313C,2(x3); 313D,1(x6); 313D,2(x2); 313D,3; 313D,4(x13); 313E,1(x4); 313E,2(x4); 313E,3(x2); 313E,5(x6); 313E,6(x7); 313E,7(x5); 313G,3(x4); 335K,5(x2); 341,4; 359B,5; 359B,16(x5); 359,17(x5).

Africa

The discussion on Augustine's African homeland became a lighting-rod within the Donatist and then the Pelagian segments of the controversy. In the first case, Augustine was considered a heathen outsider corrupted by his stay in the Roman heartland. By the time of the Pelagian uproar, the tables had turned and Augustine was now accused of being a parochially-minded African bumpkin by his more mainstream/*avant-garde* critics from closer to Constantinople and Rome. For this reason it is no surprise that 'Africa' as a theme is present *428 times in 288 places* throughout his works.

TABLE 10 *'Africa' in Augustine's writings*

Genre	# of instances	Works where the term 'Africa' is present
Anti-Manichean (380s–390s)	3	*Mor. eccl.* (x0); *Gn. adu. Man.* (x0); *Duab. anim.* (x0); *C. Fort.* (x0); *F. et symb.* (x0); *Gn. litt. imp.* (x0); *S. dom. mont.* (x0); *C. Adim.* (x0); *C. ep. Man.* (x1); *C. Faust.* (x2); *C. Fel.* (x0); *C. Sec.* (x0); *C. Prisc.* (x0)
Anti-Arian	0	*C. s. Arrian.* (x0); *Conl. Max.* (x0); *C. Max.* (x0)
Anti-Donatist (390s–420s)	155	*Ps. c. Don.* (x2); *C. ep. Parm.* (x32); *De bapt.* (x7); *C. litt. Pet.* (x21); *Cresc.* (x45); *Un. bapt.* (x1); *Brev.* (x2); *C. Don.* (x6); *Emer.* (x0); *C. Gaud.* (x2); *Cath. fr.* (x37)
Anti-Pelagian (410s–430)	13	*Pecc. mer.* (x0); *Spir. et litt.* (x0); *Nat. et gr.* (x0); *Gest. Pel.* (x0); *Gr. et pecc. or.* (x2); *Nupt. et conc.* (x0); *An. et or.* (x0); *C. ep. Pel.* (x1); *C. Iul.* (x8); *Gr. et lib. arb.* (x0); *Corrept.* (x0); *Cont.* (x0); *Perf. iust.* (x0); *Praed. sanct.* (x0); *Persev.* (x0); *C. Iul. imp.* (x2)
Letters (390s–420s) [anti-Donatist works indicated in bold]	88	*Ep.* 17(x1); 22(x1); **23**(x1); 27(x1); 31(x1); 36(x1); 42(x1); 43(x11); 44(x4); 51(x3); 55(x1); 58(x2); 64(x1); 66(x2); 73(x1); 76(x2); 78(x1); 86(x1); 87(x3); 88(x5); 89(x2); 93(x4); 97(x2); **105**(x4); **108**(x2); 118(x3); 124(x1); 126(x1); **129**(x2); **141**(x1); 166(x2); **185**(x7); 186(x1); 194(x1); 199(x1); 208(x1); 209(x2); 215(x1); 220(x1); 231(x1); 10*(x4); 23*(x1); **28***(x1)

Genre	# of instances	Works where the term 'Africa' is present
Sermons (390s–420s) [anti-Donatist works indicated in bold]	79	*s.* 45(x1); **46**(x33); **47**(x2); **88**(x3); 138(x16); 147A(x5); 162A(x9); 177(x1); 252(x1); 265F(x1); 299B(x1); 310(x1); 313C(x1); 322(x1); 324(x1); 340A(x1); 359B(x1)
Other Sermons	4	*Io. ev. tr. 6*(x1); 13(x3)
(390s–420s)	1	*Ep. Io. tr.* 10(x1)
[anti-Donatist works indicated in bold]	25	*En. in Ps.* **21**(x5); **36**(x4); 47(x1); 49(x4); 54(x1); 64(x1); 66(x2); 77(x1); **85**(x2); 120(x1); 128(x1); **147**(x1); 149(x1)
Philosophical	0	*C. acad.* (x0); *Beata vita* (x0); *Ord.* (x0); *Sol.* (x0); *Imm. anim.* (x0); *Dial.* (x0); *Reth.* (x0); *Anim. quant.* (x0); *Lib. arb.* (x0); *Vera rel.* (x0); *Div. qu.* (x0); *Mend.* (x0)
Doctrinal	17	*Util. cred.* (x0); *Ad Simp.* (x0); *De agone* (x1); *Doctr. chr.* (x0); *Disc. chr.* (x0); *Nat. bon.* (x0); *Cat. rud.* (x0); *De Trin.* (x0); *B. coniug.* (x0); *virg.* (x0); *F. et op.* (x0); *De civ. Dei* (x12); *Adult. coniug.* (x0); *C. mend.* (x0); *Ench.* (x0); *F. rerum invis.* (x0); *Haer.* (x4); *Symb. cat.* (x0)
Exegetical	0	*Exp. prop. Rm.* (x0); *Exp. Gal.* (x0); *Ep. Rm. inch.* (x0); *Ques. evan.* (x0); *Adn. Iob.* (x0); *Cons. evan.* (x0); *Gn. litt.* (x0); *Loc.* (x0); *Quaest.* (x0); *C. adu. leg.* (x0); *Cura mort.* (x0); *Dulc. ques.* (x0); *Ques. Mat.* (x0); *Adv. Iud.* (x0)
Dialogues	1	*Mag.* (x1); *De musica* (x0)
Others	13	*Conf.* (x5); *Op. mon.* (x2); *Divin. daem.* (x0); *B. uid.* (x0); *Pat.* (x0); *Retract.* (x6); *Spec.* (x0)

Augustine's use of the theme of 'Africa' is another clear example of a term that was specifically crafted and originated out of the anti-Donatist context. This explains why the term appears overwhelmingly in anti-Donatist works, sermons, and letters: *Ps. c. Don.* (x2); *C. ep. Parm.* (x32); *De bapt.* (x7); *C. litt. Pet.* (x21); *Cresc.* (x45); *Un. bapt.* (x1); *Brev.* (x2); *C. Don.* (x6); *Emer.* (x0); *C. Gaud.* (x2); *Cath. fr.* (x37); *Ep.* 23(x1); 58(x2); 87(x3); 88(x5); 89(x2); 93(x4); 105(x4); 108(x2); 129(x2); 141(x1); 185(x7); 28*(x1); *s.* 46(x33); 47(x2); 88(x3); *En. in Ps.*

21(x5); 36(x4); 85(x2); 147(x1). When one compares this lopsided anti-Donatist usage in light of how it was deployed against the Pelagians, the difference is obvious: *Pecc. mer.* (x0); *Spir. et litt.* (x0); *Nat. et gr.* (x0); *Gest. Pel.* (x0); *Gr. et pecc. or.* (x2); *Nupt. et conc.* (x0); *An. et or.* (x0); *C. ep. Pel.* (x1); *C. Iul.* (x8); *Gr. et lib. arb.* (x0); *Corrept.* (x0); *Cont.* (x0); *Perf. iust.* (x0); *Praed. sanct.* (x0); *Persev.* (x0); *C. Iul. imp.* (x2).

Here again Augustine made a very strong connection between Cyprian and a topic under heavy discussion. Altogether there are *90 occurrences in 20 places* where Augustine makes a direct link between 'Africa' and 'Cyprian'.[71] These examples show clearly what Augustine had set out to do through this entire polemical campaign: to plug into the authority of Cyprian in the way he needed to, based on the situation at hand.

The World—Mundus/Orbis

The relationship between the world and the Church was one of the defining problems within late antique Donatist Christianity, and was at the core of much of the controversy between Augustine and the Donatists, (unlike the Pelagians who had a more anthropocentric concern). In fact, this theme lay largely at the heart of the struggle to appropriate Cyprian. Cyprian's experience as a bishop came at a time when the Church in Africa was still secretive to a certain extent, and prone to persecutions in a way unmatched in other parts of the empire. Because of this reality, Cyprian's attitude to Christians as a society situated above the dread secular sphere was to have a deeply abiding effect on the African Christian mentality for centuries to come. It was the Donatists who maintained this same spirit and who clung to this normative African perspective.[72] It comes as no surprise then, to see the word *mundus/orbis* occur *884 times in 491 places.*

The thematic combination of '*mundus/orbis*' presents a curious exception to the rule thus far. These terms appear exclusively within the anti-Donatist and anti-Pelagian campaigns. Nevertheless, as a disclaimer, this example does not include the term '*saeculum*' which would probably result in a more diverse portfolio than that shown here. Nevertheless, it is clear that this area represented a specifically polemical content for use in the anti-Donatist campaign: *Ps. c. Don.* (x2); *C. ep. Parm.* (x21); *De bapt.* (x5); *C. litt. Pet.* (x45); *Cresc.* (x30); *Un. bapt.* (x5); *Brev.* (x18); *C. Don.* (x16); *Emer.* (x1); *C. Gaud.* (x10); *Cath. fr.* (x32);

---

71 *C. ep. Parm.* 3,8(x5); *De bapt.* 1,28(x2); 2,3(x5); 2,14(x2); 3,1; 3,2(x2); 3,3(x6); 3,4(x2); 3,14(x2); 4,8(x5); *Cresc.* 2,45(x2); 2,46(x2); 3,2(x5); 3,73(x4); 4,67(x3); 4,73(x3); *C. ep. Pel.* 4,21(x3); *C. Iul.* 3,31(x10); 3,32(x3); Ep. 175(x2); s. 310,1(x2); 310,2(x9); 313C,2(x3); 359B,5(x2).

72 Burns, 'Appropriating Augustine Appropriating Cyprian', 115.

TABLE 11 *'Mundus/orbis' in Augustine's writings*

Genre	# of instances	Works where the term 'mundus/orbis' is present
Anti-Manichean (380s–390s)	0	*Mor. eccl.* (x0); *Gn. adu. Man.* (x0); *Duab. anim.* (x0); *C Fort.* (x0); *F. et symb.* (x0); *Gn. litt. imp.* (x0); *S. dom. mont.* (x0); *C. Adim.* (x0); *C. ep. Man.* (x0); *C. Faust.* (x0); *C. Fel.* (x0); *C. Sec.* (x0); *C. Prisc.* (x0)
Anti-Arian	0	*C. s. Arrian.* (x0); *Conl. Max.* (x0); *C. Max.* (x0)
Anti-Donatist (390s–420s)	244	*Ps. c. Don.* (x2); *C. ep. Parm.* (x21); *De bapt.* (x5); *C. litt. Pet.* (x45); *Cresc.* (x30); *Un. bapt.* (x5); *Brev.* (x18); *C. Don.* (x16); *Emer.* (x1); *C. Gaud.* (x10); *Cath. fr.* (x32)
Anti-Pelagian (410s–430)	635	*Pecc. mer.* (x53); *Spir. et litt.* (x8); *Nat. et gr.* (x16); *Gest. Pel.* (x3); *Gr. et pecc. or.* (x15); *Nupt. et conc.* (x33); *An. et or.* (x5); *C. ep. Pel.* (x34); *C. Iul.* (x130); *Gr. et lib. arb.* (x7); *Corrept.* (x4); *Cont.* (x0); *Perf. iust.* (x17); *Praed. sanct.* (x21); *Persev.* (x10); *C. Iul. imp.* (x279)
Letters (390s–420s)	0	N/A
Sermons (390s–420s)	0	N/A
Other Sermons (390s–420s)	0	N/A
Philosophical	0	*C. acad.* (x0); *Beata vita* (x0); *Ord.* (x0); *Sol.* (x0); *Imm. anim.* (x0); *Dial.* (x0); *Reth.* (x0); *Anim. quant.* (x0); *Lib. arb.* (x0); *Vera rel.* (x0); *Div. qu.* (x0); *Mend.* (x0)
Doctrinal	0	*Util. cred.* (x0); *Ad Simp.* (x0); *De agone* (x0); *Doctr. chr.* (x0); *Disc. chr.* (x0); *Nat. bon.* (x0); *Cat. rud.* (x0); *De Trin.* (x0); *B. coniug.* (x0); *Virg.* (x0); *F. et op.* (x0); *Civ. Dei* (x0); *Adult. coniug.* (x0); *C. mend.* (x0); *Ench.* (x0); *F. rerum invis.* (x0); *Haer.* (x0); *Symb. cat.* (x0)
Exegetical	0	*Exp. prop. Rm.* (x0); *Exp. Gal.* (x0); *Ep. Rm. inch.* (x0); *Ques. evan.* (x0); *Adn. Iob.* (x0); *Cons. evan.* (x0); *Gn. litt.* (x0); *Loc.* (x0); *Quaest.* (x0); *C. adu. leg.* (x0); *Cura mort.* (x0); *Dulc. ques.* (x0); *Ques. Mat.* (x0); *Adv. Iud.* (x0)
Dialogues	0	*Mag.* (x0); *De musica* (x0)
Others	0	*Conf.* (x0); *Op. mon.* (x0); *Divin. daem.* (x0); *B. uid.* (x0); *Pat.* (x0); *Retract.* (x0); *Spec.* (x0)

and even more so in the anti-Pelagian campaign: *Pecc. mer.* (x53); *Spir. et litt.* (x8); *Nat. et gr.* (x16); *Gest. Pel.* (x3); *Gr. et pecc. or.* (x15); *Nupt. et conc.* (x33); *An. et or.* (x5); *C. ep. Pel.* (x34); *C. Iul.* (x130); *Gr. et lib. arb.* (x7); *Corrept.* (x4); *Cont.* (x0); *Perf. iust.* (x17); *Praed. sanct.* (x21); *Persev.* (x10); *C. Iul. imp.* (x279). Again, the difference between the two, that is, why there is such a strong presence of one versus the other, is based on the situation. In this case, Augustine was rebutting the Pelagian accusation that he represented a parochial African mind-set and theology. This necessitated Augustine branching out across the Roman world to Christian authorities throughout the West and East.

As with many of the other themes, Augustine also combined a consideration of '*mundus*' as well as '*orbis*' with 'Cyprian' to affect his agenda. That's why we see *69 occurrences in 20 places* where Augustine pairs the terms 'Cyprian' and '*orbis*' to elaborate on the way Cyprian's views were much more in line with Augustine's, and that the Donatists in contrast were thinking in a very local light, and ignoring the Catholic Church.[73]

Innovation—Novitas

One of the more difficult themes to assess in terms of its implications for the outcome of the Donatist/Pelagian controversies is that of innovation, or '*novitas*'. The theme arises over some *240 times in 204 places*, and is by and large present in the anti-Pelagian writings. The topic comes about when Augustine is accused by Julian of Aeclanum of essentially inventing the concept of original sin. The import of this accusation is found in the overall predicament that Augustine found himself in throughout his ministry: always accused of being the 'odd-man out' and never entirely connected to any particular place in a natural way. It was for this reason he laboured so prodigiously to vaunt his African heritage when the Donatists accused him of bringing 'innovative' doctrines to Africa which opposed the tradition of Cyprian. Against the Pelagians, Augustine was considered an African rustic and was accused of trying to inject 'Punic' doctrines into the heart of the Church under the guise of legitimate Catholic doctrine.

As the data reveals here, the presence of the term '*novitas*' is dispersed throughout Augustine's writing. Nonetheless, it is clear that this term was most frequently and abundantly used by Augustine in his polemical pursuits. This is seen in the presence of the term against the Manicheans (13 times), Arians (1), Donatists (8), and against the Pelagians (78). An explanation of why this term

73 *C. ep. Parm.* 1,6(x2); 3,24; 3,25; *De bapt.* 1,28(x2); 2,5(x3); 2,14(x2); 3,1; 3,2(x3); 3,3(x5); 3,4(x2); 4,8(x4); 5,1(x5); 5,23(x2); 6,19; 6,21; 6,68(x2); *Cresc.* 2,45(x3); 3,2; 3,3(x2); 3,64(x2); *C. Gaud.* 2,6(x2); *C. Iul.* 3,32(x3); *Ep.* 93,36(x2); *s.* 310,1; 310,2(x8); 310,3; 359B,5(x2).

TABLE 12 *'Novitas' in Augustine's writings*

Genre	# of instances	Works where the term 'novitas' is present
Anti-Manichean (380s–390s)	13	*Mor. eccl.* (x1); *Gn. adu. Man.* (x0); *Duab. anim.* (x0); *C. Fort.* (x0); *F. et symb.* (x1); *Gn. litt. imp.* (x0); *S. dom. mont.* (x0); *C. Adim.* (x0); *C. ep. Man.* (x1); *C. Faust.* (x10); *C. Fel.* (x0); *C. Sec.* (x0); *c. Prisc.* (x0)
Anti-Arian	1	*C. s. Arrian.* (x0); *Conl. Max.* (x0); *C. Max.* (x1)
Anti-Donatist (390s–420s)	8	*Ps. c. Don.* (x0); *C. ep. Parm.* (x0); *De bapt.* (x5); *C. litt. Pet.* (x1); *Cresc.* (x0); *Un. bapt.* (x1); *Brev.* (x0); *C. Don.* (x0); *Emer.* (x0); *C. Gaud.* (x1); *Cath. fr.* (x0)
Anti-Pelagian (410s 430)	78	*Pecc. mer.* (x19); *Spir. et litt.* (x8); *Nat. et gr.* (x0); *Gest. Pel.* (x0); *Gr. et pecc. or.* (x1); *Nupt. et conc.* (x3); *An. et or.* (x3); *C. ep. Pel.* (x6); *C. Iul.* (x24); *Gr. et lib. arb.* (x2); *Corrept.* (x0); *Cont.* (x0); *Perf. iust.* (x2); *Praed. sanct.* (x0); *Persev.* (x0); *C. Iul. imp.* (x9)
Letters (390s–420s) [anti-Donatist works indicated in bold]	19	*Ep.* 21(x1); 36(x1); 44(x1); 54(x1); 55(x3); 120(x1); 137(x1); 140(x2); 151(x1); 166(x1); 190(x4); 193(x1); 211(x1)
Sermons (390s–420s) [anti-Donatist works indicated in bold]	45	*s.* 88(x1); 153(x4); 155(x1); 162C(x1); 163(x1); 165(x1); 166(x1); 169(x1); 190(x1); 210(x1); 228A(x1); 229A(x1); 231(x1); 236(x1); 260(x1); 260C(x1); 267(x1); 272B(x1); 279(x1); 293(x2); 293B(x1); 294(x1); 299 (x2); 350(x2); 351(x1); 352A(x1); 353(x0); 354A(x1); 359A(x2); **359B**(x1); 360B(x1); **360C**(x3); 374(x3); 360C(x1); 376A(x1)
Other Sermons	10	*Io. ev. tr.* 21(x1); 60(x1); 97(x7); 112(x1)
(390s–420s) [anti-Donatist works indicated in bold]	19	*En. in Ps.* **10**(x1); 31(x1); **32**(x1); 38(x1); 42(x4); 59(x1); 65(x1); 75(x1); 84(x1); **95**(x1); **101**(x1); 110(x1); 118(x4);
Philosophical	3	*C. acad.* (x0); *Beata vita* (x0); *Ord.* (x0); *Sol.* (x0); *Imm. anim.* (x0); *Dial.* (x0); *Reth.* (x0); *Anim. quant.* (x0); *Lib. arb.* (x0); *Vera rel.* (x3); *Div. qu.* (x0); *Mend.* (x0)

TABLE 12 *'Novitas' in Augustine's writings* (cont.)

Genre	# of instances	Works where the term 'novitas' is present
Doctrinal	33	*Util. cred.* (x2); *Ad Simp.* (x3); *De agone* (x0); *Doctr. chr.* (x0); *Disc. chr.* (x0); *Nat. bon.* (x0); *Cat. rud.* (x4); *De Trin.* (x5); *B. coniug.* (x0); *Virg.* (x0); *F. et op.* (x0); *Civ. Dei* (x17); *Adult. coniug.* (x0); *C. mend.* (x0); *Ench.* (x2); *F. rerum invis.* (x0); *Haer.* (x0); *Symb. cat.* (x0)
Exegetical	8	*Exp. prop. Rm.* (x0); *Exp. Gal.* (x1); *Ep. Rm. inch.* (x0); *Ques. evan.* (x0); *Adn. Iob.* (x0); *Cons. evan.* (x0); *Gn. litt.* (x3); *Loc.* (x0); *Quaest.* (x3); *C. adu. leg.* (x1); *Cura mort.* (x0); *Dulc. ques.* (x0); *ques. Mat.* (x0); *Adv. Iud.* (x0)
Dialogues	2	*Mag.* (x1); *De musica* (x1)
Others	10	*Conf.* (x4); *Op. mon.* (x1); *Divin. daem.* (x0); *B. uid.* (x0); *Pat.* (x0); *Retract.* (x2); *Spec.* (x2)

features so strongly in the anti-Pelagian campaign is that both sides lobbed the accusation of doctrinal innovation against the other, and it became a matter of attrition to see who could outwit the other. It should also not be a surprise that the discussion on doctrinal innovation was integrated to a high degree in Augustine's doctrinal works: *Util. cred.* (x2); *Ad Simp.* (x3); *De agone* (x0); *Doctr. chr.* (x0); *Disc. chr.* (x0); *Nat. bon.* (x0); *Cat. rud.* (x4); *De Trin.* (x5); *B. coniug.* (x0); *Virg.* (x0); *F. et op.* (x0); *Civ. Dei* (x17); *Adult. coniug.* (x0); *C. mend.* (x0); *Ench.* (x2); *F. rerum invis.* (x0); *Haer.* (x0); *Symb. cat.* (x0).

Authority—Auctoritas

By now it is quite clear that the overriding theme for Augustine for basically the entirety of his ordained career was a search for and exploitation of authoritative sources to validate his own theological positions. This makes it seem a little low, numerically, that there are only *1258 occurrences in 1016 places* of 'authority' in Augustine's extant works. Though the examples that are present are quite clear, one would expect a higher result.

Augustine's use of the term '*auctoritas*' is unexpectedly interesting. Not only is this term used often in a polemical context, but is also quite widespread throughout the duration of his career and in the various genres that he employed. Also interesting is how this theme features early on in Augustine's

TABLE 13 *'Auctoritas' in Augustine's writings*

Genre	# of instances	Works where the term 'auctoritas' is present
Anti-Manichean (380s–390s)	170	*Mor. eccl.* (x24); *Gn. adu. Man.* (x1); *Duab. anim.* (x2); *C. Fort.* (x3); *F. et symb.* (x3); *Gn. litt. imp.* (x2); *S. dom. mont.* (x10); *C. Adim.* (x6); *C. ep. Man.* (x8); *C. Faust.* (x106); *C. Fel.* (x2); *C. Sec.* (x0); *C. Prisc.* (x3)
Anti-Arian	22	*C. s. Arrian.* (x6); *Conl. Max.* (x9); *C. Max.* (x7)
Anti-Donatist (390s–420s)	87	*Ps. c. Don.* (x0); *C. ep. Parm.* (x5); *De bapt.* (x45); *C. litt. Pet.* (x6); *Cresc.* (x19); *Un. bapt.* (x0); *Brev.* (x6); *C. Don.* (x0); *Emer.* (x0); *C. Gaud.* (x3); *Cath. fr.* (x3)
Anti-Pelagian (410s–430)	156	*Pecc. mer.* (x18); *Spir. et litt.* (x0); *Nat. et gr.* (x1); *Gest. Pel.* (x5); *Gr. et pecc. or.*(x5); *Nupt. et conc.* (x6); *An. et or.* (x8); *C. ep. Pel.* (x9); *C. Iul.* (x23); *Gr. et lib. arb.* (x0); *Corrept.* (x1); *Cont.* (x0); *Perf. iust.* (x1); *Praed. sanct.* (x5); *Persev.* (x4); *C. Iul. imp.* (x70)
Letters (390s–420s) [anti-Donatist works indicated in bold]	164	*Ep.* 1(x1); 17(x2); 22(x3); **23**(x1); 26(x1); 28(x6); **29**(x2); 40(x3); **43**(x5); 44(x2); **52**(x1); 54(x6); 55(x3); 64(x1); 71(x2); 82(x6); **89**(x4); 91(x3); **93**(x6); 102(x4); 104(x2); **108**(x1); 110(x1); 118(x9); **129**(x2); 137(x3); 138(x5); 140(x1); 143(x6); 147(x17); 149(x3); 164(x4); 167(x2); 170(x1); 173A(x2); 175(x2); 176(x1); 177(x2); 184A(x1); **185**(x4); 186(x5); 190(x1); 193(x1); 194(x2); 199(x1); 202A(x6); 204(x3); 211(x1); 228(x1); 232(x1); 237(x2); 238(x1); 262(x1); 263(x1); 265(x1); 1*(x2); 21*(x1); 22*(x2)
Sermons (390s–420s) [anti-Donatist works indicated in bold]	84	*s.* **2**(x1); 8(x1); 9(x2); 12(x2); 41(x1); 48(x2); 51(x7); **71**(x1); 72A(x2); **88**(x1); 133(x2); 145(x1); 153(x4); 159A(x1); 162C(x1); 163A(x1); **164**(x1); 198(x2); 203(x1); 212(x1); 229R(x3); 229V(x3); 229A(x1); 235(x1); **266**(x1); 294(x11); 311(x1); 322(x1); 324(x1); 326(x3); 341(x2); 348A(x1); 351(x1); 352(x1); 354A(x2); **358**(x1); **359**(x1); 361(x3); 362(x4); 363(x1); 374(x5); 375C(x1)

TABLE 13 *'Auctoritas' in Augustine's writings* (cont.)

Genre	# of instances	Works where the term 'auctoritas' is present
Other Sermons (390s–420s) [anti-Donatist works indicated in bold]	11	*Io. ev. tr.* 4(x1); 5(x1); 31(x1); 40(x1); 59(x1); 96(x3); 112(x1); 113(x1); 117(x1)
	1	*Ep. Io. tr.* 7(x1)
	54	*En. in Ps.* 3(x2); 8(x1); **10**(x1); **33**(x1); **36**(x2); 40(x1); 64(x2); **67**(x5); 69(x1); 71(x6); 72(x3); 77(x1); 81(x2); 86(x1); 87(x1); **101**(x1); 103(x9); 104(x1); 113(x2); 118(x4); 119(x2); 140(x3); 143(x1); 150(x1)
Philosophical	83	*C. acad.* (x12); *Beata vita* (x3); *Ord.* (x13); *Sol.* (x1); *Imm. anim.* (x0); *Dial.* (x1); *Reth.* (x1); *Anim. quant.* (x5); *Lib. arb.* (x12); *Vera rel.* (x14); *Div. qu.* (x9); *Mend.* (x12)
Doctrinal	206	*Util. cred.* (x28); *Ad Simp.* (x0); *De agone* (x1); *Doctr. chr.* (x23); *Disc. chr.* (x0); *Nat. bon.* (x2); *Cat. rud.* (x5); *De Trin.* (x29); *B. coniug.* (x1); *Virg.* (x6); *F. et op.* (x2); *De civ. Dei* (x104); *Adult. coniug.* (x0); *C. mend.* (x0); *Ench.* (x1); *F. rerum invis.* (x1); *Haer.* (x3); *Symb. cat.* (x0)
Exegetical	116	*Exp. prop. Rm.* (x0); *Exp. Gal.* (x5); *Ep. Rm. inch.* (x2); *Ques. evan.* (x2); *Adn. Iob.* (15); *Cons. evan.* (x24); *Gn. litt.* (25); *Loc.* (x4); *Quaest.* (x24); *C. adu. leg.* (x6); *Cura mort.* (x2); *Dulc. ques.* (x1); *Ques. Mat.* (x1); *Adv. Iud.* (x5)
Dialogues	37	*Gramm.* (x9); *Mag.* (x7); *De musica* (x21)
Others	50	*Conf.* (x32); *Op. mon.* (x4); *Divin. daem.* (x1); *B. uid.* (x3); *Pat.* (x0); *Retract.* (x9); *Spec.* (x1)

career as evidenced in the anti-Manichean controversy with 170 occurrences: *Mor. eccl.* (x24); *Gn. adu. Man.* (x1); *Duab. anim.* (x2); *C. Fort.* (x3); *F. et symb.* (x3); *Gn. litt. imp.* (x2); *S. dom. mont.* (x10); *C. Adim.* (x6); *C. ep. Man.* (x8); *C. Faust.* (x106); *C. Fel.* (x2); *C. Sec.* (x0); *C. Prisc.* (x3). To appreciate just how important this term was for Augustine's polemical activities overall, consider how it features in other polemical genres: (anti-Arian, x22): *C. s. Arrian.* (x6); *Conl. Max.* (x9); *C. Max.* (x7); (anti-Donatist, x87): *Ps. c. Don.* (x0); *C. ep. Parm.* (x5); *De bapt.* (x45); *C. litt. Pet.* (x6); *Cresc.* (x19); *Un. bapt.* (x0); *Brev.* (x6); *C. Don.* (x0);

Emer. (x0); *C. Gaud.* (x3); *Cath. fr.* (x3); (anti-Pelagian, x156): *Pecc. mer.* (x18); *Spir. et litt.* (x0); *Nat. et gr.* (x1); *Gest. Pel.* (x5); *Gr. et pecc. or.*(x5); *Nupt. et conc.* (x6); *An. et or.* (x8); *C. ep. Pel.* (x9); *C. Iul.* (x23); *Gr. et lib. arb.* (x0); *Corrept.* (x1); *Cont.* (x0); *Perf. iust.* (x1); *Praed. sanct.* (x5); *Persev.* (x4); *C. Iul. imp.* (x70). It is also clear how keen Augustine was to explain his capabilities and familiarity with the concept of '*auctoritas*' by its presence in philosophical (x83), doctrinal (x206), and exegetical works (x116).

Authority was indeed an issue at the forefront in *De bapt.* and it was there that Augustine orchestrated his first major push to claim Cyprian from the Donatists. This was the only way he could reconcile his theological proposals in a place where he stood outside the mainstream when it came to such matters as group cohesion (ritual purity, rebaptism, sacramental discipline, etc.) and identification with the local heroes. That is why it is not surprising that we see Augustine pair 'Cyprian' with '*auctoritas*' 33 times in 11 places.[74] As a result we find word pairings such as '*beati Cypriani auctoritatem*', *De bapt.* 1,29; '*auctoritate beati Cypriani*', *De bapt.* 2,1; and '*auctoritas Cypriani*', *De bapt.* 2,2(x4).

Maximian—Maximianus

As was clear after reviewing the events of the Maximianist schism in Chapter 2 and noting how that conflict impacted on the course of Augustine's anti-Donatist campaign, it should not come as a shock that Augustine repeatedly returns to Maximian throughout his many works. This was a shrewd strategic move, as it allotted him a sure weapon to prevent the Donatists from forgetting all of the theological problems that the schism had created for themselves, especially in terms of how the rest of Christian Africa perceived the legitimacy of the Donatist Church. In all, Augustine returns to the theme of '*Maximianus*' with *264 occurrences in 151 places.*

The 191 references to Maximian by Augustine make it clear that there was a decidedly *ad hoc* purpose in referring to this schismatic figure in the anti-Donatist campaign. The many instances of the term in the anti-Donatist works (191) and letters make it clear that Augustine intended to undermine the positions and actions of the Donatist leadership: *Ps. c. Don.* (x0); *C. ep. Parm.* (x5); *De bapt.* (x4); *C. litt. Pet.* (x11); *Cresc.* (x145); *Un. bapt.* (x0); *Brev.* (x11); *C. Don.* (x10); *Emer.* (x11); *C. Gaud.* (x3); *Cath. fr.* (x1); *Ep.* 43(x3); 53(x1); 88(x1); 108(x18); 128(x1); 129(x1); 141(x6); 142(x1); 185(x3).

74 *De bapt.* 2,1; 2,2(x4); 2,12(x2); 2,13(x2); 2,14(x4); 2,15; 3,4(x2); 3,5; 3,6(x2); 3,7; 4,29(x2); *Cresc.* 1,38(x2); 1,39; Ep. 93,96(x2); *Ep.* 140,13(x2); *s.* 311,3; 311,5.

TABLE 14 *'Maximianus' in Augustine's writings*

Genre	# of instances	Works where the term 'Maximianus' is present
Anti-Manichean (380s–390s)	0	*Mor. eccl.* (x0); *Gn. adu. Man.* (x0); *Duab. anim.* (x0); *C. Fort.* (x0); *F et symb.* (x0); *Gn. litt. imp.* (x0); *S. dom. mont.* (x0); *C. Adim.* (x0); *C. ep. Man.* (x0); *C. Faust.* (x0); *C. Fel.* (x0); *C. Sec.* (x0); *C. Prisc.* (x0)
Anti-Arian	0	*C. s. Arrian.* (x0); *Conl. Max.* (x0); *C. Max.* (x0)
Anti-Donatist (390s–420s)	191	*Ps. c. Don.* (x0); *C. ep. Parm.* (x5); *De bapt.* (x4); *C. litt. Pet.* (x11); *Cresc.* (x145); *Un. bapt.* (x0); *Brev.* (x11); *C. Don.* (x10); *Emer.* (x11); *C. Gaud.* (x3); *Cath. fr.* (x1)
Anti-Pelagian (410s–430)	0	*Pecc. mer.* (x0); *Spir. et litt.* (x0); *Nat. et gr.* (x0); *Gest. Pel.* (x0); *Gr. et pecc. or.*(x0); *Nupt. et conc.* (x0); *An. et or.* (x0); *C. ep. Pel.* (x0); *C. Iul.* (x0); *Gr. et lib. arb.* (x0); *Corrept.* (x0); *Cont.* (x0); *Perf. iust.* (x0); *Praed. sanct.* (x0); *Persev.* (x0); *C. Iul. imp.* (x0)
Letters (390s–420s) [anti-Donatist works indicated in bold]	42	*Ep.* **43**(x3); 44(x1); 51(x2); **53**(x1); 69(x1); 70(x7); **88**(x1); 106(x1); **108**(x18); **128**(x1); **129**(x1); **141**(x6); **142**(x1); **185**(x3)
Sermons (390s–420s) [anti-Donatist works indicated in bold]	0	N/A
Other Sermons (390s–420s) [anti-Donatist works indicated in bold]	1 13	*Io. ev. tr.* 10(x1) *En. in Ps.* 35(x1); **36**(x10); 75(x1); 124(x1)
Philosophical	2	*C. acad.* (x0); *Beata vita* (x0); *Ord.* (x0); *Sol.* (x0); *Imm. anim.* (x0); *Dial.* (x0); *reth.* (x2); *Anim. quant.* (x0); *Lib. arb.* (x0); *Vera rel.* (x0); *Div. qu.* (x0); *Mend.* (x0)

Genre	# of instances	Works where the term 'Maximianus' is present
Doctrinal	1	*Util. cred.* (x0); *Ad Simp.* (x0); *De agone* (x0); *Doctr. chr.* (x0); *Disc. chr.* (x0); *Nat. bon.* (x0); *Cat. rud.* (x0); *De Trin.* (x0); *B. coniug.* (x0); *Virg.* (x0); *F. et op.* (x0); *De civ. Dei* (x1); *Adult. coniug.* (x0); *C. mend.* (x0); *Ench.* (x0); *F. rerum invis.* (x0); *Haer.* (x1); *Symb. cat.* (x0)
Exegetical	0	*Exp. prop. Rm.* (x0); *Exp. Gal.* (x0); *Ep. Rm. inch.* (x0); *Ques. evan.* (x0); *Adn. Iob.* (x0); *Cons. evan.* (x0); *Gn. litt.* (x0); *Loc.* (x0); *Quaest.* (x0); *C. adu. leg.* (x0); *Cura mort.* (x0); *Dulc. ques.* (x0); *Ques. Mat.* (x0); *Adv. Iud.* (x0)
Dialogues	0	*Mag.* (x0); *De musica* (x0)
Others	0	*Conf.* (x0); *Op. mon.* (x0); *Divin. daem.* (x0); *B. uid.* (x0); *Pat.* (x0); *Retract.* (x0); *Spec.* (x0)

Primian—Primianus

Whilst it may seem a bit of an aside, Augustine's use of the reputation of Primian was a key polemical technique in his dealings with the Donatists, and really became one of his most important measures as he strove to bring the Donatist Church under pressure from the Roman administration, as well as from other Christians in Africa. For this reason, it is no surprise that '*Primianus*' appears *199 times in 101 places*. It is interesting, however, to note that amongst Augustine's anti-Donatist works, Primian is surprisingly underrepresented in *De bapt.* Though this might have been due to Augustine's invigorated appropriation of Cyprian, that document was nonetheless his most important anti-Donatist summary and yet contains a mere nine occurrences. Adding to this perplexing scenario, Primian's name appears a staggering 70 times in *Cresc.* and 30 times in *C. Don.*!

Much like Augustine's use of the term '*Maximianus*', his mention of Primian was cultivated in a decidedly anti-Donatist spirit. This again explains why discussing the controversial Donatist leader only occurs in anti-Donatist works (138), anti-Donatist letters (34), and anti-Donatist sermons (15): *Ps. c. Don.* (x0); *C. ep. Parm.* (x9); *De bapt.* (x4); *C. litt. Pet.* (x7); *Cresc.* (x70); *Un. bapt.* (x0); *Brev.* (x10); *C. Don.* (x30); *Emer.* (x8); *C. Gaud.* (x0); *Cath. fr.* (x0); *Ep.* 43(x6); 53(x2); 106(x2); 108(x16); 129(x2); 141(x4); 173(x2); *En. in Ps.* 36(x15).

TABLE 15 *'Primianus' in Augustine's writings*

Genre	# of instances	Works where the term 'Primianus' is present
Anti-Manichean (380s–390s)	0	*Mor. eccl.* (x0); *Gn. adu. Man.* (x0); *Duab. anim.* (x0); *C. Fort.* (x0); *F. et symb.* (x0); *Gn. litt. imp.* (x0); *S. dom. mont.* (x0); *C. Adim.* (x0); *C. ep. Man.* (x0); *C. Faust.* (x0); *C. Fel.* (x0); *C. Sec.* (x0); *C. Prisc.* (x0)
Anti-Arian	0	*C. s. Arrian.* (x0); *Conl. Max.* (x0); *C. Max.* (x0)
Anti-Donatist (390s–420s)	138	*Ps. c. Don.* (x0); *C. ep. Parm.* (x9); *De bapt.* (x4); *C. litt. Pet.* (x7); *Cresc.* (x70); *Un. bapt.* (x0); *Brev.* (x10); *C. Don.* (x30); *Emer.* (x8); *C. Gaud.* (x0); *Cath. fr.* (x0)
Anti-Pelagian (410s–430)	0	*Pecc. mer.* (x0); *Spir. et litt.* (x0); *Nat. et gr.* (x0); *Gest. Pel.* (x0); *Gr. et pecc. or.* (x0); *Nupt. et conc.* (x0); *An. et or.* (x0); *C. ep. Pel.* (x0); *C. Iul.* (x0); *Gr. et lib. arb.* (x0); *Corrept.* (x0); *Cont.* (x0); *Perf. iust.* (x0); *Praed. sanct.* (x0); *Persev.* (x0); *C. Iul. imp.* (x0)
Letters (390s–420s) [anti-Donatist works indicated in bold]	34	*Ep.* **43**(x6); **53**(x2); **106**(x2); **108**(x16); **129**(x2); **141**(x4); **173**(x2)
Sermons (390s–420s) [anti-Donatist works indicated in bold]	4	*s.* 164(x4)
Other Sermons (390s–420s) [anti-Donatist works indicated in bold]	1 15	*Io. ev. tr.* 10(x1) *En. in Ps.* **36**(x15)
Philosophical	0	*C. acad.* (x0); *Beata vita* (x0); *Ord.* (x0); *Sol.* (x0); *Imm. anim.* (x0); *Dial.* (x0); *Reth.* (x0); *Anim. quant.* (x0); *Lib. arb.* (x0); *Vera rel.* (x0); *Div. qu.* (x0); *Mend.* (x0)

Genre	# of instances	Works where the term 'Primianus' is present
Doctrinal	1	*Util. cred.* (x0); *Ad Simp.* (x0); *De agone* (x0); *Doctr. chr.* (x0); *Disc. chr.* (x0); *Nat. bon.* (x0); *Cat. rud.* (x0); *De Trin.* (x0); *B. coniug.* (x0); *Virg.* (x0); *F. et op.* (x0); *Civ. Dei* (x0); *Adult. coniug.* (x0); *C. mend.* (x0); *Ench.* (x0); *F. rerum invis.* (x0); *Haer.* (x1); *symb. cat.* (x0)
Exegetical	0	*Exp. prop. Rm.* (x0); *Exp. Gal.* (x0); *Ep. Rm. inch.* (x0); *Ques. evan.* (x0); *Adn. Iob.* (x0); *Cons. evan.* (x0); *Gn. litt.* (x0); *Loc.* (x0); *Quaest.* (x0); *C. adu. leg.* (x0); *Cura mort.* (x0); *Dulc. ques.* (x0); *Ques. Mat.* (x0); *Adv. Iud.* (x0)
Dialogues	0	*Mag.* (x0); *De musica* (x0)
Others	0	*Conf.* (x0); *Op. mon.* (x0); *Divin. daem.* (x0); *B. uid.* (x0); *Pat.* (x0); *Retract.* (x0); *Spec.* (x0)

Approaching Cyprian through Paul

Another essential aspect of Augustine's sustained anti-Donatist campaign is easily overlooked: that is, his use of scripture. His ready use of scripture to support his theology and initiatives is well known, and a great deal of research material has been produced in recent decades concerning Augustine's familiarity with and appropriation of Pauline literature. But the connection between that process and Augustine's appropriation of Cyprian has not been adequately addressed. This is problematic because tapping into the thought and authority of Paul was central for Augustine's own theological sophistication, but also because it became clear over time that without Paul, Augustine and his allies would have been unsuccessful in assuming Cyprian's authority and tradition.

To assess this process we have to return to the time of Augustine's composition of *Ep.* 21 in 391, when he disclosed to 'Pater Valeri' his need to improve his capabilities for ministry.[75] Specifically, Augustine revealed his inadequacy with

75 Aug., *Ep.* 21,3 (*WSA* II/1, 56) 'I ought to examine carefully all the remedies of his scriptures and, by praying and reading, work that he may grant my soul health suited for such dangerous tasks [the work of a cleric and ministry in the saving of souls]. I did not do this before because I did not have the time. For I was ordained at the time when we were

scripture and his need for in-depth study in order to better handle his newly-appointed duties. But what he states only opaquely is that this is a pastoral reaction to the gravitational force of the opposing Donatist Church.

Augustine was granted his wish, although exactly what happened he does not tell us. However, we know from his record that once back in action he wasted little time engaging in various pursuits. Two examples are particularly important: his invigorated anti-Donatist campaign and the proliferating use of Paul in his writings.[76] These developments were, I believe, connected. This is a crucial point, as these developments led Augustine on a particular theological course that would define his later engagements. This is even more pertinent because of Paul's distinctive role in Augustine's polemical activities (i.e., the Manichean, Donatist, and Pelagian controversies) compared with use of other biblical sources in Augustine's corpus. My exploration is limited, however, by the sparseness of research on Augustine's use of Paul against his main opponents, the Donatists.[77]

---

planning a period of retreat for gaining knowledge of the divine scriptures and wanted to arrange our affairs in order that we could have the leisure for this task'. (*CSEL* 34/1, 51): 'Debeo scripturarum eius medicamenta omnia perscrutari et orando ac legendo agere, ut idonea ualitudo animae meae ad tam periculosa negotia tribuatur. Quod ante non feci, quia et tempus non habui; tunc enim ordinatus sum, cum de ipso uacationis tempore ad cognoscendas diuinas scripturas cogitaremus et sic nos disponere uellemus, ut nobis otium ad hoc negotium posset esse'.

76 While Augustine already used Paul or Pauline concepts against Manichean enemies before his ordination as presbyter (*De magistro* (389),*De Genesi adversus Manicheos* (388/89), *De moribus ecclesiae* (388/89)), it was not until after his ordination that this trend accelerated (*Contra Fortunatum Manicheum* (392), *De duas animabus* (392/93), especially in the mid-390s with *Expositio epistulae ad Galatas* (394), *Expositio quarundum propositiionum ex epistula apostoli ad Romanos* (394/95), *Epistulae ad Romanos inchoata expositio* (394/95), Sections 66 through 68 of *De diversis quaestionibus* (395), *Ad Simplicianum* (396), *Confessiones* (397), and *Contra Faustum Manicheum* (397/99)).

77 Currently only one work per decade, roughly speaking, is produced on the polemical use of Paul in the Donatist controversy or by the Donatists themselves. In the 1950s Frend's *The Donatist Church*, 123, 307–08, 320, launched the subject into the English-speaking academic world. Not until his follow-up article 'The Donatist Church and St. Paul', in J. Ries et al. (ed.), *Le Epistole Paoline nei Manichei e Donatisti e il Primo Agostino* (Rome: 1989), 85–123, was this topic specifically broached again. In the same anthology M.G. Mara also discussed the influence of Paul in shaping Augustine's anti-Donatist thought in the Confessions, see 'L'influsso di Paolo in Agostino', 125–62; and also in 'Le Confessioni di Agostino: una confluenza di raggiunte convinzioni', *Augustinianum* 36/2 (1996), 495–509. These initial works were added to by Tilley's, *The Bible in Christian North Africa* and her examination of Donatist usage of Paul. In the 2000s there was Thomas Martin's, '*Paulus*

Augustine needed to appropriate Paul because the majority religion in Africa, the Donatist Church, had itself a tradition of appropriating Paul. If Augustine was to gain a foothold in the battle against the Donatists, he needed to learn their theological language, or at least their sources. There was a deep exegetical history of Pauline literature in North Africa. Tertullian, Cyprian, Marius Victorinus, Optatus of Milevis, and Tyconius were all individuals who dealt heavily in Paul.[78] And it should come as no surprise that Augustine would draw inspiration from all of them, Donatist or not.[79] Yet the one figure whose influence Augustine could never hope to escape was Cyprian.[80] For Catholics and Donatists alike, Cyprian was as quintessentially North African as apple pie is American. He was a Christian hero, home-grown, a bishop and a martyr.[81] What Cyprian wrote mattered, and Cyprian integrated Pauline sources liberally.[82]

Therefore Augustine needed to tap into the Cyprianic tradition and exegetical style. But the problem was Cyprian's exegesis rather explicitly vindicated key Donatist theologies,[83] and as such was not a prime polemical weapon for

---

Autem Apostolus Dicit (*Cresc.* 2.21.26): Augustine's Pauline Polemic Against the Donatists', *Augustiniana* 56/3–4 (2006), 235–59.

78 Thomas Martin, 'Pauline Commentaries', in A. Fitzgerald (ed.), *Augustine Through the Ages: An Encyclopedia* (Grand Rapids, MI: 1999), 626–27.

79 Of particular note should be the well-studied link between Augustine and the Donatist lay theologian, Tyconius (380s).

80 Indeed, the *persona* of Cyprian and the authority that went hand-in-hand with it in Roman and Punic North Africa was something which Augustine was neither able to avoid, nor fully reconcile in terms of theological positioning. An example of this was Augustine's struggle to have Cyprian's theology vindicate his own views, even though it was clear to North Africans the Donatists followed Cyprian more closely.

81 Cyprian's influence in North Africa is treated in the recent monograph of Burns, *Cyprian the Bishop*, 176. 'The Christian church in Africa would grow, in divergent and opposed ways [Donatist and Catholic], and be nourished by the life of Cyprian's church. His disciples would change and adapt much of what he defended and held dear. The Christians of Africa—Catholic and Donatist alike—held him their father and celebrated his triumph each year, with singing and dancing'.

82 The most comprehensive work to date on Cyprian's use of the bible is M.A. Fahey, *Cyprian and the Bible: A Study in Third Century Exegesis*. Cyprian references Paul 395 times in his writings (and 346 instances in the pseudo-Cyprianic texts) which number is broken down as follows: Rom. x65; 1 Cor. x104; 2 Cor. x25; Gal. x35; Eph. x68; Phil. x12; Col. x13; 1 Thes. x10; 1 Tim. x18; 2 Tim. x23x; and Tit. x10. If compared with his next most frequently used sources, the gospels of Matthew and of John, x276 and x145 respectively, the influence is evident.

83 Tilley, *The Bible in Christian North Africa*, 40–41.

the upstart Catholic. So what exactly were the exegetical themes held by Cyprian? The three most prevalent were his views that (1) the Church and the world are antithetical to each other; (2) the Church's nature is pure, and all steps must be taken to ensure its integrity; and (3) sacerdotal purity is necessary for the celebration of sacraments in order to prevent the spread of contagion. For those who have studied Donatist Christianity all three are recognisable as later central Donatist themes.[84]

All three undercurrents were strengthened by what Maureen Tilley has called Cyprian's 'literal-typological' reading of scripture.[85] His view that the world was an antagonistic force against the Church was aided by his reading in both Testaments that the Church is an association of God's elect. Terms he would use for the Church included: an enclosed garden, perfect, a bride, sealed fountain, and cistern of living water.[86] The world therefore symbolised sin, corruption, and darkness.[87] He continued this line of thought to conclude suffering and even martyrdom were signs of authentic Christian faith.[88]

Cyprian's view that the Church was a bastion of purity likewise required a contrast with the world to gain its meaning.[89] Particular nemeses were heretics and schismatics who threatened to introduce the world's poison into the Church.[90] While heretics and schismatics posed a direct risk, sinful members within the Church also risked spreading contagion within the Church.[91] To counter these threats, Cyprian mandated a rigorous Christian life,[92] whereby sinful members were to be shunned and a host of personal behaviours adopted from Paul were to be practiced: sobriety of speech,[93] courage against

84 Frend, *The Donatist Church*, esp. 315–36; Burns, *Cyprian the Bishop*, 167–69; Tilley, *The Bible in Christian North Africa*, 162–171; Gaumer, 'The Evolution of Donatist Theology as Response to a Changing Late Antique Milieu', 201–33.

85 Tilley, *The Bible in Christian North Africa*, 35–41.

86 Cant. 6,9, Cant. 6,12 in Cyp., *Ep.* 69. Cyprian tied these typologies into his christology in the same letter, using Eph. 5,25–26: 'Christ loved the Church and handed himself over on her behalf, that he might make her holy, purifying her with a bath of water'.

87 Eph. 6,12–17 in Cyp., *Ep.* 13.

88 Suffering is direct a way of being a soldier of Christ (Gal. 3,27 in Cyp., *Ep.* 62) '…all of you who have been baptised in Christ, put on Christ'. And for those who endure, victory is the prize of suffering (Rom. 8,16–17 in Cyprian. *Ep.* 58) '…we share in his sufferings so that we may share his glory'.

89 1 Cor. 10,1–2, 1 Cor. 10,6 in Cyp., *Ep.* 68,15; Gal. 3,69 in Cyp., *Ep.* 63; Eph. 5,25–26 in Cyp., *Ep.* 68 and *Ep.* 69,2.

90 2 Thes. 2,10–12 in Cyp., *Ep.* 59; 1 Tim. 4,12 in Cyp., *Ep.* 3.

91 2 Tim. 2,17 in Cyp., *Ep.* 73 and *Ep.* 59; 1 Cor. 15,33, Tit. 3:11 in Cyp., *Ep.* 59.

92 Eph. 4,27 in Cyp., *Ep.* 4.

93 Eph. 4,29 in Cyp., *Ep.* 45; 1 Cor. 6,10 in Cyp., *Ep.* 59.

the world,[94] a life of charity,[95] and so forth.[96] And yes, rebaptism would be required for those baptised in schism or heresy and coming to the true Church for the first time.[97]

For there to be a pure Church there also had to be pure ministers: '[T]he apostle warns and says "For a bishop must be blameless as being a steward of God"'.[98] This was the final piece in Cyprian's theological scheme for the Church.[99] Again drawing on the OT and also Paul,[100] Cyprian accentuated the importance of clergy especially being without sin, in order not to contaminate others.[101] But in using Paul, Cyprian extended this admonition to all Christians, with the warning that everyone has to render an explanation before God.[102]

Quantitative and Qualitative Analysis

The Cyprianic exegesis of Paul, with its focus on Church/world tension and its call for ecclesial/ministerial purity, presented a problem of adaptation for Augustine. How was he supposed to legitimately draw on Paul using the vocabulary of North African Christianity when Paul's language was already synchronised with Donatist language, so to speak? It was out of the question for Augustine to simply ignore Paul; to do so would have placed him out of vogue with Christian *literati* of his time.[103] Plus, he could ill afford to seem Manichean to his ecclesial rivals, or an aloof foreigner such as his Greek-speaking predecessor Valerius might have seemed to Donatist eyes.

94 Rom. 1,8 in Cyp. *Ep*. 30.

95 Gal. 5,14–15 in Cyp., *Ep*. 13.

96 Generosity towards the poor: 2 Cor. 8,12–13, 8,14–15, 9,6–7, 9,12, Gal. 6,10; strictness in living: Col. 2,20, 3,1–4, 1 Thes. 4,6; praying at all times: Col. 4,2.

97 Most of the sources containing Cyprian's rationale for rebaptism are contained in *Ep*. 70 and 71. See also *Ep*. 74 (Gal. 3,27; Tit. 3,5; Eph. 5,25–26) and *Ep*. 75 (1 Cor. 2,6; Gal. 3,27; Phil. 1,18).

98 Tit. 1,7 in Cyp., *Ep*. 67. Also in *Ep*. 1 (2 Tim. 2,4) 'No soldier fighting in God's service entangles himself in the anxieties of this world'.

99 The necessity for pure ministers was essential to the community model that North African Christians created for themselves. They could not conceive of a Church that was pure, while its leadership or even its members were not. Donatist Christians would carry this same concept forth in their time.

100 Cyp., *Ep*. 3,1; *Ep*. 59,5; *Ep*. 64,4; *Ep*. 65,2–3; *Ep*. 67,3; *Ep*. 72,2; *De unit*. 17 and 18.

101 1 Cor. 12,26 in Cyp., *Ep*. 17.

102 Rom. 14,12–13 in Cyp., *Ep*. 68; Gal. 6,7 in *Ep*. 67.

103 Babcock, 'Augustine's Interpretation of Romans (A.D. 394–396)', 56–57; Brown, *Augustine of Hippo: A Biography*, 151; Martin, 'Pauline Commentaries', 626.

To the question of how the young Augustine was able to make Paul his own, I found a possible and partial answer in a comparison between Augustine's use of specifically Pauline texts in the Donatist and Pelagian controversies on the one hand and Cyprian's on the other.[104] More precisely, I made a detailed map of Cyprian's Pauline references and then tracked Augustine's own usage and the areas of overlap.[105]

In all, Cyprian referred to 168 Pauline quotes, using 270 of his verses (plus there are an extra 346 instances in the pseudo-Cyprianic texts).[106] Compared with the next most used sources, the gospels of Matthew and John (178 and 117 times each respectively) the impact of Paul is significant. Of the 168 verses used by Cyprian, Augustine would himself utilise 151[107] of the same verses; with 104 of those appearing in the anti-Donatist writings.[108] His anti-Pelagian

104 To do so, I consulted the extensive scripture indexes for Augustine's works in the Donatist and Pelagian controversies. For occurrences of Paul in the anti-Donatist writings, I used the *tables des références* in the G. Finaert translations in *Œvres de Saint Augustin, Traités anti-Donatistes, Bibliothèque Augustinienne*, vols. 28–32 (Paris: 1963–1968). For the anti-Pelgian writings, I utilised the indexes contained in the R.J. Teske translations *Answer to the Pelagians I–IV*, vols. (I/23–26), *The Works of Saint Augustine: A Translation for the 21st Century* (Hyde Park, NY, 1997–1999).

105 For Cyprian's usage of Paul I consulted the scriptural index in Fahey, *Cyprian and the Bible: A Study in Third Century Exegesis*, 676–95. With those results in hand I drove my research further with the aid of the CETEDOC *Library of Christian Latin Texts, version 7 (Brepols: 2008) and Corpus Augustinianum Gissense, version 2 (Basel: 2004)*. This allowed me to analyse specific texts and find the context of the Pauline quote.

106 Fahey, *Cyprian and the Bible: A Study in Third Century Exegesis*, 43.

107 Or an 89% over-lap. These passages consist of the following: *Rom.* 1,17; 1,25–26; 1,29–32; 2,1–3; 2,4–6; 2,11; 2,12; 2,13; 2,24; 3,3–4; 3,8; 3,13–18; 3,23–24; 4,25; 5,2–5; 5,8–9; 6,6; 8,12–14; 8,16–17; 8,18; 8,24–25; 8,32; 8,35–37; 11,20–21; 11,33–36; 12,1–2; 12,19; 12,21; 13,3; 13,7–8; 13,12–13; 14,4; 14,12–13; 14,17; *1 Cor.* 1,10; 1,17–24; 1,24; 3,1–3; 3,16–17; 3,18–20; 4,7; 5,7–8; 6,7–9; 6,9–11; 6,10; 6,15; 6,18; 6,19–20; 7,1–7; 7,9; 7,29–31; 9,22; 9,24–25; 10,1–2; 10,12; 10,13; 10,33–11,1; 11,3; 11,16; 11,19; 11,26; 11,27; 12,26; 13,2–8; 13,2–5; 13,3; 13,4; 13,4–5,7–8; 13,12; 13,13; 14,29–30; 15,33; 15,36; 15,41–44; 15,47–49; 15,53; 15,53–55; *2 Cor.* 3,14–16; 5,10; 5,15; 5,17; 6,14; 9,6–7; 9,10–11; 11,14–15; 11,24; 11,29; 12,2–4; 12,7–9; *Gal.* 1,6–9; 3,6–9; 3,6; 3,21–31; 3,27; 4,4; 5,14–15; 5,17,19–24; 6,1–2; 6,7; 6,7–8; 6,10; *Eph.* 1,7; 1,18; 2,3; 2,17–18; 2,19; 4,2–3; 4,3; 4,5; 4,22–24; 5,5; 5,6–7; 5,8; 5,25–26; 5,31; 6,5–6; 6,12; *Phil.* 1,18; 1,21; 2,6–11; 2,9; 2,14–15; 2,15; 2,21; 3,19–21; 3,20–21; *Col.* 1,15; 1,18; 2,11; 3,1–4; 3,5–6; 4,2; *2 Thes.* 2,10–12; 3,6; *1 Tim.* 1,13; 4,4; 5,3–6; 5,11–12; 5,20; 6,7–10; *2 Tim.* 2,4; 2,11–12; 2,17; 2,20; 2,23–24; 2,24; 3,1–9; 4,6–8; *Tit.* 1,7; 1,15; 3,5; 3,10–11.

108 Or a 69% rate of recurrence of Cyprian's Pauline usage in the anti-Donatist writings: *Rom.*1,25–26; 1,29–32; 2,1–3; 2,13; 2,24; 3,8; 3,13–18; 4,25; 5,2–5; 8,12–14; 8,16–17; 8,18; 8,24–25; 11,20–21; 13,3; 13,7–8; 13,12–13; 14,4; 14,12–13; *1 Cor.* 1,10; 1,17–24; 3,1–3; 3,16–17; 3,18–20; 4,7; 5,7–8; 6,9–11; 6,10; 6,18; 7,1–7; 9,22; 9,24–25; 10,1–2; 10,13; 11,16; 11,19; 11,26; 11,27; 12,26; 13,2–8; 13,4–5,7–8; 13,12; 13,13; 14,29–30; 15,33; 15,53; 15,53–55; *2 Cor.* 3,14–16; 6,14; 9,10–11; 11,14–15;

works used 96 of those same verses.[109] I also analysed the number of occurrences where Augustine used the same Pauline quote in both controversies, which occurred with 45 verses.[110] In this way I found there to be greater than 50% variation between Pauline usages in the two controversies. To get a more precise account of how Augustine was handling Cyprian's Pauline exegesis, however, I looked at key passages in the construction of Cyprian's theology. This brought me to 82 central Pauline verses Cyprian used in his theological models, especially seen in his writings, the *Letters, De Lapsis, De Unitate*.[111] Of these 82 verses, Augustine would use 53 at least once in the Donatist controversy.[112] The Pelagian controversy would occasion the use of 28.[113] And in 17 unique situations, a particular verse would be used in both controversies.[114]

11,24; 11,29; 12,2–4; 12,7–9; *Gal.* 1,6–9; 3,6–9; 3,6; 3,27; 4,4; 5,17,19–24; 6,1–2; 6,10; *Eph.* 2,19; 4,2–3; 4,3; 4,5; 4,22–24; 5,5; 5,6–7; 5,8; 5,25–26; 5,31; 6,12; *Phil.* 1,18; 2,6–11; 2,15; 2,21; 3,19–21; 3,20–21; *Col.* 1,18; 2,11; 3,1–4; 3,5–6; 4,2; *2 Thes.* 3,6; *1 Tim.* 1,13; 4,4; 5,3–6; 5,20; *2 Tim.* 2,4; 2,11–12; 2,17; 2,20; 2,23–24; 2,24; 3,1–9; 4,6–8; *Tit.* 1,7; 1,15; 3,5; 3,10–11.

109 Or a 64% rate of recurrence of Cyprian's Pauline usage in the anti-Pelagian writings: *Rom.* 1,17; 1,25–26; 1,29–32; 2,4–6; 2,11; 2,12; 2,13; 3,8; 3,23–24; 4,25; 5,2–5; 5,8–9; 6,6; 8,12–14; 8,24–25; 8,32; 8,35–37; 11,33–36; 12,1–2; 12,19; 12,21; 13,3; 13,7–8; 13,12–13; 14,4; 14,17; *1 Cor.* 1,17–24; 1,24; 3,1–3; 3,16; 6,7–9; 6,9–11; 6,10; 6,15; 6,19–20; 7,1–7; 7,9; 7,29–31; 9,24–25; 10,12; 10,13; 10,33–11,1; 11,3; 11,19; 13,2–5; 13,4; 13:12; 13:13; 15,33; 15,36; 15,41–44; 15,47–49; 15,53–55; *2 Cor.* 3,14–16; 5,10; 5,15; 5,17; 6,14; 9,6–7; 11,14–15; 11,29; 12,2–4; 12,7–9; *Gal.* 3,6–9; 3,21–31; 3,27; 5,14–15; 5,17,19–24; 6,7; 6,7–8; *Eph.* 1,7; 1,18; 2,3; 2,17–18; 4,5; 5,8; 5,25–26; 6,5–6; 6,12; *Phil.* 1,21; 2,6–11; 2,9; 2,14–15; 3,19–21; 3,20–21; *Col.* 1,15; 1,18; 2,11; 3,1–4; 3:5–6; 4,2; *2 Thes.* 2,10–12; *1 Tim.* 4,4; 5,11–12; 6,7–10; *2 Tim.* 2,20; 4,6–8; *Tit.* 3,5.

110 Or a 19% rate: *Rom.* 1,25–26; 1,29–32; 2,13; 3,8; 4,25; 5,2–5; 8,12–14; 8,24–25; 13,3; 13,7–8; 14,4; 14,12–13; *1 Cor.* 1,17–24; 3,1–3; 4,7; 6,9–11; 6,10; 7,1–7; 9,24–25; 10,13; 11,19; 13,2–5; 13,3; 13,4; 13,4–5,7–8; 13,12; 13,13; 15,33; 15,53–55; *2 Cor.* 3,14–16; 6,14; 9,6–7; 11,14–15; 11,29; 12,2–4; 12,7–9; *Gal.* 3,6; 3,27; 5,17,19–24; *Eph.* 4,5; 5,8; 5,25–26; 6,12; *Phil.* 2,6–11; 3,20–21; *Col.* 1,18; 2,11; 3,1–4; 3,5–6; *1 Tim.* 4,4; *2 Tim.* 2,20; 4,6–8; *Tit.* 3,5.

111 These works were selectively chosen based on their utility in deciphering the construction of Cyprian's theology within patristic scholarship.

112 Or 65%: *Rom.* 2,24; 3,3–4; 8,16–17; 8,18; 11,20–21; 14,4; 14,12–13; *1 Cor.* 1,10; 3,16–17; 6,10; 6,18; 9,22; 9,24–25; 10,1–2; 10,13; 11,16; 11,19; 11,26; 11,27; 12,26; 13:2–8; 14,29–30; 15,33; *2 Cor.* 6,14; 11,14–15; 11,29; *Gal.* 1,6–9; 3,6–9; 3,6; 3,27; 6,1–2; *Eph.* 4,2–3; 4,3; 4,22–24; 5,5; 5,6–7; 5,25–26; 5,31; 6:12; *Phil.* 1,18; 2,6–11; 2,15; 3,20–21; *Col.* 3,5–6; *2 Thes.* 3,6; *1 Tim.* 1,13; *2 Tim.* 2,4; 2,17; 2,20; 2,24; 3,1–9; *Tit.* 1,7; 1,15; 3,5; 3,10–11.

113 Or 34%: *Rom.* 5,8–9; 8,35–37; 12,1–2; 14,4; *1 Cor.* 1,24; 3,16; 6,10; 9,24–25; 10,12; 10,33–11,1; 11,19; 13,2–5; 15,33; *2 Cor.* 6,14; 11,14–15; 11,29; *Gal.* 3,6–9; 3,27; 5,14–15; 6,7; *Eph.* 5,25–26; 6,12; *Phil.* 2,6–11; 2,15; 3,20–21; *Col.* 3,5–6; 4,2; *2 Thes.* 2,10–12; *1 Tim.* 6,7–10; *2 Tim.* 2,20; *Tit.* 3,5.

114 Or 21%: *1 Cor.* 3,16; 6,10; 9,24–25; 11,19; 13,2–5; 15,33; *2 Cor.* 6,14; 11,14–15; 11,29; *Gal.* 3,27; *Eph.* 5,25–26; 6,12; *Phil.* 2,6–11; 3,20–21; *Col.* 3,5–6; *2 Tim.* 2,20; *Tit.* 3,5.

That means that Augustine used 64% of Cyprian's Pauline texts in the Donatist controversy, whilst in the Pelagian crisis only 34%. Another benchmark I investigated was Augustine's use of cluster-verses, or those verses which Cyprian deployed three or more times.[115] I have identified 29 such clusters in Cyprian's writings. Augustine would repeat those clusters 19 times in the Donatist controversy, 13 in the Pelagian, and 6 times in both.

The numerical data I put forth is helpful, but not entirely conclusive. Not only that, but the numbers themselves do not demonstrate the process of Augustine's appropriation of Paul. They do, however, suggest a gradual movement away from dependence on the Cyprianic exegetical tradition. To reach this conclusion, I not only had to place Pauline texts side by side, but also individually analyse each passage in context. This is where I made the most important discoveries.

My principle finding was that Augustine by and large remained within Cyprian's Pauline track; a manoeuvre used to closely align himself with the tradition in Africa. Whilst Augustine certainly correlates more with Cyprian in the anti-Donatist writings, and does not take a completely different path as time progresses, all the while he is never completely successful in reaching a comfortable symbiosis with the bishop of Carthage. In other words, Augustine continued to overlap with Cyprian throughout his career. I found that the drop off in usage observed between the anti-Donatist and anti-Pelagian works is explained simply by the fact that Augustine needed to accentuate his African heritage more strongly in the earlier controversy and less so against the Pelagians.[116] I found proof of this in Augustine's Pauline exegesis when expounding Christological themes.[117] In the earlier crisis, Christology and relevant themes such as grace/*gratia* are present, but in the Pelagian controversy the themes become even more front and centre and thus required a shift in scriptural sourcing. As a result, we can trace a proliferating use of Paul

115 *Rom.* 3,3–4; 8,16–17; 8,18; *1 Cor.* 3,16; 6,19–20; 9,24–25; 11,3; 11,27; 15,33; 15,47; *Gal.* 1,10; 3,27; 6,7–8; *Eph.* 2,3; 4,23; 4,4; 4,22–24; 5,6–7; 6,11; 6,17; Col. 4,2; 2 *Thes.* 3,6; *1 Tim.* 6,7–10; 2 *Tim.* 2,4; 2,17; 2,20; *Tit.* 3,10–11.

116 This was the subject of close study in D. Weber, 'For What is so Monstrous as What the Punic Fellow says?: Reflections on the Literary Background of Julian's Polemical Attacks on Augustine's Homeland', in P.Y.-Fux, J.-M. Roessli, O. Wermelinger (eds.), *Augustinus Afer: Saint Augustin, africanité et universalité. Actes du colloque international, Alger-Annaba 1–7 avril* 2001 (Freibourg 2003), 75–82.

117 Using Pauline sources to articulate Augustine's Christological themes: *Rom.* 3–5; 3,23–24; 5,8–9; 8,35–37; *1 Cor.* 1,22–24; 15,47–49; 6,19–20; 6,9–11; 2 *Cor.* 5,10; 5,15; *Gal.* 4,4; 6,14; *Eph.* 2,17–18; *Phil.* 2,6–11; *Col.* 1,15; 1,18.

to argue Christological themes in the latter controversy as well as other themes as the context demanded.[118]

Even though Augustine continued to use the same Pauline verses as Cyprian, his theological interpretation of them did not remain stagnant.[119] I repeat this point: Augustine maintained the same Pauline verse usage but found significance in them to support his own theological stance. A difference in hermeneutical approaches is one possible explanation for this. As mentioned earlier, Cyprian, and later the Donatists, employed a literal-typological reading of the scriptures in order to make sense of the tribulations they faced in their world. By contrast, and as the late Thomas Martin pointed out,[120] Augustine readily used a seven-tiered reading of scripture. Two of those tiers, use of the *regula fidei* (rule of faith) and the hermeneutic of conversion and love,[121] go a long way towards explaining my findings. Augustine's opinion was that he could interpret Paul in a more authentic way because he read him through the mind of the universal Church, in contrast with the parochial mind-set of the Donatists.[122] He was, in short, better able to read the bible because he felt he was guided by the rule of faith used throughout the world by the Catholic Church. Another theme Augustine locked in quite early in his priesthood was that the largest stumbling block for Donatist leaders was their failure to approach Paul (or Church matters for that matter) from the angle of charity, which Augustine considered the most fundamental requirement for Christians.

With that in mind, it becomes possible to see how Augustine could be so audacious as to challenge Cyprian's Pauline exegetical tradition in Africa. Instead of being mostly concerned with the Church/world difference, and ecclesial/sacerdotal purity, Augustine could apply the same Pauline references with

118 Examples are commonly acknowledged themes such as the strength of the human will, predestination, and the salvific mediation of Christ.

119 This fits into a larger picture of Augustine as unsuccessful in fully integrating and reconciling his theological programme with Cyprian's. A clear example is found in Jonathan Yates's research on the historicity of *concupiscence* in North African Theology pre-Augustine: 'Was There "Augustinian" Concupiscence in pre-Augustinian North Africa?' *Augustiniana* 51 (2001), 39–56.

120 Thomas Martin, 'Modus Inveniendi Paulum: Augustine, Hermeneutics, and his Reading of Romans', in D. Patte and E. TeSelle (eds.), *Engaging Augustine on Romans: Self, Context, and Theology in Interpretation* (Harrisburg, PA: 2002), 63–90.

121 Martin, 'Modus Inveniendi Paulum: Augustine, Hermeneutics, and his Reading of Romans', 65–66 and 71–73.

122 Augustine would make a central element of his argument against Donatist leaders the charge that they possessed an entirely limited view of the faith, so much so that it ran contrary to the 'catholic' nature of Christianity.

different intentions. It was no longer a question of how evil the world and political society were, but one of diagnosing and curing sin and a fallen human nature.[123] Suffering was no longer a Christian obligation and merit-badge, but a divine grace reserved for the select. So too the Church was to be seen slightly differently. Though it was indeed the pure bride of Christ, it was not this because membership was exclusively reserved for the purest of the pure. It was the Church because of its relationship with Christ who purifies it through his grace. In this way it could contain wheat and chaff, gold and clay, lilies and thorns among its flock and yet remain holy.[124] Lastly, because Christ's grace is the mechanism for all sacraments and blessings, ritual efficacy was no longer the paranoid evasion of sin, but the celebration of faith. Instead of spreading contagion, rituals and sacraments conducted even by sinful clergy occasioned God's saving grace.

123 These themes would become even more prominent in the Pelagian controversy.

124 The use of these terms was the subject of study in two relevant essays: F.G. Clancy, 'St. Augustine, his predecessors and contemporaries and the exegesis of 2 Tim. 2.20', *Studia Patristica* 27 (1993), 242–48; N. Henry, 'The Lily and Thorns: Augustine's Refutation of the Donatists' Exegesis of the Song of Songs', *Revue des Études Augustiniennes* 42 (1996), 255–66.

CHAPTER 6

Sustaining Appropriation

So far in this text I have looked at how Augustine's approach to the Donatist Church was shaped and how that interaction in turn affected his thoughts on important Christian theologies. I have also shown how this chain of events inevitably brought Augustine head-to-head with the need to associate himself with an authority figure such as Cyprian, in order to gain the sort of credibility and currency he quite desperately needed in his pastoral context as shepherd of a minority organisation in Donatist Africa. This led, as observed through the course of Chapter 5, to a prolonged appropriation of Cyprian throughout his career, starting in the 390s and ending at the time of his death in 430, before his dealings with Julian of Aeclanum could be completed. As well as integrating the authority of Cyprian through his endeavours against the Donatists and then the Pelagians, it is evident, after a review of themes well-engrained throughout his career, and which receive much recognition from scholars today (e.g., truth, concupiscence, pride, etc.), that these themes were also heavily represented in the Donatist and Pelagian controversies and were often even used in conjunction with the authority of Cyprian in order to strengthen their validity.

This now leads at last to a content-based analysis of three important matters which developed as a direct result of Augustine's anti-Donatist campaign, and that had serious ramifications for his legitimate claim to appropriate Cyprian, especially through the course of the Pelagian controversy. I examine specifically: (1) Augustine's gradual condoning of state-endorsed religious coercion to effect the end of the schism; (2) his development of a more elaborate theology of grace; and (3) his pneumatology. What will be apparent to the reader throughout is that each of these developments was deeply shaped by Augustine's engagement with the Donatists, and that whilst they are not often associated with that controversy, they nonetheless show all the important indications of having their origin there. Another consequence of the Donatist campaign is the appearance of overtones which are recognisable in the Pelagian controversy later on.

The Role of Religious Coercion in Augustine's Campaigns

One of the most obvious issues over which Augustine would collide with the legacy of Cyprian and his Donatist adherents early on was that of the

 | DOI 10.1163/9789004312647_008

legitimacy of state inference in the Church. The tradition of North African Christianity was starkly opposed to the Church being any sort of mirror of the secular world, and, heaven forbid, of the pagan Roman Empire! This was a way of thinking well established by Tertullian and Cyprian, since both were leaders of Christian communities whose very existence was defined in a context of minority-status and discomfiture in the face of an otherwise non-Christian Mediterranean. The situation slowly started to change, however, with the arrival of Constantine and the startling revelation that Christians could develop an active presence in the empire. It was this development, of a rift between how things had been in Africa for scores of years and how they were becoming, which might have given sufficient cause for the emergence of a Donatist 'schism'.[1] Certainly African Christian noteworthies, such as Lactantius, had established a trend in the early-mid 300s by making a forceful argument for the legitimate integration of Christians in the Roman Empire, and especially in the Roman Legions,[2] with their recognisable presence on the African borders.

Against this mainstream development stood Donatist Christianity, the influential and quintessentially African religion. It was a religious milieu that was often fluidly divided between agrarian Punics in the interior and the more powerful Roman colonists in coastal towns, as well as Africa's fertile plantations. This line demarcated more than a division between the impoverished and the powerful, occupied and colonists; it also represented two distinct Christian traditions, whose members often viscerally rejected each other's understanding of the compatibility of the Church with the world, and who denied the legitimacy of the existence of other churches because of problems originating from the Great Persecutions (303–305), and from differing ethnic backgrounds.

A particularly marked display of this ancient tension between native Africans and Roman colonists can be seen in the way each camp attempted to coerce the other into conforming to their own view. Reaching a full appreciation of this background is complicated, however, by the fact that scholars still tend to present Augustine's involvement in the development of religious coercion against dissidents in paradigms derived from the polemical history between Catholics and Protestants, or in an over-simplified way, by portraying the onset of coercion as an outcome of the greater involvement of the state in Church

1 See the controversial insights of Timothy Barnes, 'The Beginnings of Donatism', *Journal of Theological Studies* 26/1 (1975), 13–22; and his review article, 'Was There a Constantinian Revolution?' *Journal of Late Antiquity* 2/2 (2009), 374–384.

2 For some general context, see Oliver Nicholson, 'Lactantius on Military Service', *Studia Patristica* 24 (1993), 175–183.

affairs, or because of the way bishops were becoming increasingly answerable to secular authorities.

The Changed Augustine

I have already commented that at the beginning of Augustine's ministry in North Africa he was deeply disappointed by what he considered a lack of openness to his efforts from his Donatist counterparts. This later impacted on his dealings with the Donatist leadership. It is now possible to point out how this period directly shaped Augustine's approach to coercion, and placed him at odds with the original intention of Cyprian. Before 400, Augustine supported religious freedom and dialogue. After the year 400, however, a change can be observed. From that time onwards Augustine justified the use of limited coercive measures. What can explain this change in attitude?

One explanation is found in the late 390s, when Augustine formulated views that would set the stage for his later anti-Pelagian writings on original sin, on humanity's need for grace, and on the legitimate role of correction by outside sources (e.g., God's grace, inspired authorities). Around the same time that Augustine was filtering his experiences, he was also penning his *Ad Simplicianum* (396) and Book 10 of *Confessions* (397–400), works that appear to contain early versions of his understanding of original sin, and shortly after this same period he began to produce his central anti-Donatist writings. This was probably not a coincidence. As we now know, Augustine initiated his anti-Donatist works under the influence of Optatus of Milevis, the Donatist writer, Tyconius (writing c. 370–390), and the theological influence of the Apostle Paul. These influences, combined with his developing intuitions about sin, shaped the method with which Augustine would not only criticise the Donatists, but with which he would also lay the groundwork for legitimating coercion aimed at correcting heresy, i.e., ending the Donatist Church.

At the same time, as reconstructed in Chapter 3, the series of events surrounding the Maximianist schism (the death of Parmenian (c.391/92) and the election of Primian as his successor), provided an opening for Augustine to expose the Donatists. The bishop, who by this time was analysing events and personal actions through the theological lens of a *massa damnata*, a tainted, sinful mass, concentrated on the Donatist claim to the unique sanctity of their Church by virtue of being the Church of martyrs, supposing themselves free from the infection of the *traditores*.[3] He would rhetorically ask them: '[W]hat good is it to argue for your elite lineage when it is clear your members are in fact living according to the flesh proven by the stubborn behaviour of

3 *C. ep. Parm.* 2,20 (CSEL 51, 66–68); Opt., *De Schismate* 2,20 (CSEL 26, 55–57).

Donatist leaders and the Circumcelliones,[4] selfishness in rejecting the truth contained in the Catholic Church, and a lack of love by remaining apart from the *catholica*?'[5] In other words, were these not signs of a lack of the Holy Spirit?[6] If so, what good was it to claim to be heirs of the 'blessed Cyprian'?[7] Furthermore, Augustine would add, to what end did the Donatists claim the martyr-bishop Cyprian, who himself despised schism[8] and saw the unity of the Church as the manifestation of charity, as their own? Perhaps this suggested their Church was superior to the undivided Church of Cyprian's time?[9] In this regard, the Donatists' lack of love for unity and peace caused by their schism was an indefensible example of human sinfulness and one that would allow Augustine to further exert his claim to the authority of Cyprian. Knowing full well that Cyprian condemned schism as a symbolic tearing of the seamless robe of Christ,[10] Augustine considered the pride, selfishness, and petty partisanship of the Donatists as clear results of their schism. This, it seemed, was a consequence of a fallen humanity's carnal ways.[11]

He maintained a focus on the causes and effects of schism.[12] This was particularly apt as it seemed to place him in direct succession to the thought of Cyprian, something which was less easily asserted in other subjects.[13] And it was indeed a clever manoeuvre. Augustine could ask rhetorically why the

---

4 Augustine mentions the violence of his perennial favourites, the Circumcelliones (*Ep.* 185,15 (CSEL 57, 42): 'disrupters of the existing, divinely ordained, social order'; *C. ep. Parm.* 1,19 (CSEL 51,42): 'Ubi etiam circumcellionum mentio facta est, si more suo violenter obsisterent'; *Ep.* 185,25 (CSEL 57,42): 'Sed in quorum regionibus aliaquas violentias a clericis vel circumcellionibus vel populis eorum ecclesia catholica paterentur…'); drunkenness (*Cresc.* 4,77 (CSEL 52, 577): 'Negas eas quas dixi tyrannicas vestrorum in fundis alienis dominationes et bacchationes ebrietatum'); and the intrigue, violence, and political cunning of Optatus of Thamugadi and Gildo (*C. ep. Parm.* 2,2 [CSEL 51, 45]).

5 For Augustine unity was the perfect manifestation of love; Aug. (citing Cyp., *Ep.* 73,21 [CCSL 3/C, 554–56]), in *De bapt.* 4,24 (CSEL 51, 250–51).

6 Aug., *Ep.* 185,46.

7 *De bapt.* 6,3.

8 Cyp., *De unit.* 17,15.

9 *C. ep. Parm.* 3,8.

10 Cyp., *De unit.* 7.

11 *De bapt.* 4,8 alluding to Cyprian, *De zelo et liuore* 6. The best account of Augustine's appraisal of the implications of the sin-schism relationship remains Keleher, *Saint Augustine's Notion of Schism in the Donatist Controversy*, 104–136.

12 *De bapt.* 1,16.

13 This provoked the immediate and unequivocal condemnation of Donatist leaders; M.P. Joseph, 'Heresy of the Majority: Donatist Critique of the Church-State Relationship', *Bangalore Theological Forum* 26/2 (1994), 70–77.

Donatists clung so strongly to the identity of their Church, when all the while seeming to disregard Cyprian's unquestionable appreciation of unity:[14]

> But, having considered and handled all these points, we have now come to that peaceful utterance of Cyprian at the end of the epistle, with which I am never sated, though I read and re-read it again and again, – so great is the pleasantness of brotherly love which breathes forth from it, so great the sweetness of charity in which it abounds.[15]

By rejecting Cyprian's love of unity in favour of schism, what had the Donatists done? According to Augustine, they had severed themselves from God as fallen branches from a tree or a river from its source.[16] In doing so they had committed a sacrilege,[17] were working against God who tries to bring all Christians together in the one body of Christ,[18] and had excluded themselves from salvation.[19] Augustine would be able to discern a characteristic of salvation along these lines, namely that Church identification had nothing to do with the certainty of being God's elect, but rather that grace was entirely a gift of Christ, which could be signified by love,[20] and which itself was a result of unity.[21] In opposition to such love, those who enter schism leave the light and enter darkness.[22]

Coercion in Reaction to Donatist Theology

Up to the late 390s, Augustine maintained a preference for religious freedom and dialogue with Donatist leaders. But after 400 a change of heart can be

14 *Cresc.* 2,39.

15 *De bapt.* 5,22 (CSEL 51, 280): 'Sed iam ad illa eloquia pacifica Cypriani, hoc est ad epistulae finem omnibus consideratis pertractatisque peruentum est, quae me legentem et saepe repetentem non satiant. Tanta ex eis iucunditas fraterni amoris exhalat, tanta dulcedo caritatis exuberat'.

16 Opt., *De Schismate* 2,9.

17 *C. ep. Parm.* 1,14.

18 Cyprian would use imagery of unity such as *unanimes in domo*; *De orat. Dom.* 8. For the Holy Spirit as a sign of unity, *De unit.* 9.

19 Cyp., *De unit.* 6. It is also helpful to recall at this point how interwoven salvation was with being in the Church for Cyprian, with unity as the symbol upholding and attesting to that reality: 'Quod si haeretico nec baptisma publicae confessionis et sanguinis proficere ad salutem potest, quia salus extra ecclesiam non est, quanto magis ei nihil proderit' (*Ep.* 73,21 [CCSL 3/C, 555]). See also *De unit.* 6.

20 Aug., *Ep.* 185,48–50.

21 *De bapt.* 3,21.

22 Aug., *Ep.* 190,47.

observed. From that time onwards the bishop of Hippo began to justify the use of coercive measures against Donatists. What can explain the movement from his initial, disappointed pastoral experiences towards an attitude that was far less accommodating?

Perhaps Augustine became trapped in the difficulty of handling this situation between 400 and 405, when the disappointments he had articulated in his early pastoral work began to foment, that is, when he started to engage with Donatist theology in a prolonged theological discourse as an older bishop. It was a discourse that only concluded with Augustine, as his last option, labelling the Donatists as heretics under the Theodosian anti-heresy legislation.[23] No other example is as clear of Donatist ecclesiology as utterly irreconcilable with the world. The Donatists maintained a political theology whereby they saw themselves as denizens of the City of God, (*civitas Dei*) pitted against the City of the devil (*civitas diaboli*): 'sacred and secular were two separate spheres, each contained within its own sociological milieu: the Church of the pure face to face with a hostile, persecuting world, consisting of secular society and the Roman government, and an apostate (Catholic) Church which had come to terms with them. The "secular" was irretrievably "profane"'.[24] Added to this was the fact that in the view of the Donatists, Catholics were guilty of being compromised by the influence of the world, and were now a Church of betrayers, a worldly ally of the *civitas diaboli*. This body stood in stark contrast to the Donatists themselves as the *collecta* of Israel.[25] For Augustine, the struggle thus became a matter of producing a strategy that could effectively address a demographic that vehemently rejected not only the Roman Empire (as the leading secular power), but also the Catholic Church because of its perceived collaboration with the imperial government. This is the other significant, but overlooked aspect when considering the reasons why Augustine ultimately sanctioned coercion.

---

23 This is intriguing, as Augustine is actually at odds with his predecessors on this point (specifically Optatus of Milevis). Prior to Augustine's involvement in the matter, Donatists were not considered heterodox. By arguing that the Donatists were guilty of heresy because of their use of rebaptism and self-induced schism (*schisma inveteratum*), they were punishable under the *Codex Theodosianus* (16,6,4), which carried a penalty of 4.5 kgs of gold. Such a charge was contested by Donatist bishops (*C. litt. Pet.* 2,218; *Gest. Con. Carth.* 3,193).

24 Markus, *Saeculum*, 122.

25 Such biblical typology is treated exhaustively throughout Tilley, *The Bible in Christian North Africa*.

It is important to understand the context of the Donatist perspective, however, not only for the way it affected the responses of Augustine and other Catholics, but also for an understanding of indigenous North African Christianity in late antiquity. Donatist Christians inherited a view of the Church as juxtaposed against the world. Tertullian, and especially Cyprian of Carthage, were central influences on Donatism. Cyprian's use of biblical typologies, such as the image of Noah's ark, to explain the nature of the Church, indicated a divinely selected refuge, and would resonate through future generations, as was evident at the 411 Carthage colloquium: 'nos qui ecclesiae defendimus puritatem'.[26]

After Cyprian, decades of martyr stories fortified the belief of African Christians that their Church was the one most closely identified with martyrs, though this would be less so than after 305. From the example of the martyrs, Donatists gradually articulated a number of enduring positions, such as: (1) active opposition to the world, identifiable, for example, in *Acta Maximiliani* (c. 298): 'I cannot fight [in the Roman army] [...] for I am Christian';[27] and (2) a perceived threat from the influence of the world on the Church (e.g., *The Acts of the Abitinian Martyrs* [c.304–311]):

> Some fell from faith at the critical moment by handing over to unbelievers the scriptures of the Lord and the divine testaments so they could be burned in unholy fires. But how many more in preserving them bravely resisted by freely shedding their blood for them! When the devil had been completely defeated and ruined and all the martyrs were filled with God's presence, bearing the palm of victory over suffering, they sealed with their own blood the verdict against the traitors and their associates, rejecting them from communion of the Church. For it was not right that there should be martyrs and traitors in the Church of God at the same time.[28]

26 *Gest. Con. Carth.* 3,258.

27 *Acta Maximiliani* 1,3 (Mursurillo, *Acts of the Christian Martyrs*, 244).

28 *Acts of the Abitinian Martyrs* 2 (*Tilley, The Bible in Christian North Africa*, 29), (J.-L. Maier, *Le Dossier Du Donatisme. Tome I*, 61–62): 'Et quamuis tradendo gentilibus scripturas dominicas atque testamenta divina profanis ignibus comburenda a fidei cardine cecidere nonnulli, conservando tamen ea et pro ipsis libenter suum sanguinem effundendo fortiter fecere quam plurimi. Quique pleni deo, devicto ac prostrato diabolo, victoriae palmam in passione gestantes, sententiam in traditores atque in eorum consortes qua illos ab ecclesiae communione reiecerant cuncti martyres proprio sanguine consignabant; fas enim non fuerat ut in ecclesia dei simul essent martyres et traditores'.

For Donatists, their Church was a 'garden enclosed, a sealed fountain' (Cant. 4,12),[29] the ark of salvation (Gen. 6–9) sealed against the outside world.[30] Their community was understood as the 'inside' (*intus*) and the world as 'outside' (*foris*) with light, godliness, and purity within and darkness, godlessness, and sin on the outside in the world. The 'darkness will not mix with light, gall with honey; life will not mix with death nor innocence with guilt'.[31] This background affected the Donatists, with their mindset of sensitivity towards those they considered corrupted or sinful members in their flock. Such sinful members were not just bad moral examples, but more importantly, posed a mortal threat. The *Sermon Given on the Passion of Saints Donatus and Advocatus* (c.317–21) strongly attests to the Donatists' detestation of those members, especially ordained ministers, who sinned publically, and particularly those who committed the sin of betrayal in times of persecution:

> [A certain *traditor* bishop, Eudinepisus] promoted the idea that the lapsed, the deserters of heavenly sacraments, could illicitly hold ecclesiastical office again. As much as he recently took pleasure in their weakness of faith, so now he rejoices in this fraud. He is even more secure when they are called 'bishops' or 'Christians,' than when they fell to ruin in their denial of the Christian name.[32]

This method of interpreting events would have a lasting effect on Donatist Christians. As late as 411, they maintained their view of the need to protect the purity of the Church, to separate 'the wheat from the chaff'.[33]

It is also pertinent to emphasise that the Donatist temperament seems to have been affected by the fiscal situation in North Africa. The division, both economic and geographical, between Roman culture and colonists and the

---

29 Cyp., *Ep.* 69,2, 74,11; Optatus, *De Schismate*, 1,10; 2,13; *Cres.* 1,34–40, 4,77. See also Markus, *Saeculum*, 112.

30 Aug., *Ad Catholicos Epistulae de Secta Donatistarum*, 5,9.

31 *C. litt. Pet.*, 2,92.

32 *Sermon Given on the Passion of Saints Donatus and Advocatus* 2 (Tilley, Donatist Martyr Stories, 54), (J.-L. Maier, *Le Dossier Du Donatisme. Tome 1*, 203): '...qua certissime sciuit deum gravius offendi, posse tenere lapsos illicite rursus ecclesiasticos honores quos tunc tenverant sacramentorum caelesitum desertores. Tantumdem horum falsa proditione nunc laetus quam imbecillitate fidei nuper gavisus. Immo securior modo cum quasi episcopi vel christiani dicuntur quam tunc cum nominis negatione ruerunt...'.

33 This imagery of 'wheat and tares' would gain currency throughout North Africa, as is evident in the record of the Council of Carthage in 411; see *Gest. Con. Carth.* 3,258, 1200; *Gest. Con. Carth.* 3,258, 1203–04.

native Punics, is well-studied.[34] Of particular value is David Cherry's recent insight into the expansive degree of Roman military control around and over the Donatist heartland in Numidia via a 'frontier-zone' (present-day Algeria and Tunisia). Cherry points out that the frontier-zone, rather than being a place of interaction and intermingling with the native population, tended to serve as a divide.[35] Less certain is the effect that such isolation and stagnation had in further spurring Donatist Christianity.

We now have a better realisation of the way the disparity between the two groups often spilled over into theological matters and debates. And it was with this complex scenario that Augustine would have to contend. In 400/401, after Augustine led an effort to mobilise the Catholic Church in North Africa to engage Donatists in their territories, including his own attempt at proselytisation,[36] it became apparent that his tactics had inevitably collided with the long-standing Donatist adherence to their own purity and authenticity against a 'venomous' outside world. As tensions began to rise in subsequent years, riots and other forms of violence broke out in reaction against increased Catholic interactivity.[37] This time Augustine and his team bypassed

34 A few examples are useful for a socio-political analysis: MacKendrick *The North African Stones Speak* (Chapel Hill, N.C.: University of North Carolina Press 1980); C. Lepelley, *Les cités de l'Afrique romaine au Bas-Empire*, tome I, *La permanence d'une civilisation municipal* (Paris: Coll. des Études Augustiniennes, 1979); *Les cités de l'Afrique romaine au Bas-Empire II, Notices d'histoire municipal* (Paris: Coll. des Études Augustiniennes, 1981); *Aspects de l'Afrique romaine. Les cités, la vie rurale, le christianisme, Coll. Munera. Studi storici sulla Tarda Antichità* 15 (Bari: Edipuglia, 2001). In terms of interpreting Donatism within the history of North Africa, the research of Frend, *The Donatist Church*, 1952; *Martyrdom and Persecution in the Early Church: A study of a conflict from the Maccabees to Donatus* (Oxford: Blackwell, 1965); and Markus, *Saeculum: History and Society in the Theology of St. Augustine*, still stand out, especially in terms of their influence on more recent research by Tilley, *The Bible in Christian North Africa* and Hermanowicz, *Possidius of Calama*.

35 D. Cherry, *Frontier and Society in Roman North Africa* (New York: Oxford University Press, 1998), 24–73.

36 *Cresc.* 3,66.

37 An example is when Augustine's colleague Possidius was ambushed and nearly killed by Circumcelliones under the command of a Donatist presbyter (*Cresc.* 3,50). In retaliation, the Catholic leadership submitted the matter for rectification by the secular legal system, and on a second attempt, as all of Africa awaited the outcome, it was decided by the Roman Proconsul Septimus that the presbyter's bishop (Crispinus), was responsible for the presbyters' wrongful actions. Under the laws established by Emperor Theodosius in 392, he was also found guilty of being a heretic and forced to pay the penalty of 4.5kgs of gold bullion (*Cresc.* 3,51). This event was groundbreaking in Donatist history as it was the first occurrence in which the church was declared to be heretical and an enemy of the state

an exclusively pastoral approach and had recourse to the intercession of the Roman government. At this point Augustine seems to have at last agreed with the opinion of the majority of the African bishops in this period. They considered proportionate violence a justifiable defence against the terrorist excesses of Donatists. The Donatists, regardless of the question of whether or not they were connected to the Circumcelliones, used violence against Catholic priests and churches. They liked to destroy pagan altars, idols and temples. Moreover, the bishops of North Africa were convinced that coercion could result in real conversions and restore ecclesial unity.

The mandated conversion of pagans, Manicheans and Jews did not, according to Augustine, rank as a care of the Church, since these groups were never a part of the Church. For this reason, Augustine rejected the legal suppression of pagans, Manicheans and Jews. However desirable their conversion might be, this should not take place through violence. They should be treated in a Christian way.[38] Donatists, however, were fundamentally different. Donatists were 'bad brothers, but still brothers',[39] 'bad, lost sons'.[40] Christians did not want to fight the Donatists, but on the contrary wanted the best outcome for them, namely that they re-enter into unity and share with other Christians the heritage of God.[41] To this effect, Augustine noted:

> In the first of these books [the now lost *C. partem Donati*], I said: 'I am displeased that schismatics are violently coerced to communion by the force of any secular power.' And truly, at this time, such coercion displeased me because I had not yet learned either how much evil their impunity would dare or to what extent the application of discipline could bring about their improvement.[42]

---

under the Theodosian anti-heresy legislation. This would set off a successful series of appeals to Roman legal authority, as Hermanowicz, *Possidius of Calama*, 100, notes: 'Catholic success was, therefore, largely attributable to the inherent malleability of Roman law and the tenacity of the group determined to shape it. In the struggle for souls among the residents of North Africa, the Catholics did not mind stretching either the law or the truth'.

38 *En. in Ps.* 65,5; 149,13; *s.* 90,10; *In Ep. Ioh.* 10,7; *Ep.* 91,1; *Haer.* 46,15–17.

39 *En. in Ps.* 46,31.

40 *C. ep. Parm.* 3,1.

41 *s.* 359,4.

42 *Retract.* 2,5 (CCSL 57, 93–94): 'Vorum in libro primo dixi non mihi placere ullius saecularis potestatis impetu schismaticos ad communionem uiolenter artari. Et uere mihi tunc non placebat, quoniam nondum expertus eram, uel quantum mali eorum auderet impunitas, uel quantum eis in melius mutandis conferre posset diligentia disciplinae'.

Donatists remained connected with the Church, still belonging to the Church. That is why the responsibility of the Church towards Donatists was much more pertinent than that concerning non-Christians. The Church, as the *locus veritatis*, had the duty to protect its members against error. Coercion could be a means to help erring members to recognise the truth.[43] During the period of the Carthage Conference with the Donatists (411), Augustine preached that people who refuse to be defeated by truth, are actually defeated by error. He exhorted Donatists to tear down the wall of error, so they could become brothers and sisters again. Only truth overcomes and this truth is *caritas*. It is very clear that Augustine situated this *veritas* and *caritas* exclusively within the Catholic Church.[44]

It was the very relationship of truth and love, *veritas* and *caritas*, that would mark Augustine's personal approach to his role with the Donatists. Rather than simply being an enforcer of Catholic orthodoxy against heretics, Augustine never stopped considering himself a pastor attempting to bring together his flock. Research shows that Augustine's approach, while increasingly stern towards the 390s/early 400s, was nevertheless always considered a Christic one, with spiritual-healing purposes at heart.[45] Instead of an enforcer or security guard, Augustine would not cease to see himself as a mediator, judge, teacher, and mystagogue, with the intention of being an example of Christ. It is the function of mystagogue that should be held central if we are to consider Augustine's own perception in an integral way. He considered the actions he took to correct the Donatists acts of mercy and compassion and because of his love he could not be silent.[46] This would be the redeeming feature for Augustine and his Catholic allies, a feature that they considered differentiated them from the 'seditious' Donatists.

---

43 Aug., *Ep.* 93,16.

44 *s.* 358,4–5.

45 See, for example, Paul Van Geest, '*Quid dicam de vindicando vel non vindicando*? (*Ep.* 95.3): Augustine's legitimisation of coercion in the light of his role of mediator, judge, teacher and mystagogue', in A. Geljon, R. Roukema (eds.), *Violence in Ancient Christianity: Victims and Perpetrators* (Leiden: Brill, 2014), 151–184; and '*Timor est Servus Caritatis* (*s.* 156, 13–14): Augustine's Vision on Coercion in the Process of Returning Heretics to the Catholic Church and his Underlying Principles', in A. Dupont, M. Gaumer, and M. Lamberigts (eds.), *The Uniquely African Controversy: Studies on Donatist Christianity* (Leuven: Peeters, 2015), 289–310.

46 Aug., *Ep.* 104,3,8 and *Ep.* 105,1.

Coercion, but Not Really

Augustine changed his mind around 400. And from 405 onwards it is clear that he favoured coercive measures in religious conflicts and sought support from the Roman authorities, although he remained opposed to torture and execution.[47] On 17 May 411, however, a few short weeks before the start of the famous Carthage Colloquy, he asked his community in a homily not to act as the Donatists—whom he claimed hated peace—but to treat them gently, to pray for their healing.[48] But this begs the question: what did Augustine understand by coercion? A terminological excursus gives us some clues. Augustine used the words '*correptio*' and '*correctio*,' and not the legalistic-sounding '*cohercitio*'. Augustine did not seek punishment, but instead sought helpful correction.[49] Augustine formulated this policy through a teaching/treatment vocabulary. In *Ep.* 185, he stated that Donatists should be cared for by the Church and secular authorities as patients are cared for by their doctor, corrected just as naughty children are by their father, or a woman is by her husband.[50] Christians do not persecute the non-faithful for their own satisfaction, but for the salvation and spiritual protection of the unfaithful.[51]

As a corrective measure, Augustine accepted the suspension of some legal rights of the Donatists. He allowed the prohibition of certain religious acts, worship in general, and the practice of rebaptising specifically, as tools for establishing what was right.[52] Augustine advocated two kinds of possible punishment in turn. Lashing with a stick was a possible punishment, but was to be used only during a juridical investigation and to elicit a prompt confession.[53]

47 Peter Brown, 'St. Augustine's Attitude to Religious Coercion', in J. Dunn and I. Harris (eds.), *Great Political Thinkers 3, Augustine* 1 (Cheltenham/Lyme: Elgar, 1997), 382–391; D. Burt, 'Augustine on the Morality of Violence: Theoretical Issues and Applications', in *Congresso internazionale sul S. Agostino nel XVI centenario della conversione* (Rome: Augustinianum, 1987), 25–54; M. Himbury, 'Augustine and Religious Persecution', in M. Garner and J. Martin (eds.), *St. Augustine—The Man who made the West* (Melbourne: University of Melbourne, 1990), 33–37; H. Jans, 'De verantwoording van geloofsdwang tegenover ketters volgens Augustinus' correspondenties', *Bijdragen* 22 (1961), 133–163, 247–263; E. Lamirande, *Church, State and Toleration: An Intriguing Change of Mind in Augustine* (Villanova: Villanova University Press, 1975).

48 *s.* 357,3–5.

49 *Ep.* 88,10; *Ep.* 89,6.

50 It is not the human person that is dealt with, but the vice living in that person (*Cresc.* 3,57; *C. Gaud.* 1,19).

51 *Ep.* 95,3; *Cresc.* 4,56.

52 The Edict of 12 February 405. Augustine also approves the confiscation of Donatist Church properties; *C. litt. Pet.* 1,102; *C. Gaud.* 1,50–51; *C. ep. Parm.* 2,18–20.

53 *Ep.* 133,2.

Dutiful monetary fines were another possibility. These should be a sensible amount, leaving the guilty enough to live on.[54] Augustine also approved the imperial decision to invalidate the wills and estates of obstinate Donatists.[55] He advised officials to act as gently as possible and to be lenient when the good intentions of the guilty were recognisable. This, however, does not imply that Augustine neglected crimes already committed or suggested impunity from such acts. His intention was not to punish or cause pain, but, according to him, was solely concerned with saving his opponents' eternal souls by eliciting the Catholic truth. Moreover, for Augustine being merciful was an imitation of God, who calls believers to love their enemies.[56] It was crucial that nobody be forced to convert unwillingly.[57] Inner consistency was always necessary, *but* external pressure could promote this.[58] When force was the only option left, that force should be used with the aim of inner conversion.[59]

The Catholic Justification for Coercion

Augustine based the use of legal coercion upon six justifications.[60] A first is the legal defence of Catholics against Donatist attacks.[61] Augustine's second argument is more polemical: imperial intervention and repression is justifiable because Donatists accept imperial involvement, and are actually the first to appeal to a civil authority for validation.[62] Here, Augustine reminds them of the fact that Donatists collaborated with the empire during the persecution of Julian the Apostate (360–63);[63] supported imperial repression of pagans;[64] and moreover, very violently persecuted the Maximianists.[65] Third, Augustine refutes the Donatist claim to be the true Church, because real Christians are to

54 *Ep.* 104,4.

55 *s.* 47,22.

56 *Ep.* 153,1.

57 *C. Gaud.* 1,8; 1,28.

58 *s.* 112,8.

59 *Ep.* 93,2.

60 H. Jans, 'De verantwoording van geloofsdwang tegenover ketters volgens Augustinus', 139–158.

61 *Ep.* 185,18.

62 With their approach to Constantine in April 313, the Donatists were actually the first Christian group in history to make an appeal to a Roman emperor for validation. See Merdinger, *Rome and the African Church in the Time of Augustine*, 88; Gaddis, *There is No Crime for Those Who Have Christ*, 49.

63 *Ep.* 93,12.

64 *Ep.* 93,10; *C. Gaud.* 1,51.

65 Frend, 'Augustine and State Authority', 49–73.

be recognised by the fact that they are persecuted (Mt. 5,10). Augustine replies that martyrdom is not (solely) constituted by suffering, but by a just cause. Only the one, true cause, Christ, makes a martyr, just as in the case of the martyr Cyprian. Martyrs do not fear suffering; their suffering is only an unintended consequence of their obedience to Christ and divine grace. The suffering of Donatists is nothing more than, at worst, a punishment and, at best, a charade. Moreover, the martyr's crown (*corona*) can only be attained within the true Church, from which Donatists have disinvested themselves.[66] And again, the fact that they themselves persecuted the Maximianists, renders this Donatist argument null and void.[67] The coercive 'correction' deterrent of Donatists by Catholics does not cause them harm, but is rather an antidote for their disease.[68] It is rather the Church that suffers, not the Donatists, because of their violence and mainly because of the rupture of unity they have caused.[69] Since the Donatists remain connected with the Church by their baptism, the Church suffers. Continuing, Augustine argues that the Donatists admit that the sustenance of unity is beneficial, but yet they refuse it. Through a return via coercion, they are given Christ as food and as a sign of peace. That food has to be given to them forcibly, since not giving such food would be much worse. The Church, as mother, has precisely that nurturing task: correcting, protecting, and caring for the sick.[70]

Fourth, Augustine thinks that coercion can be fruitful. External force can lead to inner consent. Afterwards, a person will be happy to have been forced to consent to what they previously did not want to accept.[71] Scripture supplies Augustine with his fifth argument. The Old Testament contains illustrations of exemplary men and women who persecuted and killed others. Elijah killed false prophets, Sarah persecuted Hagar, and Moses rebuked his rebellious Israelites.[72] Donatists, however, seem to reject the Old Testament by their deeds. Augustine replies to this with a doctrine of 'two voices' (*duae voces*). The old law of coercion was not perfect, and is of lesser importance than in the time of Moses. Yet the utility of the old law, despite its inadequacies, cannot be denied. For this reason, the situation in which Israel was forced to obey certain

66 *s.* 89,2; 108,14; 204,4; 325,2; *Ep.* 88,8; 89,2; 93,6; 105,5; 185,9; *C. Gaud.* 1,22.

67 *Ep.* 185,10.

68 *Sermo* 359,7–8: the doctor does not attack the patient, the Donatist as a person, but rather the illness: heresy.

69 , *En. in Ps.* 145,16; *Ep. ad Cath.* 20,56; *C. Gaud.* 1,25; *C. litt. Pet.* 1,102.

70 *s.* 360C,5–6.

71 *Ep.* 93,1; this is a concept that Russell, '*There is No Crime for Those Who Have Christ*', develops in-depth.

72 *Ep.* 44,9; 93,6; *C. Faust.* 22,20.

punitive laws is equal to the ecclesial situation of North Africa in the fifth century. The Jewish 'old' law and the imperial legislation against heretics are both essentially learning tools.[73] Augustine was aware of the shift between the Old and New Testaments in terms of the abolishment of capital punishment.[74] This change does not imply a total absence of punishment or violence in the New Testament as compared with the older scriptures, however. Christ himself used a violent gesture when casting out demons and scaring the money-changers out of the Jerusalem temple.[75] Also, Paul was converted by God's divine force.[76] Another biblical motif is the parable of the dinner banquet in Lk. 14,23. The parable says that the master orders his servants to make any unwilling guest enter: *compelle intrare*, by force if necessary. The banquet symbolises the unity of the Church and the unwilling guests in this comparison are the schismatics and heretics.[77]

Augustine's final argument is that civil authority has the duty to intervene in religious matters. The state has to take care of its citizens. Christian civil authorities have to defend the highest good: the Catholic faith and Church unity.[78] This reasoning is based on an interpretation of schism and heresy as a crime punishable, like all other crimes, under the auspices of imperial power and therefore punishable under the Theodosian codes.[79]

The Topic of 'Grace' in the Controversy

The anti-Donatist strategy Augustine (and his counterpart Aurelius of Carthage) developed required that the imperial bureaucracy come to identify dissidents as heretics and that they be fully punished accordingly. (This was matched with simultaneous public relations efforts to reinforce the fall-out of the Maximianist affair and to elaborate upon the violent and insurrectionist tendencies of Donatist organisers.)[80] Achieving such a classification would

73 *s*. 62,8.

74 *Ep*. 44,10.

75 Mk. 1,34; Mt. 9,32; Lk. 4,35; Mk. 11,15; Mt. 21,12; Lk. 19,45.

76 *Ep*. 24; 62; 93,5; 173,3; *Retract*. 1,6.

77 *Sermo* 112,1–8; *Ep*. 173,1; *C. Gaud*. 1,28–29.

78 *Ep*. 185,25.

79 Please refer again to the *Codex Theodosianus* (*The Theodosian Code and Novels and the Sirmondian Constitutions*), trans. C. Pharr (Princeton: Princeton University Press, 1952).

80 This three-pronged strategy is treated with a much more in-depth analysis in Brent Shaw's *Sacred Violence*, see pp. 141–45 especially. The key point to take away is that Augustine and Aurelius had arrived at this method of countering the Donatist leadership through

require more than just stating differences of opinion or targeting the other side in letters and sermons. The Donatist Church would have to be associated with an easily recognisable heretical position that could be readily explained and condemned by imperial officials and clerics alike in Ravenna, Milan, Rome, or Constantinople.

As this was still the 390s and very early in Augustine's episcopal ministry, he had to draw on a topic that had been readily familiar to him since his days in Italy: the theme of grace/*gratia*.[81] This topic would in time emerge as one of the most recognisable disputations in Augustine's theological corpus. Though this topic is often associated more with the Pelagian controversy because of its central position there, it was actually a theme that was also frequently used in the Donatist controversy, and in fact weaves the two controversies together, another expression of continuity in the thought of Augustine.[82]

That grace became a key topic in Augustine's early efforts to classify the Donatists as heretics is not altogether surprising given the period under consideration. Among his early writings, *Ad Simplicianum*, is to be regarded as one his most articulate seminal expressions of a theology of grace and was composed somewhere between 396–398. It was therefore one of the first works as a bishop,[83] from a time when Augustine was already deeply involved in the Donatist controversy.

At the heart of *Ad Simplicianum*, and what is most cogent for the crossover in the Donatist and Pelagian controversies, is Augustine's examination of Romans 9,10–29 and the story of God's preference for Jacob over Esau. In brief,

---

a process of trial and error, and would unabashedly follow this strategic approach on a long-term basis. The only caveat is that the Maximianist critique became relatively less important as the 400s turned into the 410s, as the strategy had already been quite effective in channeling imperial energies against the Donatists.

81 That grace was a major theme in Augustine's works throughout his career is beyond a doubt. By using the *CLCLT* 7.0 tool, one finds that the term '*gratia*' has 6291 occurrences in the whole Augustinian *corpus*. Of those occurrences, 133 can be located within the explicitly anti-Donatist writings. (This number does not include hits in other works not commonly described as anti-Donatist works, e.g. *Ep.* 93; 108; 215; *s.* 313E, etc.) This number is greatly expanded when one examines the anti-Pelagian and semi-Pelagian writings; which results in 1766 occurrences in those two categories.

82 Phillip Cary, *Inner Grace: Augustine in the Traditions of Plato and Paul* (Oxford: Oxford University Press, 2008).

83 A. Mutzenbecher (ed.), *Retract.*, *CCSL* 57 (Turnhout: Brepols, 1984), XVIII and *Ad Simpl.*, *CCSL* 44 (Turnhout: Brepols, 1970), XXX–XXXIII and G. Madec, *Introduction aux « Revisions » et à la Lecture des Oeuvres de Saint Augustin*, Collection des Études Augustiniennes: Série Antiquité 150 (Paris: Institut d'Études Augustiniennes, 1996).

the grace concept espoused by Augustine in this work expresses several of his theological capstones: that divine grace is the source of merit; that divine grace is the source of election to salvation; and that this grace is completely gratuitous and is undeserved by humanity, a race depraved (*massa peccati*) by inherited sin (*tradux peccati*) and original guilt (*originalis reatus*).[84]

While the nuances of grace are clearly spelt out in *Ad Simplicianum*, there is a more important dimension to the work that ties grace to the Catholic Church. Within the context of Augustine's efforts against the Donatist Church, grace and salvation are inextricably connected with the authority that is found only in the Catholic Church.

A perusal of *Ad Simplicianum* elucidates the grace-authority nexus. In several foundational passages Augustine makes certain to denote God as first and foremost the source of grace: 'This is the truth the apostle [Paul] wanted to urge; just as in another passage he says, "By the grace of God we are saved, and that not of ourselves. It is the gift of God. It is not of works…" (Eph. 2,8–9)'.[85] In another nearby section, Augustine writes:

> Grace is therefore of him who calls, and the consequent good works are of him who receives grace. Good works do not produce grace but are produced by grace. Fire is not hot in order that it may burn, but because it burns. A wheel does not run nicely in order that in may be round, but because it is round. So no one does good works in order that he may receive grace, but because he has received grace.[86]

---

84 James Wetzel, 'Simplicianum, Ad', A. Fitzgerald (ed.), *Augustine through the Ages. An Encyclopedia* (Grand Rapids/Cambridge: Wm. Eerdmans Publishing, 1999), pp. 798–799. See Carol Harrison, '"The Most Intimate Feeling of My Mind": The Permanence of Grace in Augustine's Early Theological Practice', *Augustinian Studies* 36/1 (2005), 52: 'There is, I would argue; a fundamental continuity in Augustine's thought from the very beginning which does not undergo any dramatic change when he re-reads Paul in the 390s [especially in light of the Donatist controversy]; in other words, the basic ideas of the Fall, -original sin, the weakness and inability of the will to do good without grace are present from the very beginning'.

85 Aug., *Ad Simp.*, 2,3 (*To Simplician*, trans. J.H.S. Burleigh, *Augustine: Earlier Writings* (Philadelphia: Westminster Press, 1953), 387). Augustine lays this out in a similar fashion elsewhere in *Ad Simp.*, 2,3.

86 Aug., *Ad Simp.*, 2,3 (*Augustine: Earlier Writings*, 388); *Ad Simpl.* (CCSL 44, 241): 'Vocantis est ergo gratia, percipientis vero gratiam consequenter sunt opera bona, non quae gratiam pariant, sed quae gratia pariantur. Non enim ut ferveat calefacit ignis, sed quia fervet; nec ideo bene currit rota ut rotunda sit, sed quia rotunda est. Sic nemo propterea bene operatur ut accipiat gratiam, sed quia accepit'.

Grace is issued by God, freely, and the person who receives it is called by God. Augustine also makes clear that grace precedes any good actions on the part of a Christian. But what is most germane for the purpose of this research is how Augustine crafts his concept of grace as being foremost a gift from God to be imparted through a calling (*vocatio*) which then spurs one to action:[87]

> There are two different things that God gives us, the power to will and the thing we actually will. The power to will he has willed should be both his and ours, his because he calls us, ours because we follow when called. But what we actually will he alone gives, i.e., the power to do right and to live happily for ever.[88]

Thus not only is undeserved grace the cause of faith, the desire for faith as well as faith's sustaining principle, but is also radiated by God in varying ways for the demonstration of faith in works. This is where we enter into one of the more overlooked features of *Ad Simplicianum*. Here Augustine articulates in very certain terms that there is a connection between faith and salvation through the calling of God and the authority of faithful witnesses. This is central in understanding Augustine's construction of grace and faith throughout his career: while grace is limitless, it is also to be found most abundantly and tangibly in the Church:

> Now Isaac had not conciliated God by any previous meritorious works so that his birth should have been promised, and that in Isaac 'Abraham's seed should be called' (Gen. 21,12). That means that those who are to belong to the lot of the saints in Christ who know that they are the sons of promise; who do not wax proud of their merits, but account themselves co-heirs with Christ by the grace of their calling.[89]

---

87 Aug., *Ad Simp.*, 2,3; 2,9; 2,10; 2,12 (x3); 2,21. A fair recapitulation of this is found in *Ad Simp.*, 2,9 (*Augustine: Earlier Writings*, 392): 'If God will have mercy on a man so as to call him, he will also have mercy on him that he may believe; and on him whom he in mercy bestows faith will he show compassion, i.e., will make him compassionate, so that he may also perform good works'.

88 Aug., *Ad Simp.*, 2,10 (*Augustine: Earlier Writings*, 393); *Ad Simpl.* (CCSL 44, 260): 'Aliter enim Deus praestat ut velimus, aliter praestat quod voluerimus. Ut velimus enim et suum esse voluit et nostrum, suum vocando nostrum sequendo. Quod autem voluerimus solus praestat, id est posse bene agere et semper beate vivere'.

89 Aug., *Ad Simp.*, 2,3 (*Augustine: Earlier Writings*, 387); *Ad Simpl.* (CCSL 44, 241): '…qui utique nullis operibus promeruerat Deum ut nasciturus promitteretur, ut in Isaac vocaretur semen Abrahae, id est illi pertinerent ad sortem sanctorum quae in Christo est, qui se

This elaboration on *vocatio* is a very essential component of Augustine's grace-construct, especially as it lends itself to the Donatist controversy. Grace is channelled through Christ's Church, those that are in the Church are called. Those that have been called and are located within the Church are privy to salvation. Furthermore, the desire for and imparting of grace is from God, but the actualisation of this and the reception of grace by individual people is by no means universal. Augustine explains this in his appeal to the Gospel of Matthew: 'Many are called but few are chosen' (22,14).[90]

Augustine takes this concept to another level in articulating the view that grace is made visible and manifest in the physical world through those God has already called and redeemed: vessels of salvific message, his apostles, disciples, and those that have remained in the body of Christ since. An examination of how Augustine constructs this is a profitable endeavour at this stage.

It is through the apostolic activity of the Church in its preaching, evangelisation of new regions, and celebration of sacramental rites that grace is expressed and connects people with God. Augustine's notion of *vocatio* is not directly between God and humanity, at least not routinely, but rather is communicated through the activities of the Church:

> No one believes who is not called. God calls in his mercy, and not as rewarding the merits of faith. The merits of faith follow his calling rather than precede it. 'How shall they believe whom they have not heard? And how shall they hear without a preacher?' (Rom. 10,14).[91]

So through the active proclamation of Christian preaching, people are brought to faith in God. The desire for faith and knowledge are also from God. In this way, salvation is constructed as delivered and accessed via the medium of the Church, and is not a direct transaction between individuals and God. Inherent in this *schema* is the idea that there is one Church only that can do this. Further, it is not only via the instrumentation of preaching, sermons, and

---

intellegerent filios promissionis non superbientes de meritis suis, sed gratiae vocationis deputantes quod coheredes essent Christi cum enim promissum est ut essent…'.

90 Aug., *Ad Simp.*, 2,10; 2,13 (*Augustine: Earlier Writings*, 388). This is expressed in other formulae, such as in the following in *Ad Simp.*, 2,13 (*Augustine: Earlier Writings*, 395) : 'For, although he calls many, he has mercy on those whom he calls in a way suited to them so that they may follow'.

91 Aug., *Ad Simp.*, 2,7 (*Augustine: Earlier Writings*, 391); *Ad Simpl.* (CCSL 44, 255): '*Sed ex vocante.* Nemo enim credit qui non vocatur. Misericors autem Deus vocat nullis hoc vel fidei meritis largiens, quia merita fidei sequuntur vocationem potius quam praecedunt. *Quomodo* enim *credunt quem non audierunt? Et quomodo audient sine praedicante?*'

catechesis that people are brought to grace; it is specifically through the sacraments of the Church:

> No man is to think that he has received grace because he has done good works. Rather he could not have done good works unless he had received grace through faith. A man begins to receive grace from the moment when he begins to believe in God, being moved to faith by some internal or external admonition. But the fullness and evidentness of the infusion of grace depends on temporal junctures and on sacramental rites.[92]

With that the essential ingredients for Augustine's grace-concept were in place, and provided him with a powerful line of argumentation against the Donatists. It is only within the Church—the Church that has remained in faithful unity with the apostles, Augustine's Church—that God's grace is to be encountered. While many are called, few chosen, for any group or body outside of this true Church no grace is to be found. This total grace-concept is stated in nearly complete form as follows:

> [W]e are commanded to live righteously, and the reward is set before us that we shall merit to live happily for ever. But who can live righteously and do good works unless he has been justified by faith? We are commanded to be believe that we may receive the gift of the Holy Spirit and become able to do good works by love. But who can believe unless he is reached by some calling, by some testimony borne to the truth? Who has it in his power to have such a motive present to his mind that his will shall be influenced to believe? Who can welcome in his mind something which does not give him delight? …If those things delight us which serve our advancement towards God, that is due not to our own whim or industry or meritorious works, but to the inspiration of God and to the grace which he bestows. He freely bestows upon us voluntary assent, earnest effort, and the power to perform works of fervent charity.[93]

92 Aug., *Ad Simp.*, 2,2 (*Augustine: Earlier Writings*, 405); *Ad Simpl.* (*CCSL* 44, 239): 'Incipit autem homo percipere gratiam, ex quo incipit Deo credere vel interna vel externa admonitione motus ad fidem. Sed interest, quibus articulis temporum vel celebratione sacramentorum gratia plenior et evidentior infundatur'.

93 Aug., *Ad Simp.*, 2,21 (*Augustine: Earlier Writings*, 405); *Ad Simpl.* (*CCSL* 44, 407): 'Praecipitur ut recte vivamus, hac utique mercede proposita, ut in aeternum beate vivere mereamur. Sed quis potest recte vivere et bene operari nisi iustificatus ex fide? Praecipitur ut credamus, ut dono accepto Spiritus Sancti per dilectionem bene operari possimus. Sed quis potest credere, nisi aliqua vocatione, hoc est aliqua rerum testificatione, tangatur? Quis

What remains missing from this formulation of grace theology, within the context of the Donatist controversy and pluriform Church bodies, is the means of identifying the authentic Church and therefore the font of salvation. This is where authority becomes even more critical. At this point it is helpful to recall that in the precise period that *Ad Simplicianum* was written, the rebellion of Gildo, the Roman Army commander in Africa and pivotal ally of the Donatist leadership, had reached its pinnacle. General violent insurrection against the Catholics by Donatists,[94] as well as the permissiveness of pagan cults, created an environment in which Augustine could no longer approach the Donatist Church in a genteel manner. The matter was now as much about security as it was a theological debate about the truth. There was more need than ever for Augustine to field and implement a winning strategy.

Attacking the Donatists with Authority

The realization by Augustine very early on that authority was the most crucial identifier of salvation and the authentic Church was critical in his subsequent dealings with Donatist leaders. With this insight in mind, Augustine focused his attacks against Donatist legitimacy on the source of their authority, and he did this by attacking any sense of Donatist historicity, the basis of their ecclesiology, and especially their identification with models of Christian heroism such as Cyprian of Carthage.

Augustine was already proficient in highlighting the importance of receiving faith from God through his concept of '*vocatio*.' This *vocatio* is transmitted among people through preaching, missionary efforts, and teaching. Grace is conferred exclusively within the bosom of the Church. All of this is connected, and the method by which a person comes to faith, encounters God,

---

habet in potestate tali viso attingi mentem suam, quo eius voluntas moveatur ad fidem? Quis autem animo amplectitur aliquid quod eum non delectat? Aut quis habet in potestate, ut vel occurrat quod eum delectare possit, vel delectet cum occurrerit? Cum ergo nos ea delectant quibus proficiamus ad Deum, inspiratur hoc et praebetur gratia Dei, non nutu nostro et industria aut operum meritis comparatur, quia ut sit nutus voluntatis, ut sit industria studii, ut sint opera caritate ferventia, ille tribuit, ille largitur'.

The consistency in Augustine's theological construction of grace throughout the duration of his career is remarkable. This is the topic of in-depth investigation in Carol Harrison, *Rethinking Augustine's Early Theology: an Argument for Continuity* (Oxford: Oxford University Press, 2006).

94 Aug., *Ep.* 111,1. This nadir in Catholic-Donatist relations is captured and summarized neatly in J. Merdinger, *Rome & the African Church*, 101–103. As she points out, it was with this series of events that the Donatist controversy moved from being just an ecclesial issue to a martial one, and one that the Roman Empire would have to involve itself in.

and reaches understanding, is through the authority (*auctoritas*) of witnesses to Christ, and martyrs in particular. In one of the more poignant passages in his scholarship, Robert Louis Wilken points out that faith leading to understanding is encountered in the authoritative witness of martyrs in the Church. To receive the content of faith and to understand what one believes, requires obedience and love.[95] Augustine knew this, for it was the impact of others that brought him to his faith, and he also knew that fidelity to the content of the Church's received teaching requires obedience.

This is where Augustine could connect Cyprian with the authority of the Catholic Church, for Cyprian's own witness proved that he abhorred schism from the body of Christ, Cyprian was consummate in his obedience to the faith he had received, and because of this never separated himself from the Church, even when it became filled with apostates and deniers of Christ.[96] Therefore Augustine's attack on the Donatists was an attack from authority; a sustained attack on the Donatist understanding of the Church, an understanding which was different from Cyprian's authoritative teaching and example.

Because the problem between Donatists and Catholics was, on the surface, mainly an ecclesiological one, Augustine had to dispel the engrained North African understanding of the Church in order to employ a fecund method of criticism. Donatist theology asserted two bedrock principles: (1) membership in the authentic, pure Church is necessary for salvation; and (2) only ministers untainted by ecclesial sins (specifically *traditio* or betrayal) can perform positive sacramental actions.[97] These concepts were hard-wired into North African thinking. Tertullian[98] and Cyprian[99] had clearly presented a sharp

---

95 Robert Louis Wilken, *The Spirit of Early Christian Thought: Seeking the Face of God* (New Haven, CT: Yale University Press, 2003), 183.

96 J. Patout Burns and Robin Jensen, *Christianity in Roman Africa: the Development of its Practices and Beliefs* (Grand Rapids, MI/Cambridge: Wm. Eerdmans Publishing, 2014), 602–607.

97 This is further elucidated upon in: J. Pelikan, 'An Augustinian Dilemma: Augustine's Doctrine of Grace versus Augustine's Doctrine of the Church?' *Augustinian Studies* 18 (1987), 13.

98 Tertullian, *Apologeticum* 39,4 (*CCSL* 1, 150): 'Ibidem etiam exhortationes, castigationes et censura divina. Nam et iudicatur magno cum pondere, ut apud certos de dei conspectu, summumque futuri iudicii praeiudicium est, si quis ita deliquerit, ut a communicatione orationis et conventus et omnis sancti commercii relegetur'; Tertullian also gave an early defence of the view that baptism by a heretic or other egregious sinner was invalid; *De Baptismo* 5 (*CSEL* 1, 281).

99 Cyp., *De Unit.*, 9: 'Let no one think that good men can leave the Church; it is not the grain that the wind carries away, nor the solidly rooted tree that the storm blows down: it is the

'inside-outside' or *intus-foris* paradigm of the Church and the world, in terms of which sin was seen as an easily-communicable plague and where the corrupted were to be physically separated from, or quarantined in the terrestrial Church:[100]

> Thus are the faithful proved, thus the faithless discovered; thus too even before the day of judgment, already here below, the souls of the just and unjust are distinguished, and the wheat is separated from the chaff.[101]

This orientation, claiming unrivalled fidelity to the 'one Lord, one faith, one baptism' (Eph. 4,5),[102] was strengthened in subsequent decades with the gradual emergence of an idiosyncratic North African/Donatist rite,[103] which, in its liturgical life, hagiographies, and biblical hermeneutic, codified a clear cosmological distinction between church and world.[104]

---

empty chaff that is swept away by the storm, the weakening trees that are overturned by the blast of the whirlwind…' English translation from: *The Unity of the Catholic Church, Ancient Christian Writers* [ACW] 25, trans. M. Bévenot, Mahwah, NJ, The Newman Press, 1957, 9; (CCSL 3/3A, 256): 'Nemo existimet bonos de ecclesia posse discedere: triticum non rapit ventus, nec arborem solida radice fundatam procella subvertit; inanes paleae tempestate iactantur'.

100 Robert Markus, *Christianity in the Roman World* (New York: Scribner, 1974), 111; Henry, 'The Lily and the Thorns', 258.

101 Cyp., *De Unit.* 10 (*ACW* 25, 52–53), (*CCSL* 3/A, 256): 'Sic probantur fideles, sic perfidi deteguntur, sic et ante iudicii diem hic quoque iam iustorum adque iniustorum animae dividuntur, et a frumento paleae separantur'.

102 This was a popular refrain from North Africans; Cyp., *Ep.* 70,1. This would be resourced later by Augustine; *Cresc.* 1,33 (*CSEL* 52, 353), *Un. bapt.* 10,17 (*CSEL* 53, 18).

103 It does not take an overactive imagination to theorise plausibly that these tenets of Donatist faith, well attested to in North African Christian literature and popular piety, could have been manifest in a distinctive liturgical tradition. In this regard see: J. Rives, *Religion and Authority in Roman Carthage from Augustus to Constantine*, New York, 1995, 226. Rives argues that there are grounds to hold that the African liturgy, as ancient as it was, might have been more closely identifiable with Eastern rites of the time. Also refer to H. Leclercq, *Afrique*, *DACL* 1 (1924), col. 592, where he posits that the African rite would have been the oldest of the Latin rites. This is covered summarily in: Coyle, 'The Self-identity of North African Christians in Augustine's Time', 68.

104 Evidence of this can be identified in Cyp.: *Ep.* 69 (*CCSL* 3/C, 469–496), 73 (*CCSL* 3/C, 529–562), 74 (*CCSL* 3/C, 563–580); *De rebaptismate* (*CSEL* 3/1, 69); *Sententiae Episcoporum de Haereticis Baptizandis*, §87 (*CCSL* 3/E, 107–109): 'Meam sententiam plenissime exprimit epistulae, quae ad Iubianum collegam nostrum scripta est, haereticos secundum evangelicam et apostilicam contestionem adversarios Christi et antichristos appellatos, quando ad ecclesiam venerint, unico ecclesiae baptismo baptizandos esse, ut possint fieri

The bishop of Hippo's response would therefore have to be radically different from the one North African Donatists were used to. Augustine alternatively proposed that (1) sinners are numbered among those in the Church, *per* its nature; and (2) it is not the individual minister and his status that determines whether sacraments provide salvation, but God alone. And what was the nexus of Augustine's propositions? Grace.

His model of the Church was a mixed body containing sinners and the saintly, as he found attested to in the scriptures[105] and by Cyprian.[106] What saves those in the Church is not their *de facto* membership in the authentic, pure Church in and of itself, as he claimed the Donatists proposed, but grace. Borrowing from Paul (1 Cor. 1,4–7), he insists members of the Body of Christ share in the fullness of grace, *in gratia dei quae data est vobis*, even whilst being interspersed with those in the Church lacking in grace.[107] Augustine's mixed model of Church therefore required a significant characteristic to differentiate it from the Donatists' own, namely that the unity of members is caused by

---

de adversariis amici et de antichristis christiani'. Two indispensable works on this issue are from Burns, *Cyprian the Bishop*, esp. 126–31; and *On Rebaptism: Social Organization in the Third Century Church*, 367–403. Burns illustrates the importance of the fact that African Christians identified clear cosmological boundaries between the Church associated with the bishop, and the rest of the world, including schismatics. 'Within the church, water and oil could be sanctified, the divine name could be invoked, saving faith could be professed; outside the church, water and oil were polluted by idolatry or schism, appeals to Christ were in vain, the baptismal profession contradicted…'; *Cyprian the Bishop*, 128.

105 In the Old Testament: (Mal. 1,2) Aug., *De bapt.* 1,14 (CSEL 51, 160): 'Qui autem de utero ipsius matris intus in unitate nati neglegunt gratiam quam acceperunt, similes sunt esau filio isaac, qui reprobatus est deo adtestante et dicente: Iacob dilexi, Esau autem odio habui, cum ambo ex uno concubitu concepti, ex uno utero nati sint'. In the New Testament: (1 Cor. 1,4–7) Aug., *C. Don.* 21,34 (CSEL 53, 136).

106 Cyp., *Ep.* 54,3 (CSEL 3/2, 622–623), reused in Aug., *Cresc.* 2,43 (CSEL 52, 402–403). Augustine would later use the earlier North African idea of the 'wheat and chaff', as seen on p. 4, footnote 11, in his *Ep.* 108: 'For, though we see that there are weeds in the Church, our faith and love ought not to be hampered so that we withdraw from the Church, because we see that there are weeds in the Church. We must only strive to be wheat', *Ep.* 108,10 (WSA, 74). Again, in *Ep.* 108,11 (WSA, 75): 'this law of love was promulgated by the lips of Christ the Lord, for to that love there belong the parables concerning the toleration of weeds up to the time of harvest in the unity of the field throughout the world and concerning the toleration of the bad fishes within the net up to the time of reaching the shore'. One last example, *Ep.* 108,12 (WSA, 76): '…the Lord, whether by himself or through his angels, separates the weeds from the grain [Mt. 13,24–30], the chaff from the wheat [Mt. 3,12], the vessels of anger from the vessels of mercy [Rom. 9,22–23], the goats from the sheep [Mt. 25,31], the bad fishes from the good ones [Mt. 13,47–50]'.

107 Aug., *C. Don.* 34 and 35 (CSEL 53).

love, and love is inspired by grace.[108] His view of unity was meant in terms of communion in a universalised sense, as well as a bond between the heavenly (saints already together with Christ) and terrestrial (sinful and graced members combined) existences of the Church.[109] Augustine locates evidence of this in the apostles' 'going out into the whole world through God's grace' (*quas in gratia domini proprio labore*).[110] Paul himself was a minister through grace (Rom. 15,15–19): *propter gratiam quae data est mihi a deo, ut minister sim Christi Iesu in gentibus*.[111]

Augustine's argument extends also to a rebuttal of the Donatist belief that the true Church only exists in ever-faithful Africa.[112] By rejecting the concept the Catholics were offering, Augustine turns the situation to his polemical advantage, insisting the Donatist leadership are actually denying God's work of salvation in every land, rejecting the presence of grace in the Church (God's kingdom), *gratia consecratur ecclesia*, that had been ensured through Christ's shedding of blood during his Passion.[113] By rejecting Christ's Passion they are condemning the truth, which is conferred through grace: *gratiam dei in veritate* (Col. 1,3–6).[114] If the 'grace of God is in the truth', then this truth can only be found in the Church, for it was promised by Christ that it would always be his kingdom. Ironically, by emphasising that the Church is the only source of truth and grace,[115] Augustine was claiming a key Donatist position, which is that inclusion in the Church is necessary for salvation. Polemically speaking, the bishop of Hippo could demand that if Donatists truly believed in Christ, they must believe in his promise of the kingdom. Since they were out of his

108 *C. ep. Parm.* 2,11; 3,3; 3,10; 3,26; *De bapt.* 4,12. T.J. van Bavel further illustrated that this is one readily identifiable area where Augustine rightly appropriated Cyprian. Augustine, following Cyprian's view that succession is hostile to the Holy Spirit and injurious to the unity and peace of Christ (Cyp., *De Unit.* 14; *Ep.* 59,20; *Ep.* 74,4), manifests this theology in declaring no one belongs to Christ without love (*En. in Ps.* 54, 19: *s.* 138,2) and that by breaking unity they are injuring Christ. This is so because Christ is so intimately bound up with his followers (the Church, visible and invisible), that it is no longer 'Christ' and 'us' but only an 'us,' thus forming a '*totus Christus*'; *Martyrium*, 356, 358.

109 (The visible Church), *En. in Ps.* 57,9; *Ioh. ev. Tr.* 2,2; (the invisible Church), *C. Don. Ep.* 4,7.

110 *Cresc.* 4,37.

111 *Cath.* 31.

112 *C. ep. Parm.* 1,1–2; 2,2; 3,21; *C. Gaud.* 1,22; see Robert Markus, *Donatismo e Ri-battesimo*, in *Agostino e il Donatismo: Lectio Augustini* XIX, *Settimana Agostiniana Pavese* (2003). Studia Ephemeridis Augustinianum 100 (Rome: Augustinianum, 2007), 15.

113 Aug., *Brev.* 3,20; *C. ep. Parm.* 1,12.

114 Aug., *Cath.* 45.

115 *De bapt.* 6,87.

kingdom through schism, their mutual faith in God's grace, *in Christi gratia concordemus*,[116] required that they come into unity. Without such unity, which is spawned by a right belief in the Church's population of the blessed mixed with the evil,[117] they could not share in grace,[118] since unity is a product of grace.[119]

The Working of Grace

Grace is also a central theme in Augustine's localised attack on the Donatist conception of the importance of the minister in conferring effective sacraments. This is necessary in order for him to argue that the integrity of the Church and the availability of grace are not pegged to the outward acts or faithfulness to a tradition (as he accused the Donatists of thinking), but instead are wholly reliant on God and manifest in charity.[120] It is the sign of charity which evinces God's grace and salvific presence in the Church's sacraments.

By moving away from the Donatist position on the constitution of the holiness of the Church, Augustine was required to first criticise their view of grace.[121] To do so, he compares the Donatist view with that of those who followed the Mosaic laws, believing their exterior conformity or ritual observance alone saved them from sin and placed them in God's grace.[122] There is a distinction of Law and grace[123] where intentionality determines whether one commits sin or does good. Drawing again on Paul (1 Cor. 11,29), Augustine argues that instead of concentrating on how one who eats or drinks in an unworthy

116 *Cresc.* 3,34.

117 *Cresc.* 4,37.

118 Aug., *Ioh. Ev. Tr.* 27,6.

119 Aug., *C. Don.* 28. This was, again, a point of argument taken from the arsenal of Cyprian's thought that Augustine specifically deployed against Donatist bishops: 'utentes etiam exemplo et praecepto beati Cypriani, qui collegas suos faeneratores fraudatores raptores pacis contemplatione pertulit tales nec eorum contagione factus est talis'.

120 A special feature of the Donatist controversy, which impacted on the outcome of the Pelagian crisis, was that Augustine was forced to develop his understanding of *caritas* from an individual-specific model to a wholly social consideration within the Church, and also emphatically spur his belief that the intentionality behind human acts was of prime importance in determining their goodness or badness; see Burns, *Operative Grace*, 59–60.

121 Aug., *Cath.* 49.

122 In this way Augustine distinguished between the Law (especially in the OT sense) and the new law of grace through Christ featured in the NT. The Pharisees, in their obsession with the observance of the Law, lacked the same grace in circumcision that Christ witnessed to in his humility by undergoing baptism at the hand of John the Baptist: *sacramenti gratia voluit baptizari*, *C. ep. Parm.* 2,36.

123 *Cresc.* 1,20.

way will receive negative judgment, under the new regime of grace those who eat and drink in a worthy way receive grace: *gratiam sibi manducat et bibit*.[124]

Under Augustine's proposal grace is breathed into the Church by God directly,[125] regardless of the status of the minister orchestrating the sacramental ritual.[126] Since it is Christ who actually dispenses grace,[127] especially through the sacraments, a minister can be deeply flawed, can be a 'Judas',[128] and yet can channel the grace of Christ through a sacrament, specifically baptism.[129] This does not extend to those who violate charity, and by so doing, the unity of the Church, however.[130]

The Donatist controversy also seasoned a chance for the bishop of Hippo to assert some descriptions of grace itself, and not merely discuss its origins or the method of issue. This divine grace is, borrowing once more from Paul, freely given by God (*gratuitam gratiam*) (1 Cor. 9,17),[131] miraculous (*occulta et mirabili dispensatione*),[132] dispersed latently through the work of the Holy Spirit (*occulta gratia, occulta potentia in spiritu sancto*),[133] enriches the soul (*nam gratia dei in nobis non est pauper*),[134] liberates from a life of carnal proclivities and pride,[135] cultivates further humility and conversion,[136] and instils genuine charity.[137]

The Use of Cyprian in the Donatist Controversy

A final clue in piecing together Augustine's use of grace in his polemical argumentation is his frequent recourse to Cyprian of Carthage as an authority and a witness to grace. This is a significant avenue of exploration in that we can easily identify continuity between Augustine's anti-Donatist and anti-Pelagian

---

124 *C. ep. Parm.* 2,11.

125 *C. ep. Parm.* 2,21; 2,32 ; *Cresc.* 4,16; 4,21; *De bapt.* 6,49–50; 6,69.

126 *C. ep. Parm.* 2,22.

127 *C. litt. Pet.* 1,6–7; 2,243; 3,51–52; 3,56. Augustine alternatively described the discharge of grace as a work of the Holy Spirit; *C. litt. Pet.* 3,59; 3,62.

128 *De bapt.* 5,29; 6,30; 7,54–55; *C. litt. Pet.* 3,67; *Cresc.* 2,24; 2,26.

129 *De bapt.* 1,20; 4,21; 4,31; 5,10–11; 5,14; 7,36–37; *Cresc.* 3,15.

130 *De bapt.* 1,18.

131 *C. ep. Parm.* 2,24. Alternatively, in *Ioh. Ev. Tr.* 3,10, a 'gift of God': 'ut ante susciperet gratiam, misericordem patrem opus habebat: ut praemium gratiae, iudicem iustum'.

132 *De bapt.* 2,2.

133 *C. litt. Pet.* 3,59; *Cresc.* 2,26.

134 *C. litt. Pet.* 2,202.

135 *C. litt. Pet.* 3,11: 'non illius qui me per gratiam suam et a me ipso liberavit'.

136 *Cresc.* 4,79.

137 *C. Gaud.* 1,38.

works, based on polemical necessity. However, the striking similarities in Augustine's use of Cyprian as an authority attesting to grace were precipitated by two distinct challenges. In the Donatist controversy Augustine was arguing with a group claiming to be the only authentic and genuinely-rooted Church in North Africa.[138] Therefore, for Augustine to assert an adequate level of authority against the Donatists, he would have to tap into the Donatist claim of sole possession of the unadulterated North African tradition. This could be done most effectively by usurping Donatism's exclusive hold on the teaching and legacy of Cyprian, and by refining this when doing so was advantageous for the Catholic position, whilst at the same time disregarding elements that might seem outdated or irreconcilable.

In the Pelagian conflict, appeals were made to Cyprian for a different reason. Augustine was accused of promoting a theology of grace and an anthropology that lay outside the Christian tradition, that is, they were the innovations of an African usurper.[139] His defence thus became an appropriation of Cyprian's legacy, making an attack on his own 'African' views an attack on the African Cyprian.[140] But while the need for Cyprian's authority was different in both contexts, a diachronic analysis shows they nevertheless share a nexus based on the theme of grace.

Augustine needed to affirm the special prestige awarded to Cyprian by North Africans in order to be taken seriously. It is not surprising then that he seeks to reaffirm Cyprian's standing, all the while doing so in language aimed at appropriating Cyprian's legacy. This is evident in *De baptismo* (401), which, importantly, lays out a recurring theme for Augustine's reinterpretation. Cyprian is a man of grace, expressed most solemnly in his roles as bishop

138 S. Lancel stipulates in this regard that: 'Actually, the Donatists had remained faithful to the doctrine of St Cyprian in this matter [i.e., rebaptism] whereas the rest of the African Church had renounced it following the council of Arles in 314', *Saint Augustine*, 172, and also 388–403; Alexander/ Lancel, 'Donatistae', in *Augustinus-Lexikon* II, 606–638; Brown, *Augustine of Hippo: A Biography*, 331; Merdinger, *Rome and the African Church in the Time of Augustine*, esp. part 1; Tilley, 'Augustine's Unacknowledged Debt to the Donatists', 144; Maureen Tilley, 'Cyprian', in A. Fitzgerald (ed.), *Augustine through the Ages. An Encyclopedia* (Grand Rapids, MI/Cambridge : Wm. Eerdmans Publishing, 1999), 262–264; Éric Rebillard, 'Augustin et ses autorités: l'élaboration de l'argument patristique au cours de la controverse pélagienne', *Studia Patristica* 38 (2001), 247–249.

139 Augustine's theological proposals are referred to as 'doctores nostri temporis'; Julian of Aeclanum, *Ad Turb.* 1,1 (CCSL 88, 340).

140 This is covered in depth in Matthew Gaumer, '"Poenus disputator… Non Ego, Sed Cyprianus Poenus": ¿Por qué necesitaba Agustín apropiarse de Cipriano de Cartago?' *Augustinus* 55/1 (2010), 141–64.

and martyr. Cyprian is a man of outstanding grace: *beato Cypriano, quem inter raros et paucos excellentissimae gratiae*,[141] attesting to Christ's grace through his own martyrdom[142] which likewise elevated him in grace.[143] According to Augustine, Cyprian's graced works as bishop and martyr lend the bishop of Carthage enhanced authority to teach that sacraments are avenues of God's grace independent of human dispositions,[144] (*sacramentum dei gratiae*),[145] as perfectly symbolised in John the Baptist receiving the authority to confer grace, the same grace as with which he was filled,[146] and which likewise gave life to the new regime of grace in Christ.[147] Augustine, writing in 401, states that it is Cyprian who served as a testament to the human need for humility in order to overcome pride, lust, and self-importance, all consequences of a fallen humanity,[148] for 'God withstands the proud, whilst he gives grace to the humble'.[149] Through grace Cyprian overcame 'sordid and carnal pleasures,'[150] a grace exhibited most excellently by his submission to God and his willingness to accept martyrdom (in a way mirroring Christ's own passion) for Christ's sake and not his own.

Evidence from surviving sources indicates that by the end of the first decade of the fifth century, the bishop of Hippo had found a niche in monopolising Cyprian's authority. By then Augustine had crafted a narrative and doctrinal genealogy which would be integrated into the Pelagian controversy. Cyprian is given a 'twin grace, by the way he was a bishop and the way he was a martyr'.[151] This grace allowed Cyprian as bishop to heroically defend the unity of the Church, and as martyr to give witness to his religion.[152] Not only was Cyprian killed for his confession of faith, but was, additionally, martyred for his struggle for unity within the Church:

141 *De bapt.* 6,3.

142 *De bapt.* 3,5.

143 *De bapt.* 1,29.

144 *De bapt.* 3,6. It is interesting to note how Augustine argues to redeem Cyprian's position in this regard. It is out of the abundance of grace he was given that he was able to uphold Church unity.

145 *De bapt.* 6,36.

146 *De bapt.* 5,14.

147 *De bapt.* 5,10–11. This grace functions through the auspices of the apostolic ministry; *Un. bapt.* 22.

148 (c.401) Aug., *s.* 313A,2–3.

149 *s.* 313A,4. References to Job 22,29, Jas. 4,6, 1 Pet. 5,5.

150 *s.* 313A,4.

151 (c.410) *s.* 313E,1.

152 *s.* 313E,1.

> There is also the fact that, if the fruitful branch still had something that needed pruning, it was pruned by the glorious sword of martyrdom, not because he was killed for the name of Christ, but because he was killed for the name of Christ in the bosom of unity.[153]

Augustine focuses this attack to conclude that the Donatists are in complete discontinuity with Cyprian because they disregard his central teaching on the Church, namely that it consists of both 'weeds' and 'wheat' and will remain so until Christ separates them in the end.[154]

The Use of Cyprian in the Pelagian Controversy

By the time Augustine was engaged in his anti-Pelagian efforts in the 410s, he had already mastered deployment of Cyprian as the martyr-bishop who attested through grace to the various theological positions advocated by himself. While it is already clear Augustine liberally referenced Cyprian's authority as a martyr,[155] what is less understood is that Augustine used Cyprian's martyr status in conjunction with the grace theme, the same theme he had developed for use in the Donatist controversy.

In the Pelagian controversy, Augustine readily references Cyprian as the 'most blessed martyr'[156] and as well as a bishop, and often the two in tandem:

153 (c.409–410) *Ep.* 108,9; English translation from *Letter 108*, in *WSA* II/2, 74, (*CSEL* 34/2, 621): 'Huc accedit, quoniam fructuosum sarmentum, si aliquid habebat adhuc purgandum, etiam gloriosa martyrii falce purgatum est, non quia pro Christi nomine occisus est, sed quia pro Christi nomine in gremio unitatis occisus est'. Augustine developed this line further in another source: '…observe the branch that has been pruned, the martyr Cyprian; observe the branches that have been cut off, there heretics and Donatists. Why do you people say you belong to this man, this man who bore fruit of peace and unity, who was pruned by the pruning hook or martyrdom, to obtain the crown of eternal salvation? Why do you compare yourselves to this man, heretics and Donatists, cut off from the vine by separation, defiled by your habit of headlong self-destruction? …How insane can you get, you Donatists, you rabid dogs!' *s.* 313E,6 (*WSA* III/9, 114), (*MA* 1, 541): 'Attendite ergo sarmentum purgatum, martyrem Cyprianum; attendite sarmenta amputata, haeretici et Donatistae. Quid uos ad istum dicitis pertinere, ad istum ferentem fructum pacis et unitatis, purgatum falce martyrii ad percipiendam coronam aeternae salutis? quid uos huic comparatis, haeretici et Donatistae, separatione concisi, praecipitatione coinquinati? …O insani Donatistae! O rabidi!'

154 This point is examined in detail in Dupont and Gaumer, '*Gratia Dei, Gratia Sacramenti.* Grace in Augustine of Hippo's Anti-Donatist Writings', 307–329.

155 This is the topic that is under investigation in Yates, 'Augustine's Appropriation of Cyprian the Martyr-bishop against the Pelagians', 119–135.

156 (c.419) *s.* 313D,1; see also *s.* 312,1.

'this revered bishop and venerable martyr'.[157] But more than just a bishop and martyr, in the Pelagian crisis Augustine's Cyprian is a martyr through God's grace:

> What does it mean to be clad in the breastplate of justice, and receive the shield of faith and the helmet of salvation and the sword of the Spirit which is the word of God, if not to armed by the Lord with his gifts?[158]

Augustine is also quick to emphasise that Cyprian's martyrdom was itself a consequence of grace, that is, a result of the working of God who desired:

> ...to call him when he strayed, to cleanse him when he was defiled, to form and shape him when he believed, to teach him in his obedience, to guide him in his teaching, to aid him in his fight, to crown him in his victory.[159]

The result of Cyprian's graced martyrdom is a living catechesis: 'So he taught in his life what he did; and what he did in his death is what he taught'.[160] Augustine here attributes the teaching of Cyprian to the truth of grace as Christ's

---

157 Aug., *s.* 313,1.

158 Aug., *s.* 313,3 (*PL* 38, 1423–24): 'Quid est iustitiae lorica indui, et accipere scutum fidei, et galeam salutis,et gladium spiritus, quod est uerbum dei, nisi a domino donis eius armari?' It is also worth mentioning how Augustine follows-up on this statement in the subsequent paragraph: 'Nor would it have been enough for this soldier just to be armed, unless he had also obtained help from the actual armed warrior by whom he had been armed himself'. (*PL* 38, 1424): 'Nec armari tantum sufficeret huic militi, nisi impetrasset ab armato ipso, a quo armatus fuerat, adiuuari'.

159 Aug., *s.* 312, 6 (*WSA* III/9, 84), (*PL* 38, 1422): 'Vocare errantem, mundare sordentem, formare credentem, docere oboedientem, regere docentem, adiuuare pugnantem, coronare uincentem'. See also *s.* 312,3 (*WSA* III/9, 82): 'It is I who kill, and I who make alive; I who will strike, and I who will heal (Dt. 32,39)... Behold, I have set you over nations and kingdoms, to uproot and dig up and destroy, and to rebuild and plant (Jer. 1,10). So the uprooter and planter approached that soul [Cyprian]; and he overthrew the old Cyprian, and after laying himself there as a foundation, he built up the new Cyprian in himself, and made him into a true Cyprian out of himself'.(*PL* 38, 1421): 'Ego occidam, et ego uiuere faciam; ego percutiam, et ego sanabo [Dt. 32,39]: aut frustra in futurorum figura ad Ieremiam dictum est, ecce constitui te hodie super gentes et regna, eradicare, et effodere, et perdere, et reaedificare, et plantare [Jer 1,10]. Accessit ergo ad illam animam eradicator atque plantator; et euertit ueterem Cyprianum, positoque ibi fundamento ipso se, nouum Cyprianum aedificauit in se, et uerum Cyprianum fecit ex se'.

160 *s.* 312,6.

means for humankind's salvation. For this truth Cyprian sacrificed himself, a sacrifice made possible by grace.[161] Cyprian's teaching also extended beyond that.[162] His doctrine was also a love of unity, and out of a love of peace a toleration of 'flawed' Christians to maintain its bond.[163] And like the Donatists, who were willing to disrupt Church unity for the sake of their own theological positions, the Pelagians were willing to do the same, thus making them 'enemies of grace'.[164]

For Augustine, the Pelagians were 'the new enemies of grace',[165] precisely because they were attempting to obfuscate Cyprian's teaching on grace (and thus the tradition of the Church) through a new theology or *novus theologicus*.[166] Cyprian, an instrument of grace,[167] witnessed that it is only through grace that there is reconciliation between 'the flesh and the spirit':

> The same martyr bears witness in the letter, *Mortality*, that [perfection] is not attained in this life. In it he says that the apostle Paul desired to be dissolved and to be with Christ [Phil. 2,20–24], precisely so that he might become no longer subject to sins and the failing of the flesh. How vigilant is he against your teaching that leads you to trust in your own power, as he explains this point in his letter on the Lord's Prayer! For he teaches that we should ask the Lord rather than trust in our own power so that not human strength, but divine grace [*gratia*] may produce concord between the flesh and the spirit [Gal. 5,17]. He is in full accord with the apostle who says, 'Who will set me free from the body of this death? The grace of God [*gratia Dei*] through Jesus Christ our Lord [Rom. 7,24–25].'[168]

---

161 Aug., *C. Iul.* 1,6 (*WSA* I/24, 270).

162 *s.* 312,6. Here Augustine implements one of his most revealing characterisations of Cyprian, when he refers to him as the 'most blessed Cyprian…both teacher of the art of warfare and a most glorious warrior himself'. (PL 38, 1422): '…beatissimus Cyprianus gloriosorum praeliorum doctor et gloriosus ipse praeliator'. Here Augustine is alluding to the point that Cyprian was a 'warrior of grace'.

163 *s.* 312,6.

164 Aug., *C. Iul.* 4,15; 4,16; 4,22; 5,6,24; 5,39; 6,44.

165 Aug., *Ep.* 215,1 (*CSEL* 57, 388): '…novos haereticos Pelagianos…'.

166 Augustine refers polemically to the Pelagian viewpoint as, *C. ep. Pel.* (*CSEL* 60, 543): '…recentem Pelagianorum hereticorum praesumptionem perniciem'.

167 *s.* 313,5 (WSA III/9, 88): 'Indeed, God forges potent weapons for himself against his enemies, those namely whom he makes his friends. So the soul of the blessed Cyprian was a grand claymore of God's, shining with charity, sharp with truth; used and brandished by the power of God in full war cry, what wars it settled, what bands of gainsayers it overcame with its arguments!'

168 *C. Iul.* 2,6 (*WSA* I/24, 308–309), (*PL* 44, 676–677): 'Idem quoque testis est martyr in epistola de mortalitate, ubi apostolum Paulum propterea dicit concupiscere dissolui et esse

This concept reaches its full maturity by the time of the so-called Semi-Pelagian controversy, around 427. By the end of his lifetime Augustine was still arguing against 'the new Pelagian heretics'[169] over the same issues of God's grace and its necessity for salvation. This is perhaps summed up concisely in the following: 'A person falls into the Pelagian error if he thinks that the grace of God, which alone sets a human being free through our Lord...is given in accord with some human merits'.[170] And of course Augustine would again make use of the 'blessed martyr Cyprian' to support his claim that 'we must ask from our Father...for everything that pertains to our moral conduct...so that we do not put our trust in free choice and fall away from God's grace':

> This would, of course, be a pointless act if the Church did not believe that even the evil and unbelieving wills of human beings can be converted to the good by the grace of God [*Dei gratiam in bonum posse converti*].[171]

This wording, in a sense, articulates rather well a complete synthesis of Augustine's thought on grace, a process which was developed and given nuance over a period of more than 40 years. It originally arose in a context where Augustine was desperately battling his Donatist foes, but became phenomenally successful when Augustine entered into the fray with the Pelagians.

Augustine on the Holy Spirit

So far in this chapter, we have retraced the way Augustine effectively sustained his polemic against the Donatists. When it came to developing a workable theory supporting state-sponsored religious coercion, and then another form of

---

cum Christo, ut nullis iam fieret peccatis et uitiis carnis obnoxius. Quam uero uigilanter aduersus illud dogma uestrum, quo in uestra uirtute confiditis, hoc in oratione dominica exponit? Sic enim docet, petendum id potius a domino, quam de propriis uiribus praesumendum, ut inter carnem ac spiritum non humana uirtus, sed gratia faciat diuina concordiam: consonans omnino apostolo dicenti, quis me liberabit de corpore mortis huius? Gratia dei per Iesum Christum dominum nostrum'.

169 Aug., *Ep.* 215,1.

170 *Ep.* 215,1 (*WSA* 57, 388): '...ad uos redirent aduersus nouos haereticos Pelagianos, in quorum errorem cadit, qui putat secundum aliqua merita humana dari gratiam dei, quae sola hominem liberat per dominum nostrum Iesum Christum...non iudicari hominem secundum opera sua'.

171 *Ep.* 215, 3 (*WSA* II/4, 41), (*CSEL* 57, 390): 'Quod utique inaniter fieret, nisi ecclesia crederet etiam malas atque infideles hominum uoluntates per dei gratiam in bonum posse conuerti.'

external coercion, divine grace, these concepts benefited Augustine very well. This is most evident when one acknowledges that Augustine not only maintained these ideas even after he had made the Pelagians his new chief obsession, but even expanded on them! There was a third category that Augustine utilised effectively against both groups, which it would be negligent to dismiss here: his treatment of the Holy Spirit.[172]

By the 400s and 410s, Augustine's polemical efforts against institutional Donatist Christianity had resulted in a battle-proven method for opposing those he saw as standing outside the 'Catholic truth'.[173] At the heart of this method was his arrival at the brand of the African saint *par excellence*, Cyprian the martyr-bishop. Gaining literary and argumentative control of such an authority as Cyprian, with whom contemporary North African Christians of both the Catholic and the Donatist churches identified, gave Augustine an advantage in matters pertaining to Christian piety in his corner of the empire, as it gave him a key to African hearts and minds. Indeed, by this time, nearly all of the themes and concepts that would later ignite the Pelagian controversy were already in place, a result of Augustine's prolonged involvement with the Donatists. One area, however, that remains only vaguely understood from this transitional period of Augustine's career, is his use of the theme of the Holy Spirit in a polemical manner. Understanding this theme is essential for understanding the dynamism of ancient African Christianity, as it signifies not only another area of contrast and continuity between Augustine and Cyprian, but also between Augustine and the Donatists. It also signifies the emergence of Augustine as the resurgent voice of Africa.

Cyprian's tenure as bishop of Carthage had produced strains of thought concerning the Holy Spirit that were closely paired with and influenced by his ecclesiology, which was in turn strongly affected by the persecution of the Roman imperial administration and a combative back-and-forth with the bishop of Rome. Throughout, Cyprian endeavoured to reconcile the validity of sacraments with the need to maintain the group integrity that had been broken by the reality of lapsed Church leaders reeling from the Decian persecutions.

---

172 This is comprehensively treated in M. Lamberigts, 'Augustine on the Holy Spirit in the Controversy with Julian of Aeclanum', in G. Förster, A. Grote, C. Müller (eds.), *Spiritus et Littera. Beiträge zur Augustinus-Forschung. Festschrift zum 80. Geburtstag von Cornelius Petrus Mayer* OSA (Würzburg: Augustinus, 2009), 289–315.

173 Emilien Lamirande, 'Aux origines du dialogue interconfessionnel: saint Augustin et les donatistes: vingt ans de tentatives infructueuses (391–411)', *Studia Canonica* 32 (1998), 203–228.

A net result of both forms of pressure was that Cyprian was required to make central the Holy Spirit and its role in the life of the Church.[174]

For Cyprian, the Holy Spirit was the guiding force of the Church and the source of unity for its members, far more so than the virtues and opinions of any individual bishop.[175] But the existence of public sinners within the earthly Church (those who had co-operated with the Roman authorities during the persecutions) and the need to reconcile lapsed members, collided with the North African belief that the Holy Spirit operates exclusively through graced channels, that is, through sacraments untainted by the hands of sinful ministers. Cyprian attempted to integrate these sensitive lines of thought by explaining that it was God who would later enforce justice against sinners, and to do so in the present would not be proper in the earthly Church.[176] Some 150 years later, this intuition would serve Augustine as a central talking-point in his anti-Donatist campaign.[177] Yet despite his efforts, Augustine would not overcome the extant African tradition. For ancient African Christians believed their Church was 'declared by the Holy Spirit' to be a dove, a perfect one, the bride of Christ,[178] and the ark of Noah.[179] Cyprian had reinforced this position throughout his *Ep.* 67 by drawing on OT and NT sources, which he validated by no less an authority than the Holy Spirit:

> For in the Psalms the Holy Spirit threatens men who so act with these words: *But you hate my teachings, and my words you have cast behind you. On seeing a thief you hastened to join him, and your lot you have shared*

174 Frend, *The Donatist Church*, 130–31.

175 Cyprian, *De ecclesiae catholicae unitate* [*De Unit.*], ed. M. Bévenot, *CCSL* 3/A (Turnhout, 1972), 213. M. Bévenot dates *De Unit.* to 251, making it one of Cyprian's earlier surviving works; Cyprian, *The Unity of the Catholic Church*, *ACW* 25, ed. M. Bévenot (Westminster, MD, 1957), 3 and 5.

176 Cyprian, *De lapsis* 6 (*The Lapsed*, *ACW* 25, ed. M. Bévenot (Westminster, MD, 1957), 17); *Ep.* 54,3,1–4 (*The Letters of St. Cyprian of Carthage, Volume II, Letters 28–54*, *ACW* 44, ed. G.W. Clarke, (Mahwah, NJ, 1984), 87–88); 55,15,1 (*The Letters of St. Cyprian of Carthage, Volume III, Letters 55–66*, *ACW* 46, ed. G.W. Clarke (Mahwah, NJ, 1986), 42); 55,25,1 (*ACW* 46, 49). See Peter Kaufman, 'Augustine, Evil and Donatism: Sin and Sanctity before the Pelagian Controversy', *Theological Studies* 50/1 (1990), 115–126.

177 Augustine, *C. Cresc.* 2,22; 2,48; 3,35; 3,44; 4,67; *De bapt.* 4,12. This theme would become closely associated with the 'wheat and tares' symbolism in *De bapt.* 1,4–5; 4,5; 4,18; 5,21; *Ep.* 43,22; 44,11.

178 Cyprian, *Ep.* 69,2,1 (*ACW* 46, 33), quoting Cant. 6:8; 4:12; 4:15 (see Michael Fahey, *Cyprian and the Bible*, 170). Clarke dates *Ep.* 69 to 254–257 (*ACW* 47, 158).

179 Cyprian, *Ep.* 69,2,2 (*ACW* 46, 34), quoting 1 Pt. 3:20 (Fahey, *Cyprian and the Bible*, 522).

> *with adulterers* [Ps. 50]. The Holy Spirit here reveals that they became partners and sharers in other men's sins who have joined themselves in union with sinners.[180]

Cyprian maintained that the Holy Spirit was unavailable to those remaining in serious states of public sin and as a result the true, sin-free public should distance themselves from the contagious ex-faithful: 'We must, therefore, keep watch with all vigilance so as to prevent [sinners] from returning once again for the oblation cannot be sanctified where the Holy Spirit is not present',[181] 'from those whose breasts the Holy Spirit has departed'.[182] This distinctive North African conceptualisation of the ecclesiastical-pneumatological interaction was cemented within Cyprian's lifetime.[183]

In September 256, a council debated the issue of rebaptism and the nature of the Church,[184] in which the theme of the Holy Spirit also featured centrally: 'I know of only baptism in the Church and none outside of it. It will be here, where hope truly is and certain faith, for it is surely written: One faith, one hope, one baptism [Eph. 4,5], not with heretics, where there is no hope and false faith, where all is perpetuated by lying'.[185] Another bishop from Africa speaking at the conference, Proconsularis, Successus of Abbir Germaniciana, added to the common sentiment:

> Heretics can either do nothing or do everything. It is possible to baptise, then it is also possible to confer the Holy Spirit: If it is impossible to confer the Holy Spirit, as it is they do not have it, then they cannot spiritually [genuinely] baptise. Thus, we agree it is necessary to baptise heretics.[186]

---

180 Cyp., *Ep.* 67,9,1 (*ACW* 47, 22), (*CSEL* 3/C, 460): '…cum spiritus sanctus in psalmis talibus comminentur dicens: tu atuem odisti disciplinam et abiecisti sermones meos retro. Si videbas furem, concurrebas ei et cum adulteris particulam tuam ponebas. Consortes et participes ostendit eos alienorum delictorum fieri qui fuerint delinquentibus copulati'. Clarke dates *Ep.* 67 to 254–257 (*ACW* 47, 140).

181 Cyp., *Ep.* 65,3,3–4,1 (*ACW* 46, 115). Clarke dates *Ep.* 65 to 254–257; *The Letters of St. Cyprian of Carthage, Volume III, Letters 55–66*, ed. G.W. Clarke, *ACW* 46 (Mahwah, NJ, 1986), 316.

182 Cyp., *Ep.* 66,2,2 (*ACW* 46, 117). Clarke dates *Ep.* 66 to 253–255 (*ACW* 46, 321).

183 Paul Beddoe, '*Contagio* in the Donatists and St. Augustine', *Studia Patristica* 27 (1993), 231–36.

184 Frend notes this would not be the last undivided council (pre-Donatist/Catholic schism) of Africa before the fifth-century; *The Donatist Church*, 137.

185 Bishop of Caecilius of Bltha recorded in Cyprian, *Sententiae Episcoporum de Haereticis Baptizandis* 1, *CCSL* 3/E, ed. G.F. Diercks (Turnhout, 2004), 9.

186 Cyp., *Sententiae Episcoporum* 16 (*CSEL* 3/E, 35–37): 'Haereticis aut nihil mice taut totum licet. Si possunt baptizare, possunt et sanctum spiritum dare: si autem sanctum spiritum

Cyprian himself put this plainly in a way that would have major repercussions for the tradition which the Donatists would hand down from their martyr-hero: 'My sentiment is amply expressed…[heretics] must, when they join the Church, be baptised into the Church's one baptism, so as to make enemies into friends, Christians out of anti-Christs'.[187] That the Holy Spirit operated as a significant theme in Cyprian's writings is beyond doubt; altogether Cyprian would reference the Holy Spirit 50 times in his surviving works.[188] But perhaps the greatest indication of the import of Cyprian's pneumatological rendering is not to be found in his own lifetime, but rather in the decades and centuries afterwards, especially as African Christianity would evolve into the highly stigmatised phenomenon later known as the Donatist schism.

The first records concerning the Holy Spirit to have survived from post-Cyprian North Africa are contained in the accounts of the Donatist martyrs. Given that the Donatists considered themselves the authentic heirs to Cyprian and loyal guardians of African Christianity,[189] it comes as no surprise that the ten examples contained in four separate martyrdom stories have themes which can be seen to have easily evolved from Cyprian's own pneumatology.[190] Such themes are mainly classifiable as either the Holy Spirit fortifying North African martyrs and persecuted Christians, and/or as giving the African Church the courage to resist the onslaughts of the wicked world and its persecution as embodied by the betrayers or *traditores*. Four of the ten Holy Spirit examples pertain to the Donatist insistence on their Church's separation from the contagion of evil in the world. This separation is explained as the Holy Spirit giving

---

dare non possunt, quia non habent spiritum sanctum, nec baptizare spiritaliter possunt. Propterea censemus haereticos baptizandos esse'.

187 Cyp., *Sententiae Episcoporum* 87 (CSEL 3/E, 107–09).

188 Cyp., *Ep.* 16,4; 27,3; 28,2; 41; 43; 49,2; 57,5; 59,5(x2); 59,17; 59,20; 62,2; 63,4; 63,5; 63,7; 63,8; 63,11; 63,18; 64,3; 65,4; 66,2; 67,9; 68,5; 69,2; 69,5; 69,12; 69,15; 70,1; 70,3; 72,1; 73,4; 73,12; 73,13; 73,17; 73,18; 73,19; 73,21; 73,22; 74,4; 74,5; 74,6; 75,7; 75,16; 75,18; 75,25; 76,4; 78,2; *Ad Donatum* 4; 15; *De habitu virginum* 13; *De lapsis* 27; *De unitate* 4; 6; 10; 16; 24; *De ora Dominica* 2; 5; 16; 23; 28; 34; *Ad Demetrianum* 6; 17; *De mortalitate* 11; 23; *De opere et eleemosynis* 2; 4; 5; 9; *De bono patientiae* 2; 14; 15; 16; *De zelo et livore* 8; 14; *De exhortatione martyrii* 9; 11(x2); 12.

189 J. Alexander, 'Donatism', in P. Esler (ed.), *The Early Christian World, Volume II*, 972; Robert Markus adds to this definition, that 'what we call "Donatism" is in reality nothing else than the Christianity of North Africa as it continued to survive into the fourth century…', 'Africa and the Orbis Terrarum: The Theological Problem', 321.

190 *The Passion of Saints Maxima, Donatilla and Secunda* §2; §6, in M. Tilley (ed., trans.), *Donatist Martyr Stories: The Church in Conflict in Roman North Africa*. Translated Texts for Historians 24 (Liverpool, 1996), 19; 24; *The Martyrdom of Marculus* §4 (Tilley, 80); *A Sermon on the Passion of Saints Donatus and Advocatus Given on the 4TH Day Before the Ides of March* §13 (Tilley, 59); *The Acts of the Abitinian Martyrs* §12; 16; 20; 21; 23 (Tilley, 36; 41; 45; 46; 48).

Christians the strength and fortitude to maintain their group integrity by distancing themselves from sinners and other worldly seductions, as well as giving the Church the courage and resilience it needs to defend itself against the full-scale attacks of the world via its persecutions.[191] The implications stemming from this conceptualisation were profound, as it gave a vivid justification for keeping *traditores*, or other lapsed,[192] outside the African Church, whilst also insisting that Donatists were blessed by the Holy Spirit for their rigour, rather than damned for their isolation.[193] Even more, this duality of Church/world would have a decisive impact on the work of later African luminaries such as Parmenian, Tyconius, and Augustine.

The other major classification of the Holy Spirit theme in the Donatist martyr stories was the explication of the relationship between martyrs and the Spirit. Six of the ten references to the Holy Spirit in these sources are dedicated

191 In *The Passion of Saints Maxima, Donatilla and Secunda* §2 (Tilley, 19) the separation of Church/Roman Empire is expressed in the dialogue between the martyr Maxima and Anulinus the Proconsul, where the martyr says: 'Because the Holy Spirit is in us but an evil spirit manifests itself in you'. In *The Martyrdom of Marculus* §4 (Tilley, 80) the Holy Spirit acts as the main deterrent against the devil/anti-Christ and is engaged in direct combat against the forces of the world wherever persecution is found: 'Now who could tell of the perseverance of the glorious Marculus? Who might prevail by virtue of eloquence in displaying the unheard of rage of his persecutors or the astonishing defence by Christ the Lord exhibited in the martyr? Because of this, savage ferocity was excited against him even harsher rage so that hatred of this soon-to-be martyr might now rouse the devil, and the villainy of the precursor to the Antichrist might not be concealed from the Holy Spirit'. (J.-L. Maier, *Le Dossier Du Donatisme. Tome 1*, 278): 'Hic iam constantiam Marculi gloriosi quis enarrare sufficiat? Quis eloquentiae viribus explicare praevvaleat aut inauditam persecutioris insaniam aut Christi domini circa martyrem suum praesentem stupendamque tutelam? Inde enim contra eum acriori saevitia immitis feritas concitita est, quod, et diabolum futuri iam martyris invidia stimularet et spiritum sanctum praecursoris Antichristi nequitia non lateret'.

192 *The Acts of the Abitinian Martyrs* §21 (Tilley, 46): '"If anyone communicates with the traitors, that person will have no part with us in the heavenly kingdom". And they endorsed this verdict of theirs by the authority of the Holy Spirit written in such evidence as "It is written," they said, "in the Apocalypse, 'Whoever adds to this books one part of a letter or one letter, to him will the Lord add innumerable afflictions. And whoever blots them out, so will the Lord blot out his share from the Book of Life (Rev. 22:18–19)'". (J.-L. Maier, *Le Dossier Du Donatisme. Tome 1*, 88): '"*Si quis traditoribus communicaverit, nobiscum partem in regnis caelestibus non habebi*". Et hanc sententiam suam sancti spiritus auctoritate conscriptam tali de comparatione firmabant: "*Scriptum est*, inquiunt, in Apocalypsi: 'Quicumque adiecerit ad librum istum apicem unam, adiciet dominus super illum innumerabiles plagas; et quicumque deleverit, delebit dominus partem eius de libro vitae"'.

193 *A Sermon on the Passion of Saints Donatus and Advocatus* §13 (Tilley, 59).

to pneumatological-martyrological descriptions which richly depict the working of the Spirit during times of persecution and then as the consoler and victory-maker after glorious deaths. Perhaps the most comprehensive account of early Donatist pneumatology is found in the *Acts of the Abitinian Martyrs*, where a fusion between the grace-bestowal of the Holy Spirit and the infusion of vigour martyrs needed to withstand the pain inflicted by the persecutors of the Church is witnessed in the courage displayed by persecuted Africans in withstanding the interrogation of over-scrupulous imperial officials:

> [O]ne must flee and curse the whole corrupt congregation of all the polluted people and all must seek the glorious lineage of the blessed martyrs, which is the one, holy, and true Church, from which the martyrs arise and whose divine mysteries the martyrs observe. She and she alone broke the force of infernal persecution; she preserved the law of the Lord even to the shedding of blood. In her the virtues of the people are cultivated in the presence of the Holy Spirit, saving baptism is performed, life is renewed forever. God remains ever merciful to them. The Lord Christ is here and with the Holy Spirit rejoices and is glad, victor among the confessors, conqueror among the martyrs.[194]

Given the enormous importance that African Christians placed on the Holy Spirit, especially its role as crowner of martyrs and vigilant protector of the persecuted, it is no wonder that Augustine should be forced to integrate the Holy Spirit profusely into his anti-Donatist campaign.[195] Much like the other

194 *The Acts of the Abitinian Martyrs* §23 (Tilley, 48), (J.-L. Maier, *Le Dossier Du Donatisme. Tome 1*, 91–92): 'Fugienda est ergo et exsecranda pollutorum omnium congregatio vitiosa et appetenda omnibus beatissimorum martyrum successio gloriosa quae est ecclesia una, sancta et vera catholica, ex qua martyres profecti sunt et cui martyres testamenta divina servarunt. Haec legem domini usque ad effusionem sanguinis conservavit, in hac virtutues apostolicae sancti spiritus praesentia frequentatur, baptisma salutare perficitur, vita perpetua reparatur. Semper enim illi propitious insidet dues, adest dominus Christus, collaetatur et gaudet spiritus sanctus, in confessoribus victor, in martyribus triumphator'.

195 It was this pastoral necessity that propelled Augustine to make the most of his theological manoeuvres during his anti-Donatist campaign, especially when it came to tapping into authority sources appealing to Africans, such as that of Cyprian; see R. Crespin, *Ministère et sainteté*, 38. But this not to say that his dealings with the Donatist Church were the source of Augustine's pneumatology; it is clear that as early as the late 380s (Cassiciacum Dialogues) Augustine was already developing his thoughts on the Holy Spirit; Nello Cipriani, 'Le fonti cristiane della dottrina trinitaria nei primi Dialoghi de S. Agostino', *Augustinianum* 34 (1994), 271–81. This would hold true throughout Augustine's career,

concepts Augustine would formulate against the Donatists, his thematic deployment of the Holy Spirit emerged simultaneously with his primary anti-Donatist trilogy: *Contra epistulam Parmeniani, De baptismo contra Donatistas*, and *Contra litteras Petiliani*. The first of the trilogy, *C. ep. Parm.* (c.400/01), contains the least number of references (7) but nonetheless demonstrates the direction of his polemic.[196] Among his points are that the Holy Spirit assures the safe presence of sinners in the terrestrial Church;[197] that the Donatists are exposed by the Holy Spirit as frauds for their rejection of the Catholic truth (Church unity and peace in the Holy Spirit);[198] and that the Holy Spirit works through corrupt ministers if the recipient of the sacraments is docile to the Holy Spirit's grace (since the 'Spirit cannot be stifled').[199] This foundation was expanded upon in subsequent writings, notably *De bapt.* and *C. litt. Pet.* The second of the trilogy, *De bapt.* (c. 400/01), with 29 references,[200] functions as something of a landmark, as it was the point of fusion for appropriating the authority of Cyprian of Carthage and evoking the Holy Spirit as the ultimate authority for this appropriation. The end-result of this manoeuvre, for Augustine anyway, was that rather than validating the doctrinal contagion of the

---

manifested especially in one of his three most significant doctrinal treatises, *De Trinitate*; see commentary of Edmund Hill in Augustine, *The Trinity*, WSA I/5, intro., trans., notes E. Hill, ed. J. Rotelle (Hyde Park, NY, 1991), 18–21. The importance of this work, which tightly incorporates the Holy Spirit, is under-appreciated according to T.J. van Bavel, 'To see the Ineffable by way of the inexpressible: the Trinity', in T.J. van Bavel and B. Bruning (eds.), *Saint Augustine* (Brussels: Mercatorfonds/Augustinian Historical Institute, 2007), 97–104: 'Some even consider *De trinitate* as Augustine's most original work because, in its own very characteristic manner, it illustrates the end of the classical manner of thinking and approach to life, poses new questions, and broaches new subject matter'. Considerations of the Holy Spirit would persist well into the Pelagian controversy with examples such as *C. ep. Pel.* 1,12,27; *Cont.* 20; *C. Iul. imp.* 1,107; 2,217; 2,226; Eugene TeSelle, 'Holy Spirit', in A. Fitzgerald (ed.), *Augustine through the Ages: An Encyclopedia* (Grand Rapids, MI: Wm. Eerdmans, 1999), 434–37.

196 *C. ep. Parm.* 2,15; 2,21; 2,23; 2,24; 2,26; 2,34; 3,10.

197 *C. ep. Parm.* 3,9–10.

198 *C. ep. Parm.* 2,19–20. Augustine would continue to build on the role of the Holy Spirit as the source of ecclesial unity, especially as his distinction between 'schism' and 'heresy' came into focus; *C. Cresc.* 12,15; 16,20; *Serm.* 71,19–20; 121,19–20; 128,4; 145,4; 161,6; 258,2; *In. Ioh. evang. tract.* 27,6. The premier source to consult on the role of the Holy Spirit in creating Church unity remains James Keleher, *Saint Augustine's Notion of Schism in the Donatist Controversy*.

199 *C. ep. Parm.* 2,19–20; 2,22–23; 2,30.

200 *De bapt.* 1,15; 1,18; 1,19; 3,20; 3,21; 3,23; 4,7; 4,29; 4,31; 5,28; 5,29; 5,33; 6,5; 6,6; 6,19; 6,23; 6,28; 6,29; 6,40; 6,41; 6,59; 6,60; 6,69; 6,70; 6,85; 7,72; 7,74; 7,99; 7,100.

Donatists, Cyprian and the Holy Spirit actually refute them![201] This schema is borne out in statements paralleling claims to Cyprian's authority: (1) the Holy Spirit only dwells in the Church where sins are remitted and all nations are brought into the body of Christ by the power of the Spirit;[202] (2) unity and peace are central;[203] (3) through the working of the Spirit, the potency of grace is tempered by the interior grace/or lack thereof of individuals;[204] (4) charity and peace are gifts of the Holy Spirit in the sacraments;[205] (5) God's direct grace, via the Holy Spirit, is in the sacraments;[206] and (6) humility and internal goodness are important in nurturing the working of the Spirit.[207] Throughout these uses of the Holy Spirit, Augustine constantly refers to Cyprian. He uses Cyprian's authority as the primary example of unity, a gift of the Holy Spirit's presence, to the point where Cyprian accepts martyrdom because of his commitment to safeguarding the peace and unity of the Church.

The zenith of this phenomenon is seen in *C. litt. Pet.* (c. 401/03) with some 30 references to the theme of the Holy Spirit.[208] This work expands upon Augustine's earlier pneumatology. Here we have present the argument that God is the source of all authority and grace in sacraments.[209] More specifically, it is the Holy Spirit that baptises and confers, or 'breathes' grace into the sacraments.[210] Augustine will continue that this is prefigured by John the Baptist, who baptised in the name of/and for the Holy Spirit (Jn. 1,33).[211] Concerning the Donatist view that God departs from corrupt ministers, Augustine argues that it is the Holy Spirit that guarantees grace is never absent from the sacraments, since the Spirit also cleanses ministers through fire,[212] abandoning only

201 *De bapt.* 1,1: [The Donatists] use Cyprian as a 'prop', to 'shield their error from falling before the attack of the truth'; 5,39: 'Cyprian's authority crushes the heretics' (Donatists).

202 *De bapt.* 1,15; 3,23; 6,28–29.

203 *De bapt.* 3,20; 3,21; 6,39–40; 7,99.

204 *De bapt.* 3,21; 3,23; 6,10; 6,4–5.

205 *De bapt.* 3,21; 3,23; 6,10.

206 *De bapt.* 1,18–19; 5,28–29; 5,33; 6,23; 6,70.

207 *Ead.*, 6,41; 6,59; 6,60; 7,100.

208 *C. litt. Pet.* 2,5; 2,57; 2,61; 2,72; 2,74; 2,75; 2,76; 2,77; 2,78; 2,80; 2,81; 2,82; 2,83; 2,85; 2,88; 2,91; 2,139; 2,140; 2,178; 2,247; 3,9; 3,19; 3,34; 3,36; 3,39; 3,48; 3,52; 3,58; 3,59.

209 *C. litt. Pet.* 2,57.

210 *C. litt. Pet.* 5,5; 2,72. Augustine refines this a little in saying Christ and the Holy Spirit jointly baptise; 3,58.

211 *C. litt. Pet.* 3,59.

212 *C. litt. Pet.* 2,77. Because of this purification, a pure soul in the minister is ideal, but not required; 2,82; the Holy Spirit cleans with Christ: 3,52; the Holy Spirit forgives all sins: 2,178.

hypocrites (i.e., Donatists) who reject unity and peace in the Church.[213] Only then does the Holy Spirit forsake them[214] and find abode with the embracers of unity and peace (Catholics).[215] Touching on one more criticism of the parochial African mindset, Augustine insists on the Holy Spirit as the agent that has spread the Church throughout the world from Judea,[216] guaranteeing it is 'catholic' and withheld from none,[217] and especially, is not exclusive to Africa.[218]

Finally, turning to the impact that Augustine's pneumatological considerations had on his career, and alas, on the maturation of the theology of the Holy Spirit in ancient African Christianity, an assessment is needed of the other anti-Donatist writings in his ministry. Augustine was to maintain his two major connected pneumatological concepts: (1) that the Holy Spirit is the source of grace in the sacraments and exceeds the sins of man, and (2) that the Spirit ensures the Church remains universal throughout the world as a '*catholica*'. These themes will resurface in further anti-Donatist works to prove the point: *Epistula ad Catholicos de Secta Donatistarum* (c. 402/05),[219] *Ad Cresconium grammaticum* (406/06),[220] *De unico baptismo contra Petilianum* (410/11),[221] *Ad Donatistas Post Conlationem* (412),[222] *Sermo ad Caesariensis Ecclasiae Plebem* (418),[223] and *Contra Gaudentium Donatistarum Episcopum* (419/20).[224] Augustine does not stop there, however; he expands his treatment in selected anti-Donatist *epistulae* and *sermones* as well. Among this category are: *Ep.* 23,4 (c.392); 29,5–6 (c.395); 43,1&11&22–23 (c.396/97); 44,11 (396/98); 61,2 (c.401/02); 87,1 (c.405/11); 88,9 (406/11); 89,5 (406/09); 93–6 (407/08); 173A (c.411/14); 185,1&46–50 (417); 208,1 (c.423); *Serm.* 4,2–3 (c.419/19); 10,2 (c.411); 182,1&3 (c.416); 359,1 (c.411). Combined, what this data shows us is that rather than being a mere passing fancy for Augustine, the theme of the Holy Spirit played a significant theological-polemical role in numerous anti-Donatist

213 *C. litt. Pet.* 3,39: the Holy Spirit flees hypocrites, not the sacraments; 2,61; 3,34; 3,36.

214 *C. litt. Pet.* 2,139–40: rejecting unity and peace is a sin against the Holy Spirit according to Augustine.

215 *C. litt. Pet.* 2,75.

216 *C. litt. Pet.* 2,91.

217 *C. litt. Pet.* 2,74.

218 *C. litt. Pet.* 2,76–77.

219 *Cath.* 22; 27; 30; 31; 62; 63; 65; 67; 69.

220 *Cresc.* 1,14; 2,15; 2,16; 2,17; 2,18; 2,19; 2,20; 2,21; 2,31; 3,21; 3,44; 4,10; 4,15; 4,16.

221 *Un. bapt.* 7; 13.

222 *C. Don.* 2.

223 *S. ad Caes.* 2; 4; 6.

224 *C. Gaud.* 1,22; 1,37; 1,46. 20230 14571 5659.

productions over multiple decades. When held up against the light of the totality of his anti-Donatist campaign, the data reveals that the Holy Spirit was a significant, albeit historically-neglected component of his combat arsenal. Augustine's concern about the Holy Spirit, displayed centrally against the Donatist Church, also placed him firmly within the continuum of the Roman African Christian tradition.

PART 3

Augustine's Cyprian in the Pelagian Controversy

CHAPTER 7

The Cyprian-Appropriation in the Anti-Pelagian Campaigns

Chapter 5 introduced the extent to which Augustine made use of Cyprian's authority throughout his career, and not just in the midst of his polemical combat with the Donatist leadership. It comes as something of a surprise to discover the duration of Augustine's Cyprian-appropriation, that is, that it was not exclusive to his anti-Donatist campaign, but carried on into the anti-Pelagian campaigns, from roughly 411/12 to 430. In terms of hard numbers, of the plus/minus 600 references to Cyprian in Augustine's total corpus, 95 references are made directly to Cyprian's anti-Pelagian works, which break down as follows: *Pecc. mer.* x1(–1%)[c.411];[1] *Gest. Pel.* x1(–1%)[c.416/17];[2] *Nupt. et conc.* x1(–1%)[c.419/21];[3] *C. ep. Pel.* x19(2.86%)[c.421];[4] *C. Iul.* x21(3.13%)[c.421/22];[5] *Gr. et lib. arb.* x1(–1%)[c.426/27];[6] *Corrept. x2*(–1%)[c.426/27];[7] *Praed. sanct.* x5(0.75%)[c.428/29];[8] *Persev.* x12(1.8%)[c.428/29];[9] *C. Iul. imp.* x32(4.8%)[c.429/30].[10]

This number is greatly expanded if one takes into account the considerable number of references Augustine made to Cyprian in other works during the 411/12–430 time-frame. Such works, situated within the contextual overlap of the anti-Donatist/Pelagian controversies (c. 411/12–430) are as follows: *Ep.* 98 (c.408/14),[11] *Ep.* 140 (c. 411/12),[12] *Ep.* 151 (?),[13] *Ep.* 157 (414/15),[14] *Ep.* 166

1 *Pecc. mer.* 3,10.

2 *Gest. Pel.* 25.

3 *Nupt. et conc.* 2,51.

4 *C. ep. Pel.* 4,21(x4); 4,23; 4,24; 4,25; 4,26(x2); 4,27; 4,28(x4); 4,29; 4,32(x3); 4,34.

5 *C. Iul.* 1,6; 1,22(x2); 1,32; 2,6; 2,8; 2,9; 2,18; 2,25(*x*2); 2,30; 2,33(*x*2); 2,37(*x*2); 3,31(x4); 3,32(*x*2).

6 *Gr. et lib. arb.* 26.

7 *Corrept.* 10; 12.

8 *Praed. sanct.* 8; 15; 26; 28.

9 *Persev.* 4; 7; 8(*x*2); 12; 36(x3); 43; 48; 49; 55.

10 *C. Iul. imp.* 1,6; 1,7; 1,9; 1,50; 1,52; 1,59; 1,72(*x*2); 1,106(*x*2); 1,117; 2,2(*x*2); 2,14; 2,33; 2,37; 2,73; 2,164; 4,72; 4,73; 4,109(*x*2); 4,112(*x*2); 4,113; 6,6; 6,10; 6,14(*x*2); 6,18; 6,21; 6,23.

11 *Ep.* 98,3(2).

12 *Ep.* 140,13.

13 *Ep.* 151,6.

14 *Ep.* 157,34.

 | DOI 10.1163/9789004312647_009

(spring 415),[15] *Ep*. 180 (416?),[16] *Ep*. 215 (c. 426/27),[17] *Ep*. 217 (426/28),[18] *Ep*. 259 (c. 429/30),[19] and *Ep*. 29* (c. 412/13),[20] *En. in Ps*. 80 (?),[21] s. 8 (411),[22] s. 13 (418),[23] *s*. 49 (418),[24] *s*. 114 (after 423),[25] *s*. 294 (413),[26] *s*. 309 (?)[27] *s*. 310 (?),[28] *s*. 312 (417),[29] *s*. 313D (?),[30] *s*. 313G (410/12),[31] *s*. 335K (?),[32] *s*. 341 (?).[33] But what the numerical data fails to adequately convey is the almost completely different thematic sense which Augustine gives to Cyprian's authority against his Pelagian opponents. A treatment of Augustine's thematic usage of Cyprian in his anti-Pelagian writings is thus required in order to expand on this insight.

Pelagians: Different Foes, Similar Response

This second great pastoral crisis would push Augustine to his physical and intellectual limits. Jaded and exhausted by the rigourous demands of bringing Donatist Christians into the fold, the bishop would have virtually no time to recover and re-orient himself[34] for the coming Pelagian

15 *Ep*. 166,23; 24.
16 *Ep*. 180,5.
17 *Ep*. 215,3(*x*2).
18 *Ep*. 217,2; 3(x3); 6; 22; 26.
19 *Ep*. 259,4(*x*2).
20 *Ep*. 29*,2.
21 *En. in Ps*. 80,23.
22 s. 8.
23 *s*. 13.
24 *s*. 49.
25 *s*. 114.
26 *s*. 294,19(x3).
27 *s*. 309,2(x3); 3; 5(x3); 6(x3).
28 *s*. 310,1(*x*2); 2,(x8).
29 *s*. 312,3(x6); 4; 6(*x*2).
30 *s*. 313D,1(*x*2); 2(*x*2); 4(x8).
31 *s*. 313G,3(*x*2).
32 *s*.335K,5.
33 *s*. 341,4.
34 Augustine, in *Ep*. 151,13, had appearently planned to retire to Hippo and spend his last days in study (*WSA* II/2, 387): 'I can no longer sustain the work that I have to endure in that city... For in addition to my personal infirmity, which is known to all who know me fairly well, there is also old age, which is the common infirmity of the human race. Another reason is that I decided, if the Lord is willing, to spend as much time as I am allowed by those obligations demanded of me, given the needs of the Church that I serve as my duty,

debates.[35] after the Council of 411. Whereas Donatism was an indigenous and institutionalised reality in North Africa, Augustine would find his Pelagian adversaries across the Mediterranean a less-than-concrete force to be reckoned with.[36] Furthermore, in the Donatist controversy Augustine had been challenged to demonstrate that the Catholic Church in Africa and abroad was still in line with tradition and not divorced from it by past acts of betrayal. With his Pelagian foes, Augustine would be required to defend his own point of view against the allegation that he and like-minded individuals had ruptured their connection with the Christian tradition/faith by introducing innovative concepts, and that these were indicators of his 'Manichean' or 'Punic' background. Of specific concern in the Pelagian controversy was the co-operation between God's intervention and the human being's desire, will and action, which had been kept in theological balance during the first centuries, but was now undone in favour of a notion of God's infinite and absolute omnipotence; an omnipotence with a primacy and freedom of intervention which could not be questioned or jeopardised by human free will, whatever its potential.[37] In the former controversy, Augustine's problem was that he was too connected with the Catholic Church; in the latter his problem became that he had ceased to be in communion with the tradition of the Church. To counter the accusations

---

on the task of studies pertaining to the ecclesiastical sciences, where, if it is pleasing to God's mercy, I may also do some good for future generations'. (*CSEL* 44, 392): 'Altera cause est, quod statui, si dominus uelit, quantum mihi ab aliis occupationibus, quas ecclesiae, cui proprio munere servio, necessitas flagitat, datur temporis, id totum inpendere labori studiorum ad ecclesiasticas litteras pertinentium, ubi me arbitror, si dei misericordiae placet, etiam posteris aliquid profuturum'.

35 Augustine already caught his initial distant glimpse of his future opponent Pelagius in May of 411 in Carthage and through some cordial correspondence, though they never met in person; *Gest. Pel.* 22,46 (*CSEL* 42, 100).

36 Research has shown convincingly that 'Pelagianism' as a clearly delineated controversy lacked the cohesion that Augustine ascribed to it. It was more likely an assortment of Christian scholars seeking clarity of purpose in perilous times; M. Lamberigts, 'Recent Research into Pelagianism with Particular Emphasis on the Role of Julian of Aeclanum', *Augustiniana* 52/2–4 (2002), 197; this comment is extended to the 'Semi-Pelagian' episode as well; see D. Ogliari, *Gratia et Certamen: The Relationship between Grace and Free Will in the Discussion of Augustine with the So-Called Semipelagians*. Bibliotheca Ephemeridum Theologicarum Lovaniensium 169 (Leuven: Leuven University Press, 2003), 5.

37 Ogliari, *Gratia et Certamen*, 4. Of additional note in the Pelagian debate: 'The reality of original sin, the need for baptism at any stage of life (childhood or adulthood) as a condition for being saved, the necessity and gratuity of grace over and against a religion based on merits, was defended to demonstrate that fallen man can do nothing and cannot be saved outside God's gratuitous mercy'; Ogliari, *Gratia et Certamen*, 25.

leveled against him, Augustine would interject into his defence a renewed armory of appeals to authority sources to prove that he stood within the tradition under discussion.[38] Thus, as he had done in his work against Donatist Christianity, Augustine brought Cyprian to the forefront of his argumentation.[39]

An Attack on Africa is an Attack on Cyprian

Augustine's recourse to Cyprian was necessary for many reasons, but claiming continuity with tradition was a foremost priority and will be examined here. Appeals to Cyprian in the Pelagian controversy can be categorised into two areas: (1) as a defence against Pelagius and the propositions of the Pelagian movement in general; and (2) as a means of deflecting the often incendiary rhetoric of Julian of Aeclanum.

In the first area, addressing the criticisms of Pelagius/Pelagianism, Augustine focused on defending accusations that his theology of grace and his anthropology contained concepts that were outside the Christian tradition or were innovations.[40] The crux of Pelagius's critique was 'concerned chiefly with Christian practice and its basis in free choice and human nature'.[41] Here Augustine's use of Cyprian was tempered, perhaps reflecting the initially congenial relationship with Pelagius, who at first appeared to Augustine to be a compatriot in the same faith.[42] Nonetheless, Augustine's position was at risk of being undermined in a most fundamental way. Pelagius's outrage after hearing Augustine's popular acclamation in his *Confessions* to 'Give what you

38 Others Augustine would use as authorities include: Irenaeus, Reticius of Autun, Olympius of Barcelona, Hilary of Poitiers, Ambrose of Milan, Pope Innocent, Jerome, Gregory of Nazianzus, Basil the Great, and John Chrysostom. This use of authorities is easily situated within a long Roman tradition of appealing to the past; see, in this regard, T.G. Ring, 'Auctoritas bei Tertullian, Cyprian und Ambrosius', *Cassiciacum* 29 (Würzburg: Augustinus-Verlag, 1975), 3–32.

39 Cyprian was the figure most often referred to after Ambrose of Milan; Yates, 'Augustine's Appropriation of Cyprian the Martyr-Bishop against the Pelagians', 122, esp. footnote 10ff.

40 Augustine's theological proposals are referred to as '*doctores nostri temporis*' by Julian of Aeclanum in his *Ad Turb.* 1,1 (CCSL 88), ed. L. De Coninck (Turnhout: Brepols, 1967), 340.

41 Eugene TeSelle, 'Pelagius, Pelagianism', in A. Fitzgerald, *Augustine through the Ages. An Encyclopedia* (Grand Rapids, MI/Cambridge: Wm. Eerdmans Publishing, 1999), 633.

42 Aug., *De gest. Pel.* 26, 51-29,53 (*CSEL* 42, 104–06); Aug., *Ep.* 146 (*CSEL* 43, 274): 'dominus dilectissimus', 'desideratissimus frater', 'tua benignitas'; Bonner, *St Augustine of Hippo: Life and Controversies*, 324; TeSelle, 'Pelagius, Pelagianism', 635. As Bonner also illustrates, it was only after the misunderstanding resulting from the Council of Diospolis in 415 that Augustine became more engaged in the affair and generally more aggressive; 'Pelagianism Reconsidered', *Studia Patristica* 27 (1993), 239.

command and command what you will!,'[43] initiated the beginning of a frenzy of argument over the human will, its capacity to choose goodness, and the existence of original sin. Pelagius, who would posit the possibility of human perfection,[44] and Augustine, who argued for the inability of fallen humanity to achieve excellence without the aid of God's grace,[45] quickly resorted to trading accusations that the other was dabbling in a dangerous innovation.[46]

Pelagius held that Augustine's views were African extravagances which were by their novel nature isolated from the greater Church, as proven by the fact that the East as well as the West stood in sharp opposition to what Augustine had proposed.[47] To prove this, Pelagius appealed to an array of authorities to

---

43 Aug., *Conf.* 10,40 (CCSL 27, 176): 'Da quod iubes, et iube quod vis'; Pelagius's reaction is preserved: 'Quid autem meorum opusculorum frequentius et delectabilius innotescere potuit, quam libri Confessionum mearum? Cum et ipsos ediderim antequam Pelagiana haeresis exstitisset; in eis certe dixi Deo nostro, et saepe dixi: "Da quod iubes, et iube quod vos!" Quae mea verba Pelagius Romae, cum a quodam fratre et coepiscopo meo fuissent eo praesente commemorata, ferre non potuit, et contradicens aliquanto commotius, pene cum eo qui illa commemoraverat litigavit'; *Presev.* (PL 45, ed. J.-P. Migne [Paris, 1845]), 20,53 (PL 45, 1026).

44 Aug., *Nat. et gr.* 7,8 (CSEL 60, 237): 'Nos,' inquit, 'de sola possibilitate tractamus; de qua nisi quid certum constiterit, transgredi ad aliud gravissimum esse atque extra ordinem ducimus'.

45 *Nat. et grat.* 3, 3–4,4 (CSEL 60, 235).

46 Bonner, St Augustine of Hippo: Life and Controversies, 319. Augustine would accuse those falling outside of the authority derived from Cyprian and the Church of being guilty of proposing or being: *novi haeretici, profana vocum novitas, error novitius, novitia deformitas, perversitas novitia, dogma novum, novitium, novellum, haeresis nova, pestis novitia, novitia pestilentia, novitiate praesumptiones*. See Aug., *Nupt. et conc.* 1,1 (CSEL 42, 212); 1,22 (CSEL 42, 235); 2,25 (CSEL 42, 278); 2,38 (CSEL 42, 292–93); 2,51 (CSEL 42, 307); 2,55 (CSEL 42, 312); *C. ep. Pel.* (CSEL 60, 430) 1,9; 1,11 (CSEL 60, 533); 3,15 (CSEL 60, 503); 3,25 (CSEL 60, 517); 4,4 (CSEL 60, 544); 4,12 (CSEL 60, 533); 4,20 (CSEL 60, 543); 4,24 (CSEL 60, 549); 4,26 (CSEL 60, 553); 4,32 (CSEL 60, 568); *C. Iul.*, (PL 44, 649), 1,15; 1,8 (PL 44, 615); 3,5 (PL 44, 704); 5,24 (PL 44, 798); *C. Iul. Imp.* (CSEL 85/1, 6), 1,2; 1,6 (CSEL 85/1, 9); 1,86 (CSEL 85/1, 99); 3,94 (CSEL 85/1, 419); 4,75 (CSEL 85/2, 77), 4, 122 (CSEL 85/2, 143); 5,9 (CSEL 85/2, 177); 6,3 (CSEL 85/2, 294); 6,5 (CSEL 85/2, 297). I am indebted to M. Lamberigts for these research items on Augustine's accusation of *novitas*; 'The Italian Julian of Æclanum about the African Augustine of Hippo', in P.-Y. Fux, J.-M. Roessli, O. Wermlinger (eds.), *Augustinus Afer: Saint Augustin: africanité et universalité. Actes du colloque international, Alger-Annaba, 1–7 avril 2001* (*Paradosis* 45/1), (Fribourg : Éditions Universitaires Fribourg Suisse, 2003), 91.

47 A first piece of evidence for the Eastern inspiration behind Pelagian thinkers comes from a writing of Augustine in connection with his *s.* 294, describing Pelagius's interpretation of Cyprian's *Ep.* 64, *Gest. Pel.* 11,25 (CSEL 42, 79): 'Haec sunt, quae nonnullis fratribus quidam talia sentientes ita persuadere conabantur, ut de orientalibus comminarentur

support his cause, among them Lactantius, Hilary of Poitiers, Chrysostom, Sixtus and Augustine himself.[48] It goes without saying then, that Cyprian, who enjoyed admiration in the East as well as the West, would become an even more important fixture in the Catholic counter-argumentation technique.[49]

---

ecclesiis quod, nisi qui haec tenerent, earum possent iudicio condemnari'; see also G. Bonner, *St Augustine of Hippo: Life and Controversies*, 319–20, 324. Recent research has focused on the possible particularly Eastern influences on Pelagius and 'Pelagians', especially inspired by the following passage: 'Omitto ea, quae tam scripturae sanctae, quas prophetae, quas evangelistae, quas apostolic protulerunt, quam disputatores catholica sanitate fulgentes, Iohannes Basilius Theodorus et horum similes commendaverunt…', *Ad Florum* (*CSEL* 85/1, 432), 3,111; N. Cipriani, 'L'autore dei testi pseudobasileiani riportati nel C. Iul. 1,5,16–17 e la polemica anti-agostina di Guiliano d'Eclano', *Atti del congress internazionale su s. Agostino nel XVI centenario della conversion*, I, *Studia Ephemeridis Augustinianum* 24 (1987), 439–49; N. Cipriani, 'La Presenza di Teodoro di Mopsuestia nella teologia di Guiliano d'Eclano', *Cristianesimo Latino e cultura Greco sino al sec. IV. XXI Incontro di studiosi dell'antichità cristiana (Roma, 7–9 maggio 1992)*, *Studia Ephemeridis Augustinianum* 42 (1993), 365–78; Lamberigts, 'The Italian Julian of Æclanum about the African Augustine of Hippo', 92; Lamberigts, 'Recent Research into Pelagianism with Particular Emphasis on the Role of Julian of Aeclanum', 187, 189; J. Lössl, 'A Shift in Patristic Exegesis. Hebrew Clarity and Historical Verity in Augustine, Jerome, Julian of Aeclanum and Theodore of Mopsuestia', *Augustinian Studies* 32 (2001): 157–75; J. Lössl, 'Augustine, 'Pelagianism', Julian of Aeclanum, and Modern Scholarship', *Zeitschrift für Antikes Christentum* 11 (2007), 141–42; J. Lössl, 'Julian of Aeclanum's Tractatus in Osee, Iohel, Amos', *Augustiniana* 51 (2001), 5–31; J. Lössl, *Julian von Aeclanum. Studien zu seinem Leben, seinem Werk, seiner Lehre und ihrer Überlieferung*, *Supplements to Vigiliae Christianae* 60 (Leiden: Brill, 2001), 56ff., 276ff., 292–95.

Even within the Western tradition, Pelagius would find consolation in Tertullian when criticising Augustine and his appropriation of Cyprian on the subject of original sin: 'Quid festinate innocens aetas ad remissionem peccatorum?' *De Baptismo* (*CCSL* 1/1 293); also *De Anima* 41 (*CCSL* 2/2), ed. A. Gerlo (Turnhout: Brepols, 1954), 844.

48 Aug., *Nat. et grat.* 71–85 (*CSEL* 60, 286–93).

49 Though Augustine would start off against Pelagian using Cyprian and Jerome as authorities (*Pecc. mer.* 3, 10–13, *CSEL* 60, 135–40), Ambrose would remain the single most used authority source for Augustine. His usage of Cyprian was beneficial, as it would elicit immediate familiarity from African audiences, such as when Augustine recapitulated Cyprian's *Ep.* 64,5 (*CSEL* 3/C, 424–25): 'Si etiam gravissimis delectoribus…remissa peccatorum datur et a baptismo atque gratia nemo prohibetur, quanto magis prohiberi non debat infans qui recens natus nihil peccavit, nisi quod secundum Adam carnaliter natus contagium mortis antiquae prima nativitae contraxit, qui ad remissam peccatorum accipiendam hoc ipso facilius accedit quod illi remittuntur non propria sed aliena peccata'; see *s.* 294,19 (*PL* 38, 1347–48). Refer also to E. Dassmann, 'Cyprianus', in *Augustinus-Lexikon*, Vol. 2, ed. C. Mayer (Basel: Schwabe & Co., 1996), 198: 'Auf eine erneute Flucht verzichtete er bewuβt; als geachteter Lehrer im Osten und im Westen war er bereit, das

Cyprian's recognition in East and West was, according to Augustine, attestation of the authority he carried by virtue of his martyrdom. For Augustine, Cyprian's martyr status was a trump-card *par excellence*, especially when later dealing with Julian.[50] However, the background for Augustine's use of Cyprian against Julian of Aeclanum was, by and large, a much more expansive appropriation than required against Pelagius, and Augustine's response attests to this. Julian emerged from history in the summer of 418, when, as bishop of the southern Italian see city of Aeclanum, he joined 18 or 19 other regional bishops in protesting against Pope Zosimus' turnabout condemnation of Pelagius and Caelestius, shortly after acquitting them of charges of heresy.[51] This setting, coupled with Julian's *Ad Turbantium* (a quickly-written reply to Augustine's defence of original sin [*Nupt. et con.*] against the charge the doctrine was a condemnation of marriage) propelled Augustine and Julian headlong into a polemical fight that would only end with Julian's death in 455.[52] Indeed, the entry of the topic of original sin (*peccatum originale*) was to be the pivotal moment for the final chapter in Augustine's fight to claim the authority of Cyprian.

Julian of Aeclanum: Against African Innovation

It should be noted straight away that unfortunately, according to Julian, the concept of original sin had been accepted in nearly the entire Western empire. This acceptance had happened without any consultation by a synod and was propelled by provincially-minded bishops who remained exclusively mindful of their own territories and who had in any case been forced to consent to it.[53] Indeed Julian, for whom learnedness (or erudition) was essential,[54] often

Beispiel seines Martyriums zu geben.' One must also not forget the interesting fact that Cyprian remains (even today!) the only North African in the Canon of the Roman Mass (rite I); Wiles, 'The Theological Legacy of St. Cyprian', 139.

50 *C. ep. Pel.* 4, 20 (CSEL 60, 544): '...Pelagiani heretici noui de Manicheis ueteribus hereticis nulli catholico audeant inrogare calumniam, ne tam sceleratam etiam martyri antiquo Cypriano facere conuincantur iniuriam'.

51 *C. ep. Pel.* 2,5.

52 Mathijs Lamberigts, 'Iulianus Aeclanensis', in C. Mayer (ed.), *Augustinus-Lexikon* 3, 5/6 (Basel: Schwabe & Co., 2008), 839.

53 See Julian of Aeclanum's *Epistula ad Rufum*, frg. 27–28 (CCSL 88, 340).

54 With regard to his intellectual background, see Dorothea Weber, 'Klassische Literatur im Dienst theologischer Polemik: Julian von Eclanum, Ad Florum', *Studia Patristica* 38 (2001), 503–09; J. Lössl, *Julian von Aeclanum. Studien zu seinem Lebe, seinem Werk, seiner Lehre und ihrer Überliefering* (Supplements to Vigiliae Christianae 60), (Leiden: Brill, 2001),

complained that his side was never given a fair hearing. He laboured in vain to find a council able to discuss the matter in an objective manner.[55] For Julian and his companions, what was lacking was the possibility of defending their case for the Catholic truth before *learned* judges,[56] such as John Chrysostom and Basil the Great.[57] Because of this, Julian felt his side had suffered in service of the truth.[58] At any rate, he hoped that they would no longer be harassed by slanders and defamation from the ignorant.[59] He complained about the great theological confusion that existed. He despised the fact that a horde of ignorant folk had hijacked the Church, and that as a result the authority of reason had been taken away from the Church's flock, resulting in mob-rule, or *dogma populare* (popular belief), which 'steers the ship under full sail.'[60]

In these worrisome times, the wise were outwitted by the din of the mob. This meant that Julian was on his own against the disdain of the misguided common people, 'who weigh the merit of an opinion by its success and judge that opinion to be more true which they see wins the favour of the majority'.[61] Julian bitterly remarked that such commoners sought an emotional high in defaming whatever the authority of the saints and the erudite had demonstrated,

---

74–146, esp. 101–26; Lamberigts, 'The Italian Julian of Aeclanum about the African Augustine of Hippo', esp. 85–86.

55 Julian of Aeclanum, *Ad Turbantium*, frg. 3a (*CCSL* 88, 341): '(De iudicibus) apud quos propterea (dicis) non potuisse uos agere causam uestram, quia nemo de rebus dubiis bene consultat, nisi qui ab odio, ira et amicitia uacuum pectus attulerit; quales non fuisse (dicis), qui de causa uestra iudicauerunt, quia prius eam coeperunt odisse quam nosse…'; also see frg. 3b (*CCSL* 88, 341).

56 Julian of Aeclanum, *Ad Florum* 2,1 (*CSEL* 85/1, 164): 'Commode nobis cum ageretur, si… apud eruditos iudices negotium ueritatis tueri daretur facultas…'; also 2,37 (*CSEL* 85/1, 189), where Julian, moved by mercy, asks for a trial by men, illustrious for their prudence. In his own argumentation, Julian opts for a legal and learned approach; see *Ad Florum* 5,20 (*CSEL* 85/2,201). The learned people needed could be both Christian and secular; 1, 69 (*CSEL* 85, 1, 76). With regard to Julian's position, see Jean-Marie Salamito, *Les virtuoses et la multitude. Aspects sociaux de la controverse entre Augustin et les pélagiens* (Collection Nomina), (Grenoble : Million, 2005), 208–12.

57 *Ad Turb.*, frg. 308–12 (*CCSL* 88, 392–94).

58 *Ad Turb.*, frg. 154 (*CCSL* 88, 373). Julian considered his debate a defence of the truth, now abandoned; see *Ad Turb.*, frg. 155 (*CCSL* 88, 373).

59 *Ad Florum* 2,1 (*CSEL* 85/1, 164).

60 *Ad Florum* 2,2 (*CSEL* 85/1, 164–65).

61 *Ad Florum* 2,3 (*CSEL* 85/1, 165–66): '…qui sententiae meritum de prosperitatibus ponderans eam veriorem aestimat, quam pluribus placere conspexerit'. This was already present in *Ad Turb.*, frg. 4, where Julian argued that arguments should be pondered not numbered and that a mass of blind people could not contribute to the matter under debate.

in order that they might not be remonstrated by the example of these famous authorities.[62] Continuing in this vein, Julian declared that ordinary people are comforted by the weakness caused by belief in the desires of the flesh (*concupiscentia carnis*), and feel no personal culpability.[63] And in Julian's view, whoever makes a plea in favour of a benevolent and just God, and acknowledges that human beings are able to refrain from sin and can become sanctified by virtuous living is accused of heretical thinking.[64] Therefore, Julian's desired synod was to be organised in such a way that the clamouring of the mob was excluded.[65] In fact, the mere mention of such terrorising, if the mob were to be allowed, is clearly an allusion to the condemnation drama of 418/19.[66] As was evident then, misguided bishops could only extort blind assent from the fearful and ignorant, but would never obtain validation from the erudite, for terrorism in discussion demonstrates emotional over-emphasis and a lack of rational support.[67]

Julian claimed that he could only find understanding with a few wise men.[68] To get to the Catholic truth, what was needed was a select wise group (not bureaucrats) made eminent by reason, learning and freedom, be they bishops, imperial administrators, or prefects,[69] because such wise men would not be

---

62 See *Ad Florum* 2,5 (CSEL 85/1, 166).

63 *Ad Florum* 2,6 (CSEL 85/1, 167); see also 6,3 (CSEL 85/2, 293–94) where it is said that people of the arena, circus, or the stage, because of their lustful desires, find excuses under the pretext of necessity.

64 *Ad Florum* 2,7 (CSEL 85/1, 167). Julian clearly belonged to those who believed that qualities such as work performance, virtue, and commitment, qualities that had made Rome great, would even in these Christian times inspire the Empire anew. See in this regard, P. Brown, *Pelagius and his Supporters. Aims and Environment*, in P. Brown, *Religion and Society in the Age of Saint Augustine* (London: Faber & Faber, 1972), 208–26.

65 *Ad Turb.*, frg. 6 (CCSL 88, 341).

66 For the details, see Otto Wermlinger, *Rom und Pelagius. Die theologische Position der römischen Bischöfe im pelagianischen Streit in den Jahren 411–32* (Stuttgart : Hiersemann, 1975), 196–209; Mathijs Lamberigts, 'Co-operation between Church and State in the Condemnation of the Pelagians', in T.L. Hettema & A. van der Kooij (eds.), *Religious Polemics in Context* (Studies in Theology and Religion 11), (Assen: Royal van Gorcum, 2004), 363–75.

67 *Ad Turb.*, frg. 11 (CCSL 88, 342).

68 *Ad Turb.*, frg. 154 (CCSL 88, 373): '…iactatis…de paucitate (uelut) prudentium quibus uos placere gaudetis'; also frg. 271–72 (CCSL 88, 387).

69 *Ad Turb.*, frg. 6 (CCSL 88, 341–42); frg. 271a–b (CCSL 88, 387). In frg. 271b Julian seems to have suggested that Augustine had roused hatred against him from the common ranks of workmen, sailors, bartenders, fishermen, cooks, butchers, youth dismissed from monasteries, and the ordinary run of clerics. According to Salamito, *Les virtuoses et la multitude*, 218–19; É. Rebillard, '*Dogma Populare*: Popular Belief in the Controversy between

disturbed by the ambitions and worldliness of sinners. Julian indirectly offered criteria that should be followed in order for proposals concerning the faith to qualify as authentic: they should be sustained by reason and scripture and be celebrated in the erudition of holy men, who do not impose their authority on the truth but receive their glory from upholding it.[70]

Julian in Need of a Council

Julian held that knowledge of scripture was only suited to a few erudite people.[71] Simple people, fascinated by worldy matters, could not obtain the state of mind needed and should limit themselves to the basic tenets of the faith.[72] Nonetheless, Julian found the faith of simple people endearing, for they were thoughtful enough to enter the Church by faith alone. They embraced the Catholic faith and despised any voices attempting to persuade them to the contrary.[73] Moreover, Julian had great concern for this flock, and because of their souls and his love for God's Church, refused to back down from a battle with Augustine in order to defend such Catholic faith.[74]

Augustine and Julian of Eclanum', *Augustinian Studies* 38 (2007) 175–87; also see Ilona Opelt, *Die Polemik in der christlichen lateinischen Literatur von Tertullian bis Augustin* (Bibliothek der klassischen Altertumswissenschaften, NF Reihe 2,63), (Heidelberg: Winter, 1980), 23; Andreas Kessler, *Reichtumskritik und Pelagianismus. Die pelagianische Diatribe de divitiis: Situierung, Lesetext, Übersetzung, Kommentar* (Paradosis 43), (Freiburg: Universitätsverl, 1999), 56–59.

70 *Ad Turb.*, frg. 313 (*CCSL* 88, 394): '…hanc sanam et ueram esse sententiam, quam primo loco ratio, deinde scripturarum muniuit auctoritas, et quam sanctorum uirorum semper celebrauit eruditio, qui tamen ueritati auctoritatem non suo tribuere consensu, sed testimonium et gloriam de eius suscepere consortio…' Lössl, *Julian von Aeclanum*, 110–14.; J. Lössl, 'Julian of Aeclanum's "Rationalist" Exegesis. Albert Bruckner Revisited', *Augustiniana* 53 (2003), 77–106; Salamito, *Les virtuoses et la multitude*, 210.

71 *Ad Turb.*, frg. 156 (*CCSL* 88, 373): '…difficilis paucisque conueniens eruditis sanctarum cognitio litterarum…'; and also frg. 159 (*CCSL* 88, 373).

72 *Ad Turb.*, frg. 158 (*CCSL* 88, 373); see also *Ad Florum* 2,14 (*CSEL* 85/1, 172).

73 *Ad Turb.*, frg. 158 (*CCSL* 88, 373): '…sola tamen fide ad ecclesiam Christi peruenire curarunt, ne facile obscuris quaestionibus terreantur, sed credentes Deum uerum conditorem esse hominum, indubitanter quoque teneant quia pius est, quia uerax, quia iustus; atque hanc aestimationem de illa trinitate seruantes, quicquid audierint huic conuenire sententiae, amplexentur atque collaudent, nec hoc eis ulla uis argumentationis euellat, sed detestentur omnem auctoritatem atque omnem societatem contraria persuadere nitentem'. Also refer to the comments of Rebillard, *Dogma Popolare*, 179–80.

74 *Ad Florum* 2,11 (*CSEL* 85/1, 170): '…primo benignitas, quam generi debemus humano, deinceps spes et fides, quam habemus in Deum…'.

Julian was convinced that his own position was based on reason, erudition, justice, piety and scripture; and that Augustine, with his novel doctrine, was offensive to the learned, contemptuous against the saints, and irreverent toward God.[75] Julian complained that Augustine had stirred up the common folk against him,[76] and had hidden behind them in order to avoid a man-to-man fight.[77] Instead of accepting a fair discussion on the basis of what was present in both philosophical wisdom and Catholic teaching, Augustine had rallied misguided commoners against Julian.[78] He had allied himself with women, stable-hands and imperial tribunes and had brought, with the help of his ally Alypius, 80 or more pedigree horses to Italy as a bribe.[79] Yet he would never accept the views of the genuinely erudite.[80] Every well-informed reader of my work, Julian insisted, understands that Augustine manipulates the ignorance of his supporters, who are deceived by their misconceptions and incited by Augustine's novelties.[81] Julian was adamant that if the opportunity had been

75 *Ad Florum* 1,13 (CSEL 85/1, 171): 'Nam si, ut et superior sermo patefecit et secuturus docebit, quicquid ratio est, quicquid eruditio, quicquid iustitia, quicquid pietas, quicquid testimoniorum sacrorum huic quod tuemur dogmati suffragatur, nihil aliud inimici nostri toto adipiscuntur conatu, quam ut doctis quibusque impudentissimi, sanctis contumacissimi, in Deum profanissimi comprobentur'.

76 *Ad Turb.*, frg. 251, (CSEL 88, 385); frg. 255–56; (CCSL 88, 385); frg. 314 (CCSL 88, 394).

77 *Ad Turb.*, frg. 253: '(Dicis quod) certaminis singularis oblitus in vulgus refugerim'.

78 *Ad Florum* 1,41 (CSEL 85/1, 30): 'Equidem affatim mihi tam philosophantium quam eorum qui catholici fuerunt, quod quaerimus, scripta suppeditant; sed vereor, ne refrageris et, si philosophorum ego senatum advocavero, tu continuo sellularios opifices omneque in nos vulgus accendas'. Also see Rebillard, *Dogma Populare*, 182–84.

79 *Ad Florum* 1,42 (CSEL 85, 1, 30): 'Vociferans cum feminis cunctisque calonibus et tribunis, quibus octoginta aut amplius equos tota Africa saginatos collega tuus nuper adduxit Alypius…' In 1, 74 (CSEL 85/1, 90), the following accusations of bribery can be found: offers of money, bequeathment of inheritances, of horses, and the corruption of the official powers. In 3, 35 (CSEL 85/1, 374–75), these accusations are repeated and further specified: (1) Augustine is accused of having upset all of Italy with a divisive theology, (2) he has hired people to start a rebellion in Rome, (3) has sent horses to tribunes and military officers (under the management of Alypius) that were collected from farmers from the whole of Africa at the expense of the poor, and (4) finally he has stained the reign of the emperor with the impiety of persecutions. With regard to the complaint about persecution, see *Ad Florum* 6, 2 (CSEL 85/2, 293). It is important to note that since the loss of Spain to the invading Vandal forces, Africa had become the most important supplier of horses; see Y.-M. Duval, 'Julien d'Éclane et Rufin d'Aquilée. Du concile de Rimini à la répression pélagienne. L'intervention imperial en matière religieuse', *Revue des Études Augustiniennes* 24 (1978), 243–71, esp. 250.

80 *Ad Florum* 1,43 (CSEL 85/1, 31).

81 *Ad Florum* 2,36 (CSEL 85/1, 188); and also 2, 46 (CSEL 85/1, 195); 4, 90 (CSEL 85/2, 95).

given to discuss the matter amongst learned people, Augustine would have been soundly defeated.[82] Indeed, among well-informed people,[83] none could be found who actually believed and defended the idea that, with God as the loving creator of the human body and soul, sin could pre-exist in newborns.[84] In any case, Julian hoped that over time the storm of controversy would let up and that common believers, no longer able to dictate with their loud cries, would finally be corrected by the authority of wise Christian teachers.[85]

Furthermore, Julian was upset by the way Augustine replied in *Nupt. et conc.* to his *Ad Turb*. According to Julian, his positions represented in *Ad Turb.*, were dramatically misinterpreted and misstated by Augustine for polemical gain.[86] Julian lambasted Augustine for a lack of intellectual thoroughness and for failing in the duty of authorship, an insulting accusation amongst the literary classes.[87] He accused Augustine of having incited anger by adulterating Julian's work, evidence of Augustine's dishonesty and bad intent, which had resulted in the upheaval of the common people against Julian![88] Julian continued by describing Augustine's recapitulation of *Ad Turb.* in *Nupt. et conc.* as 'the shamelessness of Numidia'. In it Augustine had condescended to say that Julian erred even though he had not read what Julian had actually written.[89] In a truncated summary of Julian's *Ad Turb.*, Augustine claimed that Julian

82 *Ad Turb.*, frg. 3a-b (*CCSL* 88, 341); frg. 6 (*CCSL* 88, 341–42); also *Ad Florum* 2,2 (*CSEL* 85/1, 164). Julian will repeat that no educated person would choose the side of Augustine; see 2,26 (*CSEL* 85/1, 180).

83 *Ad Turb.*, frg. 315 (*CCSL* 88, 394): '…de tanta multitudine assertorem non potest invenire'.

84 With regard to Julian's insistence on the goodness of God's creation, see M. Lamberigts, 'Julian of Aeclanum: A Plea for a Good Creator', *Augustiniana* 38 (1988), 5–24.

85 *Ad Florum* 5,4 (*CSEL* 85/2, 170): 'Nec illud ergo desperare vel possumus vel debemus, quoniam processu temporum tempestas excitata considat et auctoritate sapientum vulgus ignavum quod nunc perstrepit corrigatur…'.

86 See Julian's vehement reactions in *Ad Florum* 4,4 (*CSEL* 85/2, 6); 4,90 (*CSEL* 85/2, 94); Lamberigts, 'The Italian Julian of Aeclanum', 88; 92–93; also consult Dorothea Weber, 'Some Literary Aspects of the Debate between Julian of Eclanum and Augustine', *Studia Patristica* 43 (2006), 297–99.

87 *Ad Florum* 1,19 (*CSEL* 85/1, 16).

88 *Ad Florum* 1,19 (*CSEL* 85/1, 16).

89 *Ad Florum* 1,16 (*CSEL* 85/1, 13–14). On this and the following accusations, see N. Cipriani, 'La polemica antiafricana di Giuliano d'Eclano: artificio letterario o scontro di tradizione teologichi?' in *Cristianesimo e specificità regionali nel Mediterraneo latino* (*sec. IV–VI*) (Studia ephemeridis Augustinianum, 46), (Rome: Institutum patristicum Augustinianum, 1994), 147–80; Dorothea Weber, '"For What is so Monstrous as What the Punic Fellow Says?" Reflections on the Literary Background of Julian's Polemical Attacks on Augustine's Homeland', in P.-Y. Fux, J.-M. Roessli, O. Wermlinger (eds.), *Augustinus Afer: Saint Augustin: africanité et universalité. Actes du colloque international, Alger-Annaba, 1–7 avril*

was afraid to reply to the position that the baptism of children was needed for the remission of sin, according to the ancient and solid tradition of the Catholic faith.[90] In fact, Julian had clearly emphasised the need for baptism of all human beings, including infants.[91] However, the idea that infant baptism was needed because of the corrupting effects of original sin did not, according to Julian, traditionally belong to the Catholic faith (*'antiquitus tradita atque fundata'*).[92] It was a doctrine inspired by sin and pride, formulated by the heretical patriarch Mani, adopted by Marcion, Faustus, and Adimantus and their heretical disciples, and now diffused like a contagion by Augustine, the Punic usurper[93] on Italian shores.[94] As a result, Julian suggested that the idea of original sin and its theological implications were inventions, opposed to the ancient Catholic faith. Because of this violation, if only a synod were held, its judges (the voice of Catholic authority) would demand Augustine's excommunication, for he abused the faith, learning, and common sense.[95] In

---

2001 (*Paradosis* 45/1), (Fribourg: Éditions Universitaires Fribourg Suisse, 2003), 75–82. esp. 79–81; Lamberigts, 'The Italian Julian of Aeclanum about the African Augustine of Hippo'.

90 Aug., *Nupt. et conc.* 2,4 (CSEL 42, 256).

91 Jul., *Ad Turb.*, frg. 16 (CCSL 88, 344–45): 'Nos igitur in tantum gratiam baptismatis omnibus utilem aetatibus confitemur, ut cunctos qui illam non necessariam etiam paruulis putant, aeterno feriamus anathemate...Sed haec gratia non aduersatur iustitiae, quae maculas eluit iniquitatis; nec facit peccata, sed purgat, quae absoluit reos, non calumniatur innocuos. Christus enim, qui est sui operis redemptor, auget circa imaginem suam continua largitate beneficia; et quos fecerat condendo bonos, facit innouando adoptandoque meliores'.

92 *Ad Florum* 2,178 (CSEL 85/1, 297), Julian drew a line from Augustine's *tradux peccati*-doctrine to Tertullian's *tradux animarum*-doctrine, a doctrine, Julian added, that had been condemned. The link from one heresy to the other is clear!

93 *Ad Turb.*, frg. 52 (CCSL 88, 352); *Ad Florum* 1,48 (CSEL 85/1, 36–38) where Julian sarcastically describes Augustine's intelligence level and calls him a very pious priest and very capable orator; see also 3,154 (CSEL 85/1, 458); 4,75 (CSEL 85/2, 76). With regard to this well known rhetorical action, see N. Cipriani, 'Aspetti letterari dell' Ad Florum di Giuliano d'Eclano', *Augustinianum* 15 (1975), 125–67, esp. 147.

94 *Ad Florum* 1,59 (CSEL 85/1, 55): 'Non est haec fides antiquitus tradita atque fundata nisi in conciliis malignantium, inspirata a diabolo, prolata a Manicheo, celebrata a Marcione Fausto Adimanto omnibusque eorum satellitibus et nunc a te in Italiam, quod graviter gemimus, eructata'. See also 5,9 (CSEL 85/2, 177): 'Non hoc ea catholica fides credit antiquitus...' On the merits of Julian's arguments about the Manichean character of Augustine's doctrine, see M. Lamberigts, 'Was Augustine a Manichaean? The Assessment of Julian of Aeclanum', in J. van Oort, O. Wermelinger & G. Wurst (eds.), *Augustine and Manichaeism in the Latin West. Proceedings of the Fribourg-Utrecht Symposium of the International Association of Manichaean Studies* (IAMS) (Nag Hammadi and Manichaean Studies, 49), (Leiden: Brill, 2001), 113–36.

95 *Ad Florum* 1,48 (CSEL 85/1, 38); 1,114 (CSEL 85/1, 132); 3,92 (CSEL 85/1, 417–18).

short, only a synod of time-tested authorities would be able to stop Augustine's African invasion of Italy.[96] Later, in *Ad Turb.*, Julian appealed to Eastern authorities such as John Chrysostom and Serapion of Thmuis,[97] thereby placing the debate in the broader context of a Catholic faith throughout the known Roman world under siege by the throws of the Punic Augustine.

Defend the Faith from the 'Punic Menace'

Against the backdrop of the accusation from Julian of Aeclanum that Augustine and his anti-Pelagian allies were peddling contagious parochial African theology, Augustine unleashed an appropriation of Christian authority sources unprecedented in scale in his works. Given the critique of Augustine formulated by Julian, as representing a back-country Church and theology, it is obvious that Augustine considered it his mission as a Catholic bishop to defeat Julian with the help of authorities in the faith, so that Christian people would side with him against Julian's foolish novelties.[98] And just like Julian, Augustine was also a classically trained rhetorician, and that meant that he would resort to all of the rhetorical techniques at his disposal, just as he had done in driving his anti-Donatist campaign.[99]

---

96 See *Ad Florum* 6,18 (*CSEL* 85/2, 350). Both contain a very negative connotation; see Weber, '"For What is so Monstruous as What the Punic Fellow Says?"'; Cipriani, 'Aspetti letterari dell' Ad Florum di Giuliano d'Eclano', 149; Cipriani, 'La polemica antiafricana di Giuliano d'Eclano', 147.

97 See *Ad Turb.*, frg. 311–12 (*CCSL* 88, 393–94). Julian uses a valuable quote from a Latin translation of John Chrysostom's *Ad Neophytos* 6 (see *Jean Chrysostome. Huit catéchèses baptismales inédites*, ed. A. Wenger, *SC* 50 (Paris: Cerf, 1957), 151–67. For a possible Greek influence on Julian's theology, see Nello Cipriani, 'Sulle fonti orientali della teologia di Giuliano d'Eclano', in A.V. Nazzarro (ed.), *Giuliano d'Eclano el 'Hirpinia Christiana'* (Naples: Arte tipografica, 2004), 157–70. Julian incorrectly attributed the work of Serapion against the Manichees to Basil; see *Ad Turb.*, frg. 310 (*CCSL* 88, 393); Nello Cipriani, 'L'autore dei testi pseudobasiliani riportati nel C. Iulianum (1,16–17) e la polemica agostiniana di Giuliano d'Eclano', in *Congresso internazionale su S. Agostino nel XVI centenario della conversione (Roma, 15–20 settembre 1986). Atti I. Cronaca del Congresso. Sessioni generali. Sezione di studio I* (*Studia Ephemeridis Augustinianum* 24) (Rome: Institutum Patristicum Augustinianum, 1987), 439–49.

98 *C. Iul.* 2,1 (*PL* 44, 671).

99 Dorothea Weber, 'Textkritische Spezifika aus Augustins Schriften gegen Julian von Eclanum', in A. Primmer, K. Smolak, and D. Weber (eds.), *Textsorten und Textkritik. Tagungsbeiträge* (*Österreichische Akademie der Wissenschaften, Philosophisch-Historische Klasse, Sitzungsberichte* 693; *Veröffentlichungen der Kommission zur Herausgabe des Corpus der lateinischen Kirchenväter, Heft* 21), (Vienna: Österreichische Akademie der Wissenschaften, 2002), 193–209.

As noted in Chapter 3, for Augustine the authority of scripture prevailed over tradition, since scripture remained the most important rule of the faith.[100] According to Augustine, following in precedence, Church fathers should be qualified as exegetes (*divinarum scripturarum tractatores*),[101] for their commentaries are concerned with and inspired by scriptural texts. At the same time, these same orthodox fathers discuss the scriptures with great legitimacy[102] and authority.[103] What they pass on in their teaching, they themselves have learned from the apostles.[104] These teachers, authorities on the scriptures, enjoy an unparalleled authority status and are recognised for their defence of the doctrinal integrity of the Church.[105]

The faith of these doctors shows both historical continuity and geographical universality. With regard to historical continuity, Augustine cites in chronological order in *C. Iul.* 1, 5–13, quotes from his all-star panel of authorities in the faith: Irenaeus, Cyprian, Reticius of Autun, Olympius of Barcelona, Hilary of Poitiers and Pope Innocent I. Concerning the universality of what was believed, Eastern fathers are added too, namely Gregory of Nazianzus, Basil of Caesarea, John Chrysostom, and the bishops present at the synod of Diospolis

100 *C. ep. Pel.* 4,20 (*CSEL* 60, 542–43): '…ad curam nostram existimo pertinere non solum scripturas sanctas canonicas aduersus eos testes adhibere, quod iam satis fecimus, uerum etiam de sanctorum litteris, qui eas ante nos fama celeberrima et ingenti gloria tractauerunt, aliqua documenta proferre, non quo canonicis libris a nobis ullius disputatoris aequetur auctoritas, tamquam omnino non sit quod melius seu uerius ab aliquo catholico quam ab alio itidem catholico sentiatur, sed ut admoneantur qui putant istos aliquid dicere, quemadmodum de his rebus ante noua istorum uaniloquia catholici antistites eloquia diuina secuti sint, et sciant a nobis rectam et antiquitus fundatam catholicam fidem aduersus recentem Pelagianorum hereticorum praesumptionem perniciemque defendi'. And *Nupt. et conc.* 2,51 (*CSEL* 42, 307); *C. Iul.* 2,30 (*PL* 44, 694); *C. Iul. imp.* 4,112, (*CSEL* 85/2, 122). See also Germán Mártil, *La tradición en San Agustín a través de la controversia pelagiana* (Madrid: Espasa-Calpe, 1943), 175–91; Fernando Perago, '*Il valore della tradizione nella polemica tra sant'Agostine e Giuliano di Eclano*', *Annali della Facoltà di Lettere e Filosofia di Napoli* 10 (1962–63), 143–60, esp. 143; A.-M. La Bonnardière, 'Le canon des Écritures', in A.-M. La Bonnardière (ed.), *Saint Augustin et la Bible* (La Bible de tous les temps 3) (Paris: Beauchense, 1986), 287–301.

101 *Nupt. et conc.* 2,51 (*CSEL* 42, 307); *C. Iul. Imp.* 1,67 (*CSEL* 85/1, 71): 'catholici intellectores apostoli'; 2,178 (*CSEL* 85/1, 299): 'catholici doctores secundum scripturas sanctas'.

102 *C. Iul.* 2,1 (*PL* 44, 671): '…Scripturas sanctas ingenti gloria tractaverunt…'.

103 *C. Iul.* 2,19 (*PL* 44, 686).

104 *C. Iul.* 2,30 (*PL* 44, 694): '…ex apostolis ista didicerunt, et secundum apostolos ista docuerunt…'; *C. Iul. imp.* 1,67 (*CSEL* 85/1, 71): '…catholicos intellectores apostoli…'.

105 *C. Iul.* 3,1 (*PL* 44, 701): '…tot tantorumque sanctorum, et in sacris Litteris eruditorum, et in Ecclesiae regimine tam clara memoria et laude pollentium…'.

that originally condemned the Pelagian threat, since, in Augustine's view, a consensus existed between the eastern and western fathers with regard to the doctrine of original sin and its associated themes.

Cyprian: Pre-eminent Authority for the African Augustine

Not only had Cyprian refuted Pelagian ideas on original sin and the need for grace before the Pelagians were even born, as evidenced in his *Ep.* 64,[106] but his authority shone through resolutely because of his martyrdom.[107]

> Renowned teacher and glorious witness, such was your teaching, such was your warning, as such a person you have offered yourself to us to listen to and to imitate. After the other struggles with all the desires rightly were finished and the wounds healed, you fought against the last and greatest desire, the desire for this life, on behalf of the truth of Christ, and you conquered it by the abundance of his grace in you. Your crown is secure; your teaching is triumphant; by it you conquer even those who trust in their own virtue. After all, they cry out: 'We have the perfection of virtue from ourselves,' while you shout back at them: 'None are strong by their own might, but they are safe by God's own forgiveness and mercy.'[108]

---

106 É. Rebillard comments on the irony of Augustine's use of Cyprian's *Ep.* 64 to justify his stance on the baptism of children for treatment of original sin. He points out that the text of the letter clearly indicates it was a council that had agreed on the practice: 'Regarding infants, you claimed that they ought not to be baptised within a day or two after they have been born… Our episcopal council decided the matter in a far different way…' (64,1 [*CCSL* 3/C, 419]). Thus Augustine was basing his position not on Cyprian, but on a council; 'A New Style of Argument in Christian Polemic: Augustine and the Use of Patristic Citations', *Journal of Early Christian Studies* 8/4 (2000), 567.

107 Yates frames this aspect thus: 'He [Cyprian] was one of the blessed few who not only conquered the lusts and weaknesses of the flesh in his day-to-day existence, but also one who—and this is most germane to our purposes here—overcame the temptation to literally preserve his physical existence and who willingly became a martyr for the cause of Christ. Augustine all but explicitly links Cyprian's death as a martyr with the validity, and hence the value, of his teaching and of his authority. Although we are not told exactly how, it seems clear that Augustine has come to believe that the fact of Cyprian's having been chosen to become a martyr has *increased* both his authority as a teacher and the correctness of what he taught'; 'Augustine's Appropriation of Cyprian the Martyr-Bishop against the Pelagians', 128.

108 *C. Iul.* *2,25* (*PL* 44, 691): 'O doctor praeclarissime et testis gloriosissime, sic docuisti, sic monuisti, sic te audiendum, imitandumque praebuisti. Merito finitis aliis omnium cupiditatum certaminibus sanatisque vulneribus, cum extrema et omnium maxima vitae

Further more, if it is obvious that for Augustine, Cyprian stood so splendidly with the crown of martyrdom because God had made martyrdom Cyprian's vocation, and if this stood as evidence that God had condemned the Pelagian view,[109] it follows that if the Pelagians insisted on attacking Augustine and his Church, they were attacking Cyprian. And by attacking Cyprian they were offending the Church and God:

> See, I have used the words of the Punic bishop, Cyprian. You bark against him, even though he was a martyr, when you attack the most solidly grounded faith of the Church, the Church for which he shed his blood.[110]

This line of defence also worked well in tandem with another of Augustine's methods: that of making an assault on Africa an assault on Cyprian. In this way, the Pelagian, i.e., Julian's, attempt to displace the legitimacy of the claims of Africans as merely provincial musings was rendered moot by the argument that Augustine and his flock were just as African as the widely acclaimed and revered Cyprian of Carthage (although Augustine himself was Numidian, and not Punic as Cyprian had been):[111]

> But are we African pirates in opposition to you, because we are faced with a plague from abroad that must be conquered by Christ the savior and because from here we held up against you one martyr, Cyprian, by whom we prove that we are defending the ancient Catholic faith against the vain and pagan novelty of your error? What an outrage! Did the Church of God which is situated in Africa need your prayers? Did she need them when blessed Cyprian preached the doctrine which you attack? ...Your defender contemptuously labels me: 'The Punic debater.' I say: The Punic

huius cupiditate, pro Christi veritate pugnasti, et eius in te gratiae largitate vicisti. Secura est corona tua, victoriosa est doctrina tua, in qua et istos vincis qui confidunt in virtute sua. Ipsi enim clamant, 'Perfectio nobis virtutis a nobis est': tu autem reclamas, 'Nemo suis viribus fortis est, sed Dei indulgentia et misericordia tutus est'; English quote taken from Teske, *Answer to Julian* (WSA I/24, 325).

109 Yates, 'Augustine's Appropriation of Cyprian the Martyr-Bishop against the Pelagians', 131 (Footnote 33), 134.

110 *C. Iul. imp.* 1,106 (CSEL 85/1, 125): 'Ecce verbis usus sum Poeni episcopi Cypriani, contra quem tu etiam martyrem latras, cum ecclesiae fundatissimam fidem, pro qua ecclesia fusus est eius sanguis, oppugnas'; English quote taken from Teske, *Unifinished Work in Answer to Julian* (WSA I/25, 127).

111 Thascius Caecilianus Cyprianus was Carthaginian, i.e. Punic; *C. Iul.* 3,32 (PL 44, 719); *C. Iul. imp.* 1,7 (CSEL 85/1, 9); 6,6 (CSEL 85/2, 299).

debater is not me, but the Punic Cyprian, who slays you with his wound and punishes you for your accursed doctrine.[112]

Julian had attempted to use the time-tested Roman technique of disparaging an interlocutor by use of polemical attacks.[113] In this case, the highly cultivated bishop of Aeclanum[114] attempted to disqualify his African adversary by using terms such as 'Punic' (*Poenus*)[115] or 'Numidian'[116] in place of a more neutral term such as 'African' (*Afer*).[117] This usage was intended to bring to mind commonplace connotations of the Punic forces of Hannibal (*fides Punica*) from the Second Punic War (218–201 B.C.) who had occupied the Italian peninsula, as well as recall the ancient Roman prejudice dating from the first century B.C. against the perfidy of the Punics (*fides Punica*), which term by Late Antiquity had been adapted to signify an unbeliever, a pagan.[118] This ultra-heated polemical atmosphere would signal a new phase in Augustine's anti-Pelagian campaign.[119]

---

112 *C. Iul.* 3,31–32 (*PL* 44, 718–19): 'Contra vos autem, quia nobis estis pestilentia transmarina, Christo salvatore vincenda, ideone latrocinamur ex africa, quia unum martyrem hinc opponimus Cyprianum, per quem probemus antiquam nos defendere fidem catholicam, contra vestri erroris vanam profanam que novitatem? O nefas! Defuerunt Ecclesiae Dei quae in Africa constitua est, defuerunt orationes tuae, quando ista quae oppugnas, Cyprianus beatissimus praedicabat? ...'Poenus disputator,' quod me contumeliose tuus defensor appellat; Poenus, inquam, disputator, non ego, sed Cyprianus Poenus, te hoc vulnere Poenus immolat, et poenam scelerato ex dogmate sumit'; English quote taken from Teske, *Answer to Julian*, in *Answer to the Pelagians* (*WSA* I/24, 357).

113 This is covered in depth in Weber, '"For What is so Monstrous as What the Punic Fellow Says?" Supplemental Data can be Found in Dorothea Weber, '*Some Literary Aspects of the Debate between Julian of Eclanum and Augustine*', *Studia Patristica* 43 (2006), 289–302.

114 On Julian's education and upbringing, see Lössl, *Julian von Aeclanum. Studien zu seinem Leben, seinem Werk, seiner Lehre und ihrer Überlieferung*, 74–146; Lamberigts, 'The Italian Julian of Æclanum about the African Augustine of Hippo', 83.

115 For example: 'Poenus orator' (Jul., *Ad Florum* 1,48 [*CSEL* 85/1, 37]); 'Poenus tractator' (Jul., *Ad Florum* 1,7 and 1,16 [*CSEL* 85/1, 9 and *CSEL* 85/1, 13]); 'Poenus scriptor' (*Ad Florum* 1,73; 2,19; 6,18 [*CSEL* 85/1, 89; 85/1, 174; *PL* 45, 1541]); 'Poenus disputator' (*Ad Turb.* frg. 52 [*CCSL* 88, ed. L. De Coninck (Turnhout: Brepols, 1967)], 352); *C. Iul.* (*PL* 44, 719).

116 For example: 'Numidian armed with a small shield (*Numidia caetratus*)'; *C. Iul. imp.* 6,6 (*CSEL* 85/2, 298).

117 Lamberigts explains the rationale for such: 'Crucial to the genre of polemics was that the author would try to discredit the opponent in such a way that the reader would side with the author'; 'The Italian Julian of Æclanum about the African Augustine of Hippo', 85.

118 Weber, '"For What is so Monstrous as What the Punic Fellow Says?"' 81.

119 For details on the second stage of the Pelagian controversy, see Perago, 'Il valore della tradizione nella polemica tra sant'Agostine e Giuliano di Eclano', 143–60; and E. Dassmann,

The combination of such prejudice about the backwardness of the North Africans (Punics)[120] and their different Latin accent,[121] combined with Julian's literary prowess, provided the opportunity for use of a powerful literary tool against Augustine. In this sense then, it is entirely understandable that Augustine would place Cyprian even more at the forefront of his defence against the polemical onslaught wrought by Julian:

> Do not in your pride over your earthly origin scorn this Phoenician who warns and admonishes you. Do not, after all, suppose that, because you are a son of Apulia, you must surpass the Phoenicians by your origins, though you cannot surpass them by your mind. Flee, rather, the punishments, not the Phoenicians. For you cannot escape the Phoenician opponents as long as you take delight in placing your trust in your own virtue.

'Tam Ambrosius quam Cyprianus (c.Iul.imp. 4,112). Augustins Helfer im pelagianischen Streit', in D. Papandreou, W.A. Bienert, and K. Schäferdiek (eds.), *Oecumenica et Patristica. Festschrift für W. Schneemelcher* (Chambésy-Genf: Metropolie der Schweiz, 1989), 258–68. Needless to say that for pastoral reasons Augustine considered himself a man of the African Church, and had to be faithful to this tradition. See the pertinent remarks of Gerald Bonner, *Les origines africaines de la doctrine sur la chute et le péché originel, Augustinus* 12 (1967), 97–116; and also R.J. De Simone, 'Modern Research on the Sources of Saint Augustine's Doctrine of Original Sin', *Augustinian Studies* 11 (1980), 205–27. For a very critical view see Pier Franco Beatrice, *Tradux peccati. Alle fonti della dottrina agostiniana del peccato originale*, Studia Patristica Mediolanensia 8 (Milan: Vita e Pensiero, 1978).

120 Julian emphasised the stereotype of North Africans (Punics) as backward, poorly educated, and generally unwise: '…macte virtute prudentiae, nobilissime disputator, qui gradibus Punicae dialexeos, ut coendares dona, evertisi iudica, ut simulares gratiam, iustitiam subruisti, ut infamares naturam, criminatus es hominum conditorem et ita criminatus, ut non solum aliquot peccatore, sed ipsa lege peccati deus tuus nocentior appareret'; *C. Iul. imp.* 1,72 (*CSEL* 85/1, 84–85); also: 'Macte virtute sapientiae, qui novae et a te inventae primum disputationis regulis secunda primorum negatione complecteris et corpora capitibus trunca componis', 5,34 (*CSEL* 85/2, 232). Along this same line, Julian tantalised his African opponent by labeling him the 'Aristotle of the Punics' (*Aristoteles Poenorum*); *C. Iul. imp.* 3,199 (*CSEL* 85/1, 498.); *C. Iul.* 1,12 (*PL* 44, 647); 2,37 (*PL* 44, 700); 6,56 (*PL* 44, 855). Also consult Weber, '"For What Is so Monstrous as What the Punic Fellow Says?"' 79.

121 Augustine himself draws attention to the fact that his North African accent occasioned comment in Italy: *De Doctrina Christiana* (*CSEL* 32), ed. I. Martin (Turnhout: Brepols, 1962), 4,10,24 (*CSEL* 32, 132–33): 'Si enim non piguit dicere interpretes nostros: non congregabo conventicula eorum de sanguinibus, quoniam senserunt ad rem pertinere, ut eo loco pluraliter enuntiaretur hoc nomen, quod in Latina lingua singulariter tantummodo dicitur, cur pietatis doctorem pigeat imperitis moquentem ossum potius quam os dicere, ne ista syllaba non ab eo, quod sunt ossa, sed ab eo, quod sunt ora, intellegatur, ubi Africae aures de correptione vocalium vel productione non iudicant?'

For blessed Cyprian was also a Phoenician, and he said, 'We must boast over nothing when nothing is ours.'[122]

Augustine even managed to reverse Julian's cutting remarks about Africa. African Catholics were entitled to feel proud for remaining vigilant in protecting the walls of the ancient faith against the Manicheans and Donatists, and now against the intruding overseas pestilence, Pelagianism, with its new devices of destruction and uncanny attacks.[123] It was the same Punic Cyprian[124] who protected the solidly-grounded faith of the Church, for which he shed his blood,[125] with his 'small Numidian shield',[126] a shield of truth against the flaming arrows of the evil one (Eph. 6,16).[127] Indeed with the Punic Cyprian as the defender of Africa, Augustine told Julian it would behove him to stop inviting the punishment (*poena*) of the truth and leave the Punic (*Poenus*) people alone!

The authority of Cyprian would be required yet again in the Pelagian debate, this time within the context of increasingly aggressive personal attacks between Augustine and Julian. In a rather colourful barrage of attacks, the bishops alternately attempted to damage each others' credibility. These exchanges, made by both Julian and Augustine, resulted in barbs and allegations of the most serious kind, including referring to each other as: 'Lord of all donkeys' (*Patronus asinorum*),[128] 'Manichean',[129] 'curser of babies',[130] 'Pelagian windbag',[131] 'Manichean pirates',[132] '*cultor diaboli*',[133] 'quack',[134] 'brilliant gold nugget on a

122 *C. Iul. imp.* 6,18 (*CSEL* 85/2, 353): 'Noli istum Poenum monentem vel admonentem terrena inflatus propagine spernere. Non enim quia te Apulia genuit, ideo Poenos vincendos existemes gente, quos non potes mente. Poenas potius fuge, non Poenos; nam disputatores Poenos non potes fugere, quamdiu te delectat in tua virtute confidere, et beatus enim Cyprianus Poenus fuit qui dixit: 'In nullo gloriandum, quando nostrum nihil sit'. English quote taken from Teske, *Unfinished Work in Answer to Julian* (*WSA* I/25, 647).

123 *C. Iul.* 3,31 (*PL* 44, 718): 'Contra vos autem…profanamque novitatem'.

124 Augustine differentiates his Numidian identity from that of Cyprian's Punic one: '…non quidem Numidia, sed tamen Poenus ille Cyprianus…'; *C. Iul. imp.* 6,6 (*CSEL* 85/2, 299).

125 *C. Iul. imp.* 1,106 (*CSEL* 85/1, 125).

126 *C. Iul. imp.* 6,6 (*CSEL* 85/2, 298): *Numidia cetratus; caetra Numidica.*

127 *C. Iul. imp.* 6,6 (*CSEL* 85/2, 299): *in quo omnes sagittas ignitas maligni…exstinguimus.*

128 *C. Iul. imp.* 4,56 (*CSEL* 85/2, 62–63).

129 *C. Iul. imp.* 3,170 (*CSEL* 85/1, 472).

130 *C. Iul. imp.* 1,48 (*CSEL* 85/1, 36–37).

131 *s.* 181,1 and 3 (*PL* 38, 979–81).

132 Aug., *C. Iul.* 3,31 (*PL* 44, 718).

133 Jul., *Ad Turb.* frg. 57 (*CCSL* 88, 355).

134 *Ad Turb.* frg. 65 (*CCSL* 88, 357).

dunghill',[135] 'follower of the Cynics',[136] 'new physicist',[137] 'Epicurean of our time',[138] 'bedbug',[139] 'fool/idiot',[140] 'bull-headed' (*pervicax*),[141] 'committer of monstrous lies',[142] 'old and sexually inept',[143] or 'young' and 'immature'.[144] There were even deeper remarks about each other's families! Julian, with sleight of hand, opined that Augustine's view that procreation is impossible without the illness of desire may have been in part formed by Monnica, who was a *meribibula* or alcoholic.[145] Here Julian was playing on the simultaneous meanings of disease and passion when he spoke of a *morbus occultus* (hidden disease/hidden passion).[146] Augustine struck back in kind: 'I regard your parents as good Catholic Christians, and I congratulate them for having died before they saw you a heretic'.[147]

Authority and Tradition Contested

A separate round of polemical engagement would require Augustine's incorporation of Cyprian's authority more directly. Julian had expressed his annoyance with the theological items being debated in the controversy, which had,

135 *Ad Turb.* frg. 67 (CCSL 88, 357).

136 Jul., *Ad Florum* 4.43 (CSEL 85/2, 43).

137 Jul., *Ad Florum* 5.11 (CSEL 85/2, 179).

138 Jul., *Ad Florum* 1.45 (CSEL 85/1, 32).

139 Jul., *Ad Turb.* frg. 134 (CCSL 88, 368).

140 Aug., *C. Iul. imp.* 1,64 (CSEL 85/1, 61): '…cum hoc non patrocinium erroris tui, sed testimonium sit stultitae singularis…'; 1,86 (CSEL 85/1, 98): 'Ceterum duo ista quae iungis, liberum et non liberum, id est liberum et captivum, illi quidem rei de qua agitur convenire non possunt; tibi vero stultitiam singularem, impudentiam novam, impietatem veterem inesse testantur'.

141 *C. Iul.* 6,83 (PL 44, 873).

142 *C. Iul. imp.* 6,18 (CSEL 85/2, 350): '*commentorum prodiga*'.

143 *C. Iul. imp.* 3,169 (CSEL 85/1, 471): '*senex Augustine*'; *Nupt. et conc.* 1,7,8 (CSEL 42, 219–20); 1,11,13 (CSEL 42, 225); 2,21,36 (CSEL 42, 290–91).

144 Aug., *C. Iul. imp.* 3,169 (CSEL 85/1, 471): *iuvenis Iuliane.*

145 Jul., *Ad Florum* 1,68 (CSEL 85/1, 72–73): 'Quod vero adiungis morbum esse negotium nuptiarum, leniter audiri potest, si hoc solum de tuis parentibus dicas; conscius enim forte esse potes matris tuae morbi alicuius occulti, quam in libris Confessionis, ut ipso verbo utar, meribibulam vocatam esse signasti'.

146 Aug., *C. Iul. imp.* 1,68 (CSEL 85/1, 73).

147 *C. Iul. imp.* 1,68 (CSEL 85/1, 74): 'Ego vero parentes tuos tamquam catholicos christianos honorabiles habeo eisque gratulor, quod ante defuncti sunt quam haereticum te viderent'. English quote taken from: R. Teske, *Unfinished Work in Answer to Julian* (WSA I/25, 97). Augustine would repeat this polemical refrain elsewhere, urging Julian to: 'Remember your father'; *C. Iul.* 4,11 (PL 44, 741–42); 6,35 (PL 44, 841–42).

in his opinion, been forcefully imposed on Italy by the Africans,[148] and he was now witnessing the destruction of his thriving Church at the hands of such brigands (African Manicheans).[149] Worse was that, it was not even possible to hold a council to allow a fair hearing of all sides.[150] Julian's preference for validation would have taken the form of a gathering of learned (erudite) judges,[151] with such notables as John Chrysostom and Basil the Great.[152] This would provide the opportunity to discern without the interference of the insolent, ignorant, and stupid mobs[153] who had hijacked the Church and who 'steers the ship under full sail.'[154]

Indeed, for Julian such a council would have to be composed of the few who were capable of deciphering the scriptures.[155] Such men reason, learning, and liberty would have made eminent,[156] although they would be chosen on the criterion that their rationality and knowledge of the scriptures were corroborated by the erudition of holy men, and their authority was not biased towards the truth, but that they received glory and validation from their participation in truth.[157] Further, they would require independence from the presence of

148 *Cont. Iul. imp.* 1,42 and 74 (*CSEL* 84/1, 30; 89–90).

149 Jul., *Ad Turb.* frg. 51 (*CCSL* 88, 352): 'Orandus est hic Deus, frater beatissime Turbanti, consacerdos dilectissime, ut paribus etiam hac tempestate uirtutibus Ecclesiam catholicam, Filii sui sponsam, maturam, fecundam, castam, decoram, a Manichaeorum constupratione in Africa uel ex Africa latrocinantiam eruere non moretur'.

150 Julian, *Epistula ad Rufum*, frg(s). (*CCSL* 88), ed. L. De Coninck (Turnhout: Brepols, 1967), 27–28 (*CCSL* 88, 340); *Ad Turb.* frg. 2A (*CCSL* 88, 341): '(De iudicibus) apud quos propterea (dicis) non potuisse uos agere causam uestram, quia nemo de rebus dubiis bene consultat, nisi qui ab odio, ira et amicitia uacuum pectus attulerit; quales non fuisse (dicis) qui de causa uestra iudicauerunt, quia prius eam coeperunt odisse quam nosse…'; see also frg. 3B (*CCSL* 88, 341).

151 *C. Iul. imp.* 2,1 (*CSEL* 85/1, 164): 'Commode nobiscum ageretur, si aut apud eruditos iudices negotium veritatis tueri daretur facultas aut…'; see also 2,37 (*CSEL* 85/1, 189), where Julian, asks for a trial by illustrious, prudent men. Julian opts for a refined legal approach; see Pel., *Ad Florum* 5,20 (*CSEL* 85/2, 201). These learned people could be either Christian or from the world; 1,69 (*CSEL* 85/1, 76).

152 Jul., *Ad Turb.* frg. 308–12 (*CCSL* 88, 392–94).

153 Jul., *Ad Florum* 2,1 (*CSEL* 85/1, 164).

154 Jul., *Ad Florum* 2,2 (*CSEL* 85/1, 164–65).

155 Jul., *Ad Turb.* frg. 156 (*CCSL* 88, 373): '(Exaggeras, tam sit) difficilis paucisque conueniens eruditis sanctarum cognitio litterarum…'; frg. 159 (*CCSL* 88, 373).

156 Aug., *C. Iul. imp.* 3,87 (*CSEL* 85/1, 414): 'Haereat tamen id, quod sequitur, maxime prudentis animo lectoris, ut intellegat me hactenus multo remissius, quam res postulabat, egisse'. Please refer also to 3,20 (*CSEL* 85/1, 362); 4,90 (*CSEL* 85/2, 94–96); 4,95 (*CSEL* 85/2, 99–100); 5,4 (*CSEL* 85/2, 170–72); 6,14 (*CSEL* 85/2, 324–36).

157 Jul., *Ad Turb.* frg. 313 (*CCSL* 88, 394): '…hanc sanam et ueram esse sententiam, quam primo loco ratio, deinde scripturarum muniuit auctoritas, et quam sanctorum uirorum semper

coercive and boisterous crowds,[158] the type which had previously compromised the chances of Pelagians being heard, through means of mild terrorising.[159]

Augustine spared no effort to extrapolate a polemical advantage from Julian's suggestions. For this, the bishop of Hippo insinuated in no uncertain terms that the bishop of Aeclanum stood condemned of haughty arrogance,[160] elitism,[161] and of dismissing the faith of simpler, i.e., less erudite believers.[162] Augustine likewise used these circumstances to make a coherent appeal to tradition, with Cyprian again as the *sine qua non* constitutive element. This approach was effective, as Julian could not deny Cyprian's authority.[163] Here again, Augustine accentuated Cyprian's stature among the collective of many holy and erudite exemplars and teachers of the faith, one who enjoyed a consensus of the faithful,[164] and was famous among the churches in the West and East.[165] Cyprian the martyr[166] was outstanding in holiness and in teaching,[167]

---

celebrauit eruditio, qui tamen ueritati auctoritatem non suo tribuere consensu, sed testimonium et gloriam de eius suscepere consortio…'.

158 Jul., *Ad Turb.* frg. 6 (CCSL 88, 341).

159 Jul., *Ad Turb.* frg. 11 (CCSL 88, 342). Julian finds a complete lack of reasoning among such types: *Ad Florum* 6,2 (85/2, 293): 'Hoc autem in praesentiarum duabus ex causis accidit; quia et sententia Manichaeorum de criminum est probata consiliis, et excitae persecutionum procellae inopes spiritus a veritatis favore deterrent'; *C. Iul. imp.* 1,75 (CSEL 85/1, 90ff); 2,2 (CSEL 85/1, 164); 2,14 (CSEL 85/1, 172); 2,15 (CSEL 85/1, 172).

160 Augustine accuses Julian of: *libido loquendi, ianis loquacitas, vagabunda loquacitas*; *C. Iul. imp.* 3,20 (CSEL 85/1, 363); 4,57 (CSEL 85/2, 63); 5,26 (CSEL 85/2, 219–23); 5,39 (CSEL 85/2, 237–39); also see Lamberigts, 'The Italian Julian of Æclanum about the African Augustine of Hippo', 89.

161 *C. Iul.* 2,10,36 (PL 44, 699–700); 5,1,2 (PL 44, 783); 5,1,4 (PL 44, 783–84); 6,20,64 (PL 44, 862–63); *C. Iul. imp.* 2,36 (CSEL 84/1, 188); 2,51 (CSEL 84/1, 199–200).

162 *C. Iul.* 6,34 (PL 45, 841); 6,36 (PL 44, 842); *C. Iul. imp.* 2,4 (CSEL 84/1, 166).

163 As seen in Augustine's imitation of the authority's *Ad Quirinum* in his *Liber Testimoniorum*; *C. ep. Pel.* 4,21 (CSEL 60, 543); 4,25 (CSEL 60, 552).

164 *C. ep. Pel.* 6,26 (CSEL 60, 552); É. Rebillard elaborates on this, noting that by using Cyprian in the company of other remarkable holy men of late antiquity, Augustine was creating a method of arguing from patristic sources without being totally confined to the theological system of any one particular source. This could in part explain how Augustine was able to resource some of Cyprian's work differently at particular junctures in time, and also distance himself from other aspects; 'A New Style of Argument in Christian Polemic: Augustine and the Use of Patristic Citations', 578.

165 *C. ep. Pel.* 6,21 (CSEL 60, 543): 'Beatissimum, corona etiam martyrii gloriosissimum Cyprianum nec Africanis atque occidentalibus tantum, uerum et orientalibus ecclesiis fama praedicante et scripta eius longe lateque diffundente notissimum…'.

166 *Nupt. et conc.* 2,51 (CSEL 42, 308); *C. ep. Pel.* 6,21 (CSEL 60, 544); 6,24 (CSEL 60, 548); *C. Iul.* 1,6 (PL 44, 655); 2,6 (PL 44, 677); 2,18 (PL 44, 685); 3,31 (PL 44, 718); *C. Iul. imp.* 1,50 (CSEL 85/1, 44); 1,106 (CSEL 85/1, 125).

167 *C. Iul.* 1,22 (PL 44, 655); 1,32 (PL 44, 662); 2,25 (PL 44, 691); *C. ep. Pel.* 4,26 (CSEL 60, 552).

was a living apologia for the solidly-grounded faith of the Church,[168] a soldier of Christ[169] who protected the faith handed down to him,[170] a faith that clearly attests to the radical existence of original sin and humanity's dependence on grace.[171]

Thus, at the end of this particular instance of an appropriation of Cyprian by Augustine, Julian had had his own arguments and proposals reversed on him. Instead of proving that Augustine was promoting a theological innovation, the bishop of Hippo Regius used Julian's ideas against him for a literary routing. Instead of opting for secular philosophers, or '*philosophorum saecularium*'[172] as Augustine accused Julian of proposing, Augustine provided his own list of erudite and saintly men[173] from East and West and from different periods of time,[174] who formed a consensus of faith and who were informed by one another, the Church, and scripture:[175]

> They drank as milk and ate as food; they have served its milk and its food to little ones and to adults and have most clearly and bravely defended it

---

168 *C. Iul. imp.* 1,106 (CSEL 85/1, 125).

169 *C. Iul. imp.* 6,6 (CSEL 85/2, 299).

170 *C. ep. Pel.* 6,32 (CSEL 60, 658) : '…Cyprianus…demonstratur, quam sit haec, quam tenemus, fides uera uereque christiana atque catholica, sicut per scripturas sanctas antiquitus traditia sic a patribus nostris et usque ad hoc tempus…rentus atque seruata et deinceps propitio Deo retineda atque seruanada. Nam sic Cypriano et a Cypriano traditam haec atque huiusmodi ex eius litteris testimonia prolata testantur, sic autem usque ad tempora nostra seruatam…'.

171 *C. Iul. imp.* 6,21 (CSEL 85/2, 363).

172 *C. Iul. imp.* 2,4 (CSEL 85/1, 166).

173 *C. Iul. imp.* 2,37 (CSEL 85/1, 189); 4,119 (CSEL 85/2, 133): 'Quos antistites ecclesiarum cum viros sani capitis dicas…quae illi notissima consensione didicerunt atque docuerunt…'.

174 *C. Iul.* 2,37 (PL 44, 700): 'Si episcopalis synodus ex toto orbe congregaretur, mirum si tales possent illic facile tot sedere. Quia nec isti uno tempore fuerunt: sed fideles et multis excellentiores paucos dispensatores suos Deus per diversas aetates temporum, locorumque distantias, sicut ei placet atque expedire iudicat, ipse dispensat. Hos itaque de aliis atque aliis temporibus atque regionibus ab oriente et occidente congregatos vides, non in locum quo navigare cogantur homines, sed in librum qui navigare possit ad homines'; *C. Iul. imp.* 2,33 (CSEL 85/1, 186); *C. Iul.* 2,37 (PL 44, 700): 'Isti episcopi sunt, docti, graves, sancti, veritatis acerrimi defensores adversus garrulas vanitates, in quorum ratione, eruditione, libertate, quae tria bona iudici tribuisti, non potes invenire quod spernas'.

175 *C. Iul.* 1,30 (PL 44, 661); 3,32 (PL 44, 719); *C. Iul. Imp.* 4,112 (CSEL 85/2, 120); 4,119 (CSEL 85/1, 133).

> against its enemies, including you who were not born then, though they are now showing you for what you are.[176]

Indeed, by slandering Augustine's position, Julian was attacking the very erudite jury he had requested! Julian's attacks were therefore attacks on such men.[177] His only option then, according to Augustine, was acceptance and submission to the authority of those holy and learned men.[178] Therefore, Augustine argued, it was Julian who was the new heretic,[179] polluting with novelties[180] doctrines which had existed since the earliest period of the Church.[181]

Cyprian's Rank amongst Other Authorities

To demonstrate the weight associated with the authority of Cyprian as used by both parties here, it is important to analyse how Cyprian is situated within the hierarchy of authority in the course of their debate. This is so, because such an analysis clearly shows that as an authority, Cyprian was held in high regard, not only as an African hero, but as an authority within the greater universal Church of the time. But first it should be said that Augustine seldom mentions the names of his predecessors, either as individuals, as we will see further, or as a group, without an appreciative epithet.[182] The doctors he invokes are giants, worthy of being followed, as Augustine claims to do: I teach what I have learned from these holy and learned men.[183] These men were brilliant in the Catholic Church because of their search for sound doctrine. Protected and stimulated by spiritual weapons, they waged strenuous war against the heretics. After faithfully performing the labors of their ministry, they passed away

---

176 *C. Iul.* 2,37 (*PL* 44, 700): '...quam in lacte suxerunt, quam in cibo sumpserunt, cuius lac et cibum parvis magnisque ministraverunt, quam contra inimicos etiam vos tunc nondum natos, unde nunc revelamini, apertissime ac fortissime defenderunt'; English quote taken from R. Teske, *Answer to Julian*, (*WSA* I/24, 335).

177 *C. Iul. imp.* 4,73 (*CSEL* 85/2, 75–76).

178 *C. Iul.* 1,11 (*PL* 44, 647); 2,14 (*PL* 44, 684); 2,15 (*PL* 44, 684); 2,37 (*PL* 44, 700–01).

179 *Nupt. et conc.* 1,22 (*CSEL* 42, 235); 1,40 (*CSEL* 42, 251); 2,25 (*CSEL* 42, 255); 2,3 (*CSEL* 42, 278).

180 *C. Iul.* 1,4 (*PL* 44, 643); 3,1 (*PL* 44, 701).

181 *Nupt. et conc.* 2,25 (*CSEL* 42, 278).

182 *C. Iul.* 1,32 (*PL* 44, 697): 'Propter quam catholicam ueritatem sancti ac beati et in diuinorum eloquiorum pertractatione clarissimi sacerdotes, Irenaeus, Cyprianus, Reticius, Olympius, Hilarius, Ambrosius, Gregorius, Innocentius, Ioannes, Basilius, quibus addo presbyterum, velis nolis, Hieronymum, ut omittam eos qui nondum dormierunt...'.

183 *C. Iul.* 1,29–30 (*PL* 44, 661–62).

in peace.[184] Quite regularly, when giving the list of his heroes, and in order to give the impression that this is not exhaustive, Augustine adds a phrase such as, '*aliique quam plurimi*' or similar, in order to make clear to the reader that the position he is defending is held by many others.[185]

Irenaeus is the most ancient of the doctors Augustine makes use of in his debate with Julian.[186] The bishop of Lyons, who lived *non longe a temporibus apostolorum*, (not long after the time of the apostles) is described as a '*sanctus*'[187] and '*antiquus homo Dei*'.[188] Whenever Augustine presents the longer list of his authorities, Irenaeus, seemingly for chronological reasons, is placed first.[189] From Irenaeus' *Aduersus haereses*, only two texts are quoted in *C. Iul.* 1,5.[190] In Augustine's further development of the tradition argument, these texts will not really function.[191] Therefore, in my view, the function of Irenaeus in the list of the quoted Fathers seems to be limited to that of a link with

184 *C. Iul.* 1,30 (*PL* 44, 661–62): 'In Ecclesia catholica doctrinae sanae studiis claruerunt; spiritualibus armis muniti et accincti strenua contra haereticos bella gesserunt; perfuncti fideliter suae dispensationis laboribus in pacis gremio dormierunt'.

185 See *C. Iul.* 2,33 (*PL* 44, 696); 6,70 (*PL* 44, 866); *C. Iul. Imp.* 1,9 (*CSEL* 85/1, 10); 1,117 (*CSEL* 85/1, 134).

186 Concerning Augustine's knowledge of Irenaeus' work, see Berthold Altaner, 'Augustinus und Irenäus', in B. Altaner (ed.), *Kleine Patristische Schriften* (*TU* 83), (Berlin: Akademie-Verlag, 1967), 194–203; Gerard Bartelink, 'Die Beinflußung Augustins durch die griechischen Patres', in J. den Boeft & J. van Oort (eds.), *Augustiniana Traiectina. Communications présentées au Colloque International d'Utrecht* (*13–14 novembre 1986*) (Paris: Études augustiniennes, 1987), 9–24.

187 *C. Iul.* 1,32 (*PL* 44, 662).

188 *C. Iul.* 1,5 (*PL* 44, 644).

189 *C. Iul.* 2,33 (*PL* 44, 697); 2,37 (*PL* 44, 700–01); 3,32 (*PL* 44, 719); 4,72 (*CSEL* 85/2, 75); 4,73 (*CSEL* 85/2, 75).

190 *PL* 44, 644; the texts are quoted from Irenaus, *Adversus haereses*, 4,2,7; 5,19,1. Augustine used the Latin translation of this work; see Altaner, '*Augustinus und Irenäus*', 194; Edmondo Lupieri, '*Agostino e Ireneo*', *Vetera Christianorum* 15 (1978), 113–15.

191 It is odd to read in Julius Gross, *Enstehungsgeschichte des Erbsündendogmas* I (Geschichte des Erbsündendogmas), (Munich/Basel: Reinhard-Verlag, 1960), 86, that Augustine quoted Irenaeus first, because in antiquity an important role was given to the bishop of Lyons with regard to the dogma of original sin. First, I do not think that one can rightly speak of a dogma of original sin in Irenaeus. Secondly, as Augustine explicitly states, he is interested in this man because he lived not long after the time of the apostles. Finally, as already mentioned by Altaner, 'Augustinus und Irenäus', 194, one should recognise that Augustine did not use the best texts in order to substantiate his own position. But even the two texts quoted do not play any considerable role after *C. Iul* 1, which is contrary to the thesis of Altaner, 'Augustinus und Irenäus',194, n. 1.

the apostles; the second witness, the most victorious[192] Cyprian,[193] bishop,[194] outstanding doctor,[195] extraordinary soldier of Christ,[196] holy man,[197] and blessed African martyr,[198] who shed his life for the most solidly grounded faith of the Church,[199] is of much more importance for Augustine, and this for many reasons. Cyprian was a renowned commentator on the divine words in his speeches and writings,[200] teaching in the Catholic, not the Manichean, Church.[201] He was called a memorable teacher of the truth in the churches.[202] He was a model; worthy of being imitated for he fought throughout his life and doctrine for the truth of Christ and was victorious thanks to the grace of Christ.[203] He was famous not only in the churches of Africa and the West, but

192 *C. Iul.* 2,6 (*PL* 44, 676); 2,25 (*PL* 44, 690).

193 Augustine already referred to Cyprian, *Ep. 64*, in *Pecc. Mer.* 3,10 (*CSEL* 60, 135–36). Augustine added new texts to his anti-Pelagian dossier only in 418. With regard to Augustine's use of Cyprian in general, see A.A.R. Bastiaensen, 'Augustin et ses prédécesseurs latins chrétiens', in J. den Boeft and J. van Oort (eds.), *Augustiniana Traiectina. Communications présentées au Colloque International d'Utrecht (13–14 novembre 1986)* (Paris: Études augustiniennes, 1987), 25–57, see 34–36; E. Dassmann, *Cyprianus*, in C. Mayer (ed.) *Augustinus-Lexikon*, Vol. 2, 196–211; with regard to the appeal to Cyprian in the Pelagian controversy, see esp. 208–09. Unlike the appeal to Cyprian in the Donatist controversy it should be stressed that Augustine nowhere criticises Cyprian during the Pelagian controversy. With regard to the differences between Cyprian and Augustine, see, among others, Anne Pannier, 'Saint Augustin, Saint Cyprien: La postérité de deux ecclésiologies', in *Saint Augustin. Dossier conçu et dirigé par P. RANSON (Les dossiers H)* (Lausanne: L'Age d'Homme, 1988), 237–47; Mireille Labrousse, 'Le baptême des hérétiques d'après Cyprien, Optat et Augustin: influences et divergences', *Revue des études augustiniennes* 42 (1996), 223–42.

194 *C. ep. Pel.* 4,24 (*CSEL* 60, 548); *C. Iul.* 1,6 (*PL* 44, 655); *C. Iul. imp* 1,106 (*CSEL* 85/1, 125); 6,10 (*CSEL* 85/1, 313).

195 *C. Iul.* 1,22 (*PL* 44, 655); 2,9 (*PL* 44, 679).

196 *C. Iul. imp.* 6,6 (*CSEL* 85/2, 299).

197 *C. Iul.* 1,32 (*PL* 44, 662).

198 *Nupt. et Con.* 2,51 (*CSEL* 42, 308); *C. ep. Pel.* 4,21 (*CSEL* 60, 544); 4,24 (*CSEL* 60, 548); *C. Iul.* 1,6 (*PL* 44, 655); 2,6 (*PL* 44, 677); 2,18 (*PL* 44, 685); 3,31 (*PL* 44, 718). In *C. Iul. imp.* 1,50 (*CSEL* 85/1, 44), Cyprian's martyrdom gets a special emphasis, because Julian had stated that nobody was willing to give his life for the God of Augustine. In his reply, Augustine states that Cyprian not only believed in the existence of original sin, but also gave his life for his faith.

199 *C. Iul. imp.* 1,106 (*CSEL* 85/1, 125).

200 *C. ep. Pel.* 4,24 (*CSEL* 60, 549); 4,28 (*CSEL* 60, 558).

201 *C. ep. Pel.* 4,27 (*CSEL* 60, 554).

202 *C. ep. Pel.* 4,26 (*CSEL* 60, 552).

203 *C. Iul.* 1,25 (*PL* 44, 691); *C. ep. Pel.* 4,26 (*CSEL* 60, 552).

also in those of the East, and his writings were dispersed everywhere.[204] Augustine insisted that in his letters Cyprian had shown how truly Christian and Catholic is the faith which we hold (*tenemus*). 'He was my teacher and, just like me, defended doctrine of original sin', Augustine claims.[205] It is this sound faith,[206] transmitted through the scriptures from antiquity, handed down to Cyprian and transmitted by him,[207] which we must grasp and preserve today. Augustine had a very good reason to refer to Cyprian: Pelagius recognised the authority of Cyprian and wanted to imitate Cyprian's *Ad Quirinum* in his own *Liber testimoniorum*.[208] Throughout the discussion with Julian, Augustine quoted twenty-four texts from the bishop of Carthage, taken from five works and one letter.[209] As a result, Cyprian became the second most important witness in the debate with Julian, with Ambrose the first. It should be noted that the Cyprian-dossier was already complete in *C. ep. Pel.* 4.[210] However, one gets the impression that Augustine, in comparison to *C. ep. Pel.*, refers less often to Cyprian in both *C. Iul.* and *C. Iul. imp.*, probably because Julian was so negative about the Punic people.

204 *C ep. Pel.* 4,21 (CSEL 60, 543): 'Beatissimum, corona etiam martyrii gloriosissimum Cyprianum nec Africanis atque occidentalibus tantum, uerum et orientalibus ecclesiis fama praedicante et scripta eius longe lateque diffundente notissimum…' In 4,32 (CSEL 60, 568), Augustine explicitly mentions that he only quotes partially from both Ambrose and Cyprian, for otherwise his treatise would be too long.

205 *C. Iul. imp.* 6,21 (CSEL 85/2, 363).

206 *C ep. Pel.* 4,32 (CSEL 60, 569).

207 *C ep. Pel.* 4,32 (CSEL 60, 568): '…Cyprianus…demonstretur, quam sit haec, quam tenemus, fides uera uereque christiana atque catholica, sicut per scripturas sanctas antiquitus tradita sic a patribus nostris et usque ad hoc tempus…retenta atque seruata et deinceps propitio Deo retinenda atque seruanda. Nam sic Cypriano et a Cypriano traditam haec atque huiusmodi ex eius litteris testimonia prolata testantur, sic autem usque ad tempora nostra seruatam…'.

208 See *C ep. Pel.* 4,21 (CSEL 60, 543); 4,25 (CSEL 60, 552); also see François-Joseph Thonnard, 'Le témoignage de saint Cyprien', in BA 23 (Paris: Desclée de Brouwer, 1974), 824–25; Albert de Veer, 'Les relations de saint Augustin et de Pélage avec Albine, Pinien et Mélanie', in BA 22 (Paris: Desclée de Brouwer, 1975), 674–75.

209 Augustine quotes from Cyprian, *De opere et eleemosynis* 1; 3 (x2); 18; 22; *De mortalitate* 2; 4; 7; 26; *De oratione dominica* 10; 12 (x2); 14; 16;17;18; 22; 26; *Testimonia* 3,4 (x2); 3,54; *De bono patientiae* 3;11 (x2); 17; *Epistula* 64,2,4,5.

210 See the pertinent remarks of Dassmann, 'Cyprianus', in C. Mayer (ed.) *Augustinus-Lexikon*, Vol. 2, 208. For a different opinion, see Thonnard, 'Le témoignage de saint Cyprien', in BA 23, 825.

The next witnesses are Reticius of Autun[211] and Olympius of Barcelona.[212] Both bishops participated in the synod of Rome (313). In this synod, held because of the nascent Donatist controversy, with Melchiades as president,[213] Donatus, the father of the schism, was condemned and Caecilian of Carthage absolved of wrongdoing.[214] Augustine's information about these bishops' individual data is rather limited: most often the praises they receive are common to all doctors in the lists provided by Augustine.[215] On a more individual level, the only thing Augustine knew about Olympius, a man of great glory in the Church and in Christ, is that he was a Spanish bishop.[216] Reticius is called a man of great authority,[217] a man of God.[218] Given his expertise in the Donatist controversy, he deserves a place in the court Julian is asking for. Further, both bishops function as chronological links between Cyprian and Hilary.[219] One text is quoted from each of these bishops.[220]

With Hilary of Poitiers,[221] *episcopus Gallus*,[222] a holy[223] and blessed man,[224] worthy of veneration,[225] an important, well known, and extraordinary[226]

---

211 For Reticius, see Michael Fiedrowicz, 'Reticius', *Lexikon für Theologie und Kirche* 8 (Freiburg: Verlag Herder, 2000), 1132.

212 With regard to Augustine's use of Olympius, see Victoranio Menosa, 'San Agustín y Olympio, Obispo de Barcelona', *Augustinus* 25 (1980), 17–21. In *C. Iul. imp.*, Augustine will no longer appeal to Olympius.

213 See Charles Pietri and Luce Pietri (eds.), *Prosopographie de l'Italie chrétienne (313–604)* (*Prosopographie chrétienne du Bas-Empire* 2), Vol. 2 (Rome: Ecole française de Rome, 2000), s.v. 'Miltiades', 1513.

214 *C. Iul.* 1,7 (*PL* 44, 644); *C. Iul. imp.* 1,55 (*CSEL* 85/1, 52).

215 See *C. Iul.* 2,33 (*PL* 44, 697); 2,37 (*PL* 44, 700–01); 3,32 (*PL* 44, 719).

216 *C. Iul.* 1,8 (*PL* 44, 644–45).

217 *C. Iul.* 1,7 (*PL* 44, 644). Augustine bases his praise on the 'gesta ecclesiastica' of the process in Rome.

218 *C. Iul. imp.* 1,55 (*CSEL* 85/1, 52).

219 See *C. Iul.* 1,32 (*PL* 44, 662); 2,33 (*PL* 44, 697); 2,37 (*PL* 44, 700); 3,32 (*PL* 44, 719).

220 Both of these writings are lost.

221 On Augustine's use of Hilary in the Pelagian controversy, see Hanns Cristof Brennecke, 'Hilarius', in C. Mayer (ed.), *Augustinus-Lexikon* 3,3/4 (Basel: Schwabe, 2006), 341–48, esp. 344–46.

222 *C. Iul.* 1,9 (*PL* 44, 645); 1,22 (*PL* 44, 655); *C. Iul. Imp.* 2,33 (*CSEL* 85/1, 186). In *C. ep. Pel.* 4,7 (*CSEL* 60, 520), Augustine wrongly attributed a text of Ambrosiaster on Rom. 5,12 to Hilary. In this regard, see Albert de Veer, 'Saint Augustin et l'Ambrosiaster' in *BA* 23 (Paris, 1974), 817–24. According to de Veer, the text, attributed to Hilary, returns in *C. Iul. Imp.* 2,33 (*CSEL* 85/1, 186) and in 2,164 (*CSEL* 85/1, 285).

223 *C. Iul.* 1,32 (*PL* 44, 662); 2,28 (*PL* 44, 693); 2,33 (*PL* 44, 696).

224 *C. Iul.* 2,26 (*PL* 44, 691); 2,29 (*PL* 44, 693).

225 *C. Iul.* 2,8 (*PL* 44, 678).

226 *C. Iul.* 2,28 (*PL* 44, 693).

Catholic doctor[227] of the Church, highly praised among Catholic bishops, outstanding for his knowledge and reputation, we have an energetic defender (*defensor acerrimus*) of the Catholic Church against heretics.[228] It is evident that he is worthy of being a member of the court.[229] Within the list of doctors, Hilary is given a rather important place.[230] He is evidently present whenever Augustine offers a long list of all the doctors, but even in cases Augustine mentions only a few, Hilary is quite regularly on the list.[231] In this regard, one should remember that Pelagius himself quoted from Hilary in his *De natura*. By mentioning the bishop of Poitiers often, Augustine evidently wanted to show that he was in line with this Hilary. Seven texts from Hilary are quoted.[232]

227 *C. Iul. imp.* 1,71 (*CSEL* 85/1, 83).

228 *C. Iul.* 1,9 (*PL* 44, 645): 'Ecclesiae catholicae adversus haereticos acerrimum defensorem venerandum quis ignoret Hilarium episcopum Gallum? ...Hunc virum tanta in episcopis catholicis laude praeclarum, tanta notitia famaque conspicuum...'.

229 *C. Iul. imp.* 2,37 (*CSEL* 85/1, 189).

230 For a different opinion, see O'Donnell, 'The Authority of Augustine', 11.

231 *C. Iul.* 1,22 (*PL* 44, 655), (mentioned together with the Roman Innocent, the Carthaginian Cyprian, the Cappadocian Basil, the Nazianzean Gregory and the Milanese Ambrose); 2,30 (*PL* 44, 693), (together with Cyprian, Gregory and Ambrose); 2,33 (*PL* 44, 696), (explicitly mentioned, together with Cyprian and Gregory in support of Ambrose); 2,35 (*PL* 44, 698), (together with Gregory and Ambrose); 6,71 (*PL* 44, 866), (together with Gregory and Ambrose); *C. Iul. imp.* 1,9 (*CSEL* 85/1, 10), (together with Ambrose, Gregory, and Cyprian); 1,52 (*CSEL* 85/1, 47), (together with Cyprian, Ambrose, Gregory, and John Chrysostom); 1,59 (*CSEL* 85/1, 56), (together with Cyprian, Ambrose, Gregory, Basil, and John Chrysostom); 1,117 (*CSEL* 85/1, 134), (together with Ambrose, Gregory, and Cyprian); 2,33 (*CSEL* 85/1, 186), (together with Cyprian, Ambrose, and Gregory); 2,37 (*CSEL* 85/1, 189), (together with Cyprian, Ambrose, Gregory, Basil, and John); 4,109 (*CSEL* 85/2, 117).

232 *Tractatus in Psalmum* 1,1; *Tractatus in Psalmum* 51,23; *Tractatus in Psalmum* 118,27; 118,175; 118,22; *Expositio in Iob;* the seventh text is a compilation of *De Trinitate* 10,24–25 and *In Matthaeum* 10,23–24. The commentary on Job is lost; see Georges Folliet, 'Le fragment d'Hilaire 'Quas Iob litteras.' Son interprétation d'après Hilaire, Pélage et Augustin', in Edmond-René Labande (ed.), *Hilaire et son temps* (Actes du colloque de Poitiers [29 septembre–3 octobre 1968] à l'occasion du XVIe centenaire de la mort de saint Hilaire), (Paris: Études augustiniennes, 1969), 149–58; also Jean Doignon, 'Une formule-clé du fragment sur Job d'Hilaire de Poitiers, inspiré d'Origène et transmis par Augustin (*Contra Iulianum* 2,8,27)', *Vigiliae Christianae* 35 (1981), 209–21. On the compilation of *De Trinitate* and *In Matthaeum*, see Jean Doignon, 'Testimonia d'Hilaire de Poitiers dans le "Contra Iulianum" d'Augustin: Les texts, leur groupement, leur "lecture"', *Revue Bénédictine* 91 (1981), 7–19.

It will be no surprise that Ambrose is the one to whom Augustine appeals most often.[233] He is called a holy,[234] great,[235] and blessed man,[236] a man of God,[237] an excellent steward of God,[238] a lucid and clear river of eloquence,[239] steadfast in the Catholic faith,[240] and the Catholic conqueror of heretics.[241] He understands scripture,[242] is gifted with Christian wisdom,[243] is worthy of being honoured,[244] and is, in sum, a memorable Catholic doctor,[245] a *pontifex magnus*.[246] With the weight of his authority, Ambrose will destroy Julian.[247] Ambrose was Augustine's teacher,[248] and is still his solace,[249] whom he honors as a father, for Ambrose gave Augustine his birth in Christ through the Gospel.[250] With some pride, Augustine mentions that he was baptised by the bishop of

233 Of the relation between Ambrose and Augustine, studies abound; see Bastiaensen, 'Augustin et ses prédécesseurs latins chrétiens', 30–34. On the epithets given by Augustine to Ambrose, see Barbara Beyenka, 'The Names of St. Ambrose in the Works of St. Augustine', *Augustinian Studies* 5 (1974), 19–28; with regard to the topics under discussion, see Giuseppe Ferretti, *L'influsso di S. Ambrogio in S. Agostino* (Faenza: Fratelli Lega, 1951), 41–75; Claudio Basevi, 'Alle fonti della dottrina agostiniana dell' Incarnazione: l'influenza della cristologie di sant'Ambrogio', *Scripta Theologica* 7 (1975), 499–529.

234 *C ep. Pel.* 4,29 (CSEL 60, 561); 4,30 (CSEL 60, 562); 4,32 (CSEL 60, 568); *C. Iul.* 1,32 (PL 44, 662); 2,4 (PL 44, 674); 2,10 (PL 44, 680); 2,19 (PL 44, 686); 2,23 (PL 44, 689); 2,24 (PL 44, 690); 3,2 (PL 44, 702); *C. Iul. Imp.* 1,115 (CSEL 85/1, 133); 6,14 (CSEL 85/2, 329).

235 *C ep. Pel.* 4,30 (CSEL 60, 563).

236 *C. Iul.* 2,4 (PL 44, 674); 2,8 (PL 44, 678); 2,9 (PL 44, 679); 2,13 (PL 44, 683); 2,14 (PL 44, 684); 2,32 (PL 44, 695); 2,33 (PL 44, 696); *C. Iul. imp.* 1,71 (CSEL 85/1, 82); 4,108 (CSEL 85/2, 116); 6,12 (CSEL 85/2, 319).

237 *C ep. Pel.* 4,30 (CSEL 60, 563).

238 *C. Iul.* 1,10 (PL 44, 645).

239 *C. Iul.* 2,11 (PL 44, 681).

240 *C ep. Pel.* 4,29 (CSEL 60, 561); 4,30 (CSEL 60, 563).

241 *C. Iul. imp.* 4,50 (CSEL 85/1, 56).

242 *C. Iul. imp.* 1,135 (CSEL 85/1, 151); 5,25 (CSEL 85/2, 219).

243 *C. Iul. imp.* 1,71 (CSEL 85/1, 83).

244 *C ep. Pel.* 4,30 (CSEL 60, 561); *C. Iul.* 1,11 (PL 44, 647); 2,14 (PL 44, 683).

245 *C. Iul.* 2,15 (PL 44, 684); *C. Iul. imp.* 4,114 (CSEL 85/2, 125); 6,6 (CSEL 85/2, 299).

246 *C. Iul. imp.* 2,8 (CSEL 85/1, 168).

247 *C. Iul.* 2,5 (PL 44, 675).

248 *C. Iul.* 2,21 (PL 44, 688): '...Ambrosium, doctorem meum...'; *C. Iul. imp.* 1,48 (CSEL 85/1, 38): '...Ambrosius doctor meus...'; 5,25 (CSEL 85/2, 219): '...meumque doctorem'; 5,41 (CSEL 85/2, 243): 'meus doctor'.

249 *C. Iul. imp.* 4,109 (CSEL 85/2, 117).

250 *C. Iul.* 1,10 (PL 44, 645): '...quem veneror ut patrem: in Christo enim Jesu per Evangelium ipse me genuit...'.

Milan.[251] Moreover, Augustine was an eyewitness of Ambrose's efforts to defend the faith and the Roman world rightly praises him for that.[252] He heard him speak and has read his works.[253] Augustine emphasises that he is minor compared to Ambrose, but remains convinced that with regard to the doctrine of original sin, they both hold the same opinion.[254]

Needless to say, Augustine explicitly mentions that Pelagius had praised Ambrose in his treatise *Pro libero arbitrio*. In this work, Pelagius described Ambrose as the flower of the Latin authors. Furthermore, he stressed that the faith and the interpretation of scripture of the bishop of Milan was so pure that even his enemies did not dare to criticise him on these two points. For Pelagius at least, Ambrose was an uncontested authority. It is for precisely that reason that Augustine quotes from Ambrose in *Nupt. et con.* 1,40. During the controversy with Julian, Augustine will time and again confront Julian with this attitude of Pelagius towards Ambrose,[255] and will add that Julian will never find a better judge than Ambrose.[256] The fact that Ambrose was an Italian also plays a role:

---

251 *Nupt. et con.* 1,40 (CSEL 42, 251): '…beatus Ambrosius Mediolanensis episcopus, cuius sacerdotali ministerio lauacrum regenerationis accepi…'; *C. Iul.* 1,10 (PL 44, 645); *C. Iul. imp.* 1,59 (CSEL 85/1, 57); 6,21 (CSEL 85/2, 364).

252 *C. Iul.* 1,10 (PL 44, 645): 'Beatum loquor Ambrosium, cuius pro catholica fide gratiam, constantiam, labores, pericula, sive operibus sive sermonibus, et ipse sum expertus, et mecum non dubitat orbis praedicare Romanus'.

253 *C. Iul. imp.* 6,21 (CSEL 85/2, 364): 'Meus est praeceptor Ambrosius, cuius non solum libros legi, sed verba etiam loquentis audiui…'.

254 *C. Iul. imp.* 6,21 (CSEL 85/2, 364): 'Longe sum quidem impar meritis eius: sed confiteor et profiteor me in hac causa nihil ab hoc meo praeceptore differre'; also *C. Iul.* III,48, PL 44, 726: 'hoc sentio, quod sentit Ambrosius' (with regard to lust).

255 See *Gr. et pecc. or.* 1,47 (CSEL 42, 159–60). The fact that Pelagius highly esteemed Ambrose is mentioned quite often by Augustine; see also *Nupt. et con.* 1,40 (CSEL 42, 252); 2,15 (CSEL 42, 268); 2,51 (CSEL 42, 307); 2,52 (CSEL 42, 308); *C ep. Pel.* 4,29 (CSEL 60, 559–61); *C. Iul.* 1,30 (PL 44, 661); 1,35 (PL 44, 666), (Pelagius is called here Julian's bad doctor and teacher); 1,44 (PL 44, 671), (Pelagius is again called a bad doctor); 2,11 (PL 44, 681); II,15, PL 44, 684 ('quod saepe dicendum est'); II,21, PL 44, 688; II,32, PL 44, 695; *C. Iul. imp.* I,2, CSEL 85,1, p. 7; I,48, CSEL 85,1, p. 39; I,52, CSEL 85,1, p. 47; I,59, CSEL 85,1, p. 57; II,8, CSEL 85,1, p. 168 (Pelagius, excellently praising Ambrose, 'pontifex magnus', is called here heresiarch); II,36, CSEL 85,1, pp. 188–89; II,202, CSEL 85,1, p. 314; II,208, CSEL 85,1, p. 319; III,56, CSEL 85,1, p. 395; III,178, CSEL 85,1, p. 479; III,213, CSEL 85,1, p. 505; IV,10, CSEL 85,2, p. 15; IV,67, CSEL 85,2, p. 72; IV,89, CSEL 85,2, p. 93; IV,106, CSEL 85,2, p. 114; IV,118, CSEL 85,2, p. 130; VI,21, CSEL 85,2, p. 364. No wonder that Augustine exhorts Julian to imitate Ambrose, who is praised by Pelagius, rather than Pelagius himself; see *Contra Iulianum* I,11, PL 44, 646; *C. Iul. imp.* I,2, CSEL 85,1, p. 7; I,48, CSEL 85,1, p. 39; I,67, CSEL 85,1, p. 395; III,200, CSEL 85,1, p. 499.

256 *C. Iul. imp.* 1,2 (CSEL 85/1, 6–7): 'Quem vero iudicem potes Ambrosio reperire meliorem?'; see M. Zelzer, 'Quem vero iudicem potes Ambrosio reperire meliorem? (*Aug., Op. imperf.*

Julian regarded the Punic Augustine with disdain, but will now be confronted with an Italian and a Catholic.[257] From Ambrose, 44 texts taken from 12 works are quoted,[258] Ambrose thus being the most important witness for Augustine.

Innocent, holy bishop of Rome,[259] also belongs to the court of judges, and this for good reasons.[260] Under Innocent, Julian became bishop of Aeclanum. Caelestius himself had expressed his agreement with the content of Innocent's letters to the Africans.[261] Pelagius was willing to be corrected by this man who held both the chair and faith of Peter.[262] Therefore, Innocent deserves the first rank in the court of judges.[263] The same bishop had, in the letters sent to Africa, followed the positions held by the Apostolic See and the Roman Church from

---

I,2)', *Studia Patristica* 33 (1997), 280–85.

257 *C. Iul. imp.* 1,59 (CSEL 85,1, 56–57).

258 *De paradiso* 6,29,30; 10,47; 11,53; 11,54; 12,60;13,67; 15,77; *Apologia prophetae David* I,11,56 (*x*2); 11,57 (*x*2); *Expositio in Lucam* 1,37; 2,56; 2,84; 4,67; 7,27;7,73; 7,141–43; 7,234; *En. in Ps.* 48,8; *De bono mortis* 11,49; *De fuga saeculi* 1–2; 3,15; 7,39; *De paenitentia* I,13; *De Noe* 3,7; *De Isaac vel anima* 7,60; 8,65; *De Tobia* 9,33; 23,88; Thanks to Augustine, we have six texts from *De sacramento regenerationis sive de philosophia* and seven texts from *Expositio In Isaiam*, works that are otherwise lost.

259 *C. Iul.* 1,32 (PL 44, 663).

260 Although Augustine clearly considers Innocent on the African side, the correct interpretation of Innocent's own position on the topics under discussion is still matter for debate; see M. Lamberigts, 'Innocentius episcopus Romanus', in AL 3,3/4 (Basel, 2006), 613–19. In any case, in the debate with Julian, Augustine prefers to refer to Innocent's attitude towards the controversy, rather than that of Zosimus, who, to say the least, was rather unstable in his subsequent positions. However, Augustine tries to explain Zosimus' attitude as benevolent, because he still hoped for a conversion of Caelestius; see, e.g. *C. ep. Pel.* 2,5 (CSEL 60, 465). With regard to the problematic character of this explanation, see M. Lamberigts, 'Augustine and Julian of Aeclanum on Zosimus', *Augustiniana* 42 (1992), 311–30.

261 *C ep. Pel.* 2,5 (CSEL 60, 465): '…propter illud quod se papae Innocentii litteris consentire ipse responderat…'; also 2,6 (CSEL 60, 466).

262 Pelagius, *Libellus fidei* 14, (PL 45, 1718): 'In qua si minus perite aut parum caute aliquid forte positum est, emendari cupimus a te qui Petri et fidem et sedem tenes'. Augustine stresses the fact that Innocent was bishop of Rome, the place of Peter's death; see *C ep. Pel.* 2,6 (CSEL 60, 466); 2,7 (CSEL 60, 467); *C. Iul.* 1,13 (PL 44, 648).

263 *C. Iul.* 1,13 (PL 44, 648): 'Cum his etiam ipse considet, etsi posterior tempore, prior loco'. On Augustine's position, see, among others, Batiffol, *Le catholicisme de saint Augustin*, 484; Hofmann, *Der Kirchenbegriff des hl. Augustinus*, pp. 446–48; Mártil, *La tradición en san Agustín*, 210–12; Zumkeller, *Schriften gegen die Pelagianer* III, pp. 513–16; De Veer, *Primauté du pape et collegialité*, in BA 23, 748–53. Innocent was aware of this; cf. Wermelinger, *Rom und Pelagius*, 117–23. However, with one exception (*C. Iul.* 1,22, PL 44, 655), Augustine never puts Innocent on the first place in his list of giants; see, e.g., *C. Iul.* 2,33 (PL 44, 697); 2,37

the very beginning, and this along with the other churches. 'What else could he have done?' Augustine cries out.[264] His letters removed all doubt from the matter under discussion.[265] He had condemned Pelagius and Caelestius.[266] As a member of the Western Church, Julian should submit to the authority of this Western bishop.[267] In any case, it would have been better if, from his youth onwards, Julian had listened to Innocent that he might have been rescued from Pelagian snares.[268]

Although Jerome was only a priest, he deserves a place in the college of doctors, according to Augustine.[269] Jerome was a man learned in Greek and Latin, very familiar with the Hebrew language,[270] and who contributed much to the development of Catholic education in the Latin language.[271] Jerome moved from the Western to the Eastern Church. He had read most of what was written before him about the teaching of the Church and this from both sides of the world. In the matter under discussion, he shares our position, Augustine claims.[272] One gets the impression that Augustine's praise of the person of Jerome is not completely in proportion with the use the bishop of Hippo makes of him. One has to wait until *C. Iul.* 1,34 before coming across the name of Jerome. Moreover, only one text of Jerome is quoted, *In Ionam* 3,5, a text

(PL 44, 701); 3,32 (PL 44, 719). Quotes are from Innocent's letters to the Synod of Carthage (*Inter epistulas Augustini* 181,7), and Milevis (*Inter epistulas Augustini* 182,4,5).

264 *C. Iul.*1,13 (PL 44, 648): 'Quid enim potuit ille vir sanctus Africanis respondere conciliis, nisi quod antiquitus apostolica sedes et Romana cum caeteris tenet perseueranter Ecclesia?'; also see *C. ep. Pel.* 2,8 (CSEL 60, 468).

265 *C ep. Pel.* 2,5 (CSEL 60, 464); 2, 7–8 (CSEL 60, 467–68).

266 *C ep. Pel.* 2,5 (CSEL 60, 465); *C. Iul.* 2,36 (PL 44, 699).

267 *C. Iul.* 1,14 (PL 44, 648–49): 'Non est ergo cur provoces ad orientis antistites; quia et ipsi utique christiani sunt, et utriusque partis terrarum fides ista una est; quia et fides ista christiana est: et te certe occidentalis terra generauit, occidentalis regenerauit ecclesia'.

268 *C. Iul.* 1,13 (PL 44, 648).

269 On Jerome and his contacts with Augustine, see Alfons Fürst, 'Hieronymus', in C. Mayer (ed.), *Augustinus-Lexikon* 3-2/3 (Basel: Schwabe, 2004), 317–36; for his place in Augustine's tradition argument, see also De Simone, *Modern Research on the Sources of Saint Augustine's Doctrine of Original Sin*, 224–27.

270 *C. Iul.* 1,34 (PL 44, 665).

271 *C. Iul.* 2,36 (PL 44, 699).

272 *C. Iul.* 1,34 (PL 44, 665): '…ex occidentali ad orientalem transiens ecclesiam, in locis sanctis atque in litteris sacris, usque ad decrepitam vixit aetatem: omnesque vel pene omnes qui ante illum aliquid ex utraque parte orbis de doctrina ecclesiastica scripserant legit, nec aliam de hac re tenuit prompsitque sententiam.' Also in 2,33 (PL 44, 697) ('velis nolis' [Julian is inferred]) and 2,36 (PL 44, 699), Augustine explicitly mentions the fact that Jerome is a priest. Also consult Wermelinger, *Rom und Pelagius*, 276–77.

which was already used more substantially in *De peccatorum meritis et remissione* 3,12.[273] Jerome's *Dialogus aduersus Pelagianos* is not referred to, although the bishop of Hippo was aware of its existence.[274]

It seems that Augustine was conscious of the fact that the presence of both Innocent and Jerome in the court (the latter was considered his rival by Pelagius)[275] might be a problem for Julian. Indeed, the first had condemned Pelagius and Caelestius, the second had defended the Catholic faith against Pelagius in the East.[276] With regard to the first, Julian should reread what Pelagius said about this man. In the case of Jerome, Augustine states that he did not use Jerome's work against the Pelagians, but quoted from those writings from the time when he was free of all bias.[277] But even then, one cannot say that Jerome has a considerable place in Augustine's appeal to the Fathers. Further, as it becomes clear in *C. Iul. imp.* 4,88, Jerome's position in his *Dialogus aduersus Pelagianos* is a bit problematic. One might even suggest that Augustine, in a sense distanced himself from Jerome's position with regard to Pelagianism. Indeed, in *Ad Florum* 4,88,[278] Julian referred to two passages of Jerome's *Dialogus*. In the first passage, Jerome remarked that in a gospel *iuxta Hebraeos*, which was written in the Chaldaic and Syriac language, but in Hebrew letters, the mother and brothers of Jesus invited him to go with them to John the Baptist in order to receive baptism for the remission of sin. Jesus wondered why he should do so, '*Nisi forte hoc ipsum quod dixi, ignorantia est*'.[279] The conclusions drawn by Julian are not present in this text of Jerome's: Jerome did not speak of the presence of natural or voluntary sin in Christ, but, as we know, sins of ignorance were considered by Augustine signs of the existence of original sin.[280] Julian

273 *C. Iul.* 1,34 (*PL* 44, 665). See also Yvette Duval, 'Saint Augustin et le Commentaire sur Jonas de saint Jérôme', *Revue des études augustiniennes* 12 (1966), 9–40, esp. 14–21.

274 See Duval, 'Saint Augustin', 20.

275 *C. Iul.* 2,36 (*PL* 44, 699): '…quod ei tanquam aemulo inviderit.'

276 *C. Iul.* 2,36 (*PL* 44, 699): 'Ex quibus papam Innocentium et presbyterum Hieronymum retrahere fortasse tentabis: istum, quia Pelagium Coelestiumque damnavit; illum, quia in oriente contra Pelagium catholicam fidem pia intentione defendit'.

277 *C. Iul.* 2,36 (*PL* 44, 700).

278 *CSEL* 85/2, 90.

279 Jerome, *Dialogus adversus Pelagianos* 3,2 (*CCSL* 80, 99).

280 *Ad Florum* 4,88 (*CSEL* 85/2, 90): 'Verum his ut res postulabat impletis iuvat te vel mediocriter convenire, qua fiducia tu, cum Hieronymi scripta collaudes, dicas in Christo non fuisse peccatum, cum ille in eo dialogo, quem sub nomine Attici et Critoboli mira [et] ut talem fidem decebat venustate composuit, etiam quinti evangelii, quod a se translatum dicit, testimonio nitatur ostendere Christum non solum naturale, verum etiam voluntarium habuisse peccatum, propter quod se cognoverit Iohannis baptismate diluendum'.

found a much better argument against Jerome's orthodoxy in *Dialogus aduersus Pelagianos* 2,17, where Atticus (the anti-Pelagian in the dialogue), on the basis of John 7,10, makes it clear that the man Jesus is a liar: '*Iterum se negauit, et fecit quod prius negauerat*' and that this should be attributed to the flesh, '*ad carnem*'.[281] In a no-longer extant letter to Alexandria,[282] Augustine had praised Jerome's work to the extent that he claimed that Pelagius, overwhelmed by the work's scriptural references, could no longer defend the existence of free choice. However, Julian continues, Pelagius did react to this work. Anyway, Julian claims, you [Augustine] are not in agreement with scripture, and not even with the supporters of your doctrine. Julian is upset that Augustine could praise a man who was not afraid to blaspheme Christ to the point that he claimed that Christ had sinned![283] In any case, according to Julian, Jerome's view—Augustine is here called a servant (*assecla*) of Jerome—is contradicted by Ambrose, for whom Christ was always free from any lie.[284]

Although Augustine knew Jerome's work, his first reaction is to say that Julian should have quoted these texts in order to show what was wrong with Jerome's view.[285] Next, he quotes a text from Ambrose, introducing it as follows: 'I, in fact, set before you the statement, not of Jerome, but of Ambrose, and not rephrased in my own words, but expressed in his words'.[286] Further, Augustine twice explicitly recognises the possibility that Jerome might have said things that were not in line with the other illustrious teachers of the Catholic Church.[287] Finally, he admits that when anything displeases him in his own writings, as in those of his friends, he will criticise it.[288] In any case, Augustine does not think that there is any validity in Julian's accusation that he is Jerome's servant,[289] but the fact remains, Jerome gets a low profile in the debate with Julian.

281 Jerome, *Dialogus adversus Pelagianos* 2,17 (CCSL 80, 90): 'Iturum se negauit, et fecit quod prius negauerat: latrat Porphyrius, inconstantiae ac mutationis accusat, nesciens omnia scandala ad carnem esse referenda'.

282 See Yvette Duval, *Notes complémentaires. Lettre 4**, in BA 46B, *Lettres 1*-29** (Paris: Desclée de Brouwer, 1987), 430–42, esp. 434–35.

283 Jul., *Ad Florum* 4,88 (CSEL 85/2, 90–91).

284 Jul., *Ad Florum* 4,121 (CSEL 85/2, 137–38).

285 *C. Iul. imp.* 4,88 (CSEL 85/2, 91).

286 *C. Iul. imp.* 4,88 (CSEL 85/2, 91): 'Ego sane non Hieronymi sed Ambrosii nec meis commemoratam, sed verbis eius expressam sententiam tibi opposui…'.

287 *C. Iul. imp.* 4,88 (CSEL 85/2, 91); 4,89 (CSEL 85/2, 93).

288 *C. Iul. imp.* 4,88 (CSEL 85/2, 93): '…ac per hoc si quid mihi displicet, reprehendo in amici scriptis sicut in meis…'.

289 *C. Iul. imp.* 4, 122 (CSEL 85/2, 139). Augustine then repeats his argument: I need Jerome's text in order to interpret it or to reject it.

Don't Forget the Greek Fathers

According to Augustine, there was no need for Julian to appeal to Eastern bishops, for the West was the land of his birth; the Western Church was also the Church of his rebirth. Moreover, the Christian faith in both West and East was one.[290] In other words, Julian's appeal to the East will not change the situation. However, Augustine rhetorically assures Julian he will have an Eastern bishop in his court of judges, and the one he will have is Gregory of Nazianzus!

Gregory is introduced by Augustine as a man with a great name, excellent fame, and an illustrious bishop whose speeches have rightly been translated into Latin.[291] Surprisingly, Augustine does not seem to be very familiar with the biography of Gregory. In *C. Iul.* 1,19, Gregory, instead of Gregory of Nyssa, is called the brother of Basil: '*tam insignes viri…et, sicut fertur, etiam carne germani*.' The *fertur* might suggest that Augustine's information is second-hand.[292] Further, Augustine clearly does not know when Gregory wrote his books. The work *De fuga sua*, written in 362, is placed in the period when Gregory was already bishop.[293] This unfamiliarity with Gregory's life and work does not prevent Augustine from putting the Greek Catholic doctor[294] on his list of famous doctors,[295] quite often as the first of the Eastern Fathers,[296] for his doctrine is

---

290 *C. Iul.* 1,14 (*PL* 44, 648): 'Non est ergo cur provoces ad Orientis antistites; quia et ipsi utique christiani sunt, et utriusque partis terrarum fides ista una est; quia et fides ista christiana est: et te certe occidentalis terra generavit, occidentalis regeneravit ecclesia'.

291 *C. Iul.* 1,15 (*PL* 44, 649): 'Sed non tibi deerit magni nominis et fama celeberrima illustris episcopus etiam de partibus Orientis, cuius eloquia ingentis merito gratiae, etiam in linguam latinam translata usquequaque claruerunt'. The translator was likely Rufinus; see Berthold Altaner, 'Augustinus und Gregor von Nazianz, Gregor von Nyssa', in Berthold Altaner (ed.), *Kleine Patristische Schriften* (TU 83), (Berlin: Akademie-Verlag, 1967), 277–85, esp. 279. Augustine only seems to know those works of Gregory that are translated by Rufinus; see Pierre Courcelle, *Les lettres grecques en occident: de Macrobe à Cassiodore* (Paris: de Boccard, 1948), 189; also Bartelink, *Die Beinflußung Augustins durch die griechischen Patres*, 20, n. 57.

292 *C. Iul.* 1,19 (*PL* 44, 652).

293 *C. Iul. imp.* 1,69 (*CSEL* 85/1, 77); for the date of his ordination, see *Grégoire de Nazianze. Discours 1–3*, J. Bernardi (ed.), *SC* 247 (Paris: Éditions du Cerf, 1978), 17. Another proof of Augustine's unfamiliarity with Gregory's work is already present in his *Ep.* 148,10,15 (*CSEL* 44, 340–45), where he refers to Gregory, *sanctus episcopus orientalis*, quoted from work he attributed to Gregory, while the text is found in Gregory of Elvira's *De fide orthodoxa contra Arianos*. See Altaner, *Augustinus und Gregor von Nazianz, Gregor von Nyssa*, 278.

294 *C. Iul. imp.* 2,33 (*CSEL* 85/1, 186).

295 *C. Iul. imp.* 1,53 (*CSEL* 85/1, 50).

296 See *C. Iul.* 2,33 (*PL* 44, 697); 2,37 (*PL* 700–01) (*x*2); 3,32 (*PL* 44, 719); *C. Iul. imp.* 1,59 (*CSEL* 85/1, 59); 2,37 (*CSEL* 85/1, 189); 4,72 (*CSEL* 85/2, 75); 4,73 (*CSEL* 85/2, 75).

in harmony with that of his brothers and co-doctors.[297] Julian would be better off listening to Gregory than to Caelestius.[298] In the debate with Julian, Augustine quotes in all six texts, taken from the *Apologia pro sua fuga* and five *Orationes*.[299]

Quite rhetorically, Augustine asks Julian if Gregory alone is not sufficient to demonstrate the authority of the Eastern bishops: he is a great man, but Gregory is well aware that all he said he had learned from the Christian faith. He is famous and venerated by the faithful, but only because they know that what he has taught is in accord with the rule of the truth.[300] In order to 'satisfy' Julian, Augustine deliberately adds a second Eastern witness, Basil of Caesarea, an authority recognised by Julian himself.[301]

Given Julian's recognition of the authority of Basil (and Chrysostom),[302] Augustine wants to prove that, through the works of these men, he can refute Julian.[303] Like the other doctors, Basil is called a holy, learned, and famous man, a Christian bishop.[304] Although translations are available, Augustine prefers to offer his own word-by-word translation from the Greek of a sermon of Basil's on fasting in order to remain more faithful to the original text.[305] By quoting

297 *C. Iul.* 2,7 (*PL* 44, 677).

298 *C. Iul. imp.* 1,67 (*CSEL* 85/1, 71).

299 *Apologia pro sua fuga* 2,91; *Oratio* 17,5; 36,15; 38,4; 38,17; 41,14.

300 *C. Iul.* 1,16 (*PL* 44, 650): 'Est quidem tanta persona, ut neque ille hoc nisi ex fide christiana omnibus notissima diceret, nec illi eum tam clarum haberent atque venerandum, nisi haec ab illo dicta ex regula notissimae veritatis agnoscerent'.

301 *C. Iul.* 1,16 (*PL* 44, 650): 'Sed si vis addimus huic et sanctum Basilium, imo velis nolis addendus est, maxime quia et tu de libro eius, quem scripsit adversus Manichaeos, in quarto volumine huius operis tui aliquid putasti esse ponendum, quod ad causam peccati originalis per unum intrantis in mundum, et per omnes homines transeuntis omnino non pertinet'. With regard to Augustine's use of the work of Basil, see Berthold Altaner, 'Augustinus und Basilius der Große', in B. Altaner (ed.)., *Kleine Patristische Schriften* (TU 83), (Berlin: Akademie-Verlag, 1967), 269–76; Bartelink, *Augustin und die griechischen Patres*, 19–20; It is clear that Augustine only knows this pseudo-Basilian work through his reading of Julian; see Lössl, *Intellectus gratiae*, 336, n. 134. With regard to the rhetorical aspect, see Weber, *Some Literary Aspects of the Debate between Julian of Eclanum and Augustine*, 293.

302 *C. Iul.* 1,35 (*PL* 44, 666): '...sic et tu loquentibus tibi tot venerabilibus viris...episcopis Basilio et Ioanne, quos tu quoque in sanctis eruditis veridica attestatione posuisti...'.

303 See *C. Iul.* 6,69 (*PL* 44, 865).

304 See *C. Iul.* 1,16 (*PL* 44, 650), (sanctus); 1,35 (*PL* 44, 666), (Christian bishop); 2,33 (*PL* 44, 697), (one of the *clarissimi sacerdotes*); 2,37 (*PL* 44, 700), (one of the learned, earnest, holy, and sharp defenders of the faith).

305 *C. Iul.* 1,18 (*PL* 44, 652): 'Quod etsi reperi interpretatum, tamen propter diligentiorem veri fidem, verbum e verbo malui transferre de Graeco.'

Basil he wants to make clear that if Julian had read this author more carefully, he would not have quoted a text from Basil that had nothing to do with the topic under discussion.[306] Apart from reinterpreting the texts as offered by Julian, Augustine quotes two texts from Basil himself, texts he knows through translation, but one of the two he wrongly attributes to Chrysostom.[307]

It is well known that John Chrysostom was highly esteemed, not only in the inner circle of Julian's family and friends, but also by Pelagius, who, in his debate with Augustine, had already referred to Chrysostom.[308] Further, Julian had referred to Chrysostom's *Oratio ad Neophytos* as a support for his own position that baptism of infants was not needed for the remission of original sin.

---

306 *C. Iul.* 1,18 (*PL* 44, 652); that the text quoted by Julian is not relevant for the dispute, is repeated in 1,30 (*PL* 44, 661).

307 *Sermo I De ieiunio* 1, 3–4; *Oratio* 13,2 (attributed to Chrysostom); see Altaner, *Augustinus und Basilius der Große*, 274–75.

308 See *Nat. et grat.* 76 (*CSEL* 60, 291). With regard to the sympathy of the Pelagians for Chrysostom, see Brown, *Pelagius and his Supporters*, 214–16. Anianus of Celada, regularly associated with Pelagius, translated quite a number of Chrysostom's works; see Berthold Altaner, 'Altlateinische Übersetzungen von Chrysostomusschriften', in B. Altaner (ed.), *Kleine patristische Schriften* (TU 83), (Berlin: Akademie-Verlag, 1967), 416–36, esp. 418; also see Bartelink, *Augustin und die griechischen Patres*, 22–23. On Anianus, see Christoph Breuer-Winkler, 'Anianus', *Lexikon für Theologie und Kirche* 1 (1993), 677; Pietri and Pietri, *Prosopographie de l'Italie chrétienne (313–604)*, s.v. 'Annianus', 141–42. Charles Pietri, 'Esquisse de conclusion. L'aristocratie chrétienne entre Jean de Constantinople et Augustin d'Hippone', in Charles Kannengiesser (ed.), *Jean Chrysostome et Augustin (Actes du colloque de Chantilly, 22–24 septembre 1974)* (Théologie historique 35), (Paris: Beauchesne, 1975), 283–305, pays much attention to the contacts between the different noble families in East and West, and their relations to both Chrysostom and Augustine. Augustine came rather late in contact with the writings of Chrysostom; see Berthold Altaner, *Augustinus und Chrysostomus*, in B. Altaner (ed.), *Kleine Patristische Schriften* (TU 83), (Berlin: Akademie-Verlag, 1967), 302–11, esp. 303: 'Wir gewinnen den Eindruck, daß Augustinus auch damals (414/415) noch keine Schriften des Konstantinopeler Bischofs kannte'; also Bartelink, *Augustin und die griechischen Patres*, 22–23. On Chrysostom, Augustine, and the Pelagian controversy, see François-Joseph Thonnard, 'Saint Jean Chrysostome et saint Augustin dans la controverse pélagienne', *Revue des Études byzantines* 25 (1967), 189–218; R. Brändle, 'La ricezione di Giovanni Crisostomo nell' opera di Agostino', in *Giovanni Crisostomo: Oriente e Occidente tra IV e V secolo. XXXIII Incontro di studiosi dell' antichità Cristiana. Roma, 6–8 maggio 2004* (Studia Ephemeridis Augustinianum 93) (Rome: Institutum Patristicum Augustinianum, 2005), 885–95, esp. 888–95; M. Zelzer, 'Giovanni Crisostomo nella controversia tra Giuliano d'Eclano e Agostino', in *Giovanni Crisostomo: Oriente e Occidente tra IV e V secolo. XXXIII Incontro di studiosi dell' antichità Cristiana. Roma, 6–8 maggio 2004* (Studia Ephemeridis Augustinianum 93) (Rome: Institutum Patristicum Augustinianum, 2005), 927–32.

According to Julian, John denied that original sin existed in newly-born children.[309] It is Augustine's challenge to prove that this 'friend' of the Pelagians held positions similar to his own view,[310] and, indeed, in *C. Iul.* 1, no other author receives so much attention as Chrysostom (ten lengthy chapters!). John must be a member of the court, for the 'young' Julian thought he had found in John's writings arguments against the views held by so many and great colleagues of John.[311] Augustine explicitly states that if Julian was right, John's position could never have been preferred over that of so many great people with regard to a subject that the Christian faith and Catholic Church have never changed their opinions about. But, as one might expect, this eventuality is immediately excluded.[312] This position is substantiated with a whole series of texts taken from John's Homily 10 on Romans, in order to conclude that John is far from Julian's way of argumentation, for he does not deviate from the Catholic way of thinking.[313]

Just like the other members of Augustine's court of judges, John is called blessed and holy,[314] a bishop of excellent glory.[315] Learned in the Catholic faith and teaching,[316] he is its defender.[317] With regard to the interpretation of Rom. 5,12, he is said to stand more clearly than daylight in the truth of the Catholic faith.[318] With regard to the foundations of faith, Chrysostom holds the same

309 Jul., *Ad Turb.*, frg. 312 (CCSL 88, 393–94).

310 Augustine carefully reads the Greek original and presents then a 'verbum e verbo' for the Latin translation of the text; see *C. Iul.* 1,26 (PL 44, 658).

311 *C. Iul.*1,23 (PL 44, 656): 'Ecce etiam ipsum numero illi adiungo sanctorum. Ecce inter meos testes, vel inter nostros constituo iudices, quem putasti patronum tuum… Ingredere, sancte Ioannes, ingredere, et conside cum fratribus tuis, a quibus te nulla ratio et nulla tentatio separavit. Opus est et tua, et maxime tua sententia: quoniam in tuis litteris iste iuvenis invenisse se putat, unde tot tantorumque coepiscoporum tuorum se arbitratur percellere et evacuare sententias'.

312 *C. Iul.* 1,23 (PL 44, 656).

313 *C. Iul.* 1,28 (PL 44, 660); 1,30, (PL 44, 661); also 1,33 (PL 44, 663).

314 See *C. Iul.* 1,22 (PL 44, 655); 1,23 (PL 44, 656); 1,27, (PL 44, 658); 1,28 (PL 44, 660); 1,29 (PL 44, 661); 2,17 (PL 44, 685); 2,18 (PL 44, 685); *C. Iul. imp.* 6,9 (CSEL 85/2, 309); 6,26 (CSEL 85/2, 390).

315 *C. Iul. imp.* 6,7 (CSEL 85/2, 302).

316 *C. Iul.* 1,26 (PL 44, 658).

317 *C. Iul.* 1,28 (PL 44, 660): '…magno christianae fidei atque huius catholici dogmatis defensori…'.

318 *C. Iul.* 1,27 (PL 44, 658–59). Augustine seems to have the whole tenth homily of John on Romans at his disposal for he explicitly states: 'Quod totum quia longum est huic opera intexere, pauca inde contingam'.

ideas as the others.[319] Augustine quotes thirteen texts from six works attributed to Chrysostom. However, three of the quotations are taken from works wrongly attributed to Chrysostom.[320]

The last members of the court of judges are the fourteen bishops, present at the Synod of Diospolis. At first sight, the incorporation of these bishops in the court might be a surprise, for indeed, Pelagius had been acquitted by them. However, Augustine offers a series of good reasons why these bishops deserve a seat in the court of judges. These Eastern bishops all in the same way - '*uno eodemque modo*' - believe that all human beings are subjected to the sin of the first man.[321] As one they set Pelagius free because the latter had condemned those who stated that even children without baptism could possess eternal life.[322] Augustine is convinced that he believes what they believe, holds what they hold, teaches what they teach and preaches what they preach.[323] They judged all together in one place and thus really functioned as an assembly.[324] Further, Augustine time and again stresses that Pelagius' acquittal was motivated by the fact that, fearing a condemnation, he also condemned positions now under discussion. Augustine regularly suggests that Pelagius deceived the bishops at Diospolis,[325] who took him for a Catholic because they were only human, and understood Pelagius' comments according to the Catholic faith: '*secundum catholicam fidem*'.[326] In any case, the documentation makes clear that Augustine did not really know that much about the individual profiles of

319 *C. Iul.* 1,22 (*PL* 44, 655).

320 *Homiliae ad Neophytos in Genesim* 3,6;3,21; 9,4; 9,14; *De Lazaro resuscitato*; *In triduanam resurrectionem*; *Epistula ad Olympiam* 10,3; *Homilia in Epistulam ad Romanos* 10,1;10,2; 10,3; *Oratio* 13,2. Augustine attributes Basil's *Oratio* 13, the pseudo-Chrysostom sermon on the ressurection, and (Pseudo)-Potamius of Lissabon's sermon *De Lazaro resuscitato* to Chrysostom; cf. Altaner, *Augustinus und Johannes Chrysostomus*, 309–10. On the questionable attribution of the sermon to Potamius, see Zelzer, *Giovanni Crisostomo nella controversia tra Giuliano d'Eclano e Agostino*, 931–32.

321 *C. Iul.* 1,20 (*PL* 44, 654).

322 *C. Iul.* 1,32 (*PL* 44, 663).

323 *C. Iul.* 1,20 (*PL* 44, 654): '...quod credunt credo, quod tenent teneo, quod docent doceo, quod praedicant praedico...'.

324 *C. Iul.* 1,19 (*PL* 44, 652): '...quos uno loco simul inventos in istum consessum introducere valeamus...'.

325 *C ep. Pel.* 2,10 (*CSEL* 60, 470). Augustine suggests that Pelagius had condemned the statement that one receives grace according to one's merits, but that in his later writings he would have repeated this position he had first condemned. Similar critiques one will find in *C. Iul.*1,19 (*PL* 44, 653); *C. Iul. imp.* 4,43 (*CSEL* 85/2, 46). For an evaluation of Pelagius' attitude, see Wermelinger, *Rom und Pelagius*, 78–87.

326 *C. Iul.* 1,19 (*PL* 44, 651–52).

these bishops.[327] The importance of these bishops' testimony is already modest in *C. Iul.*, and becomes marginal in the *C. Iul. imp.*[328]

The profile of the predecessors is clear: they are men of great faith, stay within a tradition, represent chronological and geographical coherence and continuity in doctrine, possess authority, know how to cope with heresies, and are worthy of belonging to the college of judges Julian has constantly requested.[329]

Application and Function of the Appeal to Predecessors

According to Augustine, the type of judges Julian is searching for are highly trained experts in the liberal arts and familiar with the philosophers of this world.[330] Julian is accused of promoting a few of the secular philosophers[331] and Julian's problem is that he wants to have learned judges to the point that he no longer wants Catholic Christian judges.[332] In this context, it is interesting to note that Augustine was in no way impressed by the erudition of the pagan philosophers invoked by Julian; certainly they were wise and learned men, but not truly righteous, for not living by faith in Christ.[333] By searching for dialecticians, Julian wants to be seen as a clever, learned, and bad philosopher, as well as a dialectician, and, Augustine adds ironically,[334] seeks to avoid ecclesiastical judges.[335] What Julian misses are the eyes of faith of great and important people such as Ambrose, Cyprian, and all the other doctors of the Church.[336] Julian misses a lack of believing carefulness. Not willing to be nourished by the grace of Christ, he is unable to come to those things which have been hidden from the wise and prudent and have been revealed to the little ones.[337]

Julian wants to award himself the palm of victory against the many bishops of God who, before Augustine, had learned and taught in the Church of Christ.

---

327 Diospolis 11; 14; 17 (Wermelinger, *Rom und Pelagius*, 296–97).

328 This give nuance to Wermelinger's observation in *Rom und Pelagius*, 275 somewhat: 'Die anfängliche Zurückhaltung gegenüber Diospolis schwindet im augustinischen Schrifttum immer mehr'. In fact, only Diospolis 11 and 14 will be quoted in *C. Iul. imp.*

329 *C. Iul.* 2,8 (*PL* 44, 678).

330 *C. Iul. imp.* 2,1 (*CSEL* 85/1, 164); and also *C. Iul.* 3,2 (*PL* 44, 702).

331 *C. Iul. imp.* 2,4 (*CSEL* 85/1, 166).

332 *C. Iul. imp.* 2,1 (*CSEL* 85/1, 164).

333 *C. Iul.* 4,17 (*PL* 44, 745).

334 *C. Iul. imp.* 6,18 (*CCSL* 85/2, 351).

335 *C. Iul. imp.* 2,36 (*CSEL* 85/1, 188).

336 *C. Iul. imp.* 2,73 (*CSEL* 85/1, 217).

337 *C. Iul.* 2,3 (*PL* 44, 673).

The new heretic[338] wants to pollute with novelties this most strongly founded and ancient Catholic faith.[339] He wants to attract people to the novelty of his error.[340] Typical of such heretics is that they obscure with their interpretations what has always been clear.[341] Therefore, Augustine does not believe that reason, sound erudition, justice, piety, and scripture support Julian's position.[342]

Augustine invokes his authorities in order to show that his doctrine is supported by all the doctors of the Church (although he can only present the position of a few of them),[343] for he is convinced that the doctrine of original sin is not his own invention, but a doctrine held by the Catholic faith from its very beginning.[344] Erudition is important for Augustine: as seen in the presentation of the individual judges of the court; he mentions regularly that they are learned doctors. These people cannot be reckoned with the common ranks of workmen, soldiers, schoolboys, sailors, bartenders, fishermen, cooks and butchers, youths dismissed from monasteries, men from the ordinary run of clerics, or people who cannot judge doctrines through the categories of Aristotle; in sum, the sorts of people Julian was complaining about. When Julian uses descriptors such as country folk and people of the theater, he must see that he is attributing these qualifications to people like Cyprian and Ambrose and so many learned writers, companions in God's kingdom of heaven.[345] Someone like Ambrose, Augustine insists, is not simply someone from the common folk, those ignorant masses Julian looks down upon. Ambrose is a man Julian is in

338 *Nupt. et con.* 1,22 (*CSEL* 42, 235): '…noui haeretici…'; also 1,40, (*CSEL* 42, 251); 2,3 (*CSEL* 42, 255); 2,25 (*CSEL* 42, 278). On the use of such accusations in polemics, see Opelt, *Die Polemik in der christlichen lateinischen Literatur*, 158. It is quite evident that Julian was furious and upset when reading this accusation; cf. *Ad Turb.*, frg. 10 (*CCSL* 88, 342). Julian lamented this by calling Augustine a new heretic; Augustine was stirring up the common folk; frg. 251 (*CCSL* 88, 385). However, Julian used the same strategy.

339 *C. Iul.* 3,1 (*PL* 44, 701).

340 *C. Iul.* 1,4 (*PL* 44, 643).

341 *C. Iul. imp.* 1,22 (*CSEL* 85/1, 18): 'Novit enim, quemadmodum soleant haec verba apostolica quae praetermisit accipere catholicorum corda fidelium, quae verba tam recta et tanta luce fulgentia tenebrosis et tortuosis interpretationibus novi haeretici obscurare et depravare moliuntur'.

342 *C. Iul. imp.* 2,13 (*CSEL* 85,1, 171).

343 *C. Iul.* 1,5 (*PL* 44, 643).

344 *Nupt. et con.* 2,25 (*CSEL* 42, 278).

345 See *C. Iul.* 2,37 (*PL* 44, 700): 'Numquid Irenaeus, et Cyprianus, et Reticius, et Olympius, et Hilarius, et Gregorius, et Basilius, et Ambrosius, et Ioannes, de plebeia faece sellulariorum, sicut Tulliane iocaris, in vestram invidiam concitati sunt?'; *C. Iul. imp.* 2,14 (*CSEL* 85/1, 172): 'Vide sane, quemadmodum rurales et theatrales dicas Cyprianum et Ambrosium et tot eruditos in regno Dei scribas, socios eorum'.

no sense equal to in the worldly literature which Julian is so proud of: Ambrose is the person *par excellence* who meets the standards requested by Julian.[346] Moreover, with regard to the quality of his ecclesiastical writings, one should simply read the praise of Pelagius![347]

Because Julian has requested a small group of learned people, Augustine regularly emphasises that the judges he presents are indeed that small group of learned people requested.[348] These people meet the standards of reason, erudition and freedom Julian asked for.[349] This board of doctors from Africa, Gaul, Italy, and Greece[350] defend the catholic truth, and meet the standards requested by Julian, for they are 'bishops of the Church' and 'men of sound minds'.[351] They form the neutral and objective court of learned people that Julian wanted.[352] Living before the outbreak of the controversy, possessing sound doctrine, they can judge the question under discussion without any party politics.[353] Julian could not hope to find a synod of such high quality or better judges than these

346 *C. Iul. imp.* 2,1 (*CSEL* 85/1, 164): 'Talis hic erat Ambrosius, quem iudicem si non refugis, dubitare non debes iustissime te esse damnatum…'.

347 *C. Iul. imp.* 2,36 (*CSEL* 85/1, 188–89): 'Ambrosius est ille, non quicumque de vulgo, cuius imperitam multitudinem non valentem de tuis disputationibus iudicare nimis alta cervice et proterva fronte contemnis; Ambrosius est, inquam, cui nulla ex parte in ipsis litteris saecularibus, de quibus multum inflaris, aequaris; in ecclesiasticis vero quis ille sit, audi vel lege Pelagium doctorem tuum…' See also *C. Iul. imp.* 2,8 (*CSEL* 85/1, 168).

348 See *C. Iul.* 1,31 (*PL* 44, 662): 'Sed ecce, quo te introduxi, conventus sanctorum istorum non est multitudo popularis: non solum filii, sed et patres Ecclesiae sunt'; 2,36 (*PL* 44, 699): 'Verum quia te delectat, non numerare multitudinem, sed appendere paucitatem; exceptis iudicibus Palaestinis, qui haeresim vestram in absoluto Pelagio damnaverunt, quem timore compressum Pelagiana ipsa dogmata damnare coegerunt, decem episcopos iam defunctos et unum presbyterum tibi huius causae opposui iudices, qui de illa cum hic viuerent iudicaverunt. Si vestra consideretur paucitas, multi sunt: si multitudo catholicorum episcoporum, perpauci sunt'.

349 *C. Iul.* 2,37 (*PL* 44, 700): 'Isti episcopi sunt, docti, graves, sancti, veritatis acerrimi defensores adversus garrulas vanitates, in quorum ratione, eruditione, libertate, quae tria bona iudici tribuisti, non potes invenire quod spernas'.

350 *C. Iul. imp.* 2,33 (*CSEL* 85/1, 186).

351 *C. Iul. imp.* 4,119 (*CSEL* 85/2, 133): 'Quos antistites ecclesiarum cum viros sani capitis dicas;…quae illi notissima consensione didicerunt atque docuerunt…'.

352 *C. Iul.* 2,34 (*PL* 44, 698): '…ad hanc tamen causam tales erant…: nullas nobiscum vel vobiscum amicitias attenderunt, vel inimicitias exercuerunt; neque nobis neque vobis irati sunt, neque nos neque vos miserati sunt. Nec nos nec vos eis noti fueramus, et eorum pro nobis latas contra vos sententias recitamus'. See also Weber, *Some Literary Aspects of the Debate between Julian of Eclanum and Augustine*, 294.

353 *C. Iul.* 3,42 (*PL* 44, 723): 'In qua vellem quidem egregios iudices non repudiares, quos tibi meis superioribus libris sana doctrina eruditos, sine ullo studio partium de hac causa sententias protulisse monstravi'.

men.[354] Augustine does not neglect to mention that John Chrysostom and Basil, who were qualified by Julian himself as learned, belong to his court.[355]

They are learned representatives of what is also held by their colleagues and the *whole* Church of Christ,[356] from its very beginning. The Church's belief in original sin and the need of baptism for all, including babies, belongs to the very ancient, authoritative Catholic faith, is based upon scripture, and is very well known through the celebrations of the Church.[357] The defence of this venerable faith of the Church belongs to the essence of the Catholic resistance to the Pelagians.[358] These authorities did not live at the same time, but at different periods and in distant places, yet still holding the same, orthodox doctrine. They are gathered from the East and from the West, and their writings are still available.[359] They include men from the rising of the sun to its setting, some from the past, others nearer to Augustine's era; some have already passed away, others are still living at time of writing.[360] These men *taught what they had learned in the Church*:

> They drank as milk and ate as food; they have served its milk and its food to little ones and to adults and have most clearly and bravely defended it against its enemies, including you who were not born then, though they are now showing you for what you are.[361]

354 *C. Iul. imp.* 2,37 (*CSEL* 85/1, 189).

355 *C. Iul.* 1,33 (*PL* 44, 663): 'Postremo sanctus episcopus Joannes...quam tu sicut sanctum eruditumque laudasti...'; 1,35 (*PL* 44, 666): '...et episcopis Basilio et Joanne, quos tu quoque in sanctis eruditis veridica attestatione posuisti...'.

356 *C. Iul.* 6,11 (*PL* 44, 828–29).

357 *C ep. Pel.* 3,26 (*CSEL* 60, 519): 'Sed hoc dico tam manifestum esse secundum scripturas sanctas originale peccatum atque hoc dimitti lavacro regenerationis in parvulis tanta fidei catholicae antiquitate atque auctoritate firmatum, tam clara ecclesiae celebritate notissimum...'.

358 *C ep. Pel.* 4,29 (*CSEL* 60, 559): '...catholicis, qui eis pro antiquissima et firmissima ecclesiae fide resistant...'; see also *Nupt. et con.* 1,1 (*CSEL* 42, 211–12); 2,15 (*CSEL* 42, 268); *C. Iul. imp.* 3,61 (*CSEL* 85/1, 400).

359 *C. Iul.* 2,37 (*PL* 44, 700): 'Si episcopalis synodus ex toto orbe congregaretur, mirum si tales possent illic facile tot sedere. Quia nec isti uno tempore fuerunt: sed fideles et multis excellentiores paucos dispensatores suos Deus per diversas aetates temporum, locorumque distantias, sicut ei placet atque expedire iudicat, ipse dispensat. Hos itaque de aliis atque aliis temporibus atque regionibus ab oriente et occidente congregatos vides, non in locum quo navigare cogantur homines, sed in librum qui navigare possit ad homines'.

360 *C. Iul.* 1,20 (*PL* 44, 654): '...a solis ortu usque ad occasum tot ac tantos catholicae fidei doctores et defensores, antiquos et nostrae aetati contiguos, dormientes et manentes...'; see also *C. Iul. imp.* 4,7 (*CSEL* 85/2, 12).

361 *C. Iul.* 2,37 (*PL* 44, 700): '...quam in lacte suxerunt, quam in cibo sumpserunt, cuius lac et cibum parvis magnisque ministraverunt, quam contra inimicos etiam vos tunc nondum

In other words, these men were both children of the Church and fathers of the Church. They were nourished by the Church's truth, defended it, and through their books are continuing to defend it against people like Julian: 'It was through the efforts of these men that the Church, after the death of the apostles, was still able to grow, for these men planted, watered, built, shepherded and nourished the Church, which has taken fright at the profane words of your novelty...'[362]

Reaching a Consensus

Between these men there is a great consensus,[363] a consensus that cannot be called a '*conspiratio perditorum*'.[364] As Catholic co-disciples and co-doctors, they believed that through one person sin came into the world and passed to all.[365] Their consensus with regard to original sin is very important for Augustine.[366] He stresses that they were in agreement with each other, with scripture, and with the Catholic faith.[367] Therefore, Augustine can never accept that Julian might try to separate one of Augustine's doctors from the rest of the group. In defence of his case, Julian had appealed to John Chrysostom,[368] and, incorrectly, to Basil.[369] With regard to the essentials of the faith, it is not possible that John, Julian's authority, held an opinion different from that of colleagues such as the Roman Innocent, the Carthaginian Cyprian, the Cappadocian Basil, the Nazianzean Gregory, or the Milanese Ambrose.[370] The one who dares to question the truth of 1 Cor. 15, 21–22, is destroying what we believe in Christ, that is, that Christ is the saviour of children, that he is the sole saviour, and that, without his flesh and blood, one cannot have life. According to

natos, unde nunc revelamini, apertissime ac fortissime defenderunt'. For the translation, see *WSA* I/24, 335.

362 *C. Iul.* 2,37 (*PL* 44, 700): 'Talibus post apostolos sancta ecclesia plantatoribus, rigatoribus, aedificatoribus, pastoribus, nutritoribus creuit. Ideo profanas voces vestrae novitatis expavit...' The translation is taken from *WSA* I/24, 335.

363 *C. Iul.* 1,30 (*PL* 44, 661); 3,32 (*PL* 44, 719); *C. Iul. imp.* 4,119 (*CSEL* 85/1, 133).

364 *C. Iul.* 1,34 (*PL* 44, 665); also 6,69 (*PL* 44, 865): '...sanctorum et eruditorum Ecclesiae catholicae partum pius fidelisque consensus...' For Julian's complaint, see *Ad Turb.*, frg. 313 (*CCSL* 88, 394).

365 *C. Iul. imp.* 1,126 (*CSEL* 85/1, 139): 'Sic quippe intellexit (Ambrosius) cum ceteris condiscipulis et condoctoribus suis sine ulla dubitatione catholicis...'.

366 See *C. Iul.* 3,32 (*PL* 44, 719); *C. Iul. imp.* 1,52 (*CSEL* 85,1, 48).

367 *C. Iul. imp.* 4,112 (*CSEL* 85/2, 120).

368 *Ad Turb.*, frg. 308 (*CCSL* 88, 392); frg. 311–12 (*CCSL* 88, 393–94).

369 *Ad Turb.*, frg. 309–10 (*CCSL* 88, 392–93).

370 *C. Iul.* 1,22 (*PL* 44, 655); see Rebillard, 'Augustin et ses autorités', 260–61.

Augustine, '*Hoc sensit, hoc credidit, hoc didicit, hoc docuit et Joannes*'. Here Augustine accuses Julian of transforming John's words into his own doctrine.[371] Augustine admits that these doctors and defenders of the Catholic rule of faith can differ, without harming the integrity of the faith. Augustine is willing to accept that the Catholic defenders of the rule can have different opinions about problems that do not belong to the essence of faith. He quite frankly admits that one doctor can be better and more faithful to the truth than another, but he will never accept that a person such as Chrysostom would ever hold salvation without Christ was possible, for this has to do with the foundations of faith. If there are differences, they are to be situated on a different level from the one that has to do with these foundations.[372]

What these men learned and taught can in no way be described as stupid or impious, as was suggested by Julian with regard to Augustine's doctrine. Reversing Julian's critique, Augustine claims that through the Lord who governs his Church mercifully, the Catholic faith has been so vigilant that neither the stupid, impious doctrine of the Pelagians nor that of the Manicheans have been received.[373] Those who rejected them are saintly and educated men, Catholics, as is proved by their fame in the whole Church.[374] Reacting against Julian's complaints about coercion, Augustine replies that one cannot deny that people like Cyprian and Ambrose—*beatissimis et in fide catholica excellentissimis viris*—overthrew the heresy even before it came into existence with such clarity that one can hardly find a clearer answer to these heretics. Augustine is therefore not convinced that a synod, as requested by Julian, is needed:

---

371 *C. Iul.* 1,22 (*PL* 44, 655).

372 *C. Iul.* 1,22 (*PL* 44, 655): 'Alia sunt, in quibus inter se aliquando etiam doctissimi atque optimi regulae catholicae defensores, salva fidei compage non consonant, et alius alio de una re melius aliquid dicit et verius. Hoc autem unde nunc agimus, ad ipsa fidei pertinet fundamenta'. Skilful debater as he was, Jul., *Ad Florum* 4,112 (*CSEL* 85/2, 119) referred to Augustine's *Nat. et grat.* 71. in order to show that when Pelagius appealed to Ambrose and Cyprian, Augustine had replied that he was not bound by the authority of these people. Augustine had even suggested that their eventually incorrect views were wiped out by progress toward the better life. Julian accused Augustine of staining the reputation of these men by associating them with his own case, although their positions could easily be explained through clear and benevolent argumentation. It should be said that Augustine's reply is not really convincing: I do not see why Julian might have refuted Pelagius' and his own heresy as a result of these statements; see *C. Iul. imp.* 4,112 (*CSEL* 85/2, 119). In the text Julian referred to, Augustine implicitly accepts the authority of those Pelagius appealed to, but rejects Pelagius' arguments; see Rebillard, 'Augustin et ses autorités', 253–57.

373 *C ep. Pel.* 4,33 (*CSEL* 60, 569).

374 *C ep. Pel.* 4,33 (*CSEL* 60, 569): 'Ecce sancti et docti viri, fama totius ecclesiae contestante catholici…'.

it is quite rare to find heresies which need a synod in order that they might be condemned.[375] Augustine does not see any reason why the Christian governors should doubt the ancient Catholic faith and give space and time to an examination by the Pelagians. They would be better off coercing the Pelagians![376] Augustine even goes a step further. He accuses Julian of either not knowing the thoughts and the statements of these Catholic teachers, or if he does, that he is trying to deceive those not familiar with these teachers.[377]

Like his predecessors, such as Ambrose, Augustine, with his modest ability, tries to build people up by exhortation, entreatment, and correction, but like Ambrose and all his great companions, he holds and states the same opinion about original sin.[378] It is to men such as Irenaeus, Cyprian, Hilary, Ambrose, Basil, and John Chrysostom that Augustine wants to cling in the communion of faith, which he seeks to defend against the idle words and calumnies of Julian: 'Look to these catholic eyes and open your eyes!', Augustine cries out.[379] He asks Julian ironically whether he dares to say that when people hear the Pelagians, they will be set afire for virtue, but when they hear these great and good men, they will be broken by despair and refuse to long for perfection.[380] You, Augustine continues, honour the saints of God, the patriarchs, the prophets, and apostles through the praise of nature, whilst these lights of the Church (the Pelagians) dishonor them by their blame of nature, for they claim that one must fight against the innate evil of concupiscence in order to maintain the good of chastity.[381] By God's grace, this evil must be overcome through conflict, and thereafter, through the last rebirth healed.[382] 'Is the light called darkness', Augustine asks, 'and the darkness light to the point that Pelagius, Caelestius,

375 *C ep. Pel.* 4,34 (CSEL 60, 569–70).

376 *C. Iul. imp.* 1,10 (CSEL 85,1, 11): 'Absit a christianis potestatibus terrenae rei publicae, ut de antiqua catholica fide dubitent et ob hoc oppugnatoribus eius locum et tempus examinis praebeant ac non potius in ea certi atque fundati talibus quales vos estis inimicis eius disciplinam coercitionis imponant'; also *C. Iul. imp.* 2,103 (CSEL 85/1, 235), where Augustine states that once a heresy is condemned by bishops, the Christian civil power should coerce it, not examine it again.

377 *C. Iul.* 1,29 (PL 44, 661).

378 *C. Iul. imp.* 4,119 (CSEL 85/2, 133): 'Et nos pro modulo nostro populos aedificamus hortando obsecrando arguendo, quod fecit Ambrosius; et tamen de originali peccato hoc sentimus et dicimus, quod sensit et dixit Ambrosius, nec solus, sed cum aliis magnis consortibus suis'; 4,122 (CSEL 85/2, 141): 'Illud scilicet originale peccatum, quod vos negatis cum Pelagio, nos vero cum Ambrosio confitemur'.

379 *C. Iul. imp.* 4,73 (CSEL 85/2, 76); see also 4,97 (CSEL 85/2, 102).

380 *C. Iul.* 2,30 (PL 44, 693).

381 *C. Iul.* 2,30 (PL 44, 693); see also 2,70 (PL 44, 866).

382 *C. Iul.* 2,30 (PL 44, 693–94).

and Julian can see, whilst Hilary, Gregory, and Ambrose are blind?'[383] It will be evident that Julian must, or at least should, deny this. Therefore, he must take into account the views of these latter men.[384] Because of the already-mentioned request of Julian for a few wise men, Augustine only mentions three persons here: Hilary, Gregory, and Ambrose. Indeed, Julian had suggested that if Augustine were forced to appear for judges, he would not know what to do or whence to flee, since he would not find anything with which to meet Julian's arguments. If Julian wants to weigh something, he should weigh the views of these few men: 'I do not want there be so many that it is a bother for you to count them, but they are not lightweight so that many disdain to weigh them'.[385] In the presence of Hilary, Gregory, and Ambrose, Julian cannot say that Augustine is too weak to object to Julian. These few men, authorities in the matter, are sufficient to answer Julian's accusations. Therefore Augustine flees from the Pelagian darkness to the bright Catholic light of Hilary, Gregory, and Ambrose.[386]

If Julian concedes that what Augustine has presented from the writings of Ambrose, Cyprian, or other Catholics is true, he must recognise original sin.[387] If he refuses to return to the true faith, he will be confronted with these standards of truth. Augustine appears surprised that Julian seems unaware that the critique he has formulated against Augustine and his view on original sin is also a critique against these many and great doctors of the Church, who lived excellent lives, defended the faith against the heresies of their times, and passed away before the coming of the Pelagian resistance to the doctrine of original sin.[388] Slandering Augustine means slandering these great men.[389] Julian is accused of attacking the lights of the city of God, people he would do better to follow instead of attacking,[390] for they recognised that God is the creator of all that exists. They honored marriage, they proclaimed that in baptism through Christ all sins are forgiven, they believed in a just God, in the human capacity for virtue and perfection through God's grace, without thereby denying the doctrine of original sin.[391] Proclaiming the doctrine of original sin did not hinder these men in their attempts to mistrust their own virtue, to

383 *C. Iul.* 2,35 (*PL* 44, 698).
384 *C. Iul.* 2,35 (*PL* 44, 698–99).
385 *C. Iul.* 2,35 (*WSA* I/24, 333), (*PL* 44, 699).
386 *C. Iul.* 2,35 (*PL* 44, 698–99).
387 *C. Iul. imp.* 4,113 (*CSEL* 85/2, 122).
388 *C. Iul.*1,11 (*PL* 44, 646); 2,30 (*PL* 44, 694).
389 *C. Iul. imp.* 4,73 (*CSEL* 85/2, 75–76).
390 *C. Iul.* 1,11 (*PL* 44, 647).
391 *C. Iul.* 2,19 (*PL* 44, 686), (on the basis of texts of Ambrose); 2,32 (*PL* 44, 695); *C. Iul. imp.* 4,117 (*CSEL* 85/2, 129).

live chaste lives, to overcome vice, and to fight as exemplary soldiers of Christ, overcoming the works of the devil.[392] Therefore Augustine is convinced that Julian will never be able to live a better life than these men[393] from whom he is deviating by denying that Christ is also the redeemer of little children.[394] He invites Julian to be open to the teaching of these men in order to return to the truth.[395] Augustine hopes that Julian will be healed by the statements and the authority of these holy men.[396]

Augustine's Faith is that of the Multitude, for it is Christian and Catholic

Augustine accepts that his faith is also a *dogma populare*, a doctrine of the people, because he and the faithful are the Church of him who is called Jesus, who saves his people from their sins. To this Church belong not only people like Ambrose and Cyprian, but also Julian's father: faith did not create such people but found them.[397] However, it should be clear that Augustine cannot accept that deprecating language should be used to ridicule the faith of the common people and their leaders, the bishops: for they all taught what they had learned! Julian should realise that the multitude of Christians despise the new heresy,[398] for it cannot give a sufficient answer to the suffering of babies. Only the doctrine of original sin and its acceptance can offer a valid answer.[399] Furthermore, when Julian complains that Augustine is stirring up the common people against him by saying that these new heretics denied that rebirth through baptism was needed for the redemption of babies from the power of the devil, Augustine wonders whether this is not a sign that this Catholic faith is so popular and firmly implanted in society that even ordinary people

---

392 *C. Iul.* 2,24 (*PL* 44, 690).

393 *C. Iul. imp.* 1,70 (*CSEL* 85/1, 79).

394 *C. Iul. imp.* 1,118 (*CSEL* 85/1, 135).

395 *C. Iul.* 2,14 (*PL* 44, 684); 2,15 (*PL* 44, 684).

396 *C. Iul.* 2,37 (*PL* 44, 700–01).

397 *C. Iul. imp.* 2,2 (*CSEL* 85/1, 165). One should not focus too much on the expression *dogma populare* as meaning 'popular': Augustine considers this faith of the people to be the faith of the Church, its leaders and its believers. Faith is universal and is *found* by the faithful, not created by them. See the pertinent remarks of Rebillard, 'Dogma populare', 185–86.

398 *C. Iul.* 2,36 (*PL* 44, 699): '…sed nec ego te ullius multitudinis numerositate perturbo; quamvis propitio Deo, de hac fide, cui contradicitis, catholica sanum sapiat etiam multitudo; in qua usquequaque plurimi, ubi possunt, quomodo possunt, sicut divinitus adiuvantur, vana vestra argumenta confutant'.

399 *C. Iul.* 5,4 (*PL* 44, 784).

notice it.[400] Augustine is convinced that Julian, whilst detesting the common folk—this countless multitude of believers[401]—does not realise that he will accomplish nothing with these people. For all, rich and poor, high and low, learned and unlearned, men and women,[402] are firmly grounded in the truth and the antiquity of the Catholic faith,[403] and know why mothers all over the world run to the Church in order to have their babies baptised.[404] What the 'learned' debater Julian [does] not see with all his 'knowledge', is crystal clear to the common people![405]

In reaction to Julian's complaint that Augustine can only raise the murmuring of the people as an argument, Augustine stresses that this murmuring rests upon the authority of so many doctors,[406] thus linking the doctors' authority and the faith of the common people.[407] Further, Augustine can claim that if Julian came to the essence of the matter under discussion, it would be clear not only to the learned, but also to the ordinary Christian faithful, that he is a new heretic.[408] Augustine is in no way impressed by Julian's boasting

400 *C. Iul.* 6,22 (*PL* 44, 835).

401 *C. Iul. imp.* 6,3 (*CSEL* 85/2, 294).

402 *C. Iul.* 1,31 (*PL* 44, 662): 'Divites et pauperes, excelsi atque infimi, docti et indocti, mares et feminae noverunt quid cuique aetati in baptismate remittatur'.

403 *C. Iul.* 6,34 (*PL* 44, 841): 'Sed nimirum tua disputata considerans, nihil te talibus argumentis apud populum in catholicae fidei veritate et antiquitate fundatum agere potuisse vel posse sensisti'; also 6,36 (*PL* 44, 842).

404 *C. Iul.* 1,31 (*PL* 44, 662): 'Unde etiam matres quotidie toto orbe terrarum non ad Christum tantum, id est, ad unctum; sed ad Christum Iesum, id est, etiam salvatorem cum parvulis currunt'. Texts such as the one quoted here make clear that Augustine, when speaking of the faith of the multitude, stresses the universality of their faith, and not so much, as suggested by Salamito, the popular character of the faith; Jean-Marie Salamito, *Les virtuoses et la multitude. Aspects sociaux de la controverse entre Augustin et les pélagiens* (Collection Nomina), (Grenoble: Millon, 2005), 211–12; 226–32. See the sharp critique of Rebillard, 'Dogma Populare', 181–82. On the use of liturgical rites as an argument in the Pelagian controversy, see J.-A. Vinel, 'L'argument liturgique opposé par Saint Augustin aux Pélagiens', *Questions liturgiques* 68 (1987), 209–41, see esp. 215–24.

405 *C. Iul.* 1,36 (*PL* 44, 699); 6,22 (*PL* 44, 835–36): 'Necesse quippe fuerat, quidquid in parvulis suis ageret, quod attinet ad mysteria christiana, omnes nosse Christianos… Antequam essem natus huic mundo, et antequam essem renatus Deo, multa catholica lumina vestras futuras tenebras redarguendo praevenerunt…'; *C. Iul. imp.* 3,104 (*CSEL* 85/1, 424): 'O stulti haeretici novi'.

406 *C. Iul.* 6,69 (*PL* 44, 865).

407 *C. Iul.* 1,31 (*PL* 44, 662): 'Sed ecce, quo te introduxi, conventus sanctorum istorum non est multitudo popularis: non solum filii, sed et patres ecclesiae sunt'.

408 *C. Iul. imp.* 3,183 (*CSEL* 85/1, 482).

of small numbers and maintaining that Augustine's doctrine only pleases the majority,[409] especially when this majority is Catholic and disapproves of the Pelagian heresy.[410] Using an argument *ad hominem*, Augustine reminds Julian not to forget that it is these common folk that he himself has found in the Church.[411]

In passing, it should be said that in *C. ep. Pel.*, a work known to Julian, Augustine himself also suggests that the Pelagians, these new heretics, even after an explicit condemnation, still try to tempt by their writings the hearts of the less cautious or less educated.[412] By interjecting the din of others' questions, they hide their unbelief from human beings who are simpler or slower or less learned in the sacred scriptures.[413] They terrify the weak and those less well-trained in scripture lest they be in conflict with the Pelagians.[414] Also in *C. Iul.*, Augustine insists that protection of the faithful, especially of the weaker ones, is needed for those terrified by Julian's arguments and for those less well-trained in scripture, should they be confronted by Julian.[415] In other words, Augustine himself warns his readers to be careful with these misleaders of simple people.[416]

In passing and without further development, he writes, it should be remembered that only a few people are really intelligent and studious enough to seek knowledge about the human and divine; there is a great multitude of slow and lazy beings, who for Augustine are proof that our nature is indeed vitiated because of Adam's fall.[417]

---

409 *C. Iul. imp.* 2,3 (CSEL 85/1, 166).

410 *C. Iul. imp.* 2,4 (CSEL 85/1, 166).

411 *C. Iul. imp.* 2,2 (CSEL 85/1, 165).

412 *C ep. Pel.* 1,2 (CSEL 60, 424): 'Noui quippe heretici, inimici gratiae Dei, quae datur pusillis et magnis per Iesum Christum dominum nostrum, etsi iam cauendi euidentius apertiore inprobatione monstrantur, non tamen quiescunt scriptis suis minus cautorum uel minus eruditorum corda temptare'.

413 *C ep. Pel.* 3,24 (CSEL 60, 516): '…inmittunt aliarum nebulas quaestionum, in quibus eorum apud homines simpliciores siue tardiores siue sanctis litteris minus eruditos inpietas delitiscat'.

414 *C. Iul.* 2,1 (PL 44, 672).

415 *C. Iul.* 2,2 (PL 44, 672).

416 Augustine does not always react when Julian ridicules the common folk; see *C. Iul.* 5, 2–3 (PL 44, 783).

417 See *C. Iul. imp.* 5,1 (CSEL 85/2, 166): 'Nempe tanta raritas ingeniosorum et studiosorum, per quae duo ad humanarum divinarumque rerum scientiam pervenitur, et tanta multitudo tardorum et desidiosorum, satis indicat in quam partem suo tanquam pondere feratur ipsa natura, quam negatis esse vitiatam'.

Neither a Manichean nor a Punic Faith

Julian quite often accuses Augustine of still being an *African Manichean*. He fears that the Catholic Church might be ravished by Manichean robbers from Africa, and he insists with Turbantius that one should pray to God that He might save his Church.[418] According to Julian, Augustine's positions are not in line with the faith rooted in antiquity and handed down to the present time. Time and again, Augustine refutes the accusation that his faith might be Manichean. He reminds Julian that such accusations are typical of heretics: the same procedure was followed by Jovinian at the time.[419] It is no surprise that the new heretics give new names to Catholics (Augustine thinks here of the term *traducianus*). This has already happened in the past.[420]

If this faith, as Julian suggests, is a *dogma populare*, it can never be Manichean, for the Manichean madness, like that of the Pelagians, is only present in a few and it does not attract many.[421] Julian must be aware that if the doctrine of original sin is a Manichean idea,[422] this is the doctrine that has been confessed and professed by the great men who learned it in Christ's Church at the time of their first formation and who, once bishops, continued to teach it in the Church of Christ. Julian should be aware that he is attacking many great defenders and doctors of the Catholic Church![423] With regard to the councils

418 See *Ad Turb.m*, frg. 51 (CCSL 88, 352).

419 *Nupt. et con.* 2,38 (CSEL 42, 292): 'Nec ego id dico, quod isti hoc sentiant; uerumtamen per Jouinianum catholicis Manicheos obicientem non esse hoc nouum noui haeretici recognoscant'; *C. Iul.* 1,4 (PL 44, 643); see Rebillard, 'Augustin et ses autorités', 258.

420 *C. Iul. imp.* 1,6 (CSEL 85/1, 9).

421 *C. Iul. imp.* 6, 2–3 (CSEL 85/2, 293–94); see also 2, 2–3 (CSEL 85/1, 165–66), with regard to the small number of the Manicheans. This *theme* is well known in the Christian controversy literature; see Opelt, *Die Polemik in der christlichen lateinischen Literatur von Tertullian bis Augustin*, 230–31.

422 Within the discussion about the *dogma populare*, it is interesting to see that Augustine also complains that Julian is disgracing Augustine's name among the '*imperiti*'; *C. Iul.* 2,1 (PL 44, 671).

423 *C. Iul.* 1,12 (PL 44, 648): 'Sed qua confidentia id dicere audebis, homo qui dicis Manichaeum esse sensum, confiteri ex Adam trahere nascentes originale peccatum; quod isti confessi atque professi sunt quod in Christi Ecclesia suorum rudimentorum tempore didicerunt, quod Christi Ecclesiam suorum honorum tempore docuerunt…'; 2,1 (PL 44, 671): '…quot et quantis viris, Ecclesiae sanctis clarisque doctoribus, Manichaeorum crimen impingas…'; *C. Iul. imp.* 1,2 (CSEL 85/1, 2): 'Post commemorationem quippe doctorum catholicorum quos Manicheos facis—mihi sub hoc crimine obiciendo, quod illi in catholica ecclesia didicerunt atque docuerunt— …'; *C. Iul. imp.* 4,113 (CSEL 85/2, 113–14): 'cur ergo me dicis, quod illum esse non dicis, cum hoc ille tanto ante dixerit, quod ego nunc dico, atque in hac sententia propter quam Manichaeum me dicis, mihi et illi sit causa communis? …cur

of the wicked, Augustine asks Julian whether the latter dares to call the agreement of so many Catholics and teachers of the Church, standing in the ancient Catholic truth before him, a council of the wicked?[424] The faith of somebody like Ambrose is true, sound, rooted in antiquity, handed down to us and for all these reasons, Augustine adds, it is also my faith.[425] Accusing Augustine of Manicheism is to also accuse his predecessors of Manicheism[426] or Traducianism.[427] Julian should know that all his slander not only hurts Augustine, but also Augustine's predecessors, and by doing so gives proof that he belongs with the new heretics.[428] Augustine continues: 'I did not spit it out upon Italy… Rather, I received the bath of rebirth from this bishop of Italy who preached and taught this faith'.[429] If 'I am a disciple of Mani, then Ambrose is also one;

---

in una eademque sententia, quam dicit ille, dico ego, non est Manicheus ille, sed ego?'; *C. Iul. imp.* 4,120 (CSEL 85/2, 134): 'Prorsus si illum non dicis, nec me debes dicere; si autem me dicendum putas, et illum cogeris dicere, et illos omnes magnos ecclesiae claros que doctores, qui de peccato originali, propter quod me Manichaeum dicis, ea dicunt sine ulla obscuritate vel ambiguitate quae dico, ut in primo et secundo sex librorum meorum, quos contra quatuor tuos edidi, satis euidenter ostendi'; also refer to 1,135, (CSEL 85/1, 151); 4,119 (CSEL 85/1, 133); 4,120 (CSEL 85/1, 135).

424 *C. Iul. imp.* 1,59 (CSEL 85/1, 56).

425 *C. Iul. imp.* 1,59 (CSEL 85/1, 57): 'Ecce non est eorum, sed est Ambrosii; quia vera est, quia sana est, quia ut dixi antiquitus tradita atque fundata est, haec et mea est'. See also 1,109 (CSEL 85/1, 129): '…Ambrosius utique, non ut Manicheus, quo nomine tales qualis ille fidei fuerat criminaris, sed ut catholicus intellexit Apostolum…'; 1,115 (CSEL 85/1, 133): 'Hoc non dixit haereticus immundus Manicheus, sed catholicus sanctus Ambrosius'; also 1,52 (CSEL 85/1, 47); 4,118 (CSEL 85/2, 130): 'Originale peccatum cum Ambrosio confitemur…' 4,50 (CSEL 85/1, 56): 'Nec Apollinarista nec Manicheus fuit, sed haereticorum catholicus expugnator Ambrosius…' Sometimes Augustine quotes a text from one of his giants and rhetorically asks: is this man a Manichean?; see, e.g., *C. Iul. imp.* 1,123 (CSEL 85/1, 137).

426 *C. Iul. imp.* 6,33 (CSEL 85/2, 428–29); see also *C. Iul.* 1,11 (PL 44, 647); *C. Iul. imp.* 2,9 (CSEL 85/1, 169).

427 *C. Iul. imp.* 1,6 (CSEL 85/1, 9).

428 *C. Iul. imp.* 1,9 (CSEL 85/1, 10); with regard to Cyprian and Ambrose, see already *C. ep. Pel.* 4,24, (CSEL 60, 548–49); 4,32 (CSEL 60, 569); also see *C. Iul.* 2,4 (PL 44, 674); 2,11 (PL 44, 681), (with regard to Ambrose); 2,37 (PL 44, 701); *C. Iul. imp.* 1,9 (CSEL 85/1, 10); 4,109 (CSEL 85/2, 117).

429 *C. Iul. imp.* 1,59 (CSEL 85/1, 57): 'Non ego hanc in Italiam, quod vos gemere dicitis, eructaui, sed potius ab isto episcopo Italiae hanc praedicante et docente lauacrum regenerationis accepi'.

but he is not',[430] for he held anti-Manichean positions.[431] If I, Augustine, am in line with Ambrose, why do you accuse me of Manicheism?[432] With his accusations, Julian makes of these many great men false defenders and doctors of the Catholic faith.[433] Some of them had never heard of Manicheism![434] It is monstrous and crazy to suggest that the Manichean error had already deceived Cyprian long before the name of Mani had even been heard in Roman territory.[435] These men were instead standing in the oldest tradition of the Church.[436] Augustine himself does not need the help of Mani or Faustus, for his position is not only supported by the prophets and the apostles, but also by his predecessors in the Church, very sound in faith, very sharp in mind, very rich in learning, and renowned in reputation.[437] Augustine stresses that he

430 *C. Iul. imp.* 1,66 (CSEL 85/1, 65): 'Si enim ego hinc sum discipulus Manichei, hoc est et ille; non est autem hoc ille…'; 4,88 (CSEL 85/2, 91): 'Ubi cernis esse consequens, ut si ego propter hanc sententiam sum Manichaeus, sit et Ambrosius; quia uero ille non est, neminem faciat vel ostendat ista sententia Manichaeum'; also 1,48 (CSEL 85/1, 39–40); 2,2 (CSEL 85/1, 165); 2,9 (CSEL 85/1, 169); 2,21 (CSEL 85/1, 176); 2,31 (CSEL 85/1, 185); 2,164 (CSEL 85/1, 285); 2,207 (CSEL 85/1, 318): 'Doctores catholici, non Manichei deceptores…'; 2,208 (CSEL 85/1, 319); 4,75 (CSEL 85/2, 77); 4,113 (CSEL 85/2, 113); 4,118 (CSEL 85/2, 130); 4,122 (CSEL 85/2, 141).

431 *C. Iul.* 1,44 (PL 44, 671); *C. Iul. imp.* 4,109 (CSEL 85/1, 116–17).

432 *Nupt. et Con.* 2,15 (CSEL 42, 267): 'Si ergo illum Manicheum dicere non audetis, nos, cum in eadem causa eadem sententia fidem catholicam defendamus, cur dicitis Manicheos?'; see also *C. ep. Pel.* 4,33 (CSEL 60, 569): 'Unde apparet istos doctores catholicos longe a Manicheorum sensibus alienos. Et tamen asserunt originale peccatum…'; *C. Iul. imp.* 4,109 (CSEL 85/2, 117): 'Quod ergo credit Ambrosius, hoc et ego; quod autem Manicheus, nec ille nec ego. Quid est quod tu niteris me separare ab Ambrosio et coniungere Manicheo?… cur non ambos a Manicheis dignaris abiungere?', also 4,108 (CSEL 85/2, 116). See also Dassmann, 'Tam Ambrosius quam Cyprianus', 362.

433 *C. Iul.* 1,36 (PL 44, 666).

434 *C. Iul.* 3,32 (PL 44,719). In *Nup. et Con.* 2,51 (CSEL 42, 308), Augustine explicitly refers here to Cyprian: '…numquid et gloriosissimae coronae Cyprianus dicetur ab aliquo non solum fuisse, sed vel esse potuisse Manicheus, cum prius iste sit passus, quam illa in orbe Romano pestis adparuit?'

435 *C. Iul.* 3,31 (PL 44, 718).

436 *Nupt. et con.* 2,51 (CSEL 42, 308).

437 *C. Iul. imp.* 4,72 (CSEL 85/2, 74–75); also *Nupt. et con.* 2,51 (CSEL 42, 307–08), (with regard to Ambrose and Cyprian); *C. Iul. imp.* 1,6 (CSEL 85/1, 9); 4,108 (CSEL 85/1, 116). It is interesting to see that Julian's argumentation was very much on the same lines. He also claimed that he was in line with scripture, the prophets, evangelists, apostles and catholic thinkers known for their '*catholica sanitas*', in his case John Chrysostom, Basil, and Theodore of Mopsuestia; see *Ad Florum* 3,111 (CSEL 85/1, 432).

stands in a continuous line.[438] Before Augustine, there was Ambrose, who was not a Manichee. Before Ambrose there were Hilary and Gregory, who were certainly no Manichees. Before them there were Cyprian and many others, who, again, were no Manichees.[439] Not without exaggeration he can speak of '*meus est Cyprianus, meus est Hilarius, meus est Ambrosius, meus est Gregorius, meus est Basilius, meus est Iohannes Constantinopolitanus; hi omnes et alii socii eorum eadem sentientes, quos commemorare longum est, mei sunt*'.[440]

Using, like Julian, the metaphor of a fight, Augustine states that Ambrose's Catholic faith, and I with him,[441] will defeat in the name and the power of Christ both the Manicheans and the Pelagians.[442] Therefore, both Mani and Julian, confronted with scripture (John) and tradition (Ambrose), would be better off silent.[443] It would be better for Julian to learn from Ambrose from whence the evil of carnal concupiscence comes, in order not to help the Manichees, as he is now doing,[444] whilst slandering the Catholics.[445] Indeed, the Catholic bishops are able to give an adequate answer to the question of where evil comes from, an answer that Julian cannot give.[446]

In a passage full of irony, Augustine wonders whether Ambrose, if he were still alive in those days, might come to realise that he was a Manichee, whilst listening to Pelagius and hearing that the struggle between flesh and spirit was not, as he had taught, the result of Adam's transgression, something

---

438 For the latter, to whom Gregory will be opposed, see *C. Iul. imp.* 1,69 (*CSEL* 85/1, 76).

439 *C. Iul. imp.* 1,117 (*CSEL* 85/1, 134): 'Ante me erat Ambrosius, qui non erat Manicheus, ante ipsum Hilarius, Gregorius, ante hos Cyprianus et ceteri, quos commemorare longum est, qui non erant Manichei'; also 1,9 (*CSEL* 85/1, 10).

440 See *C. Iul. imp.* 1,52 (*CSEL* 85/1, 47–48).

441 *C. Iul. imp.* 6,14 (*CSEL* 85/2, 334–35).

442 *C. Iul. imp.* 3,178 (*CSEL* 85/1, 480); and also 3,181 (*CSEL* 85/1, 481); 3,187 (*CSEL* 85/1, 490): '… quoniam catholica fide in Christi nomine atque virtute utrosque vincit Ambrosius'; 2,213 (*CSEL* 85/1, 504): 'Non esse Ambrosium Manicheum, qui fidei catholicae invictissimus et Manicheos prostravit et vos…'; 4,112 (*CSEL* 85/2, 120); see also 5,5 (*CSEL* 85/2, 173); 5,41 (*CSEL* 85/2, 243): 'tuus destructor'; 5,43 (*CSEL* 85/2, 246–47); 6,8 (*CSEL* 85/1, 305): 'Quo telo inevitabili et insuperabili veritatis, et Manicheus obtruncatur, et tu'; 6,37 (*CSEL* 85/2, 445); already in *C. Iul.* 2,5 (*PL* 44, 675).

443 *C. Iul. imp.* 4,23 (*CSEL* 85/1, 25).

444 *C. Iul. imp.* 4,28 (*CSEL* 85/2, 28); 4,42 *CSEL* 85/2, 43; 4,50 (*CSEL* 85/2, 56); 4,64 (*CSEL* 85/2, 69); 4,70 (*CSEL* 85/2, 74); 5,20 (*CSEL* 85,2, 202); 6,6 (*CSEL* 85/2, 299); 6,8 (*CSEL* 85/2, 304); 6,14 (*CSEL* 85/1, 331). See also Agostino Trapè, 'Un celebre testo de Sant'Agostino sull' 'Ignoranza e la difficoltà' (*Retract.* I,9,6) et *l'Opus imperfectum Contra Iulianum*', in *Augustinus Magister* 2 (Paris: Études augustiniennes, 1954), 795–803.

445 *C. Iul. imp.* 4,56 (*CSEL* 85/2, 62).

446 *C. Iul. imp.* 6,14 (*CSEL* 85/2, 330–31).

he would no longer dare to say *'sub vobis magistris'*.[447] Obeying Julian, he would have forbidden the rites of exhortation and exsufflation and would have been expelled from the Catholic Church, together with Julian.[448] Yet of course, this could never happen. If Ambrose were still alive, he would react even more vehemently and authoritatively than Augustine for the Catholic faith and the grace of God (*pro catholica fide et pro Dei gratia vel aequitate*).[449]

Since Julian has called Augustine a Punic debater, Augustine will not only refer to Cyprian—he is the real Punic debater, not me, Augustine retorts—but also to the other doctors. Only one of the holy men comes from Africa, the others from elsewhere. If the Manicheans would have defiled the Church through these holy bishops of God and renowned doctors, which Church gave birth to Julian?[450] How can Julian accuse these men, who are on so many matters in consensus, of Manicheism?[451] Stop accusing us of Manicheism, he says, in order not to injure the venerable martyr Cyprian,[452] who, together with his colleagues at the time, through a conciliar decision had already condemned the Pelagians who would only come years later.[453] Long before the Manichean pestilence came to Africa, Cyprian had already confessed the doctrine of original sin,[454] teaching what he had learned in the African Church.

Instead of constantly accusing Augustine of Manicheism, Julian would do better to join Augustine in following Ambrose,[455] for he, with his colleagues, stands like Augustine in the Catholic truth.[456] Augustine cannot understand that Pelagius and Caelestius have such a great influence on Julian that he dares

---

447 *C. Iul. imp.* 4,114 (*CSEL* 85/2, 123–24); a similar procedure but now adapted to Julian in 4,120 (*CSEL* 85/2, 135).

448 *C. Iul. imp.* 4,120 (*CSEL* 85/2, 135).

449 *C. Iul. imp.* 4,114 (*CSEL* 85/2, 124–25).

450 *C. Iul. imp.* 3,32 (*PL* 44, 719).

451 *C. Iul. imp.* 1,55 (*CSEL* 85/1, 52): 'Numquid Manicheus fuit iste Reticius?'

452 *C ep. Pel.* 4,21, (*CSEL* 60, 544); also see 4,32 (*CSEL* 60, 569).

453 *C ep. Pel.* 4,23 (*CSEL* 60, 546); with regard to Augustine's respect for counciliar decisions, see Hermann Josef Sieben, *Die Konzilsidee der Alte Kirche* (Paderborn: Schöningh, 1979), 68–102.

454 *C ep. Pel.* 4,24 (*CSEL* 60, 549): '...antequam terras nostras vel tenuissimus odor Manicheae pestilentiae tetigisset...'.

455 *C. Iul. imp.* 5,30 (*CSEL* 85/1, 229): 'Desine ergo mihi magistrum apponere Manicheum, sed mecum potius sequere Ambrosium...'.

456 *C. Iul.* 2,5 (*PL* 44, 675): '...cum hoc dicere me videas, quod ille dixit...'; *C. Iul. imp.* 4,122 (*CSEL* 85/2, 143): 'Ego tamen in hac causa, in qua tibi de originali peccato multum videor detestandus, et Manicheo potius coaequandus, cum Ambrosio sum, velis nolis, quem Io-

to label these judges and defenders of the Catholic faith Manichees. Because of Julian's denial of the doctrine of original sin, he is a stronger and mightier enemy of Christ's cross and God's grace than of people like Ambrose.[457] In any case, even if Julian dares to call one of these men Manichees, he certainly will not dare to give this name to Christ.[458]

Just as Julian displayed his Italian 'nationalistic' feelings, Augustine does not hesitate to show that he is proud of his African background and his African predecessor Cyprian. When Julian suggests that the Catholic Church has been ravished by the Manichean pirates from Africa,[459] Augustine reverses the accusation. He first stresses that Catholics react against Manichees, Donatists, and other heretics or enemies of the Christian and Catholic name in Africa.[460] He describes the Pelagian heresy as a scourge from overseas, a *transmarina pestilentia*, a robbery against which he places Cyprian, through whom he wants to defend the Catholic faith against the vain and profane novelty of the Pelagian error.[461] Indeed, it is Julian himself who speaks against the most ancient Catholic faith.[462] Using military vocabulary (like Julian), Augustine claims that Julian constructs new machines and prepares new attacks against the walls of the most ancient truth. I am not, as you say, the Punic debater, but Cyprian, who will punish you for your impious doctrine, he declares.[463] Augustine does not believe, as suggested by Julian, that his faith is to be compared to a small Numidian shield (*caetra Numidica*). It is a genuinely complete shield of truth!

---

vinianus Manicheum dicebat…'; see also 6,41 (CSEL 85/2, 464) concerning carnal concupiscence as the result of the fall of the first man.

457 *C. Iul. imp.* 2,56 (CSEL 85/1, 395).

458 *C. Iul.* 1,13 (PL 44, 648), regarding Innocent.

459 *Ad Turb.*, frg. 51 (CCSL 88, 352).

460 *C. Iul.* 3,31 (PL 44, 718).

461 *C. Iul.* 3,31 (PL 44, 718): 'Contra vos autem, quia nobis estis pestilentia transmarina, Christo salvatore vincenda, ideo ne latrocinamur ex Africa, quia unum martyrem hinc opponimus Cyprianum, per quem probemus antiquam nos defendere fidem catholicam, contra vestri erroris vanam profanamque novitatem?' On the use of the term pestilence as a polemical motive, see Opelt, *Die Polemik in der christlichen lateinischen Literatur*, 158.

462 *C. Iul.* 3,31 (PL 44, 718–19): '…contra antiquissimam catholicam fidem…'.

463 *C. Iul.* 3,32 (PL 44, 719): 'Sed quantumlibet tergiverseris, O haeresis Pelagiana, quae contra muros antiquissimae veritatis novas construis machinas, novas moliris insidias: Poenus disputator, quod me contumeliose tuus defensor appellat; Poenus, inquam, disputator, non ego, sed Cyprianus Poenus, te hoc vulnere poenus immolat, et poenam scelerato ex dogmate sumit'; also *C. Iul. imp.* 1,7 (CSEL 85/1, 9); 6,23 (CSEL 85/2, 378). See also Dassmann, 'Tam Ambrosius quam Cyprianus', 160.

With this shield, the Punic Cyprian,[464] an outstanding soldier of Christ, was already armed against the Pelagians. When Julian ironically calls Augustine the most notable debater who, by the steps of his Punic dialectics, has destroyed judgment, Augustine refers to Cyprian, a Punic person in whom Julian will not dare to mock Punic dialectics.[465] Julian should realise that, whilst barking against the Punic bishop and martyr Cyprian, he is attacking the most solidly-grounded faith of the Church for which this martyr shed his blood.[466] Quite evidently, Julian's hint about the Punic wars does not escape Augustine, but he is not really impressed by it. Because Julian was born in Apulia, he might think that he surpasses the Punic people, but he will never surpass them with his mind. Julian should better flee the punishments (*poena*) than the Punic (*Poenus*) people. Indeed, he will never escape his Punic opponents as long as he trusts in his own virtue, for the Punic Cyprian claimed that we must boast over nothing, for nothing is ours.[467]

Keeping Score: Appropriation by the Numbers

In the end, Augustine's appropriation of Cyprian, or at least the scientific analysis thereof, is a numbers game. In Chapter 5 numerous charts revealed in over 600 uses the division and allotment of the Cyprian theme in Augustine's efforts. Furthermore, I integrated a global thematic cartography that categorised the main theological or rhetorical themes present throughout Augustine's career. This effort, though designed to leave room for further analysis and comparison, demonstrated the extent to which key themes (such as *concupiscentia*, *gratia*, Africa, *superbia*, etc.) were used. It was clear that many of the themes that Augustine later became renowned for featured heavily in the anti-Donatist and anti-Pelagian campaigns. However, what is still missing is a complete accounting of where Cyprian's writings, and not just his ideas or traditions, were quoted or otherwise utilised in Augustine's own writings. That is presented as follows:

464 Augustine clearly distinguishes between his own Numidian background and the Punic Cyprian: '…non quidem Numida, sed tamen Poenus ille Cyprianus…'; *C. Iul. imp.* 6,6 (CSEL 85/2, 299).

465 *C. Iul. imp.* 1,72 (CSEL 85/1, 85).

466 *C. Iul. imp.* 1,106 (CSEL 85/1, 125).

467 *C. Iul. imp.* 6,18 (CSEL 85/2, 353): 'Non enim quia te Apulia genuit, ideo Poenos vincendos existimes gente, quos non potes mente. Poenas potius fuge, non Poenos: nam disputatores Poenos non potes fugere, quamdiu te delectat in tua virtute confidere; et beatus enim Cyprianus Poenus fuit, qui dixit, in nullo gloriandum, quando nostrum nihil sit'.

As a means of disseminating this data, it is important to note a few characteristics of the Cyprian sources that Augustine chooses to quote directly and with which to advocate his own positions. First, it is clear that Augustine generally utilises individual sources of Cyprian separately against the Donatists and the Pelagians. In other words, Cyprian's individual writings mostly appear in one or the other controversy. Examples of Cyprian's writings used by Augustine in the Donatist controversy and not in the Pelagian controversy are: *De lapsis* (*De bapt.* 4,12; *C. ep. Parm.* 3,14(x2); *Cresc.* 2,18; 3,40; 4,33; *Ep.* 93,47; 98,3(x3); 108,10); *De ecclesiae catholicae unitate* (*C. Gaud.* 2,2; 2,14; *Cresc.* 2,42(x2); 3,64; 3,73); *De zelo et livore* (*De bapt.* 4,11(x2)); *Sententiae episcoporum* (see list for detailed list); *Ep.* 11 (*De bapt.* 4,3(x2); 4,16; 4,19; 6,60; *Cresc.* 2,18; *Ep.* 157,34); *Ep.* 54 (*C. Don.* 9; 11; 28; 37; *C. Gaud.* 2,3; 2,4; 2,5(x2); 2,10; 2,14; 2,43; 2,45; 2,48; 3,35; 3,73; 4,67; *Ep.* 108,10); *Ep.* 55 (*Ep.* 93,41; *De bapt.* 4,17; 4,18); *Ep.* 69 (*De bapt.* 6,10; 7,97; 7,98); *Ep.* 70 (*De bapt.* 5,29); *Ep.* 71 (*De bapt.* 2,2; 2,5; 2,13(x2); 2,14); *Ep.* 73 (*Cresc.* 2,41; *De bapt.* 2,14; 2,18; 2,41; 3,7; 3,17(*x*2); 3,23; 4,7(x2); 4,8(*x*2); 4,9; 4,10; 4,11; 4,16; 4,24(x2); 5,1; 5,2; 5,3; 5,4; 5,8; 5,14; 5,22; 5,39; 6,10(x3); 7,31; 7,49); *Ep.* 74 (*Cresc.* 3,2; *De bapt.* 5,34; 5,37).

On the other hand, examples of Cyprian's works used by Augustine in support of his anti-Pelagian writings exclusively are as follows: *De dominica oratione* (*C. ep. Pel.* 4,25(x4); 4,27(x2); *C. Iul.* 2,6; *C. Iul. imp.* 1,72; *Corrept.* 10; *Persev.* 4(x2); 7; 8; 12); *Opere et eleemmosynis* (*C. ep. Pel.* 4,21(x2); 4,27(*x*2); 4,28; *C. Iul.* 2,25); *De Mortalitate* (*C. ep. Pel.* 4,25(x5); *Praed. sanct.* 28(x2)); and *Testimoniorum* (*C. ep. Pel.* 4,25; 4,26; 4,27; *C. Iul. imp.* 6,18; *Persev.* 36(x3) 43; 48; 49).

What these divergences in Augustine's use of Cyprian's work seem to indicate is that Augustine does indeed refer to Cyprian in a contextually-based manner. Proof of this is observed in the thematic importance of each Cyprian source in advancing Augustine's particular arguments in the Donatist and Pelagian controversies respectively. For example, Augustine's references to Cyprian's works in *De lapsis* and *De ecclesiae catholicae unitate* (and Augustine does not refer to those works against the Donatists) are clearly used only against the Donatists, because Augustine is advocating an ecclesiological agenda to show that it is he who agrees with Cyprian and not the Donatists, who claim Cyprian's authority in matters of the nature of the Church. A more elaborate example of this contextually-based utilisation of Cyprian's works by Augustine is seen in *Sententiae episcoporum*. While this is not a work by Cyprian alone (it is a compendium of North African bishops at a third century council), it is clearly being used by Augustine to augment the historicity of Donatist claims to authenticity based on legitimate episcopal pedigree. Also, at this point, Augustine goes to great lengths to relativise what he considers Cyprian's error in supporting rebaptism of the lapsed. He is able to satisfy this endeavour by asserting that Cyprian was less culpable because his colleagues also supported rebaptism.

In the case of the anti-Pelagian campaign, Augustine would have exclusive recourse to certain works of Cyprian for a similar reason, but with a differing objective. As the Pelagians presented a different set of challenges to Augustine's theology, he had to find in Cyprian's writings another substratum to support his views. A fine example of this is in *De dominica oratione*, where Augustine is quite visibly drawing on Cyprian to benefit a particular theology of grace that is effective against the Pelagians. This is also keenly seen again in *Opere et eleemmosynis*, where Augustine is definitively placing his own theology of grace in continuity with an authority such as Cyprian. A more complex usage of Cyprian's works is found in Augustine's integration of *De Mortalitate* in the Pelagian controversy. The sections Augustine uses are mostly concerned with creating a tenable Christian worldview and approach to the secular world. Upon reading the sections that Augustine quotes, one is instantly struck by how closely such examples parallel the historical Donatists' conception of the relationship between Christians and the world. *De Mortalitate* is replete with exhortations for Christians to be ready in their defence against the influences of the world. Most important is Cyprian's insistence on focusing on the perfection of the life to come and having the fortitude to resist the pitfalls of this world. This entire worldview seems to be at variance with the theology advocated by Augustine in *De civ. Dei*, so it is somewhat of a surprise that Augustine uses this source against the Pelagians. One possible explanation for this anomaly is that Augustine sought to motivate his flock to be resilient against the attempts of the Pelagian 'enemy' to coerce orthodox Christians to follow the Pelagian way. Regardless, it remains true throughout that Augustine's use of Cyprian's works in his own writings was contextually-based and formed responses to individual challenges from Donatists and Pelagians separately.

Summary Remarks

As a means of concluding this section on the use of Cyprian's authority in the Pelagian controversy, it is helpful to briefly reflect on what has been covered and uncovered in these pages. As noted in the beginning, little has been made of what seems to be a most interesting phenomenon; namely, that in the breadth of two of the most heated controversies of his career, Augustine would at times have to assume and subvert the exclusivist claims upon the legacy of Cyprian by his opponents, whilst also disregarding elements of the Cyprianic tradition that were less compatible with his own position. At other times, Augustine would use Cyprian as a defence and source of validation before those who recognised the authority of the martyr-bishop of Carthage, even if the opposing party had a rightful connection to the legacy of Cyprian as Catholic Christians.

In the course of this book, an attempt has been made to begin unraveling this matter. This has allowed us to observe how Augustine used Cyprian's authority against the Donatists. Facing a highly organised and influential group such as they were, Augustine undermined his opponents by denying their claim to be heirs of Cyprian. He did this by forcefully arguing their innovation in interpreting Cyprian's stance on baptism/rebaptism, ecclesiology, concepts of Church unity, and by savaging them with regard to how they lived their lives as opposed to how they said they should (the Circumcelliones were, to Augustine, the least profound example of a community of saints).

Against the Pelagians it was no longer Augustine who needed to argue to usurp the claim to Cyprian. Having mostly vanquished his foes, the Donatists, he now used Cyprian's name to defend his views from personal attacks concerning his theology and ethnicity and against the allegation he had ruptured the Christian tradition. As opposed to the first controversy where Augustine eagerly refined Cyprian's works in order to critique the North African practice of rebaptism; with the Pelagians, Augustine would elicit from the same authority 'proof' that belief in original sin and total reliance on God's grace were age-old precepts of Christianity. Augustine again used Cyprian to castigate his interlocutors. They claimed to represent the faith of the Church as it is dispersed in the West and East, but how could that be if Cyprian was revered in both East and West and it is quite clear his work supports Augustine's position? Likewise, attempts by the Pelagians to signal the eccentric African character of Augustine's theology as isolated from the rest of the Church were frustrated by an Augustine most willing to argue that such statements were attacks on Africa, of which Cyprian the martyr was a part, and for which Church he had shed his blood. Even Julian of Aeclanum's polemical give-and-take with Augustine was thwarted as Augustine made his defence out of a closer connection with the African/Punic Cyprian.

TABLE 16 *Use of Cyprian's writings by Augustine*

Cyprian's work	# of instances	Where Augustine quotes Cyprian
Ad Don. 1	1	*Doct. Christ.* 4,31
—, 3	1	*s.* 312,2
—, 4	1	*s.* 312,2
Ora. Dom. 12	5	*C. ep. Pel.* 4,25; 4,27; *Corrept.* 10; *Persev.* 4(x2)
—, 14	1	*C. ep. Pel.* 4,25
—, 16	4	*C. ep. Pel.* 4,25; *C. Iul.* 2,6; *C. Iul. imp.* 1,72; *Retract.* 1,3
—, 17	1	*C. ep. Pel.* 4,25
—, 18	2	*C. ep. Pel.* 4,25; *Persev.* 7
—, 22	2	*C. ep. Pel.* 4,27; *Persev.* 8
—, 25	1	*Persev.* 12
—, 26	2	*C. ep. Pel.* 4,25
Opere et eleem. 1	1	*C. ep. Pel.* 4,21
—, 3	3	*C. ep. Pel.* 4,27; 4,28; *C. Iul.* 2,25
—, 18	1	*C. ep. Pel.* 4,27
—, 22	1	*C. ep. Pel.* 4,21
Fort. 13	1	*s.* 305A,2
Hab. Virg. 3	1	*Doct. Christ.* 4,47
—, 15	1	*Doct. Christ.* 4,49
—, 23	1	*Doct. Christ.* 4,47
Idol.	1	*De bapt.* 6,87
De lap. 6	10	*Adult. conj.* 1,31(x2); *De bapt.* 4,12; *C. ep. Parm.* 3,14(x2); *Cresc.* 2,18; 3,40; 4,33; *Ep.* 93,47; 108,10
—, 9	3	*Ep.* 98,3(x3)
Mort. 2	1	*C. ep. Pel.* 4,25
—, 3	1	*Praed. sanct.* 28
—, 4	2	*C. ep. Pel.* 4,25
—, 5	2	*C. ep. Pel.* 4,25
—, 7	2	*C. ep. Pel.* 4,25
—, 15	1	*Praed. sanct.* 28
—, 26	2	*C. ep. Pel.* 4,25
Test. 3,4	11	*C. ep. Pel.* 4,25; 4,26; *C. Iul. imp.* 6,18;

TABLE 16 *Use of Cyprian's writings by Augustine* (cont.)

Cyprian's work	# of instances	Where Augustine quotes Cyprian
		Persev. 36(x3); 43; 48; 49; *Retract.* 2,1
—, 3,54	1	*C. ep. Pel.* 4,27
Unit. eccl. 5	6	*C. Gaud.* 2,2
		C. Gaud. 2,14
		Cresc. 2,42(x2)
		Cresc. 3,64
		Cresc. 3,73
Zel. 1	1	*De bapt.* 4,11
—, 4	2	*De bapt.* 4,11
Dat. 3	1	*C. ep. Pel.* 4,25
—, 11	1	*C. ep. Pel.* 4,22
—, 17	1	*C. ep. Pel.* 4,22
Sent. Episc. Pref.	22	*De bapt.* 2,3; 2,6; 2,7; 2,15; 2,20; 3,1; 3,14; 3,15(x4); 4,11; 6,9; 6,10; 6,12; 6,48; 7,3(x2); 7,7; 7,49; *Cresc.* 3,2(x2)
—, 1	3	*De bapt.* 6,11; *De bapt.* 6,12(x2)
—, 2	1	*De bapt.* 6,14
—, 3	1	*De bapt.* 6,15
—, 5	5	*De bapt.* 6,19(x5)
—, 6	1	*De bapt.* 6,20
—, 7	3	*De bapt.* 6,23(x3)
—, 8	2	*De bapt.* 6,24; 6,25
—, 9	1	*De bapt.* 6,26
—, 10	1	*De bapt.* 6,28
—, 11	1	*De bapt.* 6,30
—, 12	2	*De bapt.* 6,32; 6,33
—, 13	1	*De bapt.* 6,34
—, 14	2	*De bapt.* 6,36; 6,37
—, 15	3	*De bapt.* 6,38; 6,39(x2)
—, 16	1	*De bapt.* 6,40
—, 17	1	*De bapt.* 6,42
—, 18	2	*De bapt.* 6,46; 6,48
—, 19	1	*De bapt.* 6,49
—, 20	1	*De bapt.* 6,51
—, 21	1	*De bapt.* 6,53
—, 22	2	*De bapt.* 6,55; 6,56

Cyprian's work	# of instances	Where Augustine quotes Cyprian
—, 23	1	*De bapt.* 6,57
—, 24	1	*De bapt.* 6,59
—, 25	1	*De bapt.* 6,67
—, 26	1	*De bapt.* 6,63
—, 27	2	*De bapt.* 6,65; 6,66
—, 28	2	*De bapt.* 3,8; 6,67
—, 29	1	*De bapt.* 6,69
—, 30	2	*De bapt.* 3,9; 6,71
—, 31	1	*De bapt.* 6,73
—, 32	1	*De bapt.* 6,75
—, 33	2	*De bapt.* 6,77; 6,78
—, 34	1	*De bapt.* 6,79
—, 35	1	*De bapt.* 6,81
—, 36	1	*De bapt.* 6,83
—, 37	1	*De bapt.* 6,85
—, 38	4	*De bapt.* 7,2; 7,3(x3)
—, 39	2	*De bapt.* 7,4; 7,5
—, 40	3	*De bapt.* 7,6; 7,7(x2)
—, 41	1	*De bapt.* 7,8
—, 42	1	*De bapt.* 7,10
—, 43	1	*De bapt.* 7,12
—, 44	1	*De bapt.* 7,14
—, 45	1	*De bapt.* 7,16
—, 46	1	*De bapt.* 7,18
—, 47	1	*De bapt.* 7,20
—, 48	1	*De bapt.* 7,22
—, 49	1	*De bapt.* 7,24
—, 50	1	*De bapt.* 7,26
—, 51	1	*De bapt.* 7,28
—, 52	2	*De bapt.* 7,30; 7,31
—, 53	1	*De bapt.* 7,32
—, 54	1	*De bapt.* 7,34
—, 55	1	*De bapt.* 7,36
—, 56	3	*De bapt.* 3,10(x2); 7,38
—, 57	1	*De bapt.* 7,40
—, 58	1	*De bapt.* 7,42
—, 59	1	*De bapt.* 7,44
—, 60	1	*De bapt.* 7,46

TABLE 16 *Use of Cyprian's writings by Augustine* (cont.)

Cyprian's work	# of instances	Where Augustine quotes Cyprian
—, 61	1	*De bapt.* 7,48
—, 62	1	*De bapt.* 7,50
—, 63	2	*De bapt.* 3,11; 7,52
—, 64	1	*De bapt.* 7,54
—, 65	1	*De bapt.* 7,56
—, 66	1	*De bapt.* 7,58
—, 67	1	*De bapt.* 7,60
—, 68	1	*De bapt.* 7,62
—, 69	1	*De bapt.* 7,64
—, 70	1	*De bapt.* 7,66
—, 71	1	*De bapt.* 7,68
—, 72	1	*De bapt.* 7,70
—, 73	1	*De bapt.* 7,72
—, 74	1	*De bapt.* 7,74
—, 75	1	*De bapt.* 7,76
—, 76	1	*De bapt.* 7,78
—, 77	2	*De bapt.* 3,12; 7,80
—, 78	1	*De bapt.* 7,82
—, 79	1	*De bapt.* 7,84
—, 80	1	*De bapt.* 7,86
—, 81	1	*De bapt.* 7,88
—, 82	1	*De bapt.* 7,90
—, 83–85	1	*De bapt.* 7,92
—, 86	1	*De bapt.* 7,94
—, 87	1	*De bapt.* 7,96
Ep. 11,1	7	*De bapt.* 4,3(x2); 4,16; 4,19; 6,60; *Cresc.* 2,18; *Ep.* 157,34
—, 54,2	1	*C. Gaud.* 2,10
—, 54,3	19	*C. Don.* 9; 11; 28; 37; *C. Gaud.* 2,3; 2,4; 2,5(x2); 2,10; 2,14; 2,43; 2,45; 2,48; 3,35; 3,73; 4,67; *Ep.* 108,10; *Retract.* 2,28
—, 55,2	1	*Ep.* 93,41
—, 55,25	1	*De bapt.* 4,18
—, 55,27	1	*De bapt.* 4,7
—, 63,2–4	1	*Doct. Chr.* 4,45

Cyprian's work	# of instances	Where Augustine quotes Cyprian
—, 64,2	1	*C. ep. Pel.* 4,23
—, 64,4	1	*C. ep. Pel.* 4,23
—, 64,5	1	*C. ep. Pel.* 4,23; *C. Iul.* 1,6; 1,22; 3,31; *s.* 294,19
—, 69,5	2	*De bapt.* 7,97; 7,98
—, 69,12	1	*De bapt.* 6,10
—, 70,2	1	*De bapt.* 5,29
—, 71,3	4	*De bapt.* 2,2; 2,5; 2,13(x2)
—, 71,4	1	*De bapt.* 2,14
—, 73,1	1	*De bapt.* 7,31
—, 73,3	2	*De bapt.* 3,17(x2)
—, 73,7	1	*De bapt.* 3,23
—, 73,13	5	*De bapt.* 4,7(x2); 4,8(x2); 4,9
—, 73,14	2	*De bapt.* 4,10; 4,16
—, 73,15	1	*De bapt.* 4,20
—, 73,16	1	*De bapt.* 4,21
—, 73,21	2	*De bapt.* 4,24(x2)
—, 73,23	10	*De bapt.* 2,14; 2,18; 3,7;5,1; 5,2; 5,3; 5,4; 5,39; 7,49; *Cresc.* 2,41
—, 73,24	1	*De bapt.* 5,8
—, 73,25	1	*De bapt.* 5,14
—, 73,26	6	*De bapt.* 4,11; 5,22; 6,10(x3)
—, 74,5	1	*Cresc.* 3,2
—, 74,10	1	*De bapt.* 5,34
—, 74,11	1	*De bapt.* 5,37

CHAPTER 8

General Conclusions

This work has followed Augustine's appropriation of Cyprian, a process that ran through the entirety of his career. Events that started with his ordination as a priest in 391, and carried on until his death in 430, were recapitulated in these pages, with consideration also given to Cyprian's ongoing appeal to North African Christians in the centuries thereafter.

The beginning of the book was concerned with the earliest years of Augustine's ordained ministry. Through a careful analysis of selected works, such as *Ep.* 19, 20, 21, 23, 29, and *Conf.* Chapter 10, I recaptured the vocational crisis Augustine underwent at the start, which I surmise to have been his reaction to a perceived lack of interest from his fellow North Africans in his passion for the Catholic truth. Eventually this frustration manifested itself in increasing criticisms of the Donatists by way of themes that he would deploy throughout his career. Works that were closely examined were *Ep.* 22, 23, 29, 32, 33, 34, 35, 43, 44, 49, 51, 52, 53. The most important themes to come out of this period of the 390s were the pride (*superbia*) of the Donatists; the provincialism of 'Africa' and its desired separation from the world (in opposition to Augustine's biblical exegesis); the notion that schism is worse than heresy; the idea that public sinners are to be tolerated for the sake of Church unity; and an early critique of the Donatist leadership's actions in the course of the Maximianist schism (390s).

Up to this point no surviving records show that Augustine had as yet stumbled upon Cyprian as an authority against the Donatists. But he was heading in that direction. As the year 400 approached, the anti-Donatist campaign intensified, with an increase in polemical language and themes appearing in Augustine's letters and sermons. A look at *s.* 37, 252, 271, 292, 313E, *En. in Ps.* 54, *Ex.* 2 of 21, *Ex.* 2 of Ps. 33, *En. in Ps.* 54, *En. in Ps.* 57 revealed that he continued aggressively criticising the Donatists for being influenced by concupiscence, arrogance, and pride, and for therefore rejecting Christ because of their insistence on the exclusive integrity of their own, local and African Church. As these polemically-charged trends developed, it was possible to carefully retrace the seminal moments of Cyprian's influence in the surviving accounts. This was done through an assessment of an array of works written between 394–400: *Doct. Chr.* (where the first direct mention/appeal to Cyprian was made), *Conf.* and *C. Faust.* But establishing the precise moment of appropriation was a difficult task, since this was based on a collection of sermons that are difficult to date precisely: i.e., *s.* 37, 305A, 313A, 313B, 313C, 313E. Each of

 | DOI 10.1163/9789004312647_010

these sermons contains language clearly aimed at appropriating Cyprian's authority. Of the many sermons that are believed to have been delivered in this period, this group presents the most promising primary examples of Augustine's use of Cyprian against the Donatists; though they are obviously not the first specifically anti-Donatist works, an honour which falls to *Ps. c. part. Don.* (393), *C. ep. Donati heretici* (393/94), and *C. partem Donati* (397). A special analysis was made of *s.* 37 and 313E, which showed that if the dating of both could be clarified, a picture would emerge of Augustine becoming capable of using Cyprian's authority early on, earlier than the surviving anti-Donatist treatises in fact. All of this is remarkable, given that Augustine launched into his effort of appropriating Cyprian with virtually no precedent, since Optatus of Milevis (from whom he borrowed much of his scheme for the anti-Donatist campaign) had not tried to do so himself.

The final instalment of part one was a consideration of the impact that the intra-Donatist Maximianist schism (390s) had upon Augustine's efforts overall. At the heart of this matter was the outrage surrounding the election of Primian to replace the beloved Donatist primate Parmenian of Carthage (in 392/93). When a Carthaginian deacon, Maximian, became the figurehead of a protest movement, this outrage was manifest in regional councils and mutual excommunications. But Augustine seized the moment when Primian and his allies were reconciled with the Maximianists without requiring rebaptism, the cause of the original Donatist-Catholic split. Augustine launched into his attack on this seeming hypocrisy, which was only instigated when the Donatists attempted to curry the favour of the Roman administration in Africa by asking them to step in and end the Maximianist debacle. The polemical gold-mine this request opened up for Augustine was further enriched when, in 398/99, Roman joint-forces pursued and executed Count Gildo and the Donatist bishop, Optatus of Thamugadi, two individuals who were later personified by Augustine as the consummate Donatist leaders.

The second segment of this book covered Augustine's appropriation of Cyprian once he had entered into his full-blown anti-Donatist campaign. This began in 400/01 when he started producing his anti-Donatist trilogy: *C. ep. Parm*, *De bapt.*, and *C. litt. Pet.* With these works, Augustine began a sustained appropriation of Cyprian that would only end with his death. He used a combination of flattering accolades such as *beatus*, *sanctus*, martyr, *exemplum*, *auctoritas*, most graced and tolerant, along with anti-Donatist themes he had already firmly established by then, including examples such as Donatist concupiscence, stubbornness, pride, and arrogance. Going beyond this, Augustine moved to pull Cyprian's legacy away from the claims of the Donatist leadership, saying that their rejection of unity was a rejection of all that Cyprian had stood for. In this way Augustine sought to displace the Donatists' claim of heredity to Cyprian's authority and in its stead assert his own claim to pedigree with the hero-martyr of Carthage. Indeed, of the more than 600 references Augustine would make to Cyprian, his central argument remained throughout that the Donatists had disavowed Cyprian's teaching and spirit by their refusal to reconcile with Catholics in Africa. This meant any discussion on rebaptism, the efficacy of sinful ministers in lieu of divine grace, and the relation between the Church and the Roman Empire, which the Donatist controversy is well-known for, came down to Augustine's argument that the Donatist leadership had rejected Cyprian's example and therefore forfeited any legitimate claim to his authority.

From this point an analysis follows of the way that Augustine not only sustained his appropriation, but also how he attempted to merge both his and Cyprian's teachings into one coherent Catholic narrative. He did this in a number of ways: through the adoption of Cyprian's own biblical vocabulary via similar Pauline usage (of the 168 Pauline verses used by Cyprian, Augustine would use 151); through a rather novel promotion of imperially-backed coercion of non-compliant Donatists; through a new theology of grace that focused more on individual holiness and less on group integrity as North Africans had traditionally done; and through a pneumatology that was critical of the Donatists' defiance of unity with the Catholics. The results of these new proposals by Augustine were mixed. On the one hand, these new theologies certainly placed Cyprian's authority on Augustine's side, since he had the luxury of writing as the victor and his diagnosis was credibly regarded as historical truth for a millennia and a half thereafter, but on the other, it is unmistakable that in nearly all of those areas where Augustine tried to expand upon Cyprian's authority, Cyprian's own original intention and context were contrary to the purposes that Augustine intended. It was only by sheer determination, endurance, and a constant process of appeal that Augustine could seemingly overcome this rift. This was achieved not only by references to Cyprian in Augustine's treatises, but perhaps more importantly, by commanding the conversation through his letters and sermons to audiences and recipients in Africa and throughout the Roman world.

This process of appropriating Cyprian reached its pinnacle, not in the heated African winds of the Donatist controversy, since that never came to an end as such, but rather as that crisis merged into the Pelagian affair after 411/12. In this new fight, the scarred veteran fighter Augustine, found himself placed in a scenario unlike that in which he was placed during the height of the anti-Donatist campaign. Here the bishop of Hippo was taking regular criticism in the form of stinging personal attacks and polemical insinuations from his self-anointed Pelagian foes, especially Julian of Aeclanum, for being 'too African' and for peddling 'African novelties and heresies'. In this situation Augustine's appropriation of Cyprian reached a mature stage, since not only did he have to deflect the personal commentaries of Julian, but he also had to simultaneously situate his views within a continuum of authority in the Latin and Greek-speaking churches. Here the importance of Cyprian was evident and it is clear that Cyprian remained the most important authority within his work (with the exception of his spiritual father and role-model Ambrose),[1] because Cyprian was not only respected in Africa, but also abroad—quite in contrast to Ambrose, who was at this point venerated mostly in Italy and the northern rim of the Mediterranean. And despite Augustine's intensive appropriation of Cyprian throughout the duration of his career, the martyr-hero of Carthage remained the indispensible Christian figure for Africans. For several centuries after Augustine's time, veneration of Cyprian remained a steadfast phenomenon in chapels, basilicas, and crypts throughout North Africa, even as Roman and Byzantine influence diminished and Islam eventually took hold in the former Roman breadbasket. Though they were not 'Donatists' in the sense in which Augustine would have labelled them, Christians in early medieval North Africa remained true sons and daughters of Cyprian, and hence, the extended family of the Donatist Christians.

Lingering Questions

Even after such an exhaustive study of Augustine's full-blown effort to appropriate the authority of Cyprian, questions rightfully and inevitably remain. For one, it is hard to avoid the impression that Augustine invented the entire

1 Of course, one cannot forget that even this comparison must be nuanced, since Augustine related differently to Cyprian and Ambrose. Cyprian was the undisputed African authority Augustine strived to associate himself with, according to the context he was embedded in at the time (whether it was the anti-Donatist or anti-Pelagian campaigns). But Ambrose was much more for Augustine, who mentions proudly that Ambrose was his teacher (*C. Iul. imp.* 1,48 (*CSEL* 85/1, 38): '...Ambrosius doctor meus...'; 2,21 (*PL* 44, 688): '...Ambrosium, doctorem meum...'; 5,25 (CSEL 85/2, 219): '...meumque doctorem...'; 5,41 (CSEL 85/2, 243): '...meus doctor...'), father in faith (*C. Iul. imp.* 1,10), baptiser (*Nupt. et con.* 1,40 (CSEL 42, 251): '...beatus Ambrosius Mediolanensis episcopus, cuius sacerdotali ministerio lauacrum regenerationis accepi...'; *C. Iul. imp.* 1,10; 1,59; 6,21), and his solace (*C. Iul. imp.* 4,109). One cannot but question if this filial loyalty and reverence might have been one of Augustine's prime motivators against the Donatists and the Pelagians throughout his career, in terms of which Augustine assumed an aura of duty and mission to defend what Ambrose had taught him?

Donatist vs. Catholic distinction, in the same sort of way that the Pelagian and 'Semi-Pelagian' controversies came about.[2] Though Optatus of Milevis had laboured hard to draw a distinction between 'Catholics' and 'Donatists' in the 380s, especially based on the controversy surrounding the Diocletian persecution in the early 300s and the resulting episcopal elections of Caecilian and Majorinus, such complaints were rather rare before the Augustinian era. Even so, the distinctions that Augustine and his allies insisted upon seem to be so minute as to have drawn only half-hearted reaction from meaningful respondents. It was only in rare circumstances that the so-called Donatists retaliated faintly. It is my supposition that the more the ecclesial council and imperial records are explored by future researchers, the greater will be the evidence of an even smaller formal distinction between the alleged parties. But to Augustine's credit, although I have tried my best to counteract the sparseness of records from the 'Donatist' side, he nonetheless succeeded in creating a vast distinction between 'orthodox Catholics' and 'heretical Donatists' which has endured even till the twenty-first century. My supposition is that North African Christians had much more in common than Augustine and his allies suggest, which we can see in the generations after his death, where the motivation for survival and the protection of livelihoods bypassed any distinction proposed by higher clergy and the political classes, as had always been the case in North Africa. This is not to say that Donatist Christianity did not exist as such. That it did is well proven by the imperial interventions in 405 and 411. But the degree to which one or other side was a 'majority' or a 'minority' will need to be reexamined through the application of recent archaeological input.

In the matter of the authenticity of the Donatist-Catholic distinction, there remains the question of the reception of Cyprian of Carthage in Africa and the rest of the Roman Empire before and after Augustine. Too often, beyond the investigation of the Pelagian controversy, treatment of Cyprian remains solely concerned with Africa. It is obvious that some research is warranted to see if there was any ambivalence in Cyprian's reception after his death, much as there was during the controversies during his lifetime.

More importantly, this work has attempted to make connections between Augustine's appeal to Cyprian and statically-proven trends. While these connections were overwhelmingly demonstrated in Chapter 5, a treasure-trove remains in the data. By simply analysing the information provided here it is possible to show the continuities/discontinuities in the appropriation of Cyprian

2 Again, refer to M. Lamberigts, 'Recent Research into Pelagianism with Particular Emphasis on the Role of Julian of Aeclanum', 197; and Ogliari, *Gratia et Certamen: The Relationship between Grace and Free Will in the Discussion of Augustine with the So-called Semipelagians*, 5.

and the themes that Augustine crafted to sustain this appropriation. It would be an interesting sideline to explore when/where/why Augustine pursued the theme of 'Africa' sceptically against the Donatists, and then welcomingly against the Pelagians. What does this say about his growth as a theologian and bishop? Likewise, there are hosts of themes that were in one of the controversies but not in the other, for example, Church or *ecclesia* (important against the Donatists, not against the Pelagians); flesh or *caro* (seminally present with the Donatists, but massively present against the Pelagians); and grace or *gratia* (carefully used against the Donatists, but a major concept in the anti-Pelagian battle). This shows Augustine's deployment of themes was decided contextually, something that deserves substantial treatment in the future.

Augustine's Cyprian: Final Thoughts

At the end of the day, Cyprian's authority remained quintessentially North African; he was a hero for mainstream Christians (whatever group that might have been, depending on the century: Catholic, Donatist, Byzantine, and so forth), as well as for the persecuted minority of the period. Though this book has been partly critical of Augustine's long-term success in appropriating Cyprian as an authority and a judge, on Augustine's side and in light of the tenacious grip native North Africans had on the Carthaginian martyr-bishop's fame, the fact is that Augustine would succeed in incorporating Cyprian fully into the Catholic camp in the centuries after his death via the canon of saints.

Though the results of the long-term appropriation of Cyprian are complex, what can be most readily seen is the success Augustine had in interpreting Cyprian's authority within the scope of his own career. This assessment is based on the fact that when Augustine walked into his ordination as a priest, he had no previous experience of working with the legacy of Cyprian, or at least none that is observable in surviving evidence. I have retraced how, within a few years of his ordination, Augustine had sometimes waded haphazardly into Cyprian's legacy, though it remains unclear if this was by accident or design. The impact of this initial anti-Donatist appropriation is clear enough, however, when reconstructing how this development entered into Augustine's polemical repertoire to become a central feature of his campaign to sequester the Donatist hierarchy and assert the prominence of his own Catholic Church. As Augustine began to use Cyprian's authority more intensively, a scenario arose wherein this authority was employed to defend positions that were opposed to Cyprian's original third-century intent. This became clear as Augustine came to focus on ecclesiology and sacramentology, especially concerning the Church/world relationship, the reality of the presence of sinful Christians in the Church, the legitimacy of religious coercion by the Roman Empire in pursuit of enforcing orthodoxy, and a doctrine of grace (the earlier African emphasis was placed on group integrity, whilst Augustine's was more on anthropological and individual concerns).

But even more than serving as a cornerstone for Augustine's various theological arguments in the period of his anti-Donatist campaign, Cyprian's authority became more concrete as Augustine's war with the rival Donatist Church dragged on. In Augustine's letters and sermons especially, Cyprian became a symbol and method for targeting African listeners and readers. In this the beginning of his career, and indeed throughout, Augustine's preoccupation was to elucidate the Catholic truth for his contemporaries. This meant that Augustine found in Cyprian the perfect advocate to complement scripture and the authority of other figures. This manoeuvre moved to front and centre of Augustine's efforts in the wake of the Maximianist schism in the 390s, as Augustine became profoundly more emboldened. By the time he launched his fully-fledged campaign against the Donatists with his anti-Donatist trilogy, *Contra epistulam Parmeniani*, *De baptismo contra Donatistas*, and *Contra litteras Petiliani*, Cyprian's authority had become a completely indispensible part of Augustine's approach. The overall record of Augustine's Cyprian-appropriation demonstrates this clearly, with over 600 references throughout his career, second only to his appeal to Ambrose of Milan, yet more evenly distributed throughout the duration of Augustine's career.

This phenomenon of appropriation became even more pronounced when Augustine launched into his decades-long quarrel with his self-appointed Pelagian nemeses. Cyprian again became one of Augustine's most indispensible authority sources, in ways that mirror his appropriation against the Donatists. In this case, however, the outcome of appropriation would serve an entirely different purpose. Unlike the scenario Augustine faced in the anti-Donatist campaign, where he had desperately sought validation for his Catholic views against the accusation of being foreign to the African tradition, in the anti-Pelagian effort Augustine faced withering criticisms (especially from Julian of Aeclanum) that he was peddling novelties and heretical filth. Interlocutors such as Julian, likewise masters of the traditional Roman rhetorical style, savaged Augustine for proposing Punic nonsense. So, in this latter phase of his career, Augustine was accused of being too African! Cyprian's authority in this case was used to safeguard Augustine's views as both truly African as well as universally recognised in the East and the West.

But in the end Augustine could not fully reconcile the fact that, despite his best multi-decade appropriation of Cyprian, there were fundamental variances between their perspectives and contexts. Though history has placed them on the same side, at least in liturgical art, Christian hagiography, and the canons of many Christian churches, North African adherents of the Christian religion in late antiquity would surely have observed some level of idiosyncrasy in finding the two towering personalities as members of the same team. Indeed, Augustine's appropriation of Cyprian symbolises the very complexity of the historical Augustine himself. Never completely content in his native homeland, nor in his adopted Italian seedbed, Augustine's life was defined by evolving tensions and a nuanced identity that has perplexed us till this day. The duality of his universality, stemming from being a Roman world-citizen together with his pulsing home-grown African blood, would cause more trouble for Augustine than he could possibly have appreciated when he first set out from the African shores, under the shadow of that shrine to Cyprian recorded in his *Confessions*. When he finally came home he was a changed man, at peace, and with a newly-converted heart. Yet for the rest of his industrious life Augustine would be torn between these two worlds, and Cyprian would remain forever on the tip of his tongue in articulating this. Through the remainder of his days, Augustine would rely on Cyprian as an authority and a source of validation. Indeed, more than just a footnote or after-thought, Augustine's Cyprian is as much a part of Augustine's story as the bishop of Hippo himself.

Bibliography

Primary Sources

1 *Works of Augustine*

De bapt. De baptismo contra Donatistas, ed. M. Petschenig, CSEL 51/1 (Vienna: Tempsky, 1909).

Brev. Breviculus Collationis cum Donatistis, ed. M. Petschenig, CSEL 53/3 (Vienna: Tempsky, 1910).

Cath. Ad Catholicos fratres [*Epistula ad Catholicos de Secta Donatistarum*], CSEL 52/2 (Vienna: Tempsky, 1909).

C. ep. Parm. Contra epistulam Parmeniani, ed. M. Petschenig, CSEL 51/1(Vienna: Tempsky; Leipzig: Freytag, 1908).

Civ. Dei. De civitate Dei, ed. B. Dombart and A. Kalb, CCSL 47–48 (Turnhout: Brepols, 1955).

Conf. Confessiones, ed. L. Verheijen, CCSL 27 (Turnhout: Brepols, 1981).

C. Don. Ad Donatistas Post Conlationem [*Contra Partem Donati post Gesta; Contra Donatistas*], ed. M. Petschenig, CSEL 53/3 (Vienna: Tempsky, 1910).

Correct. De Correctione Donatistarum [*Ep. 185*], ed. A. Goldbacher, CSEL 57 (Vienna: Tempsky, 1911).

Cresc. Ad Cresconium grammaticum partis Donati [*Cont. Cresc.*], ed. M. Petschenig, CSEL 52/2 (Vienna: Tempsky, 1909).

Doc. Chr. De doctrina Christiana, ed. I. Martin, CCSL 32 (Turnhout: Brepols, 1962).

C. ep. Pel. Contra duas epistulas Pelagianorum, ed. C. Urba and I. Zycha, CSEL 60 (Vienna: Tempsky, 1962).

Emer. Gesta cum Emerito Donatistarum Episcopo, ed. M. Petschenig, CSEL 53/3 (Vienna: Tempsky, 1910).

En. Ps. Enarrationes in Psalmos, ed. E. Dekkers and J. Fraipoint, CCSL 38–40 (Turnhout: Brepols, 1956).

Ep. Epistula/Epistulæ, ed. A. Goldbacher, CSEL 34, 44, 57–58; ed. J. Divjak, CSEL 88 (Vienna: Tempsky, 1895–1923); (Vienna: Tempsky, 1981).

C. Gaud. Contra Gaudentium Donatistarum Episcopum, ed. M. Petschenig, CSEL 53/3 (Vienna: Tempsky, 1910).

Gr.lib. arb. De gratia and libero arbitrio, ed. J.-P. Migne, PL 44 (Paris: Migne, 1861).

Gest. Pel. De gestis Pelagii, ed. C. Urba and I. Zycha, CSEL 42 (Vienna: Tempsky, 1902).

Haer. De haeresibus, ed. R. Vanderplaetse and C. Beukers, CCSL 46 (Turnhout: Brepols, 1969).

Ioh.ev. tr. In Iohannis euangelium tractatus, ed. R. Willems, CCSL 36 (Turnhout: Brepols, 1954).

C. Iul. Contra Iulianum, ed. J.-P. Migne, PL 44 (Paris: Migne, 1845).

C. Iul. Imp. Contra Iulianum opus imperfectum, ed. M. Zelzer, CSEL 85/1–2 (Vienna: Hoelder-Pichler-Tempsky, 1974, 2004).

C. litt. Pet. Contra litteras Petiliani, ed. M. Petschenig, CSEL 52/2 (Vienna: Tempsky, 1909).

Nat. et grat. De natura et gratia , ed. C. Urba and J. Zycha, CSEL 60 (Vienna: Tempsky, 1913).

Nupt. et Con. De Nuptiis et concupiscentia ad Valerium, ed. C. Urba and J. Zycha, CSEL 42 (Vienna: Tempsky, 1902).

Pecc. Mer. De peccatorum meritis et remissione peccatorum et de baptismo paruulorum, ed. C. Urba and J. Zycha, CSEL 60 (Vienna: Tempsky, 1913)., CSEL 60.

Ps. c. Don. Psalmus contra partem Donati, ed. M. Petschenig, CSEL 51/1 (Vienna: Tempsky, 1908).

Ad Simplic. De diversis quaestionibus ad Simplicianum, ed. A. Mutzenbecher, CCSL 44 (Turnhout: Brepols, 1970).

Serm. Sermo/Sermones, ed. J.-P. Migne, PL 38–39; ed. C. Lambot, CCSL 41 (Paris: 1845); (Turnhout: Brepols, 1961).

Serm. Caes. Sermo ad Caesariensis Ecclesiae plebem, ed. M. Petschenig, CSEL 53/3 (Vienna: Tempsky, 1910).

Un. bapt. De unico baptismo contra Petilianum ad Constantinum, ed. M. Petschenig, CSEL 53/3 (Vienna: Tempsky, 1910).

Retract. Retractationum, ed. A. Mutzenbecher, CSEL 57 (Turnhout: Brepols, 1984).

Cetedoc Library of Christian Latin Texts, version 7, mod. P. Tombeur (Turnhout: Brepols, 2008).

Corpus Augustinianum Gissense 2.0, ed. C. Mayer (Basel: Zentrum für Augustinus-Forschung in Würzburg/Kompetenzzentrum für elektronische Erschlieβung-und Publikations-verhafen in den Geisteswissenschaften an der Universität Trier/ Schwabe Verlag, 2005).

2 *Works of Cyprian*

Epistulae 1–57 [*Ep.*], ed. G.F. Diercks, CCSL 3/B (Turnhout: Brepols, 1996).

Epistulae 58–81 [*Ep.*], ed. G.F. Diercks, CCSL 3/C (Turnhout: Brepols, 1996).

De rebaptismate, ed. W. Hartel, CSEL 3/1 (Vienna: C. Geroldi, 1868).

Sententiae Episcoporum de Haereticis Baptizandis, ed. G.F. Diercks, CCSL 3/E (Turnhout: Brepols, 2004).

De ecclesiae catholicae unitate [*De Unit.*], ed. M. Bévenot, CCSL 3/A (Turnhout: Brepols, 1972).

3 *Other Ancient Sources*

Actes de la Conférence de Carthage en 411, ed., intro. S. Lancel, SC 194, 195, 224, 373 (Paris: Les Éditions du Cerf, 1972–1991).

Balduinius, Franciscus, *Deliberatio Africanæ historiæ ecclesiasticæ, sive Optati Mileuitani libri VII. ad Parmenianum de schismate donatistarum. Victoris Vticensis libri III. de persecutione Vandalica in Africa. Cum annotationibus ex Fr. Balduini, ...Commentariis rerum ecclesiasticarum* (Paris: Claudium Fremy, 1569).

Casaubonus, Merici, *Optati Mel. de schismate Donatistarum libri VII. In eosd. notae et emendationes Merici Casauboni* (London: Flesher, 1631).

Concilia Africae A.345–A.525, ed. C. Munier, CCSL 149 (Turnhout: Brepols, 1976).

Eusebius of Caesarea, *Historia Ecclesiastica* [*Histoire Ecclésiastique*] *II, Livres V–VII*, ed. G. Bardy (Paris: Les Éditions du Cerf, 1955).

Julian of Aeclanum, *Ad Florum*, ed. M. Zelzer, CSEL 85/1 (Vienna: Hoelder-Pichler-Tempsky, 1974).

Julian of Aeclanum, *Ad Turbantium*, ed. L. De Coninck, CCSL 88 (Turnhout: Brepols, 1976a).

Julian of Aeclanum, *Epistula ad Rufum*, ed. L. De Coninck, CCSL 88 (Turnhout: Brepols, 1976b).

Optatus of Milevis, *De Schismate Donatistarum*, ed. C. Ziwsa, CSEL 26 (Prague/Vienna: Tempsky; Leipzig: Freytag, 1893).

Tertullian, *De anima* ed. A. Gerlo CCSL 2/2 (Turnhout: Brepols, 1954a).

Tertullian, *Apologeticum*, ed. A. Kroymann, CCSL 1 (Turnhout: Brepols, 1954b).

Tertullian, *De Baptismo*, ed. Kroymann A. CCSL 1 (Turnhout: Brepols, 1954c).

Tyconius, *Liber Regularum* [*The Books of Rules of Tyconius*], *Texts and Studies* 3/1, trans. F. Crawford Burkitt (Cambridge: Cambridge University Press, 1894).

Translations of Primary Sources

Musurillo, H. (trans., intro.), *The Acts of the Christian Martyrs* (Oxford: Clarendon Press, 1972).

Augustine, *To Simplician*, trans. J.H.S. Burleigh, *Augustine: Earlier Writings* (Philadelphia: Westminster Press, 1953a), 370–406.

Augustine, *The Usefulness of Belief*, trans. J.H.S. Burleigh, *Augustine: Earlier Writings* (Philadelphia: Westminster Press, 1953b), 284–323.

Augustine, *Contre la Lettre de Parménien trois livres*, trans. G. Finaert, intro., notes Y. Congar, BA 28 (Brugge: Desclée de Brouwer, 1963a).

Augustine, *Lettre aux Catholiques au Sujet de la Secte des Donatistes* [*Ad Cath.*], trans. G. Finaert, intro., notes Y. Congar, BA 28 (Brugge: Desclée de Brouwer, 1963b).

Augustine, *Psaume Contre le Parti de Donat* [*Ps. c. Don.*], trans. G. Finaert, intro., notes Y. Congar, BA 28 (Brugge: Desclée de Brouwer, 1963c).

Augustine, *Révisions, Livre I, chapitre XX*, [*Retract.*], trans. G. Finaert, intro., notes Y. Congar, BA 28 (Brugge: Desclée de Brouwer, 1963d).

Augustine, *Sept Livres sur le Baptême*, trans. G. Finaert, intro., notes G. Bavaud, BA 29 (Brugge: Desclée de Brouwer, 1964).

Augustine, *L'Affaire de Gaudentius de Thamugadi*, trans. G. Finaert, intro., notes E. Lamirande, BA 32 (Brugge: Desclée de Brouwer, 1965a).

Augustine, *Compte Rendu Abrégé de la Conférence avec les Donatistes*, trans. G. Finaert, intro., notes E. Lamirande, BA 32 (Brugge: Desclée de Brouwer, 1965b).

Augustine, *Discours aux Fidèles de l'Église de Césarée* [*Sermo ad Caesariensis Ecclasiae Plebem*] trans. G. Finaert, intro., notes E. Lamirande, BA 32 (Brugge: Desclée de Brouwer, 1965c).

Augustine, *Procès-Verbal de la Conférence avec Emeritus Évêque des Donatistes*, trans. G. Finaert, intro., notes E. Lamirande, BA 32 (Brugge: Desclée de Brouwer, 1965d).

Augustine, *Un Livre aux Donatistes après la Conférence*, trans. G. Finaert, intro., notes E. Lamirande, BA 32 (Brugge: Desclée de Brouwer, 1965e).

Augustine, *Contre les Lettres de Petilianus*, trans. G. Finaert, BA 30 (Brugge: Desclée de Brouwer, 1967).

Augustine *Livre sur l'Unique Baptême*, trans. G. Finaert, intro., notes A.C. de Veer, BA 31 (Brugge: Desclée de Brouwer, 1968a).

Augustine, *Résponse a Cresconius, Grammairien et Donatiste*, trans. G. Finaert, intro., notes A.C. de Veer, BA 31 (Brugge: Desclée de Brouwer, 1968b).

Augustine, *Sermons I (1–19), On the Old Testament*, ed. J.E. Rotelle, trans., notes E. Hill, intro. M. Pellegrino, WSA III/1 (Hyde Park, NY: New City Press, 1990a).

Augustine, *Sermons II (20–50), On the Old Testament*, ed. J.E. Rotelle, trans., notes E. Hill, WSA III/2 (Hyde Park, NY: New City Press, 1990b).

Augustine, *Sermons III (51–94), On the New Testament*, ed. J.E. Rotelle, trans., notes E. Hill, WSA III/3 (Hyde Park, NY: New City Press, 1991).

Augustine, *Sermons III/4 (94A–147A), On the New Testament*, WSA III/4 (Hyde Park, NY: New City Press, 1992a).

Augustine, *Sermons III/5 (148–183), On the New Testament*, ed. J.E. Rotelle, trans., notes E. Hill, WSA III/5 (Hyde Park, NY: New City Press, 1992b).

Augustine, *Sermons III/6 (184–229Z), On the Liturgical Seasons*, ed. J.E. Rotelle, trans., notes E. Hill, WSA III/6 (Hyde Park, NY: New City Press, 1993a).

Augustine, *Sermons III/7 (230–272B), On the Liturgical Seasons*, ed. J.E. Rotelle, trans., notes E. Hill, WSA III/7 (Hyde Park, NY: New City Press, 1993b).

Augustine, *Sermons III/8 (273–305A), On the Saints*, ed. J.E. Rotelle, trans., notes E. Hill, WSA III/8 (Hyde Park, NY: New City Press, 1994a).

Augustine, *Sermons III/9 (306–340A), On the Saints*, ed. J.E. Rotelle, trans., notes E. Hill, WSA III/9 (Hyde Park, NY: New City Press, 1994b).

Augustine, *Sermons III/10 (341–400), On Various Subjects*, ed. J.E. Rotelle, trans., notes E. Hill, WSA III/10 (Hyde Park, NY: New City Press, 1995a).

Augustine, *Arianism and Other Heresies: Heresies, Memorandum to Augustine, To Orosius in Refutation of the Priscillianists and Origenists, Arian Sermon, Answer to an Arian Sermon, Debate with Maximianus Answer to Maximianus, Answer to an Enemy of the Law and the Prophets*, WSA I/18, trans. R. Teske (Hyde Park, NY: New City Press, 1995b).

Augustine, *Teaching Christianity*, trans., notes, intro. E. Hill, ed. J.E. Rotelle, WSA I/11 (Hyde Park, NY: New City Press, 1996).

Augustine, *Sermons III/11, Newly Discovered Sermons*, ed. J.E. Rotelle, trans., notes E. Hill, WSA III/11 (Hyde Park, NY: New City Press, 1997a).

Augustine, *The Confessions*, intro., trans. notes M. Boulding, ed. J. Rotelle, *WSA* I/1 (Hyde Park, NY: New City Press, 1997b).

Augustine, *Against the Two Pelagian Letters*, trans. R. Teske, ed. J. Rotelle WSA I/24 (Hyde Park, NY: New City Press 1998.

Augustine, *Answer to Julian*, trans. R. Teske, ed. J. Rotelle, WSA I/24 (Hyde Park, NY: New City Press, 1998a).

Augustine, *De Nuptiis et Concupiscentia ad Valerium*, trans. R. Teske, ed. J. Rotelle, WSA I/24 (Hyde Park, NY: New City Press, 1998b).

Augustine, *Unfinished Work in Answer to Julian*, trans. R. Teske, ed. J. Rotelle, WSA I/25 (Hyde Park, NY: New City Press, 1998c).

Augustine, *Unfinished Work Against Julian*, trans., intro. Notes R. Teske, ed. J. Rotelle, WSA I/25 (Hyde Park, NY: New City Press, 1999).

Augustine, *Exposition of the Psalms* 1–32, trans. M. Boulding, ed. J. Rotelle, WSA III/15 (Hyde Park, NY: New City Press, 2000a).

Augustine, *Exposition of the Psalms*, trans. R. Teske, ed. J. Rotelle, WSA III/16 (Hyde Park, NY: New City Press, 2000b).

Augustine, *Exposition of the Psalms*, trans. R. Teske, ed. J. Rotelle, WSA III/17 (Hyde Park, NY: New City Press, 2001a).

Augustine, *Letters 1–99*, trans. R. Teske, ed. J.E. Rotelle, *WSA* II/1 (Hyde Park, NY: New City Press, 2001b).

Augustine, *Exposition of the Psalms*, trans. R. Teske, ed. J. Rotelle, WSA III/18 (Hyde Park, NY: New City Press, 2002).

Augustine, *Augustine's Commentary on Galatians: Introduction, Text, Translation, and Notes* [*Epistulae ad Galatas expositio*], ed., trans., notes Eric Plumer (New York: Oxford University Press, 2003a).

Augustine, *Exposition of the Psalms*, trans. M. Boulding, ed. B. Ramsey, WSA III/19 (Hyde Park, NY: New City Press, 2003b).

Augustine, *Letters 100–155* (*Epistulae*), trans. R. Teske, ed. B. Ramsey, *WSA* II/2 (Hyde Park, NY: New City Press, 2003c).

Augustine, *Exposition of the Psalms*, trans. M. Boulding, ed. B. Ramsey, WSA III/20 (Hyde Park, NY: New City Press, 2004a).

Augustine, *Letters 156–210 (Epistulae)*, trans. R. Teske, ed. B. Ramsey, *WSA* II/3 (Hyde Park, NY: New City Press, 2004b).

Augustine, *Letters 211–270, 1*–29* (Epistulae)*, trans. R. Teske, ed. B. Ramsey, *WSA* II/4 (Hyde Park, NY: New City Press, 2005).

Cyprian, *The Lapsed*, trans. M. Bévenot, ACW 25 (Westminster, MD: The Newman Press, 1957a).

Cyprian, *The Unity of the Catholic Church*, trans. M. Bévenot, ACW 25 (Westminster, MD: The Newman Press, 1957b).

Cyprian, *The Letters of St. Cyprian of Carthage [Ep.], Volume I, Letters 1–27*, trans. G.W. Clarke, ACW 43 (Mahwah, NJ: Newman Press, 1984a).

Cyprian, *The Letters of St. Cyprian of Carthage, Volume II, Letters 28–54*, trans. G.W. Clarke, ACW 44 (Mahwah, NJ: Newman Press, 1984b).

Cyprian, *The Letters of St. Cyprian of Carthage, Volume III, Letters 55–66*, trans. G.W. Clarke, ACW 46 (Mahwah, NJ: Newman Press, 1986).

Cyprian, *The Letters of St. Cyprian of Carthage, Volume IV, Letters 67–82*, trans. G.W. Clarke, ACW 47 (Mahwah, NJ: Newman Press, 1989).

Donatist Martyr Stories: The Church in Conflict in Roman North Africa, trans., intro., notes Maureen Tilley, *Translated Texts for Historians* 24 (Liverpool: Liverpool University Press, 1996).

Eusebius of Caesarea, *Historia Ecclesiastica II, Livres V–VII*, ed. G. Bardy (Paris: Les Éditions du Cerf, 1955).

Jean Chrysostome, *Huit catéchèses baptismales inédites*, ed. A. Wenger, *SC* 50 (Paris: Cerf, 1957).

Optatus of Milevis, *Against the Donatists*, trans., ed. Mark Edwards, *Translated Texts for Historians* 27 (Liverpool: Liverpool University Press, 1997).

Pontius, *Vita Cypriani*, in M. Pellegrino (ed.), *Ponzio: Vita e martirio de San Cipriano, Verba Seniorum* 3 (Alba: Pia Società *San* Paolo, 1955).

Possidius of Calama, *The Life of Saint Augustine*, intro., notes M. Pellegrino, ed. J.E. Rotelle, *Saint Augustine Series* (Villanova, PA: Augustinian Press, 1988).

Theodosius, *Codex Theodosianus* (*The Theodosian Code and Novels and the Sirmondian Constitutions*), trans. C. Pharr (Princeton, NJ: Princeton University Press, 1952).

Tyconius, *The Books of Rules*, trans. W.S. Babcock, *Texts and Translations* 31. *Early Christian Literature Series* 7 (Atlanta: Scholars Press, 1989).

Secondary Literature

Alexander, James, 'A Note on the Interpretation of the Parable of the Threshing Floor at the Conference of Carthage of A.D. 411', in *Journal of Theological Studies* 24 (1973), 512–19.

Alexander, James, 'The Motive for a Distinction between Donatus of Carthage and Donatus of Casae Nigrae', *Journal of Theological Studies* 31/2 (1980), 540–47.

Alexander, James, 'Aspects of Donatist Scriptural Interpretation at the Conference of Carthage of 411', *Studia Patristica* 15 (1984), 125–30.

Alexander, James, 'Count Taurinus and the Persecutors of Donatism', *Zeitschrift für Antikes Christentum* 2 (1998), 247–67.

Alexander, James, 'Donatism', in P.F. Esler (ed.), *The Early Christian World*, vol. 2 (New York/London: Routledge, 2000), 952–74.

Alexander, James, and S. Lancel, 'Donatistae', in C. Mayer (ed.), *Augustinus-Lexikon*, vol. 2 (Basel: Schwabe & Co., 1999), 607–38.

Altaner, Berthold, 'Augustinus und Gregor von Nazianz, Gregor von Nyssa', in B. Altaner (ed.), *Kleine Patristische Schriften* (TU 83) (Berlin: Akademie-Verlag, 1967a), 277–85.

Altaner, Berthold, 'Augustinus und Irenäus', in B. Altaner (ed.), *Kleine Patristische Schriften* (TU, 83) (Berlin: Akademie-Verlag, 1967b), 194–203.

Arnauld, Dominique, *Histoire du Christianisme en Afrique: Les sept premiers siècles* (Paris: Éditions Karthala, 2001).

Babcock, William, *Historia Carthaginensis Collationis sive disputationis de ecclesia, olim habitae inter Catholics et Donatistas* (Paris: Claudium Fremy, 1566).

Babcock, William, 'Augustine's Interpretation of Romans (A.D. 394–396)', *Augustinian Studies* 10 (1979), 55–74.

Babcock, William, 'Augustine and Tyconius: A Study in the Latin Appropriation of Paul', *Studia Patristica* 17/3 (1982), 1209–215.

Barnes, Timothy, 'The Beginnings of Donatism', *Journal of Theological Studies* 26/1 (1975), 13–22.

Barnes, Timothy, Review Article: "Was There a Constantinian Revolution?" *Journal of Late Antiquity* 2/2 (2009), 374–84.

Baronius, *Annales Ecclesiastici, Avctore Cæsare Baronio* [...] *Tomus primus* [– *duodecimus*] [...], *tomes 3–5* (Cologne: Johann Gymnich IV, 1588–1607).

Bartelink, Gerard, 'Die Beeinflußung Augustins durch die griechischen Patres', in J. den Boeft and J. van Oort (eds.), *Augustiniana Traiectina. Communications présentées au Colloque International d'Utrecht (13–14 novembre 1986)* (Paris: Études augustiniennes, 1987), 9–24.

Basevi, Claudio, 'Alle fonti della dottrina agostiniana dell' Incarnazione: l'influenza della cristologie di sant'Ambrogio', *Scripta Theologica* 7 (1975), 499–529.

Bastiaensen, A.A.R., 'Augustin et ses prédécesseurs latins chrétiens', in J. den Boeft and J. van Oort (eds.), *Augustiniana Traiectina. Communications présentées au Colloque International d'Utrecht (13–14 novembre 1986)* (Paris: Études augustiniennes, 1987), 25–57.

Beatrice, Pier Franco, *Tradux peccati. Alle fonti della dottrina agostiniana del peccato originale*, Studia Patristica Mediolanensia 8 (Milan: Vita e Pensiero, 1978).

Beaver, R. Pierce, 'The Donatist Circumcelliones', *Church History* 4 (1935), 123–33.

Beaver, R. Pierce, 'The Organization of the Church of Africa on the Eve of the Vandal Invasion', *Church History* 5 (1936), 168–81.

Beddoe, Paul, '*Contagio* in the Donatists and St. Augustine', *Studia Patristica* 27 (1993), 231–36.

Beddoe, Paul, 'L'Afrique vandale et byzantine', *Antiquité tardive* 10 (2003), 13–179.

Benedict, David, *History of the Donatists, History of the Donatists with Notes*. The Dissent and Nonconformity Series 12 (Providence, RI: Nickerson, Sibley & Co., 1875. Reprinted by The Baptist Standard Bearer, Inc., Paris, AR).

Benson, E.W., *Cyprian: His Life, His Times, His Work* (London: Macmillan, 1897).

Bernet, Anne, *Les chrétientés d'Afrique: Des origines à la conquête arabe* (Versailles: Éditions de Paris, 2006).

Bernino, Domenico, *Historia di tutte l'heresie descritta da Domenico Bernino* (Venice: Presso Paolo Baglioni, 1711).

Bévenot, Maurice, 'A Bishop is Responsible to God Alone (St. Cyprian)', *Recherches de Science Religieuse* 39 (1951–52), 397–415.

Bévenot, Maurice, 'Épiscopat et Primauté chez S. Cyprien', *Ephemerides Theologicae Lovanienses* 42/1 (1966), 176–95.

Bévenot, Maurice, 'Cyprian and his Recognition of Cornelius', *Journal of Theological Studies* 28/2 (1977), 346–59.

Bévenot, Maurice, 'Cyprian's Platform in the Rebaptism Controversy', *Heythrop Journal* 19/2 (1978), 123–42.

Bévenot, Maurice, 'Sacerdos' as Understood by Cyprian', *Journal of Theological Studies* 30/2 (1979), 413–29.

Beyenka, Barbara, 'The Names of St. Ambrose in the Works of St. Augustine', *Augustinian Studies* 5 (1974), 19–28.

Biersack, M., 'Bellarmin und die « Causa Baii »', in M. Lamberigts, L. Kenis (eds.), *L'Augustinisme à l'Ancienne Faculté de Théologie de Louvain, Bibliotheca ephemeridum theologicarum Lovaniensium* 111 (Leuven: Peeters, 1994), 167–78.

Bindemann, Carl, *Der heilige Augustinus*, sections 2–3 (Berlin: Hermann Schultze, 1844–1869).

Böhringer, Georg Friedrich, *Die Kirche Christi in Biographien* (Zürich: Verlag van Meyer & Zeller, 1845).

Bonner, Gerald, 'How Pelagian was Pelagius?' *Studia Patristica* 9 (1966), 350–58.

Bonner, Gerald, 'Les origines africaines de la doctrine augustinienne sur la chute et le péché originel', *Augustinus* 12 (1967), 97–116.

Bonner, Gerald, 'Rufinus of Syria and African Pelagianism', *Augustinian Studies* 1 (1970), 31–47.

Bonner, Gerald, *Augustine and Modern Research on Pelagianism* (Villanova, PA: Villanova University Press, 1972).

Bonner, Gerald, 'Augustine, the Bible and the Pelagians', in P. Bright (ed., trans.), *Augustine and the Bible* (Notre Dame, IN: University of Notre Dame Press, 1986a), 227–42.

Bonner, Gerald, *St Augustine of Hippo: Life and Controversies* (Norwich: Canterbury Press, 1986b).

Bonner, Gerald, 'Christus Sacerdos: The Roots of Augustine's Anti-Donatist Polemic', in A. Zumkeller (ed.), *Signum Pietatis* 40. Festgabe für Cornelius Petrus Mayer OSB zum 60 Geburtstag, *Cassiciacum* 40 (Würzburg: Augustinus Verlag, 1989), 325–39.

Bonner, Gerald, 'Baptismus paruulorum', in C. Mayer (ed.), *Augustinus-Lexikon* 1, 3/4 (Basel: Schwabe & Co., 1990), 592–602.

Bonner, Gerald, 'Caelestius', in C. Mayer (ed.), *Augustinus-Lexikon* 1, 5/6 (Basel: Schwabe & Co., 1992a), 693–98.

Bonner, Gerald, 'Pelagianism and Augustine', *Augustinian Studies* 23 (1992b), 33–51.

Bonner, Gerald, 'Pelagianism Reconsidered', *Studia Patristica* 27 (1993a), 237–41.

Bonner, Gerald, 'Augustine and Pelagianism', *Augustinian Studies* 24 (1993b), 24–47.

Bonner, Gerald, 'Concupiscentia', in C. Mayer (ed.), *Augustinus-Lexikon* 1, 7/8 (Basel: Schwabe & Co., 1994), 1113–122.

Bonner, Gerald, 'Correptione et gratia, De', in A. Fitzgerald (ed.), *Augustine through the Ages. An Encyclopedia* (Grand Rapids/Cambridge: Wm.B. Eerdmans Publishing, 1999a), 245–46.

Bonner, Gerald, 'Dic Christi Veritas Ubi Nunc Habitas: Ideas of Schism and Heresy in the Post-Nicene Age', in W.E. Klingshirn and M. Vessey (eds.), *The Limits of Ancient Christianity: Essays on Late Antique Thought and Culture in Honor of R.A. Markus* (Ann Arbor, MI: University of Michigan Press, 1999b), 63–79.

Bonner, Gerald, 'Dono perseuerantiae, De', *in* A. Fitzgerald (ed.), *Augustine through the Ages. An Encyclopedia* (Grand Rapids/Cambridge: Wm. Eerdmans Publishing, 1999c), 287.

Bonner, Gerald, 'Duas epistulas Pelagianorum, Contra', in A. Fitzgerald (ed.), *Augustine through the Ages. An Encyclopedia* (Grand Rapids/Cambridge: Wm. Eerdmans Publishing, 1999d), 288–89.

Bonner, Gerald, 'Gratia et libero arbitrio, De', in A. Fitzgerald (ed.), *Augustine through the Ages. An Encyclopedia* (Grand Rapids/Cambridge: Wm. Eerdmans Publishing, 1999e), 400–01.

Bonner, Gerald, 'Julianum, Contra', in A. Fitzgerald (ed.), *Augustine through the Ages. An Encyclopedia* (Grand Rapids/Cambridge: Wm. Eerdmans Publishing, 1999f), 480.

Bonner, Gerald, 'Julianum opus imperfectum, Contra', in A. Fitzgerald (ed.), *Augustine through the Ages. An Encyclopedia* (Grand Rapids/Cambridge: Wm. Eerdmans Publishing, 1999g), 480–81.

Bonner, Gerald, 'Nuptiis et concupiscentia, De', in A. Fitzgerald (ed.), *Augustine through the Ages. An Encyclopedia* (Grand Rapids/Cambridge: Wm. Eerdmans Publishing, 1999h), 592–93.

Bonner, Gerald, 'Praedestinatione sanctorum, De', in A. Fitzgerald (ed.), *Augustine through the Ages. An Encyclopedia* (Grand Rapids/Cambridge: Wm. Eerdmans Publishing, 1999i), 699.

Bonner, Gerald, 'Schism and Unity', in I. Hazlett (ed.), *Early Christianity: Origins and Evolution to AD600, in Honour of W.H.C. Frend* (London: SPCK, 1991j).

Bord, J.-B., 'L'autorité de saint Cyprien dans la controverse baptismale, jugée d'après saint Augustin', *Revue d'Histoire Ecclésiastique* 18 (1922), 445–68.

Botha, Chris, 'The Extinction of the Church in North Africa', *Journal of Theology for Southern Africa* 57 (1986), 24–31.

Bowder, Diana, *The Age of Constantine and Julian* (London: Paul Elek Books, 1978).

Brennecke, Hanns Cristof, 'Hilarius', in C. Mayer (ed.), *Augustinus-Lexikon* 3–3/4 (Basel: Schwabe, 2006), 341–48.

Brent, Allen, 'Cyprian's Reconstruction of the Martyr Tradition', *Journal of Ecclesiastical History* 53/2 (2002), 41–268.

Bright, Pamela, '"The Preponderating Influence of Augustine": A Study of the Epitomes of the *Book of Rules* of the Donatist Tyconius', in P. Bright (ed., trans.), *Augustine and the Bible* (Notre Dame, IN: University of Notre Dame Press, 1986), 109–28.

Bright, Pamela, 'Donatist Bishops' in *Augustine through the Ages, An Encyclopedia*, ed. A. Fitzgerald (Grand Rapids, MI: Wm. Eerdmans Publishing, 1999), 281–84.

Brisson, J.-P., *Autonomisme et christianisme dans l'Afrique romaine de Septime Sévère à l'invasion vandale* (Paris: De Boccard, 1958).

Brown, Peter, 'Religious Coercion in the Later Roman Empire: The Case of North Africa', *History* 48 (1963), 283–305. Reprinted in P. Brown, *Religion and Society in the Age of Augustine* (London: Faber & Faber, 1972), 301–31.

Brown, Peter, 'St. Augustine's Attitude Towards Religious Coercion', *Journal of Roman Studies* 54 (1964), 107–16. Reprinted in P. Brown, *Religion and Society in the Age of Augustine* (London: Faber & Faber, 1972), 260–78.

Brown, Peter, 'Review of: Enim Tengström, *Donatisten und Katholieken: Soziale, Wirtschaftliche und Politische Aspekten einer Nordafrikanischen Kirchenspaltung* (Studia Graeca et Latina Gothoburgensia, xviii). Göteborg: Acta Universitatis Gothoburgensis, 1964', *Journal of Roman Studies* 55 (1965), 281–83. Reprinted in P. Brown, *Religion and Society in the Age of Augustine* (London: Faber & Faber, 1972), 335–38.

Brown, Peter, 'Approaches to the Religious Crisis of the Third Century A.D.', *English Historical Review* 83 (1968a), 542–48. Reprinted in P. Brown, *Religion and Society in the Age of Augustine* (London: Faber & Faber, 1972), 74–93.

Brown, Peter, 'Christianity and Local Culture in Late Roman Africa', *Journal of Roman Studies* 58 (1968b), 85–95. Reprinted in P. Brown, *Religion and Society in the Age of Augustine* (London: Faber & Faber, 1972), 279–300.

Brown, Peter, '*Pelagius and his Supporters. Aims and Environment*', in P. Brown, *Religion and Society in the Age of Saint Augustine* (London: Faber & Faber, 1972), 208–26.

Brown, Peter, *Augustine of Hippo: A Biography*, revised edition (Berkeley/Los Angeles: University of California Press, 2000).

Buonaiuti, Ernesto, *Il Cristianesimo nell'Africa Romana* (Bari: Guis. Laterza & Figli, 1928).

Burns, J. Patout, 'Augustine's Role in the Imperial Action against Pelagius', *Journal of Theological Studies* 30 (1979), 67–83.

Burns, J. Patout, 'Appropriating Augustine Appropriating Cyprian', *Augustinian Studies* 36/1 (2005), 113–30.

Burns, J. Patout, 'The Interpretation of Romans in the Pelagian Controversy', *Augustinian Studies* 10 (1979), 43–54.

Burns, J. Patout, *The Development of Augustine's Doctrine of Operative Grace, Collection des Études Augustiniennes – Série Antiquité* 82 (Paris: Études Augustiniennes, 1980).

Burns, J. Patout, 'On Rebaptism: Social Organization in the Third Century Church', *Journal of Early Christian Studies* 1/4 (1993a), 367–403.

Burns, J. Patout, 'Social Context in the Controversy between Cyprian and Stephen', *Studia Patristica* 24 (1993b), 38–44.

Burns, J. Patout, 'Grace', in A. Fitzgerald (ed.), *Augustine through the Ages. An Encyclopedia* (Grand Rapids, MI/Cambridge: Wm. Eerdmans Publishing, 1999), 391–98.

Burns, J. Patout, 'The Eucharist as the Foundation of Christian Unity in North African Theology', *Augustinian Studies* 32/1 (2001), 1–23.

Burns, J. Patout, *Cyprian the Bishop* (London/New York: Routledge, 2002).

Burns, J. Patout, 'Establishing Unity in Diversity', *Perspectives in Religious Studies* 32/4 (2005), 381–99.

Burns, J. Patout, and Robin Jensen, *Christianity in Roman Africa: the Development of Its Practices and Beliefs* (Grand Rapids, MI/Cambridge: Wm. Eerdmans Publishing, 2014).

Burt, D., 'Augustine on the Morality of Violence: Theoretical Issues and Applications', *Congresso internazionale su S. Agostino nel XVI centenario della conversione* (Rome, 1987), 25–54.

Callistus, Georgius, *Accedit Georgii Calixti, S. Theo. Doct. et in Acad. Julia Prof. primarii, in eorundem librorum lectionem Introductionis fragmentum edente Frid. Ulrico Calixto* (Helmstedt: F. Chayer, 1657).

Cameron, Michael, 'Augustine's Use of the Song of Songs against the Donatists', in F. Van Fleteren and J.C. Schnaubelt (eds.), *Augustine: Biblical Exegete* (New York: Peter Lang, 2001), 99–127.

Cameron, Michael, 'Valerius of Hippo: A Profile', *Augustinian Studies* 40/1 (2009), 5–26.

Cary, Phillip, *Inner Grace: Augustine in the Traditions of Plato and Paul* (Oxford: Oxford University Press, 2008).

Cenzon Santos, Maria A., *Baptismal Ecclesiology of St. Augustine: A Theological Study of His Antidonatist Letters* (Rome: Athenaeum Romanum Sanctae Crucis, 1990).

Chadwick, Henry, 'Orthodoxy and Heresy from the Death of Constantine to the Eve of the First Council of Ephesus', in A. Cameron and P. Garnsey (eds.), *The Cambridge Ancient History, Volume XIII. The Late Empire, A.D. 337–425* (Cambridge: Cambridge University Press, 1998).

Chadwick, Henry, 'Donatism', in *The Church in Ancient Society: From Galilee to Gregory the Great* (New York: Oxford University Press, 2001), 382–93.

Chadwick, Henry, 'Augustine', in F. Young, L. Ayres, A. Louth (eds.), *The Cambridge History of Early Christian Literature* (Cambridge: Cambridge University Press, 2004), 328–41.

Chapman, H. John, 'Donatists', in C. Herbermann, et al (eds.), *The Catholic Encyclopedia*, vol. V (New York: Robert Appleton Co., 1909), 121–29.

Chapman, H. John, 'Pélage et le Texte de S. Paul', in *Revue d'Histoire Ecclésiastique* 18 (1922), 469–81.

Christern, J., *Das frühchristliche Pilgerheiligtum von Tebessa: Architektur und Ornamentik einer spätantiken Bauhütte in Nordafrika* (Wiesbaden: Steiner Verlag, 1976).

Cipriani, Nello, 'Aspetti letterari dell'Ad Florum di Giuliano d'Eclano', *Augustinianum* 15 (1975), 125–67.

Cipriani, Nello, 'L'autore dei testi pseudobasiliani riportati nel C. Iulianum (I,16–17) e la polemica agostiniana di Giuliano d'Eclano', in *Congresso internazionale su S. Agostino nel XVI centenario della conversione (Roma, 15–20 settembre 1986). Atti I. Cronaca del Congresso. Sessioni generali. Sezione di studio* I (*Studia Ephemeridis Augustinianum* 24) (Rome: Institutum Patristicum Augustinianum, 1987), 439–49.

Cipriani, Nello, 'La Presenza di Teodoro di Mopsuestia nella teologia di Guiliano d'Eclano', in *Cristianesimo Latino e cultura Greco sino al sec. IV. XXI Incontro di studiosi dell'antichità cristiana (Roma, 7–9 maggio 1992)*, *Studia Ephemeridis Augustinianum* 42 (1993), 365–78.

Cipriani, Nello, 'La polemica antiafricana di Giuliano d'Eclano: artificio letterario o scontro di tradizione teologichi?' in *Cristianesimo e specificità regionali nel Mediterraneo latino (sec. IV–VI)* (Studia ephemeridis Augustinianum, 46) (Rome: Institutum Patristicum Augustinianum, 1994a), 147–80.

Cipriani, Nello, 'Le fonti cristiane della dottrina trinitaria nei primi Dialoghi de S. Agostino', *Augustinianum* 34 (1994b), 271–81.

Cipriani, Nello, 'L'altro Agostino di G. Lettieri', *Revue des études augustiniennes* 48 (2002), 249–65.

Cipriani, Nello, 'Sulle fonti orientali della teologia di Giuliano d'Eclano', in A.V. Nazzarro (ed.), *Giuliano d'Eclano e l'Hirpinia Christiana"* (Naples: Arte tipografica, 2004), 157–70.

Clancy, Finbarr G., 'St. Augustine, his predecessors and contemporaries, and the exegesis of 2 Tim. 2.20', *Studia Patristica* 27 (1993), 242–48.

Clark, Gillian, 'Desires of the Hangman: Augustine on Legitimized Violence', in H.A. Drake (ed.), *Violence in Late Antiquity: Perceptions and Practices* (Aldershot, UK: Ashgate Publishing, 2006), 137–46.

Congar, Yves, 'Introduction Générale', in G. Finaert (ed.), *Œuvres de Saint Augustin* 28 (*Bibliothèque augustinienne*), *Traités Anti-Donatistes I* (Paris: Desclée de Brouwer, 1963).

Contreras, E., 'Sententiae episcoporum numero LXXXVII de haereticis baptizandis', *Augustinianum* 27 (1987), 407–21.

Cowdrey, H.E.J., 'The Dissemination of St. Augustine's Doctrine of Holy Orders during the Later Patristic Age', *Journal of Theological Studies* 20/2 (1969), 448–81.

Coyle, J. Kevin, 'The Self-identity of North African Christians in Augustine's Time', in P.-Y. Fux, J.-M. Roessli, O. Wermlinger (eds.), *Augustinus Afer: Saint Augustin: africanité et universalité. Actes du colloque international, Alger-Annaba, 1–7 avril 2001*(*Paradosis* 45/1) (Fribourg: Éditions Universitaires Fribourg Suisse, 2003), 61–73.

Coyle, J. Kevin, 'Particularities of Christianity in Roman Africa', *Studia Patristica* 39 (2006), 13–26.

Crawley Quinn, Josephine, '"Roman Africa?" *"Romanization"?' Digressus Supplement* 1 (2003), 7–34.

Dassmann, E., 'Glaubenseinsicht – Glaubensgehorsam. Augustinus über Wert und Grenzen der "auctoritas"', in H. Waldenfels et al (eds.), *Theologie – Grund und Grenzen. Festgabe für Heimo Dolch zur Vollendung des 70 Lebensjahres* (Paderborn: Schöningh, 1982), 255–71.

Dassmann, E., 'Tam Ambrosius quam Cyprianus (c.Iul.imp. 4,112). Augustins Helfer im pelagianischen Streit', in D. Papandreou, W.A. Bienert, and K. Schäferdiek (eds.), *Oecumenica et Patristica. Festschrift für W. Schneemelcher* (Chambésy-Genf: Metropolie der Schweiz, 1989), 258–68.

Dassmann, E., 'Cyprianus', in C. Mayer (ed.) *Augustinus-Lexikon*, vol. 2 (Basel: Schwabe & Co., 1996), 196–211.

Dearn, Alan, 'The *Passio S. Typasii Veterani* as a Catholic Construction of the Past', *Vigiliae Christianae* 55/1 (2001), 86–98.

Dearn, Alan, 'Voluntary Martyrdom and the Donatist Schism', *Studia Patristica* 39 (2006), 27–32.

De Bruyne, T., '*Enarrationes in Psalmos* prêchées à *Carthage*', *Miscellanea Augustiniana* II (1976), 321–25.

Decret, F., *Le Christianisme en Afrique du Nord Ancienne* (Paris: Éditions du Seuil, 1996).

De Labriolle, P., 'Pourquoi saint Augustin a-ti-il rédigé des Confessiones?' *Bulletin de l'Association Guillaume Budé* (1926), 34–39.

De Simone, R.J., 'Modern Research on the Sources of Saint Augustine's Doctrine of Original Sin', *Augustinian Studies* 11 (1980), 205–27.

De Veer, Albert, 'L'exploitation du schisme maximianiste par saint Augustin dans sa lutte contre le Donatisme', *Recherches augustiniennes* 3 (Paris: Études Augustiniennes, 1965), 219–37.

De Veer, Albert, 'Les relations de saint Augustin et de Pélage avec Albine, Pinien et Mélanie', in *BA* 23 (Paris: Desclée de Brouwer, 1974a), 671–75.

De Veer, Albert, 'Saint Augustin et l'Ambrosiaster', in *BA* 23 (Paris: Desclée de Brouwer, 1974b), 817–24.

Dewart, Joanne McW., The Christology of the Pelagian Controversy', *Studia Patristica* 17/3 (1982), 1221–244.

Diesner, H.-J., 'Methodisches und Sachliches zum Circumcellionentum', *WZHalle* 8 (1959), 1009–016.

Diesner, H.-J., 'Die Periodisierung des Circumcellionentums', *WZHalle* 11 (1962), 1329–338.

Director of National Intelligence, *Global Trends 2025: A Transformed World* (Washington, D.C.: Office of the Director of National Intelligence, National Intelligence Council, 2008).

Dodaro, Robert, 'The Theologian as Grammarian: Literary Decorum in Augustine's Defense of Orthodox Discourse', *Studia Patristica* 38 (2001), 70–83.

Dodaro, Robert, 'Augustine's Revision of the Heroic Ideal', *Augustinian Studies* 36/1 (2005), 141–57.

Doignon, Jean, 'Testimonia d'Hilaire de Poitiers dans le 'Contra Iulianum' d'Augustin: Les texts, leur groupement, leur 'lecture', *Revue Bénédictine* 91 (1981a), 7–19.

Doignon, Jean, 'Une formule-clé du fragment sur Job d'Hilaire de Poitiers, inspiré d'Origène et transmis par Augustin (*Contra Iulianum* 2,8,27)', *Vigiliae Christianae* 35 (1981b), 209–21.

Donaldson, Stuart A., *Church Life and Thought in North Africa A.D. 200* (Cambridge: Cambridge University Press, 1909).

Doyle, Daniel Edward, *The Bishop as Disciplinarian in the Letters of St. Augustine.* Patristic Studies, vol. 4 (New York: Peter Lang, 2002).

Doyle, Daniel Edward, 'Spread throughout the World: Hints on Augustine's Understanding of Petrine Ministry', *Journal of Early Christian Studies* 13/2 (2005), 233–46.

Drake, H.A., *Constantine and the Bishops: The Politics of Intolerance* (Baltimore/London: The Johns Hopkins University Press, 2000).

Drecoll, Volker, *Die Entstehung der Gnadenlehre Augustins, Beiträge zur historischen Theologie* 109 (Tübingen: Mohr Siebeck, 1999).

Drecoll, Volker, 'Gratia', in C. Mayer (ed.), *Augustinus-Lexikon*, vol. 3 (Basel: Schwabe & Co., 2004), 182–242.

Dunn, Geoffrey, 'Clement of Rome and the Question of Roman Primacy in the Early African Tradition', *Augustinianum* 43 (2003a), 5–24.

Dunn, Geoffrey, 'Cyprian and his college: Patronage and the episcopal synod of 252', *Journal of Religious History* 27/1 (2003b), 1–13.

Dunn, Geoffrey, 'Heresy and Schism According to Cyprian of Carthage', *Journal of Theological Studies* 55/2 (2004a), 551–74.

Dunn, Geoffrey, 'The White Crown of Works: Cyprian's Early Pastoral Ministry of Almsgiving in Carthage', Church History 73/4 (2004b), 715–40.

Dunn, Geoffrey, 'Validity of Baptism and Ordination in the African response to the "Rebaptism" Crisis: Cyprian of Carthage's Synod of Spring 256', *Theological Studies* 67 (2006), 257–74.

Dunn, Geoffrey, *Cyprian and the Bishops of Rome: Questions about Papal Primacy in the Early Church, Early Christian Studies* 11 (Strathfield, Aus.: St. Paul's Publications, 2007).

Dunn, Geoffrey, 'The Reception of the Martyrdom of Cyprian of Carthage in Early Christian Literature', in J. Leemans (ed.), *Martyrdom and Persecution in Late Antique Christianity: Festschrift Boudewijn Dehandschutter, Bibliotheca Ephemeridum Theologicarum Lovaniensium* 241 (Leuven: Peeters, 2010), 65–86.

Du Pin, Louis Ellies, *Nouvelle bibliotheque des auteurs ecclesiastiques* [...]. *Tome III. Des auteurs ducinquiéme siecle de l'eglise* (Paris: André Pralard, 1690).

Du Pin, Louis Ellies, *De schismate Donatistarum libri septem, ad...codices et veteres editiones collati...Quibus accessêre Historia Donatistarum...nec non geographia episcopalis Africae* (Paris: André Pralard, 1700a).

Du Pin, Louis Ellies, *Monumenta vetera ad Donatistarum Historiam pertinenta* (Paris: André Pralard, 1700b).

Dupont, Anthony, 'Continuity or Discontinuity in Augustine? Is There an 'Early Augustine' and What Does He Think on Grace?' *Ars Disputandi* 8 (2008), 67–79.

Dupont, Anthony, 'Saint Augustin et le Commentaire sur Jonas de saint Jerome', *Revue des études augustiniennes* 12 (1966), 9–40.

Dupont, Anthony, 'Julien d'Eclane et Rufin d'Aquilee. Du concile de Rimini a la repression pelagienne. L'intervention imperial en matiere religieuse', *Revue des Études Augustiniennes* 24 (1978), 243–71.

Dupont, Anthony, 'Notes complementaires. Lettre 4*', in *BA* 46B, *Lettres 1*–29** (Paris: Desclee de Brouwer, 1987), 430–42.

Dupont, Anthony, and Matthew Gaumer, '*Gratia Dei, Gratia Sacramenti.* Grace in Augustine of Hippo's Anti-Donatist Writings', *Ephemerides Theologicae Lovanienses* 86/4 (2010), 307–29.

Duval, Y.-M. 'Saint Augustin et le Commentaire sur Jonas de saint Jérôme', *Revue des études augustiniennes* 12 (1966), 9–40.

Duval, Y.-M. 'Julien d'Éclane et Rufin d'Aquilée. Du concile de Rimini à la répression pélagienne. L'intervention imperial en matière religieuse', *Revue des Études Augustiniennes* 24 (1978), 243–71.

Duval, Y.-M. 'Notes complémentaires. Lettre 4*', in *BA* 46B, *Lettres 1*–29** (Paris: Desclée de Brouwer, 1987), 430–42.

Eber, Jochen, '*De Baptismo – Über die Taufe Augustinus*', book review in *European Journal of Theology* 16/2 (2007), 122–24.

Ellingsen, M., *The Richness of Augustine: His Contextual & Pastoral Theology* (Louisville, KY: Westminster/ John Knox Press, 2005).

Eno, Robert, 'Some Nuances in the Ecclesiology of the Donatists', *Revue des études augustiniennes* 18/1–2 (1972), 46–50.

Eno, Robert, 'The Work of Optatus as a Turning Point in the African Ecclesiology', *The Thomist* 37/4 (1973), 668–85.

Eno, Robert, 'Holiness and Separation in the Early Centuries', *Scottish Journal of Theology* 30 (1977), 523–42.

Eno, Robert, 'Doctrinal Authority in Saint Augustine', *Augustinian Studies* 12 (1981), 133–72.

Eno, Robert, 'The Significance of the Lists of Roman Bishops in the Anti-Donatist Polemic', *Vigiliae Christianae* 47/2 (1993), 158–69.

Eno, Robert, 'Authority', in A. Fitzgerald (ed.), *Augustine through the Ages. An Encyclopedia* (Grand Rapids, MI/Cambridge: Wm. Eerdmans Publishing, 1999a), 80–82.

Eno, Robert, 'Epistulae', in A. Fitzgerald (ed.), *Augustine through the Ages. An Encyclopedia* (Grand Rapids, MI/Cambridge: Wm. Eerdmans Publishing, 1999b), 299–305.

Eno, Robert, 'Optatus of Milevis', in A. Fitzgerald (ed.), *Augustine through the Ages. An Encyclopedia* (Grand Rapids, MI/Cambridge: Wm. Eerdmans Publishing, 1999c), 596–97.

Errington, R.M., *Roman Imperial Policy from Julian to Theodosius* (Chapel Hill, NC: University of North Carolina Press, 2006).

Evans, Robert, *One and Holy: The Church in Latin Patristic Thought* (London: SPCK, 1972).

Evans, Robert, 'Augustine on Exegesis against the Heretics', in F. Van Fleteren and J.C. Schnaubelt (eds.), *Augustine: Biblical Exegete* (New York: Peter Lang, 2001), 145–56.

Fahey, Michael, *Cyprian and the Bible: A Study in Third-Century Exegesis, Beiträge zur Geschichte der Biblischen Hermeneutik* 9 (Tübingen: J.C.B. Mohr (Paul Siebeck), 1971).

Faul, D., 'Sinners in the Holy Church: A Problem in the Ecclesiology of St. Augustine', Studia Patristica 9 (1966), 404–15.

Fenger, Anne-Lene, 'Zur Beurteilung der Ketzertaufe durch Cyprian von Karthago und Ambrosius von Mailand', in E. Dassmann and K. Suso Frank (eds.), *Pietas: Festschrift für Bernhard Kötting, Jahrbuch für Antike und Christentum Ergänzungsband* 8 (Münster: Aschendorf, 1980), 179–97.

Ferguson, Everett, *Baptism in the Early Church: History, Theology, and Liturgy in the First Five Centuries* (Grand Rapids, MI/Cambridge: Wm. Eerdmans Publishing, 2009).

Ferguson, Niall, 'Complexity of Collapse: Empires on the Edge of Chaos', *Foreign Affairs* 89/2 (2010), 18–32.

Fernández, Damián, 'Cipriano de Cartago y la autoridad en la Iglesia del siglo III', *Cuaderno de Teología* 18 (1999), 211–24.

Ferretti, Giuseppe, *L'influsso di S. Ambrogio in S. Agostino* (Faenza: Fratelli Lega, 1951).

Fiedrowicz, Michael, 'Reticius', *Lexikon für Theologie und Kirche* 8 (Freiburg: Verlag Herder, 1999), 1132.

Fischer, Joseph, 'Die ersten Konzilien im römischen Nordwest-Afrika', in E. Dassmann and K. Suso Frank (eds.), *Pietas: Festschrift für Bernhard Kötting, Jahrbuch für Antike und Christentum Ergänzungsband* 8 (Münster: Aschendorf, 1980), 217–27.

Fitzgerald, Allan, *Augustine through the Ages: An Encyclopedia* (Grand Rapids, MI/ Cambridge: Wm. Eerdmans Publishing, 1999).

Fitzgerald, Allan, 'Augustine the Preacher', in *Saint Augustine*, ed. T.J. van Bavel (Brussels: Mercatorfonds/Augustinian Historical Institute, 2007), 143–50.

Fitzgerald, Allan, 'When Augustine was Priest', *Augustinian Studies* 40/1 (2009), 37–48.

Fitzgerald, Paul J., 'A Model for Dialogue: Cyprian of Carthage on Ecclesial Discernment', Theological Studies 59 (1998), 236–53.

Flash, Kurt, Logik des Schreckens. Augustinus von Hippo, De diversis quaestionibus ad Simplicianum I 2. *Deutsche Erstübersetzung von Walter Schäfer. Herausgegeben und erklärt von Kurt Flasch. Zweite, verbesserte Auflage mit Nachwort (Excerpta classica* 8) (Mainz: Dieterich Verlagsbuchhandlung, 1995).

de Foigny, Jacques, *Epistre ou le Livre de St. Augustin de l'Unité de l'Eglise, contre Petilien, Evesque Donatiste, avec certaines observations pour entendre les lieux plus difficiles* (Rhiems: Jean de Foigny, 1567).

Folliet, Georges, 'Le fragment d'Hilaire 'Quas Iob litteras'. Son interprétation d'après Hilaire, Pélage et Augustin', in Edmond-René Labande (ed.), *Hilaire et son temps* (Actes du colloque de Poitiers [29 septembre-3 octobre 1968] à l'occasion du XVIe centenaire de la mort de saint Hilaire) (Paris: Études augustiniennes, 1969), 149–58.

Frend, William, 'The *Cellae* of the African Circumcellions', *Journal of Theological Studies* 3/1 (1952a), 87–89.

Frend, William, *The Donatist Church: A Movement of Protest in Roman North Africa* (Oxford: Clarendon Press, 1952b, reprinted 1970).

Frend, William, 'Church and State in Latin Theology: A Review and Discussion', *Modern Churchman* 1/3 (1958), 172–80.

Frend, William, 'Donatismus', *Reallexikon für Antike und Christentum* 4 (1959), 128–47.

Frend, William, 'The Roman Empire in the Eyes of Western Schismatics during the Fourth Century A.D.', in *Extraits des Miscellanea Historiae Ecclesiasticae Stockholm 1960* (Louvain: Imprimerie E. Warny, 1961a).

Frend, William, 'The Seniores Laici and the Origins of the Church in North Africa', *Journal of Theological Studies* 12/2 (1961b), 280–84.

Frend, William, 'Constantine's Settlement with the Church and its Legacy', *Modern Churchman* 6/1 (1962), 32–46.

Frend, William, *Martyrdom and Persecution in the Early Church: A Study of the Conflict from the Macabees to Donatus* (Oxford: Basil Blackwell, 1965).

Frend, William, 'Circumcellions and Monks', *Journal of Theological Studies* 20/2 (1969a), 542–49.

Frend, William, 'Liberalism in the Early Church', *Modern Churchman* 13/1 (1969b), 28–40.

Frend, William, 'Heresy and Schism as Social and National Movements', in D. Baker (ed.), *Schism, Heresy and Religious Protest* (Cambridge: Cambridge University Press, 1972), 37–56.

Frend, William, *The Rise of Christianity* (London: Darlon, Longman, & Todd, 1984).

Frend, William, 'Prelude to the Great Persecution: The Propaganda War', *Journal of Ecclesiastical History* 38/1 (1987), 1–18.

Frend, William, 'Augustine and State Authority. The Example of the Donatists', in G. Francesco, R.A. Markus, and M. Forlin Patrucco (eds.), *Agostino d'Ippona, "Quaestiones disputatae"* (Palermo: Augustinus, 1989a), 49–73.

Frend, William, 'The Donatist Church and St. Paul', in J. Ries, F. Decret, W.H.C. Frend, and M.G. Mara (eds.), *Le Epistole Paoline nei Manichei I Donatisti e il Primo Agostino, Sussidi Patristici 5* (Roma: Istituto Patristico Augustinianum, 1989b), 87–123.

Frend, William, 'Donatism', in E. Ferguson (ed.), *Encyclopedia of Early Christianity*, 2nd edition, vol. 1 (New York: Garland Publishing, 1997a), 343–46.

Frend, William, 'Donatus the Great (d.355)', in E. Ferguson (ed.), *Encyclopedia of Early Christianity*, 2nd edition, vol. 1 (New York: Garland Publishing, 1997b), 347.

Frend, William, 'Donatus 'paene totam Africam decepit'. How?' *Journal of Ecclesiastical History* 48/4 (1997c), 611–27.

Frend, William, *Orthodoxy, Paganism and Dissent in the Early Christian Centuries, Variorum Collected Studies Series* (Aldershot, UK, 2001).

Frend, William, and K. Clancy, 'The Winning of the Countryside', *Journal of Ecclesiastical History* 18/1 (1967), 1–14.

Frend, William, and K. Clancy, 'When Did the Donatist Schism Begin?' *Journal of Theological Studies* 27/1 (1977), 104–09.

Fürst, Alfons, 'Hieronymus', in C. Mayer (ed.), *Augustinus-Lexikon* 3–2/3 (Basel: Schwabe, 2004), 317–36.

Gaddis, Michael, *There is No Crime for Those Who Have Christ: Religious Violence in the Christian Roman Empire* (Berkeley/Los Angeles/London: University of California Press, 2005).

Gangauf, Theodore, *Metaphysische Psychologie des heiligen Augustinus* (Augsburg: Karl Kollmann, 1852).

Garcia, Ruben Dario, 'San Cipriano y el Donatismo en la polémica antidonatista de San Agustín: Estudio historico-pastrístico', *Teologia* 13 (1976), 5–49.

Garnier, Jean, *Dissert. vii. quibus integra continentur Pelagianorum hist. Opera quaecumque extant/prodeunt nunc primum studio Joannis Garnieri...qui notas etiam ac dissertationes addidit* (Paris: Sebastianum Mabre-Cramoisy, 1673).

Garnsey, Peter and Caroline Humfress, *The Evolution of the Late Antique World* (Cambridge: Orchard Academic, 2001).

Gaumer, Matthew Alan, 'The Evolution of Donatist Theology as Response to a Changing Late Antique Milieu', *Augustiniana* 58/3–4 (2008), 201–33.

Gaumer, Matthew Alan, 'Coerción religiosa patrocinada por el Estado: su contexto en Norte áfrica donatista y el cambio de la actitud de Agustín hacia aquélla', *Augustinus* 54/2 (2009), 345–71.

Gaumer, Matthew Alan, 'The Election of Primian of Carthage: The Beginning of the End of Donatist Christianity?', *Zeitschrift für Antikes Christentum* 17 (2012), 290–308.

Gaumer, Matthew Alan, 'The Development of the Concept of Grace in Late Antique North Africa (Its Context within the Donatist & Pelagian Debates)', *Augustinianum* 50/1 (2010a), 163–87.

Gaumer, Matthew Alan, '"Poenus disputator...Non Ego, Sed Cyprianus Poenus": ¿Por qué necesitaba Agustín apropiarse de Cipriano de Cartago?' *Augustinus* 55/1 (2010c), 141–64.

Gaumer, Matthew Alan, and Anthony Dupont, 'Donatist North Africa and the Beginning of Religious Coercion by Christians: A New Analysis', La Ciudad de Dios 223–2 (2010b), 445–66.

Gieseler, Johann Karl Ludwig, *Kirchengeschichte*, vol. 2 (Bonn: A. Marcus, 1845).

Gotoh, Atsuko, '*Circumcelliones*: The Ideology behind Their Activities', in Toru Yuge and Masaoki Doi (eds.), *Forms of Control and Subordination in Antiquity* (Leiden/New York/Tokyo: Brill/University of Tokyo Press, 1988), 303–11.

Granfield, Patrick, 'Episcopal Elections in Cyprian: Clerical and Lay Participation', *Theological Studies* 37/1 (1976), 41–52.

Grasmück, Ernst Ludwig, *Coercitio: Staat und Kirche im Donatistenstreit* (Bonn: Ludwig Röhrscheid Verlag, 1964).

Greenslade, S.L., *Church & State from Constantine to Theodosius* (London: SCM Press, 1954).

Gross, Julius, *Enstehungsgeschichte des Erbsündendogmas* I (Geschichte des Erbsündendogmas) (Munich/Basel: Reinhardt-Verlag, 1960).

Grossi, Vittorino, 'Gli Scritti di Agostino Prosbitero (391–396), le Motivazioni Principali', http://www.cassiciaco.it/navigazione/scriptorium/settimana/1991/grossi.html (L'Associazione storico-culturale Sant'Agostino, 1991).

Grossi, Vittorino, 'Baptismus', in C. Mayer (ed.), *Augustinus-Lexikon*, vol. 1 (Basel: Schwabe & Co., 1996), 583–91.

Gryson, R., *Répertoire général des auteurs ecclésiastiques latins de l'antiquité et du haut moyen âge, Tome I* (Freiburg: Verlag Herder, 2007).

Hamilton, Andrew, 'Cyprian and Church Unity', *Pacifica* 8 (1995), 9–21.

Hamilton, Louis, 'Possidius' Augustine and Post-Augustinian Africa', *Journal of Early Christian Studies* 12/1 (2004), 85–105.

Harrison, Carol, *Augustine: Christian Truth and Fractured Humanity, Christian Theology in Context* (New York: Oxford University Press, 2000a).

Harrison, Carol, 'The Rhetoric of Scripture and Preaching: Classical decadence or Christian aesthetic?' in R. Dodaro and G. Lawless (eds.), *Augustine and His Critics: Essays in Honour of Gerald Bonner* (London: Routledge, 2000b), 214–29.

Harrison, Carol, '"The Most Intimate Feeling of My Mind": The Permanence of Grace in Augustine's Early Theological Practice', *Augustinian Studies* 36/1 (2005), 51–58.

Harrison, Carol, *Rethinking Augustine's Early Theology: An Argument for Continuity* (Oxford: Oxford University Press, 2006).

Harrison, Carol, 'The early works (386–96)', in *Saint Augustine,* ed. T.J. van Bavel (Brussels: Mercatorfonds/Augustinian Historical Institute, 2007), 165–80.

Harrison, Simon, 'Truth, Truths', in A. Fitzgerald (ed.), *Augustine through the Ages: An Encyclopedia* (Grand Rapids, MI: 1999), 852–53.

Heather, Peter, *The Fall of the Roman Empire* (London: Macmillan, 2005/London: Pan Books, 2006).

Heather, Peter, 'Why Did the Barbarian Cross the Rhine?' *Journal of Late Antiquity* 2/1 (2009), 3–29.

Henry, Nathalie, 'The Lily and the Thorns: Augustine's Refutation of the Donatist Exegesis of the Song of Songs', *Revue des Études Augustiniennes* 42/2 (1996), 255–66.

Hermanowicz, Erika, 'Catholic Bishops and Appeals to the Imperial Court: A Legal Study of the Calama Riots in 408', *Journal of Early Christian Studies* 12/4 (2004), 481–521.

Hermanowicz, Erika, *Possidius of Calama: A Study of the North African Episcopate* (New York: Oxford University Press, 2008).

Herrera, Robert, 'A Shattered Mirror: The Presence of Africa in Augustine's Exegesis', in F. Van Fleteren and J.C. Schnaubelt (eds.), *Augustine: Biblical Exegete* (New York: Peter Lang, 2001), 175–88.

Himbury, M., 'Augustine and Religious Persecution', in M. Garner and J. Martin (eds.), *St. Augustine – The Man who made the West* (Melbourne, 1990), 33–37.

Hogrefe, Arne, *Umstrittene Vergangenheit: Historische Argumente in der Auseinandersetzung Augustins mit den Donatisten* (Berlin: Walter de Gruyter, 2009).

Holmes, D. Nicholas, *Augustini liber de moderate coercendis haereticis ed Bonifacium Comitem. Nic. Bergius Revalensis Holmiae* (Leipzig: Enaeus Holmiae 1696).

Hombert, Pierre-Marie, *Gloria gratiae. Se glorifier en Dieu, principe et fin de la théologie augustinienne de la grâce.* Collection des Études Augustiniennes, Série Antiquité 148 (Paris: Études augustiniennes, 1996).

Hombert, Pierre-Marie, *Nouvelles Recherches de chronologie augustinienne, collection des études augustiniennes, Série Antiquité* 163 (Paris: Institut d'études augustiniennes, 2000).

Humphries, Mark, *Early Christianity* (New York: Routledge, 2006).

Hunt, D., 'The Church as a Public Institution', in A. Cameron and P. Garnsey (eds.), *The Cambridge Ancient History, Volume XIII. The Late Empire, A.D. 337–425* (Cambridge: Cambridge University Press, 1998), 242.

Hunter, David G., 'Augustine and the Making of Marriage in Roman North Africa', *Journal of Early Christian Studies* 11/1 (2003), 63–85.

Hunter, David G., *Marriage, Celibacy, and Heresy in Ancient Christianity: The Jovinianist Controversy* (New York: Oxford University Press, 2007).

Ittig, Thomas, *De Haeresiarchis Aevi Apostolici Et Apostolico Proximi* (Leipzig: Lanckisius, 1690–1703).

Jacobi, Iustus Ludwig, *Die Lehre des Pelagius* (Leipzig: Friedrich Fleisher, 1842).

James, 'Aspects of Donatist Scriptural Interpretation at the Conference of Carthage of 411', *Studia Patristica* 15 (1984), 125–30.

James, 'Count Taurinus and the Persecutors of Donatism', *Zeitschrift für Antikes Christentum* 2 (1998), 247–67.

James, and S. Lancel, 'A Note on the Interpretation of the Parable of the Threshing Floor at the Conference of Carthage of A.D. 411', in *Journal of Theological Studies* 24 (1973), 512–19.

James, and S. Lancel, 'The Motive for a Distinction between Donatus of Carthage and Donatus of Casae Nigrae', *Journal of Theological Studies* 31/2 (1980), 540–47.

James, and S. Lancel, 'Donatism', in P.F. Esler (ed.), *The Early Christian World*, vol. 2 (New York/London: Routledge, 2000), 952–74.

Jans, H., 'De verantwoording van geloofsdwang tegenover ketters volgens Augustinus' correspondenties', *Bijdragen* 22 (1961), 133–63, 247–63.

Jansenius, Cornelius, *Augustinus, sive doctrina S. Augustini de humanae naturae sanitate, aegritudine, medicina, adv. Pelagianos et Massilienses* (Leuven: Iacobi Zegeri, 1640).

Joseph, M.P., 'Heresy of the Majority: Donatist Critique of the Church-State Relationship', *Bangalore Theological Forum* 26/2 (1994), 70–77.

Kannengiesser, Charles, 'Augustine and Tyconius: A Conflict of Christian Hermeneutics in Roman Africa', in P. Bright (ed., trans.), *Augustine and the Bible* (Notre Dame, IN: University of Notre Dame Press, 1986), 149–77.

Kaufman, Peter, 'Augustine, Evil and Donatism: Sin and Sanctity before the Pelagian Controversy', *Theological Studies* 50/1 (1990), 115–26.

Kaufman, Peter, 'Redeeming Politics: Augustine's Cities of God', in D. Donnelly (ed., intro.) *The City of God: A Collection of Critical Essays* (New York: Peter Lang, 1995), 75–92.

Kaufman, Peter, 'Donatism Revisited: Moderates and Militants in Late Antique North Africa', *Journal of Late Antiquity* 2/1 (2009), 131–42.

Keleher, James, *Saint Augustine's Notion of Schism in the Donatist Controversy*, *Dissertationes ad Lauream* 34 (Mundelein, IL: University of St. Mary of the Lake Seminary Press, 1961).

Kessler, Andreas, *Reichtumskritik und Pelagianismus. Die pelagianische Diatribe de divitiis: Situierung, Lesetext, Übersetzung, Kommentar* (Paradosis 43) (Freiburg: Universitätsverl, 1999).

Kriegbaum, Bernhard, *Kirche der Traditoren oder Kirche der Märtyrer: Die Vorgeschischte des Donatismus* (Innsbruck: Tyrolia-Verlag, 1986).

Kriegbaum, Bernhard, 'Die Donatistischen Konzilien von Cebarsussa (393) and Bagai (394)', *Zeitschrift für Katholische Theologie* 124 (2002), 267–77.

Kugler, Robert, 'Tyconius's *Mystic Rules* and the Rules of Augustine', in P. Bright (ed., trans.), *Augustine and the Bible* (Notre Dame, IN: University of Notre Dame Press, 1986), 129–48.

Kunzelmann, A., 'Die Chronologie der Sermones des Hl. Augustinus', in J. Wilpert, et al (ed.), *Miscellanea Agostiniana: testi e studi publicata a cura dell'ordine eremitano di S. Agostino nel XV centenario dalla morte del santo dottore, vol. II, Studi Agostiniani* (Rome: Tipografia Poliglotta Vaticana, 1931), 417–520.

La Bonnardière, Anne-Marie, '*Les Enarrationes in Psalmos prêchées par saint Augustin* à l'occasion des fêtes de martyrs', *Recherches Augustiniennes* 7 (1971), 73–104.

La Bonnardière, Anne-Marie, 'La Prédication d'Augustin sur les Psaumes à Hippone', *AEPHE.R* 86 (1977), 337–42.

La Bonnardière, Anne-Marie, 'The Bible and Polemics', in P. Bright (ed., trans.), *Augustine and the Bible* (Notre Dame, IN: University of Notre Dame Press, 1986), 183–207.

Labrousse, Mireille, 'Le baptême des hérétiques d'après Cyprien, Optat et Augustin: influences et divergences', *Revue des études augustiniennes* 42 (1996), 223–42.

Lamberigts, Mathijs, 'Les évêques pélagiens déposés, Nestorius et Ephèse', *Augustiniana* 35 (1985), 264–80.

Lamberigts, Mathijs, 'Some Remarks on the Critical Edition of the Preserved Fragments of Julian of Aeclanum', *Recherches de théologie ancienne et médiévale* 54 (1987), 238–39.

Lamberigts, Mathijs, 'Julian of Aeclanum: A Plea for a Good Creator', *Augustiniana* 38 (1988), 5–24.

Lamberigts, Mathijs, 'Julien d'Éclane et Augustin d'Hippone. Deux conceptions d'Adam', in B. Bruning, M. Lamberigts, and J. Van Houtem (eds.), *Collectanea Augustiniana. Mélanges T.J. van Bavel, Bibliotheca ephemeridum theologicarum Lovaniensium* 92 (Leuven: Peeters, 1990), 373–410.

Lamberigts, Mathijs, 'Augustine and Julian of Aeclanum on Zosimus', *Augustiniana* 42 (1992), 311–30.

Lamberigts, Mathijs, 'Augustinus' Confessiones. Enkele beschouwingen', *Kleio* 23 (1993a), 24–46.

Lamberigts, Mathijs, 'Julian of Aeclanum on Grace. Some Considerations', *Studia Patristica* 27 (1993b), 342–49.

Lamberigts, Mathijs, 'Julián de Eclano sobre la gracia. Algunas reflexiones', *Augustinus* 40 (1995), 169–77.

Lamberigts, Mathijs, 'Julian of Aeclanum and Augustine on the Origin of the Soul', *Augustiniana* 46 (1996), 243–60.

Lamberigts, Mathijs, 'Iulianus IV (Iulianus von Aeclanum)', *Realenzyklopädie für Antike und Christentum* 19 (1999a), 483–505.

Lamberigts, Mathijs, 'Caelestius, Innocent I, Cornelius, Julian of Eclanum, Predestination', in A. Fitzgerald (ed.), *Augustine through the Ages. An Encyclopedia* (Grand Rapids, MI/Cambridge: Wm. Eerdmans Publishing, 1999b), 129; 473–74; 483–84; 499–500; 689–90.

Lamberigts, Mathijs, 'Pélage. La réhabilitation d'un hérétique', in J. Pirotte and E. Louchez (eds.), *Deux mille ans d'histoire de l'Église. Bilan et perspectives historiographiques, Revue d'histoire ecclésiastique* 95/3 (2000), 97–111.

Lamberigts, Mathijs, 'Julien d'Éclane', in *Dictionnaire d'Histoire et Géographie Ecclésiastiques* 164 (2001a), 515–19.

Lamberigts, Mathijs, 'Was Augustine a Manichaean? The Assessment of Julian of Aeclanum', in J. van Oort, O. Wermelinger, and G. Wurst (eds.), *Augustine and Manichaeism in the Latin West. Proceedings of the Fribourg-Utrecht Symposium of the International Association of Manichaean Studies (IAMS), Nag Hammadi and Manichaean Studies* 49 (Leiden: Brill, 2001b), 113–36.

Lamberigts, Mathijs, 'Recent Research into Pelagianism, with Particular Emphasis on the Role of Julian of Aeclanum', *Augustiniana* 52 (2002), 175–98.

Lamberigts, Mathijs, '*The Italian Julian of Aeclanum about the African Augustine of Hippo*', in P.-Y. Fux, J.-M. Roessli, and O. Wermelinger (eds.), *Augustinus Afer. Saint Augustin. Africanité et universalité (Actes du colloque international Alger-Annaba, 1–7 avril 2001), Paradosis* 45/1 (Fribourg: Éditions Universitaires Fribourg Suisse, 2003), 83–93.

Lamberigts, Mathijs, 'Augustine on Predestination. Some Quaestiones Disputatae Revisited', *Augustiniana* 54 (2004a), 279–305.

Lamberigts, Mathijs, 'Co-operation between Church and State in the Condemnation of the Pelagians', in T.L. Hettema and A. van der Kooij (eds.), *Religious Polemics in Context, Studies in Theology and Religion* 11 (Assen, NL: Royal van Gorcum, 2004b), 363–75.

Lamberigts, Mathijs, 'Competing Christologies: Julian and Augustine on Jesus Christ', *Augustinian Studies* 36/1 (2005a), 159–94.

Lamberigts, Mathijs, 'In Defence of Jesus Christ. Augustine on Christ in the Pelagian Controversy', *Augustinian Studies* 36 (2005b), 159–94.

Lamberigts, Mathijs, 'Innocentius episcopus Romanus', in C. Mayer (ed.), *Augustinus-Lexikon* 3 (Basel: Schwabe & Co., 2006a), 613–19.

Lamberigts, Mathijs, 'The Presence of 1 Cor. 4,7 in the anti-Pelagian Works of Augustine', *Augustiniana* 56 (2006b), 373–99.

Lamberigts, Mathijs, 'Julian von Aeclanum und seine Sicht der Gnade. Eine Alternative?' in C. Mayer, A.E.J. Grote and C. Müller (eds.), *Gnade – Freiheit – Rechtfertigung. Augustinische Topoi und ihre Wirkungsgeschichte* (*Internationales Kolloquium zum 1650. Geburtstag Augustins vom 25. bis 27. November 2004 zu Mainz*), *Akademie der Wissenschaften und der Literatur. Abhandlungen der geistes- und sozialwissenschaftlichen Klasse* 2007/3 (Mainz/Stuttgart, 2007), 95–122.

Lamberigts, Mathijs, 'Iulianus Aeclanensis', in C. Mayer (ed.), *Augustinus-Lexikon* 3, 5/6 (Basel: Schwabe & Co., 2008a), 836–47.

Lamberigts, Mathijs, 'Pelagius and Pelagians', in S. Ashbrook Harvey and D. Hunter (eds.), *Oxford Handbook of Early Christian Studies* (Oxford: Oxford University Press, 2008b).

Lamberigts, Mathijs, 'Augustine on the Holy Spirit in the Controversy with Julian of Aeclanum', in G. Förster, A. Grote, and C. Müller (eds.), *Spiritus et Littera. Beiträge zur Augustinus-Forschung. Festschrift zum 80. Geburtstag von Cornelius Petrus Mayer OSA* (Würzburg: Augustinus, 2009), 289–315.

Lamirande, E., 'Argument tiré par Augustin du schisme des Maximianistes', in *Œuvres de Saint Augustin* 32 (*Bibliothèque augustinienne*), *Traités Anti-Donatistes V* (Paris, 1965).

Lamirande, E., *La situation ecclésiologique des Donatistes d'après saint Augustin* (Ottawa: Éditions de l'université d'Ottawa, 1972).

Lamirande, E., *Church, State and Toleration: An Intriguing Change of Mind in Augustine* (Villanova: Villanova University Press, 1975).

Lamirande, E., 'Coercitio', in C. Mayer (ed.), *Augustinus-Lexikon* (Basel: Schwabe & Co., 1996), 1038–046.

Lamirande, E., 'Aux origines du dialogue interconfessionnel: saint Augustin et les donatistes: vingt ans de tentatives infructueuses (391–411)', *Studia Canonica* 32 (1998), 203–28.

Lancel, Serge, *Actes de la Conférence de Carthage en 411. Tome I–II: Texte et traduction de la capitulation générale et des Actes de la Première Séance*, *Sources chrétiennes* 194 (Paris: Les Éditions du Cerf, 1972).

Lancel, Serge, '*Breuiculus conlationis cum Donatistis*', in C. Mayer (ed.) *Augustinus-Lexikon*, vol. 1 (Basel: Schwabe & Co., 1986–1994), 681–84.

Lancel, Serge, 'Conlatio Carthaginiensis', in C. Mayer (ed.), *Augustinus-Lexikon*, vol. 1 (Basel: Schwabe & Co., 1986–1994), 1204–209.

Lancel, Serge, 'Donatistas (Contra–)', in C. Mayer (ed.), *Augustinus-Lexikon*, vol. 2 (Basel: Schwabe & Co., 1996–2002a), 639–44.

Lancel, Serge, 'Epistulam Parmeniani (Contra–)', in C. Mayer (ed.), *Augustinus-Lexikon*, vol. 2 (Basel: Schwabe & Co., 1996–2002b), 1078–084.

Lancel, Serge, *Saint Augustine*, trans. A. Nevill (London: SCM Press, 2002).

Lancel, Serge, *Pax et Concordia. Chrétiens des premiers siècles en Algérie (IIIe–VIe siècles)* (Alger: Institut des Sources chrétiennes, 2003).

Lancel, Serge, 'The Donatist Dispute', in T.J. van Bavel and B. Bruning (eds.), *Saint Augustine* (Brussels: Mercatorfonds/Augustinian Historical Institute, 2007a), 193–203.

Lancel, Serge, 'Saint Augustine, an African bishop serving his people', in T.J. van Bavel and B. Bruning (eds.), *Saint Augustine* (Brussels: Mercatorfonds/Augustinian Historical Institute, 2007b).

Lancel, Serge, and J. Alexander, 'Donatistae', in C. Mayer (ed.), *Augustinus-Lexicon*, vol. 2 (Basel: Schwabe & Co., 1999), 607–22.

Lane Fox, Robin, *Pagans and Christians* (London: Penguins Books, 1986).

Laurance, John D., 'Eucharistic Leader according to Cyprian of Carthage: A new Study', *Studia Liturgica* 15/2 (1982–83), 66–75.

Lenski, Noel E., 'Evidence for the *Audentia episcopalis* in the New Letters of Augustine', in Ralph Mathisen (ed.), *Law, Society, and Authority in Late Antiquity* (New York: Oxford University Press, 2001), 83–97.

Lepelley, Claude, *Les cités de l'Afrique romaine du Bas-Empire 1–2* (Paris: Études Augustiniennes, 1979–1981).

Lepelley, Claude, *Iuvenes et circoncelliones. Les derniers sacrifices humains de l'Afrique antique, Antiquités africaines* 15 (1980), 261–71.

Lepelley, Claude, 'Augustin dans l'Afrique romaine de son temps: Les continuités avec la cité classique', in C. Mayer and K.H. Chelius (eds.), *Internationales Symposion über den Stand der Augustinus-Forschung vom 12. bis 16. April 1987 im Schloß Rauischholzhausen der Justus-Liebig-Universität Gießen, Cassiciacum* 39/1 (1989), 169–98.

Lepelley, Claude, 'Circumcelliones', in C. Mayer (ed.) *Augustinus-Lexikon*, vol. 1 (Basel: Schwabe & Co., 1996).

Lettieri, Gaetano, *L'altro Agostino. Ermeneutica e retorica della grazia dalla crisi alla metamorfosi del De doctrina christiana* (Brescia: Morcelliana, 2001).

Lewis, Gordon, 'Violence in the Name of Christ: The Significance of Augustine's Donatist Controversy for Today', *Journal of the Evangelical Theological Society* 14/2 (1971), 103–10.

Leydecker, Melchior, *Historia Ecclesiastica Africana* (Utrecht: Luchtmans, 1687).

Leydecker, Melchior, *Ext. cum Commentariis uberrimis et utillisimis in Melchioris Lydeckeri Historia illustrata Ecclesiae Africanae, cujus totum paene tomum secundum constituit inscriptum: Tomus secundus ad Librum Augustini de Unitate Ecclesiae contra Donatistas, de principiis Ecclesiæ Africanæ, illiusque fide in Articulis de Capite Christo et Ecclesia, de Unitate et Schismate, plurimisque Religionis Christianae capitibus agit. Ultrajecti apud viduam Guil. Clerck. Aurelii Augustini, Episcopi Hipponensis, Liber de Unitate Ecclesiae contra Donatistas* (Utrecht: Luchtmans, 1690).

Long, Thomas, *History of the Donatists* (London: Walter Kettilby, 1677).

Lössl, Josef, *Intellectus Gratiae. Die erkenntnistheoretische und hermeneutische Dimension der Gnadenlehre Augustins von Hippo, Supplements to Vigiliae Christianae* 38 (Leiden/New York/Köln, 1997).

Lössl, Josef, *'Julian von Aeclanum. Studien zu seinem Leben, seinem Werk, seiner Lehre und ihrer Überlieferung', Vigiliae Christianae* 60 (Leiden: Brill, 2001).

Lössl, Josef, 'Julian of Aeclanum's "Rationalist" Exegesis. Albert Bruckner Revisited', *Augustiniana* 53 (2003), 77–106.

Lössl, Josef, 'Augustine, "Pelagianism", Julian of Aeclanum, and Modern Scholarship', *Zeitschrift für Antikes Christentum* 11 (2007), 129–50.

Lupieri, Edmondo, *'Agostino e Ireneo', Vetera Christianorum* 15 (1978), 113–15.

Lütcke, Karl-Heinrich, *„Auctoritas" bei Augustin* (Stuttgart: W. Kohlhammer Verlag, 1968).

Lütcke, Karl-Heinrich, 'Auctoritas', in C. Mayer (ed.), *Augustinus-Lexikon*, vol. 1 (Basel: Schwabe & Co., 1996), 498–510.

Mac Gaw, C.G., *Le problème du baptême dans le schisme donatiste* (Paris: De Boccard, 2008).

MacKendrick, Paul, *The North African Stones Speak* (Chapel Hill, NC: University of North Carolina Press, 2000).

MacMullen, Ramsay, *Christianity and Paganism in the Fourth to Eight Centuries* (New Haven, CT: Yale University Press, 1997).

Madec, G., 'Sur une nouvelle introduction à la pensée d'Augustin', *Revue des études augustiniennes* 28 (1982), 100–11.

Madec, G., 'Augustinus – ist er der genius malignus Europas?' in P. Koslowski (ed.), *Europa imaginieren. Der europäische Binnenmarkt als kulturelle und wirtschaftliche Aufgabe, Studies in Economic Ethics and Philosophy* (Berlin: Springer-Verlag, 1992), 298–312.

Madec, G., *Introduction aux « Revisions » et à la Lecture des Oeuvres de Saint Augustin*, Collection des Études Augustiniennes: Série Antiquité 150 (Paris: Institut d'Études Augustiniennes, 1996).

Maier, J.-L., *Le dossier du Donatisme.* 1 : *Des origines à la mort de Constance II (303–361), Texte und Untersuchungen zur Geschichte der altchristlichen Literatur* 134 (Berlin: Akademie Verlag, 1987).

Maier, J.-L., *Le dossier du Donatisme.* 2 : *De Julien l'Apostat à Saint Jean Damascène (361–750), Texte und Untersuchungen zur Geschichte der altchristlichen Literatur* 135 (Berlin: Akademie Verlag, 1989).

Mandouze, André, *Prosopographie de l'Afrique Chrétienne (303–533). Prosopographie Chrétienne du Bas-Empire 1* (Paris: Éditions du CNRS, 1982).

Marcone, A., 'Late Roman Social Relations', in A. Cameron and P. Garnsey (eds.), *The Cambridge Ancient History, Volume XIII. The Late Empire, A.D. 337–425* (Cambridge: Cambridge University Press, 1998).

Markus, Robert, *Saeculum: History and Society in the Theology of St. Augustine* (Cambridge: Cambridge University Press, 1970).

Markus, Robert, 'Christianity and Dissent in Roman North Africa: Changing Perspectives in Recent Work', in D. Baker (ed.), *Schism, Heresy, and Religious Protest, Studies in Church History 9* (Cambridge: Cambridge University Press, 1972), 21–36.

Markus, Robert, 'The legacy of Pelagius: orthodoxy, heresy and conciliation', in Rowan Williams (ed.), *The Making of Orthodoxy: Essays in Honour of Henry Chadwick* (Cambridge: Cambridge University Press, 1989), 214–34.

Markus, Robert, *The End of Ancient Christianity* (Cambridge: Cambridge University Press, 1990).

Markus, Robert, 'Donatus, Donatism', in A. Fitzgerald (ed.), *Augustine through the Ages. An Encyclopedia* (Grand Rapids, MI/Cambridge: Wm. Eerdmans Publishing, 1999), 284–87.

Markus, Robert, 'Africa and the Orbis Terrarum: The Theological Problem', in F.Z. Bouayed (ed.), in *Le philosophe algérien Saint Augustin africanité et universalité: actes du premier colloque international Alger – Annaba, 1–7 avril 2001, Tome 2* (Algiers: Publications du Haut Conseil Islamique, 2004), 101–09.

Markus, Robert, *Christianity and the Secular* (Notre Dame, IN: University of Notre Dame Press, 2006).

Markus, Robert, 'Donatismo e Ri-battesimo', in *Agostino e il Donatismo: Lectio Augustini XIX*, Settimana Agostiniana Pavese (2003), *Studia Ephemeridis Augustinianum* 100 (Rome: Augustinianum, 2007).

Mártil, Germán, *La tradición en San Agustín a través de la controversia pelagiana* (Madrid: Espasa-Calpe, 1943).

Martin, Thomas, *Rhetoric and Exegesis in Augustine's Interpretations of Romans 7:24–25A, Studies in Bible and Early Christianity* 47 (Lewiston, NY: The Edwin Mellen Press, 2001).

Martin, Thomas, 'Modus Inveniedi Paulum: Augustine, Hermeneutics, and his Reading of Romans', in D. Patte and E. TeSelle (eds.), *Engaging Augustine on Romans: Self, Context, and Theology in Interpretation, Romans through History and Cultures Series* (Harrisburg, PA: Trinity Press International, 2002), 63–90.

Martin, Thomas, '*Paulus Autem Apostolus Dicit* (*Cresc.* 2.21.26): Augustine's Pauline Polemic against the Donatists', *Augustiniana* 56/3–4 (2006), 235–59.

Martroye, F., 'Une tentative de révolution sociale en Afrique. Donatistes et circoncellions', *Revue des questions historiques* 76 (1904), 353–416.

Martroye, F., 'Circoncellions', *DACL* 3/2 (1914), 1692–1710.

Mayer, Cornelius, 'Taufe und Erwählung – Zur Dialektik des sacramentum-Begriffes in der antidonatistischen Schrift Augustins: De baptismo', in C. Mayer and W. Eckermann (eds.), *Festschrift: P. Dr. theol. Dr. phil. Adolar Zumkeller OSA zum 60. Geburtstag*, *Cassiciacum* 30 (1975), 22–42.

McGowan, Andrew, 'Rethinking Agape and Eucharist in early North African Christianity', *Studia Liturgica* 34 (2004), 165–76.

Menosa, Victoranio, 'San Agustín y Olympio, Obispo de Barcelona', *Augustinus* 25 (1980), 17–21.

Merdinger, Jane, *Rome & the African Church in the Time of Augustine* (New Haven, CT: Yale University Press, 1997).

Merdinger, Jane, 'On the Eve of the Council of Hippo, 393: The Background to Augustine's Program for Church Reform', *Augustinian Studies* 40/1 (2009), 27–36.

Mettepenningen, Jürgen, 'Más allá del déficit de teología (1930–1965): La "nouvelle théologie" y el redescubrimiento de Agustín', *Augustinus* 55 (2010a), 165–84.

Mettepenningen, Jürgen, *Nouvelle Théologie – New Theology: Inheritor of Modernism, Precursor of Vatican II* (London: T&T Clark, 2010b).

Milman, Henry Hart, *History of Latin Christianity: Including That of the Popes to the Pontificate of Nicolas V* (New York: Sheldon, 1862).

Monceaux, Paul, *Histoire littéraire de l'Afrique chrétienne: depuis les origines jusqu'a l'invasion arabe, tome une, Tertullien et les origines* (Paris: Éditions Ernest Leroux, 1901).

Monceaux, Paul, *Histoire littéraire de l'Afrique chrétienne: depuis les origines jusqu'a l'invasion arabe, tome deuxième, Saint Cyprien et son temps* (Paris: Éditions Ernest Leroux, 1902).

Monceaux, Paul, 'L'Église donatiste avant saint Augustin', *Revue de l'histoire des religions* 60 (1909), 3–63.

Monceaux, Paul, 'L'Église donatiste au temps de saint Augustin', *Revue de l'histoire des religions* 61 (1910), 20–77.

Monceaux, Paul, 'L'Église donatiste après saint Augustin', *Revue de l'histoire des religions* 63 (1911a), 148–94.

Monceaux, Paul, 'L'Église donatiste. Organisation et caractères', *Revue de l'histoire des religions* 63 (1911b), 257–95.

Monceaux, Paul, *Histoire littéraire de l'Afrique chrétienne: depuis les origines jusqu'a l'invasion arabe, tome sixième, Saint Augustin et le donatisme* (Paris: Éditions Ernest Leroux, 1922–1923).

Monceaux, Paul, *Histoire littéraire de l'Afrique chrétienne: depuis les origines jusqu'a l'invasion arabe, tome septième, Saint Optat et les premiers écrivains donatistes* (Paris: Éditions Ernest Leroux, 1923).

Morceli, Stefano Antonio, *Africa christiana in tres partes distribute*, vol. 2 (Brescia: Officina Bettoniana, 1816–17).

Moreton, M.J., 'Rethinking the Origin of the Roman Canon', *Studia Patristica* 26 (1993), 63–66.

Mühlsteiger, Johannes, ‚Donatismus und die verfassungrechtlichen Wirkungen einer Kirchenspaltung‘, *ZRG Kan.Abt.* 85 (1999), 1–59. Reprinted in Konrad Breitsching and Wilhelm Rees (eds.), *Tradition-Wegweisung in die Zukunft* (Berlin: Dunker&Humbolt, 2001), 681–739.

Müller, Julius, *Die christliche Lehre von der Sünde* (Wroclaw: Verlag von Josef Max, 1838).

Müller, Julius, *Der Pelagianismus* (Berlin: Verlag von Wilhem Schultze, 1854).

Müller, Hildegund and M. Fiedrowicz, 'Enarrationes in Psalmos', in C. Mayer (ed.), *Augustinus-Lexikon*, vol. 2 (Basel: Schwabe & Co., 2001), 804–58.

Munier, Charles, 'Carthage: Councils', in E. Ferguson (ed.), *Encyclopedia of Early Christianity* I, 2nd edition (New York: Garland Publishing, 1999), 146–48.

le Nain de Tillemont, Louis Sebastien, *Mémoires pour servir à l'histoire ecclésiastique des six premiers siècles jusfifiez par les citations des auteurs originaux*, vol. 13 (Brussels: Eugene Henry Fricx, 1732a).

le Nain de Tillemont, Louis Sebastien, *Memoires pour servir a l'histoire Ecclésiastique, Tom. I, Histoire du schisme des Donatistes, où l'on marque aussi tou ce qui regarde' l'Eglise d 'Afrique depuis l'an 305, jusques en l'an 391 que S. Augustin fut fait Prestre.* (Paris: Charles Robustel, 1732b).

le Nain de Tillemont, Louis Sebastien, *Tom. XIII. La Vie de Saint Augustin, dans laquelle on trouvera l'histoire des Donatistes de son temps, et celle des Pelagiens* (Paris: Charles Robustel, 1732c).

Naylor, Phillip, *North Africa: A History from Antiquity to the Present* (Austin, TX: University of Texas Press, 2009).

Nicholson, Oliver, 'Lactantius on Military Service', *Studia Patristica* 24 (1993), 175–83.

de Noris, Henry, *Historia pelagiana et dissertatio de synodo V oecumenica, in qua origenis ac Theodori Mopsuesteni pelagiani erroris auctorum justa damnatio exponitur et Aquileiense schisma describitur ; additis vindiciis Augustianis...contra pelagianos* (Leuven: Henricum Schelte, 1673, reprinted in 1702).

Norsius, Henricus, *Opera omnia nunc prim. collecta et ordinata*, four vol. (Verona: Tumermani, 1729–32).

Norton, Peter (ed.), *Episcopal Elections 250–600: Hierarchy and Popular Will in Late Antiquity* (New York: Oxford University Press, 2007).

Nthamburi, Zablon, 'The Relevance of Donatism for the Church in Africa Today', *Afer* 23/4 (1981), 215–20.

Ocker, Christopher, 'Augustine, Episcopal Interests, and the Papacy in Late Roman Africa', *Journal of Ecclesiastical History* 42/2 (1991), 179–201.

O'Donnell, James J., 'The Inspiration for Augustine's *De Civitate Dei*', *Augustinian Studies* 10 (1979), 75–79.

O'Donnell, James J., 'The Authority of Augustine', *Augustinian Studies* 22 (1991), 7–35.

O'Donnell, James J., *Augustine: A New Biography* (New York: Harper-Perennial, 2006).

O'Donnell, James J., 'Augustine the African' (2007), from: http://www9.georgetown.edu/faculty/jod/twayne/aug1.html.

O'Donovan, Oliver, *The Desire of the Nations: Rediscovering the Roots of Political Theology* (Cambridge: Cambridge University Press, 1996).

O'Donovan, Oliver, and Joan Lockwood O'Donovan (eds.), *From Irenaeus to Grotius: A Sourcebook in Christian Political Thought 100–1625* (Grand Rapids, MI/Cambridge: Wm. Eerdmans, 1999).

Ogliari, Donato, *Gratia et Certamen: The Relationship between Grace and Free Will in the Discussion of Augustine with the So-Called Semipelagians, Bibliotheca Ephemeridum Theologicarum Lovaniensium* 169 (Leuven: Peeters, 2003).

Opelt, Ilona, *Die Polemik in der christlichen lateinischen Literatur von Tertullian bis Augustin* (Bibliothek der klassischen Altertumswissenschaften, NF 2,63) (Heidelberg: Winter, 1980).

Orsi, Giuseppe Agostino, *Della Istoria Ecclesiastica descritta da F. Guiseppe Agostino Orsi*, vols. 4–5 (Rome: Roma nella stamperia di Pallade appresso Niccolò e Marco Pagliarini, 1741–49).

Overbeck, M., 'Augustin und die Circumcellionen seiner Zeit', *Chiron* 3 (1973), 457–63.

Pannier, Anne, 'Saint Augustin, Saint Cyprien: La postérité de deux ecclésiologies', in *Saint Augustin. Dossier conçu et dirigé par P. RANSON* (*Les dossiers H*) (Lausanne: L'Age d'Homme, 1988), 237–47.

Pelikan, Jaroslav, *The Christian Tradition: A History of the Development of Doctrine, Vol. 1: The Emergence of the Catholic Tradition (100–600)* (Chicago: University of Chicago Press, 1971).

Penn, Michael, 'Ritual Kissing, Heresy and the Emergence of Early Christian Orthodoxy', *Journal of Ecclesiastical History* 54/4 (2003), 625–40.

Perago, Fernando, '*Il valore della tradizione nella polemica tra sant'Agostine e Giuliano di Eclano*', *Annali della Facoltà di Lettere e Filosofia di Napoli* 10 (1962–1963), 143–60.

Perler, Othmar, *Le "De unitate" (chap. IV–V) de saint Cyprien, interprété par Saint Augustin* (Freiburg: *Gesammelte Aufsätze*, 1990), 75–98.

Pietri, Charles, and Luce Pietri (eds.), *Prosopographie de l'Italie chrétienne (313–604)* (*Prosopographie chrétienne du Bas-Empire* 2), vol. 2 (Rome: Ecole française de Rome, 2000).

Rankin, David, 'Class Distinction as a Way of Doing Church: The Early Fathers and the Christian Plebs', *Vigilae Christianae* 58 (2004), 298–315.

Ratzinger, Joseph, *Volk und Haus Gottes in Augustines Lehre von der Kirche, Münchener Theologische Studien* 7 (München: Karl Zink Verlag München, 1954).

Ratzinger, Joseph, *Europa: I suoi fondamenti oggi e domani* (Milan: Edizioni San Paolo, 2004).

Ratzinger, Joseph, and Marcello Pera, M.F. Moore (trans.), *Without Roots: The West, Relativism, Christianity, Islam* (New York: Basic Books, 2007).

Rebenich, Stefan, 'Christian Asceticism and Barbarian Incursion: The Making of a Christian Catastrophe', *Journal of Late Antiquity* 2/1 (2009), 49–59.

Rebillard, Éric, 'Sermones', in A. Fitzgerald (ed.), *Augustine through the Ages. An Encyclopedia* (Grand Rapids, MI/Cambridge: Wm. Eerdmans Publishing, 1999), 773–92.

Rebillard, Éric, 'A New Style of Argument in Christian Polemic: Augustine and the Use of Patristic Citations', *Journal of Early Christian Studies* 8/4 (2000), 559–78.

Rebillard, Éric, 'Augustin et ses autorités: l'élaboration de l'argument patristique au cours de la controverse pélagienne', *Studia Patristica* 38 (2001).

Rebillard, Éric, '*Dogma Populare*: Popular Belief in the Controversy between Augustine and Julian of Eclanum', *Augustinian Studies* 38/1 (2007), 175–87.

Rebillard, Éric, 'The West (2): North Africa', in S. Ashbrook Harvey and D.G. Hunter (eds.) *The Oxford Handbook of Early Christian Studies* (New York: Oxford University Press, 2008), 303–22.

Rees, B.R., *Pelagius: A Reluctant Heretic* (Woodbridge: Boydell and Brewer, 1988).

Rees, B.R. (trans., intro., notes), *The Letters of Pelagius and his Followers* (Woodbridge: Boydell and Brewer, 1991).

Rees, B.R., *Pelagius: Life and Letters* (Woodbridge: Boydell and Brewer, 1998).

Ribbeck, Ferdinand, *Donatus und Augustinus oder der erste entscheidende Kampf zwischen Separatismus und Kirche. Ein Kirchenhistorischer Versuch von Ferdinand Ribbeck* (Elberfeld: Bädeker, 1857).

Rigby, Paul, 'Original Sin', in A. Fitzgerald (ed.), *Augustine Through the Ages. An Encyclopedia* (Grand Rapids, MI/Cambridge: Wm. Eerdmans Publishing, 1999), 607–14.

Riggs, David, 'Placing the Christian Basilicas of Pre-Constantinian North African in Their Proper Architectural Context', *Studia Patristica* 39 (2006), 103–07.

Ring, T.G., 'Auctoritas bei Tertullian, Cyprian und Ambrosius', *Cassiciacum* 29 (Würzburg: Augustinus-Verlag, 1975), 3–32.

Ring, T.G., 'Bruch oder Entwicklung im Gnadenbegriff Augustins? Kritische Anmerkungen zu K. Flasch, Logik des Schreckens. Augustinus von Hippo, Die Gnadenlehre von 397', *Augustiniana* 44 (1994), 31–113.

Rist, John, *Augustine: Ancient thought Baptized* (Cambridge: Cambridge University Press, 1994).

Rives, J.B., *Religion and Authority in Roman Carthage from Augustus to Constantine* (New York: Oxford University Press, 1995).

Rolandus, J., 'No Easy Reconciliation: St Cyprian on Conditions for Re-integration of the Lapsed', *Journal of Theology for Southern Africa* 92 (1995), 23–31.

Rondet, H., 'Bulletin d'histoire de la théologie, études augustiniennes', *Recherches de Science Religieuse* 37 (1950), 619–33.

Rondet, H., 'Essais sur la chronologie des «Enarrationes in Psalmos» de saint Augustin', *Bulletin de Littérature Ecclésiastique* 61 (1960), 199–202.

Roux, Adrianus, *Dissertatio de Aurelio Augustino, adversario Donatistarum* (Leiden: H. Gebhard, 1838).

Ruether, Rosemary Radford, 'Augustine and Christian Political Theology', *Interpretations* 29/3 (1975), 252–65.

Russell, F., 'Persuading the Donatists: Augustine's Coercion by Words', in W.E. Klingshirn and M. Vessey (eds.), *The Limits of Ancient Christianity: Essays on Late Antique Thought and Culture in Honor of R.A. Markus* (Ann Arbor, MI: University of Michigan Press, 1999).

Sage, Michael, *Cyprian, Patristic Monograph Series* 1 (Cambridge, MA: The Philadelphia Patristic Foundation, 1975).

Athanase Sage, 'Péché originel. Naissance d'un dogme', *Revue des études augustiniennes* 13 (1967), 211–48.

Salamito, Jean-Marie, *Les virtuoses et la multitude. Aspects sociaux de la controverse entre Augustin et les pélagiens* (Collection Nomina) (Grenoble, 2005), 208–12.

Scalise, Charles J., 'Exegetical Warrants for Religious Persecution: Augustine vs. the Donatists', *Review and Expositor* 93 (1996), 497–506.

Schaff, Philip, 'The Pelagian Controversy', in the *Bibliotheca Sacra* 18 (1848), 205–43.

Schaff, Philip, 'The Donatist Schism', in *History of the Christian Church*, vol. III. *Nicene and Post-Nicene Christianity: From Constantine the Great to Gregory the Great, AD 311–600* (Grand Rapids, MI: Wm. Eerdmans Publishing, 1910), 360–73.

Schelstrate, Emmanuel, *Ecclesia Africana* (Paris: Fredericum Leonard, 1679, reprinted in Antwerp: 1780).

Schindler, Alfred, 'Die Unterscheidung von Schisma und Häresie in Gesetzgebung und Polemik gegen den Donatismus (mit einer Bemerkung zur Datierung von Augustinus Schrift: Contra epistulam Parmerniani', in E. Dassmann and K. Suso Frank (eds.), *Pietas: Festschrift für Berhnard Kötting, Jahrbuch für Antike und Christentum Ergänzungsband* 8 (Münster: Aschendorf, 1980), 228–36.

Schindler, Alfred, 'L'Histoire du Donatisme considérée du point de vue de sa propre théologie', *Studia Patristica* 17/3 (1982), 1306–315.

Schindler, Alfred, 'Die Theologie der Donatisten und Augustins Reaktion', in C. Mayer and K.H. Chelius (eds.), *Internationales Symposion über den Stand der Augustinus-Forschung vom 12. bis 16. April 1987 im Schloß Rauischholzhausen der Justus-Liebig-Universität Gießen, Cassiciacum* 39/1 (1989), 131–48.

Schindler, Alfred, 'Baptismo (De-)', in C. Mayer (ed.), *Augustinus-Lexikon*, vol. 1 (Basel: Schwabe & Co., 1996), 573–82.

Schlüssler Fiorenza, Francis, 'Political Theology as Foundational Theology', in *The Catholic Theological Society of America Proceedings of the Thirty-Second Annual Convention* 32 (Toronto, 1977), 142–77.

Schönmann, Karl, '*S. Augustini liber sex Epistola de Unitate Ecclesiae contra Petiliani Donat. Epistolam, Argumentiis, Notis atque Analysi illustrata, studio Justi Caluini*', in K. Schönmann *Bibliotheca historico-literaria patrvm Latinorvm. A Tertvlliano principe vsqve ad Gregorivm M. et Isidorvm Hispalensem. Ad Bibliothecam Fabricci Latinam accomodata* (Leipzig: Weidmannia (Lipsiae), 1792–94).

Schröckh, Johann Mattheus, *Christliche Kirchengeschichte* (Leipzig: Schwickert, 1784–1786).

Shaw, Brent D., 'Who were the Circumcellions?' in A.H. Merrills (ed.), *Vandals, Romans, and Berbers: New Perspectives on late Antique North Africa* (Aldershot, UK: Ashgate Publishing, 2004), 227–58.

Shaw, Brent D., 'Bad Boys: Circumcellions and Fictive Violence', in H.A. Drake (ed.), *Violence in Late Antiquity: Perceptions and Practices* (Aldershot, UK: Ashgate Publishing, 2006), 179–96.

Shaw, Brent D., *Sacred Violence: African Christians and Sectarian Hatred in the Age of Augustine* (Cambridge: Cambridge University Press, 2011).

Sidebottom, Harry, *Ancient Warfare: A Very Short Introduction* (New York: Oxford University Press, 2001).

Sieben, Hermann Josef, *Die Konzilsidee der Alte Kirche* (Paderborn: Schöningh, 1979).

Simonis, Walter, *Ecclesia Visibilis et Invisibilis: Untersuchungen zur Ekklesiologie und Sakramentenlehre in der afrikanischen Tradition von Cyprian bis Augustinus, Frankfurter Theologische Studien* 5 (Frankfurt am Main: Josef Knecht Verlag, 1970).

Smither, Edward, 'An Unrecognized and Unlikely Influence? The Impact of Valerius of Hippo on Augustine', *Irish Theological Quarterly* 72 (2007), 251–64.

Solignac, Aimé, 'Introduction aux Confessions', in *BA* 13, Œuvres *de Saint Augustine, Les Confessions I–VII* (Paris: Desclée de Brouwer, 1962), 45–54.

Storren, J. Ph., *Ansführlicher und gründlicher Bericht von den Namen, Ursprung, v.s.w. der Donatisten* (Frankfurt-am-Main: J.Ph. Storren, 1723).

Strauss, A. and J. Corbin, *Basics of Qualitative Research: Techniques and Procedures for Developing Grounded Theory* (Thousand Oaks, CA: Sage, 1998).

Stuckwisch, D. Richard, 'Principles of Christian Prayer from the Third Century: A Brief Look at Origen, Tertullian and Cyprian with Some Comments on Their Meaning for Today', *Worship* 71/1 (1997), 2–18.

Taylor, John H., 'St. Cyprian and the Reconciliation of Apostates', *Theological Studies* 3/1 (1942), 27–46.

Tedesco, Diana Rocco, 'Donatismo: un movimiento de Resistencia del sigli IV', *Cuaderno de Teología* 22 (2003), 257–77.

Teissier, Henri, *Histoire des Chrétiens d'Afrique du Nord : Libye-Tunisie-Algérie-Maroc* (Paris: Desclée, 1991).

Tengström, Emin, *Donatisten und Katholiken: soziale, wirtschaftliche und politische Aspecten einer Nordafrikanischen Kirchenspaltung* (Göteborg: Elanders Boktryckeri Aktiebolag, 1964).

Teselle, Eugene, *Augustine the Theologian* (New York: Herder & Herder, 1970).

Teselle, Eugene, 'Rufinus the Syrian, Caelestius, Pelagius: Explorations in the Prehistory of the Pelagian Controversy', *Augustinian Studies* 3 (1972), 61–95.

Teselle, Eugene, 'Pelagianism Reconsidered', *Studia Patristica* 27 (1993).

Teselle, Eugene, 'Holy Spirit', in A. Fitzgerald (ed.), *Augustine through the Ages: An Encyclopedia* (Grand Rapids, MI: Wm. Eerdmans, 1999a), 434–37.

Teselle, Eugene, 'Pelagius, Pelagianism', in A. Fitzgerald (ed.), *Augustine through the Ages. An Encyclopedia* (Grand Rapids/Cambridge: Wm. Eerdmans Publishing, 1999b), 633–40.

Their, S., 'Kirche bei Pelagius', in *Patristische Texte und Studien* 50 (Berlin & New York, 1999) in *Vigiliae Christianae* 57 (2003), 224–27.

Thonnard, François-Joseph, 'Le témoignage de saint Cyprien', in *BA* 23 (Paris: Desclée de Brouwer, 1974), 824–25.

Tilley, Maureen, 'The Ascetic Body and the (Un) Making of the World of the Martyr', *Journal of the American Academy of Religion* 59/3 (1991a), 467–79.

Tilley, Maureen, 'Dilatory Donatists or Procrastinating Catholics: The Trial at the Conference of Carthage', *Church History* 60/1 (1991b), 7–19.

Tilley, Maureen, 'Understanding Augustine Misunderstanding Tyconius', *Studia Patristica* 27 (1993), 405–08.

Tilley, Maureen, *The Bible in Christian North Africa: The Donatist World* (Minneapolis, MN: Fortress Press, 1997a).

Tilley, Maureen, 'From Separatist Sect to Majority Church: The Ecclesiologies of Parmenian and Tyconius', *Studia Patristica* 33 (Leuven: Peeters, 1997b), 260–65.

Tilley, Maureen, 'The Sign Value of Donatist Baptismal Architecture or Baptisteries Rebaptized', *American Academy of Religion Seminar on the Practice of Christianity in Roman North Africa* (1997c), 1–14.

Tilley, Maureen, 'Sustaining Donatist Self-identity: From the Church of the Martyrs to the Collecta of the Desert', *Journal of Early Christian Studies* 5/1 (1997d), 21–35.

Tilley, Maureen, 'Anti-Donatist Works', in A. Fitzgerald (ed.), *Augustine through the Ages: An Encyclopedia* (Grand Rapids, MI/Cambridge: Wm. Eerdmans Publishing, 1999a), 34–39.

Tilley, Maureen, 'Baptism', in A. Fitzgerald (ed.), *Augustine through the Ages. An Encyclopedia* (Grand Rapids/Cambridge: Wm. Eerdmans Publishing, 1999b), 84–92.

Tilley, Maureen, 'Baptismo, De', in A. Fitzgerald (ed.), *Augustine through the Ages. An Encyclopedia* (Grand Rapids, MI/Cambridge: Wm. Eerdmans Publishing, 1999c), 91–92.

Tilley, Maureen, 'Cyprian of Carthage', in A. Fitzgerald (ed.), *Augustine through the Ages. An Encycolpedia* (Grand Rapids, MI/Cambridge: Wm. Eerdmans Publishing, 1999d), 262–64.

Tilley, Maureen, 'Donatistas post conlationem, Contra', in A. Fitzgerald (ed.), *Augustine through the Ages: An Encyclopedia* (Grand Rapids, MI/Cambridge: Wm. Eerdmans Publishing, 1999e), 281.

Tilley, Maureen, 'Donatist Bishops', in A. Fitzgerald (ed.), *Augustine through the Ages: An Encyclopedia* (Grand Rapids, MI/Cambridge: Wm. Eerdmans Publishing, 1999f), 281–84.

Tilley, Maureen, 'The Collapse of a Collegial Church: North African Christianity on the Eve of Islam', *Theological Studies* 62/1 (2001a), 3–22.

Tilley, Maureen, 'Theologies of Penance during the Donatist Controversy', *Studia Patristica* 35 (2001b), 330–37.

Tilley, Maureen, 'Augustine's Unacknowledged Debt to the Donatists', in P.-Y. Fux, J.-M Roessli, and O. Wermlinger (eds.), *Augustinus Afer: Saint Augustin: africanité et universalité. Actes du colloque international, Alger-Annaba, 1–7 avril 2001, Paradosis* 45/1 (Fribourg: Éditions Universitaires Fribourg Suisse, 2003), 141–48.

Tilley, Maureen, 'North Africa', in Margaret Mitchell and Frances Young (eds.), *The Cambridge History of Christianity,* vol. I, *Origins to Constantine* (Cambridge: Cambridge University Press, 2006), 380–96.

Tilley, Maureen, 'When Schism Becomes Heresy in Late Antiquity: Developing Doctrinal Deviance in the Wounded Body of Christ', *Journal of Early Christian Studies* 15/1 (2007), 1–21.

Torrance, Iain, 'They Speak to Us across the Centuries, 2. Cyprian', *The Expository Times* 108/12 (1997), 356–59.

Trapè, Agostino, 'Un celebre testo de Sant'Agostino sull "Ignoranza e la difficoltà" (Retract. I,9,6) e ***l'Opus imperfectum Contra Iulianum', in *Augustinus Magister* II (Paris: Études augustiniennes, 1954), 795–803.

Trigg, J.W., 'Martyrs and Churchmen in Third-Century North Africa', *Studia Patristica* 15 (1984), 242–54.

Turner, H.E.W., *The Pattern of Christian Truth: A Study in the Relationship between Orthodoxy and Heresy in the Early Church,* Bampton Lectures 1954 (London: A.R. Mowbray & Co. Ltd., 1954).

Ubiña, José Fernández, 'San Cipriano y el Imperio', *Estudios Eclesiásticos* 57 (1982), 65–81.

Valesius, Henricus, *Historia ecclesiastica Eusebii Pamphili, Socratis scholastici, Hermiae Sozomeni, Theodoriti episcopi Cyri et Evagrii scholastici* (Paris: Petri le Petit, 1659).

Van Bavel, T.J., 'The Cult of the Martyrs in St. Augustine. Theology versus Popular Religion?' in M. Lamberigts and P. Van Deun (eds.), *Martyrium in Multidisciplinary Perspective. Memorial Louis Reekmans, Bibliotheca Ephemeridum Theologicarum Lovaniensium* 117 (Leuven: Peeters, 1995), 351–61.

Van Bavel, T.J., 'To see the Ineffable by way of the inexpressible: the Trinity', in T.J. van Bavel (ed.), *Saint Augustine* (Brussels: Mercatorfonds, 2007), 97–104.

Van der Meer, F., *Augustine the Bishop: The Life and Work of a Father of the Church,* trans. Brian Battershaw and G.R. Lamb (London: Sheed & Ward, 1961).

Van Eijl, E.J.M., 'Michael Baius (1513–1589)', *Louvain Studies* 5 (1975), 287–91.

Van Eijl, E.J.M., 'La controverse louvaniste autour de la grâce et du libre arbitre à la fin du XVIe siècle', in M. Lamberigts and Leo Kenis (eds.), *L'augustinisme à l'ancienne faculté de théologie de Louvain, Bibliotheca ephemeridum theologicarum Lovaniensium* 111 (Leuven: Peeters, 1994), 207–82.

Van Geest, Paul, 'Pectus ardet Evangelica pietate, et pectori respondet oratio: Augustine's Neglect of Cyprian's Striving for Sincerity', in H. Bakker, P. van Geest, and H. Van Loon (eds.), *Cyprian of Carthage: Studies in His Life, Language, and Thought*, *Late Antique History and Religion* 3 (Leuven: Peeters, 2010), 203–25.

Van Geest, Paul, '*Quid dicam de vindicando vel non vindicando*? (*ep*. 95.3): Augustine's legitimisation of coercion in the light of his role of mediator, judge, teacher and mystagogue', in A. Geljon, R. Roukema (eds), *Violence in Ancient Christianity: Victims and Perpetrators* (Leiden: Brill, 2014), 151–184.

Van Geest, Paul '*Timor est Servus Caritatis* (*s*. 156,13–14): Augustine's Vision on Coercion in the Process of Returning Heretics to the Catholic Church and his Underlying Principles', in A. Dupont, M. Gaumer, and M. Lamberigts (eds.), *The Uniquely African Controversy: Studies on Donatist Christianity* (Leuven: Peeters, 2015), 289–310.

Vanneste, A., 'Le « De prima hominis justicia » de M. Baius. Une relecture critique', in M. Lamberigts and Leo Kenis (eds.), *L'Augustinisme à l'Ancienne Faculté de Théologie de Louvain, Bibliotheca ephemeridum theologicarum Lovaniensium* 111 (Leuven: Peeters, 1994), 123–66.

Verbraken, P.-P., *Études Critiques sur les Sermons Authentiques de Saint Augustin, Instrumenta Patristica* 12 (Steenbrugge, Bel.: Abbatia S. Petri/Martinus Nijhoff, 1976).

Vossius, Gerhard Johannes, *Historia Pelagiana sive Historiae de controversies quas Pelagius ejusque reliquiae moverunt* (Amsterdam: Adrianum Vlacq, 1618).

Walch, Christian Wilhelm Franz, *Entwurf einer vollständigen Historie der Ketzereien, Spaltungen und Religionsstreitigkeiten, bis auf die Zeiten der Reformation*, see Section 4 (Leipzig: M.G. Weidmanns Erben und Reich, 1768).

Walch, Christian Wilhelm Franz, *Ketzerhistorie* (Leipzig: M.G. Weidmanns Erben und Reich, 1770).

Ward-Perkins, Bryan, *The Fall of Rome and the End of Civilization* (Oxford: Oxford University Press, 2005).

Weber, Dorothea, 'Klassische Literatur im Dienst theologischer Polemik: Julian von Eclanum, Ad Florum', *Studia Patristica* 38 (2001), 503–09.

Weber, Dorothea, 'Textkritische Spezifika aus Augustins Schriften gegen Julian von Eclanum', in A. Primmer, K. Smolak, and D. Weber (eds.), *Textsorten und Textkritik. Tagungsbeiträge* (*Österreichische Akademie der Wissenschaften, Philosophisch-Historische Klasse, Sitzungsberichte* 693; Veröffentlichungen der Kommission zur Herausgabe des Corpus der lateinischen Kirchenväter, Heft 21) (Vienna: Österreichische Akademie der Wissenschaften, 2002), 193–209.

Weber, Dorothea, '"*For What is so Monstrous as What the Punic Fellow Says?*" Reflections on the Literary Background of Julian's Polemical Attacks on Augustine's Homeland', in P.-Y. Fux, J.-M. Roessli, and O. Wermelinger (eds.), Augustinus Afer. *Saint Augustin. Africanité et universalité* (*Actes du colloque international*

Alger-Annaba, 1–7 avril 2001), *Paradosis* 45/1 (Fribourg: Éditions Universitaires Fribourg Suisse, 2003), 75–82.

Weber, Dorothea, 'Some Literary Aspects of the Debate between Julian of Eclanum and Augustine', *Studia Patristica* 43 (2006), 289–302.

Weinrich, W.C., 'Cyprian, Donatism, Augustine, and Augustana VIII: Remarks on the Church and the Validity of Sacraments', *Concordia Theological Quarterly* 55/4 (1991), 267–96.

Wermelinger, Otto, *Rom und Pelagius. Die theologische Position der römischen Bischöfe im pelagianischen Streit in den Jahren 411–432* (Stuttgart : Hiersemann, 1975).

Wermelinger, Otto, 'Neure Forschungskontroversen um Augustinus und Pelagius', in C. Mayer and K.H. Chelius (eds.), *Internationales Symposion über den Stand der Augustinus-Forschung vom 12. bis 16. April 1987 im Schloß Rauischholzhausen der Justus-Liebig-Universität Gießen, Cassiciacum* 39/1 (1989), 189–218.

Wetzel, James, 'Simplicianum, Ad', in A. Fitzgerald (ed.), *Augustine through the Ages. An Encyclopedia* (Grand Rapids/Cambridge: Wm. Eerdmans Publishing, 1999), 798–99.

Whittaker, C.R., and Peter Garnsey, 'Rural Life in the Later Roman Empire', in A. Cameron and P. Garnsey (eds.), *The Cambridge Ancient History, Volume XIII. The Late Empire, A.D. 337–425* (Cambridge: Cambridge University Press, 1998).

Wickert, Ulrich, *Sacramentum Unitatis: Ein Beitrag zum Verständnis der Kirche bei Cyprian* (Berlin: Walter de Gruyter, 1971).

Wickham, Lionel, 'Pelagianism in the East', in Rowan Williams (ed.), *The Making of Orthodoxy: Essays in Honour of Henry Chadwick* (Cambridge: Cambridge University Press, 1989), 200–13.

Wiggers, Gustav Friederich, *Versuch einer pragmatischen Darstellung des Augustinismus und Pelagianismus nach ihrer geschichtlichen Entwickelung* (Hamburg: Perthes, 1833).

Wiles, M.F., 'The Theological Legacy of St. Cyprian', *Journal of Ecclesiastical History* 14/2 (1963), 139–49.

Wilken, Robert Louis, *The Spirit of Early Christian Thought: Seeking the Face of God* (New Haven, CT: Yale University Press, 2003).

Willis, Geoffrey, *Saint Augustine and the Donatist Controversy* (London: SPCK, 1950).

Witsius, *Miscellaneorum Sacrorum libri*, two vols. (Amsterdam: Ioannem van Ghemmert, 1692).

Wörter, Friedrich, *Der Pelagianismus nach seinem Ursprung und seiner Lehre* (Freiburg: Wagner, 1866).

Wundt, Max, 'Zur Chronologie augustinischer Schriften', *Zeitschrift für die neutestamentliche Wissenchaft und die Kunde der älteren Kirche* 21 (1922), 128–35.

Yates, Jonathan, 'Was There "Augustinian" Concupiscence in Pre-Augustinian North Africa?' *Augustiniana* 51 (2001), 39–56.

Yates, Jonathan, 'The Epistle of James in Augustine and his Pelagian Adversaries. Some Preliminary Observations', *Augustiniana* 52 (2002), 273–90.

Yates, Jonathan, 'Augustine's Appropriation of Cyprian the Martyr-Bishop against the Pelagians', in J. Leemans (ed.), *More than a Memory: the Discourse of Martyrdom and the Construction of Christian Identity in the History of Christianity, Annua Nuntia Lovaniensia* 51 (Leuven: Peeters, 2005), 119–35.

Yates, Jonathan, 'De nuptiis et concupiscentia I: A Pauline Exegetical Milestone or Status quo ante?' in M. Lamberigts and J. Yates (eds.), *Sicut scripsit apostolus: The Text of the Apostle Paul in Augustine and his Pelagian Opponents (411–430), The Bible in Ancient Christianity Series* (Leiden/Boston: Brill, 2009).

Yates, Jonathan, 'The Use of the Bible in the North African Martyrological Polemics of Late Antiquity', in J. Leemans (ed.), *Martyrdom and Persecution in Late Antique Christianity: Festschrift Boudewijn Dehandschutter, Bibliotheca Ephemeridum Theologicarum Lovaniensium* 241 (Leuven: Peeters, 2010), 393–419.

Zarb, S.M., *Chronologia Enarrationum s. Augustini in Psalmos* (Valetta*: St. Dominic's Priory,* 1948).

Ziche, Hartmut, 'Making Late Roman taxpayers Pay: Imperial Government Strategies and Practice', in H.A. Drake (ed.), *Violence in Late Antiquity: Perceptions and Practices* (Aldershot,UK: Ashgate Publishing, 2006), 127–36.

Zumkeller, A., 'Eph. 5, 27 im Verständnis Augustins und seiner donatistischen und pelagianischen Gegner', *Augustinianum* 16 (1976), 457–474.

Index

Printed in the United States
By Bookmasters